QuickBooks®
Pro 2013:
Comprehensive

TRISHA CONLON
Chemeketa Community College

LABYRINTH
LEARNING™

Berkeley, CA

QuickBooks Pro 2013: Comprehensive
by Trisha Conlon

Copyright © 2014 by Labyrinth Learning

Labyrinth Learning
2560 9th Street, Suite 320
Berkeley, California 94710
800.522.9746
On the web at lablearning.com

President:
Brian Favro

Product Development Manager:
Jason Favro

Managing Editor:
Laura Popelka

Production Editor:
Margaret Young

Production Manager:
Rad Proctor

eLearning Production Manager:
Arl S. Nadel

Editorial/Production Team:
Donna Bacidore, Everett Mike Cowan,
Sandy Jones

Indexing: Joanne Sprott

Interior Design:
Mark Ong, Side-by-Side Studios

Cover Design:
Words At Work

ITEM: 1-59136-477-9
ISBN-13: 978-1-59136-477-1

Manufactured in the United States of America.

10 9 8 7 6 5 4 3 2 1

Contents in Brief

Table of Contents

Quick Reference Tables

PAYROLL TASKS

PHYSICAL INVENTORY TASKS

REPORT TASKS

Preface

QuickBooks® Pro 2013: Comprehensive provides essential coverage of QuickBooks 2013 software. Topics covered include basic accounting principles, backing up files, creating companies, working with vendors, working with customers, banking with QuickBooks, customizing QuickBooks, classes, the accounting cycle, physical inventory, payroll, estimates and time tracking, balance sheet accounts, budgets, closing the books, adjusting entries, and more.

For almost two decades, Labyrinth Learning has been publishing easy-to-use textbooks that empower educators to teach complex subjects quickly and effectively, while enabling students to gain confidence, develop practical skills, and compete in a demanding job market. We add comprehensive support materials, assessment and learning management tools, and eLearning components to create true learning solutions for a wide variety of instructor-led, self-paced, and online courses.

Our textbooks follow the *Labyrinth Instruction Design,* our unique and proven approach that makes learning easy and effective for every learner. Our books begin with fundamental concepts and build through a systematic progression of exercises. Quick Reference Tables, precise callouts on screen captures, carefully selected illustrations, and minimal distraction combine to create a learning solution that is highly efficient and effective for both students and instructors.

This course is supported with *comprehensive instructor support* materials that include printable solution guides for side-by-side comparisons, test banks, customizable assessments, customizable PowerPoint presentations, detailed lesson plans, preformatted files for integration to leading learning management system, and more.

Visual Conventions

This book uses many visual and typographic cues to guide students through the lessons. This page provides examples and describes the function of each cue.

`Type this text`	Anything you should type at the keyboard is printed in this typeface.
	Tips, Notes, and Warnings are used to draw attention to certain topics.
Command→ Command→ Command, etc.	This convention indicates a Ribbon path. The commands are written: Ribbon Tab→Command Group→Command→Subcommand.
FROM THE KEYBOARD Ctrl+S to save	These margin notes indicate shortcut keys for executing a task described in the text.
NEW! 2013	Features new to this edition of the software are indicated with this icon.
Visualize!	If there is an Intuit video related to the QuickBooks topic being discussed, this convention will point you to it.

Exercise Progression

The exercises in this book build in complexity as students work through a lesson toward mastery of the skills taught.

- **Develop Your Skills** exercises are introduced immediately after concept discussions. They provide detailed, step-by-step tutorials.
- **Reinforce Your Skills** exercises provide additional hands-on practice with moderate assistance.
- **Apply Your Skills** exercises test students' skills by describing the correct results without providing specific instructions on how to achieve them.
- **Critical Thinking** exercises are the most challenging. They provide generic instructions, allowing students to use their skills and creativity to achieve the results they envision.

Acknowledgements

We are grateful to the instructors who have used Labyrinth titles and suggested improvements to us over the many years we have been writing and publishing books. This book has benefited greatly from the reviews and suggestions of the following instructors.

Teresa Allen, *Tyler Junior College*

Kim Anderson, *Elgin Community College*

Marcia Bercot, *SkillSource*

Ed Bonner, *National Career Skills Institute*

David Campbell, *Northern Virginia Community College*

Lori Chambers, *Manhattan Area Technical College*

Nancy Dugan, *Eastern Iowa Community Colleges*

Valorie Duvall, *South Plains College*

Nancy Escudero, *Small Business Development Center (SBDC)*

Saria Fox, *Asher College*

Evangelina Gallegos-Garner, *South Texas Vocational Institute*

Theresa Hagelbarger, *Villa Park High School*

Diane Hageman, *San Mateo Adult School*

Penny Hahn, *Henderson Community College*

Amanda Hayman, *Technical College of the Lowcountry*

Scott Hibbs, *Madison Area Technical College*

Lorene Hintz, *Great Northern Development Corp.*

Stacy Jemmott-Hunt, *Midlands Technical College*

Connie Keim, *Upper Valley Career Center (JVS) and Troy High School*

Tynia Kessler, *Lake Land College*

Dave Kiley, *Muskegon Community College*

Lee Kirk, *Utah Valley University*

Dawn Krause, *Macomb Community College*

Kathryn Langston, *Ozarka College*

Gayle Larson, *Highline Community College*

Kathy Lavieri, *Great Oaks Institute of Technology and Career Development*

Gabriele Lenga, *Truckee Meadows Community College*

Pieri Levandofsky, *Medina County Career Center*

Sue Lobner, *Nicolet Area Technical College*

Teresa Loftis, *San Bernardino Adult School*

Claire Moore, *Placer Adult Education*

Leah Morrison, *Hawkeye Community College*

LoAnn Nelson, *Lake Region State College*

Patti Norris, *Central Oregon Community College*

Allan O'Bryan, *Rochester Community and Technical College*

Monika Olsen, *Acalanes Adult Education*

John Oppenheim, *OneOC*

Larry Overstreet, *College Of DuPage*

Beth Quimby, *River Valley Community College*

Floydette Rector, *Mt. Tabor High School*

David Reilly, *Forest Hill Community High School*

Delvan Roehling, *Ivy Tech Community College*

Charles Rovner, *Ulster County Community College*

Crystalynn Shelton, *UCLA Extension*

Stanley Snyder, *Colorado Mountain College*

Rita Thayer, *Sandusky City Schools*

Charles Thompson, *Edison State College*

Norma Tyler, *Central Tech*

Keith Wallace, *Billings Public School District 2*

Randy Watkins, *Contra Costa College*

Sonora White, *Caddo Kiowa Technology Center*

Mary Ann Whitehurst, *Southern Crescent Technical College*

John D. Williams, *University of New Mexico – Taos*

Peter Young, *San Jose State University*

U N I T

1

Essential Skills

Essential Skills

QuickBooks is an Intuit software program designed to help small- and medium-sized businesses keep their books easily and accurately. In this unit, you will first be introduced to the software and basic file-management tasks. In the second lesson you will learn how to properly set up a company file. The next three lessons will take you through working with vendors, customers, and banking tasks in QuickBooks. The final lesson in this unit will help you deal with errors and some of the unpleasantries of running a business (writing off bad debt and dealing with NSF checks) before you learn to customize reports and templates for your company.

Introducing QuickBooks Pro

LESSON OBJECTIVES

After studying this lesson, you will be able to:

- Discuss basic accounting concepts
- Determine if QuickBooks is right for your business
- Manage basic QuickBooks files
- Open a portable company file
- Back up a company file

QuickBooks has become the software of choice for many owners of small- and medium-sized businesses. No doubt, this is due to the multitude of functions and features that the software offers the smaller company. In this lesson, you will explore the various editions of QuickBooks and determine which is right for you. You will also examine what goes on behind the scenes and why it is so important for you to have a basic understanding of accounting. Finally, you will be introduced to some QuickBooks basics that are vital to your success as a QuickBooks user, and you will learn how to access valuable supplemental training tools right in your QuickBooks software.

Student Resources   http://labyrinthelab.com/qb13

Discovering What's New in QuickBooks 2013

Each year, Intuit introduces a new version of QuickBooks with new-and-improved features. As you work through this book, you will see these new aspects of the software called to your attention with a special icon.

 This is how you will be able to identify new or improved QuickBooks features.

The following list outlines some of the new QuickBooks 2013 features as well as the lesson in which each is introduced. (The main change from QuickBooks 2012 is the total revamp of the user interface!)

- New Icon Bar (Lesson 1, Introducing QuickBooks Pro)
- New App Center (Lesson 1, Introducing QuickBooks Pro)
- A centralized location for displaying information in the Customer, Vendor, and Employee Centers (Lesson 3, Working with Vendors)
- Ribbons and tabs in transaction windows (Lesson 3, Working with Vendors)
- Customization of up to eight contact fields for customers, vendors, and employees (Lesson 3, Working with Vendors)
- A feature that allows you, as a QuickBooks user, to collect invoice payments online (Lesson 8, Dealing with Physical Inventory)
- New user interface (throughout this book)

 Later in this lesson you will learn about the video tutorials available through the QuickBooks Learning Center. Once you have learned how to access tutorials, you will have a chance to view the "What's New in 2013" tutorial.

Presenting QuickBooks Pro

QuickBooks is a software program that allows companies to:

- Keep track of customers, vendors, employees, and other important entities
- Process sales transactions and cash receipts
- Process purchase transactions and payments to vendors
- Run payroll
- Track and sell inventory
- Run end-of-period financial reports
- Track assets (what you own) and liabilities (what you owe)
- Keep track of bank accounts
- Collaborate with accountants easily and efficiently

Types of Companies That Use QuickBooks Pro

QuickBooks Pro works well for different types of companies in a variety of industries. Ideally, your company should not have more than twenty employees and $1 million in annual revenue if you plan to use QuickBooks Pro (these are not strict rules, but guidelines). If your company is larger, you may want to consider using QuickBooks Enterprise Solutions. One type of business that QuickBooks Pro is not suited for is manufacturing, but Intuit has produced both Premier and Enterprise editions of QuickBooks especially for the manufacturing industry.

Aside from these issues, QuickBooks Pro can be customized and works well for many businesses, including not-for-profit organizations.

Editions of QuickBooks

Before you purchase your copy of QuickBooks, you should evaluate what you need QuickBooks to do for you. There are several editions of QuickBooks, all of which perform the basic tasks required for small-business bookkeeping. This book requires at the minimum the use of QuickBooks Pro, but it can be used with the Premiere edition as well. If you are using a different edition, your screen may look a little bit different from what is displayed throughout this book. Intuit also creates a QuickBooks edition for Mac users, which is similar to the Windows-based version in functions yet looks different due to the differences in the two platforms.

Versions, as Compared to Editions

Now, don't let yourself become confused by the difference between editions and versions of QuickBooks. Intuit creates a new version of QuickBooks each year (such as QuickBooks 2011, 2012, or 2013). Each new version provides additional features that are new for that year. This book is designed for QuickBooks 2013, but once you learn how to use the features QuickBooks offers, it will be easy to switch between versions.

With each version, Intuit creates a multitude of editions from which a company may choose (such as QuickBooks Simple Start, QuickBooks Pro, QuickBooks Premier, and QuickBooks Enterprise Solutions). There are also online editions of QuickBooks available that, for a monthly fee, allow you to access your company QuickBooks files via the Internet. Take a look at the student resource center for this book (http://labyrinthelab.com/qb13) to determine which edition will work best for your company.

Other Tools from Intuit

Intuit creates other tools that are a part of the "Quicken family" and are used by small businesses. You may find that software such as Quicken Home & Business or Quicken Rental Property Manager might be a better tool to track your small business' finances. To learn more about these other options produced by Intuit, browse over to the company's website at http://www.intuit.com.

The Online Editions of QuickBooks

Many companies are now using the online editions (Simple Start, Essentials, and Plus) of QuickBooks. The online versions look very similar to the traditional desktop editions but have some unique features, such as:

- The ability to access QuickBooks from any computer with Internet access, as well as from many popular smart phones
- A way for users in multiple or remote locations to easily utilize a single file
- Automatic online backups

In addition, there is no need to worry about technological problems associated with desktop product installation and support when using QuickBooks online.

All of the users of a company file can access it through the web with a username and password, and all users work with the same up-to-date company file. It is recommended that you have a high-speed Internet connection to utilize these editions. The online editions, as with the desktop editions, allow you to set up users and determine the access level for each one.

The online interface is very similar to that of QuickBooks Pro, so once you learn the basics of the program from studying this book, you will be able to transfer your knowledge to the online editions. It is similar to learning to drive a Ford and then driving a Toyota—you will just need to familiarize yourself with the differences before you take off! You also have the ability to import your company data from a desktop edition of QuickBooks into your online account. You do not purchase software for an online edition but, instead, pay a monthly fee. Not all features are available in the online editions, though, so it is best to compare the different editions on the Intuit website in order to determine which is best suited for your company's needs. You can find a link to the online edition comparison as well as current pricing in the student resource center for this book (http://labyrinthelab.com/qb13).

QuickBooks App Center and Add-Ins

In QuickBooks 2013, the new App Center features tools that can help increase your efficiency with QuickBooks.

The QuickBooks App Center is a web-based resource with tools to help you manage your business more effectively.

This is the window that appears when you click the Web and Mobile Apps task icon in the Company area of the Home page.

This link leads to the web page for the full App Center.

Types of Tasks

There are many types of tasks you can perform with QuickBooks. The tasks can be broken down into two main categories: those that affect the accounting behind the scenes (activities and company setup) and those that do not (lists and reporting). The following table lists the four basic types of tasks covered in this book.

Task	Function
List (Database)	A list allows you to store information about customers, vendors, employees, and other data important to your business.
Activities	This feature affects what is happening behind the scenes. Activities can be easily entered on forms such as invoices or bills.
Company Setup	This feature takes you through the steps necessary to set up a new company in QuickBooks.
Reports	QuickBooks provides many preset reports and graphs that are easily customizable to meet your needs.

Understanding Basic Accounting

Many business owners use QuickBooks to keep their own books and attempt to just learn the software. QuickBooks is quite intuitive, but you will find yourself running into problems if you don't understand the accounting basics on which QuickBooks is based. If you want to make sure you have a more solid understanding of accounting, you may wish to consider the book, *The ABCs of Accounting, 2nd Edition*, also published by Labyrinth Learning.

An Accountant's Worst Nightmare (or Greatest Dream?)

Picture yourself as an accountant who has just received a QuickBooks file from a client. The client has no idea how accounting works and, to him, debit and credit are just types of plastic cards he carries in his wallet. In his file you find duplicate accounts in the Chart of Accounts, accounts created as the wrong type, items posted to incorrect accounts, accounts payable inaccuracies, and payroll inaccuracies (to name just a few problems).

Now, as an accountant, you can consider this a nightmare because you will have to run numerous diagnostics to find all the mistakes (which could have been easily avoided if your client learned how to use QuickBooks properly in the first place) or a dream because your billable hours will increase at a rapid rate.

This scenario is exactly the reason why you, as the client, need to learn what happens behind the scenes in QuickBooks, as well as how to use the day-to-day functions of the software. By having a better understanding of the accounting and how to do things properly in the program, you will reduce the number of hours your accountant will have to spend and, thereby, save yourself the accountant fees in the end!

What's Up with GAAP?

GAAP stands for *generally accepted accounting principles*. These are accounting rules used to prepare, present, and report financial statements for a wide variety of entities. The organization that creates the rules is called the FASB (Financial Accounting Standards Board). Publicly owned companies need to follow these rules unless they can show that doing so would produce information that is misleading. It is wise for the small-business owner to adhere to GAAP. These rules work to make taxation fair as it affects small-business owners.

As GAAP attempt to achieve basic objectives, they have several basic assumptions, principles, and constraints (described below). Throughout the book you will see reminders of how GAAP apply to tasks that you are completing in QuickBooks via the "Flashback to the GAAP" feature.

Principle	Description
Business entity principle	The business is separate from the owners and from other businesses. Revenues and expenses of the business should be kept separate from the personal expenses of the business owner.
The assumption of the going concern	The business will be in operation indefinitely.
Monetary unit principle	A stable currency is going to be the unit of record.
Time-period principle	The activities of the business can be divided into time periods.
Cost principle	When a company purchases assets, it should record them at cost, not fair market value. For example, an item worth $750 bought for $100 is recorded at $100.
Revenue principle	Publicly traded companies (not always sole proprietorships) record when the revenue is realized and earned, not when cash is received (accrual basis of accounting).
Matching principle	Expenses need to be matched with revenues. If a contractor buys a specific sink for a specific bathroom, it is matched to the cost of remodeling the bathroom. Otherwise, the cost may be charged as project expense. This principle allows a better evaluation of the profitability and performance (how much did you spend to earn the revenue?).
Objectivity principle	The statements of a company should be based on objectivity.
Materiality principle	When an item is reported, its significance should be considered. An item is considered significant when it would affect the decision made regarding its use.
Consistency principle	The company uses the same accounting principles and methods from year to year.
Prudence principle	When choosing between two solutions, the one that will be least likely to overstate assets and income should be selected.

INTRODUCING "BEHIND THE SCENES"

Throughout this book you will see a special section called "Behind the Scenes" whenever you are learning about an activity performed within QuickBooks. This section will go over the accounting that QuickBooks performs for you when you record a transaction. Please note that the account names used in this feature use QuickBooks, rather than traditional accounting, nomenclature.

Accrual vs. Cash Basis Accounting

There are two ways that companies can choose to keep the books. The method you choose to implement depends on the nature of your business. QuickBooks makes it easy for you to produce reports utilizing either method, and your data entry will be the same regardless of which method you choose. Talk to your accountant or tax advisor to determine which method you have been using (for an existing business) or should use (for a new business).

Accrual Basis

In the accrual basis of accounting, income is recorded when the sale is made and expenses recorded when accrued. This method is often used by firms and businesses with large inventories. As you just learned from the GAAP table, this is the basis you need to use for publicly traded corporations.

Essential Skills

Cash Basis

In the cash basis of accounting, income is recorded when cash is received and expenses recorded when cash is paid. This method is commonly used by small businesses and professionals involved in occupations that are not publicly traded.

> **FLASHBACK TO GAAP: REVENUE**
>
> Remember that publicly traded companies should record when the revenue is realized and earned—not when cash is received (accrual basis of accounting).

Where to Find More Help

You can learn more about accounting fundamentals in Appendix A, Need to Know Accounting, at the back of this book. It provides some basic definitions, theories, and a link to a web page with online resources. More in-depth coverage of accounting concepts can be found in the Labyrinth Learning book, *The ABCs of Accounting, 2nd Edition*.

In Appendix A, Need to Know Accounting, you will find information on:

■ The accounting equation

■ Debits and credits

■ Types of accounts and normal balances

Introducing the Integrative Case Studies

In Lessons 1–6, you will explore the operations of a company called Chez Devereaux Salon and Spa for the Develop Your Skills exercises. This company provides hair care and spa services to clients. In Lessons 7–12, you will work with Rock Castle Construction, a construction company that deals with both service and inventory items.

You will further hone your QuickBooks skills with Reinforce Your Skills exercises that deal with Tea Shoppe at the Lake, a café and small retail store, and with Apply Your Skills exercises that deal with Wet Noses Veterinary Clinic. The Develop Your Skills exercises focus on using the Home page to perform tasks, while the Reinforce Your Skills exercises primarily use the menu bar since that is a preference for some QuickBooks users. Once you are on your own with QuickBooks, you should use whichever method(s) you prefer.

The exercises that you will complete for Chez Devereaux, Tea Shoppe at the Lake, and Wet Noses are set in the time frame of May through July 2013. Rock Castle Construction exercises are set in the time frame of December 2014 through January 2015. Each exercise step that includes a date will have you set the correct date within these time frames.

At the end of each lesson there are also Critical Thinking exercises that will challenge you further. Sort Through the Stack exercises sit you down at the desk of a woman who runs a not-for-profit organization. You will "look through" all of the papers at her desk and make the necessary entries into QuickBooks. Tackle the Tasks exercises allow you to further practice your skills using the Develop Your Skills company file, and the culminating WebQuests send you to the Internet to learn more about QuickBooks and accounting.

How to Use This Book and the Student Files

You may be curious about the large number of student exercise files that come with this book and how using this book as a learning tool compares to working with your own company file. The following questions and answers should help to set you in the right direction!

Why is there a different company file for each exercise?

When you are learning QuickBooks, it is much easier to follow the instructions if your screen matches the illustrations in the book (or your instructor's screen). Having a fresh file at the beginning of each lesson helps ensure that mistakes naturally made by students learning new material do not compound and cause a disconnect between student files and the example illustrations.

A fresh company file for each lesson also means that the lessons in this book can be completed in any order.

What if I want to use one file that continues from lesson to lesson?

You also have the option to use a file that continues from lesson to lesson. You can use each of the end-of-lesson exercise files this way from Lesson 3 onward. This means that once you complete the Reinforce Your Skills exercise in Lesson 3, you can then use the file for Lessons 4–12 in order. The same is true for the Apply Your Skills exercises. To use the same company file for the Develop Your Skill exercises from Lesson 3 onward, you must also complete the "Tackle the Tasks" Critical Thinking exercise at the end of each lesson before continuing to the next lesson. That is, you must complete the Lesson 3 Develop Your Skills exercises and Critical Thinking 3.2 before moving on to the Lesson 4 Develop Your Skills exercises.

Is this how I will work in QuickBooks in "real life"?

No, using a separate file for each type of task (e.g., working with vendors, customers, inventory, etc.) is *not* how you will operate in "real life." In the real world, you will have *one* company file only. The multiple company files are for training purposes only.

Do I have to complete the lessons in the order presented in the book?

No, this book is entirely modular, and you can approach the lessons in any order you choose. For instance, some people feel that the discussion of how to create a company should come after a full discussion of the basics of the software (i.e., after Lesson 5), rather than where it is placed in this book. Lessons may be worked through in any order. Fresh company files provided for each lesson make this possible.

Why do portable company files take so long to restore? What can I do while waiting for a file to restore?

Portable company files are compressed files that QuickBooks must "inflate" before you can use them. Think of the "space bags" you may have seen on an infomercial. Using a vacuum to remove all of the air from a space bag, you can fit some thirty sweaters into a shoebox. (Okay, this is a stretch, but hopefully you get the idea!) This is akin to QuickBooks creating a portable company file. Opening the seal and letting the air back in is like what happens when you restore a portable company file. It takes time for QuickBooks to prepare the portable company files just as it takes time for air to seep back into a space bag so the sweaters can return to their normal volume. If you are using an old computer system or a USB drive, the process will take longer than it will if you have a newer system.

Many users are not happy about waiting for the restore process to occur, but it is a necessity. You may want to begin a lesson by restoring the portable company file first so you can read the concepts discussions while it restores.

What if I want to work with "real" company files rather than portable company files?

You can download either company files or portable company files for this course. Remember that company files will take longer to download and will use more space on your storage drive. On the plus side, you need not restore them in order to use them. For every portable company file there is also a regular company file—except for the Develop Your Skills exercise in Lesson 1, as the first task teaches you how to restore a portable company file.

 Follow the exercise directions based on the file type you are using.

How do I "print to PDF"?

Many instructors request students to print reports as PDF files. This makes it easier to submit your work and it saves paper. To print to PDF, first create and display the report. Next, issue the print command and choose to print to a *.pdf file. What you choose in the Printer field may not exactly match this figure. The key is to print to a *.pdf file type.

Managing Basic QuickBooks Files

Before you can begin working with a QuickBooks file, you need to understand some basic file-management operations. This section will cover how to launch the program, store files, and restore QuickBooks portable company files.

Launching the Program

There is more than one way to do just about everything on a computer, and launching QuickBooks is no exception. Each computer is set up a little differently and may have different options for launching the program depending on shortcuts that have been created. Ask your instructor how he wishes for you to launch QuickBooks in your computer lab. Depending on the version of Windows you are running, QuickBooks will be found in the All Programs or Programs menu accessed via the Start button. Or there may be a shortcut to QuickBooks on the Windows Desktop.

 "There is more than one way to do just about everything on a computer" is not meant to confuse you! You will be introduced to various ways to perform tasks in QuickBooks. Choose whichever methods work best for you.

Types of QuickBooks Files

There are three different types of files in which you can store your QuickBooks data: company files, backup files, and portable company files. The type of file that you will utilize when working with your business is the company file. A backup file is used to store a copy of your data in case your main file becomes corrupted and needs to be restored. A portable company file is much smaller than both company and backup files and is a convenient way to send your company information by email.

There are two other QuickBooks file types that play important support roles for your company data. A network data file has a file extension of .nd, and it contains important configuration data. A transaction log has a file extension of .tlg, and it can help you to recover any data entered after the last backup operation you have performed.

Your company file can be stored anywhere on your computer. The QuickBooks default storage location is the QuickBooks folder for the current version you are using.

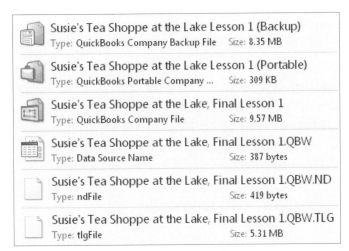

Susie's Tea Shoppe at the Lake Lesson 1 (Backup)
Type: QuickBooks Company Backup File   Size: 8.35 MB

Susie's Tea Shoppe at the Lake Lesson 1 (Portable)
Type: QuickBooks Portable Company ...   Size: 309 KB

Susie's Tea Shoppe at the Lake, Final Lesson 1
Type: QuickBooks Company File   Size: 9.57 MB

Susie's Tea Shoppe at the Lake, Final Lesson 1.QBW
Type: Data Source Name   Size: 387 bytes

Susie's Tea Shoppe at the Lake, Final Lesson 1.QBW.ND
Type: ndFile   Size: 419 bytes

Susie's Tea Shoppe at the Lake, Final Lesson 1.QBW.TLG
Type: tlgFile   Size: 5.31 MB

Backup and portable company files contain all data stored from the company file—just compressed. These files are substantially smaller than company files, and portable company files are great for sending by email. The other, "auxiliary," files do not store company data, but they do have important support functions.

Even though .nd and .tlg. files do not allow you to work with your company information, do *not* delete them. This can affect the integrity of your company data.

Opening and Restoring QuickBooks Files

In order to open a QuickBooks company file, or to restore either a backup or portable company file, you access the command via the File menu. QuickBooks doesn't save files as other applications like word-processing programs do. When you enter transactions, they are saved automatically to the QuickBooks file. To save a QuickBooks file for backup purposes, you create a compressed file—either a backup or portable company file. The act of decompressing a backup or portable company file for use is called restoring.

Open or Restore Company

What type of file do you want to open or restore?

○ Open a **c**ompany file
  - Open a regular company file (.qbw)
  - Open an Accountant's Copy working file (.qba)

○ Restore a bac**k**up copy
  - Restore a backup file (.qbb)
  - Restore files from an online backup

○ Restore a **p**ortable file
  - Re-create a company file that was stored as a portable file (.qbm)

When you open or restore a company file from the File menu, you must choose the file type you are accessing.

QUICK REFERENCE	OPENING AND RESTORING QUICKBOOKS DATA FILES
Task	**Procedure**
Open a QuickBooks company file	■ Choose File→Open or Restore Company. ■ Choose Open a company file; click Next. ■ Navigate to and select the desired file; click Open.
Restore a backup file	■ Choose File→Open or Restore Company. ■ Choose Restore a backup copy; click Next. ■ Navigate to the desired backup copy, either locally or online; click Next. ■ Locate the backup copy you wish to restore; click Open. ■ Click Next, choose the save-to location, and then click Save.
Restore a portable company file	■ Choose File→Open or Restore Company. ■ Choose Restore a portable file; click Next. ■ Navigate to the portable file you wish to restore; click Open. ■ Click Next, choose the save-to location, and then click Save. ■ Be patient as the file restores! Click OK to acknowledge the successful restoration.

DEVELOP YOUR SKILLS 1.1
Restore a Portable Company File

In this exercise, you will restore a QuickBooks portable company file.

Before You Begin: Navigate to the student resource center at http://labyrinthelab.com/qb13 to download the student exercise files for this book. Two versions of the files are available—portable company files and company files.

In the following step, you may see one of two editions of QuickBooks installed on your computer: Pro or Premier. This book works with both of these editions, so choose whichever edition is installed.

1. Click the **Start** button, choose **All Programs**, choose **QuickBooks**, and then choose **QuickBooks 2013**.

   A "splash screen" displays the version of QuickBooks you are launching and opens the program window. If this is the first time you have used the QuickBooks installation on this computer, you will see a QuickBooks Setup window.

2. Choose **File**, and then choose the **Open or Restore Company** command.

In the future, a menu bar command like this will be written as Choose File→Open or Restore Company.

QuickBooks displays the Open or Restore Company window.

3. Click in the circle to the left of **Restore a portable file**.

4. Click **Next**.

5. Follow these steps to restore your file:

Ⓐ Navigate to the location of the downloaded student files.

Ⓑ Click to select the **Chez Devereaux Salon and Spa, Lesson 1 (Portable)** file.

Ⓒ Click the **Open** button.

6. Click **Next**, and then follow these steps to determine where the resulting company file will be located:

Ⓐ Navigate to your file storage location.

Ⓑ Replace Lisa's name with your own (e.g., the author's filename would be Trish's Chez Devereaux Salon and Spa, Lesson 1).

Ⓒ Click the **Save** button.

It may take a few moments for the portable company file to open. The QuickBooks window opens with the Chez Devereaux Salon and Spa company file ready to go. Leave this window open for the next exercise.

7. Click **OK** to close the QuickBooks Information window.

8. Click **No** in the Set Up External Accountant User window, if necessary.

9. Close the **Accountant Center** window, if necessary.
For the exercises in this book you can restore a portable company file or open a company file. This exercise showed you how to restore a portable company file. Use this process as applicable moving forward.

Working with the QuickBooks Window

There are many screen elements with which you are probably familiar if you have ever worked with a Windows-based PC. Many of the elements remain very similar regardless of the program in which you are operating. The elements in common are the title bar and quick-sizing buttons. In addition, many programs utilize menu and tool/Icon Bars that you can see in QuickBooks.

Viewing the QuickBooks Window

The QuickBooks window features many components designed to help you complete all of the tasks necessary to effectively manage your business.

Click a button on the menu bar to see a drop-down menu of options specific to that button.

The title bar shows the company name and the QuickBooks version/edition you are using.

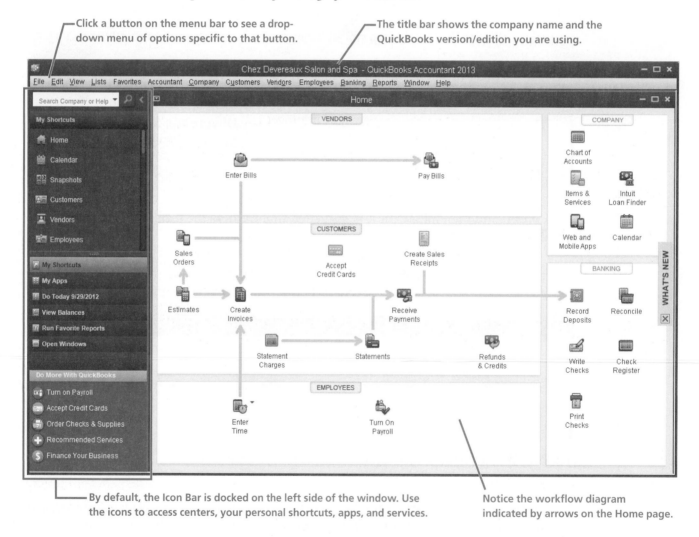

By default, the Icon Bar is docked on the left side of the window. Use the icons to access centers, your personal shortcuts, apps, and services.

Notice the workflow diagram indicated by arrows on the Home page.

Flowing Through the Home Page

The workflow diagram on the Home page is indicated by arrows going from one task icon to another. It is important to follow the diagram so as not to run into trouble. Some instances of trouble that you may encounter are listed below.

- If you write a check rather than pay a bill (for which a bill has been entered), you will overstate expenses.
- If you make a deposit rather than receive a payment for an invoiced amount, you will overstate income.

Sales tax errors can also occur by not following the proper flow outlined on the Home page.

The Icon Bar

The Icon Bar in QuickBooks 2013 has been upgraded and looks very different compared to previous versions.

The new Icon Bar provides a quick way to access QuickBooks centers, snapshots, shortcuts, apps, and services. It is docked on the left side of the QuickBooks window by default, but you can move it to the top of the window or hide it altogether.

All commands accessible on the Icon Bar and Home page can be found through the menu bar, but the opposite is not also true. (They would be a bit too crowded!)

QuickBooks Calendar

The QuickBooks Calendar allows you to keep up with deadlines. This feature also integrates a to-do list so you can keep track of your calendar and tasks in one handy place. The calendar can be accessed via the Company area of the Home page or via the Icon Bar.

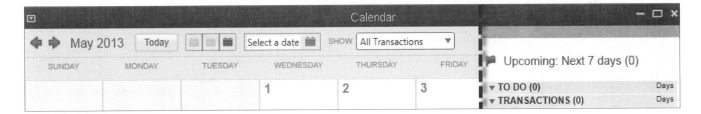

Controlling the QuickBooks Display

If you cannot see the Icon Bar, you can turn it on through the View menu. To show or hide the Icon Bar, choose View→Icon Bar from the menu bar.

The Icon Bar is docked to the left side of the screen.

Note where you can go to customize the Icon Bar.

To single-click or double-click—that is the question. Make it a rule to always single-click first; double-click only if the single-click doesn't work. Most students are "happy double-clickers," and this can get you into trouble (especially if you double-click a toggle button, which is like flipping a light switch up and down and then wondering why the light doesn't stay on). Remember, you always single-click a button and a hyperlink!

Customizing the Home Page

QuickBooks allows users to customize the Home page based on their preferences and how they use the software. The task icons displayed on the Home page will change when a user makes changes to certain preferences. For instance, if a user decides to track inventory in QuickBooks and so turns on the "Inventory and purchase orders are active" preference, additional task icons will be added to the Vendor area of the Home page to assist with the inventory-related tasks. You will learn how to change this preference in Lesson 8, Dealing with Physical Inventory. Changes to other preferences that result in changes to the Home page will be dealt with throughout this book as well.

When you change a preference that will alter the content of the Home page, QuickBooks displays a warning message first.

In addition, you can choose to not display some of the task icons that you may not use as often. The commands will still be available through the menu, just not accessible via a task icon on the Home page.

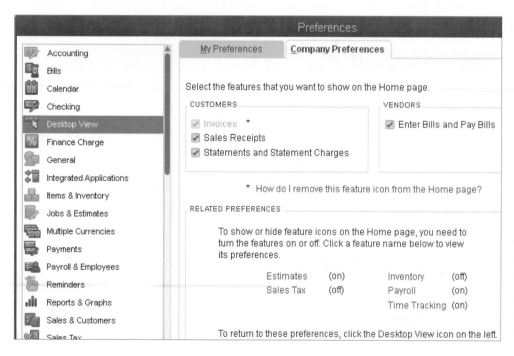

On the Company Preferences tab in the Desktop View category, you can choose to not display certain task icons on the Home page. Add them back at any time by returning to the Preferences window and reselecting the option.

QuickBooks Learning Center Tutorials

Sure to be a valuable resource during your study is the QuickBooks Learning Center. It features a large number of instructional QuickBooks videos that are great learning tools for many students. You will find yourself directed to these tutorials through the new "Visualize!" element in this book. Develop Your Skills 1.2 includes steps to show you how to access a video. In this book you will see a special icon and text whenever a QuickBooks Learning Center tutorial is available (see below).

 Tab: Thank you for upgrading
Topic: What's New in 2013

In addition, QuickBooks provides help for some topics that are not in video format. When you choose one of these topics in the Learning Center, a web page with more information will open.

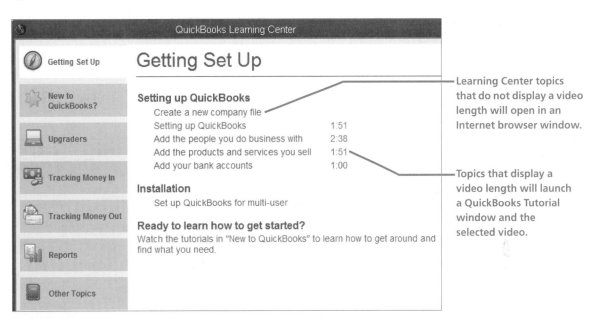

Learning Center topics that do not display a video length will open in an Internet browser window.

Topics that display a video length will launch a QuickBooks Tutorial window and the selected video.

Exiting QuickBooks

When you are finished working with QuickBooks, you will need to close the company file and the program. This can be accomplished by clicking the Close button at the top-right corner of the QuickBooks window or by selecting File→Exit.

QuickBooks displays a warning message when you click the Close button at the top-right corner of the window. Notice that you can choose to not have this message appear again.

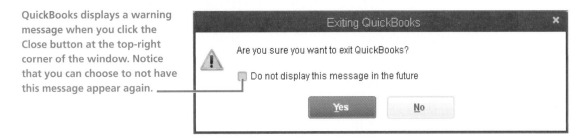

Close All Windows with One Command

If you have a lot of windows open and wish to close them all simultaneously, QuickBooks makes it easy with the Close All command. This command can be accessed by choosing Windows from the menu bar.

Task Icon ToolTips

There are many task icons on the Home page. As you customize your QuickBooks file, you may see more or fewer appear, depending on how you use the program. If you are not sure what a certain task item is used for, simply "mouse over" it (place your mouse pointer over the icon and hold it still, without clicking), and a ToolTip that explains what the task will accomplish for you will appear.

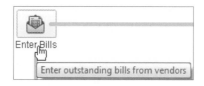

Notice that when you "mouse over" the Enter Bills task icon, a ToolTip appears to explain what task you can accomplish if you click the icon.

DEVELOP YOUR SKILLS 1.2
Explore the QuickBooks Window

In this exercise, you will have a chance to explore the QuickBooks window.

1. Click the **Vendors** button on the Home page.
   The Vendor Center will open, from where you can work with the vendors on your list, manage various vendor transactions, and create new vendors.

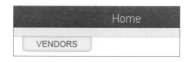

2. Choose **Lists→Chart of Accounts**.
   The Chart of Accounts window opens. This is an example of a list in QuickBooks. It lists the various accounts this company utilizes.

3. Click the **Snapshots** icon on the Icon Bar.
   The Company Snapshot window opens.

4. Choose **Window**.
   Notice that all four of the open windows are listed.

5. Click the **Chart of Accounts** item.
   The Chart of Accounts window appears on top of the other windows and is active. Look at the windows you have opened within QuickBooks and notice that each one has its own set of quick-sizing buttons (Close, Restore/Maximize, Minimize), which you can use to control the display of each window within the QuickBooks program window.

6. Click the **Close** [×] button for the Chart of Accounts window.

7. Choose **Window→Close All**.
   This command will close all open windows for you so you don't have to go chasing "Xs" around the screen! Notice that the Home page is closed since it is a window, but that the Open Windows List is still displayed since it is not.

8. Open the Home page by choosing **Company→Home page**.

9. Choose **View→Hide Icon Bar**.
   QuickBooks no longer displays the Icon Bar.

Exit and Reopen QuickBooks

10. Choose **File→Exit**. Click **No** in the Automatic Backup window, if necessary.
    The QuickBooks window closes.

11. Choose **Start→All Programs→QuickBooks→QuickBooks 2013**.
    Notice that QuickBooks opens the file that you were last working on and that the Icon Bar is not visible.

12. Click **No** in the Set Up an External Accountant User window, if necessary.

13. Close the **Accountant Center** window, if necessary.

14. **Maximize** the QuickBooks program window, if necessary.

15. Choose **View→Left Icon Bar**.
    The Icon Bar reappears.

Mouse Around the Home Page

16. Mouse over the task icon for the following tasks on the Home page, and then write the ToolTips in the spaces provided. If you do not wish to write in the book, print the Mouse Around the Home Page worksheet from the student resource center.

    ■ Chart of Accounts

    _____

    _____

    ■ Create Invoices

    _____

    _____

    ■ Pay Bills

    _____

    _____

    ■ Reconcile

    _____

    _____

17. Submit your responses to step 16 based on the guidelines provided by your instructor.

Explore the QuickBooks Learning Center

Throughout this book, the "Visualize!" feature will point you to QuickBooks video tutorials. These steps will show you how to access these tutorials.

18. Choose **Help→Learning Center Tutorials**.

19. Follow these steps to view a tutorial that will show you how to get around in QuickBooks:

Ⓐ Click **New to QuickBooks?**

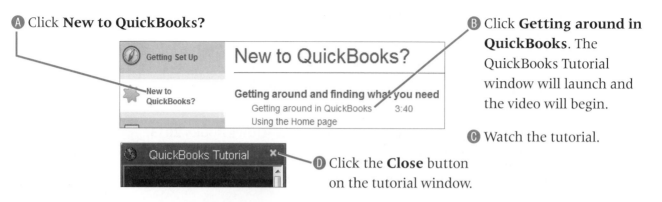

Ⓑ Click **Getting around in QuickBooks**. The QuickBooks Tutorial window will launch and the video will begin.

Ⓒ Watch the tutorial.

Ⓓ Click the **Close** button on the tutorial window.

20. Click the [Go to QuickBooks] button.
Leave QuickBooks open with the Home page displayed for the next exercise.

In the future, you will see text like followingthe to direct you to available videos.

Tab: New to QuickBooks?
Topic: Getting Around in QuickBooks

Backing Up and Updating Your Company File

You have already learned how to restore a portable company file. Now you will learn how to create a backup file. If you have ever lost a file or had your computer "crash" on you, you can surely understand the importance of backing up your data!

When working in QuickBooks, you cannot save your file as you may be used to doing in programs such as Microsoft® Word. Transactions are automatically saved to your company file as you enter them, so the backup operation will back up the entire file.

How often you back up your file is up to you, but you should not let too much time go between backups. If you lose your company file and are forced to restore the backup copy, you will have to enter all of the transactions since your last backup.

Backup Location

Do not back up your company file to your hard drive or where your main company file is stored. Choose an alternate backup location such as a network drive, USB drive, external hard drive, or the QuickBooks' online backup option. If you back up your file to a USB drive or some other removable media, make sure to store the backup copy someplace other than where the original file is physically located. For instance, do not set the backup disc on the PC where the original file is, just in case something such as fire or water damage occurs at the physical location.

Intuit Data Protect

To ensure the security of your QuickBooks data in the event of human error, natural disaster, or a computer crash, you may wish to use Intuit Backup Data. This online service allows you to recover your data in the event you lose your working company file. Data is encrypted and backed up automatically each day to secure servers. You can also use the service to back up other important files, such as reports and contracts, or personal items, such as valuable photos. Learn more about Intuit Data Protect through the File menu bar command. There is a fee associated with this service.

 If your data is not backed up properly, Intuit Data Protect cannot help you. Make sure to back up your data properly!

When to Save a Backup Copy

In QuickBooks, you can choose when to back up your company file. QuickBooks allows you to choose among three options:

- Save it now
- Save it now and schedule future backups
- Only schedule future backups

The future backup options make it easy to back up your company file on a regular basis without having to remember to physically issue the command. If you choose scheduled backups, make sure the backup location is available to QuickBooks at the scheduled times. For instance, ensure that you have your USB flash drive available if that is your backup location.

Updating Your QuickBooks Company File

Earlier in this lesson you learned about the different editions of QuickBooks that are available for purchase each year. In addition, Intuit releases free updates for your QuickBooks software throughout the life of the version. (At some point, Intuit will announce that they will no longer support each version of QuickBooks based on the length of time since it was released.) These updates are available for download over the Internet and may include such things as a new service, a maintenance release, a new feature, or something else relevant to your company.

The easiest way to stay abreast of these updates is to have QuickBooks automatically check for and download them for you through the Automatic Update feature.

Verifying the QuickBooks Release Number

You can easily find out which release number you are working with for your current version of QuickBooks by tapping the F2 key. This will launch a Product Information window that displays not just the release number, but also a lot of other information about your QuickBooks file. In addition, if you choose to open the Update QuickBooks window from the Help menu, you can also find your release number displayed at the top of that window.

FROM THE KEYBOARD
Tap F2 to display the QuickBooks Product Information window

Task	Procedure
Create a portable company file	■ Choose File→Create Copy. ■ Choose Portable company file; click Next. ■ Choose your file storage location; click Save. ■ Click OK to allow QuickBooks to close and reopen your file. ■ Click OK to acknowledge the portable company file creation.
Create a backup file	■ Choose File→Back Up Company→Create Backup. ■ Choose to create a local or online backup; click Next. ■ Choose your file storage location; click OK. ■ Choose when you wish to create the backup copy; click Next. ■ Ensure the location for the backup file is correct; click Save. ■ Click OK to acknowledge the backup file creation.
Start Intuit Data Protect	■ Choose File→Back Up Company→Setup/Activate Online Backup. ■ View the web page with information about Intuit Data Protect that opens.
Set up QuickBooks to automatically update	■ Choose Help→Update QuickBooks. ■ Click the Options tab; choose Yes to Automatically Update your QuickBooks file. ■ Click Close.
Update QuickBooks manually	■ Choose Help→Update QuickBooks. ■ Click the Update Now tab; click to select/deselect the updates you wish to receive. ■ Click Get Updates.
Determine the release number of QuickBooks	■ Choose Help→Update QuickBooks. ■ With the Overview tab displayed, look at the top right of the Update QuickBooks window for the release number, or tap F2 to view the full Production Information window.

Back Up Your QuickBooks Data File

In this exercise, you will create a backup copy of your company file. Ask your instructor where he wants you to back up your file. A cloud storage option is used in this example.

1. Choose **File→Back Up Company→Create Local Backup**.

2. Verify that **Local Backup** is selected, and then click **Next**.

3. Click the **Browse** button.

4. Choose your file storage location in the **Browse for Folder** window. (The drive or folder name will probably be different from the one shown here.)

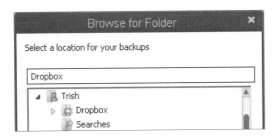

If you are not sure where to save your backup copy, ask your instructor.

5. Click the **OK** button two times.
   If you have chosen to save the file to the same drive on which the company file is stored, QuickBooks will display a warning window.

6. Read the information in the QuickBooks window, and then click the **Use this location** option, if necessary.

7. Choose **Save it now**, and then click **Next** again.

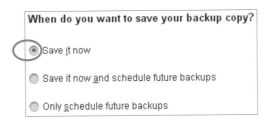

A Save Backup Copy window will appear and should display the file storage location you chose in step 4.

8. Ensure that the correct file storage location is displayed, and then click **Save**.
   QuickBooks will first verify that your file is not corrupted and will then create a backup copy in the location you specified.

9. Click **OK** to acknowledge the information window that tells you a backup file has been created.

10. Choose the appropriate option for your situation:
    - If you are continuing on to the next lesson or to the end-of-lesson exercises, leave QuickBooks open.
    - If you are finished working in QuickBooks for now, choose **File→Exit**.

Concepts Review

Concepts Review   http://labyrinthelab.com/qb13

To check your knowledge of the key concepts introduced in this lesson, complete the Concepts Review quiz by going to the URL listed above.

Reinforce Your Skills

In all of the Reinforce Your Skills exercises, you will be working with a company called Tea Shoppe at the Lake. This business sells food and drinks and provides catering services. Susie Elsasser is the proprietor of the business. You will assist Susie in a variety of QuickBooks tasks as you work your way through this book.

REINFORCE YOUR SKILLS 1.1
Find Your Way Around QuickBooks

In this exercise, you will take a look at Susie's QuickBooks company file. You will begin by opening a portable company file.

1. Start **QuickBooks**, if necessary.

2. Choose **File→Open or Restore Company**.

3. Choose to **Restore** a portable file, and then click **Next**.

4. Follow these steps to select the file to restore:

Ⓐ Navigate to your file storage location.

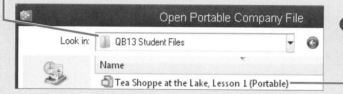

Ⓑ Double-click to select **Tea Shoppe at the Lake, Lesson 1 (Portable)**.

Double-clicking the filename works the same as if you had single-clicked the filename and then clicked the Open button.

5. Click **Next** to move to the next screen.

6. Follow these steps to choose where to locate your new company file:

Ⓐ Navigate to your file storage location.

Ⓑ Here, type your name in front of the company name.

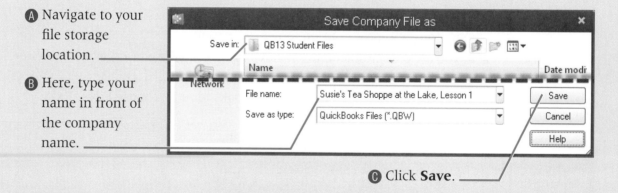

Ⓒ Click **Save**.

There is a long pause as QuickBooks opens the portable company file.

7. Click **OK** in the QuickBooks Information window, if necessary.
QuickBooks opens the company file and displays the Home page.

Navigate in the Company File

Now you will explore the QuickBooks window.

8. Click the **Items & Services** task icon in the Company area of the Home page.
   QuickBooks displays the Item List window.

9. Click the **Customers** button on the Icon Bar.

10. Choose **Vendors→Enter Bills**.
    QuickBooks displays the Enter Bills window, ready for you to enter a bill from a vendor.

11. Click **App Center** on the Icon Bar.
    A "QuickBooks Connect" Internet browser window launches with information.

12. Choose **Window→Item List**.

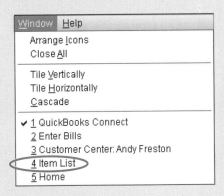

   The Item List window appears on top of the other open windows. Notice that all open windows are listed at the bottom of the Window menu list. Clicking on one of them will make that window active.

13. Choose **Window→Close All**.
    The Close All command closes all open windows, including the Home page.

14. Click the **Home** icon on the Icon Bar.
    QuickBooks displays the Home page.

Tab: New to QuickBooks?
Topic: Using the Home Page

Get to Know QuickBooks Better

Before you begin this section of the exercise, print or save the Get to Know QuickBooks Better worksheet from the student resource center.

15. Complete the Get to Know QuickBooks Better worksheet.

16. Submit your worksheet based on the guidelines provided by your instructor.

17. Choose the appropriate option for your situation:
    - If you are continuing on to the next lesson or the rest of the end-of-lesson exercises, leave QuickBooks open.
    - If you are finished working in QuickBooks for now, choose **File→Exit**.

Work with T-Accounts

In this exercise, you will use your accounting knowledge. You may wish to refer to Appendix A for assistance, or if you have a copy of Labyrinth's The ABCs of Accounting, 2nd Edition, *that would be a helpful resource as well.*

You can either write directly in the book or download the Work with T-Accounts worksheet from the student resource center.

1. Below or on your printed worksheet, write the following account names at the tops of the T charts.
   - Bank Service Charges
   - Food Sales
   - Checking Account
   - Loan for Delivery Vehicle
   - Prepaid Insurance
   - Retained Earnings

2. Next to each account, write the account types (asset, liability, equity, income, or expense).

3. Label the debit and credit side of each T.

4. Place an **NB** on the appropriate side of the T to indicate the normal balance of each account.

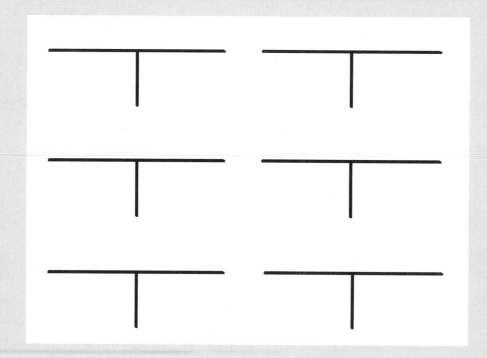

5. Submit your work based on the guidelines provided by your instructor.

Apply Your Skills

In all of the Apply Your Skills exercises, you will be working with a company called Wet Noses Veterinary Clinic run by Dr. Sadie James, DVM. She is a small-animal vet specializing in dogs and cats.

Restore a Backup File and Explore QuickBooks

In this exercise, you will restore a backup file (up to this point you have been working with portable company files) and take a look at Dr. Sadie James' QuickBooks company file.

1. Start **QuickBooks**.

2. Restore the **Wet Noses Veterinary Clinic, Lesson 1** backup company file. Name the restored company file **[Your first name]'s Wet Noses Veterinary Clinic, Lesson 1**.
   You are restoring a backup *file here, not a portable company file.*

3. Open the following windows using any of the methods described in this lesson.
   - Create Invoice
   - Item List
   - Customer Center
   - Chart of Accounts
   - Pay Bills
   - Company Snapshot

4. Display the **Item List** window above the other open windows.
   Next you will create a screen capture to submit to your instructor. Two options are presented. Use the option as directed by your instructor.

Option 1: Capture Your Work Using Microsoft Word

5. Tap PrtScn, and then launch **Microsoft Word**.
   Your screen capture is automatically copied to the Window's Clipboard, ready for pasting.

6. Display a blank document, and then press Ctrl + v.
   Your screen capture is pasted into the Word document.

7. Save your Word document as **[Your first name]'s AYS Lesson 1 Capture** and submit it according to the guidelines provided by your instructor.

8. Choose the appropriate option for your situation:
   - If you are continuing on to the next lesson or the rest of the end-of-lesson exercises, leave QuickBooks open.
   - If you are finished working in QuickBooks for now, choose **File→Exit**.

Option 2: Complete a Worksheet to Capture Your Work

5. Print or save the **Capture Your Work** worksheet from the student resource center.

6. Complete and then submit the worksheet according to the guidelines provided by your instructor.

7. Choose the appropriate option for your situation:

   - If you are continuing on to the next lesson or the rest of the end-of-lesson exercises, leave QuickBooks open.

   - If you are finished working in QuickBooks for now, choose **File→Exit**.

Get a Grasp on Accounting Principles

In this exercise, you will use your accounting knowledge to brainstorm the accounts that would be required for the business that you will be working with in the Apply Your Skills exercises throughout the rest of this book.

You can either write directly in the book or download the Get a Grasp on Accounting Principles worksheet from the student resource center.

1. Think about a veterinary practice. On the printed worksheet or in the following space, list the accounts that you feel would be required on the business's Chart of Accounts.

2. In the second column, list the type of account for each.

3. In the third column, state whether the normal balance for the account would be a debit or a credit.

Account Name	Account Type (Asset, Liability, Equity, Income, Expense)	Normal Balance (DR/CR)

4. Submit your work based on the guidelines provided by your instructor.

Critical Thinking

1.1 Use the Web as a Learning Tool

Throughout this book, you will be provided with an opportunity to use the Internet as a learning tool by completing WebQuests. According to the original creators of WebQuests, as described on their website (WebQuest.org), a WebQuest is "an inquiry-oriented activity in which most or all of the information used by learners is drawn from the web." To complete the WebQuest projects in this book, navigate to the student resource center at http://labyrinthelab.com/qb13 and choose the WebQuest for the lesson on which you are currently working. The subject of each WebQuest will be relevant to the material found in the lesson.

WebQuest Subject: Learn more about QuickBooks versions and determine which one is most appropriate for your business

Creating a Company

LESSON OBJECTIVES

After studying this lesson, you will be able to:

- Plan and create a company
- Edit your QuickBooks preferences and customize a company file
- Enter opening balances and historical transactions
- Run list reports and find help for QuickBooks
- Set up QuickBooks users
- Understand closing the books "QuickBooks style"

N ow that you have had a chance to explore the QuickBooks window and learn about how to work with QuickBooks files, it is time to create a company file. By taking the knowledge that you gain from this lesson and coupling it with what you will learn in the rest of the book, you will be ready at the end of your QuickBooks studies to create a file for your own company.

Chez Devereaux Salon and Spa

Lisa Devereaux is a new small-business owner who has opened a small but upscale salon and spa in a serene wooded setting. She has three multi-licensed cosmetologists and one licensed massage therapist who will rent the space needed for creating quality services. There are three styling chairs for hair services and one private room available for massages and private waxing services.

Before creating this company, Lisa's friend Adrianna told her about QuickBooks and what it could do for her new company in terms of saving time and improving efficiency. Adrianna suggested that Lisa write down some important information in a checklist before starting her QuickBooks company.

Chez Devereaux Salon and Spa
Company Checklist for QuickBooks

Address:

444 North Pelham St.

Rhinelander, WI 54501

Fiscal year: January

Tax form: 1040

Accounting basis: Cash

Federal EIN: 99-9999999

State ID: 999-9999-9

Phone:

715.555.4010

715.555.4015 fax

Need from accountant: Chart of accounts, what should I use for items?

Vendors: need names, addresses, account numbers, and payment terms for each

Customers: need names and contact information, payment terms, and account numbering system

Start date: 4/30/2013

Lisa has written out the information she needs to have handy to start her new company file.

Planning and Creating a Company

Before you begin to set up your QuickBooks company, it is important to do some careful planning. You must think about the information you want to get from QuickBooks before you begin. As with many situations, garbage in will equal garbage out!

Choosing Your Start Date

Choosing the start date that is right for you is important. Very ambitious people may think they want to start their QuickBooks file the day they started their company. This is a nice idea, but not very practical for a busy or cost-conscious entrepreneur.

Keep in mind that you must enter all transactions for your company (invoices, checks, bills paid, etc.) from the start date forward. If you choose a date too far in the past, this process will take a long time to complete.

You should strive to start your QuickBooks company file at the beginning of a month, a quarter, or your fiscal year. You may want to discuss this matter with your accountant to help determine the best and most practical starting date for your business. The actual start date should be the last day of the prior period rather than the first day of the current period; for example, we will use 4/30/13 rather than 5/1/13.

The Five Ps

Sit down and think about what you want QuickBooks to do for you. It is difficult to go back and add a new field for every customer or change every transaction! A little planning at the beginning can save you a lot of time in the future. Think about the five Ps (Prior Planning Prevents Poor Performance) as you get ready to start your company and take into account the needs of all of the stakeholders involved. What type of information will each stakeholder need to be able to interact efficiently with your business? Potential stakeholders may include your accountant, customers, vendors, employees, stockholders, partners, etc.

How Many Companies Should You Create?

Generally, the best guideline is to set up a separate QuickBooks company file for each tax return you will file.

> **FLASHBACK TO GAAP: BUSINESS ENTITY**
>
> Remember that the business is separate from the owners and from other businesses. Revenues and expenses of the business should be kept separate from the personal expenses of the business owner. Also, revenue and expenses for separate companies must be kept separate from the other companies that may be operated by the same owner.

Creating a New QuickBooks File

There are several ways you can go about creating your new QuickBooks file. Look at the following list to determine which one will work best for your situation.

- Create a company from scratch
- Upgrade from a previous version of QuickBooks
- Convert from a different QuickBooks edition
- Convert a Quicken file
- Convert a Peachtree© file

Choosing a Setup Path

When creating a new company, QuickBooks makes it easy for you to select from a variety of options. Express Start is the easiest method; use the Detailed Start method if you wish to fine-tune your company file as you set it up.

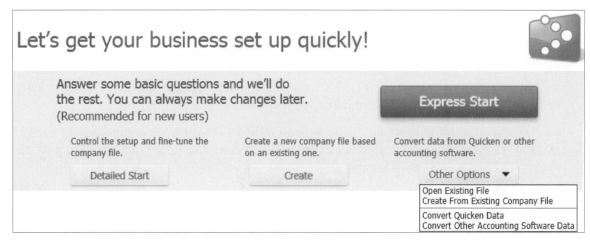

In this window, choose the method for creating a company that works best for you.

Express Start

New in QuickBooks 2012 was the Express Start option for company setup. It allows you to provide a minimum amount of information and get started with QuickBooks right away. Once you have entered the Express Start information and your company file is created, QuickBooks helps you set up the rest of the information needed to run your business. You will use this method in the Develop Your Skills exercises in this lesson.

Detailed Start (Easy Step Interview)

A click of the Detailed Start button takes you to the EasyStep Interview window. Here you provide more information when creating your company file. You will use this method in a Reinforce Your Skills exercise at the end of the lesson.

Using an Old QuickBooks File as a Template for a New File

If you wish to create your new company file based on an older one, QuickBooks will allow you to keep the lists and preferences from the old file while removing the old, unneeded transactions. Some QuickBooks users prefer to keep a separate company file for each fiscal year of the business, and being able to keep preferences and list data while removing transactions makes this easy.

To complete this task, you must clean up your company data from the old file using the Clean Up Company Wizard. Be sure you have a large window of time available before you start this process, as it can take some time to clean up a large file. QuickBooks will create a backup and archive copy of your file as a part of this process, as well as verify file integrity. You will work with the cleanup process in Lesson 12, Reporting, Closing the Books, and Adjusting Entries, as it is also used by many companies to clean up a company file after closing the books.

Converting Data to Start a New Company File

An additional option available to you when creating a new company file is to convert an existing file from Quicken or other accounting software data.

A Setup Checklist

There are some items that you should gather before you begin to set up your company. Review the checklist of items to collect in the student resource center for this book at http://labyrinthelab.com/qb13.

A Quick Payroll Primer

You will be introduced to running payroll in QuickBooks in Lesson 9, Using QuickBooks for Payroll. If you choose to create your new company using the Detailed Start method, you need to understand a bit about how QuickBooks deals with payroll first.

If you wish to include an addition or deduction on an employee's paycheck, you must first set it up as a payroll item. During the EasyStep interview you will have an opportunity to create payroll items. If you will be using QuickBooks for payroll and wish to set it up during the setup process (you can also set this up after the fact if you choose, and that process will be covered in Lesson 9), you will need to have the following information ready.

- Information for each employee: name, address, social security number, and withholding information (from their W-4)
- All "additions" that will be found on a paycheck, such as salaries, hourly wages, and bonuses
- All payroll taxes the employees are required to pay
- All payroll taxes you, as the employer, are required to pay
- Any additional deductions you will be withholding from paychecks, such as investment plan contributions or child support payments

Your Starter Chart of Accounts

During the setup process, QuickBooks will ask you to search for the business type that your company most closely resembles. QuickBooks will use your choice to create a Chart of Accounts close to what you need. (It will take you less time to edit it to fit your unique business than to start from scratch.) QuickBooks will also create profile lists based on your selection. You will work with the customer and vendor profile lists in Lesson 3, Working with Vendors. Choose carefully here, as you cannot go back and change the business type option.

In order to ensure your books are set up properly, you should talk to your accountant to make sure that your chart of accounts is set up correctly. A quick conversation and small bill now can prevent a large bill in the future.

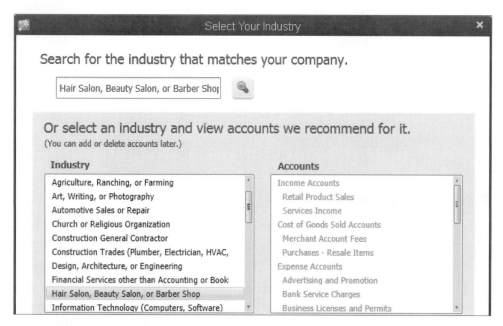

QuickBooks has several predefined company chart of accounts for specific industries that will help users in those or similar industries streamline their setup processes.

Once you select a business type during the setup process, you cannot change it later. You can edit and delete accounts and list entries, though.

Account Beginning Balances

If you have an existing company for which you are setting up QuickBooks, you should enter the balances of all asset and liability accounts during the setup process (although you can also enter them in the registers later). These account beginning balances are termed "opening balances" in QuickBooks. You will learn more about entering and editing these balances later in the lesson.

After you create your first balance sheet account, QuickBooks will create an Opening Balance Equity account, in which the account beginning balances you enter will be placed. Asset beginning balances credit the account, while liability beginning balances debit it. This account is created so you can have a balance sheet that is accurate from the start even if you haven't entered all assets and liabilities for your company.

TYPES OF ACCOUNTS IN QUICKBOOKS		
Account Type	**Example**	**Normal Balance**
Bank	Checking Account	Debit
Accounts Receivable	Accounts Receivable	Debit
Other Current Asset	Prepaid Rent	Debit
Fixed Asset	Machinery	Debit
Other Asset	Long Term Notes Receivable	Debit
Accounts Payable	Accounts Payable	Credit
Credit Card	Silver Falls Bank Visa	Credit
Other Current Liability	Short Term Loan	Credit

TYPES OF ACCOUNTS IN QUICKBOOKS (continued)

Account Type	Example	Normal Balance
Long Term Liability	Auto Loan	Credit
Equity	Opening Balance Equity	Credit
Income	Sales	Credit
Cost of Goods Sold	Cost of Goods Sold	Debit
Expense	Telephone Expense	Debit
Other Income*	Interest Income	Credit
Other Expense*	Corporate Taxes	Debit

* Other Income and Other Expense accounts are used to track income and expenses that are not the result of normal day-to-day business operations.

QUICK REFERENCE   CREATING A NEW COMPANY FILE

Task	Procedure
Create a new company in QuickBooks	▪ Go through the checklist to make sure you have all necessary information. ▪ Plan what you want QuickBooks to do for you. ▪ Choose File→New Company. ▪ Choose the method you want to use to set up your company file.
Edit information for a new company	▪ Choose Company→Company Information. ▪ Edit the information in the Company Information window.
Create a new company file based on a prior one, keeping list data and preferences	▪ Choose File→Utilities→Clean Up Company Data. ▪ Choose to either remove all transactions as of a specific date or all transactions in the file. ▪ Continue through the wizard screens. ▪ Click Begin Cleanup. ▪ Click OK to close the "message;" click Create Back Up.

DEVELOP YOUR SKILLS 2.1
Create a New Company

In this exercise, you will use Express Start to set up the company for Chez Devereaux Salon and Spa.

1. Launch **QuickBooks**.

2. Choose **File→New Company**.

3. Click the **Express Start** button.

Express Start

4. Follow these steps to enter the first set of company data:

Ⓐ Type **Chez Devereaux Salon and Spa**.

Ⓑ Tap Tab, and then type **hair**.

Ⓒ Click to select **Hair Salon, Beauty Salon, or Barber Shop**.

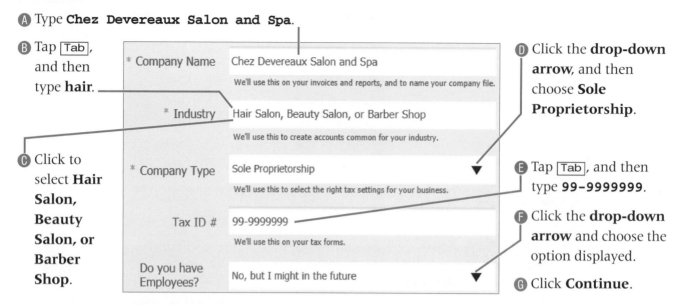

Ⓓ Click the **drop-down arrow**, and then choose **Sole Proprietorship**.

Ⓔ Tap Tab, and then type **99-9999999**.

Ⓕ Click the **drop-down arrow** and choose the option displayed.

Ⓖ Click **Continue**.

5. Follow these steps to enter your business contact information:

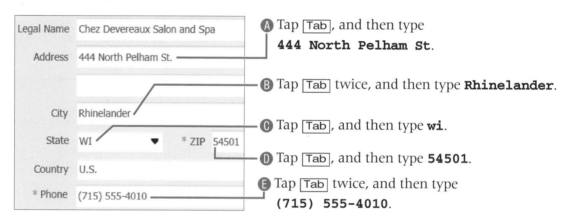

Ⓐ Tap Tab, and then type **444 North Pelham St**.

Ⓑ Tap Tab twice, and then type **Rhinelander**.

Ⓒ Tap Tab, and then type **wi**.

Ⓓ Tap Tab, and then type **54501**.

Ⓔ Tap Tab twice, and then type **(715) 555-4010**.

In this window, you will need to type the phone number and address just as you wish them to appear on forms—including punctuation such as parentheses, dashes, or periods. Take care to spell everything correctly when entering this company information. Imagine how embarrassing it would be to send out invoices, bills, and other correspondence with your own company name and information incorrect!

6. Click **Preview Your Settings**.
QuickBooks will open the Preview Your Company Settings window, where you can choose where to save your file.

| Preview Your Settings |

7. Click the **Company File Location** tab, and then click **Change Location**.

| Change Location |

8. Choose your file storage location in the **Browse for Folder** window, and then click **OK**.

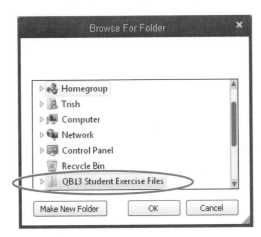

9. Click **OK** again, and then click **Create Company File**.
   QuickBooks creates your new company file, which will take a minute or so. Once the file is created, the QuickBooks Setup window will appear.

10. Click **Start Working**.
    We will be adding information in the next several lessons, but not right now.

    The Quick Start Center, which is designed to help you perform basic tasks, will appear. We will be working from the QuickBooks Home page as we progress through this book, so this window is not necessary.

11. Click the **Close** button at the top-right corner of the Quick Start Center window.
    The QuickBooks Home page for your new company file will be displayed. Leave it open and continue to the next topic.

Editing Your QuickBooks Preferences

The way you interact with QuickBooks is controlled by the preferences you select. The Preferences window has twenty-one categories of preferences you can set or modify so Quick-Books can work more efficiently for your company.

Use these tabs to switch between company and personal preferences with a click of the mouse.

Here are the twenty-one preference categories.

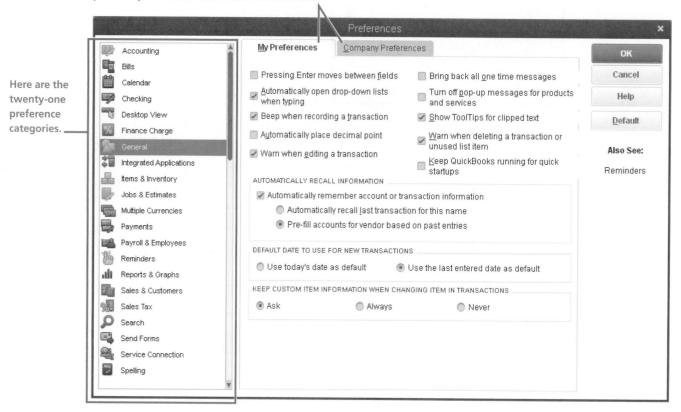

Notice the many General preferences each individual user can choose. Each option will affect how the individual interacts with QuickBooks.

 Tab: Getting Set Up
Topic: Setting up QuickBooks

Company vs. Personal Preferences

Each category has two tabs on which changes to preferences can be set: the Company Preferences tab and the My Preferences (personal) tab. Company preferences are controlled by the administrator. They determine how the entire company interacts with QuickBooks. Personal preferences are controlled by each individual user. They dictate interactions between Quick-Books and that one user only.

The following illustrations show an example of a company and a personal preference.

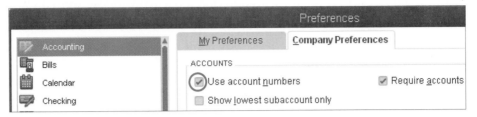

Changes made by an administrator affect all users. Here, administrator turned on the preference to use account numbers. In the Chart of Accounts, there would then be an account number associated with each account.

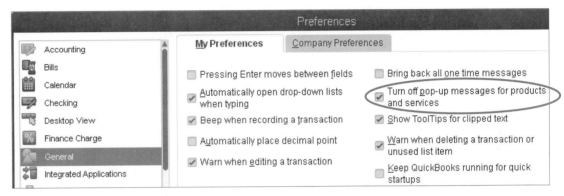

Here, a user can change the setting for pop-up messages on the My Preferences tab that will affect only her individual QuickBooks user login.

Setting a Company Preference: Account Numbers

Many businesses use account numbers for the accounts in their Chart of Accounts. You will be using account numbers as you work with the company file for Chez Devereaux Salon and Spa. Account numbers are somewhat standard within the accounting world. "Somewhat" means that each account type begins with the same number, but the accounts listed within the account type are not universally numbered. Examine the following table to understand how account numbers work. Note that account numbers have a minimum of four characters, and you can use five or six. For instance, a Checking account (which is an asset) could be numbered 1000, 10000, or 100000. This book will use five-digit account numbers.

Account number starts with:	Type of account	Example
1	Asset	Checking Account
2	Liability	Accounts Payable
3	Equity	Retained Earnings
4	Income	Retail Product Sales
5	Cost of Goods Sold	Purchases – Resale Items
6	Expenses	Utilities Expense
7	Other Income	Interest Income
8	Other Expense	Sales Tax Penalty

Setting a Personal Preference

In many of the Preferences categories, an individual user can choose from a variety of options. In the following exercise, you will choose to turn off all pop-up messages for products and services.

QUICK REFERENCE	EDITING BASIC QUICKBOOKS PREFERENCES
Task	**Procedure**
Edit QuickBooks file preferences	▪ Choose Edit→Preferences.
	▪ Click the category (listed on the left side of the window) in which you wish to make a change.
	▪ Choose either the Company Preferences or My Preferences tab.
	▪ Make any necessary changes.
	▪ Click OK to save the new preferences.

DEVELOP YOUR SKILLS 2.2

Change Your Preferences

In this exercise, you will turn on the account number preference for the company and turn off pop-up messages for the user.

Whether to turn on the use of account numbers is a company preference, is set by the company administrator, and cannot be changed by other users.

1. Choose **Edit→Preferences**.

2. Follow these steps to turn on the account numbers preference:

Ⓐ Click **Accounting**.   Ⓑ Click the **Company Preferences** tab.

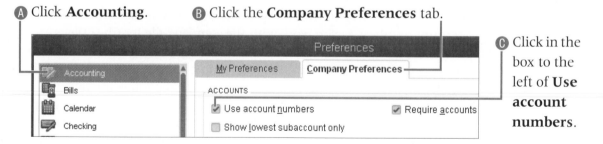

Ⓒ Click in the box to the left of **Use account numbers**.

The Show lowest subaccount only preference will be introduced in Lesson 11, Working with Balance Sheet Accounts and Budgets.

3. Click **OK** to accept the new preference.

Change a Desktop View Personal Preference

Now, you will turn off pop-up messages.

4. Choose **Edit→Preferences**.

5. Follow these steps to choose to turn off pop-up messages for products and services:

Ⓐ Click **General**.   Ⓑ Ensure that the **My Preferences** tab is displayed.

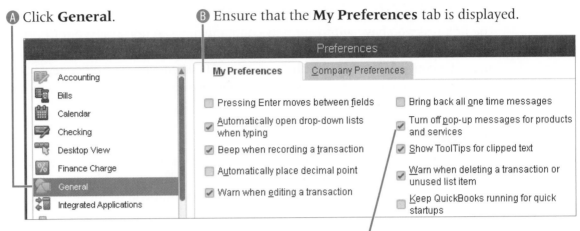

Ⓒ Click to place a checkmark in the box to turn off pop-up messages.

6. Click **OK** to accept the new preference.
Leave the QuickBooks window open and continue with the next topic.

Customizing a Company File

During the setup process, QuickBooks allows you to choose a business type similar to your own. It is up to you to take this generic file and customize it to fit your company.

Modifying the Lists in a New File

You will need to look at several lists after you set up your new QuickBooks company to ensure they are correct. If any of them are incorrect or incomplete, you will need to edit, delete, or add entries to them. These lists include the following:

- The Chart of Accounts
- The Customers & Jobs List
- The Vendor List
- The Item List
- Customer & Vendor Profile Lists

- The Fixed Asset Item List
- The Employees List
- The Payroll Items List
- The Price Level List

Entries in these lists can be created during the EasyStep interview. If you choose to skip the interview, you will need to populate these lists once the company has been created.

The Chart of Accounts

The Chart of Accounts is composed of all of the asset, liability, equity, income, and expense accounts your company utilizes. You use the Chart of Accounts list window to create new accounts, edit existing accounts, and delete unused accounts.

Customizing the Chart of Accounts

The first task you have with your new company file is to fine-tune your Chart of Accounts. If you are using QuickBooks for an existing business, you will want to talk to your accountant and get a copy of your current Chart of Accounts. If you are starting a new business, you may also want to contact your accountant for guidance on how best to set up your Chart of Accounts for your unique company.

Adding Accounts

When you add an account to the Chart of Accounts, make sure to select the correct account type, as this is one of the most prevalent errors accountants find in their clients' QuickBooks files. Keep in mind that your "behind the scenes" action will be incorrect if the wrong account type is selected.

To Edit or Delete—That Is the Question...

The generic Chart of Accounts that QuickBooks provides will have some accounts you probably won't need for your unique business. You can choose to either rename (edit) these accounts or delete them. Renaming an account is appropriate if you are working with the same account type. Deleting is appropriate if you no longer need additional accounts of the same type.

Moving and Sorting Accounts Within the List

You can change the order in which accounts appear within your Chart of Accounts. By default, QuickBooks alphabetizes accounts by type. The Chart of Accounts is structured so that assets are listed first, liabilities second, equity accounts third, income accounts fourth, cost of goods sold accounts fifth, and expense accounts last. This structure must remain intact; you can only move accounts around within their own type. Moving list items works the same way in the various lists in QuickBooks—by clicking and dragging the diamond to the left of the list entry.

If you move your accounts and later decide you want them alphabetized by type once again, QuickBooks allows you to resort the list. Resorting the list restores the QuickBooks default.

Subaccounts

To keep precise records, you may wish to use QuickBooks subaccounts. For instance, to keep the number of expense accounts within reason, you are likely to utilize only one telephone expense account for all of your telephone lines. To track expenses more closely, though, you may want to have separate accounts for your office phone, office fax, and cellular phone. Subaccounts are a great way to track these separate expenses while keeping the number of expense accounts down.

When you run Profit & Loss reports and budgets, you have the option to expand the report (show subaccounts) to show detail or collapse the report (show only main accounts) for brevity.

Using Classes in QuickBooks

In Lesson 7, Introducing the Accounting Cycle and Using Classes, you will go into depth in regards to using classes in QuickBooks. Classes allow you to track income and expenses for one specific aspect of your company, and they are not tied to any particular customer, job, vendor, or item. For right now, understand that if you choose to use classes for your own business, the best option is to set them up when you create your new company file.

QUICK REFERENCE	CUSTOMIZING THE CHART OF ACCOUNTS
Task	**Procedure**
Add an account	■ Click the Account menu button; choose New.
	■ Choose the correct account type; click Continue.
	■ Enter all necessary information.
	■ Click Save & Close or Save & New.
Edit an account	■ Single-click the account you wish to edit.
	■ Click the Account menu button; choose Edit.
	■ Make any necessary changes; then click Save & Close.
Delete an account	■ Single-click the account you wish to delete.
	■ Click the Account menu button and choose Delete; click OK to confirm.
Create a subaccount	■ Click the main account for which you wish to create a subaccount.
	■ Click the Account menu button; choose New.
	■ Choose the correct account type; click Continue.
	■ Type the name of the subaccount; click in the box for Subaccount of.
	■ Click the drop-down arrow, click the main account from the list, and then click OK.
Move an account	■ Click the account you want to move.
	■ Place your mouse pointer over the diamond to the left of the account name until you see a four-way arrow.
	■ Click and drag the account to the new location within the same account type.
Re-sort accounts	■ Click the Account menu button; choose Re-sort.

DEVELOP YOUR SKILLS 2.3
Make the File Fit Your Business

In this exercise, you will take the generic Chart of Accounts created for Chez Devereaux Salon and Spa and make it fit the needs of the company.

The first task is to add an account that Lisa needs but that was not provided in the generic Chart of Accounts, Checking.

FROM THE KEYBOARD
Ctrl+a to open the Chart of Accounts

1. Click the **Chart of Accounts** task icon in the Company area of the Home page.
   QuickBooks opens the generic Chart of Accounts created for you. Notice the account numbers that you turned on in the previous exercise.

Chart of
Accounts

FROM THE KEYBOARD

Ctrl+n to create a new account.

2. Follow these steps to create the new account:

Ⓐ Click the **Account** menu button at the bottom left of the window.

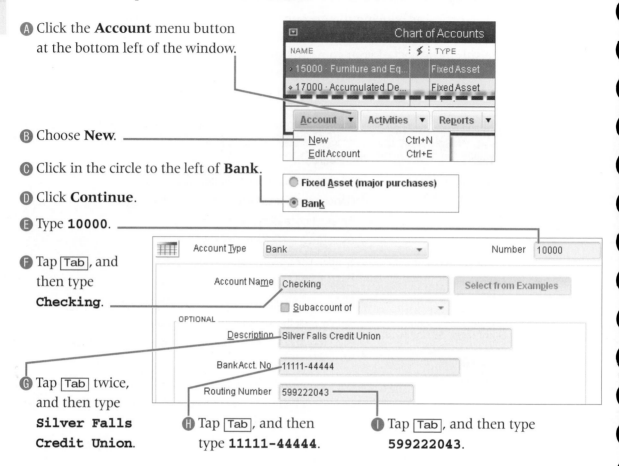

Chart of Accounts

NAME	𝄢	TYPE
◇ 15000 · Furniture and Eq...		Fixed Asset
◇ 17000 · Accumulated De...		Fixed Asset

Account ▼ **Activities** ▼ **Reports** ▼

New　　　Ctrl+N
Edit Account　　Ctrl+E

Ⓑ Choose **New**.

Ⓒ Click in the circle to the left of **Bank**.

○ **Fixed Asset (major purchases)**
◉ **Bank**

Ⓓ Click **Continue**.

Ⓔ Type **10000**.

Account Type ___Bank___ ▼　　　Number ___10000___

Account Name ___Checking___　　**Select from Examples**

☐ Subaccount of ___ ▼

OPTIONAL

Description ___Silver Falls Credit Union___

Bank Acct. No ___11111-44444___

Routing Number ___599222043___

Ⓕ Tap Tab, and then type **Checking**.

Ⓖ Tap Tab twice, and then type **Silver Falls Credit Union**.

Ⓗ Tap Tab, and then type **11111-44444**.

Ⓘ Tap Tab, and then type **599222043**.

3. Click **Save & Close**.

4. Click **No** in the Set Up Online Services window.
Take a look at your Chart of Accounts window and notice the new Checking account at the top of the list.

Edit an Account

In Lesson 4, Working with Customers, you will learn how to create items and route them to the proper account in the Chart of Accounts. For now, you will rename the sales account to which you will direct one of the service items.

5. Scroll down the Chart of Accounts, if necessary, and then single-click the **Services Income** account.

FROM THE KEYBOARD

Ctrl+e to edit the selected account

6. Click the **Account** menu button, and then choose **Edit Account**.

7. Follow these steps to rename the account:

Ⓐ Click in front of *Services Income*, and then type **Hair**.

Ⓑ Click between *salon* and *services*, and then type **hair**.

Ⓒ Click **Save & Close**.

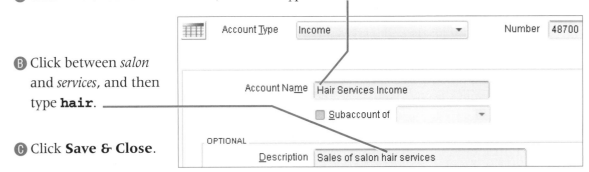

Delete an Account

8. Scroll to the bottom of the Chart of Accounts window, and then single-click the **Ask My Accountant** account.

9. Click the **Account** menu button, and then choose **Delete Account**.

10. Click **OK** in the Delete Account window.
    Since you cannot undo an account deletion, QuickBooks verifies your choice.

FROM THE KEYBOARD
Ctrl+d to delete the selected account

Create Subaccounts

Lisa wants to track her telephone expenses more carefully, so she has decided to use subaccounts.

11. Single-click **Telephone Expense** in the Chart of Accounts.

12. Click the **Account** menu button, and then choose **New**.

13. Follow these steps to create your new subaccount:

Ⓐ Click in the circle to the left of **Expense**.

Ⓑ Click **Continue**.

Ⓒ Type **68110** as the Number.

Ⓓ Tap Tab, and then type **Office Phone**.

Ⓔ Click in the box to the left of **Subaccount of**.

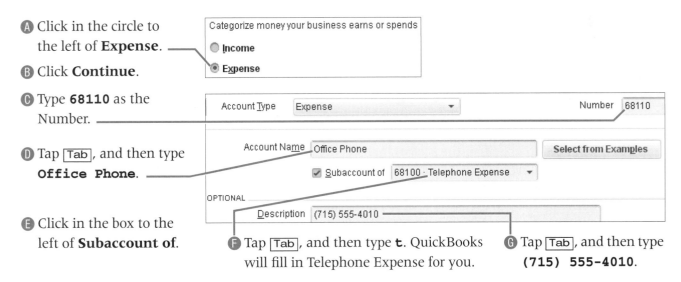

Ⓕ Tap Tab, and then type **t**. QuickBooks will fill in Telephone Expense for you.

Ⓖ Tap Tab, and then type **(715) 555-4010**.

14. Click **Save & New** to add your new subaccount and leave the window open to add another one.

15. Follow **step 13 C–G** to add the following additional subaccounts for Telephone Expense, clicking **Save & New** after creating the first additional subaccount.

Account Number	Subaccount Name	Description
68120	Fax Line	(715) 555-4015
68130	Cell Phone	(715) 555-1011

16. Click **Save & Close** to create the last new subaccount and close the window.

17. Close the **Chart of Accounts** window.

Working with Opening Balances and Historical Transactions

If you chose a start date for your company that was not the first day you were in business, it is important to enter all of the historical transactions and opening balances in your file.

Entering and Editing Account Opening Balances

You need to make sure that you have the correct opening balances in QuickBooks for all of your accounts. There are five different methods by which you can enter opening balances. The type of account that you are dealing with determines which method, or combination of methods, will work the best. The five methods available are:

- EasyStep Interview (for bank accounts only)
- Journal entries
- Forms (for individual transactions)
- Registers
- Lists (lump sums can be entered when creating entries)

Editing a Beginning Balance

If you need to correct a beginning balance that you entered, you will not be able to do it through the EasyStep Interview or the Edit Account window. In order to accomplish this task, you need to use either the account register or a journal entry (journal entries will be covered in Lesson 12, Reporting, Closing the Books, and Adjusting Entries). For example, if you incorrectly entered $15,000 as the opening balance for the Savings account when you created it, you will need to open the Savings account register by double-clicking the account in the Chart of Accounts and change the amount in that window.

Entering Historical Transactions for an Account

There are two different ways that you can enter historical transactions into your QuickBooks file. Transactions can be entered either individually or in a summary journal entry.

Entering Historical Transactions Individually

If you wish to enter your transactions individually, you must have all of the data for each one. It is very important that you enter them in the correct order. Check out the following illustration to see the correct order for historical transaction entry.

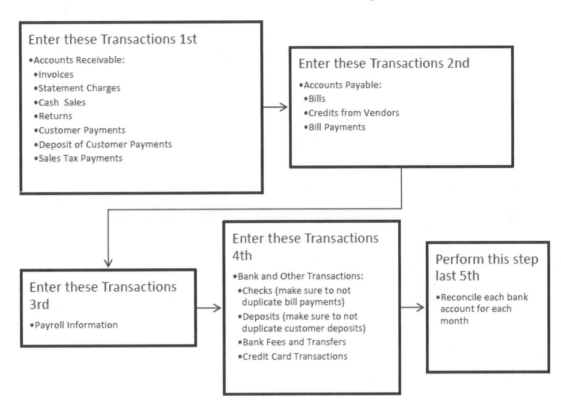

Enter these Transactions 1st

- Accounts Receivable:
  - Invoices
  - Statement Charges
- Cash Sales
- Returns
- Customer Payments
- Deposit of Customer Payments
- Sales Tax Payments

Enter these Transactions 2nd

- Accounts Payable:
  - Bills
  - Credits from Vendors
  - Bill Payments

Enter these Transactions 3rd

- Payroll Information

Enter these Transactions 4th

- Bank and Other Transactions:
  - Checks (make sure to not duplicate bill payments)
  - Deposits (make sure to not duplicate customer deposits)
  - Bank Fees and Transfers
  - Credit Card Transactions

Perform this step last 5th

- Reconcile each bank account for each month

Making a Summary Journal Entry

In a summary journal entry, you will not enter the details of individual transactions; you will only enter the total amounts. In this lesson, you will edit an opening balance in a register.

QUICK REFERENCE	ENTERING HISTORICAL TRANSACTIONS
Task	**Procedure**
Edit an account opening balance	▪ Open the register for the account. ▪ Drag to select the opening amount. ▪ Type the correct amount; click Record.
Enter historical transactions individually	▪ Gather the information for all of the historical transactions. ▪ Enter all accounts receivable transactions and then accounts payable transactions using the proper QuickBooks forms. (Follow the order shown above.) ▪ Enter outstanding payroll information. (For more information regarding payroll, see Lesson 9, Using QuickBooks for Payroll.) ▪ Enter outstanding "bank and other" transactions. (Follow the order shown above.) ▪ Reconcile each bank account for each month chronologically.
Make a summary journal entry to account for historical transactions	▪ Gather the information for all historical transactions. ▪ Determine each account that is affected, whether the net effect is a debit or a credit, and the total amount. ▪ Choose Company→Make General Journal Entries. ▪ Enter each of the affected accounts and the amount of the debit/credit. ▪ Ensure that debits equal credits. (QuickBooks will not allow you to record the journal entry until they do!) ▪ Record the journal entry.

DEVELOP YOUR SKILLS 2.4
Deal with an Opening Balance

In this exercise, you will work with a register to deal with an adjustment to the opening balance for the Checking account, since it was not entered when you created the account. The account you will credit in this transaction is 30000•Open Balance Equity (the whole account name is cut off due to the size of the field).

1. Click the **Check Register** task icon in the Banking area of the Home page.
   There is only one bank account at this time, so the Checking register will open automatically for you.

Check
Register

2. Follow these steps to enter the opening balance for the Checking account:

Ⓐ Type **042913** in the Date field.

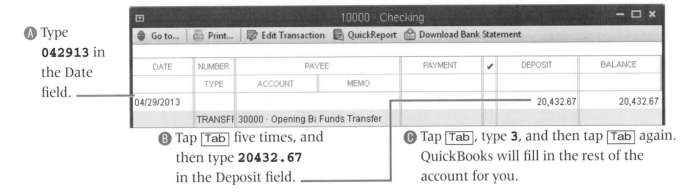

Ⓑ Tap ⎄Tab⎄ five times, and then type **20432.67** in the Deposit field.

Ⓒ Tap ⎄Tab⎄, type **3**, and then tap ⎄Tab⎄ again. QuickBooks will fill in the rest of the account for you.

The Memo will fill in automatically when you record the transaction.

3. Click the **Record** button at the bottom of the register window. Click **Yes** in the Future Transactions window, if necessary.

4. Close the **Checking** register window.

Finding Help in QuickBooks

There will be times when you will need to be able to find answers to questions you have about QuickBooks on your own. QuickBooks has a built-in help feature as well as a "coaching" feature that can come to your rescue in these circumstances.

The "Have a Question?" Window

The "Have a Question?" window is a separate window you can launch to search for help. This window is contextual, which means its contents change depending on the active window. For instance, if you choose to launch it while you have the Chart of Accounts window open, the results will relate to that window. Review the following figure.

Type keywords here and then view the topics found below. In this case, no words were necessary as the window was launched when the Home page was active.

Suggested answers are presented in two categories (How To and Community) identified by these icons.

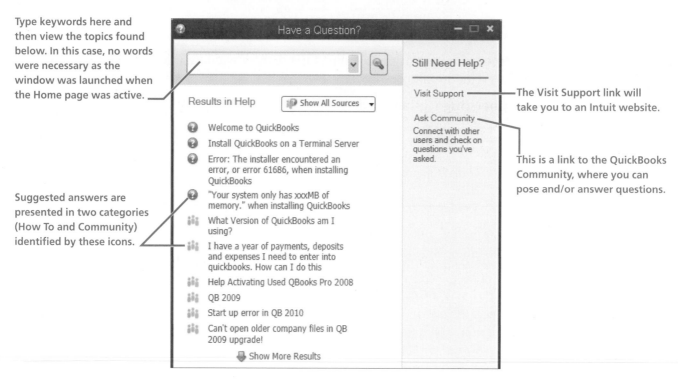

The Visit Support link will take you to an Intuit website.

This is a link to the QuickBooks Community, where you can pose and/or answer questions.

The Persistent Search Bar

The persistent search bar, which is a feature on the Icon Bar, allows you to search the company file (the results will be displayed in a Search window) or to search through help topics (the results will be displayed in the "Have a Question?" window). You will learn how to use the Search window in more detail in Lesson 6, Correcting and Customizing in QuickBooks.

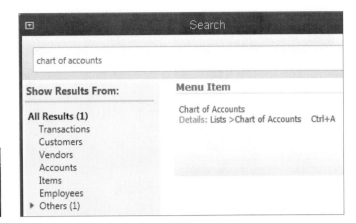

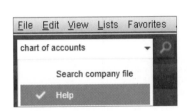

If you choose to search the company file, a Search window will show the results of the search.

If you choose to search for help, the "Have a Question?" window will display the results.

Help Articles

Once you see a result in the "Have a Question?" window that you feel is relevant to your needs, click on it. The Help Article window will launch with the information you selected displayed. For instance, here you can see the result of clicking the *Understand your chart of accounts* topic in the How To section of the "Have a Question?" window.

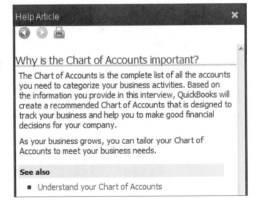

The Quick Start Center

Earlier in this lesson, you closed the Quick Start Center window that appeared after you created your new company file. This feature is available to you whenever you need it. The command to launch it can be found on the Help menu. This center helps you to perform basic tasks and is another place to access the tutorials to help you learn more about working in QuickBooks.

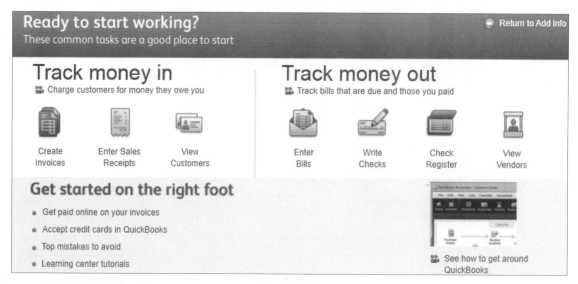

Notice that the Quick Start window is organized in sections to help you track money both coming into and leaving your business. It also features ways to start your QuickBooks experience right and to get more from the software once you are up and running.

QUICK REFERENCE	FINDING HELP FOR QUICKBOOKS
Task	**Procedure**
Search for help with the "Have a Question?" window	■ Choose Help→QuickBooks Help. ■ Type the relevant keyword(s); click Search. ■ Click the result you desire to see. It will be displayed in a Help Article window.
Search for help with the persistent search bar	■ Click in the persistent search bar; type the relevant keyword(s). ■ Choose to search for Help; click Search. ■ Click the result you desire to see. It will be displayed in a Help Article window.
Search your QuickBooks file with the persistent search bar	■ Click in the persistent search bar; type the relevant keyword(s). ■ Choose to Search company file; click Search.
Ask a question of another QuickBooks user	■ Choose Help→QuickBooks Help. ■ Click the Ask Community link. (An Internet browser will launch.) ■ Type the question you wish to pose to other users; click Ask. ■ If you feel up to the challenge, you may wish to answer a question for another user as well!
Print a help topic	■ Search for the topic of your choice; click to display it in the Help Article window. ■ Click the Print Topic button at the top left of the Help Article window. ■ Set your printer and print options; click Print.
Open the Quick Start Center window to view a tutorial	■ Choose Help→Quick Start Center. ■ Click the hyperlink to the desired tutorial.

Search for Help

In this exercise, you will use the Search help feature in QuickBooks.

FROM THE KEYBOARD
F1 to open the "Have a Question?" window

Essential Skills

1. Choose **Help→QuickBooks Help**.
   The "Have a Question?" window will display.

2. Follow these steps to search for a help topic:

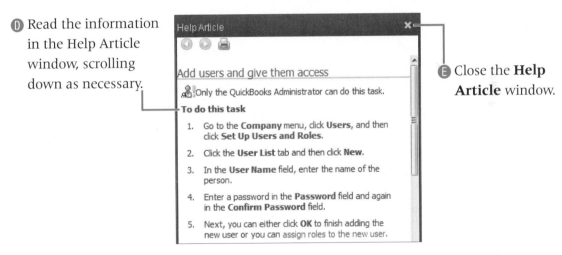

Ⓐ Click here, and then type **user access**.

Ⓑ Click the **Search** button.

Ⓒ Click this topic.

Your chosen topic will be displayed in the Help Article window that appears.

The results displayed may be in a different order on your screen.

Ⓓ Read the information in the Help Article window, scrolling down as necessary.

Ⓔ Close the **Help Article** window.

3. Close the **"Have a Question?"** window.

Setting Up Users

When your company grows, and you hire additional employees, you may decide that you need to allow certain employees access to your QuickBooks file.

Administrators and Users

Before you can set up any users for your QuickBooks file, you must set up an administrator who will control the access of all users. You can assign a password for each person with access to your file. The administrator controls all company preferences in the Preferences window. Users have the ability to change only their own personal preferences. QuickBooks allows you to set up unlimited users for your company file, although the number that can access the file at any one time depends on your QuickBooks license agreement.

The External Accountant user has access to all areas of QuickBooks except those that contain confidential customer information. An External Accountant can conduct reviews of your file and separate the changes from those of other users. Only an administrator can create an External Accountant user.

Restricting Access

When you decide to give employees access to your QuickBooks company file, you may not want them to see all of your company's financial information. You can choose to restrict each individual user's access to specific areas of QuickBooks.

There are nine areas for which you can give access rights to a user. Lisa has asked Bill to help out at Chez Devereaux Salon and Spa with sales and product ordering, so she will need to set him up as a user with limited access. This illustration

Access for user: Bill

This user has the following access rights. Click the Leave button to return.

AREA	CREATE	PRINT	REP...
Sales and Accounts Receivable	Y	Y	Y
Purchases and Accounts Payable	Y	N	N
Checking and Credit Cards	N	N	n/a
Time Tracking	N	N	N
Payroll and Employees	N	N	N
Sensitive Accounting Activities	N	N	N
Sensitive Financial Reports	N	N	n/a

displays those areas. In this example, Bill has access to all areas of sales and accounts receivable (creating new transactions, printing forms, and running reports) and can create new purchase and accounts payable transactions.

Setting Passwords

It is very important to make sure you have a password that is not easy for others to guess and yet that is easy for you to remember. Once you set your username and password, the Change QuickBooks Password window allows you to change your password whenever you wish (recommended every 90 days) and to set or change your secret "challenge question" that will allow you to retrieve a forgotten password. This challenge question should not have an answer with which others are familiar.

Working with QuickBooks in a Multi-User Environment

QuickBooks provides a way for more than one user to access a company file at the same time. In QuickBooks Pro and Premier, up to five users can have simultaneous access to the file. Most tasks that you usually do can be completed in multi-user mode, but there are some that must be performed in single-user mode.

You cannot do the following in multi-user mode:

- Create a new company file
- Set or edit a closing date
- Rebuild, clean up, or verify the file
- Create or work with accountant's copies
- Merge, delete, and sort list information
- Change company preferences
- Export and import data

 Tab: Getting Set Up
Topic: Set up QuickBooks for multi-user

QUICK REFERENCE	SETTING UP USERS AND PASSWORDS
Task	**Procedure**
Set up an administrator name and password	■ Choose Company→Set Up Users and Passwords→Set Up Users. ■ Select Admin; click Edit User. ■ Type the username and password, entering the password twice to verify. ■ Set the challenge question and answer, if desired; click OK.
Change an administrator password	■ Choose Company→Set Up Users and Passwords→Change your password. ■ Type a complex password; retype it to verify you did it correctly. ■ Set the challenge question and answer, if desired; click OK.
Set up users	■ Choose Company→Set Up Users and Passwords→Set Up Users. ■ Click Add User. ■ Type the username and password; click Next. ■ Follow the steps in the "Set up user password and access" screens to customize the access for the user. ■ View the new user's access rights; click Finish.
Switch between multi-user/single-user modes	If you are in single-user mode and wish to switch to multi-user mode: ■ Choose File→Switch to Multi-user Mode. If you are in multi-user mode and wish to switch to single-user mode: ■ Choose File→Switch to Single-user Mode.

Set Up Users for a Company

In this exercise, you will help Lisa set up Bill as a user for the Chez Devereaux Salon and Spa company file. The first step is to set her own password as the administrator.

1. Choose **Company→Set Up Users and Passwords→Set Up Users**.

2. Click **Edit User**.

3. Follow these steps to set up Lisa's administrator account and password:

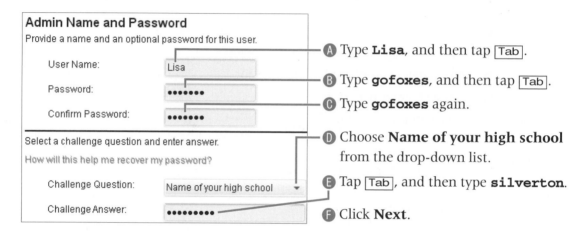

Ⓐ Type **Lisa**, and then tap ⌧Tab.

Ⓑ Type **gofoxes**, and then tap ⌧Tab.

Ⓒ Type **gofoxes** again.

Ⓓ Choose **Name of your high school** from the drop-down list.

Ⓔ Tap ⌧Tab, and then type **silverton**.

Ⓕ Click **Next**.

4. Click **Finish**.

   Notice that you do not need to change the access areas for the administrator. She has access to everything in the company file!

Add a User

Now that the administrator is set up, you can set up individual users.

5. Click the **Add User** button in the User List window; then follow these steps to add Bill as a user:

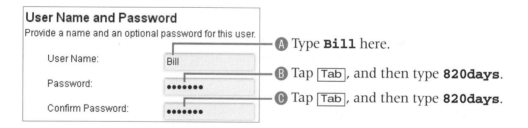

Ⓐ Type **Bill** here.

Ⓑ Tap ⌧Tab, and then type **820days**.

Ⓒ Tap ⌧Tab, and then type **820days**.

6. Click **Next** twice.

   Each time you click Next as you move through the "Set up user password and access" screens, you can change the access for the user in one of nine areas.

7. Click to choose **Full Access** for the Sales and Accounts Receivable option; click **Next**.

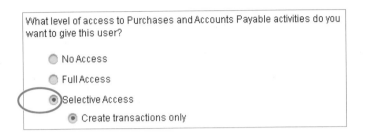

8. Click in the circle to the left of **Selective Access** for Purchases and Accounts Payable.

What level of access to Purchases and Accounts Payable activities do you want to give this user?

○ No Access

○ Full Access

◉ Selective Access

    ◉ Create transactions only

The Create transactions only option will be automatically selected.

9. Click **Finish**; then click **OK** in the Warning window, if necessary.
   Notice that Bill has been added to the User List.

10. Click **View User**.
    You will see a summary of the access you have given to Bill. You can change this at any time by opening the User List, clicking on Bill, and then clicking the Edit User button.

11. Click the **Leave** button in the View user access window.

12. Close the **User List**.

Closing the Books and Running List Reports

You will not actually close the books yet, but it is important to understand how QuickBooks deals with this task, so it will be covered now. You will, however, find the need to produce list reports early on in your QuickBooks experience. For instance, your accountant may wish to see a list of the accounts you have set up for your business to ensure all is well before you get too far down the road. QuickBooks reports can provide you with a wealth of information about your company. You will learn a lot more about how to use these reports in Lesson 12, Reporting, Closing the Books, and Adjusting Entries.

Keeping the End in Mind

You are not required to "close the books" in QuickBooks, but you can choose to if you like. When you close the books, QuickBooks:

■ Transfers the net income or net loss to Retained Earnings

■ Restricts access to transactions prior to the closing date by requiring a password

■ Allows you to clean up your data

Only the company file administrator can set a closing date and allow or restrict access to prior-period transactions by a user. You will have an opportunity to close the books and complete the full accounting cycle in Lesson 12, Reporting, Closing the Books, and Adjusting Entries. For now, it is important for you to keep in mind how QuickBooks operates at the end of an accounting period.

The Report Center

There are many preset reports available for you to use in QuickBooks. They are broken into three main categories: list, summary, and transaction. The Report Center is a tool in Quick-Books that allows you to learn about different types of reports without having to create them by trial and error. It includes sample reports and descriptions of the type of information each report provides.

Contributed Reports

Contributed reports are specialized reports submitted by users and integrated into the Report Center. You can search for specialized reports by your industry type, and you can even rate a report for other users to see how valuable it is to you.

These tabs allow you to view standard QuickBooks reports, your memorized reports, your favorite reports, your recently displayed reports, and reports contributed by other users.

These three buttons allow you to change how you view Report Center information.

Here are the different categories of reports available.

The main section displays the different available reports. Here you are viewing information about a contributed report.

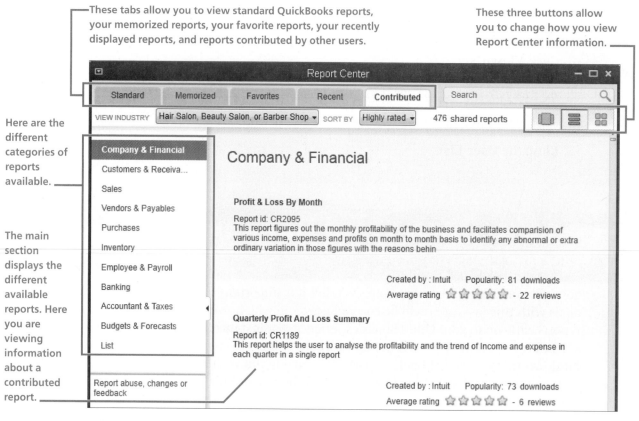

Visualize! **Tab:** Reports
Topic: Reports

List Reports in QuickBooks

One category of reports that you can access are list reports. They simply display the information that is found in your various QuickBooks lists in an easy-to-read format.

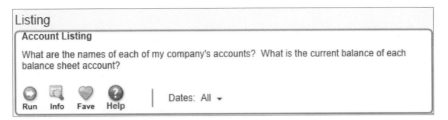

When you view the Report Center in List View, you will see a question that the report will answer below the name of the report. This will come in handy when you are completing the Apply Your Skills exercises, where you will be expected to "answer questions with reports!"

Viewing Sample Report Images

An additional feature available in the Report Center is the ability for you to view what a report will look like without having to actually produce the report.

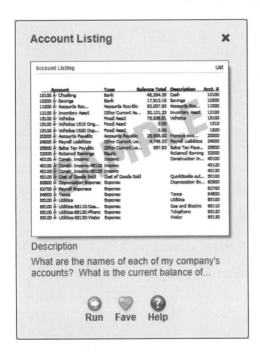

When you click the Info button for a report, a sample of what the report will look like is displayed.

QUICK REFERENCE	PRODUCING LIST REPORTS
Task	**Procedure**
Display an Account Listing report	▪ Choose Reports→Report Center.
	▪ Choose List as the report category.
	▪ Scroll down; click Account Listing.
	▪ Click the Run report button.

Produce a List Report

In this exercise, Lisa will create a report for her accountant that displays the accounts in her Chart of Accounts.

1. Choose **Reports→Report Center**.

2. Follow these steps to display the report:

Ⓐ Click the **List View** button.

Ⓑ Click **List**.

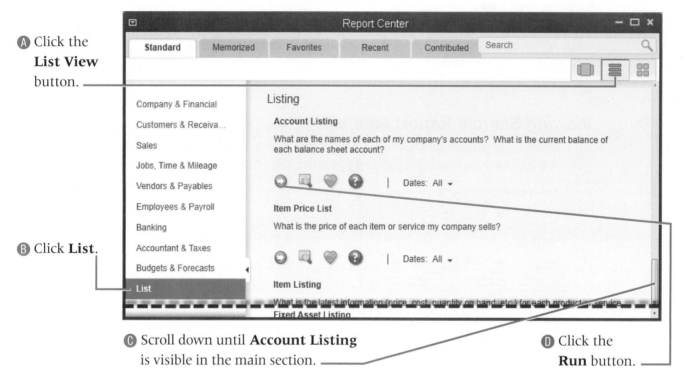

Ⓒ Scroll down until **Account Listing** is visible in the main section.

Ⓓ Click the **Run** button.

A report displaying all of the accounts in your Chart of Accounts is displayed.

3. Close the **Account Listing** report and **Report Center** windows.

4. Choose the appropriate option for your situation:

FROM THE KEYBOARD
Alt + F4 to exit from QuickBooks

■ If you are continuing on to the next lesson or to the end-of-lesson exercises, leave QuickBooks open.

■ If you are finished working in QuickBooks for now, choose **File→Exit**.

Concepts Review

Concepts Review   http://labyrinthelab.com/qb13

To check your knowledge of the key concepts introduced in this lesson, complete the Concepts Review quiz by going to the URL listed above.

Reinforce Your Skills

Set Up a New QuickBooks Company

In this exercise, you will use Detailed Start to set up the company for Tea Shoppe at the Lake.

1. If necessary, launch **QuickBooks**.

2. Choose **File→New Company**.

3. Click the **Detailed Start** button in the QuickBooks Setup window.
   The Easy Step Interview window displays.

4. Refer to the information on the following page to complete the EasyStep Interview for Susie.

5. Once the information is entered, click **Go to Setup** to complete the interview.
   The "You've got a company file!" screen appears in the QuickBooks Setup window.

6. Click **Start working**.

7. Click the **Close** button on the Quick Start Center window.

EASYSTEP INTERVIEW INFORMATION

Field	Data
Company/Legal Name	**Tea Shoppe at the Lake**
Tax ID (Federal Employee Identification Number)	**99-9999999**
Address	**316 Swan Drive** **Lake San Marcos, CA 92078**
Phone	**(760) 555-3759**
Fax	**(760) 555-3758**
Industry Type	Restaurant, Caterer, or Bar
Company Organization	Sole Proprietorship
First Month of Fiscal Year	January
Administrator Password	**Tea4Two** (remember that passwords are case-sensitive)
File Name	**[Your first name]'s Tea Shoppe at the Lake, Lesson 2** (e.g. Susie's Tea Shoppe at the Lake, Lesson 2)
What Is Sold?	Services Only
Sales Tax	No
Estimates	No
Billing Statements	No
Invoices	Yes
Progress Invoicing	No
Bill Tracking	Yes
Time Tracking	No
Employees	No
Multiple Currencies	No (this option is not available in all versions)
Start Date	**01-31-2013**
Income & Expense Accounts	Start with the accounts provided

REINFORCE YOUR SKILLS 2.2

Change Preferences

In this exercise, you will change two preferences in the file you just created for Tea Shoppe at the Lake.

You will begin by turning on the account number preference so that when you create and edit accounts, you can enter the numbers.

Before You Begin: Make sure you have completed Reinforce Your Skills 2.1.

1. Choose **Edit→Preferences**.

2. Choose the **Accounting** category.

3. Click the **Company Preferences** tab.

4. Click in the box to turn on the **Use account numbers** preference.

5. Click **OK**.

Display Additional Task Icons on the Home Page

Susie would like to be able to create sales receipts in QuickBooks, so you will make the Create Sales Receipts task icon visible on the Home page.

6. Choose **Edit→Preferences**.

7. Choose the **Desktop View** category.

8. Click the **Company Preferences** tab.

9. Click in the box to the left of **Sales Receipts** in the Customers area of the window.

10. Click **OK** to change the preference, and then click **OK** again to close the window.

REINFORCE YOUR SKILLS 2.3

Work with the Chart of Accounts

In this exercise, you will add, edit, and delete accounts as well as add subaccounts in the Chart of Accounts.

Add a New Account

Susie wants to add her Checking account.

1. Choose **Lists→Chart of Accounts**.

2. Click the **Account** menu button, and then choose **New**.
   The account menu button can be found in the bottom-left of the Chart of Accounts window.

3. Choose **Bank** as the account type; click **Continue**.

4. Type **10000** in the Number field, tap `Tab`, and then type **Checking** as the Name.

5. Click **Save & Close**; click **No** in the Set Up Online Services window.

Edit an Account

Susie wants to change the name of the Restaurant Supplies account.

6. Scroll, if necessary, and right-click on the **53100•Restaurant Supplies** account; then choose **Edit Account** from the shortcut menu.

7. Change the name of the account to **Shoppe** Supplies, and then click **Save & Close**.

Delete an Account

Susie has decided that she doesn't need the Uniforms expense account, so you will delete it for her.

8. Scroll down, if necessary, and single-click on account **68500•Uniforms**.

9. Click the **Account** menu button, and then choose **Delete Account**.

10. Click **OK** to confirm the deletion.

Add Subaccounts

You will now add two subaccounts for the Utilities account: Gas & Electric and Water.

11. Click the **Account** menu button, and then choose **New**.

12. Choose **Expense** as the account type; click **Continue**.

13. Enter **68610** as the Number and **Gas & Electric** as the Name.

14. Make it a subaccount of **68600•Utilities**.

15. Click **Save & New**, and then create one additional subaccount for Utilities: **68620•Water**.

16. Click **Save & Close**; then close the **Chart of Accounts** window.

REINFORCE YOUR SKILLS 2.4

Produce a List Report

In this exercise, you will create an Account Listing report for Susie to show her the work that you have completed on her Chart of Accounts.

1. Choose **Reports→List→Account Listing**.

2. Take a look at the report and make sure that all of the **Chart of Accounts** work you did in the last exercise is correct.

3. Either print the report or save it as in PDF, based on your instructor's direction.

4. Submit the report based on the guidelines provided by your instructor.

5. Close the **Account Listing** report.

6. Choose the appropriate option for your situation:
   - If you are continuing on to the next lesson or the rest of the end-of-lesson exercises, leave QuickBooks open.
   - If you are finished working in QuickBooks for now, choose **File→Exit**.

Apply Your Skills

Create and Customize a New Company File

In this exercise, you will create a QuickBooks company file for Dr. Sadie James, DVM. You should use the Express Start method to set up the company.

1. Use the following information to set up a new company file for Dr. James. Save the file in your default file location, naming it **[Your first name]'s Wet Noses Veterinary Clinic, Lesson** 2.

Company/Legal Name	**Wet Noses Veterinary Clinic**
Tax ID Number	**99-9999999**
Address	**589 Retriever Drive**
	Bothell, WA 98011
Phone	**(425) 555-2939**
Income tax form	LLP
Fiscal Year first month	January
Company Type	Medical, Dental, or Health Service
Employees	No employees yet—will have in future

Remember that with this method of new company setup, QuickBooks will automatically save the file to the default location with the default name unless you choose to change it by previewing your settings.

2. Click **Start Working** in the QuickBooks Setup window.

3. Close the **Quick Start Center** window.

Change Account Preferences

In this exercise, you will set preferences for Wet Noses. You will not turn on account number preferences for this company, as you will operate this company without using them.

1. Open the **Preferences** window.

2. Choose to turn off **pop-up messages for products and services**.

3. Choose to have QuickBooks show a full list of the **To Do Notes** when you open the company file.
   Hint: Look in the Reminders category.

4. Choose to turn off **date warnings**.
   Hint: Look in the Accounting category.

5. Close the **Preferences** window.

Modify the Chart of Accounts

In this exercise, you will modify the Chart of Accounts for the company you just created.

1. Open the **Chart of Accounts**.

2. Add two new **Bank** accounts: **Checking** and **Savings**.

3. Add a new **income** account: **Boarding Income**.

4. Add a new **expense** account: **Boarding Food and Supplies**.

5. Change the name of the Vaccines and Medicines account to **Pharmaceuticals**.

6. Add two **subaccounts** for Pharmaceuticals: **Vaccines** and **Medicines**.

7. Delete the **Uniforms** account.

Answer Questions with Reports

In this exercise, you will answer questions for Dr. James by running reports. You may wish to display the Report Center in List View to help you answer the questions. Ask your instructor if you should print the reports, print (save) them as PDF files, export them to Excel, or simply display them on the screen.

1. Dr. James' accountant has asked if the Chart of Accounts has been set up correctly. Produce a report that will show all of the accounts that have been set up for the company.

2. Before Dr. James begins working with customers and vendors, her accountant asks if the proper terms have been set up for her to use on invoices and bills. Display a report that will show her what terms are currently set up for the company.

3. Submit your reports based on the guidelines provided by your instructor.

4. Choose the appropriate option for your situation:

   ■ If you are continuing on to the next lesson or the Critical Thinking exercises, leave QuickBooks open.

   ■ If you are finished working in QuickBooks for now, choose **File→Exit**.

Critical Thinking

In the course of working through all of the Critical Thinking exercises, you will be utilizing various skills taught in this and previous lesson(s). Take your time and think carefully about the tasks presented to you. Turn back to the lesson content if you need assistance.

2.1 Sort Through the Stack

You have been hired by Mary Minard to help her with her organization's books. She is the owner of Monkey Business, a nonprofit organization that provides low-income students with help in preparing for college placement exams and applying for scholarships. You have just sat down at her desk and found a pile of papers. It is your job to sort through the papers and make sense of what you find, entering information into QuickBooks whenever appropriate and answering any other questions in a word-processing document saved as **Critical Thinking 2.1**. Remember, you are digging through papers on a desk, so it is up to you to determine the correct order in which to complete the tasks.

Following are the notes on the papers you find.

- An email from her accountant: Set up Chart of Accounts, use Non-Profit as industry type, and add Grant Revenue as an income account.
- A bank statement from Salem First National Bank dated 6/30/2013. Checking account #21375-01, ending balance $5,462.11; Savings account #21375-20, ending balance $18,203.54.
- A handwritten sticky note: Need for three volunteers (Cheryl, Rick, and Susan) to have access to entering donor revenue. How can I make sure they can do this but don't have access to other areas in QuickBooks? Will I need a password or something?
- A scrap of paper with the following written on it: Fiscal year July-June.
- A scribbled phone message from Mary's accountant: Make sure to use account numbers when you set up in QuickBooks.
- The following message on a sticky note: Is there a reminders list to keep me on track???
- Another email from Mary's accountant: Make sure to not have the starting date the day you started the organization…would be too much information to enter. How about 6/30/2013 instead since it is the end of the fiscal year?
- A copy of last year's taxes: Form 990, Federal EIN 99-9999999.
- A piece of company letterhead with the following information: Monkey Business 1775 Fidelis Blvd., Salem, OR 97305; Phone (503) 555-5239; FAX (503) 555-6979.

2.2 Tackle the Tasks

Now is your chance to work a little more with Chez Devereaux Salon and Spa and apply the skills that you have learned in this lesson to accomplish additional tasks. Open or restore the **Critical Thinking 2.2** company or portable company file from your file storage location, and then complete the following tasks. (Remember that the username is "Lisa" and the password for the file is "gofoxes"!)

Add Accounts	▪ Add the following bank account: 10200•Savings
	▪ Add the following income account: 48800•Nail Services
	▪ Add the following expense account: 61500•Client Refreshments
Add Subaccounts	▪ Add the following subaccounts to the Utilities account: 68610•Gas & Electric, 68620•Water
Change Account Opening Balance	▪ Change the Savings account opening balance to $17,382.35, as of 4/30/13
Search for Help	▪ Use the QuickBooks help feature to learn how to enter a bill from a vendor
Change Preferences	▪ Choose to show the Reminders List when opening a company file (hint: Reminders/My Preferences)
	▪ Turn off the two date warnings (hint: Accounting/Company Preferences)
Create a List Report	▪ Create a list report that shows all of the Terms available (these list entries were automatically added when you created the company)

2.3 Use the Web as a Learning Tool

Throughout this book, you will be provided with an opportunity to use the Internet as a learning tool by completing WebQuests. According to the original creators of WebQuests, as described on their website (WebQuest.org), a WebQuest is "an inquiry-oriented activity in which most or all of the information used by learners is drawn from the web." To complete the WebQuest projects in this book, navigate to the student resource center and choose the WebQuest for the lesson on which you are currently working. The subject of each WebQuest will be relevant to the material found in the lesson.

WebQuest Subject: Working with QuickBooks in a multi-user environment

Working with Vendors

LESSON OBJECTIVES

After studying this lesson, you will be able to:

- Work with the Vendor Center and List
- Create and use custom fields
- Use Customer & Vendor Profile Lists
- Enter bills, pay bills, and write checks
- Produce vendor reports and QuickBooks graphs

T racking expenses properly is very important for your financial statements as well as for keeping your vendors happy! A vendor is essentially anyone to whom you pay money. However, this does not include employees. A vendor could be the electric company, the organization to which you pay taxes, a merchandise supplier, or subcontractors you pay to do work for your customers. QuickBooks allows you to produce 1099 tax forms for subcontractors at the end of the year. In this lesson, you will examine the QuickBooks lists, activities, and reports that allow you to effectively deal with vendors.

Student Resources   http://labyrinthelab.com/qb13

Chez Devereaux Salon and Spa

Lisa Devereaux, the owner of Chez Devereaux Salon and Spa, just began using QuickBooks. She needs to work on the Vendor List before she can track her expenses by entering bills, paying bills, and writing checks. Once she has established her list of vendors, she will be able to choose them from drop-down lists in the various vendor forms. Lisa will also learn how to produce reports that will provide relevant vendor information.

Lisa can access the Vendor List and activities (entering and paying bills) from the Vendor Center. In the following illustration you can see the Vendor Center. In total, there are four centers: Customer, Vendor, Employee, and Report. Centers allow you to view a snapshot of information; in this case, it's an all-in-one look at an individual vendor's information, bills, and payments. You can also initiate a new transaction for the selected vendor from the center.

┌─These let you create new list entries, enter new transactions,   ┌─Information and links to reports for
  print a vendor's information, and export information.   the selected vendor are shown here.

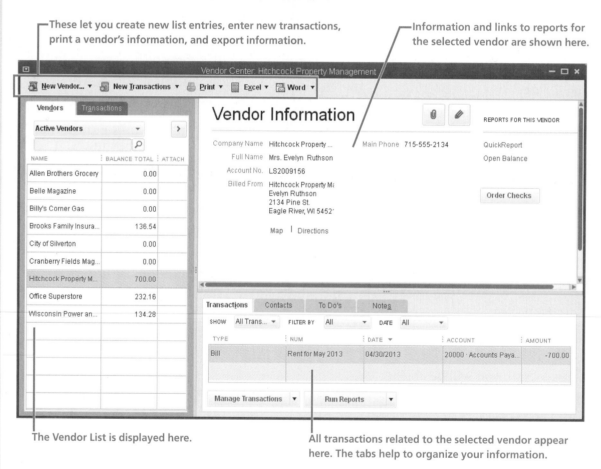

The Vendor List is displayed here.   All transactions related to the selected vendor appear
                                      here. The tabs help to organize your information.

The Vendor Center window displays the Vendor List as well as a snapshot view of the selected vendor.

Exploring the Vendor Center

In Lesson 1, Introducing QuickBooks Pro, you were introduced to the four types of tasks you will work with in QuickBooks throughout this book (lists, activities, company setup, and reports). Information is stored in QuickBooks through the use of lists. Lists allow you to store information that can be easily filled into forms by using drop-down arrows or by beginning to type the entry and letting QuickBooks fill in the rest. Lists comprise the database aspect of QuickBooks; the Vendor List can even be exported to contact management software such as Microsoft® Outlook.

Tab: Tracking Money Out
Topic: Expenses overview; Building blocks of recording expenses

Each individual vendor record tracks information organized into five tabs: Address Info, Payment Settings, Tax Settings, Account Settings, and Additional Info. You can also create custom fields for information unique to your business. In addition, with QuickBooks 2013, you can customize eight different contact fields. Keep in mind that the more information you enter for each vendor, the better prepared you will be later when you learn how to customize reports because you can sort, group, and filter your reports using the information in the vendor records. The Vendor List is an integrated part of the Vendor Center.

Here you can add vendors to the list.

Here you can create transactions for the selected vendor.

The Attach button lets you attach files to the selected vendor record.

This button opens the Edit Vendor window so you can modify information.

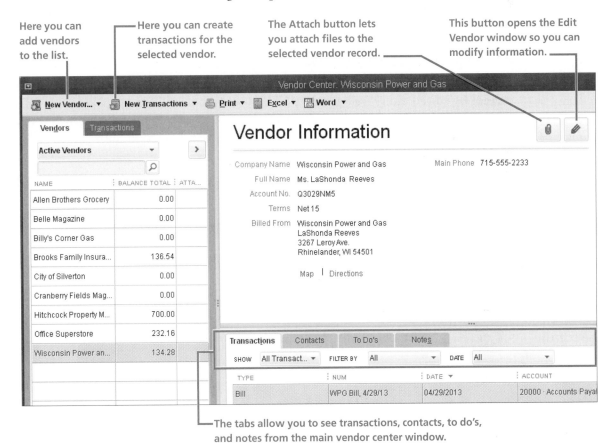

The tabs allow you to see transactions, contacts, to do's, and notes from the main vendor center window.

In QuickBooks 2013, information in the Customer, Vendor, and Employee Centers is more centralized and can help users be more efficient and effective when working with the main lists.

 Tab: New to QuickBooks?
Topic: Using Centers

Managing the Vendor List

List-management tasks are performed similarly for the various lists in QuickBooks. The exact procedure that you follow will depend on whether the list is integrated into a QuickBooks center (Customers & Jobs, Vendors, Employees) or is accessible via the List option on the menu bar. The lists that are integrated into a center are not accessible separately via the menu bar.

Creating a New Vendor

To start entering vendor transactions, you must first enter your vendors into the Vendor List. You can enter vendors directly into the list, in the Add/Edit Multiple List Entries window (which you will learn more about in Lesson 8, Dealing with Physical Inventory), or "on the fly" in forms such as Enter Bills and Write Checks and then select Quick Add or Setup from the pop-up window. Remember that subcontractors should be set up as vendors, not as employees.

Editing an Existing Vendor

Once created, the vendor can always be edited through the Vendor Center. The only item that cannot be edited after you have created and saved a new vendor is the opening balance (it must be adjusted through the accounts payable register). When you change the information for a vendor, including the vendor's name, it will be reflected in both future and past transactions.

Each of these tabs holds additional
fields to track vendor information.

Clicking the drop-down arrow on the customizable
contact fields produces a list of options for each.

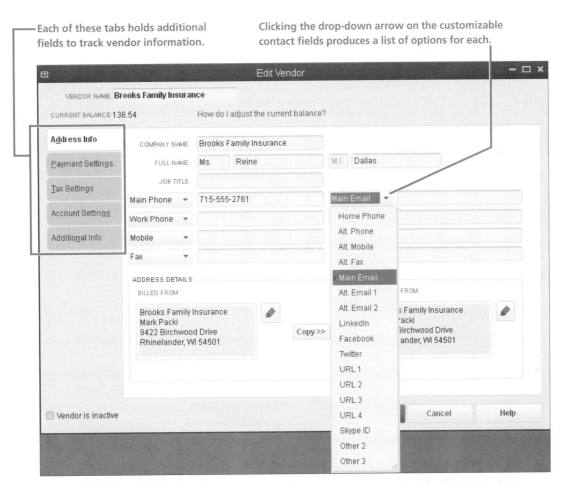

The Edit Vendor window allows you to enter a large amount of information for an individual vendor.
The eight contact fields are highly customizable.

Deleting a Vendor

You can delete a vendor from the Vendor List as long *as you have not used it in a transaction*. If you
have used it in a transaction, you can make it inactive, but you cannot delete it until after you
close the books for a period and clean up your company's data.

Tab: Getting Set Up
Topic: Add the people you do business with

QUICK REFERENCE	MANAGING THE VENDOR LIST
Task	**Procedure**
Edit an existing vendor	▪ Open the Vendor Center. ▪ Double-click the vendor you need to edit. ▪ Make the desired changes; click OK.
Add a new vendor	▪ Open the Vendor Center. ▪ Click the New Vendor button on the toolbar. ▪ Enter the necessary information; click OK.
Delete a vendor	▪ Open the Vendor Center. ▪ Click the vendor you wish to delete. ▪ Choose Edit→Delete Vendor; click OK.

Manage the Vendor List

In this exercise, you will manage the Vendor List for Chez Devereaux Salon and Spa. The first step is to open QuickBooks, and then either open a company file or restore a portable company file.

1. Start **QuickBooks 2013**.

   If you downloaded the student exercise files in the portable company file *format, follow Option 1 below. If you downloaded the files in the* company file *format, follow Option 2 below.*

Option 1: Restore a Portable Company File

2. Choose **File→Open or Restore Company**.

3. Click in the circle to the left of **Restore a portable file**, and then click **Next**.

4. Follow these steps to restore your file:

Ⓐ Navigate to your file storage location.

Ⓑ Click to select the **Chez Devereaux** portable file for this lesson.

Ⓒ Click **Open**.

5. Click **Next**, and then follow these steps to determine where the resulting company file will be located:

Ⓐ Navigate to your file storage location.

Ⓑ Replace Lisa's name with your own (e.g., the author's filename would be Trish's Chez Devereaux Salon and Spa, Lesson 3).

Ⓒ Click **Save**.

It may take a few moments for the portable company file to open. Once it does, continue with step 7.

Option 2: Open a Company File

2. Choose **File→Open or Restore Company**.

3. Ensure that **Open a company file** is selected.

4. Follow these steps to open the company file:

Ⓐ Navigate to your file storage location.

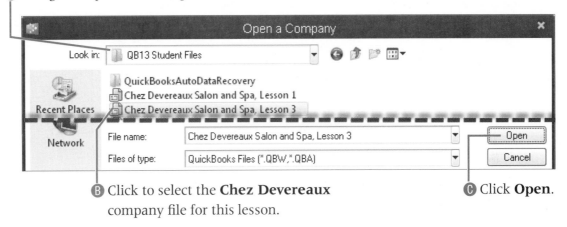

Ⓑ Click to select the **Chez Devereaux** company file for this lesson.

Ⓒ Click **Open**.

The QuickBooks company file opens.

5. Click **OK** to close the QuickBooks Information window.

6. Click **No** in the Set Up External Accountant User window, if necessary.

Edit an Existing Vendor

The first step in modifying a vendor record is to open the Vendor Center so you can view the Vendor List.

FROM THE KEYBOARD
Ctrl+e to open the selected list item to edit

7. Click the **Vendors** button in the Vendors area of the Home page.

8. Double-click **Brooks Family Insurance** to open it for editing.

 When you double-click a record on the Vendor List, QuickBooks opens it for editing. You could also single-click the vendor you wish to open and then click the Edit Vendor button.

9. Change the name to **Ms. Reine Dallas**.

 In QuickBooks, you can use the same text editing techniques you use in word-processing programs. Simply select the text to be replaced by clicking and dragging the mouse pointer over it and then type the replacement. You can also use the Delete or Backspace keys on your keyboard.

10. Click **OK** to accept the change.

Add a New Vendor

Next you will help Lisa to add a new vendor to the list.

11. Click the **New Vendor** button on the toolbar, and then choose **New Vendor** from the menu.

12. Follow these steps to enter the information for the vendor:

 You will not need to change the Opening Balance date unless you enter an amount for the opening balance, as the information is only used when accompanied by an amount.

Ⓐ Type **Stacey's Beauty Supply**.

Ⓑ Tap `Tab` three times, and then type **Stacey's Beauty Supply**.

Ⓒ Tap `Tab` and type **Ms.**, tap `Tab` and type **Stacey**, and then tap `Tab` twice and type **del Campo**.

Ⓓ Tap `Tab`, and then type **Manager**.

Ⓔ Tap `Tab` twice, and then type **715-555-6660**.

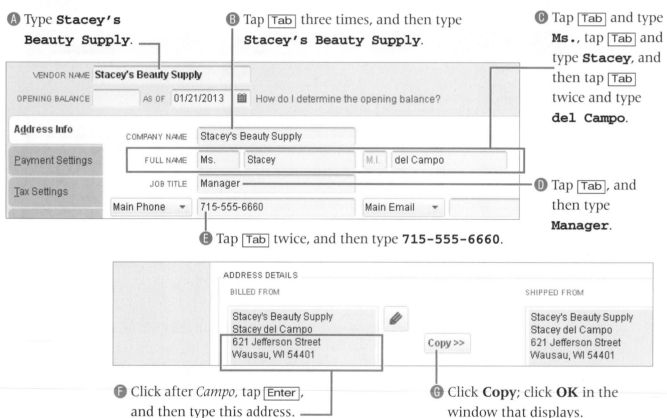

Ⓕ Click after *Campo*, tap `Enter`, and then type this address.

Ⓖ Click **Copy**; click **OK** in the window that displays.

 Tapping `Enter` in a field with multiple lines (such as the Billed From Address field) takes you to the next line. Tapping `Enter` while working in a single line field (such as Name or Phone) is equivalent to clicking the default button in the window (the blue button)—in this case, the OK button.

13. Follow these steps to add the additional vendor information:

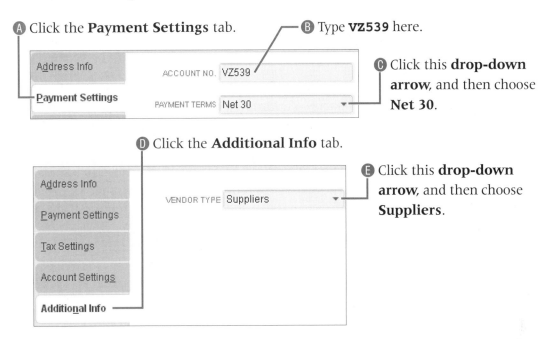

A Click the **Payment Settings** tab.

B Type **VZ539** here.

C Click this **drop-down arrow**, and then choose **Net 30**.

D Click the **Additional Info** tab.

E Click this **drop-down arrow**, and then choose **Suppliers**.

14. Click **OK** to complete the new vendor record.

Delete a Vendor

Lisa has not purchased anything from Billy's Corner Gas yet, and the company has just gone out of business. You will now delete this company from the Vendor List.

15. Single-click the **Billy's Corner Gas** record in the Vendor List to select it.

16. Choose **Edit→Delete Vendor**.

QuickBooks asks you to confirm the deletion. QuickBooks wants to ensure that you don't delete anything by accident; it will always ask you to confirm deletions.

17. Click **OK** to confirm the deletion.

In the next step, you will close the Vendor Center window within QuickBooks. Do not click the Close button for the QuickBooks window, as it will exit the program rather than simply close the center window!

18. Close the **Vendor Center** window.

Working with Customer & Vendor Profile Lists

When you created your new QuickBooks company and chose a type of company on which to base it, QuickBooks gave you a generic Chart of Accounts and populated your Customer & Vendor Profile Lists with entries relevant to your chosen company type. You will see many of these profile lists in the forms and lists you will work with in this book.

Table of Customer & Vendor Profile Lists

Look at the profile lists that QuickBooks provides to track customer and vendor information, as well as the examples of forms and lists in which you may find them appearing as fields.

NAME OF LIST	YOU MAY FIND THIS LIST AS A FIELD ON…
Sales Rep List	■ Customer & Job List (Additional Info tab) ■ Create Invoices form
Customer Type List	■ Customer & Job List (Additional Info tab)
Vendor Type List	■ Vendor List (Additional Info tab)
Job Type List	■ Customer & Job List (Job Info tab)
Terms List	■ Vendor List ■ Create Invoices form
Customer Message List	■ Enter Sales Receipts form
Payment Method List	■ Receive Payments form
Ship Via List	■ Create Invoices form (product or custom template)
Vehicle List	■ Enter Vehicle Mileage window

Making the Lists Work for You

Using the Customer & Vendor Profile Lists can help you in many ways. You can even use a list for a purpose other than that for which it was intended. For instance, your company may not ship products, so you have no need for the Ship Via field. You can use this field to track an additional aspect of your company. You cannot create your own profile list, so you need to maximize the profile lists QuickBooks provides to track all information needed by your company.

The benefit of fully utilizing these lists is that they can be included on reports and custom form templates. This means that if you want to focus a marketing effort on your residential customers, you can create a report and filter out all customer types other than residential.

Task	Procedure
Open a profile list	▪ Choose Lists→Customer & Vendor Profile Lists→[the name of the list you need].
Edit a profile list entry	▪ Double-click the entry you need to edit. ▪ Make any necessary changes; click OK.
Create a new profile list entry	▪ Right-click within the list; choose New. ▪ Enter all relevant information; click OK.
Delete a profile list entry	▪ Click the entry to be deleted. ▪ Use [Ctrl]+[d] to delete the entry, clicking OK to confirm the deletion.

DEVELOP YOUR SKILLS 3.2
Work with Customer & Vendor Profile Lists

In this exercise, you will work with the Customer Message, Vendor Type, and Customer Type Lists. You can use these procedures with any other profile list as well.

1. Choose **Lists→Customer & Vendor Profile Lists→Customer Message List**.

2. Double-click **Thank you for your business**.

3. Replace the current message with the following:

   We truly appreciate your business.

   When you open the message for editing, the current message is selected (highlighted); it will be replaced when you type the new message.

4. Click **OK** to save the new message.
   Now you can select this message on the Create Invoices and Enter Sales Receipt forms that you will learn about in the next lesson.

5. Close the **Customer Message List** window.

Create a New Profile List Entry
You will now help Lisa to add a new customer type.

6. Choose **Lists→Customer & Vendor Profile Lists→Customer Type List**.

7. Click the **Customer Type** menu button, and then click **New**.

8. Follow these steps to complete the new list entry:

Ⓐ Type **From Chamber**.

Ⓑ Click **OK**.

Notice that you can create customer subtypes as well. For instance, if you were a member of two chambers, you could have them listed as subtypes of the entry you just created.

9. Close the **Customer Type List**.

Essential Skills

Delete a Profile List Entry

Lisa has decided that she doesn't want to have both Suppliers and Supplies on the Vendor Type List, so you will delete one for her. Since you used Suppliers when you created the vendor entry, you will delete Supplies.

10. Choose **Lists→Customer & Vendor Profile Lists→Vendor Type List**.

11. Single-click **Supplies**.

12. Click the **Vendor Type** menu button and choose **Delete Vendor Type**; click **OK** to confirm the deletion.

13. Close the **Vendor Type List**.

Creating Custom Fields

You will work with many forms in QuickBooks, and you may choose to send some of these forms to customers and vendors. QuickBooks provides many standard forms (such as invoice, purchase order, and sales receipt), but you can also choose to create your own forms or modify the standard Intuit forms. In order to use custom fields on a form, you must create your own rather than use one of the standard forms provided by QuickBooks (you can also make a copy of a standard Intuit form and customize it).

Adding Custom Fields

Before you can use custom fields in reports, you must first set them up in the lists where they belong. You can set up custom fields for Customers:Jobs, Vendors, Employees, and Items. You can either populate custom fields in the lists or enter the information directly on the forms where they appear.

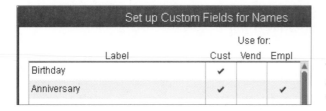

The Set up Custom Fields for Names window allows you to create custom fields for three lists: Customers & Jobs, Vendors, and Employees.

NOTE Custom fields are available for all types of items except for subtotals, sales tax items, and sales tax groups.

QUICK REFERENCE	WORKING WITH CUSTOM FIELDS

Task	Procedure
Create custom fields for customers, vendors, and employees	■ Open the Vendor Center (this works the same for the other centers); double-click to open a vendor's record. ■ Click the Additional Info tab; click the Define Fields button. ■ Type the field names. ■ Click in the column(s) below the list(s) where you want to see each field displayed; click OK. ■ Enter the new field information into the vendor record; click OK.
Create custom fields for items	■ Open the Item List; double-click to open an item for editing. ■ Click the Custom Fields button; click the Define Fields button. ■ Type the labels you wish to use. ■ Click in the box to the left of each label that you want to activate; click OK. ■ Enter any custom field information you want to see automatically appear on forms; click OK twice.

DEVELOP YOUR SKILLS 3.3

Create and Fill Custom Fields

In this exercise, you will help Lisa create custom fields to track additional information and for her to use on custom templates in the future.

1. Choose **Customers→Customer Center**.

2. Double-click **Holly Rose** in the Customers & Jobs List at the left.

3. Click the **Additional Info** tab.

4. Click the **Define Fields** button in the Custom Fields section of the window.

5. Follow these steps to set up two custom fields:

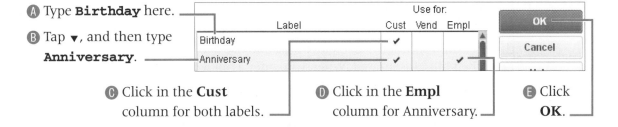

Ⓐ Type **Birthday** here.

Ⓑ Tap ▾, and then type **Anniversary**.

Ⓒ Click in the **Cust** column for both labels.

Ⓓ Click in the **Empl** column for Anniversary.

Ⓔ Click **OK**.

QuickBooks may display an information window indicating that you can use the custom fields in templates.

6. Click **OK** to acknowledge the prompt, if necessary.

7. Click in the **Birthday** field and type **5/21/69**.

8. Click **OK** to accept the changes and close the Edit Customer window.

9. Close the **Customer Center** window.

Create and Fill an Item Custom Field

You will now add a custom field for items and use it on a non-inventory item.

10. Choose **Lists→Item List**.

11. Scroll down, and then double-click **Hairspray**.
    The Edit Item window will open for Hairspray.

12. Click the **Custom Fields** button. Click **OK** to continue to the Custom Fields for Hairspray window if QuickBooks displays an Information window.

13. Click the **Define Fields** button.

14. Follow these steps to add the custom field:

A Type **Hold** in the Label column.　　**B** Click in the **Use** column to the right of Hold.　　**C** Click **OK**.

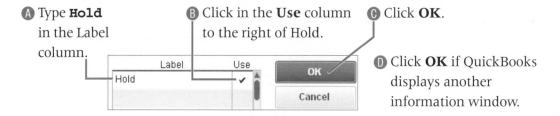

D Click **OK** if QuickBooks displays another information window.

15. Click **OK**.
    QuickBooks closes the Custom Fields for Hairspray window. You did not type in a "hold" here because you will add it to the individual forms instead. If you wish, you can type the custom field information into the Custom Fields for Hairspray window and have it appear on each form or report you create that displays the field.

16. Click **OK** to close the Edit Item window.

17. Close the **Item List**.

Entering Bills

Once you have set up your initial Vendor List, you can begin to enter spending transactions. In this section, you will learn to enter bills and use accounts payable, which is the account credited when bills are entered. When you enter a bill, you *must* specify a vendor because accounts payable will be credited by the transaction.

Entering Vendor Information on Bills

After you select your vendor from the drop-down list at the top of the form, QuickBooks automatically fills the relevant information for that vendor into the appropriate fields on the Enter Bills window. If you wish to enter a bill for a new vendor not yet entered into the Vendor List, QuickBooks will allow you to create the new record "on the fly."

When entering bills, you need to decide if the expenditure is for an expense or items that you will add to your inventory. The following illustration displays the primary features of the Enter Bills window.

In this lesson you will deal only with expenses. You will learn about QuickBooks' inventory features in Lesson 8, Dealing with Physical Inventory.

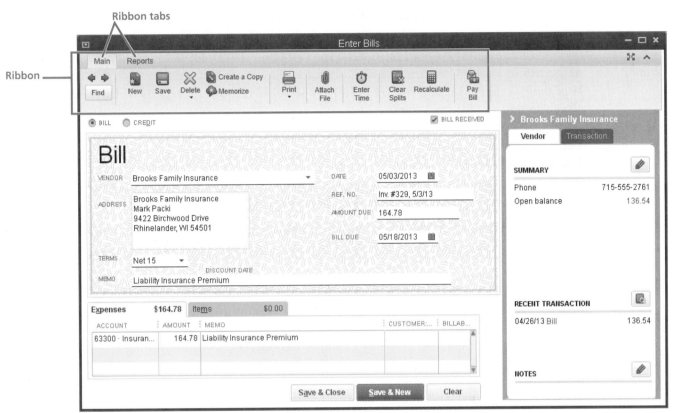

On the right side of the Enter Bills window is a snapshot of information for the selected vendor.

 Ribbons appear at the top of all transaction windows in QuickBooks 2013. The Ribbon tabs group commands by function.

Importance of Entering Reference Numbers and Memos

When entering a bill, it is very important to enter reference information or the bill number in the Ref. No. field and notes in the Memo fields. This information displays in reports and can aid you if you are looking for a duplicate bill number.

Making Changes to Vendor Information on Forms

Whenever you make a change to a vendor's information on a form such as the Enter Bills window, QuickBooks asks if you want to make that change permanent. If you choose Yes, QuickBooks will change the vendor's record. If you choose No, the new information will appear only on the current form; the permanent record remains unchanged.

Allowing List Entries to Fill In

When your insertion point is in a field that draws from a list, you can simply begin to type the entry that you want to choose from the list. QuickBooks will search down the list and fill in the entry for you. This fill-in feature is not case-sensitive, so you can type in lowercase even though the list entry will fill in with the proper capitalization (if you entered it with proper capitalization in the list).

Entering a Vendor "On the Fly"

When you type a new entry into a field that draws from a list, QuickBooks gives you the opportunity to add the record to the list. You can choose to Quick Add the new record (the name will be entered into the list without accompanying information, which you can add at a later date) or to complete a full setup (a New Vendor window appears in which you can type all of the relevant information).

Tab: New to QuickBooks?
Topic: Using forms

Choosing Accounts to Prefill Information

In QuickBooks, when you set up a vendor, you have the option to choose up to three expense accounts for which information will fill in when you make a payment. By setting up expense account information to be prefilled, you can make tracking expenses easier and faster.

When you enter a vendor's name in the Enter Bills, Write Checks, or Enter Credit Card Charges windows, QuickBooks fills in the expense account names for you. This allows you to then enter the amounts to be debited to each expense account. By prefilling information, you can make sure that you use the same expense account(s) each time you use a particular vendor. You can always choose to override the default accounts that are filled in by changing them in the individual transaction window. If there are fewer than three expense accounts for a vendor, just leave the additional account prefill fields blank.

Passing On Expenses to Customers

When you enter a bill, you may be purchasing equipment or supplies for which you wish to pass on the expense to the customer. QuickBooks allows you to easily indicate which expenses are to be billed to a customer by providing a "Billable?" column in the Enter Bills window. Simply ensure that there is a checkmark in the column; it will be easy to create a customer invoice for the item(s).

The Cost of Goods Sold comprises expenses that are directly related to the manufacture of products or services that the company sells. Some expenses that might be considered Cost of Goods Sold are labor, raw materials, depreciation, and overhead. You cannot pass on the Cost of Goods Sold to a customer (it is instead incorporated into the final price of the product), so make sure that you use the proper type of account (expense) if the costs are to be billed to your customer. You will have an opportunity to actually create an invoice for billable costs in Lesson 7, Introducing the Accounting Cycle and Using Classes.

FLASHBACK TO GAAP: COST

Remember that when a company purchases assets, it should record them at cost, not fair market value. For example, if you bought an item worth $750 for $100, the item should be recorded at $100.

Going Behind the Scenes

If you recall in Lesson 1, Introducing QuickBooks Pro, there is a special feature in this book that allows you to take a peek at the accounting that QuickBooks is doing for you when you enter information into forms. In the following illustration, you will find the first instance of the "Behind the Scenes" feature. Remember that the names used in this feature are the account names QuickBooks uses, not traditional accounting nomenclature. If you would like to learn more about basic accounting principles and what the "behind the scenes stuff" is all about, you may want to check out another Labyrinth Learning book, *The ABCs of Accounting, 2nd Edition*.

BEHIND THE SCENES

When entering bills, QuickBooks takes care of all of the accounting for you. Here is an illustration of the accounting going on behind the scenes.

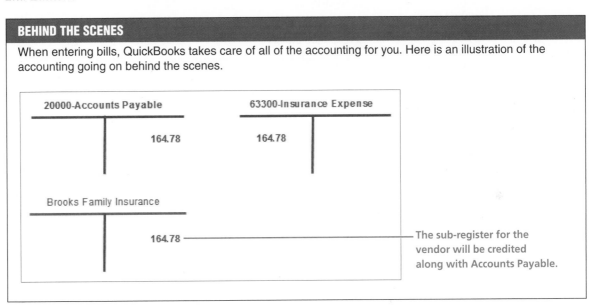

The sub-register for the vendor will be credited along with Accounts Payable.

Behind the Scenes (BTS) Brief

This book includes a feature to help you further understand the accounting that occurs behind the scenes. Labeled "BTS Brief," these accounting notes will appear within Develop Your Skills exercises. As an example (though not associated with an exercise), the BTS Brief for the transaction described in the Behind the Scenes table above would be:

BTS BRIEF

63300•Insurance Expense DR 164.78; 20000•Accounts Payable CR <164.78>

In this feature, DR indicates a debit and CR indicates a credit. CR amounts display with brackets.

Task	Procedure
Enter a bill for an existing vendor	▪ Open the Enter Bills window; select a vendor.
	▪ Enter the amount of the bill; ensure that the terms are correct.
	▪ Expense the bill.
	▪ If desired, select a customer to whom you wish to pass on the expense; click OK.
Enter a bill for a vendor not on the Vendor List	▪ Open the Enter Bills window, fill in the Vendor field, and choose to Quick Add or Set Up.
	▪ Enter the amount of the bill and the terms for the vendor.
	▪ Expense the bill.
	▪ If desired, select a customer to whom you wish to pass on the expense; click OK.

DEVELOP YOUR SKILLS 3.4

Enter Bills

In this exercise, you will enter bills and track expenses.

First you will enter the insurance bill that Lisa just received into QuickBooks.

1. Click the **Enter Bills** task icon in the Vendors area of the Home page.

2. Click the **Vendor drop-down button**, and then choose **Brooks Family Insurance**.

Look at the form and notice that the vendor's terms fill in for you from the underlying list and that the due date is calculated.

3. Tap ⌜Tab⌝ to move to the date field; then, follow these steps to create a bill for Brooks Family Insurance:

Ⓐ Type **050313** here.

Ⓑ Tap ⌜Tab⌝, and then type **Inv. #329, 5/3/13**.

Ⓒ Tap ⌜Tab⌝, and then type **164.78**.

Ⓓ Tap ⌜Tab⌝ three times, and then type this memo.

Ⓔ Click in the **Account** column, and then type **i** to choose **Insurance Expense**.

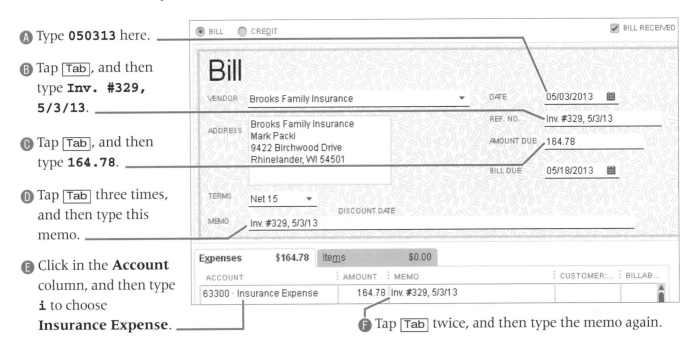

Ⓕ Tap ⌜Tab⌝ twice, and then type the memo again.

When you typed "i," QuickBooks filled in Insurance Expense *from the underlying list for you (in this case, the Chart of Accounts) and replaced the default entry* 69800•Uncategorized Expenses.

When you type in a date field, you do not need to include the slash marks. QuickBooks will format the date properly for you once you move to the next field.

4. Click the **Save & New** button.
QuickBooks records your bill transaction by crediting Accounts Payable and debiting the expense(s) you chose in the Account column (in this case, 63300•Insurance Expense). The Enter Bills window stays open for the next step.

BTS BRIEF

63300•Insurance Expense DR 164.78; 20000•Accounts Payable CR <164.78>

Enter a Bill for a Vendor Not on the Vendor List

When you enter a vendor name that is not on the Vendor List, QuickBooks allows you to add it to the Vendor List.

5. Make sure the **insertion point** is in the Vendor field at the top of a new bill. Type **Willamina Telephone Company**, and then tap ⌜Tab⌝.
A Vendor Not Found window will appear.

6. Click **Set Up**; then, follow these steps to create the new vendor:

Ⓐ Tap `Tab` three times, and then type **Willamina Telephone Company** again.

Ⓑ Tap `Tab`; fill in the **Full Name** and **Job Title** fields as shown, tapping `Tab` to move from field to field.

Ⓒ Tap `Tab` twice, and then type **715-555-1008**.

Ⓓ Click after *France*, tap `Enter`, and then type this address.

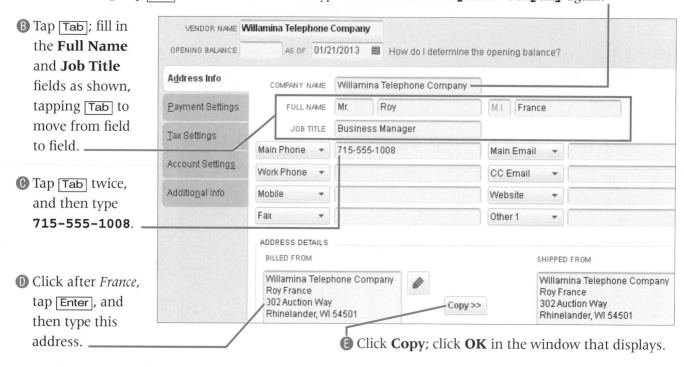

Ⓔ Click **Copy**; click **OK** in the window that displays.

Ⓕ Click the **Payment Settings** tab.　Ⓖ Type **BL-2273** here.

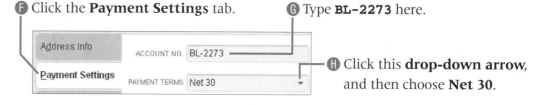

Ⓗ Click this **drop-down arrow**, and then choose **Net 30**.

7. Follow these steps to set up an account to prefill for this vendor and to add additional information:

By choosing an account to prefill for this vendor, you will not have to replace Uncategorized Expenses when you complete the bill entry.

Ⓐ Click the **Account Settings** tab.

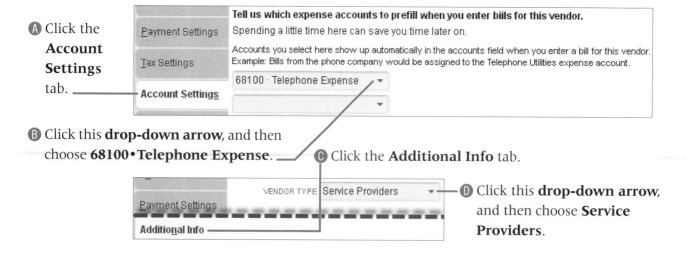

Ⓑ Click this **drop-down arrow**, and then choose **68100•Telephone Expense**.　Ⓒ Click the **Additional Info** tab.

Ⓓ Click this **drop-down arrow**, and then choose **Service Providers**.

8. Click **OK** to accept the information for the new vendor.
   You could also Quick Add the vendor, in which case you would need to return to the Vendor List later and edit the entry to include all of the vendor information in your company file.

9. Finally, follow these steps to finish entering the bill:

 Ensure that **05/03/2013** is the date displayed. ——————————————

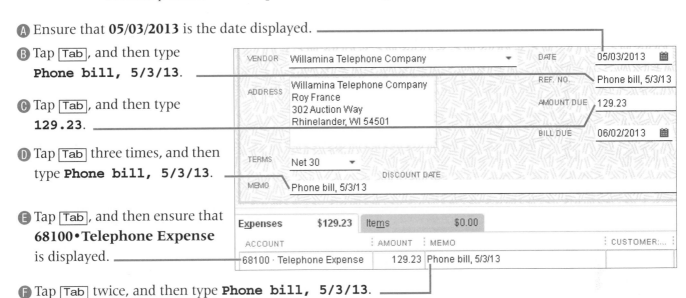

Ⓐ Ensure that **05/03/2013** is the date displayed.

Ⓑ Tap Tab, and then type
Phone bill, 5/3/13.

Ⓒ Tap Tab, and then type
129.23.

Ⓓ Tap Tab three times, and then
type **Phone bill, 5/3/13**.

Ⓔ Tap Tab, and then ensure that
68100•Telephone Expense
is displayed. ——————————————

Ⓕ Tap Tab twice, and then type **Phone bill, 5/3/13**. ——————————————

Rather than typing the information for the reference number and memo fields three times, you can drag to select the information in the Ref. No. field, copy it, and then paste it in the two Memo fields.

TIP

BTS BRIEF

68100•Telephone Expense DR 129.23; 20000•Accounts Payable CR <129.23>

10. Click **Save & Close** to record the bill.

Essential Skills

Paying Bills

Once you have entered your bills, you will need to pay them in a timely manner. In Quick-Books you use the Pay Bills window to debit accounts payable. The other half of the equation (the account that will be credited) depends on the account from which you withdraw funds (or charge, in the case of bill payment by credit card). The Pay Bills window shows all bills due in chronological order by due date. If you wish, you can choose Due on or before and set a date by which to arrange the list. You also have the option to pay only a portion of what you owe on a particular bill by editing the value in the Amt. To Pay column.

When you have used the Enter Bills window, make sure you use the Pay Bills window to issue the payment—*not* the Write Checks window! If you use the Write Checks window, you will expense the purchase twice and not "clear out" the entry in the accounts payable account.

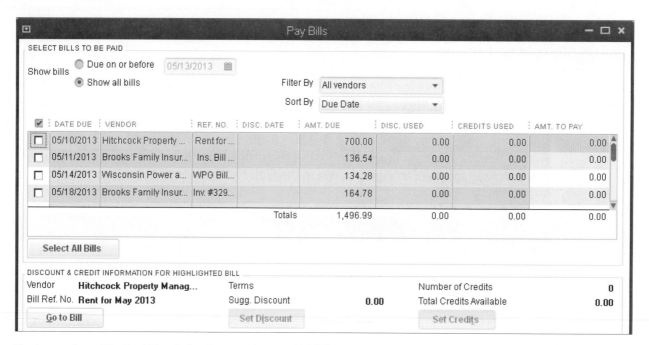

The top portion of the Pay Bills window lets you choose which bills to pay as well as notes any discount and credit information for the selected bill.

Visualize! **Tab:** Tracking Money Out
Topic: Entering and paying bills

Payment Details

At the bottom of the Pay Bills window, you must make three important choices regarding your payment: Payment Date, Payment Method, and Payment Account.

QuickBooks allows you to choose the payment options for each bill.

- **Payment Date**—Make sure you select the date you want the payment to be reflected in your bank and Accounts Payable accounts.
- **Payment Method**—You can choose how you will pay the bill. If you choose to pay by check, you must select whether you will print the check or write it by hand. You will learn how to print checks in the Writing Checks section. You can also choose to pay your bill by credit card. In order to pay by credit card, you must have a credit card account set up. Then you can choose it from the Payment Method drop-down list.
- **Payment Account**—You can select to pay the bill from any bank account you have set up. When you select an account, QuickBooks will show you the ending balance for the account so you can ensure you have enough money to pay the bill. Make sure to select the proper account, as it will be credited behind the scenes!

The Payment Summary Window

Once you have chosen to pay the selected bills in the Pay Bills window, QuickBooks will display a Payment Summary window. There are three options made available to you from this window: pay another bill, print checks, or close the window.

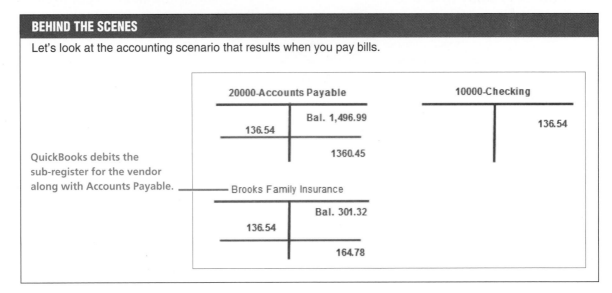

Task	Procedure
Pay a bill	■ Open the Pay Bills window; select the desired bill.
	■ Select the account from which you wish to make the payment, along with the payment method and date.
	■ Click Pay & Close or Pay & New.
Pay a partial amount on a bill	■ Open the Pay Bills window; select the desired bill.
	■ Enter the bill amount in the Amt. To Pay column.
	■ Select the account from which you wish to make the payment, along with the payment method and date.
	■ Click Pay & Close or Pay & New.

DEVELOP YOUR SKILLS 3.5

Pay Bills

In this exercise, you will pay bills that have been entered into QuickBooks.

Lisa is ready to pay one of the bills for Brooks Family Insurance. She will complete this task by using the Pay Bills window because the bill was originally entered in the Enter Bills window and, therefore, is "sitting" in Accounts Payable.

1. Click the **Pay Bills** task icon on the Home page.
   The Pay Bills window opens with the Show All Bills option selected at the top of the window.

Pay Bills

2. Follow these steps to pay the insurance bill:

Ⓐ Click in the box beside the bill due on **5/11/13** for **Brooks Family Insurance**.

Ⓑ Click the **calendar button** in the Payment Date field, and then click to choose **5/11/13**.

☑	DATE DUE	VENDOR	REF. NO.	DISC. DATE	AMT. DUE	DISC. USED	CREDITS USED	AMT. TO PAY
☐	05/10/2013	Hitchcock Property ...	Rent for ...		700.00	0.00	0.00	0.00
☑	05/11/2013	Brooks Family Insur...	Ins. Bill ...		136.54	0.00	0.00	136.54
☐	05/14/2013	Wisconsin Power a...	WPG Bill...		134.28	0.00	0.00	0.00
☐	05/18/2013	Brooks Family Insur...	Inv. #329...		164.78	0.00	0.00	0.00
				Totals	1,496.99	0.00	0.00	136.54

[Clear Selections]

DISCOUNT & CREDIT INFORMATION FOR HIGHLIGHTED BILL

Vendor	**Brooks Family Insurance**	Terms	**Net 15**	Number of Credits	**0**
Bill Ref. No.	**Ins. Bill 4/2013**	Sugg. Discount	**0.00**	Total Credits Available	**0.00**
[Go to Bill]		[Set Discount]		[Set Credits]	

Ⓒ Ensure that **Check** is chosen as the payment method.

PAYMENT

Date	Method		Account
05/11/2013 📅	Check ▼	⦿ To be printed	10000 · Checking ▼
		○ Assign check number	**Ending Balance** 20,157.93

Ⓓ Ensure that **To be printed** is the option chosen here.

Ⓔ Ensure that **10000•Checking** is the account displayed here.

Ⓕ Click the **Pay Selected Bills** button.

3. Click **Pay More Bills** in the Payment Summary window.

Pay a Partial Amount on a Bill

Lisa spoke with her landlord; she made an agreement to pay $500 of the rent due now and the rest in one week. You will help her to pay a partial amount of a bill due.

4. Follow these steps to pay a portion of the Hitchcock Property Management bill:

Ⓐ Click to place a checkmark for the **Hitchcock Property Management** bill.

☑	DATE DUE	VENDOR	REF. NO.	DISC. DATE	AMT. DUE	DISC. USED	CREDITS USED	AMT. TO PAY
☑	05/10/2013	Hitchcock Property ...	Rent for ...		700.00	0.00	0.00	500.00
☐	05/14/2013	Wisconsin Power a...	WPG Bill...		134.28	0.00	0.00	0.00
☐	05/18/2013	Brooks Family Insur...	Inv. #329...		164.78	0.00	0.00	0.00
☐	05/28/2013	Office Superstore	Off Supp...		232.16	0.00	0.00	0.00
				Totals	1,360.45	0.00	0.00	500.00

Ⓑ Drag to select the total amount in the **Amt. To Pay** column and type **500**.

5. Click the **Pay Selected Bills** button to complete the transaction.

6. Click **Pay More Bills** in the Payment Summary window.
Take a look at the current bills to be paid. Notice that the bill for Hitchcock Property Management is still on the list, but only for the remaining amount due of $200.

7. Close the **Pay Bills** window.

Writing and Printing Checks

If you are using the cash basis of accounting, you do not have to use the enter bills and pay bills features of QuickBooks—even though these are useful features for managing cash flow. Instead, you can simply write a check to pay for your expenditures when they are due and expense them properly.

Remember that if you use the enter bills feature, you must use the pay bills feature for the bills you have entered! If you don't, your expenses will be overstated, and you will have funds "hanging out" in Accounts Payable and getting you into trouble.

As with the Pay Bills window, you must decide from which account to issue the check and whether to print or handwrite the check.

The following illustration displays the primary features of the Write Checks window.

You can choose from which account to write the check, if applicable.

Notice that a check number displays if one has been assigned and the Print Later option is not checked.

This area looks like a typical check. The "Pay to the Order of" field will draw from all of your name lists.

Here you can expense your purchase just as you did in the Enter Bills window. You can also pass on expenses to customers or jobs.

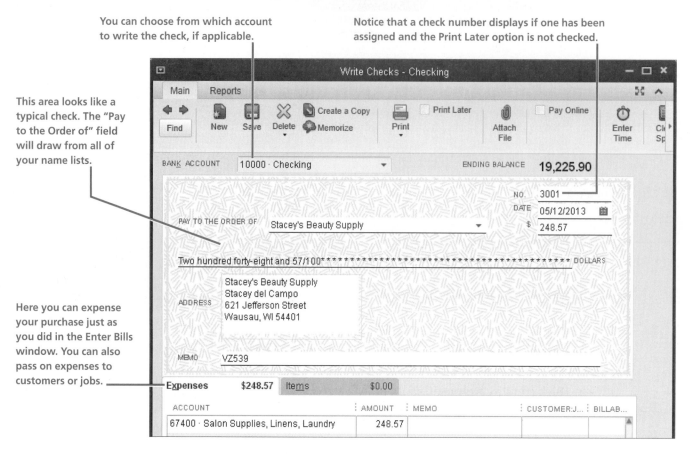

Visualize! **Tab:** Paying Money Out
Topic: Write checks

Printing Checks

When you choose to print your checks in the Pay Bills and Write Checks windows, QuickBooks will "hold" all of them in a queue until you are ready to print a batch of them. You can issue the command to print a batch of checks from the menu bar, or you can click the Print Checks task icon in the Banking area of the Home page.

From this window, you can choose exactly which checks from your batch to print.

BEHIND THE SCENES

The behind the scenes accounting that occurs when you write a check is a hybrid of the two previous transactions (Enter Bills and Pay Bills), with the elimination of Accounts Payable, the middle man.

67400-Salon Supplies, Linens, Laundry		10000-Checking	
248.57			248.57

QUICK REFERENCE	WRITING CHECKS
Task	**Procedure**
Write a check to be printed	▪ Open the Write Checks window; choose the payee. ▪ Type the amount of the check; ensure the Print Later box is checked. ▪ Select the proper expense account(s) on the Expense tab; select a customer if you wish to pass on the expense. ▪ Click Save & Close or Save & New.
Record a handwritten check	▪ Open the Write Checks window; choose the payee. ▪ Type the amount of the check; ensure there is a *not* a checkmark in the Print Later box. ▪ Type the check number in the "No." field at the top of the window. ▪ Select the proper expense account(s) on the Expense tab; select a customer if you wish to pass on the expense. ▪ Click Save & Close or Save & New.
Print a batch of checks	▪ Choose File→Print Forms→Checks. ▪ Select the checks you wish to print from the Select Checks to Print window; click OK. ▪ Select the correct options in the Print Checks window, ensuring the correct first check number is entered; click OK.

Write and Print Checks

In this exercise, Lisa will pay for expenses with both printed and handwritten checks.

Write
Checks

1. Click the **Write Checks** task icon in the Banking area of the Home page.

FROM THE KEYBOARD

Ctrl+w to open the
Write Checks window
Spacebar to check/
uncheck a selected
checkbox

2. Follow these steps to complete the check:

Ⓐ Click in the
   Print Later box.

Ⓑ Tap Tab, and then
   type **051213** here.

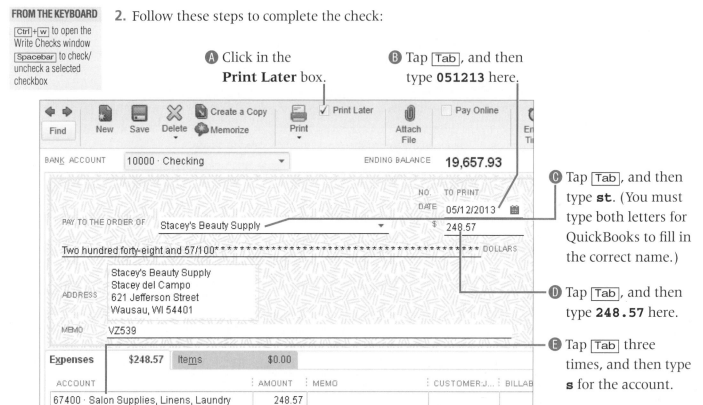

Ⓒ Tap Tab, and then type **st**. (You must type both letters for QuickBooks to fill in the correct name.)

Ⓓ Tap Tab, and then type **248.57** here.

Ⓔ Tap Tab three times, and then type **s** for the account.

QuickBooks automatically fills in the vendor's account number into the Memo field of the check.

BTS BRIEF

67400•Salon Supplies, Linens, Laundry DR 248.57; 10000•Checking CR <248.57>

3. Click **Save & New** to record this check and leave the Write Checks window open.

Record a Handwritten Check

You may not always be at your computer when you wish to write a check. In this situation, Lisa has taken her checkbook shopping and needs to record the handwritten check.

4. Click to remove the checkmark from the **Print Later** box.

The check number field can be edited once this checkmark is removed.

5. Follow these steps to record the handwritten check:

Ⓐ Tap `Tab`, and then type **1101**.　　Ⓑ Tap `Tab`, and ensure that **05/12/2013** is the date displayed.

Ⓒ Click here, type **Cost Club**, tap `Tab`, and then choose to **Quick Add** the new vendor.

Ⓓ Type **183.46** as the amount.

Ⓔ Click here, and then type **o**.

Ⓕ Tap `Tab`, and then type **53.86**.

Ⓖ Click here, type **c1**, and then tap `Tab`.

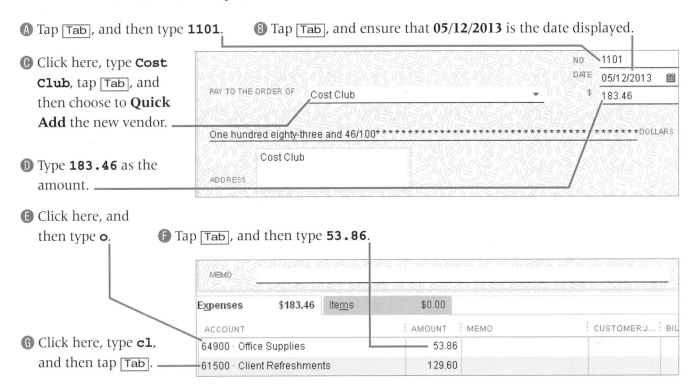

Notice that the expenditure was split between multiple expense accounts and that QuickBooks filled in the remaining amount based on the amount you entered on the first line.

BTS BRIEF
64900•Office Supplies DR 53.86; 61500•Client Refreshments DR 129.60; 10000•Checking CR <183.46>

6. Click the **Save & Close** button to complete the transaction.

Print a Batch of Checks

Once you have indicated that checks are to be printed, you need to issue a separate command to print them.

7. Click the **Print Checks** task icon in the Banking area of the Home page.

If you don't see the Print Checks task icon, use the sizing arrow to make the Home page larger or choose File→Print Forms→Checks.

Print Checks

8. Tap `Tab`, and then type **3000** as the first check number.
By default, all of the checks will be selected.

9. Click the checkmark to the left of the **Brooks Family Insurance** to deselect it.

✓	DATE	PAYEE	AMOUNT
	05/11/2013	Brooks Family Insurance	136.54
✓	05/11/2013	Hitchcock Property Manage...	500.00
✓	05/12/2013	Stacey's Beauty Supply	248.57

10. Click **OK**.

The Print Checks window will appear.

If you wish to be "green," you can choose to not physically print the checks in the next step by choosing to print to PDF or to just preview how they would appear if printed.

11. Ensure that **Voucher** is chosen as the check style and then click **Print**.

QuickBooks will display a Print Checks - Confirmation window. Here you have the opportunity to reprint any checks that did not print correctly or to troubleshoot the order in which your checks printed.

12. Click **OK** in the Print Checks - Confirmation window.

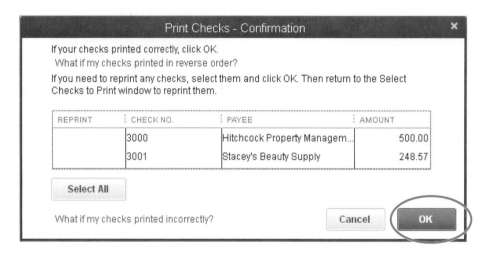

Notice that there are links to help you if your checks do not print correctly.

Producing Vendor Reports

Once you have recorded your vendor-related transactions, QuickBooks has many reports that you can produce to view your data. In Lesson 2, Creating a Company, you learned about list reports. The other two general types of reports are listed below.

- Summary reports subtotal your data and provide a summary.
- Transaction reports show each transaction that makes up the subtotal found in a summary report.

If you wish to see all transactions grouped by vendor, there are two different reports you can run. The Vendor Balance Detail report (found in the Vendors & Payables category) shows only those transactions affecting Accounts Payable (transactions entered and paid as "bills"). The Expense by Vendor reports (both summary and detail, found in the Company & Financial category) show transactions made by all payment methods.

The Report Window Toolbar

The Vendor Balance Summary report toolbar is shown in the following illustration. When viewing other reports, you may also see additional buttons specific to certain reports.

Some of the basic functions that the toolbar buttons allow you the ability to do include:

- Change and memorize the settings for the report
- Print or email the report; clicking the Print button will also allow you to choose to preview how the report will appear in printed form before you issue the command to print it
- Export the report to Microsoft Excel
- Share the report with other users as a template

QuickReports

QuickReports can be run from the various center windows. They show all transactions recorded in QuickBooks for a particular list record. You will use this report to get a quick snapshot of all vendor transactions for Hitchcock Property Management in the Develop Your Skills exercise.

QuickZoom

QuickBooks has a great feature called QuickZoom. This feature allows you to zoom through underlying sub-reports until you reach the form where the data was originally entered. This can be extremely useful if you have questions as to where a figure in a report comes from.

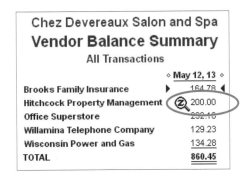

The zoom pointer indicates that you can double-click to dive deeper into your data. The number of layers to zoom through depends on the type of report (or graph) with which you started. Here, a double click would show all transactions that led to the $200 balance for Hitchcock Property Management.

Task	Procedure
Produce a QuickReport	■ Open the center with the record on which you wish to run the report. ■ Click the list entry. ■ Click the QuickReport link at the right of the center window. ■ Set the correct date range.
Produce a vendor-related report using the Report Center	■ Choose Reports→Report Center. ■ Choose Vendors & Payables as the report category. ■ Click on the report you wish to produce in the main section of the Report Center. ■ Click the Display report button.
Print or preview a report	■ Display the report you wish to print or preview. ■ Click the Print button on the toolbar. ■ Click Preview or Print.

DEVELOP YOUR SKILLS 3.7

Produce Vendor Reports

In this exercise, you will produce a vendor QuickReport, a vendor summary report, and a vendor detail report.

1. Click the **Vendors** button on the Icon Bar.

2. Single-click **Hitchcock Property Management** to select it.
   You must always select the list item on which you wish to run a QuickReport.

3. Click the **QuickReport** link at the right of the Vendor Center window.
   If you cannot see the QuickReport link, use the sizing arrows to make the window wider.

4. Change the date range to **All** by typing **a** to select All from the Dates list.

Chez Devereaux Salon and Spa
Vendor QuickReport
All Transactions

Type	Date	Num	Memo	Account	Clr	Split	Debit	Credit
Hitchcock Property Management								
Bill	04/30/2013	Rent...	Rent for May...	20000 · Accounts...		67100 · Rent...		700.00
Bill Pmt -Check	05/11/2013	3000	LS2009156	10000 · Checking		20000 · Acco...		500.00

A vendor QuickReport will display all transactions for a selected vendor within a designated date range.

When you first display a report, the Dates field is selected. Typing *a* chooses All from the Dates list.

5. Close the **Vendor QuickReport** and the **Vendor Center** windows.

Create a Vendor Summary Report and Use QuickZoom

You will now create a report that shows what you owe all vendors. Then you will use QuickZoom to see the details of where a balance originated.

6. Choose **Reports→Vendors & Payables→Vendor Balance Summary**.
   You can generate reports through the Report Center or the menu bar with the same result. The report will be displayed with the date range of All selected, as it is the default for this particular report.

7. Place your mouse pointer over the amount listed for Brooks Family Insurance until you see the **zoom pointer**, and then **double-click**.
   A Vendor Balance Detail report will be displayed that shows the transactions leading to the balance for Brooks Family Insurance. You can also display a Vendor Balance Detail report directly by choosing it from the menu bar or Report Center.

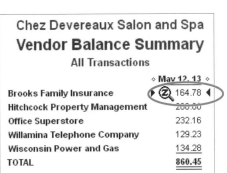

8. Place your mouse pointer over the Bill date 5/3/13 that you entered for this vendor until you see the **zoom pointer**, and then **double-click**.

Type	Date	Num	Account	Amount	Balance
Brooks Family Insurance					
Bill	04/26/2013	Ins. B...	20000 · Accounts...	136.54	136.54
Bill	05/03/2013	Inv. #...	20000 · Accounts...	164.78	301.32
Bill Pmt -Check	05/11/2013		20000 · Accounts...	-136.54	164.78
Total Brooks Family Insurance				164.78	164.78
TOTAL				**164.78**	**164.78**

Chez Devereaux Salon and Spa
Vendor Balance Detail
All Transactions

The Enter Bills window will open with the bill that you entered for this vendor earlier in this lesson.

9. Choose **Window→Close All**.
   Click No if asked to memorize any of the reports displayed.

Display a Vendor Detail Report

Now you will create a report that lists the details for all of the unpaid bills in Accounts Payable.

10. Choose **Reports→Vendors & Payables→Unpaid Bills Detail**.

11. Tap ⓐ to set the date range to All.
    The Unpaid Bills Detail report will be displayed, listing the five unpaid bills totaling $860.45.

12. Close the report, clicking **No** when asked if you want to memorize it.

Working with QuickBooks Graphs

QuickBooks provides several graphs along with the preset reports. QuickBooks graphs are accessible through the Reports option on the menu bar or through the Report Center.

Types of QuickBooks Graphs

Following are the six graphs provided by QuickBooks. If you can't find a graph that suits your needs, you always have the option of exporting a report to Microsoft Excel and using the Excel charting features to create additional charts and graphs.

The graphs provided in QuickBooks include:

- Income and Expense
- Sales
- Net Worth
- Accounts Payable
- Accounts Receivable
- Budget vs. Actual

The Graph Toolbar

The Graph toolbar displays different buttons depending on which graph you have created. Once you have created your graph, you can use the Graph toolbar to do a variety of tasks such as:

- Customize your graph by date
- Choose how to view your data
- View your next group of information
- Print your graph
- Refresh the data contained within your graph (if you have made changes to your data since the graph was created)

For some graphs, there are also buttons at the bottom of the window that allow you to choose how to view the pie chart data at the bottom of the window (e.g., by Income or by Expense).

QuickZooming with Graphs

The QuickZoom feature you used previously in this lesson for reports is also available with graphs. You simply double-click on a portion of a graph (when you see the QuickZoom pointer) to zoom in and see where the data comes from.

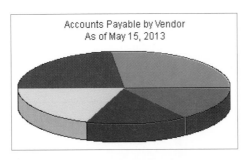

Accounts Payable by Vendor
As of May 15, 2013

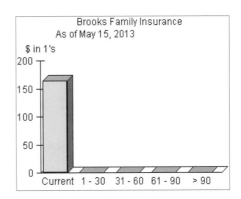

Brooks Family Insurance
As of May 15, 2013

$ in 1's

Current 1 - 30 31 - 60 61 - 90 > 90

Chez Devereaux Salon and Spa
A/P Aging QuickZoom
As of May 15, 2013

◇ Type ◇	Date ◇	Num ◇	Due Date ◇	Aging ◇	Open Balance
Brooks Family Insurance					
Bill	05/03/2013	Inv. #...	05/18/2013		164.78
Total Brooks Family Insurance					164.78

Notice that when you QuickZoom on a pie chart, you see a bar graph. When you QuickZoom on a bar graph, you see a report showing where the data originated.

QUICK REFERENCE	CREATING AN ACCOUNTS PAYABLE GRAPH
Task	**Procedure**
Produce an Accounts Payable graph	Choose Reports→Vendors & Payables→Accounts Payable Graph.

DEVELOP YOUR SKILLS 3.8
Create QuickBooks Graphs

In this exercise, you will create a graph that will depict what is in your Accounts Payable account. You will use QuickZoom to drill down to the source of the data for one vendor.

1. Choose **Reports→Vendors & Payables→Accounts Payable Graph**.

2. Follow these steps to set the date for the graph:

Ⓐ Click the **Dates** button on the graph toolbar.

Ⓑ Type **051513**, and then tap Tab.

Ⓒ Click **OK**.

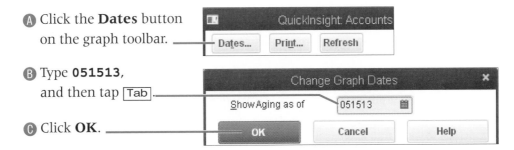

QuickInsight: Accounts

Dates... Print... Refresh

Change Graph Dates

Show Aging as of 051513

OK Cancel Help

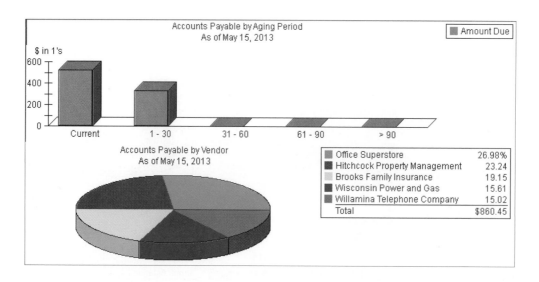

The Accounts Payable graph will be displayed with all balances owing as of May 15.

3. Place your mouse pointer over the yellow slice that shows the balance due to Brooks Family Insurance, and then hold down the right mouse button.
   Holding down the mouse button allows you to see the dollar amount corresponding to the "pie slice."

4. Double-click on the pie slice for **Brooks Family Insurance**.
   A bar graph will appear showing just the amount for the selected vendor.

5. Double-click on the bar graph showing the current amount owed to the vendor.
   An A/P Aging report will be displayed.

6. Double-click on the **bill dated 5/3/13** for Brooks Family Insurance.
   The Enter Bills window will be displayed. This is as far as QuickZoom will go!

7. Choose **Window→Close all**.

8. Choose **Company→Home Page**.

9. Choose the appropriate option for your situation:

   ■ If you are continuing on to the next lesson or to the end-of-lesson exercises, leave QuickBooks open.

   ■ If you are finished working in QuickBooks for now, choose **File→Exit**.

Concepts Review

Concepts Review   http://labyrinthelab.com/qb13

To check your knowledge of the key concepts introduced in this lesson, complete the Concepts Review quiz by going to the URL listed above.

Reinforce Your Skills

Before you begin the Reinforce Your Skills exercises, complete one of these options:

- *Open* **[Your name] Tea Shoppe at the Lake, Lesson 1** *or Tea Shoppe at the Lake, Lesson 3 from your file storage location.*
- *Restore* **Tea Shoppe at the Lake, Lesson 3 (Portable)** *from your file storage location. If you need to review how to restore a portable company file, take a peek at Develop Your Skills 3.1. Make sure to place your name as the first word in the company filename (e.g., Susie's Tea Shoppe at the Lake, Lesson 3).*

REINFORCE YOUR SKILLS 3.1
Manage the Vendor List

In this exercise, you will work with the Vendor List for Tea Shoppe at the Lake. You will edit an existing vendor, create a new vendor, and delete a vendor.

To begin, Valley Insurance Company has changed its name to Vista Insurance Company. You will help Susie to make that change in QuickBooks.

1. Choose **Vendors→Vendor Center**.

2. Double-click **Valley Insurance Company** to open it for editing. (Scroll down, if necessary.)

3. Change the vendor's name to **Vista Insurance Company**.
   You will have to change the name in five separate places, including on the Payment Settings tab. This new name will be reflected in all transactions that deal with this vendor—past and present.

4. Click **OK** to accept the change.

Add a New Vendor

Susie has decided to start selling some new candies that she has discovered. You will set up the company as a vendor.

5. Click the **New Vendor** button, and then choose **New Vendor**.

6. Enter the following information to create a new vendor.

Company Name	**Carmela's Old Fashioned Candies**
Contact Name	**Ms. Carmela Hutch, Owner**
Address	**525 E. San Marcos Road** **San Marcos, CA 92069**
Phone	**760-555-9438**
Fax	**760-555-9455**
Type	Suppliers
Terms	Net 15
Account #	**84-976**

7. Click **OK** to accept the new vendor record.

Delete a Vendor

8. Click **Carlsbad Restaurant Supply** to select it.

9. Choose **Edit→Delete Vendor**.

10. Click **OK** to confirm the deletion.

11. Close the **Vendor Center** window.

REINFORCE YOUR SKILLS 3.2

Create and Populate Custom Fields

In this exercise, you will create and populate a custom field.

1. Choose **Customers→Customer Center**.

2. Double-click to open **Suzanne Stevens** for editing.

3. Click the **Additional Info** tab, and then click the **Define Fields** button.

4. Type **Favorite Drink** as a label, and then place a check in the **Cust** column to the right of the label.

5. Click **OK** twice to accept the new custom field.

6. Click in the **Favorite Drink Custom Field** for Suzanne, and then type **Soy latte w/ honey**.

7. Click **OK** to close the Edit Customer window.

8. Close the **Customer Center**.
   The custom field will now be available for all customers.

REINFORCE YOUR SKILLS 3.3

Enter and Pay Bills

In this exercise, you will enter a bill Susie just received. You will also pay all bills due by a certain date for Susie.

1. Choose **Vendors→Enter Bills**.

2. Click the **drop-down arrow** and choose **San Marcos Gas & Electric** as the Vendor.

3. Set the date to **5/19/2013**, and then enter **May 2013 G & E Bill** as the memo and ref. no.

4. Type **$173.54** as the amount, and choose **Utilities** as the account.

5. Click the **Save & Close** button to enter the transaction and close the window.

Pay a Bill

6. Open the Pay Bills window by choosing **Vendors→Pay Bills**.

7. Choose all bills that are due on or before **5/21/2013** (you should find four).

8. Set the date to **5/21/13**, and choose to print the checks.

9. Click **Pay Selected Bills** to record the payments and close the window.

10. Click **Done** in the Payment Summary Window.

Write and Print Checks

In this exercise, you will write a check for an expense and print the checks you have created.

1. Choose **Banking→Write Checks**.

2. Set the check to print later.

3. Set the date to **5/20/2013**.

4. Type **San Diego County** into the Pay to the Order of field and choose to **Quick Add** it to the Vendor List.

5. Type **$125** as the amount and **Business License, 2013** as the memo.

6. Select **Business Licenses and Permits** as the account.

7. Click **Save & Close** to accept the transaction and close the window.

Print a Batch of Checks

8. Choose **File→Print Forms→Checks**.
   Notice that, by default, QuickBooks selects all checks; you can change this if you need to.

9. Ensure that **Checking** is the bank account and that **1104** is the first check number.

10. Click **OK** to move to the Print Checks window.
    At this point you can verify that the correct printer and check style are selected. Now, either "stay green" and print the checks to a PDF file or physically print the checks using an available printer.

11. Click **Print** once you have chosen how you will print the checks.

12. Click **OK** in the Print Checks - Confirmation window.

Create Vendor Reports

In this exercise, you will run a vendor report for Tea Shoppe at the Lake.

1. Choose **Reports→Vendors & Payables→Transaction List by Vendor**.

2. Set the date range to **All**.

3. Submit your report based on the guidelines provided by your instructor.

4. Choose **Window→Close All**.

5. Choose the appropriate option for your situation:
   - If you are continuing on to the next lesson or the rest of the end-of-lesson exercises, leave QuickBooks open.
   - If you are finished working in QuickBooks for now, choose **File→Exit**.

Apply Your Skills

Before you begin the Apply Your Skills exercises, complete one of these options:

- *Open* **[Your name] Wet Noses Veterinary Clinic, Lesson 1** *or* **Wet Noses Veterinary Clinic, Lesson 3** *from your file storage location.*

- *Restore* **Wet Noses Veterinary Clinic, Lesson 3 (Portable)** *from your file storage location. Make sure to place your name as the first word in the company filename (e.g., Sadie's Wet Noses Veterinary Clinic, Lesson 3). If you need to review how to restore a portable company file, see Develop Your Skills 3.1.*

APPLY YOUR SKILLS 3.1

Work with the Vendor List and Vendor Type List

In this exercise, you will manage the Vendor List for Wet Noses.

1. Using the following information, create three new **Vendor List** entries.

Name	Casey's Consulting	Take a Walk	Billy's Van Service
Address	902 Creekview Dr. Kirkland, WA 98034	13602 75th Ave NE Seattle, WA 98132	9501 NE 182nd Pl Bothell, WA 98011
Phone	425-555-9569	206-555-9433	425-555-4477
Fax	425-555-9568	206-555-9434	425-555-4478
Contact Name	Ms. Casey Scripps	Ms. Shannon High	Mr. Billy Ranch
Job Title	Owner	Walker	President
Type	Consultant	Service Providers	Service Providers
Terms	Due on Receipt	Net 15	Net 15
Account Number	JR154	VET87	BB23

2. Edit the **Puget Sound Power Company** vendor record to display **Shaunda Jones** as the contact.

3. Add the following vendor types to the existing vendor records, adding a new entry to the **Vendor Type List** when necessary:

- Wyland Broadband: Service Providers
- Northshore Water Company: Utilities
- Oberg Property Management: Service Providers
- Puget Sound Power Company: Utilities
- Seattle Vet Supply: Suppliers
- Whoville Office Supplies: Supplies
- Brian's Pet Taxi: Service Providers

APPLY YOUR SKILLS 3.2
Create Custom Fields

In this exercise, you will create a custom field and populate it for customers.

1. Open the **Customer Center**.

2. Double-click **Becky Karakash:Dog-Spencer**, and then click the **Additional Info** tab.

3. Click the **Define Fields** button.

4. Add the following **Labels** for Customers: **Species**, **Breed**, **Color**, and **Gender**.

5. Click **OK** twice to add the new custom fields.

6. Fill in the custom fields for Spencer using the following information:
   - Species: **Canine**
   - Breed: **Golden Retriever**
   - Color: **Light Brown**
   - Gender: **Male**

7. Click **OK** to close the Edit Job window.

8. Close the **Customer Center**.

APPLY YOUR SKILLS 3.3
Perform Vendor Transactions

In this exercise, you will deal with expenses incurred by Wet Noses.

1. On 7/2/2013, Dr. James received a bill from Seattle Vet Supply for $3,813.58. It should be broken down by account as follows: $1,773.25 for medical supplies, $1,056.92 for vaccines, and $983.41 for medicines. The ref. no./memo is: Inv. #77-9-56.

2. Enter a bill received on 7/8/2013 from Northshore Water Company for **$210.67**. The ref. no./memo is **Water Bill, 7/2013**.

3. On 7/18/2013, a bill was received from Puget Sound Power Company for **$241.33**. The ref. no./memo is **Power Bill, 7/2013**.

4. Enter a bill received on 7/21/2013 from Wyland Broadband for **$159.44**. It should be broken down by account as follows: $55.99 for Internet service and $103.45 for Telephone service. The ref. no./memo is **Int/Phone July 2013**.

5. On 7/21/2013, Sadie decided to sit down and pay her bills. Pay all of the bills due on or before 7/22/2013. You will print the checks later.

6. Choose **Done** in the Payment Summary window.

Write and Print Checks

7. Dr. James took all of her employees out for a working lunch at Laura's Café on 7/11/2013. The total cost was **$84.35**. She wrote a check at the restaurant, using check number 1418.

8. Print all checks in the queue using 1419 as the first check number.

Answer Questions with Reports

In this exercise, you will answer questions for Dr. James by running reports. You may wish to display the Report Center in List View to help you answer the questions. Ask your instructor if you should print the reports, print (save) them as PDF files, export them to Excel, or simply display them on the screen.

1. Are any of the bills overdue?

2. Is there a way to see all of the transactions for each vendor for the month of July 2013?

3. I would like to have a list of the phone numbers for all of the vendors. Can you create one for me?

4. Can I see a graph of the total amount owed and the amount by vendor as of July 31, 2013?

5. Submit your reports based on the guidelines provided by your instructor.

6. Choose the appropriate option for your situation:
   - If you are continuing on to the next lesson or the Critical Thinking exercises, leave QuickBooks open.
   - If you are finished working in QuickBooks for now, choose **File→Exit**.

Critical Thinking

In the course of working through the following Critical Thinking exercises, you will be utilizing various skills taught in this and previous lesson(s). Take your time and think carefully about the tasks presented to you. Turn back to the lesson content if you need assistance.

3.1 Sort Through the Stack

Before You Begin: Restore the **Monkey Business, Lesson 3 (Portable)** *file from your storage location. (Remember that you are to leave the password field blank for Mary.) You also have the option of opening either the final file from Critical Thinking 2.1 or Monkey Business, Lesson 3 from your storage location.*

You have been hired by Mary Minard to help her with her organization's books. She is the owner of Monkey Business, a nonprofit organization that provides low-income students with help in preparing for college placement exams and applying for scholarships. You have just sat down at her desk and found a pile of papers. It is your job to sort through the papers and make sense of what you find, entering information into QuickBooks whenever appropriate and answering any other questions in a word-processing document saved as **Critical Thinking 3-1**. Remember, you are digging through papers on a desk, so it is up to you to determine the correct order in which to complete the tasks.

- Sticky note: New source for books—Enter Woods Publishing Company as a vendor: 921 Pamela Lake Drive, Salem, OR 97301; 503.555.2211; Terms—Net 30; Contact—Pam Woods.
- Bill: From Salem Power and Light, dated 7/3/2013, for $94.57, due 7/13/2013.
- Canceled check: Written to USPS for stamps on 7/2/2013 for $25.10, number 1003.
- Note: Would like to track employee anniversaries. How can I do that?
- Scribbled on a scrap of paper: I need a report that shows all of the bills that have been entered into QuickBooks.
- Packing slip and bill: Materials received for a FAFSA seminar; need to enter the bill for $124.32, payable to Chandler Distributors, dated 7/1/2013, terms Net 15. (Mary is not tracking inventory in QuickBooks!)
- Carbon copies of checks: Used to pay Salem Power and Light (#1004, 7/7/2013, for full amount) and Chandler Distributors (#1005, 7/7/2013, for full amount).
- Note: We have "customers" who are referred to us by the school district. Can we include them in the customer type list?
- Bill: From Willamette Cable for Internet and Phone service, dated 7/5/2013, for $112.65, due 7/15/2013.
- Printed email message from accountant: Please send a report that shows the amount owed to each vendor as of 7/10/2013.
- Bill: From Jones Brothers' Pizza for food provided at an event, dated 7/8/2013, payment due on receipt, for $67.21.

3.2 Tackle the Tasks

Now is your chance to work a little more with Chez Devereaux Salon and Spa and apply the skills that you have learned in this lesson to accomplish additional tasks. Open or restore the **Critical Thinking 3.2** company or portable company file from your file storage location, or open the company file you used in the Develop Your Skills exercises for this lesson. Then, enter the following tasks.

Add a Vendor	Enter the following vendor:
	■ Midwest Salon Unlimited 6439 Washington Square, Wausau, WI 54401
	■ Contact: Abby Gibbs, Manager, 715-555-9922
	■ Acct #: PR203X, Type: Suppliers, Terms: Net 15
Delete Profile List Entries	Delete Retail and Wholesale from the Customer Type List
Enter a Bill	Enter the following bill from Midwest Salon Unlimited:
	■ Dated: 05/14/2013; Amt. $63.27; Memo- Inv. #17-222
	■ Acct: 67400•Salon Supplies, Linens, Laundry
Pay Bills	■ Pay all bills due during the month of May.
	■ Payment date: 05/18/2013; checks to be printed
Write and Print Checks	■ Write a check on 5/17/13 to Allen Brothers Grocery for $36.21 for Office Supplies, choose for it to be printed later.
	■ Print all checks waiting in the queue, first check #3002.
Display Reports	Display reports that will answer the following questions:
	■ Which bills are due?
	■ What is my company's current balance with each vendor?
	■ What is the contact information and current balance for each vendor?

You may use the company file from this exercise for the Develop Your Skills exercise in Lesson 4 if you wish.

3.3 Use the Web as a Learning Tool

Throughout this book, you will be provided with an opportunity to use the Internet as a learning tool by completing WebQuests. According to the original creators of WebQuests, as described on their website (WebQuest.org), a WebQuest is "an inquiry-oriented activity in which most or all of the information used by learners is drawn from the web." To complete the WebQuest projects in this book, navigate to the student resource center and choose the WebQuest for the lesson on which you are currently working. The subject of each WebQuest will be relevant to the material found in the lesson.

WebQuest Subject: Making profile lists and custom fields work for you

Working with Customers

LESSON OUTLINE

Working with the Customer Center
Understanding and Creating Items
Creating Invoices
Receiving Payments
Entering Sales Receipts
Integrating with Microsoft Word
Working with Customer-Related and P&L Reports
Concepts Review
Reinforce Your Skills
Apply Your Skills
Critical Thinking

LESSON OBJECTIVES

After studying this lesson, you will be able to:

- Use the Customer Center and Customers & Jobs List
- Create service and non-inventory items
- Create Word documents based on QuickBooks lists
- Create invoices and receive payment on them
- Enter sales receipts
- Work with customer-related and profit and loss reports

L et's face it. The best part of being in business is creating and developing relationships with customers. After all, who doesn't enjoy receiving payment for a job well done? Intuit describes a customer as "any person, business, or group that buys or pays for the services or products that your business or organization sells or provides." When working with QuickBooks, you can consider a customer anyone who pays you funds. This simple definition will help you if you have a unique business, such as a not-for-profit organization that doesn't normally use the term "customer." The job feature is an optional aspect of QuickBooks, but the feature can be extremely helpful if you have more than one project for a customer. In this lesson, you will examine QuickBooks' lists, activities, and reports that allow you to effectively deal with customers.

Chez Devereaux Salon and Spa

Lisa has learned from her friend Adrianna that the next step she needs to complete is to set up her company to track customers and sales transactions. She will begin by working on her Customers & Jobs List, which is a part of the Customer Center. Once her customers have been entered, she will be able to create transactions for them. In order to create sales transactions such as invoices and sales receipts, though, she must first create items that will be used to direct income into the proper accounts behind the scenes. Finally, Lisa will create reports that will tell her about her customer-related transactions as well as a profit and loss report that will show the profitability of the business.

Lisa can access the Customers & Jobs List, and all of the transactions concerning a customer, from the Customer Center. The following illustration shows the Customer Center with Holly Rose selected.

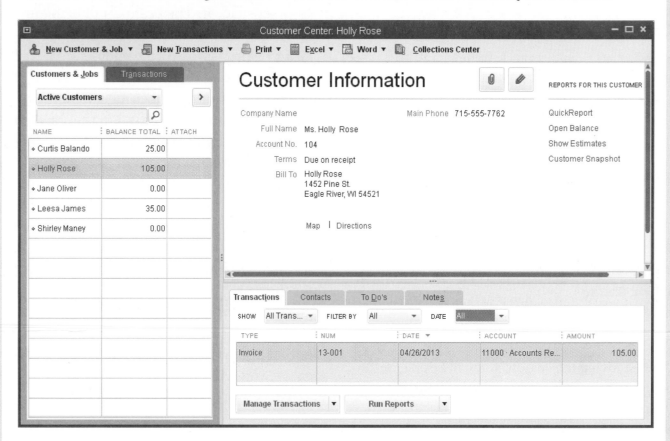

In this lesson, you will also help Lisa create a letter for a customer using the list data from QuickBooks merged with a template from Microsoft Word.

Visualize!   **Tab:** Tracking Money In
Topic: Sales overview; Building blocks of sales

Working with the Customer Center

When opened, the Customer Center gives you a quick look at all of your customers. If you recall from the introduction, a customer is anyone who pays you funds. This general definition is useful because it applies to all types of organizations, even those that do not have "customers" in the traditional sense, such as not-for-profits.

Remember that QuickBooks uses lists to organize your company's information. Lists allow you to store information that you can easily fill into forms by using drop-down arrows or by just starting to type the entry and letting QuickBooks fill in the rest. Lists comprise the database aspect of QuickBooks. As an option, the Customers & Jobs List can be exported to contact management software such as Microsoft Outlook.

The Customer Center window provides you with the following information:

- The name of each customer and any jobs that have been created
- The balance that each customer owes
- Information for the selected customer or job
- Transactions affecting the selected customer or job

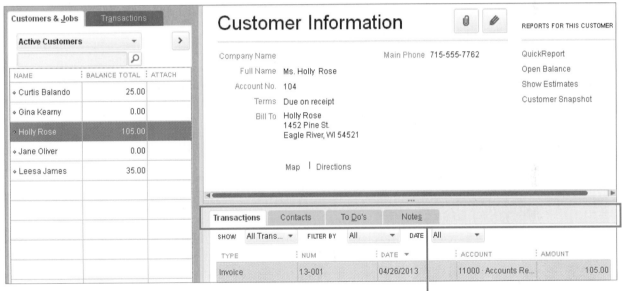

The Customer Information window displayed to the right of the Customers & Jobs List relates to the selected customer record.

These tabs help track information for each customer.

The Customers & Jobs List tracks a lot of information for each customer and each job. This information is organized onto five tabs: Address Info, Payment Settings, Sales Tax Settings, Additional Info, and Job Info. If you have jobs assigned to a customer, you will see only three tabs. You will manage the jobs in the separate job records. If you want to track information that does not already have a field, you can create Custom Fields to customize QuickBooks for your unique business, as you learned about in the previous lesson. Remember, the more information you enter for each customer, the more flexibility you will have later when you learn how to customize reports. When you utilize fields, you can sort, group, and filter your reports using those fields. You can access the Customers & Jobs List through the Customer Center.

Managing the Customers & Jobs List

The list management techniques that you learned about in Lesson 3, Working with Vendors are very similar for the Customers & Jobs List as well as the Employees List. The next three concepts will serve as a review of creating, editing, and deleting Customers & Jobs, Vendors, and Employees List entries.

Creating a New Customer

To enter customer transactions, you must first enter your customers into the Customers & Jobs List. Customers can be entered at any time and can even be entered "on the fly" into the customer field on forms such as Create Invoices and Enter Sales Receipts; you will then have to select Quick Add or Setup from the pop-up window. Once you have added a customer to the list, you can create individual jobs for that customer.

Editing an Existing Customer

Once you have created a customer, you can always go back and edit that customer through the Customer Center. The one item that cannot be edited after you have created and saved a new customer is the opening balance (it must be adjusted through the customer register).

Deleting a Customer

You can delete a customer or job from the Customers & Jobs List *as long as you have not used it in a transaction*.

Making a Customer Inactive

If you have a customer with whom you are no longer working, you cannot *delete* him from the Customers & Jobs List if he has been involved in any transactions. What you can do is make him *inactive*.

You can also make list entries inactive in the other lists if they are no longer used. The benefit of making list entries inactive is that they will no longer clutter your lists. If you find you need a list entry again, you can reactivate it.

Merging List Entries

Occasionally, you may find that you have two records created for the same list entry. Quick-Books allows you to merge these duplicated entries into one. You perform the merge by editing one of the entries and changing its name to exactly match the other. The two entries will permanently become one once you complete the merge. All prior transactions with the merged list entry will reflect the change in name.

Merging list entries *cannot* be undone!

Adding/Editing Multiple List Entries

You can manage the customer, vendor, and item lists all in one location. And, you can choose to type the list entries or paste them from Microsoft Excel. In this lesson, you will enter one entry at a time in the Vendor List. In Lesson 8, Dealing with Physical Inventory, you will work with the Add/Edit Multiple List Entries feature.

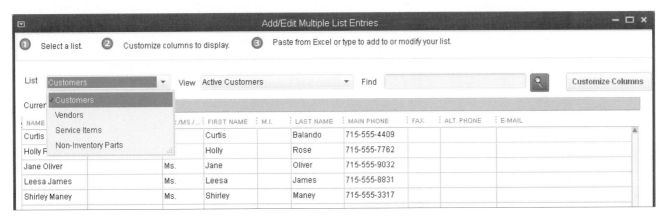

The Add/Edit Multiple List Entries window lets you quickly add and edit multiple list entries.
Note that Inventory Parts is not displayed here because the feature is not yet turned on.

The QuickBooks Lead Center

The QuickBooks Lead Center is a feature that provides you with a tool to track potential sales leads. Within the Lead Center, you can track outstanding tasks, contact information for the leads, location information, and notes related to your interactions and knowledge of the sales lead.

Working with Non-Profit Organizations

You use QuickBooks to work with non-profit organizations just as you do with for-profit companies. Intuit also offers a specialized edition, QuickBooks Premier, designed especially for non-profits. In this book you have been working with a non-profit organization, Monkey Business, in the Critical Thinking exercises.

When working with non-profits in QuickBooks, take care with the term "customer." QuickBooks defines a customer as anyone who pays you funds. So, with a non-profit, donors are customers. They should be entered in the Customers & Jobs List. You can also use the customer and vendor profile lists in creative ways to track aspects of a non-profit organization.

Task	Procedure
Edit an existing customer/job	▪ Open the Customer Center; double-click the desired customer or job. ▪ Make the change(s) in the field(s); click OK.
Add a new customer	▪ Open the Customer Center; click the New Customer & Job button, and then choose New Customer. ▪ Enter all of the customer's information; click OK.
Add a new job	▪ Open the Customer Center; single-click the desired customer. ▪ Click the New Customer & Job button; choose Add Job from the menu. ▪ Enter all of the information for the job; click OK.
Delete a customer/job	▪ Open the Customer Center; single-click the desired customer or job. ▪ Choose Edit→Delete Customer:Job. ▪ Click OK to confirm the deletion.
Make a list entry inactive	▪ Open the center in which the list entry is located. ▪ Right-click the desired list entry, and then choose Make Inactive.
Merge list entries	▪ Open the center in which the list entries are located. ▪ Double-click the list entry you wish to merge with another. ▪ Change the name of the entry to exactly match the entry into which you wish to merge; click OK.
Access the Lead Center	▪ Choose Customers→Lead Center.

DEVELOP YOUR SKILLS 4.1

Manage the Customers & Jobs List

In this exercise, you will manage the Customer List. The first step is to open QuickBooks, and then either open a company file or restore a portable company file.

1. Start **QuickBooks 2013**.

   If you downloaded the student exercise files in the portable company file *format, follow Option 1 below. If you downloaded the files in the* company file *format, follow Option 2 below.*

If you choose, you may use the final company file from Critical Thinking 3.2. In this case, open the Critical Thinking 3.2 company file from your default storage location in Option 2 below.

Option 1: Restore a Portable Company File

2. Choose **File→Open or Restore Company**.

3. Restore the **Chez Devereaux** portable file for this lesson from your file storage location, placing your name as the first word in the filename (e.g., Lisa's Chez Devereaux Salon and Spa, Lesson 4).

   It may take a few moments for the portable company file to open. Once it does, continue with step 4.

Option 2: Open a Company File

2. Choose **File→Open or Restore Company**, ensure that **Open a regular company file** is selected, and then open the **Chez Devereaux** company file for this lesson from your file storage location.
   The QuickBooks company file will open.

3. Click **OK** to close the QuickBooks Information window. If necessary, click **No** in the Set Up External Accountant User window.

Edit an Existing Customer

FROM THE KEYBOARD
Ctrl+J to open the Customer Center

The first step in performing any Customers & Jobs list management task is to open the Customer Center.

4. Click the **Customers** button located in the Customers area of the Home page.

5. Single-click to select **Jane Oliver** in the Customers & Jobs List.
   You must first select the customer you wish to edit.

6. Click the **Edit Customer** button in the Customer Information area of the Customer Center.

The Edit Customer window will open for Jane Oliver.

7. Correct the phone number to read **715-555-9030**.

8. Click **OK** to accept the change.

Add a New Customer

Now you will add a new customer to the Customers & Jobs List.

9. Click the **New Customer & Job** button, and then choose **New Customer**.

10. Follow these steps to fill in the information on the Address Info tab:

Ⓐ Type **Gina Kearny**.

Ⓑ Fill in the **Full Name** fields as shown, tapping ⌈Tab⌉ to move from field to field.

Ⓒ Type **715.555. 1645** here.

Ⓓ Click after *Kearny,* tap ⌈Enter⌉, and then type this address.

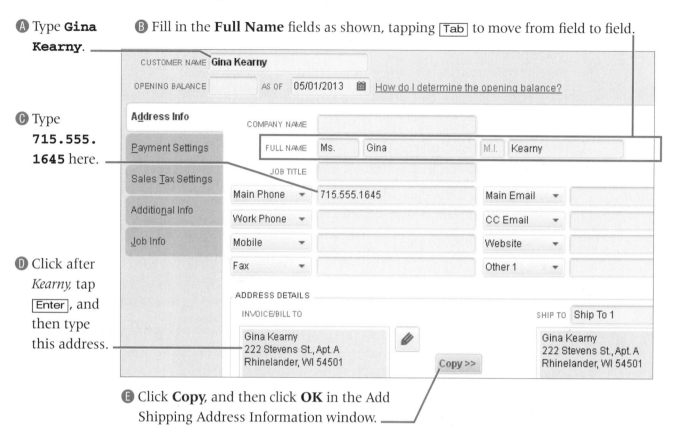

Ⓔ Click **Copy**, and then click **OK** in the Add Shipping Address Information window.

11. Click the Payment Settings tab, and then follow these steps to add information:

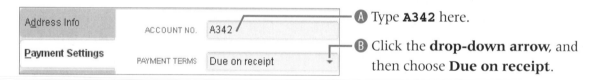

Ⓐ Type **A342** here.

Ⓑ Click the **drop-down arrow**, and then choose **Due on receipt**.

12. Click the Additional Info tab, and then follow these steps to add information:

Ⓐ Click the **drop-down arrow**, and then choose **From advertisement**.

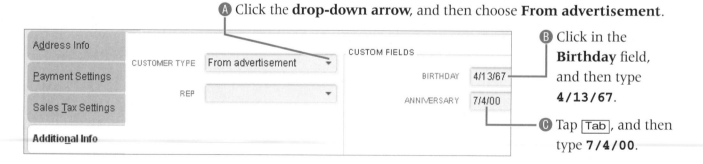

Ⓑ Click in the **Birthday** field, and then type **4/13/67**.

Ⓒ Tap ⌈Tab⌉, and then type **7/4/00**.

The custom fields are not formatted date fields, so you must enter the date as you wish it to appear.

13. Click **OK** to complete the new customer record.

Make a Customer Inactive

Customer Shirley Maney has moved out of state. As such, you know you will not be doing business with her. You can make her inactive so her name will no longer appear in the Customers & Jobs List (unless you choose to show the customers who are inactive).

14. Right-click on **Shirley Maney,** and then choose **Make Customer:Job Inactive**.
    You will no longer see Shirley displayed on the Customers & Jobs List.

15. Click the **View drop-down arrow,** and then choose **All Customers**.
    Notice that when you choose to view all customers, you see the inactive customers listed with an "X" next to their names and jobs.

16. Click the **View drop-down arrow** again, and then choose **Active Customers**.

Merge List Entries

Customer Leesa James has been entered twice by mistake. You will now help Lisa merge the two list entries into one.

17. Double-click the list entry for **Leesa James**.
    You must always open the incorrect entry (or the one that is "going away") for editing when you are merging list entries.

18. Type **Leesa James** in the Customer Name field.

You must type the name exactly as it appears in the list or it will not merge into the other entry! You change the name in the Customer Name field only, not elsewhere in the Edit Customer window.

19. Click **OK**.
    QuickBooks displays a message asking if you would like to merge the duplicate list entries. Remember, clicking Yes is a permanent action! If you did not receive the Merge pop-up window, check your spelling. You must enter the name you want it to merge into perfectly.

20. Click **Yes** to permanently merge the two entries. Click **Yes** a second time in the Merge window to acknowledge the comment about the Ship To entry, if necessary.
    Leesa James will no longer be displayed on the Customers & Jobs List, and all transactions for Leisa James will appear with Leesa James displayed as the customer.

21. Close the **Customer Center,** leaving the Home page displayed.

Understanding and Creating Items

Before you can create an invoice, you must create items to be included on the invoice. You will now learn how to create items for service and non-inventory items. An item is defined in QuickBooks as something that a company buys, sells, or resells in the course of business.

When you create a new item, you need to provide QuickBooks with very important information. When an item is sold, it directs the sales to the proper income account based on the information you entered when you created the item. The Item List will be studied in more depth in Lesson 8, Dealing with Physical Inventory, when you begin to work with inventory. In this lesson, you will access the Item List through the Home page.

This search feature can come in handy if you have a large number of items through which you may need to look to find a specific item.

This column shows the item names. This is what you will enter into a form to choose the item.

NAME	DESCRIPTION	TYPE	ACCOUNT	ON SA...	PRICE	AT...
CS-C	Color Services - Color	Service	48700 · Hair Services Income		60.00	
CS-Hcap	Color Services - Highlights...	Service	48700 · Hair Services Income		60.00	
CS-Hfoil	Color Services - Highlight ...	Service	48700 · Hair Services Income		80.00	
CS-IF	Color Services - Individual ...	Service	48700 · Hair Services Income		3.00	
HC	Haircut	Service	48700 · Hair Services Income		25.00	
PW-lh	Permanent Wave - Long H...	Service	48700 · Hair Services Income		90.00	
PW-sh	Permanent Wave - Short H...	Service	48700 · Hair Services Income		65.00	
SB	Shampoo/Blow Out	Service	48700 · Hair Services Income		15.00	
SE	Special Event Styling	Service	48700 · Hair Services Income		35.00	
Conditioner	Salon Envy Conditioner	Non-inventory...	67400 · Salon Supplies, Linens, Laundry		6.23	
Gel	Salon Envy Gel	Non-inventory...	67400 · Salon Supplies, Linens, Laundry		4.78	
Hairspray	Salon Envy Hairspray	Non-inventory...	67400 · Salon Supplies, Linens, Laundry		4.96	
Mousse	Salon Envy Mousse	Non-inventory...	67400 · Salon Supplies, Linens, Laundry		5.17	
Shampoo	Salon Envy Shampoo	Non-inventory...	67400 · Salon Supplies, Linens, Laundry		5.67	

Look for _____ in All fields ▼   Search   Reset   ☐ Search within res

Item ▼   Activities ▼   Reports ▼   Excel ▼   Attach   ☐ Include inactive

The Item List displays all items that can be included on sales forms.

TYPES OF ITEMS	
Item Type	**Description**
Service	For services you charge for or purchase (e.g., specialized labor, consulting hours, or professional fees)
Non-inventory Part	For goods you buy but don't track (e.g., office supplies) or materials for a specific job that you charge back to the customer
Inventory Part	For goods you purchase, track as inventory, and resell
Other Charge	For miscellaneous labor, material, or part charges (e.g., delivery charges, setup fees, or service charges)
Subtotal	Totals all items above it on a form up to the last subtotal; to apply a percentage discount or surcharge to many items
Group	Quickly enters a group of individual items on an invoice
Discount	Subtracts a percentage or fixed amount from a total or subtotal; do not use for an early payment discount
Payment	Records a partial payment at the time of sale; reduces the amount owed on an invoice
Sales Tax Item	Calculates a single sales tax at a specific rate that you pay to a single tax agency
Sales Tax Group	Calculates and individually tracks two or more sales tax items that apply to the same sale; customer sees only the total sales tax

Service Items

Service items are used in QuickBooks to track services that you both sell to others and purchase from them. They can be used to track time that employees spend on a certain customer's project and then be easily passed on to a customer using the QuickBooks time-tracking feature as well. This use of service items will be covered in Lesson 10, Working with Estimates and Time Tracking.

Non-Inventory Items

Non-inventory part items are for things that a business buys but doesn't stock as inventory. You can use purchase orders to obtain non-inventory items if you wish to track items that are used in your business but not resold to customers, such as brushes, shampoo, and hairspray. You will learn more about purchase orders in Lesson 8, Dealing with Physical Inventory. You can also purchase non-inventory items through the Enter Bills window by utilizing the Items tab. In order to track both purchase and sales information for an item, you need to identify that the item is "used in assemblies or is purchased for a specific customer:job" in the New or Edit Item window.

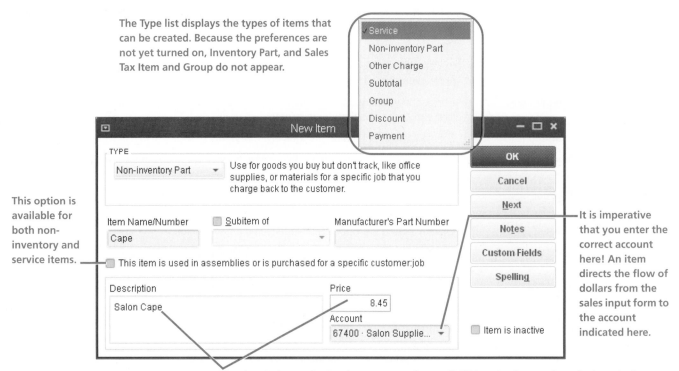

The Type list displays the types of items that can be created. Because the preferences are not yet turned on, Inventory Part, and Sales Tax Item and Group do not appear.

This option is available for both non-inventory and service items.

It is imperative that you enter the correct account here! An item directs the flow of dollars from the sales input form to the account indicated here.

The description and price that you enter here will fill in sales forms when the item is chosen.

NOTE

When you enter an item on a QuickBooks form, you can override the price that you have recorded in the Item List. If you don't have standard pricing and find that you enter specialized pricing more than you use a default price, you may wish to leave the Price field as zero in the Item List and fill it in on each form created.

Introducing Sales Tax Items

In some states, sales tax is collected on services provided. However, this is the exception rather than the rule. In this book, dealing with sales tax will be introduced in Lesson 8, Dealing with Physical Inventory, when you begin to work with the inventory tracking and product resale. In order to charge sales tax on a sales form, it must first be set up as an item.

Make sure that when you deal with sales tax, you take some time to learn about how the sales tax laws are set up in your jurisdiction. Some states do not collect sales tax at all. For states that do, there is variation among what is taxed. What it comes down to is that you must know the sales tax laws where you do business before you set up sales tax for your company.

Using Subitems

If you wish to track your items in a more detailed fashion, you can use subitems. They can be created for any item on your Item List and can be useful on reports to determine aspects of your business such as profitability. You might use subitems in your company file to:

- Differentiate between broad categories of products/services and individual items within them
- Manage pricing levels for volume discounts
- Differentiate between measurements (see the following figure)
- Track multiple vendors for an item

When using subitems, you state an item with no price for the main item, and then list prices for the subitems beneath it.

If Lisa chose to charge a different price for haircuts for long hair versus short hair, she could set up subitems to track the different service prices.

 Tab: Getting Set Up
Topic: Add the products and services you sell

QUICK REFERENCE	CREATING ITEMS
Task	**Procedure**
Create a new item	▪ Open the Item List.
	▪ Click the item menu button, choose New, and then choose the desired item type.
	▪ Enter an item name, description, and price.
	▪ Select the account (income for a service item, expense, or cost of goods sold for a non-inventory item) to which you want the purchase of the item directed.
Turn on the QuickBooks sales tax feature	▪ Choose Edit→Preferences.
	▪ Click the Sales Tax category at the left of the window; click the Company Preferences tab.
	▪ Click in the circle to the left of Yes in the "Do you charge sales tax?" section.
	▪ Select your most common sales tax item. If necessary, create the sales tax item.
	▪ Select when you owe sales tax and how often you must pay it; click OK.
Create a sales tax item	▪ Open the Item List, click the Item menu button, and then click New.
	▪ Choose Sales Tax Item as the type of item (the sales tax preference must be set up first).
	▪ Type the name and description for the item.
	▪ Set the tax rate and agency to which you pay the tax; click OK.

Create Items

In this exercise, you will create both a service and a non-inventory item.

FROM THE KEYBOARD

Ctrl+n to open a New Item window from the Item List

1. Click the **Items & Services** task icon in the Company area of the Home page.

2. Click the **Item** menu button and choose **New** from the menu.

3. Tap Tab and the default service item type, **Service**, is chosen automatically.

4. Follow these steps to create a new service item:

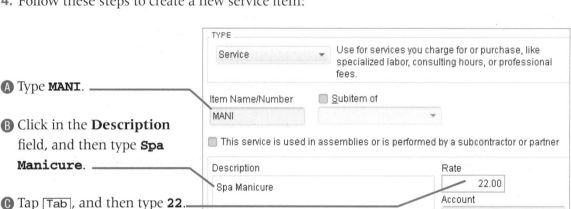

Ⓐ Type **MANI**.

Ⓑ Click in the **Description** field, and then type **Spa Manicure**.

Ⓒ Tap Tab, and then type **22**.

Ⓓ Click the **drop-down arrow**, and then choose **48800•Nail Services Income** from the list.

Ⓔ Click **Next**.

The new item will be added to the Item List and the New Item window will remain open so you can create another item.

Set Up a Non-Inventory Item

5. Follow these steps to create a new non-inventory part:

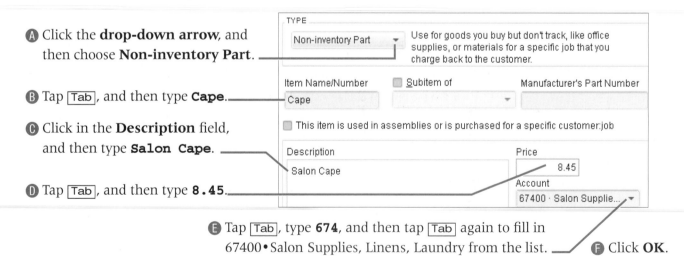

Ⓐ Click the **drop-down arrow**, and then choose **Non-inventory Part**.

Ⓑ Tap Tab, and then type **Cape**.

Ⓒ Click in the **Description** field, and then type **Salon Cape**.

Ⓓ Tap Tab, and then type **8.45**.

Ⓔ Tap Tab, type **674**, and then tap Tab again to fill in 67400•Salon Supplies, Linens, Laundry from the list.

Ⓕ Click **OK**.

6. Close the **Item List** window.

Creating Invoices

Once you have set up your initial Customers & Jobs List, you can begin to enter sales transactions. In this section, you will learn to create invoices and use accounts receivable, which is the account debited when invoices are created. When you create an invoice, you *must* specify a customer because accounts receivable (along with the customer's individual sub-register) will be debited by the transaction. Invoicing a customer is also known as a customer making a purchase "on account."

After you select your customer from the drop-down list at the top of the form, all of the relevant information you entered in that customer's record will fill into the appropriate fields on the Create Invoices window. If you wish to create an invoice for a new customer not yet entered into the Customers & Jobs List, QuickBooks will allow you to create the new list record "on the fly," just as you did for vendors.

This menu shows all entries in the Customers & Jobs list from which you may choose.

This menu shows the available invoice templates. You can customize the existing templates or create your own templates from scratch.

This column section of the invoice deals specifically with the items the customer purchases.

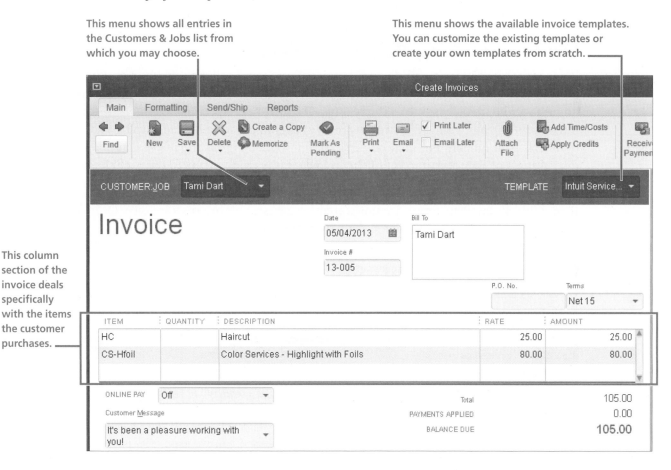

 Visualize!

Tab: Tracking Money In
Topic: Create an invoice

When you created your customer records, you entered a lot of information about each customer that will automatically fill into invoices when the customer is chosen. You have the option of changing that information when you create an invoice, though. If you change a customer's information in the Create Invoices window, QuickBooks will ask if you want to make the change permanent before recording the transaction.

If you click Yes, QuickBooks will change the customer information in the Customers & Jobs List.

If you click No, the new information will appear on the current invoice, but the Customers & Jobs List record will remain unchanged.

If you click Cancel, QuickBooks will return you to the Create Invoices window.

Entering Customers Not Already on the Customers & Jobs List

You can enter customers "on the fly" in sales forms just as you did with vendors in the last lesson by simply typing them into the Customer:Job field. Once you enter the customer that is not in the Customers & Jobs List, you will have an option to Quick Add or Setup the new customer before completing the rest of the form.

Understanding Payment Terms

Payment terms dictate an agreement between buyer and seller as to when and how much is to be paid for a product or service. In the case of a "Net 30" payment term, the net (or entire) amount of the invoice is due in thirty days. There are also discount payment terms (discussed in Lesson 8, Dealing with Physical Inventory) that allow for a discount to be taken if the invoice is paid quickly. For instance, 2% 10 Net 30 means that the buyer can take a 2 percent discount off of the total amount of the invoice if it is paid within 10 days, or the net amount is due to the seller in 30 days.

By default, if payment terms are not stated for a customer or on an invoice, QuickBooks will set the payment due date to be ten days from the date of sale.

Choosing the Correct Form

In this section, you are learning about invoices. There are other ways of notifying customers that they have a balance due. The following table describes the three main forms you can use.

COMPARING CUSTOMER FORMS	
Form	**When to Use**
Invoices	Use this when a customer does not make a payment at the time of service and/or receipt of product. The invoice amount is held in Accounts Receivable.
Sales Receipts	Use this when a customer makes a payment at the time of service and/or receipt of product. Accounts Receivable is not affected. You will learn more about sales receipts later in this lesson.
Statements	Use this to leave a balance in the customer's Accounts Receivable account without creating an invoice. For example, if you have a customer for whom you do multiple jobs throughout the month, you can gather the charges and send one statement for all of them. You will learn more about statements in Lesson 6, Correcting and Customizing in QuickBooks.

Form Templates

When you first install QuickBooks, Intuit provides you with various templates, such as the Intuit Service Invoice, Intuit Product Invoice, Intuit Professional Invoice, and Intuit Packing Slip. You can continue to use these invoices as they are, create custom invoices to meet your specific needs, or download templates from the QuickBooks website. In this section, you will work with one of the default invoice forms—the Intuit Service Invoice. The creation and customization of form templates will be covered in Lesson 6, Correcting and Customizing in QuickBooks.

BEHIND THE SCENES

When creating invoices, QuickBooks takes care of all of the accounting for you. Following is an illustration of the accounting that goes on behind the scenes for the second invoice you will create in the following exercise.

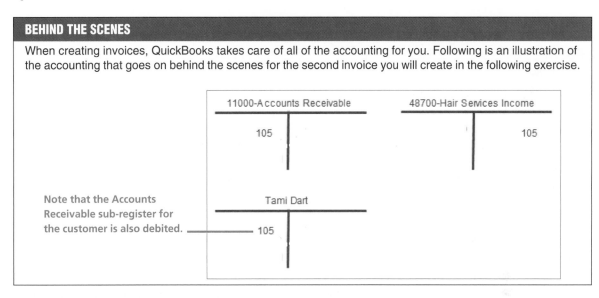

Note that the Accounts Receivable sub-register for the customer is also debited.

11000-Accounts Receivable	48700-Hair Services Income
105	105

Tami Dart
105

QUICK REFERENCE   CREATING INVOICES

Task	Procedure
Create an invoice	▪ Open the Create Invoices window.
	▪ Choose an existing customer or type a new customer.
	▪ Choose the correct date and terms.
	▪ Fill in the item(s) for which you wish to bill your customer, including the correct quantity for each item.
	▪ Choose a customer message, if desired; click Save & Close or Save & New.

DEVELOP YOUR SKILLS 4.3
Create Invoices

In this exercise, you will create invoices for customers. Gina Kearny has just come in with her daughter for manicures and haircuts. You have agreed to grant her terms of "Net 15," which means that her bill will be due in 15 days.

FROM THE KEYBOARD

Ctrl+i to open the Create Invoices window

1. Click the **Create Invoices** task icon in the Customers area of the Home page.

2. Click the **Customer:Job** field **drop-down arrow** at the top of the window, and then choose **Gina Kearny** from the Customers & Jobs List.

Create Invoices

Invoice

Notice that the customer's address and terms fill in for you from the underlying list.

3. Tap `Tab` two times, type **050213**, and then tap `Tab`.

4. Type **13-004** as the Invoice #.

5. Follow these steps to complete the invoice:

Ⓐ Click the **drop-down arrow**, and then choose **Net 15**.

Ⓑ Tap `Tab`,
type **m**,
tap `Tab`, and
then type **2**.

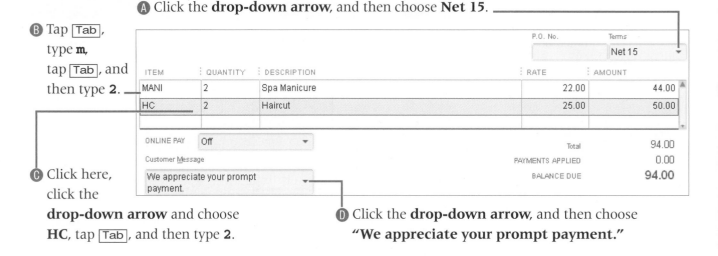

Ⓒ Click here,
click the
drop-down arrow and choose
HC, tap `Tab`, and then type **2**.

Ⓓ Click the **drop-down arrow**, and then choose
"We appreciate your prompt payment."

Once you select the item, the description, rate, and amount information fill in for you from the Item List. QuickBooks automatically calculates the total amount by multiplying the quantity by the rate. If you need to adjust the rate, you can replace the rate that filled in from the Item List, and QuickBooks will recalculate the amount once you move your insertion point to another field on the invoice form.

BTS BRIEF

11000•Accounts Receivable DR 94.00; 48800•Nail Services Income CR <44.00>; 48700•Hair Services Income CR <50.00>

---

6. Click the **Save & New** button; then, click **No** in the Name Information Changed window.
A Name Information Changed window appeared since you changed the terms for the customer.

Create an Invoice for a New Customer

A new customer, Tami Dart, has stopped by the salon. You will add her as a new customer "on the fly" while creating the invoice for her. Your insertion point should be in the Customer:Job field at the top of a new invoice. If this is not the case, choose Customers→Create Invoices.

7. Type **Tami Dart**, and then tap `Tab`.
The Customer:Job Not Found window will be displayed.

8. Click **Quick Add** in the Customer:Job list window.

Tami Dart is not in the Customer:Job list.

To automatically add Tami Dart to the Customer:Job list, click QuickAdd.
You can enter more detailed information later.

To enter the detailed information now, click Set Up (usually not required).

9. Tap ⌷Tab⌷ to go to the Date field, and then tap ⊞ until the date reads **05/04/2013**.

10. Follow these steps to complete the invoice:

FROM THE KEYBOARD

⊞ to increase the date by one day at a time
⊟ to decrease the date by one day at a time
⌷t⌷ in a Date field to enter today's date

Ⓐ Click the **drop-down arrow** and choose **Net 15**. ————

Ⓑ Click in the **Item** column, and then type **hc** to choose it from the list.

			P.O. No.	Terms
				Net 15 ▾

ITEM	QUANTITY	DESCRIPTION	RATE	AMOUNT
HC —		Haircut	25.00	25.00
CS-Hfoil		Color Services - Highlight with Foils	80.00	80.00

ONLINE PAY	Off ▾	Total	105.00
Customer Message		PAYMENTS APPLIED	0.00
It's been a pleasure working with you! ▾		BALANCE DUE	**105.00**

Ⓒ Click below **HC**, and then click the **drop-down arrow** and choose **CS-Hfoil** from the list.

Ⓓ Tap ⌷Alt⌷ + ⌷m⌷, and then type **i**.

If the quantity is one item, you do not have to enter anything in the Quantity field. It is up to you if you choose to do so.

FROM THE KEYBOARD

⌷Alt⌷+⌷m⌷ to move to the Customer Message field

 TIP

When you see a field name that has an underlined letter, you can tap the ⌷Alt⌷ key as well as the underlined letter to move to that field quickly.

BTS BRIEF

11000•Accounts Receivable DR 105.00; 48700•Hair Services Income CR <105.00>

11. Click **Save & Close**; then, click **Yes** in the Name Information Changed window.

Receiving Payments

Once you have created invoices, you need to be able to accept the payments on them from your customers. In QuickBooks, you will use the Receive Payments window to credit Accounts Receivable and the appropriate customer sub-register. The other half of the equation (the account that will be debited) depends on how you treat the payments you receive.

It is very important to use the payments received window to enter payments received from invoiced customers. If you don't, the invoices will remain open, and your income and the amounts in accounts receivable will be overstated.

The Undeposited Funds Account

If you typically collect payments from more than one source before making a deposit, you will want to choose to group all payments in QuickBooks using the Undeposited Funds account. QuickBooks automatically creates this Other Current Asset account for you.

The default setting is for all payments received and cash sales to be placed in the Undeposited Funds account. You can change this preference in the Payments category of the Edit Preferences window.

Once you are ready to make a deposit to the bank, you will use the Make Deposit window, where you can select the payments in the Undeposited Funds account that you wish to deposit. You will learn about making deposits in QuickBooks in the next lesson.

Tab: Tracking Money In
Topic: Receiving and depositing payments

BEHIND THE SCENES

Let's look at accounting scenarios that result when you receive payments.

11000-Accounts Receivable		12000-Undeposited Funds	
Bal. 374.48			
	99.17	99.17	
275.31			

Using the Undeposited Funds account when receiving a customer payment

11000-Accounts Receivable		10000-Checking	
Bal. 374.48			
	99.17	99.17	
275.31			

Depositing a customer payment directly into a bank account

QUICK REFERENCE	RECEIVING PAYMENTS
Task	**Procedure**
Receive a payment	■ Open the Receive Payments window.
	■ Choose the customer from whom you are receiving a payment.
	■ Enter the correct date and the amount received.
	■ Choose the correct payment method and enter any reference or check number information.
	■ Apply the payment to the correct invoice(s).
	■ Click Save & Close or Save & New.

DEVELOP YOUR SKILLS 4.4

Receive Payments

In this exercise, you will deal with payments received from invoiced customers.

You have just received a payment from Gina Kearny.

1. Click the **Receive Payments** task icon in the Customers area of the Home page. *The Receive Payments window opens with the insertion point in the Received From field.*

2. Follow these steps to enter a customer payment:

Ⓐ Click this **drop-down arrow** and choose **Gina Kearny**.

Ⓑ Tap ⎯Tab⎯, and then type **94**.

Ⓒ Tap ⎯Tab⎯, and then type **050713** as the Date.

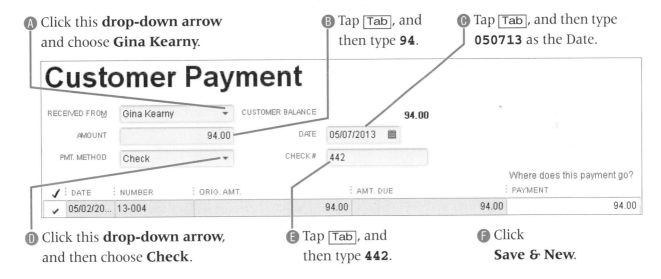

Ⓓ Click this **drop-down arrow**, and then choose **Check**.

Ⓔ Tap ⎯Tab⎯, and then type **442**.

Ⓕ Click **Save & New**.

Notice that when you typed the amount, QuickBooks automatically applied it to the invoice listed. If you had multiple invoices displayed, QuickBooks would first apply the payment to the invoice that was for the exact amount. If no invoices matched the amount, it would be applied to invoice(s) beginning with the oldest one.

BTS BRIEF
12000•Undeposited Funds DR 105.00; 11000•Accounts Receivable CR <105.00>

Receive a Partial Payment

Holly Rose just sent in $50 to apply to her outstanding invoice. You will receive this payment.

3. Type **h**, and then tap `Tab`.

4. Follow these steps to complete the payment receipt:

A Type **50** in the **Amount** field.

B Tap `Tab`, and then tap `+` to change the date to 5/9/13.

C Tap `Tab` twice, and then type **892**.

QuickBooks applies the payment to the outstanding invoice. The next time you select Holly Rose as the customer in the Receive Payments window, QuickBooks will show that there is a balance due of $55.00. Notice that QuickBooks gives you an option as to how to deal with underpayments on invoices while you're still in the Receive Payments window.

BTS BRIEF

12000•Undeposited Funds DR 50.00; 11000•Accounts Receivable CR <50.00>

5. Click **Save & Close** once you have ensured that you have entered all information correctly.

Entering Sales Receipts

As discussed earlier, you can use either of two forms to enter sales transactions. You have already learned how to create invoices and about the effect that they have behind the scenes. Now you will learn how to enter sales when payment is received up front.

A company does not have to choose one method of recording sales transactions and stick with it. Both forms can be used for the same company, depending on the situation at hand. When entering a sales receipt, you do not have to enter a customer (as accounts receivable is not affected) although you may want to enter customers to produce more meaningful sales reports. You have the option of adding a customer "on the fly" in the Enter Sales Receipts window just as you do when creating invoices.

As with the Receive Payments window, you can set a preference in order to be able to choose whether to group your payment with other funds waiting to be deposited or directly deposit it in the bank. The default option is to place all payments in the Undeposited Funds account. If you change the preference, you will need to choose into which account to deposit each payment.

When this option is deselected in the Preferences window, you will be able to choose which asset account the payment will go to.

The Deposit To field that appears on the Create Sales window appears when the preference is not to automatically place deposits into the Undeposited Funds account

You should notice how the Enter Sales Receipt form differs from the Create Invoices form and is essentially a combination of the Create Invoices and Receive Payments windows.

Visualize!

Tab: Tracking Money In
Topic: Sales receipts

"JIT" Customer and Transaction History

There are two tabs on the history panel that allow you to view information about the active transaction. The history panel allows you to view information just when you need it ("just in time"), without your having to leave the transaction and go to the Customer or Vendor Center to find it.

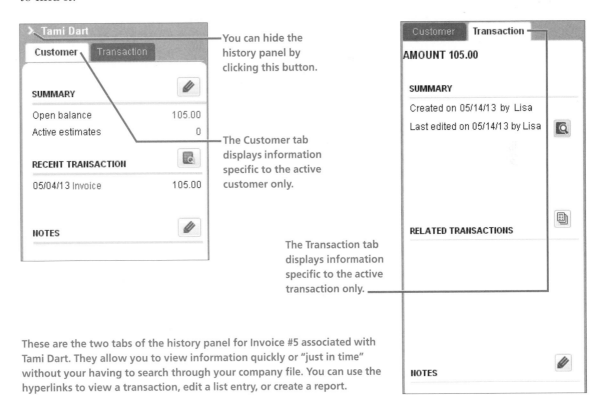

You can hide the history panel by clicking this button.

The Customer tab displays information specific to the active customer only.

The Transaction tab displays information specific to the active transaction only.

These are the two tabs of the history panel for Invoice #5 associated with Tami Dart. They allow you to view information quickly or "just in time" without your having to search through your company file. You can use the hyperlinks to view a transaction, edit a list entry, or create a report.

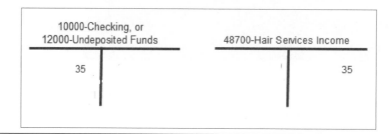
QUICK REFERENCE	ENTERING CASH SALES
Task	**Procedure**
Enter a cash sale	▪ Open the Enter Sales Receipts window and choose a customer, if desired.
	▪ Enter the date of the transaction, payment method, and reference/check number.
	▪ Enter the items and quantity sold.
	▪ Select a message for the customer, if desired.
	▪ Click Save & Close or Save & New.

DEVELOP YOUR SKILLS 4.5

Enter Cash Sales

In this exercise, you will receive payment at the time of the sale.

1. Click the **Create Sales Receipts** task icon in the Customers area of the Home page.
   The Enter Sales Receipts window opens with the insertion point in the Customer:Job field.

Create Sales Receipts

2. Type **t** to bring up Tami Dart, and then tap ⎡Tab⎤ two times.

3. Follow these steps to complete the sale:

Ⓐ Use ⊞ to change the date to **5/14/13**.

Ⓑ Tap [Tab], and then type **SR-13-003**.

Ⓒ Tap [Tab] two times, and then type **1539**.

Ⓓ Tap [Tab], and then type **ch**.

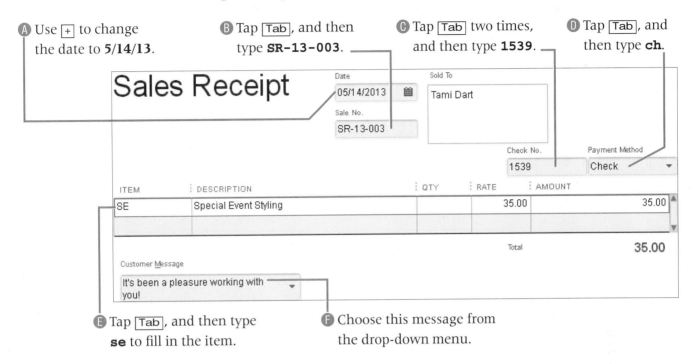

Sales Receipt

Date 05/14/2013

Sale No. SR-13-003

Sold To Tami Dart

Check No. 1539

Payment Method Check

ITEM	DESCRIPTION	QTY	RATE	AMOUNT
SE	Special Event Styling		35.00	35.00

Total **35.00**

Customer Message
It's been a pleasure working with you!

Ⓔ Tap [Tab], and then type **se** to fill in the item.

Ⓕ Choose this message from the drop-down menu.

BTS BRIEF

12000•Undeposited Funds DR 35.00; 48700•Hair Services Income CR <35.00>

---

4. Click **Save & New**.

Your insertion point should be in the Customer:Job field of a new Enter Sales Receipt window.

Record a Sales Receipt Without a Specified Customer

Since Accounts Receivable is not affected when you enter a cash sale, you can create a sales receipt without choosing a customer. This may come in handy if you sell something to someone just once and don't need that customer listed in your Customers & Jobs List. In this exercise, Lisa worked with another stylist to style hair for a wedding party.

5. Tap [Tab] two times to move to the date field.

6. Follow these steps to complete the sales receipt:

Ⓐ Verify that the date is set to **5/14/13**.

Ⓑ Tap [Tab] four times, and then type **c** to fill in **Cash** as the payment method.

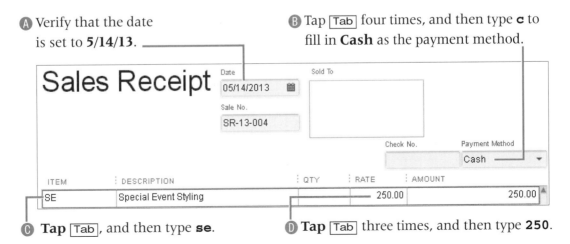

Sales Receipt

Date 05/14/2013

Sale No. SR-13-004

Sold To

Check No.

Payment Method Cash

ITEM	DESCRIPTION	QTY	RATE	AMOUNT
SE	Special Event Styling		250.00	250.00

Ⓒ **Tap** [Tab], and then type **se**.

Ⓓ **Tap** [Tab] three times, and then type **250**.

7. Click **OK** in the Price Level/Billing Rate Level window, if necessary.

8. Click **Save & Close**.

This transaction will debit Undeposited Funds and credit Hair Services Income, but there will be no customer tracked. The purpose of selecting a customer for a sales receipt is to ensure that you can produce meaningful customer reports, such as Sales by Customer Summary, if they are important to your business.

Integrating with Microsoft Word

QuickBooks works very well with a variety of Microsoft Office Suite programs. For instance, you can import and export lists from Outlook, export reports to Excel (which you will learn more about in Lesson 12, Reporting, Closing the Books, and Adjusting Entries), and merge data from QuickBooks with a Word document to produce letters for those with whom you work.

The option to create letters with Word is accessible from the Company menu.

QUICK REFERENCE	CREATING MICROSOFT WORD LETTERS THROUGH QUICKBOOKS
Task	**Procedure**
Create a letter for customers with QuickBooks data	■ Choose Company→Prepare Letters with Envelopes→Customer Letters. ■ Choose to copy the letter templates to your QuickBooks program folder, if necessary. ■ Follow the steps displayed to complete the letter(s).

Produce QuickBooks Letters with Word

In this exercise, you will produce a letter for one of your new customers, Gina Kearny, thanking her for her business and letting her know about a special deal just for her.

In order to complete this exercise, you must have a copy of Microsoft Word installed on your computer. If you do not have Word installed, skip this exercise and continue to the next topic.

1. Choose **Company→Prepare Letters with Envelopes→Customer Letters**.

2. Click **Copy** in order to place a copy of the QuickBooks letter templates in your default storage location, if necessary.
   The Letters and Envelopes window will appear with all of your customers displayed. You will be creating a letter for one customer only.

3. Follow these steps to choose to create a letter only for Gina Kearny:

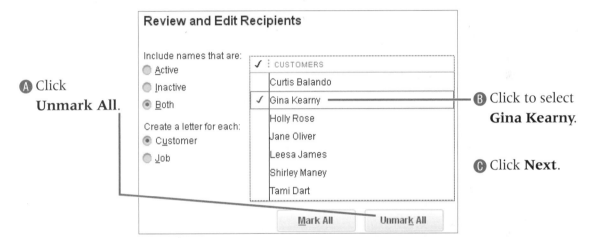

Ⓐ Click **Unmark All**.

Ⓑ Click to select **Gina Kearny**.

Ⓒ Click **Next**.

You will now have a chance to choose from a template or to create or edit your own template.

4. Scroll to the bottom of the list, and then click **Thanks for business (service)**.

5. Click **Next**.

6. Follow these steps to set how you want to sign off on the letters:

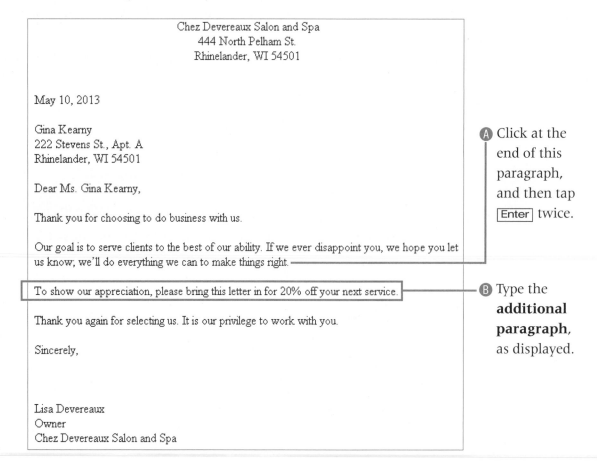

Enter a Name and Title

For letters with fields for signature and title, enter how you want to sign off.

Name   Lisa Devereaux ————————————— Ⓐ Type **Lisa Devereaux**.

Title   Owner ————————————————— Ⓑ Tap Tab , and then type **Owner**.

When you click Next:

Ⓒ Click **Next**.

- Letters will be created in a single Microsoft Word Document
- Each letter will start on a new page
- Editing your letters will not affect the original letter template
- You can continue working in QuickBooks and choose to print envelopes

QuickBooks will create the letter and launch Microsoft Word for you. If required information was missing from your customer record(s), you would see a "QuickBooks Information Is Missing" window explaining how to resolve the issue. Your letter will appear in a Microsoft Word window.

7. Follow these steps to modify the letter:

Chez Devereaux Salon and Spa
444 North Pelham St.
Rhinelander, WI 54501

May 10, 2013

Gina Kearny
222 Stevens St., Apt. A
Rhinelander, WI 54501

Dear Ms. Gina Kearny,

Thank you for choosing to do business with us.

Our goal is to serve clients to the best of our ability. If we ever disappoint you, we hope you let us know; we'll do everything we can to make things right. ———— Ⓐ Click at the end of this paragraph, and then tap Enter twice.

To show our appreciation, please bring this letter in for 20% off your next service. ———— Ⓑ Type the **additional paragraph**, as displayed.

Thank you again for selecting us. It is our privilege to work with you.

Sincerely,

Lisa Devereaux
Owner
Chez Devereaux Salon and Spa

8. Read the information presented regarding how to print the letters and envelopes, and then click **Next**.

The Envelope Options window will appear.

Print Letters and Envelopes

Your options for printing letters and envelopes are:

- Print letters you've created by selecting Print in the Microsoft Word File menu
- Print envelopes in Microsoft Word by selecting Next on this screen
- Choose not to print envelopes by selecting Cancel on this screen

Envelope Size:

Size 10   (4 1/8 x 9 1/2 in)   ▼

☑ Print return address

Chez Devereaux Salon and Spa
444 North Pelham St.
Rhinelander, WI 54501

Printer: Canon Inkjet MX310 series

CHOOSE ENVELOPE OPTIONS HERE

Select:
- envelope size
- return address
- delivery point barcode

Click OK and then select fonts and printing options on the next dialog.

The envelope will appear in Word.

9. Click **OK** in the Envelope Options window in Word after making sure the printer options are correct.

10. Close all **Word windows**, and then close the QuickBooks Letters and Envelopes window.

Working with Customer-Related and P&L Reports

You learned in the last two lessons that there are many preset reports you can run to display vendor transactions and list information. The same is true for customer- and company-related transactions.

Now that you have recorded both income and expenses for May, you will be able to run a meaningful profit and loss (P&L) report. It is important to make sure all income and expense transactions are entered so that income is matched to expenses for the period you are reporting. A P&L is a financial report that can be found in the Company & Financial category of the Report Center window. The P&L report will reflect all transactions that have affected income and expense accounts.

FLASHBACK TO GAAP: TIME PERIOD

Remember that it is implied that the activities of the business can be divided into time periods.

FLASHBACK TO GAAP: MATCHING

Remember that expenses need to be matched with revenues.

Visualize!

Tab: Reports
Topic: Profit & Loss statement

DEVELOP YOUR SKILLS 4.7

Produce Customer-Related and P&L Reports

In this exercise, you will help Lisa create customer and profit and loss reports. QuickBooks provides a report for you that displays all unpaid invoices. You will produce this for Lisa now.

1. Click the **Reports** button on the Icon Bar, scrolling down if necessary.

2. Follow these steps to create an Open Invoices report:

Ⓐ Click to choose **List View.**

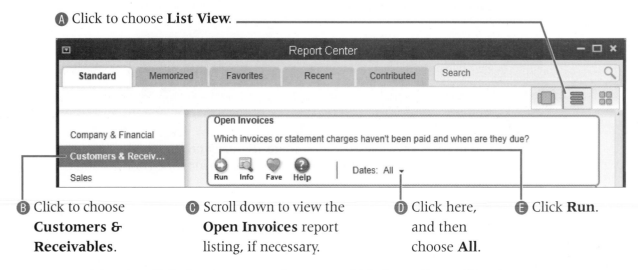

Ⓑ Click to choose **Customers & Receivables**.

Ⓒ Scroll down to view the **Open Invoices** report listing, if necessary.

Ⓓ Click here, and then choose **All**.

Ⓔ Click **Run**.

QuickBooks will display the Open Invoices report, which shows all unpaid invoices.

3. Close the **Open Invoices** report and the **Report Center**.

Create a Profit and Loss Report

Lisa would now like to see if the company had a net income or loss for May based on the transactions entered.

4. Choose **Reports→Company & Financial→Profit & Loss Standard**.
Remember, you can display all reports available through the Report Center via the menu bar as well.

5. Follow these steps to set the correct date range:

Ⓐ Tap ⟨Tab⟩ to reach the From field, and then type **050113**.

Ⓑ Tap ⟨Tab⟩, type **053113**, and then tap ⟨Tab⟩ again.

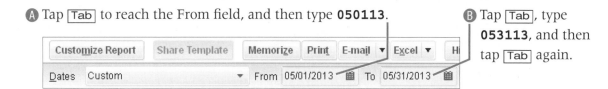

You will see a report that shows your total income and expenses for the time period along with the resulting net income (or loss). The income portion of your report should match the illustration at right. Notice that the date range is set to Custom on the toolbar. QuickBooks gives you the option to set the exact date range you desire in your reports.

Chez Devereaux Salon and Spa	
Profit & Loss	
May 2013	
	◇ May 13 ◇
▼ Income	
48700 · Hair Services Income	▶ 440.00 ◀
48800 · Nail Services Income	44.00
Total Income	484.00
Gross Profit	484.00

6. Close the **Profit & Loss** report, choosing not to memorize the report.

7. Choose the appropriate option for your situation:

- If you are continuing on to the next lesson or to the end-of-lesson exercises, leave QuickBooks open.
- If you are finished working in QuickBooks for now, choose **File→Exit**.

Concepts Review

Concepts Review   http://labyrinthelab.com/qb13

To check your knowledge of the key concepts introduced in this lesson, complete the Concepts Review quiz by going to the URL listed above.

Essential Skills

Reinforce Your Skills

Before you begin the Reinforce Your Skills exercises, complete one of these options:

■ *Open* **[Your name]'s Tea Shoppe at the Lake, Lesson 3** *or Tea Shoppe at the Lake, Lesson 4 from your file storage location.*

■ *Restore* **Tea Shoppe at the Lake, Lesson 4 (Portable)** *from your file storage location. If you need to review how to restore a portable company file, take a peek at Develop Your Skills 3.1. Make sure to place your name as the first word in the company filename (e.g., Susie's Tea Shoppe at the Lake, Lesson 4).*

REINFORCE YOUR SKILLS 4.1
Manage Your Customers & Jobs List

In this exercise, you will create, edit, and delete Customers & Jobs List entries for Susie.

1. Choose **Customers→Customer Center**.

2. Double-click **Lisa Mills** to open it for editing.

3. Change the customer's name to **Lisa Silvers**.
   You will have to change the name in four separate locations. You can use the Copy button to copy the Bill to Address to the Ship to Address field. This customer's name will change in all of the transactions that Lisa was involved in, as well as in all of her future transactions.

4. Click **OK** to accept the change.

Add a New Customer

5. Click the **New Customer & Job** button, and then choose **New Customer**.

6. Use the following information to set up the new customer, making sure to select the correct tab to enter each piece of information.

Name	`Karen Douglas`
Address	`4673 South Stayton Way, San Marcos, CA 92069`
Phone	`760-555-8137`
Fax	`760-555-8237`
Type	`Catering`
Terms	`Net 15`
Account Number	`214`

7. Click **OK** to accept the new record.

Delete a Customer Record

8. Single-click **Andy Freston** to select the name.

9. Choose **Edit→Delete Customer:Job**.

10. Click **OK** to confirm the deletion.

11. Close the **Customer Center** window.

Work with Service Items

In this exercise, you will create a service item so you can use it on a sales form. It may seem strange, but a restaurant is technically considered a service business! Susie will be adding a catering service to her business, so you will set up the item for her now.

1. Choose **Lists→Item List**.

2. Click the **Item** menu button and choose **New** from the drop-down menu.

3. Create the following service item:

Item Name	`Catering`
Description	`Off-site Event Catering`
Rate	`[Leave this blank; you will fill it in for each job]`
Account	`Catering Sales`

4. Click **OK** to accept the new item and close the window.

5. Close the **Item List**.

Enter Sales Transactions

In this exercise, you will create invoices and sales receipts for Tea Shoppe at the Lake.

1. Choose **Customers→Create Invoices**.

2. Choose **Karen Douglas** as the customer.

3. Set the date to read **6/3/2013**, and then choose to use the **Intuit Service Invoice Template**.

4. Click in the **Item** column of the invoice and choose **Catering** as the item.

5. Tap Tab twice, delete the existing entry, and then type **Catering for Parents' 50th Anniversary**.

6. Tab Tab, and then type **$750** in the **Rate** column.

7. Tap Tab; click **OK** in the Price Level/Billing Rate Level window, if necessary.

8. Select **We appreciate your prompt payment** in the Customer Message field.

9. Click **Save & Close** to record the transaction and close the **Create Invoices** window.

10. Click **No** in the QuickBooks Information window about the Payment Interview, if necessary, choosing to not display the message in the future.

Enter a Sales Receipt

Now you will enter a sales receipt to account for the food and beverage sales.

11. Choose **Customers→Enter Sales Receipts**.

12. Set the date to read **6/4/2013**.

13. Click the **Item** column of the sales receipt and choose **Food** as the item.

14. Enter $**804** as the rate.

15. Click in the **Item** column below the Food entry, and choose **Beverages** as the item.

16. Enter $**1594** as the rate.
    The item section of your sales receipt should match the following figure.

ITEM	DESCRIPTION	QTY	RATE	AMOUNT
Food	Weekly Food Sales		804.00	804.00
Beverage	Weekly Beverage Sales		1,594.00	1,594.00

17. Enter the following food and beverage sales for the month of June:
    - 6/11/13: Food $**881**; Beverage $**1,633**
    - 6/18/13: Food $**871**; Beverage $**1,617**
    - 6/25/13: Food $**865**; Beverage $**1,629**

18. Click **Save & Close** to record the transaction and close the Enter Sales Receipts window.

REINFORCE YOUR SKILLS 4.4

Receive Payments

In this exercise, you will receive the payment for the invoice you created earlier.

1. Choose **Customers→Receive Payments**.

2. Choose **Karen Douglas** from the Received From field.

3. Enter **750** for the amount.

4. Set the date to read **6/11/2013**.

5. The payment was written on check number **592**.

6. Click **Save & Close**.

REINFORCE YOUR SKILLS 4.5

Run Customer-Related and P&L Reports

In this exercise, you will run three reports for Susie, beginning with a QuickReport.

1. Open the **Customer Center**.

2. Single-click **Karen Douglas** to select it.

3. Click the **QuickReport** link at the far right of the window.

4. Set the date range to **All**.
   You will see a report that shows all of the transactions for Karen Douglas.

5. Choose **Window→Close All**.

Create a List Report and Edit a Customer Record

6. Choose **Reports→Customers & Receivables→Customer Phone List**.

7. Using your QuickZoom pointer, double-click **Karen Douglas**.
   QuickBooks will open an Edit Customer window, from where you can make any changes to the customer's information.

8. Change Karen's phone number to **760–555–8037**; click **OK**.

9. Choose **Window→Close All**.

Create a Profit & Loss Report

10. Choose **Reports→Company & Financial→Profit & Loss Standard**.

11. Type **a** to set the date range to **All**.

12. Close the report, choosing not to memorize it.

13. Choose the appropriate option for your situation:

   ■ If you are continuing on to the next lesson or the rest of the end-of-lesson exercises, leave QuickBooks open.

   ■ If you are finished working in QuickBooks for now, choose **File→Exit**.

Apply Your Skills

Before you begin the Apply Your Skills exercises, complete one of these options:

- *Open* **[Your Name] Wet Noses Veterinary Clinic, Lesson 3** *or* **Wet Noses Veterinary Clinic, Lesson 4** *from your file storage location.*

- *Restore* **Wet Noses Veterinary Clinic, Lesson 4 (Portable)** *from your file storage location. Make sure to place your name as the first word in the company filename (e.g., Sadie's Wet Noses Veterinary Clinic, Lesson 4). If you need to review how to restore a portable company file, see Develop Your Skills 3.1.*

APPLY YOUR SKILLS 4.1

Set Up a Customers & Jobs List

In this exercise, you will work on the Customers & Jobs List for Wet Noses. If you wish, you may explore the Add/Edit Multiple List Entries feature and use it to complete this exercise. It will be fully introduced in Lesson 8, Dealing with Physical Inventory.

1. Open the **Customer Center**.

2. Set up the following customers for Wet Noses Veterinary Clinic:

Name	Edison York	LaShonda Reeves	Ellie Sanders
Address	7931 NE 176th St. Bothell, WA 98011	11908 100th Pl. NE Kirkland, WA 98034	302 Northshore Blvd. Bothell, WA 98011
Phone	425-555-4401	425-555-3953	425-555-7731
Type	From advertisement	Referral	From advertisement
Terms	Due on receipt	Due on receipt	Due on receipt
Account Number	D22	C94	D34
Pet Type & Name	Dog-Hummer	Cat-Squeakers	Dog-Lucy
(Create as a Job for each customer)	Species-Canine	Species-Feline	Species-Canine
	Breed-German Shepherd	Breed-Tabby	Breed-Labradoodle
	Color-Brown	Color-Gray	Color-Black
	Gender-Male	Gender-Male	Gender-Female

3. Close the **Customer Center**.

Set Up Items

In this exercise, you will set up service and non-inventory items.

1. Set up the following service items:

Item Name	Boarding	Dental
Description	Overnight Boarding	Dental Cleaning
Rate	35.00	45.00
Account	Nonmedical Income	Fee for Service Income

2. Set up the following non-inventory item:

Item Name	Treats
Description	Treats for patients—by the box
Rate	18.43
Account	Boarding Food & Supplies

3. Close the **Item List** window.

Work with Customer Transactions

In this exercise, you will complete sales transactions and receive payments for Wet Noses' customers.

Record Sales Transactions

You will start by helping Dr. James to record invoices and cash sales. Enter the sales information and update the Additional Info tab for the job to capture the custom field information for each pet.

1. On 6/1/13, Emily Dallas brought her male black lab, Cowboy, in for an Exam, Vaccine Injection Fee, and Rabies Vaccine. Invoice her for this and enter her pet's information on the Additional Info tab of her customer record. Terms are Net 15; choose to save the new terms for the customer.

2. On 6/2/13, Kimberly Wurn brought her female calico cat (the breed is domestic short hair, or DSH), Princess, in for a New Patient Exam, Vaccine Injection Fee, Feline DHC, and FIV/FeLV. She paid cash, so create a sales receipt for her and enter her pet's information on the Additional Info tab of her customer record.

3. On 6/3/13, Becky Todd brought her black and white male Jack Russell Terrier dog, Jedi, in for an Exam requiring Venipuncture, ACTH Stimulation Test, CBC Chem, and a Kennel fee. Create an invoice for her and enter her pet's information on the Additional Info tab of her customer record.

4. On 6/4/13, Millie Schumann brought her male orange and white domestic short hair kitten, Smelly, in for an Exam and Pre-A Blood Work. She paid cash, so create a sales receipt for her.

Accept Customer Payments

You will now receive the payments for customer invoices that have been recorded.

5. On 6/7/13, you received check #773 for $56.90 from Emily Dallas as payment for invoice #173.

6. On 6/8/13, you received check #2310 for $284.21 from the County Animal Shelter as payment for invoice #163.

Answer Questions with Reports

In this exercise, you will answer questions for Dr. James by running reports. You may wish to display the Report Center in List View to help you answer the questions. Ask your instructor if you should print the reports, print (save) them as PDF files, export them to Excel, or simply display them on the screen.

1. How much did Sadie's company make during the month of May?

2. Are there any unpaid invoices?

3. What transactions has Wet Noses had with each customer during June 2013?

4. What was the net income for May 2013?

5. What are the prices for each item?
   Hint: One report will show them all.

6. Submit your reports based on the guidelines provided by your instructor.

7. Choose the appropriate option for your situation:

   ■ If you are continuing on to the next lesson or the Critical Thinking exercises, leave QuickBooks open.

   ■ If you are finished working in QuickBooks for now, choose **File→Exit**.

Critical Thinking

In the course of working through the following Critical Thinking exercises, you will be utilizing various skills taught in this and previous lesson(s). Take your time and think carefully about the tasks presented to you. Turn back to the lesson content if you need assistance.

4.1 Sort Through the Stack

Before You Begin: Restore the **Monkey Business, Lesson 4 (Portable)** *file from your storage location. (Remember that you are to leave the password field blank for Mary.) You also have the option of opening either the final file from Critical Thinking 3.1 or Monkey Business, Lesson 4 from your storage location.*

You have been hired by Mary Minard to help her with her organization's books. She is the owner of Monkey Business, a nonprofit organization that provides low-income students with help in preparing for college placement exams and applying for scholarships. You have just sat down at her desk and found a pile of papers. It is your job to sort through the papers and make sense of what you find, entering information into QuickBooks whenever appropriate, and answering any other questions in a word-processing document saved as **Critical Thinking 4.1**. Remember, you are digging through papers on a desk, so it is up to you to determine the correct order in which to complete the tasks.

- Sticky note: We now also receive funding from the Hanson Family Trust. Would we set them up as a customer? The information for the trust is 900 SE Commercial St., Salem, OR 97306; 503.555.9331; contact, Richard Hanson.

- A handwritten note: We will be providing SAT Prep services to private schools and organizations to raise additional funds for the organization. Can we set up a service item directed to 47250•Service to Outside Orgs? (You will need to set this account up as a subaccount for 47200•Program Income.) Set the amount to zero as it will be entered at the time of "sale."

- Note: How would we set up the students who participate in our program? They don't pay us money, so are they customers or is there another list we can include them on? Enter the following students when you find an answer: Leslie Goldsmith, Greg Harrison, Taylor Morrissey, and Sampson Disher.

- Scribbled on a scrap of paper: Provided an SAT Prep seminar on 7/9/2013 at St. Martin's Catholic School, received check #3821 for $1,100. Can we enter this receipt of cash into QuickBooks?

- A letter from the House Foundation: They will be providing a $5,000 grant (not yet received) to the organization to work with students from rural schools in Yamhill County. Set up the new customer, who is located at 552 Sheridan Avenue, Yamhill, OR 97148.

- Handwritten invoice: College 101 workshop to be held at Lakeside Christian School on 7/27/2013 for $985. Due Net 15. (Hint: You will need to set up College 101 as an Item directed to 47250-Service to Outside Orgs.)

- Scribbled note from Mary: Can you produce a report for me that shows all of the donors and customers for Monkey Business?

- A handwritten question: I don't have customers, but I do have donors and grants... How do I set them up if QuickBooks just has customers?

4.2 Tackle the Tasks

Now is your chance to work a little more with Chez Devereaux Salon and Spa and apply the skills that you have learned in this lesson to accomplish additional tasks. Open or restore the **Critical Thinking 4.2** company or portable company file from your file storage location, or open the company file you used in the Develop Your Skills exercises for this lesson. Then, enter the following tasks.

Add a Customer	Add the following customer: Blaise Kennedy, 1021 Miller St., Minoqua, WI 54548 • 715-555-8921 • Referral • Due on Receipt • # A350 Birthday 6/14/72 • Anniv. 7/22/99
Create Items	Service item: PEDI • Spa Pedicure • $40 • 48800•Nail Services Income. Service item: MSG • Hour Massage • $85 • 48900•Spa Services Income (you will need to set up a new account). Non-inventory item: Brush • Salon Brush • $3.67 • 67400•Salon Supplies, Linens, Laundry. Non-inventory item: Towels • Dozen Color Safe Towels • $15 • Salon Supplies, Linens, Laundry.
Create Invoices	Blaise Kennedy • 5/23/13 • 2 Pedicures • 2 Massages Jane Oliver • 5/25/13 • Manicure • Pedicure • Haircut
Create Sales Receipts	Leesa James • 5/22/13 • Manicure • Color • Haircut • Check #692 Curtis Balando • 5/24/13 • Massage • Cash
Receive Payments	Receive full payment for invoice #13-003 from Leesa James, Check #1632, 5/23/13 Receive full payment for invoice #13-005 from Tami Dart, Check #872, 5/25/13
Generate Reports	Create a report that will show the contact information for all of your customers.

 You may use the company file from this exercise for the Develop Your Skills exercises in the next lesson if you wish.

4.3 Use the Web as a Learning Tool

Throughout this book, you will be provided with an opportunity to use the Internet as a learning tool by completing WebQuests. According to the original creators of WebQuests, as described on their website (WebQuest.org), a WebQuest is "an inquiry-oriented activity in which most or all of the information used by learners is drawn from the web." To complete the WebQuest projects in this book, navigate to the student resource center and choose the WebQuest for the lesson on which you are currently working. The subject of each WebQuest will be relevant to the material found in the lesson.

WebQuest Subject: Charging sales tax for services and different types of payment receipt options

Banking with QuickBooks

LESSON OBJECTIVES

After studying this lesson, you will be able to:

- Create bank accounts
- Make deposits into bank accounts
- Transfer funds
- Manage credit card transactions
- Reconcile accounts
- Create banking reports
- Use online banking with QuickBooks

Any business must be able to work with bank accounts and the funds contained within to be able to operate effectively. If you utilize credit cards for your business, you will need to know how to work with them as well. In this lesson, you will learn all about dealing with bank and credit card accounts in QuickBooks, from creating them to running reports about them. You will also have an opportunity to explore a little about banking online with QuickBooks.

Chez Devereaux Salon and Spa

Lisa has been getting comfortable performing the basic vendor and customer transactions in Quick-Books. One of the individuals who rents space at her salon, Bill, is now going to take over the books because Lisa has gotten quite busy with her customers and marketing her new company. Bill will take over creating bank accounts, tracking banking transactions, dealing with credit card transactions, and reconciling both the bank and credit card accounts.

In addition, Bill is interested in exploring how online banking with QuickBooks works.

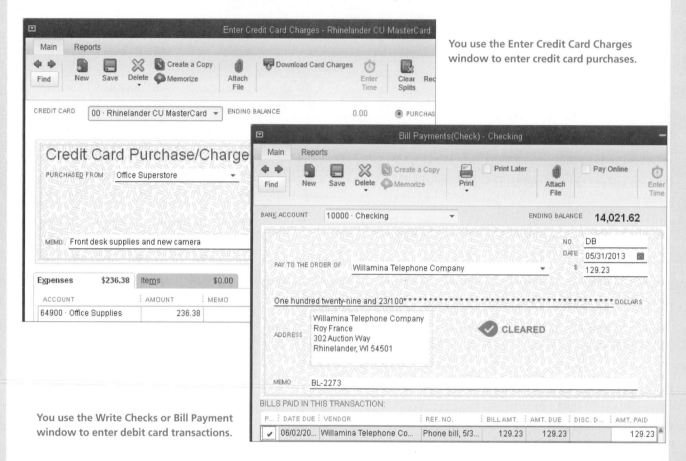

You use the Enter Credit Card Charges window to enter credit card purchases.

You use the Write Checks or Bill Payment window to enter debit card transactions.

Creating Bank Accounts

The accounts you will work with in this lesson are assets (bank accounts) and liabilities (credit cards). There are two types of bank accounts you will deal with: Checking and Savings. Petty cash accounts will be covered in Lesson 11, Working with Balance Sheet Accounts and Budgets.

Accessing Banking Activities in QuickBooks

The banking area on the Home page displays task icons for many of the activities you will perform in this lesson. The rest of the activities can be accessed via the menu bar.

Notice that you can begin the reconciliation process by either clicking the task icon in the Banking area of the Home page or by choosing an option from the menu bar. However, to transfer funds and perform online banking activities, you must use the menu bar.

The Chart of Accounts

Remember from Lesson 2, Creating a Company that the Chart of Accounts is composed of all of the asset, liability, equity, income, and expense accounts your company utilizes. In that lesson, you learned how to create new accounts, edit existing accounts, and delete unused accounts. QuickBooks responds differently when you double-click items in the Chart of Accounts, depending on the type of account, as explained in the following table.

When you double-click this type of account...	QuickBooks responds by...
Any balance sheet account (asset, liability, or equity)	Opening an account register for that account (Exception: The Retained Earnings account, which is a specially created account without a register; you will get a QuickReport when you double-click this account)
Any income or expense account	Creating an account QuickReport

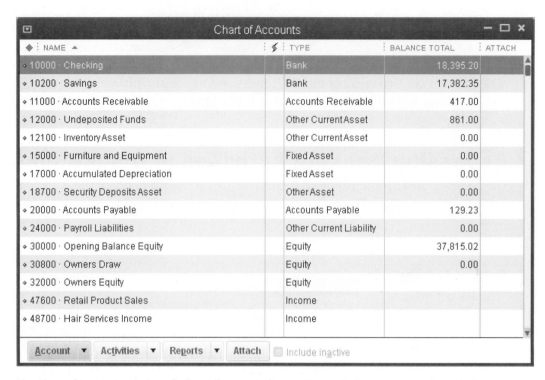

NAME ▲	⚡	TYPE	BALANCE TOTAL	ATTACH
◇ 10000 · Checking		Bank	18,395.20	
◇ 10200 · Savings		Bank	17,382.35	
◇ 11000 · Accounts Receivable		Accounts Receivable	417.00	
◇ 12000 · Undeposited Funds		Other Current Asset	861.00	
◇ 12100 · Inventory Asset		Other Current Asset	0.00	
◇ 15000 · Furniture and Equipment		Fixed Asset	0.00	
◇ 17000 · Accumulated Depreciation		Fixed Asset	0.00	
◇ 18700 · Security Deposits Asset		Other Asset	0.00	
◇ 20000 · Accounts Payable		Accounts Payable	129.23	
◇ 24000 · Payroll Liabilities		Other Current Liability	0.00	
◇ 30000 · Opening Balance Equity		Equity	37,815.02	
◇ 30800 · Owners Draw		Equity	0.00	
◇ 32000 · Owners Equity		Equity		
◇ 47600 · Retail Product Sales		Income		
◇ 48700 · Hair Services Income		Income		

Account ▼   Activities ▼   Reports ▼   Attach   ☐ Include inactive

The Chart of Accounts window displays all accounts for a company. It shows balances for all balance sheet accounts but not for income, cost of goods sold, and expense accounts. Accounts are listed alphabetically by type (unless you manually rearrange them). The highlighted account (Checking here) will be affected if you issue any command.

Creating and Editing Accounts

You have already learned the basics regarding creating and editing accounts in the Chart of Accounts. In this lesson, you will look specifically at the basic accounts used in banking: Bank and Credit Card. Remember that you will use the same editing techniques used in a word-processing program to edit account information.

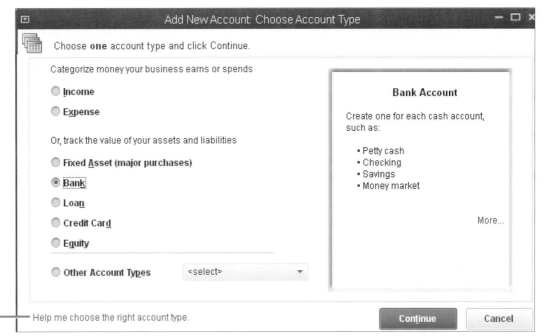

This link, when clicked, launches a Help window to assist you in choosing the correct type of account to create.

The Add New Account window will help to ensure that you choose the correct type of account when creating a new one. Notice how, when an account type is selected on the left, you see a description of how it is used on the right to assist you in choosing the correct type.

Tab: Getting Set Up
Topic: Add your bank accounts

Working with an Account Register

Each balance sheet account (except for Retained Earnings) has its own register, which is a record of all transactions pertaining to the account. A QuickBooks register looks like the check register you may already keep for your personal checking account. The running balance automatically recalculates as you record each new transaction.

When you double-click within a transaction in a register, QuickBooks takes you to the source of the transaction (similar to the QuickZoom feature). For instance, if you double-click the check transaction for Midwest Salon Unlimited in the following illustration, QuickBooks opens the Bill Payments (Check) - Checking window with all information for the transaction displayed.

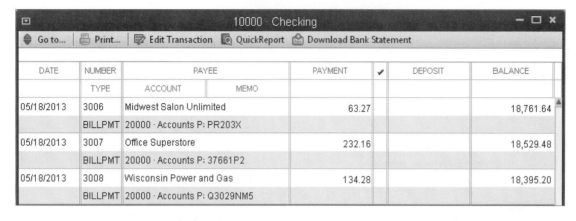

Notice that each transaction in the register includes two lines. The header at the top consists of two lines and describes what is found in each field.

QUICK REFERENCE — WORKING WITH BANKING ACCOUNTS

Task	Procedure
Open an account register	■ Open the Chart of Accounts.
	■ Double-click the balance sheet account for the register you wish to view.

DEVELOP YOUR SKILLS 5.1
Work with Banking Accounts

In this exercise, you will help Bill work with banking accounts and view a register. The first step is to open QuickBooks, and then either open a company file or restore a portable company file.

1. Start **QuickBooks 2013**.

   If you downloaded the student exercise files in the portable company file *format, follow Option 1 below. If you downloaded the files in the* company file *format, follow Option 2 below.*

If you choose, you may use the final company file from Critical Thinking 4.2. In this case, open the Critical Thinking 4.2 company file from your default storage location in Option 2 below.

Option 1: Restore a Portable Company File

2. Choose **File→Open or Restore Company**.

3. Restore the **Chez Devereaux** portable file for this lesson from your file storage location, placing your name as the first word in the filename (e.g., Lisa's Chez Devereaux Salon and Spa, Lesson 5).

   It may take a few moments for the portable company file to open. Once it does, continue with step 4.

Option 2: Open a Company File

2. Choose **File→Open or Restore Company**, ensure that **Open a regular company file** is selected, and then open the **Chez Devereaux** company file for this lesson from your file storage location.

   The QuickBooks company file will open.

3. Click **OK** to close the QuickBooks Information window. If necessary, click **No** in the Set Up External Accountant User window.

Edit an Existing Account

4. Click the **Chart of Accounts** task icon in the Company area of the Home page.

5. Follow these steps to edit the account:

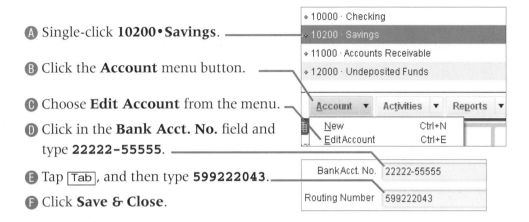

Ⓐ Single-click **10200·Savings**.

Ⓑ Click the **Account** menu button.

Ⓒ Choose **Edit Account** from the menu.

Ⓓ Click in the **Bank Acct. No.** field and type **22222-55555**.

Ⓔ Tap Tab, and then type **599222043**.

Ⓕ Click **Save & Close**.

Create a New Account

You will now create a new credit card account that will be used later in this lesson. The Chart of Accounts window should still be open. If it isn't, choose Lists→Chart of Accounts.

6. Click the **Account** menu button, and then choose **New**.

7. Follow these steps to create the new credit card account:

Ⓐ Click to choose the **Credit Card** type.

Ⓑ Click **Continue**.

Ⓒ Type **21000**.

Ⓓ Tap Tab, and then type **Rhinelander CU MasterCard**.

8. Click **Save & Close**; click **No** in the Set Up Online Services window.

FROM THE KEYBOARD

Ctrl+r to open a register

9. Double-click **10000•Checking** in the Chart of Accounts window, scrolling up if necessary.

10. Double-click anywhere within the **first two lines** of the **5/18/2013 Wisconsin Power and Gas** transaction.

DATE	NUMBER	PAYEE		PAYMENT	✔	DEPOSIT	BALANCE
	TYPE	ACCOUNT	MEMO				
05/18/2013	3006	Midwest Salon Unlimited		63.27			18,761.64
	BILLPMT	20000 · Accounts P: PR203X					
05/18/2013	3007	Office Superstore		232.16			18,529.48
	BILLPMT	20000 · Accounts P: 37661P2					
05/18/2013	3008	Wisconsin Power and Gas		134.28			18,395.20
	BILLPMT	20000 · Accounts P: Q3029NM5					

QuickBooks will take you to the Bill Payments (Check) – Checking window.

11. Choose **Window→Close All**.
All QuickBooks windows will close.

Making Deposits

If you have utilized the Undeposited Funds account (as you did in the last lesson), you will need to take one more step to move your payments to your bank account. This step is accomplished through the Make Deposits window. The Make Deposits window can also be used when you make a sale and do not need a sales receipt, or when you want to deposit a lump sum that will credit an income account and debit your bank account.

Reviewing the Undeposited Funds Account

In Lesson 4, Working with Customers, you learned that funds received through the Receive Payments and Enter Sales Receipts windows are deposited into the Undeposited Funds account by default. Think of it as a "holding tank" that stores all of the funds you have collected together until you are ready to make a deposit. In this section, you will learn how to empty the Undeposited Funds account.

If you have payments sitting in your Undeposited Funds account and you click the Record Deposits task icon on the Home page, you will get the Payments to Deposit window. Here you can choose which payments you wish to deposit.

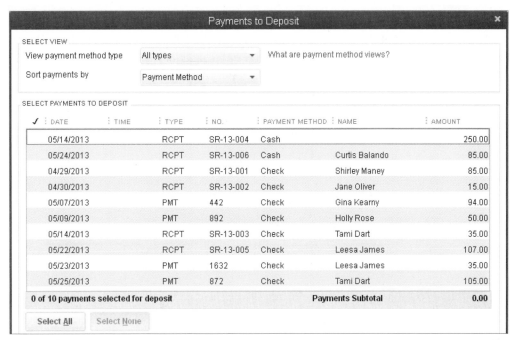

The Payments to Deposit window

You can always click OK if you are not ready to deposit the payments shown in the Payments to Deposit window yet still need to work with the Make Deposits window.

By clicking this drop-down arrow, you can select any bank account that you have set up in QuickBooks.

The Memo fields are optional, but keep in mind that you can display your memos on reports.

If you wish to keep cash back from the deposit, you can indicate that here. You will learn about petty cash in Lesson 11, Working with Balance Sheet Accounts and Budgets.

The Make Deposits window. You can click the Print button to print a detailed report of your deposits, including deposit slips if you choose to purchase and use them.

If you make deposits from your Undeposited Funds account, the following accounting will occur behind the scenes.

12000-Undeposited Funds		10000-Checking	
Bal. 871.82		871.82	
	871.82		
0.00			

If you use the Make Deposits window to record sales, the accounting involved is as follows.

48800-Nail Services Income		10000-Checking	
	100	100	

QUICK REFERENCE	MAKING DEPOSITS
Task	**Procedure**
Make a deposit from the Undeposited Funds account	■ Choose Banking→Make Deposits.
	■ Choose the payment(s) you wish to deposit; click OK.
	■ Choose the correct bank account and date for the deposit.
	■ Click Save & Close or Save & New.
Make a deposit directly to a bank account	■ Choose Banking→Make Deposits; click OK if the Payments to Deposit window appears.
	■ Choose the correct bank account and date for the deposit.
	■ Enter all of the deposit information including the customer (if desired), account, payment method, and amount.
	■ Click Save & Close or Save & New.

DEVELOP YOUR SKILLS 5.2

Use the Make Deposits Window

In this exercise, you will work with the Make Deposits window to deposit funds from the Undeposited Funds account and to make a deposit without a sales form.

1. Click the **Home** button on the Icon Bar.

2. Click the **Record Deposits** task icon in the Banking area of the Home page.

3. Click the **Select All** button; QuickBooks will place a checkmark to the left of all ten payments waiting to be deposited.

Notice that after you click the Select All button, it is grayed out. It is no longer a valid selection since all payments are already selected.

4. Click **OK** to accept the payments for deposit and move on to the Make Deposits window.

5. Click the **drop-down arrow** for the **Deposit To** field, and then choose **10000•Checking**; click **OK** in the Setting Default Accounts window, if necessary.

6. Tap Tab, and then type **052613** as the date.

BTS BRIEF

10000•Checking DR 861.00; 12000•Undeposited Funds CR <861.00>

---

7. Click the **Save & New** button to make the deposit to your Checking account. Leave the Make Deposits window open for the next step.
   Your insertion point should be in the Deposit To field of a clear Make Deposits window. If this is not the case, choose Banking→Make Deposits.

Make a Deposit Without Specifying a Customer

Lisa worked at a church fundraiser and provided $20 manicures, for which she received $10 for each one and donated the remaining $10. Since there were multiple customers whom she does not want to track individually, she will make a deposit to Checking, directly crediting Nail Services Income.

8. Tap Tab to move to the Date field.

9. Follow these steps to complete the deposit:

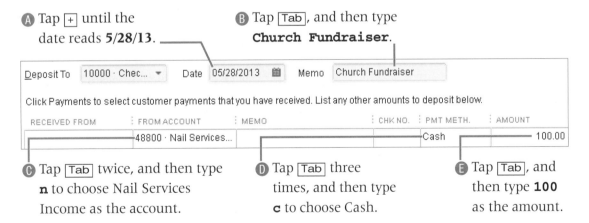

Ⓐ Tap ＋ until the date reads **5/28/13**.

Ⓑ Tap Tab, and then type **Church Fundraiser**.

Ⓒ Tap Tab twice, and then type **n** to choose Nail Services Income as the account.

Ⓓ Tap Tab three times, and then type **c** to choose Cash.

Ⓔ Tap Tab, and then type **100** as the amount.

Note that you don't fill in an item in this form, but you do fill in the account. Remember that an item is used to direct funds to the underlying account. You cannot leave the From Account field blank because you must specify the account that will be credited since you will be debiting a bank account with the deposit.

10. Click **Save & Close**; your deposit will be recorded, and the window will close.

Transferring Funds

Most people have transferred money between their bank accounts. QuickBooks has a feature that allows you to record this transfer. If you use online banking, you can even set QuickBooks to perform the transfer for you when you go online.

Since you are transferring funds between two asset accounts, you want to debit the account that is increasing and credit the account that is decreasing. Look at the following T-accounts to visualize this transaction.

FLASHBACK TO GAAP: MONETARY UNIT

Remember that it is assumed a stable currency is going to be the unit of record.

BEHIND THE SCENES

In this illustration, you are transferring funds from the Checking account to the Savings account.

10200-Savings		10000-Checking	
5,000			5,000

QUICK REFERENCE	TRANSFERRING FUNDS BETWEEN ACCOUNTS
Task	**Procedure**
Transfer funds	■ Choose Banking→Transfer Funds.
	■ Choose the account from which you wish to draw the funds.
	■ Choose the account to which you wish to send the funds.
	■ Type the amount to be transferred and, if you wish, a memo.
	■ Click Save & Close or Save & New to record the transfer.

Transfer Funds Between Accounts

In this exercise, Bill will transfer funds between the Checking and Savings accounts.

1. Choose **Banking→Transfer Funds**.

2. Follow these steps to complete the funds transfer:

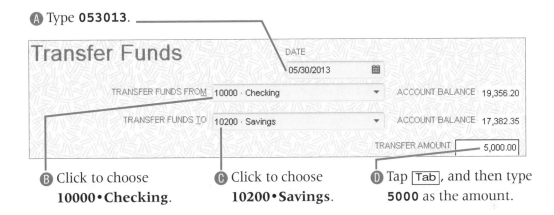

Ⓐ Type **053013**.

Ⓑ Click to choose **10000•Checking**.

Ⓒ Click to choose **10200•Savings**.

Ⓓ Tap ⟨Tab⟩, and then type **5000** as the amount.

Notice that QuickBooks displays the account balances of the accounts involved in the transfer so you can verify sufficient funds are available.

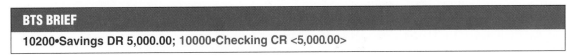

BTS BRIEF

10200•Savings DR 5,000.00; 10000•Checking CR <5,000.00>

3. Click **Save & Close** to record the transaction.

Essential Skills

Managing Credit and Debit Card Transactions

Credit cards give business owners an easy way to track their expenses. QuickBooks allows you to track credit card transactions just as you track checking and savings account transactions. You can set up as many credit card accounts as you need; then, simply choose the account you want to work with in the Enter Credit Card Charges window.

If you use your personal credit cards occasionally for business purposes, you should not enter them in QuickBooks as business credit cards. Only create accounts for business credit cards.

Credit card transactions are classified as either a charge (when you make a purchase) or a credit (when you make a return). As you will use the same form for both types, you need to choose the correct type when entering transactions.

You can choose from all of your credit card accounts.

You choose whether you are recording a purchase or a refund. Purchase/Charge will be selected by default when you open the window.

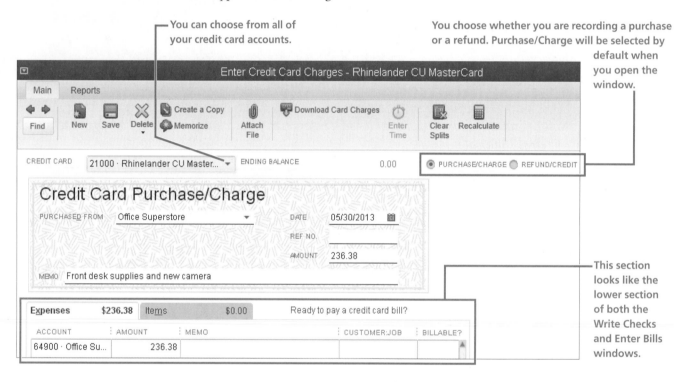

This section looks like the lower section of both the Write Checks and Enter Bills windows.

Type of Account and Normal Balance

A credit card is a liability, so its normal balance is a credit. This means you credit the account when you make a purchase (a "charge") and debit the account when you make a payment (a "credit").

The term credit is a bit confusing at this point, as you will debit your credit card account if you enter a "credit" transaction. However, if you think of it from the perspective of the merchant, it makes perfect sense!

Pay a Bill with a Credit Card

If you have entered a bill into QuickBooks, you do have the option to pay it with a credit card. Make sure that you use the Pay Bills window to accomplish the task, though, as you must remove the amount from Accounts Payable!

 If you use a credit card to pay a bill that you entered through the QuickBooks Enter Bills window, you must use the Pay Bills window when you pay it—or expenses and Accounts Payable will be overstated!

Dealing with Debit Card Transactions

When you make a purchase or pay a bill with a debit card, funds are taken directly from your checking account, which is different than what occurs for credit card purchases. Use the Write Checks window to handle debit card transactions. If you use the Enter/Pay Bills windows in QuickBooks, you can continue to use them when working with debit card purchases. This means that if you have entered a bill in QuickBooks and then choose to use a debit card to pay it, you must enter that payment through the Pay Bills window. Otherwise, the expenses will be overstated and you will leave the bill hanging out in Accounts Payable.

When you enter a debit card transaction in the Write Checks window, indicate it by entering a code such as "DB" in the No. field.

Other Types of Transactions Affecting the Checking Account

In addition to debit card transactions, you may have other ones that draw funds from the checking account as well. For instance, ATM cards and a service such as PayPal™ can directly withdraw funds from your bank account. All of these transactions will be entered using the Write Checks window; you just need to create common codes that will be used in the No. field to record each type of transaction. Common codes include DB for debit card, ATM for an ATM card transaction, and PP for a PayPal payment. You do not have to use the codes suggested here; however, you should choose one code for each type of transaction and stick with it!

A purchase credits the credit card account, as shown here.

21000-Rhinelander CU MasterCard		64900-Office Supplies	
	236.38	236.38	

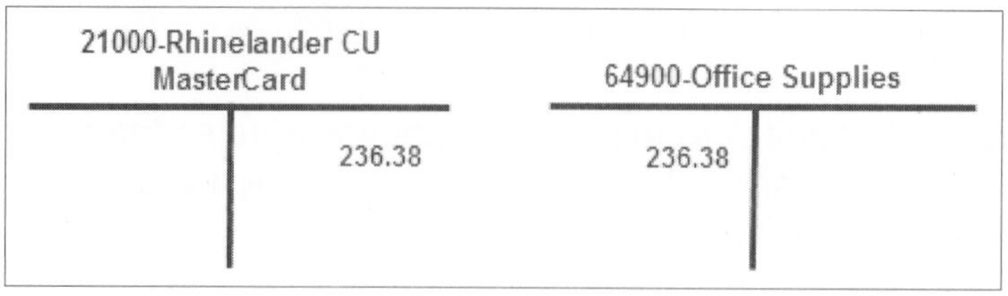

A payment debits the credit card account, as shown here.

21000-Rhinelander CU MasterCard		10000-Checking	
195.35			195.35

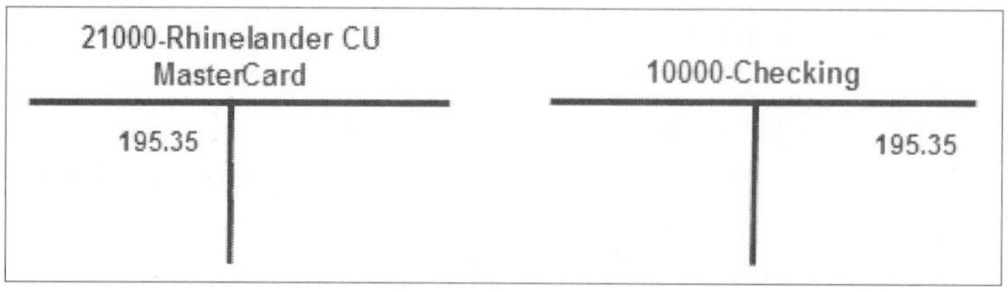

When you use a credit card to pay a bill, the following occurs behind the scenes for you.

21000-Rhinelander CU MasterCard		20000-Accounts Payable	
	129.23	129.23	

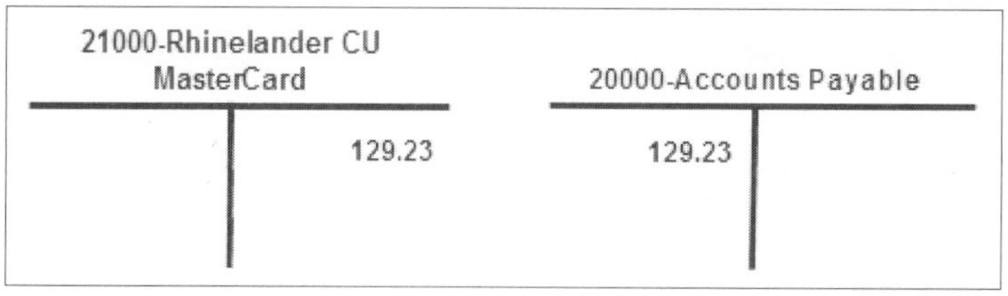

When you use a debit card to purchase office supplies, the following occurs behind the scenes for you.

64900-Office Supplies		10000-Checking	
100.00			100.00

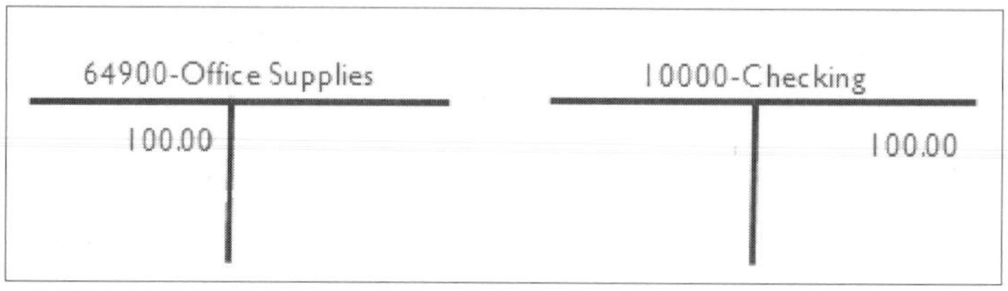

QUICK REFERENCE	RECORDING CREDIT AND DEBIT CARD TRANSACTIONS
Task	**Procedure**
Record a credit card transaction	■ Choose Banking→Enter Credit Card Charges.
	■ Choose the account to record a purchase or refund to.
	■ Enter the transaction information.
	■ Click Save & Close or Save & New.
Record a debit card transaction	■ Choose Banking→Write Checks.
	■ Select the bank account to which the debit card is linked.
	■ Enter "DB" or the code you have chosen in the No. field.
	■ Enter information into the payee, amount, and memo fields.
	■ Ensure the proper expense/asset accounts are indicated on the Expense and/or Item tab.
	■ Click Save & Close or Save & New.
Record a debit card transaction for a bill already entered into Accounts Payable	■ Choose Vendors→Pay Bills.
	■ Select the bill you wish to pay by debit card.
	■ Set the date and account to which the debit card is linked.
	■ Choose to Assign check number in the Payment Method area; click Pay Selected Bills.
	■ Type your code in the Assign Check Numbers window; click OK.
	■ Click Done in the Payment Summary window.

DEVELOP YOUR SKILLS 5.4

Manage Credit Card Transactions

Lisa needs to purchase some supplies for the front desk. She has also decided to purchase a digital camera so she can start a portfolio of her special event work.

In this exercise, you will help Bill enter a credit card purchase and a return, as well as pay a bill with a credit card.

1. Click the **Enter Credit Card Charges** task icon in the Banking area of the Home page.
   Since you have only one credit card set up at this time, the information will fill in to the Credit Card field. If you had multiple cards, you would need to choose the appropriate one before entering other information.

Enter Credit Card Charges

2. Follow these steps to record the credit card charge:

Ⓐ Tap Tab three times, and then type **o** to fill in Office Superstore.

Ⓑ Tap Tab, and then type **053013** as the date.

Ⓒ Tap Tab twice, and then type **236.38** as the amount.

Ⓓ Tap Tab, and then type **Front desk supplies and new camera** in the Memo field.

Ⓔ Tap Tab, and then type **o** to fill in Office Supplies as the account.

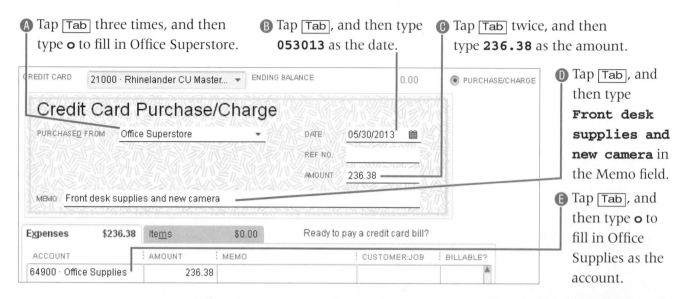

3. Click the **Save & New** button.

Record a Credit Card Return

In the next transaction, Lisa returns a calculator she purchased at Office Superstore, as she realized she didn't need it once she got back to the salon.

4. Follow these steps to record the credit card refund:

Ⓐ Click to choose the **Refund/Credit** option.

Ⓑ Tap Tab, and then type **o**.

Ⓒ Tap Tab, and then use **+** to change the date to **5/31/13**.

Ⓓ Tap Tab twice, and then type **41.03**.

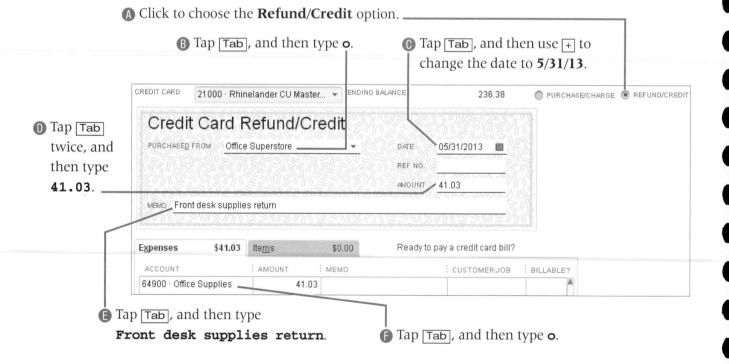

Ⓔ Tap Tab, and then type **Front desk supplies return**.

Ⓕ Tap Tab, and then type **o**.

5. Click the **Save & Close** button.
   QuickBooks records the transaction and closes the Enter Credit Card Charges window.

Pay a Bill with a Debit Card

You can record a bill paid by debit card in QuickBooks, although you must use the Pay Bills window in order to properly affect Accounts Payable.

6. Click the **Pay Bills** task icon in the Vendors area of the Home page.

7. Follow these steps to pay a bill with a debit card:

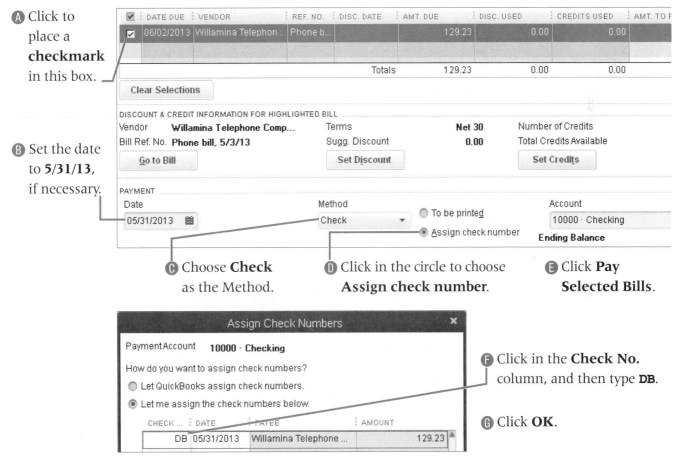

Ⓐ Click to place a **checkmark** in this box.

Ⓑ Set the date to **5/31/13**, if necessary.

Ⓒ Choose **Check** as the Method.

Ⓓ Click in the circle to choose **Assign check number**.

Ⓔ Click **Pay Selected Bills**.

Ⓕ Click in the **Check No.** column, and then type **DB**.

Ⓖ Click **OK**.

When you pay a bill with a debit card, you are affecting the Checking account, so you will need to assign the transaction the "check number" that you use for all debit card transactions. In the scenario above, that would be "DB."

8. Click **Done** in the Payment Summary window.
   QuickBooks records the bill payment, debiting Accounts Payable and crediting Checking for you.

Reconciling Accounts

It is important to make sure that your account records in QuickBooks match those of the bank. The process of matching your accounts to the bank statements you receive is called *reconciliation*.

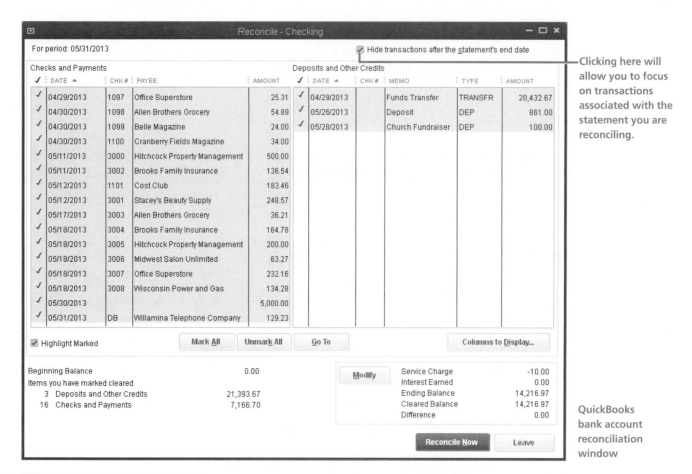

Clicking here will allow you to focus on transactions associated with the statement you are reconciling.

QuickBooks bank account reconciliation window

QuickBooks' Reconciliation Features

You should be aware of some important reconciliation features in QuickBooks. You can save your reconciliation reports in PDF so they are ready to send via email and are viewable with the free Adobe Reader program (also known as Acrobat Reader). In QuickBooks Pro, when you reconcile a new statement, the reconciliation report replaces the prior report with the new month's information. You should save each report as a PDF file to a storage location such as your hard drive or a network drive if you are using the Pro edition. In QuickBooks Premier and Enterprise editions, QuickBooks stores all reconciliation reports as PDF files for you, and you can access them through QuickBooks at any time.

Locating Discrepancies

QuickBooks also provides a feature that helps you locate discrepancies if there is a difference in balances during the reconciliation process. You can run a Reconciliation Discrepancy Report that lists transactions affecting the reconciliation balance. The types of transactions that can affect the balance are:

- Deleted transactions
- A change to a previously cleared amount
- Transactions that were manually un-cleared in the register
- Transactions in which the date was changed to a different statement period

When Your Accounts Don't Match

It is important to take the time when performing reconciliations to ensure there are no errors. As you clear each transaction, make sure the amounts are exactly the same. It is very frustrating when you get to the end of the transactions, and they don't balance.

 Once you have cleared transactions through the reconciliation process, it is important to *not* change them. Changes may alter your starting balance for the next reconciliation. If you find yourself in such a situation, you can run a Reconciliation Discrepancy report to find the problem(s).

Problem Resolution Process

If you do find yourself in the unfavorable situation of finishing your reconciliation without balancing, consider the following suggestions:

- Look for a transaction that is exactly the same amount as the difference and ensure whether or not it should be cleared.
- Determine whether you are missing a deposit or a payment by looking at the totals of each on the bank statement and the QuickBooks reconciliation window.
- Compare the number of transactions on the bank statement to the number of cleared transactions in QuickBooks.
- Verify the individual amount of each transaction on the bank statement and compare it to the amounts you have in QuickBooks.
- Determine whether it is a bank error (the bank may have recorded a transaction for the wrong amount). If it is a bank error, you can create an adjustment transaction in QuickBooks, notify the bank, and then reverse the adjustment transaction after the bank corrects the error.
- Run a Reconciliation Discrepancy report to see if any changes were made to previously cleared transactions. If changes were made to previously cleared transactions, undo the last reconciliation and redo it.

Reconciling Credit Cards

You can reconcile your credit cards the same way as you reconcile your bank account, although you access the command through the Chart of Accounts.

Once you have reconciled the credit card, you have the option to pay any amount due. You can choose to either write a check or enter a bill for the payment. QuickBooks takes the balance due on the credit card and fills it in to either the Enter Bills or the Write Checks window. If you don't plan to pay the entire amount owed, you can change the amount manually.

FLASHBACK TO GAAP: ASSUMPTION OF A GOING CONCERN

Remember that it is assumed that the business will be in operation indefinitely.

QUICK REFERENCE	RECONCILING BANK AND CREDIT CARD ACCOUNTS
Task	**Procedure**
Reconcile a bank account	■ Choose Banking→Reconcile. ■ Choose the account you wish to reconcile; enter the statement date and ending balance. ■ Enter any service or finance charges; click Continue. ■ Compare the QuickBooks transactions to the bank statement; mark off cleared transactions. ■ Once the difference between QuickBooks and the bank statement is zero, click Reconcile Now.
Reconcile a credit card	■ Choose Lists→Chart of Accounts; single-click the desired credit card account. ■ Click the Activities button at the bottom of the window; choose Reconcile Credit Card. ■ Choose the account; enter the statement date and ending balance. ■ Enter any service or finance charges; click Continue. ■ Compare the QuickBooks transactions to the bank statement; mark off cleared transactions. ■ Once the difference between QuickBooks and the bank statement is zero, click Reconcile Now.

Reconcile Accounts

In this exercise, you will reconcile accounts in QuickBooks.

First, you will prepare to help Bill reconcile the checking account for Chez Devereaux Salon and Spa. The bank statement for this account that you will use to complete the reconciliation is displayed here.

Before You Begin: You will be working with a bank statement and a credit card statement. You can use the illustrations shown, or you can print them from your file storage location. The files are labeled DYS 5.5 Checking Statement and DYS 5.5 Credit Card Statement.

Silver Falls Credit Union
487 Merrifield Avenue
Rhinelander, WI 54501

Statement of Account Prepared For:
Chez Devereaux Salon and Spa
444 North Pelham St.
Rhinelander, WI 54501

Account Number: 11111-44444

Statement Period: May 1 - May 31, 2013

Total Deposits:	$998.20		Total Payments:	$7,047.47
Beginning Balance:	$20,432.67		Ending Balance:	$14,216.97

Transactions:

Date	Transaction type	Payment	Deposit	Balance
5/1/2013	Beginning Balance			$20,432.67
5/2/2013	Check #1097	25.31		$20,407.36
5/3/2013	Check #1098	54.89		$20,352.47
5/6/2013	Check #1099	24.00		$20,328.47
5/7/2013	Check #1100	34.00		$20,294.47
5/13/2013	Check #3001	500.00		$19,794.47
5/16/2013	Check #3002	136.54		$19,657.93
5/17/2013	Check #1101	183.46		$19,474.47
5/17/2013	Check #3000	248.57		$19,225.90
5/19/2013	Check #3003	36.21		$19,189.69
5/20/2013	Check #3004	164.78		$19,024.91
5/23/2013	Check #3005	200.00		$18,824.91
5/23/2013	Check #3008	134.28		$18,690.63
5/24/2013	Check #3007	232.16		$18,458.47
5/25/2013	Check #3006	63.27		$18,395.20
5/26/2013	Deposit		861.00	$19,256.20
5/30/2013	Deposit		100.00	$19,356.20
5/30/2013	Transfer to Savings	5,000.00		$14,356.20
5/31/2013	Debit purch-Willamina	129.23		$14,226.97
5/31/2013	Service Charge	10.00		$14,216.97
	Ending Balance			14,216.97

---

1. Click the **Reconcile** task icon in the Banking area of the Home page.
   QuickBooks displays the Begin Reconciliation window.

Reconcile

2. Using the illustration of the bank statement provided or the one you printed, follow these steps to prepare for reconciliation:

Ⓐ Ensure that **10000•Checking** is the account displayed.

Ⓑ Tap Tab, and then type **053113**.

Ⓒ Tap Tab, and then type **14216.97**.

Ⓓ Tap Tab, and then type **10**.

Ⓔ Tap Tab, and then type **053113**.

Ⓕ Tap Tab, and then type **b**. QuickBooks will fill in **60400•Bank Service Charges** as the account.

> Select an account to reconcile, and then enter the ending balance from your account statement.
>
> | Account | 10000 · Checking ▾ |
> | Statement Date | 05/31/2013 📅 |
> | Beginning Balance | 0.00 |
> | Ending Balance | 14,216.97 |
>
> What if my beginning balance doesn't match my statement?
>
> Enter any service charge or interest earned.
>
> | Service Charge | Date | Account |
> | 10.00 | 05/31/2013 📅 | 60400 · Bank Service Charges ▾ |

There will be a difference in the beginning balance between this window and the bank statement because this is the first reconciliation performed since you started your QuickBooks company file.

3. Click **Continue** to move to the Reconciliation-Checking window.
The Reconciliation-Checking window shows all transactions waiting to be cleared.

Reconcile a Checking Account

Now that you have finished the prep work, it is time to begin the actual reconciliation.

4. Click to place a checkmark to hide all transactions after the statement's end date.

5. Click in the √ **(checkmark)** column to the left of each transaction in QuickBooks that is also on the bank checking statement displayed above step 1.
When you are finished, your Reconciliation-Checking window should match the following illustration.

For period: 05/31/2013 ☑ Hide transactions after the statement's end date

Checks and Payments				Deposits and Other Credits				
√	DATE ▲	CHK #	PAYEE	AMOUNT	√	DATE ▲	CHK #	MEMO	TYPE	AMOUNT

√	DATE ▲	CHK #	PAYEE	AMOUNT	√	DATE ▲	MEMO	TYPE	AMOUNT
√	04/29/2013	1097	Office Superstore	25.31	√	04/29/2013	Funds Transfer	TRANSFR	20,432.67
√	04/30/2013	1098	Allen Brothers Grocery	54.89	√	05/26/2013	Deposit	DEP	861.00
√	04/30/2013	1099	Belle Magazine	24.00	√	05/28/2013	Church Fundraiser	DEP	100.00
√	04/30/2013	1100	Cranberry Fields Magazine	34.00					
√	05/11/2013	3000	Hitchcock Property Management	500.00					
√	05/11/2013	3002	Brooks Family Insurance	136.54					
√	05/12/2013	1101	Cost Club	183.46					
√	05/12/2013	3001	Stacey's Beauty Supply	248.57					
√	05/17/2013	3003	Allen Brothers Grocery	36.21					
√	05/18/2013	3004	Brooks Family Insurance	164.78					
√	05/18/2013	3005	Hitchcock Property Management	200.00					
√	05/18/2013	3006	Midwest Salon Unlimited	63.27					
√	05/18/2013	3007	Office Superstore	232.16					
√	05/18/2013	3008	Wisconsin Power and Gas	134.28					
√	05/30/2013			5,000.00					
√	05/31/2013	DB	Willamina Telephone Company	129.23					

6. Look at the **"Difference"** at the bottom right of the window to see if you have successfully reconciled your account.

The goal when you perform a reconciliation is for the Difference to be 0.00. The Difference is calculated by determining the difference between the transactions on the bank statement and those that you have marked cleared in QuickBooks.

Beginning Balance	0.00	Modify	Service Charge	-10.00
Items you have marked cleared			Interest Earned	0.00
3 Deposits and Other Credits	21,393.67		Ending Balance	14,216.97
16 Checks and Payments	7,166.70		Cleared Balance	14,216.97
			Difference	0.00

7. Click the **Reconcile Now** button; then, click **OK** in the Information window.

There is a pause as QuickBooks records the marked transactions as cleared.

8. Click **Close** to choose to not produce a report at this time.

You will learn about reconciliation reports in the next section.

Prepare to Reconcile a Credit Card Account

The process of reconciling a credit card account is quite similar to the process you just used to reconcile a bank statement. You can either use the illustration provided below or the one you may have printed before starting this exercise.

Rhinelander Credit Union
1932 Eagle Creek Drive
Rhinelander, WI 54501

MasterCard Statement Prepared For:
Chez Devereaux Salon and Spa
444 North Pelham St.
Rhinelander, WI 54501

Account Number: XXXX XXXX XXXX 7777

Statement Period: May 1 - May 31, 2013

Total Charges:	$236.38		Total Payments:	$41.03
Beginning Balance:	$0.00		Ending Balance:	$195.35

Transactions:

Date	Description	Charge	Credit	Balance
	Beginning Balance			$0.00
5/30/2013	Office Superstore	236.38		$236.38
5/31/2013	Office Superstore		41.03	$195.35
5/31/2013	Periodic Finance Charge	0		$195.35
	Ending Balance			$195.35

9. Choose **Lists→Chart of Accounts**.

10. Single-click **21000•Rhinelander CU MasterCard** to select it.

11. Click the **Activities** button at the bottom of the Chart of Accounts window, and then choose **Reconcile Credit Card** from the menu.

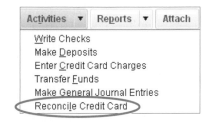

12. Using the credit card statement you just printed or the illustration provided, follow these steps to prepare for reconciliation:

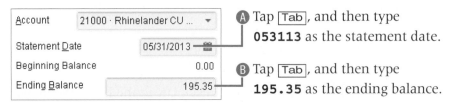

Ⓐ Tap [Tab], and then type **053113** as the statement date.

Ⓑ Tap [Tab], and then type **195.35** as the ending balance.

13. Click **Continue** to begin reconciling.

Reconcile the Credit Card Account

14. Click in the √ (checkmark) column to the left of each transaction in QuickBooks that is also on the credit card statement displayed above step 9.
    When you are finished, your Reconcile Credit Card – Rhinelander CU MasterCard window should match the following illustration.

Charges and Cash Advances				Payments and Credits					
√	DATE ▲	REF #	PAYEE	AMOUNT	√	DATE ▲	REF #	MEMO	TYPE	AMOUNT
√	05/30/2013		Office Superstore	236.38	√	05/31/2013		Front desk supplies r...	CC CRED	41.03

15. Look at the **"Difference"** to see if it is zero.
    If you do not have a difference of zero, look back at the Problem Resolution Process section on page 177 for troubleshooting ideas as to how to resolve the difference.

16. Once the Difference is displayed as 0.00, click the **Reconcile Now** button.
    QuickBooks will clear all of the marked transactions, and since you have a balance due on the credit card, a Make Payment window will be displayed.

Write a Check to Make a Payment on the Credit Card Account

You can either enter a bill for the payment amount or write a check. You will help Bill to write a check in this exercise.

17. Choose the **Write a check for payment now** option.

18. Click **OK** to continue.
    There is a pause as QuickBooks records the cleared transactions. A congratulatory message will appear.

> **Make Payment**
>
> The outstanding balance on this account is $195.35. To pay all or a portion of this amount, select the payment type and click OK. To leave the balance in the reconciled account, click Cancel.
>
> Payment
> ● Write a check for payment now
> ○ Enter a bill for payment later

19. Click the **Close** button in the Select Reconciliation Report window to bypass creating a report.
    QuickBooks displays the Write Checks – Checking window with much of the information already filled in for you.

20. Follow these steps to complete the check:

Ⓐ Click to place a checkmark here. ⎯⎯⎯⎯⎯⎯⎯⎯⎯⎯⎯⎯⎯⎯⎯

Ⓑ Click here, and then type **Rhinelander Credit Union**. ⎯⎯⎯

Ⓒ Tap [Tab], and then Quick Add the credit union as a new vendor.

Ⓓ Tap [Tab] two times, and then type **MasterCard ending in 7777**. ⎯⎯⎯

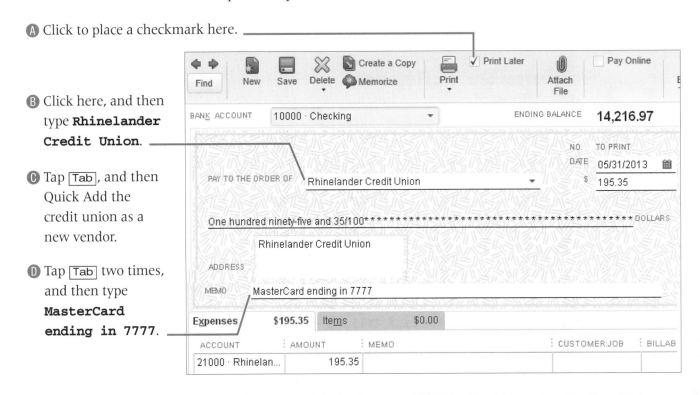

BTS BRIEF

21000•Rhinelander CU MasterCard DR 195.35; 10000•Checking CR <195.35>

---

21. Click **Save & Close** to record the check and close the window.

22. Close the **Chart of Accounts** window.

Working with Banking and Balance Sheet Reports

In this section, you will learn about reports that can tell you stories about your banking activities in QuickBooks as well as those that display information about your balance sheet accounts (asset, liability, and equity). You will also have an opportunity to look at the snapshots available in QuickBooks. In previous versions of QuickBooks, there was just one "snapshot" available to give you general information about your company. Now, you can also access snapshots relative to payments and customers.

Banking Reports

The QuickBooks banking feature comes with preset reports for you to use to get answers from your data. Banking reports deal with answers to questions such as:

■ What are all of the transactions involving a specific payee?

■ What checks have not cleared the bank as of the last bank statement?

- Which payments still need to be deposited?
- Where can I find a list of all transactions that affect my checking account?
- What changes in transactions may affect my next reconciliation?

Register QuickReports

Register QuickReports are run right from a register window. Once you have selected a transaction and clicked the QuickReport button, you will receive a report that shows all transactions for the payee of the selected transaction.

Chez Devereaux Salon and Spa
Register QuickReport

Accrual Basis — **All Transactions**

	Type	Date	Num	Memo	Account	Clr	Split	Amount
Hitchcock Property Management								
	Bill Pmt -Check	05/11/2013	3000	LS2009156	10000 · Checking	✔	20000 · Acco...	-500.00
	Bill Pmt -Check	05/18/2013	3005	LS2009156	10000 · Checking	✔	20000 · Acco...	-200.00
	Total Hitchcock Property Management							-700.00
TOTAL								**-700.00**

This is an example of a register QuickReport based on Chez Devereaux Salon and Spa's transactions with Hitchcock Property Management.

Reconciliation Reports

Reconciliation reports show transactions that have cleared as well as those that have yet to clear the bank. QuickBooks allows you to save reconciliation reports in PDF.

Alternatives to Printing Reports

Of course you can send any report to the printer. QuickBooks also gives you additional options for storing or working with a report:

- **Email:** QuickBooks can convert the report to PDF, which can be viewed with the free Adobe Reader program. This allows viewing of the report exactly as it would print even to those who do not have QuickBooks. In QuickBooks 2011, this feature was improved. When you choose to email a form or report to a customer, the form or report will automatically be converted to PDF for you.

- **Export:** QuickBooks can export the report to Microsoft Excel so you can use Excel's powerful spreadsheet features to work with your data.

Saving Reports and Forms as PDF

PDF copies of QuickBooks reports and forms make emailing forms and reports convenient for you. They are also a great way to create copies to save for your own records. You learned about printing a file to PDF in the How do I "print to PDF"? section of Lesson 1 (page 12).

DEVELOP YOUR SKILLS 5.6

Produce Banking Reports and a PDF Copy of a Report

In this exercise, you will help Bill produce two banking reports and save one of them as a PDF file.

In the last exercise, you reconciled the checking account for Chez Devereaux Salon and Spa. Now you will produce a report that documents this task.

1. Choose **Reports→Banking→Previous Reconciliation**.

2. Ensure **10000•Checking** is displayed and that the circle to the left of Detail is selected.

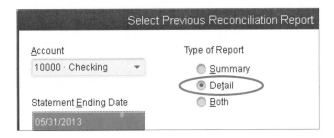

3. Click the **Display** button to produce the report.
   QuickBooks generates this report as a PDF file that can be saved, printed, and/or emailed.

4. Close the **Reconciliation Detail** report window.

Run a Register QuickReport

You will now create a report based on information contained within your Checking account.

5. Click the **Check Register** task icon in the Banking area of the Home page.

6. Click **OK** to choose the **10000•Checking** account.
   The Chez Devereaux Salon and Spa Checking register will be displayed.

Check Register

7. Follow these steps to produce the register QuickReport:

Ⓐ Scroll up until the **5/11/13** transaction for **Hitchcock Property Management** is visible.

Ⓑ Single-click anywhere within the **two-line transaction**.

Ⓒ Click the **QuickReport** button on the toolbar.

DATE	NUMBER	PAYEE		PAYMENT	✓	DEPOSIT	BALANCE
	TYPE	ACCOUNT	MEMO				
04/30/2013	1100	Cranberry Fields Magazine		34.00	✓		20,294.47
	CHK	62500 · Dues and £ renew magazine su					
05/11/2013	3000	Hitchcock Property Management		500.00	☑		19,794.47
	BILLPMT	20000 · Accounts P: LS2009156					
05/11/2013	3002	Brooks Family Insurance		136.54	✓		19,657.93
	BILLPMT	20000 · Accounts P: WBS58					

Toolbar: ◆ Go to... | 🖨 Print... | 📝 Edit Transaction | 📷 QuickReport | 📄 Download Bank Statement

FROM THE KEYBOARD
Ctrl+q to display a QuickReport

A report will be displayed that shows all of the transactions from the checking register for Hitchcock Property Management. Notice the various buttons on the toolbar that you can use to print, email, export, and perform other tasks with this report. Leave this report open for the next step.

Produce a PDF Copy of a Report

Now you will help Bill save a PDF copy of this report. You will save it in your default file location.

8. Make sure that the QuickReport for **Hitchcock Property Management** is still the active window; then, choose **File→Save as PDF** from the main QuickBooks menu bar. *A Save document as PDF window will appear.*

9. Follow these steps to save a copy of the report as a PDF file:

Ⓐ Navigate to your file storage location.

Ⓑ Replace what is in the File name field with `QuickReport-HPM.pdf`.

Ⓒ Click **Save**.

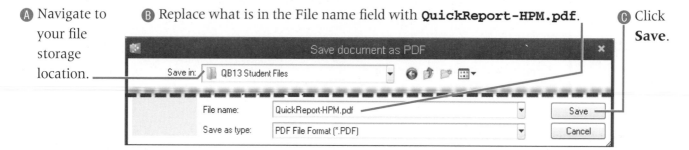

QuickBooks will process the command, saving a copy of the file to your default file location.

10. Choose **Window→Close All**.

Balance Sheet Reports

In Lesson 4, Working with Customers, you learned how to produce one of the main company reports, Profit & Loss. In this section, you will look at another vital report, the balance sheet report. Extensive coverage of the reports produced at the end of a reporting period for a company can be found in Lesson 12, Reporting, Closing the Books, and Adjusting Entries.

Types of Accounts Displayed on a Balance Sheet Report

A balance sheet report displays all of your asset, liability, and equity accounts (hence the designation the "balance sheet accounts"). You can customize your report to show only the accounts you wish to display.

Tab: Reports
Topic: Balance sheet

Company Snapshot

The Company Snapshot window gives you a quick view of your company's bottom line in one convenient place. You can customize it to include "at-a-glance" reports that are most important to your company. The Company Snapshot can be accessed via a button on the Icon Bar or by choosing Reports→Company Snapshot from the menu bar. The Company Snapshot will show information only within a preset date range. If you don't see anything displayed, it is likely because the date for which you are performing the exercise is past the date range available through the snapshot.

Tab: Reports
Topic: Company Snapshot

Browse for content panels to include in your Company Snapshot.

Bring back any removed panels, reset any date range changes, and remove any added panels.

This menu provides options to print, print preview, or save as an image your content panel data.

Information in the Company Snapshot is contained within content panels, each with its own Close button.

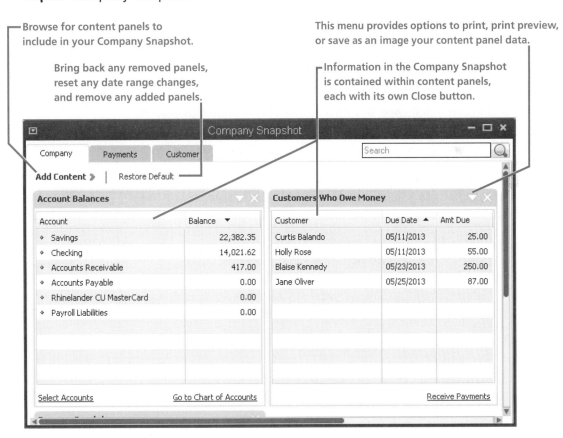

You can customize the Company Snapshot to display information that is of value to you. Notice the three tabs at the top of the window that allow you to switch between the three snapshot views.

Task	Procedure
Produce a balance sheet report	▪ Choose Reports→Company & Financial→Balance Sheet Standard.
Produce a Company Snapshot	▪ Choose Reports→Company Snapshot. ▪ Customize the snapshot to meet your needs.

DEVELOP YOUR SKILLS 5.7

View a Balance Sheet Report and a Company Snapshot

In this exercise, you will create both a balance sheet report and a company snapshot for Chez Devereaux Salon and Spa.

When you create a balance sheet report, it will be based as of a certain date rather than for a period of time (as is the case for a Profit & Loss report).

1. Choose **Reports→Company & Financial→ Balance Sheet Standard**.

2. Tap ⎡Tab⎤, type **053113**, and then tap ⎡Tab⎤ again. *QuickBooks displays a balance sheet report showing the asset, liability, and equity account balances as of May 31, 2013.*

3. Close the **Balance Sheet** window, choosing not to memorize the report.

Display and Customize the Company Snapshot

You will now help Bill delete a content panel from the company snapshot and then restore the default.

4. Choose **Reports→Company Snapshot**.
   Depending on the actual date that you perform this exercise, you may or may not have information displayed since all of
   the transactions we have entered up to this point are dated in May 2013. Don't worry about the data displayed in the content panel for this exercise, but rather how to manipulate it.

Chez Devereaux Salon and Spa
Balance Sheet
As of May 31, 2013

	◇ May 31, 13 ◇
▼ASSETS	
▼ Current Assets	
▼ Checking/Savings	
10000 · Checking	▶ 14,021.62 ◀
10200 · Savings	22,382.35
Total Checking/Savings	36,403.97
▼ Accounts Receivable	
11000 · Accounts Receivable	417.00
Total Accounts Receivable	417.00
Total Current Assets	36,820.97
TOTAL ASSETS	36,820.97
▼LIABILITIES & EQUITY	
▼ Equity	
30000 · Opening Balance Equity	37,815.02
Net Income	-994.05
Total Equity	36,820.97
TOTAL LIABILITIES & EQUITY	36,820.97

5. Follow these steps to remove a content panel from the snapshot:

Ⓐ Click the **Close** button to remove the Income and Expense Trend panel.

Ⓑ Click **OK** in the Remove Content window.

Notice that once you have removed the Income and Expense Trend panel, the Account Balances panel "snaps" up into the vacated space. You will now restore the default content panels to the snapshot.

6. Click the **Restore Default** link above the Account Balances panel.

7. Click **Yes** in the Restore Default window.

8. Close the **Company Snapshot** window.

9. Once you are finished learning about Banking Online with QuickBooks, choose the appropriate option for your situation:

   ■ If you are continuing on to the next lesson or to the end-of-lesson exercises, leave QuickBooks open.

   ■ If you are finished working in QuickBooks for now, choose **File→Exit**.

Banking Online with QuickBooks

There are a variety of tasks that can be carried out online with QuickBooks. You can manage your documents, bank online, and pay bills online to name a few.

QuickBooks Doc Center

The Doc Center allows you to store electronic documents on your local computer, network drive, or other storage location accessible from your computer station that can be attached to your QuickBooks transactions and customer, vendor, and employee list items for no additional fee. You will learn more about this powerful feature in Lesson 7, Introducing the Accounting Cycle and Using Classes.

Notice the Attach buttons available in the Vendor Information area of the Vendor Center and on the toolbar of the Enter Credit Card Charges window.

Downloading Statements and Transactions

If your financial institution provides online account access for QuickBooks, you can download bank and credit card transactions directly into QuickBooks. This can save you a bunch of time because you will not have to manually enter transactions, but rather just accept them into QuickBooks—ensuring they are correct and linked to the appropriate accounts as you go.

You can also transfer funds online using QuickBooks, providing that both accounts are at the same financial institution.

Paying Your Bills Online

Another timesaving task you can complete online, providing your financial institution offers the service, is bill payment. This feature allows you to enter a bill in QuickBooks, and then carry out the actual payment online.

You must have your vendor set up correctly to pay bills online, which means that the following fields must be set up in the Vendor List: name, address, phone number, and account number.

Preparing for Online Banking with QuickBooks

Before you can use the online banking features in QuickBooks, you must complete an application with your financial institution and receive a confirmation letter with a personal identification number (PIN) in the mail. Charges for this service vary by financial institution. Contact your financial institution to find out the charges and functionality with QuickBooks.

QUICK REFERENCE	GOING ONLINE WITH QUICKBOOKS
Task	**Procedure**
Open the Doc Center	■ Choose Company→Documents→Doc Center.
Set up an account for online access	■ Contact your financial institution and complete an application for QuickBooks online services.
	■ Choose Banking→Online Banking→Setup Account for Online Services once you have received the PIN from your financial institution.
	■ Progress through the steps in the Setup Account for Online Services interview.

Concepts Review

Concepts Review   http://labyrinthelab.com/qb13

To test your knowledge of the key concepts introduced in this lesson, complete the Concepts Review quiz by going to the URL listed above.

Reinforce Your Skills

Before you begin the Reinforce Your Skills exercises, complete one of these options:

- *Open* **[Your name]'s Tea Shoppe at the Lake, Lesson 4** *or Tea Shoppe at the Lake, Lesson 5 from your file storage location.*
- *Restore* **Tea Shoppe at the Lake, Lesson 5 (Portable)** *from your file storage location. If you need to review how to restore a portable company file, take a peek at Develop Your Skills 3.1. Make sure to place your name as the first word in the company filename (e.g., Susie's Tea Shoppe at the Lake, Lesson 5).*

REINFORCE YOUR SKILLS 5.1
Work with Bank Accounts and Make a Deposit

In this exercise, you will take care of the banking tasks for Tea Shoppe at the Lake. Since Susie's business checking account does not earn interest, she has decided to open a money market account. You will begin by helping her set up this account.

1. Choose **Lists→Chart of Accounts**.

2. Click the **Account** menu button and choose **New**.

3. Choose **Bank** as the account type, and then click **Continue**.

4. Type **Money Market** as the new account name.

5. Click **Save & Close**, choosing **No** in the Set Up Online Services window.

6. Close the **Chart of Accounts** window.

Transfer Funds Between Accounts

Since the money market account earns interest, Susie has decided to transfer some funds from her checking account into it.

7. Choose **Banking→Transfer Funds**.

8. Set the date to **6/1/13**.

9. Choose **Checking** as the Transfer Funds From account.

10. Choose **Money Market** as the Transfer Funds To account.

11. Type **10000** as the transfer amount.

12. Click **Save & Close** to record the transfer and close the window.

Make Deposits

Susie did a cooking demonstration for a local organization. She needs to deposit the fee she earned into her checking account along with the funds that are currently in the Undeposited Funds account. You will do this in two separate steps.

13. Choose **Banking→Make Deposits**.

14. Select all five of the payments in the **Payments to Deposit** window, and then click **OK**.

15. Ensure **Checking** is the Deposit To account. Click **OK** if the default account information window appears in order to acknowledge it and move to the Make Deposits window.

16. Set the deposit date as **6/25/13**, and then click **Save & New**.

17. Change the Date for the next deposit to **6/27/13**, tap Tab, and then type **cooking demonstration** as the memo.

18. Click in the **From Account** column, and then type **cat** to fill in Catering Sales as the income account.
Remember, you do not have to enter a customer, but you must enter an income account!

19. Enter the payment in the form of a check: number **753** for **$800**.
Your screen should resemble the following illustration.

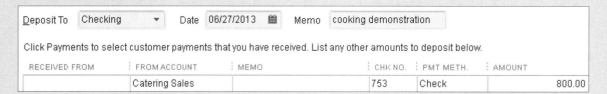

20. Click **Save & Close** to record the transaction and close the window.

Reconcile a Bank Account

The bank statement has just arrived. In this exercise, you will reconcile Tea Shoppe at the Lake's Quick-Books account. You may print your own statement (RYS 5.2 Bank Statement) from your file storage location or refer to the illustration shown after step 2.

1. Choose **Banking→Reconcile**.

2. Use the back statement to reconcile the Checking account for Susie.

ROP Credit Union
487 Merrifield Avenue
Lake San Marcos, CA 92078

Statement of Account Prepared For:
  The Tea Shoppe at the Lake
  Susie Elsasser
  316 Swan Drive
  Lake San Marcos, CA 92078

Account Number: 555-777

Statement Period: May 1 - May 31, 2013

Total Deposits: $9,878.00	Total Payments: $11,990.86
Beginning Balance: $13,953.99	Ending Balance: $18,149.64

Transactions:

Date	Transaction type	Payment	Deposit	Balance
	Beginning Balance			$13,953.99
5/6/2012	Check #1102	1,000.00		$12,953.99
5/7/2012	Deposit		2,510.00	$15,463.99
5/7/2012	Check #1081	55.73		$15,408.26
5/7/2012	Check #1082	779.00		$14,629.26
5/7/2012	Check #1083	163.00		$14,466.26
5/7/2012	Check #1084	186.00		$14,280.26
5/7/2012	Check #1085	124.00		$14,156.26
5/7/2012	Check #1086	202.63		$13,953.63
5/14/2012	Deposit		2,463.00	$16,416.63
5/14/2012	Check #1087	175.00		$16,241.63
5/14/2012	Check #1088	175.00		$16,066.63
5/14/2012	Check #1089	130.00		$15,936.63
5/14/2012	Check #1090	84.99		$15,851.64
5/20/2012	Check #1103	1,000.00		$14,851.64
5/20/2012	Check #1104	125.00		$14,726.64
5/21/2012	Deposit		2,500.00	$17,226.64
5/21/2012	Check #1105	782.00		$16,444.64
5/21/2012	Check #1106	349.00		$16,095.64
5/21/2012	Check #1107	170.00		$15,925.64
5/21/2012	Check #1108	171.00		$15,754.64
5/28/2012	Deposit		2,405.00	$18,159.64
5/31/2012	Service Charge	10.00		$18,149.64
	Ending Balance			$18,149.64

Pay attention to the following hints when you reconcile:

- *Make sure to set the reconciliation date to 5/31/2013.*
- *In the Begin Reconciliation window, make sure to enter the ending balance and the service charge.*
- *In the Reconcile-Checking window, make sure to mark only those transactions that have cleared the bank (and are on the bank statement) and that have zero differences before you click Reconcile Now.*
- *If the difference is not zero, see the Problem Resolution Process section on page 177.*

3. Choose to not create a reconciliation report now.

Manage Credit Card Transactions

In this exercise, you will help Susie set up and use her new Visa credit card in QuickBooks.

1. If necessary, choose **Lists→Chart of Accounts**.

2. Click the **Account** menu button and choose **New** from the context menu.

3. Choose **Credit Card** as the account type, and then click **Continue**.

4. Name the new account **ROP CU Visa**.

5. Click **Save & Close** to enter the new account and close the window, choosing **No** when asked if you want to set up online services.

Enter a Credit Card Charge

Susie is purchasing new aprons for the business. She is not sure of the color for one of the aprons, so she will purchase two and later return one of them.

6. Choose **Banking→Enter Credit Card Charges**, and ensure that the **ROP CU Visa** is selected.

7. Tap ⌐Tab⌐ three times, and then type **Betty's Boutique** as the vendor. Tap ⌐Tab⌐ again, and then choose to **Quick Add** the boutique as a vendor.

8. Set the date to **6/2/13**, tap ⌐Tab⌐ twice, and then type **$150** as the amount.

9. Click in the **Account** column and choose **Uniforms & Linens** as the expense account.

10. Click **Save & New** to record the transaction.

Enter a Credit Card Credit

Now you will process the uniform return for Susie. The Enter Credit Card Charges window should still be open from the last step; if it isn't, choose Banking→Record Credit Card Charges→Enter Credit Card Charges.

11. Choose **Betty's Boutique** as the vendor.

12. Set the date to **6/6/13**.

13. Choose the **Refund/Credit** option to show it is a return.

14. Type **$30** as the amount and ensure that **Uniforms & Linens** is the account.

15. Click **Save & Close** to record the refund and close the window.

Produce Banking and Balance Sheet Reports

Susie wants to run some banking reports to get answers from her data. In this exercise, you will help her do just that. Susie has already performed the reconciliation, and she asks you to print the reconciliation report.

1. Choose **Reports→Banking→Previous Reconciliation**.

2. Choose to create a **Summary** report for the reconciliation you just performed (statement ending date of 5/31/2013).

3. Click **Display** to produce the report.

4. Preview how the report will print, and then close the **Reconciliation Summary** window.

Run a Deposit Detail Report

Susie would like to see all of her bank deposits for June, so she will run a report to display them.

5. Choose **Reports→Banking→Deposit Detail**.

6. Tap ⌷Tab⌷, and then type **060113**; tap ⌷Tab⌷, and then type **063013**.

7. Click the Refresh button on the report toolbar.
   You will see a report that displays the details for each deposit in June.

If you tap ⌷Tab⌷ after changing the date, QuickBooks will automatically refresh the report for you, too.

8. Choose **File→Save as PDF**.

9. Choose to save a copy of the report in your default storage location, naming it **June 2013 Deposits**.

10. Close the **Deposit Details** report window, clicking **No** when asked to memorize the report.

Display a Balance Sheet Report

11. Choose **Reports→Company & Financial→Balance Sheet Standard**.

12. Tap ⌷a⌷ to change the date range to All.

13. Choose **Window→Close All**.

14. Choose the appropriate option for your situation:

    ■ If you are continuing on to the next lesson or the rest of the end-of-lesson exercises, leave QuickBooks open.

    ■ If you are finished working in QuickBooks for now, choose **File→Exit**.

Apply Your Skills

Before you begin the Apply Your Skills exercises, complete one of these options:

- *Open* **[Your name] Wet Noses Veterinary Clinic, Lesson 4** *or* **Wet Noses Veterinary Clinic, Lesson 5** *from your file storage location.*

- *Restore* **Wet Noses Veterinary Clinic, Lesson 5 (Portable)** *from your file storage location. Make sure to place your name as the first word in the company filename (e.g., Sadie's Wet Noses Veterinary Clinic, Lesson 5). If you need to review how to restore a portable company file, see Develop Your Skills 3.1*

APPLY YOUR SKILLS 5.1
Manage Banking and Deposits

In this exercise, you will help Dr. James with some basic banking tasks.

1. Open the **Chart of Accounts** and create two new accounts for Wet Noses: a bank account named **Money Market** and a credit card account named **American Express**. Choose to not set up online services for either account.

2. Open the **Make Deposits** window and choose to deposit all four payments from the Undeposited Funds account into your Checking account on 6/8/13.

3. Open the **Transfer Funds** window and transfer $30,000 from Checking to Money Market on 6/10/13.

Enter Credit Card Transactions

In this exercise, you will now enter transactions into the credit card account you just created.

1. Open the **Enter Credit Card Charges** window.

2. Enter the following **American Express** charges for the month.
   Quick Add any vendors not on the Vendor List and use your best judgment in selecting an expense account.

Date	Vendor	Amount	Memo
6/1/13	Thrifty Grocery	$26.73	Bottled water and soda for office
6/4/13	Glen's Handyman Service	$108.70	Office repairs
6/4/13	Malimali Hardware Store	$43.20	Supplies for office repairs
6/8/13	Labyrinth Veterinary Publications	$94.85	Reference books
6/11/13	Thrifty Grocery	$18.49	Refreshments for office
6/14/13	Bothell Pet Supply Co.	$115.43	Boarding supplies
6/14/13	Murray Gardening Service	$60.00	Monthly garden maintenance
6/20/13	Beezer Computer Repair	$145.00	Computer repair
6/20/13	Bothell Pet Supply Co.	-$38.29	Return-Boarding supplies
6/22/13	Laura's Café	30.21	Business lunch with partner

3. Close the **Enter Credit Card Charges** window when you are finished.

Reconcile a Credit Card Account

In this exercise, you will reconcile the American Express account.

1. Open the **Chart of Accounts** and begin the process to reconcile the **American Express** account using the following illustration.

American Express
6539 Beck Place
New York, NY 07852

Credit Card Statement Prepared For:
  Wet Noses Veterinary Clinic
  589 Retriever Drive
  Bothell, WA 98011

Account Number: 3333-888888-55555

Statement Period: May 21 - June 20, 2013

| Total Charges: | $612.48 | Total Credits: | $38.29 |
| Beginning Balance: | $0.00 | Ending Balance: | $574.19 |

Transactions:

Date	Description	Charge	Credit	Balance
	Beginning Balance			$0.00
5/1/2010	Thrifty Grocery	26.73		$26.73
5/4/2010	Glen's Handyman	108.70		$135.43
5/4/2010	Malimali Hardware Store	43.20		$178.63
5/8/2010	Laby Vet Pub	94.85		$273.48
5/11/2010	Thrifty Grocery	18.49		$291.97
5/14/2010	Bothell Pet Supply	115.43		$407.40
5/14/2010	Murray Gardening Service	60.00		$467.40
5/20/2010	Beezer Computer	145.00		$612.40
6/20/2013	Bothell Pet Supply		38.29	$574.11
	Periodic Finance Charge	0		$574.11
	Ending Balance			$574.11

---

2. When you have completed the reconciliation, write a check to **American Express** for the entire amount on 6/22/2013, choosing for it to be printed later. Then, display a **summary reconciliation report**.

Answer Questions with Reports

In this exercise, you will answer questions for Dr. James by running reports. You may wish to display the Report Center in List View to help you answer the questions. Ask your instructor if you should print the reports, print (save) them as PDF files, export them to Excel, or simply display them on the screen.

1. What are the details of the checks that have been written during June 2013?

2. What transactions were not cleared when the American Express account was reconciled?

3. Is it possible to get a detailed list of all deposits for June 2013?

4. Are there any missing or duplicate check numbers in the Checking account?

5. What is the balance of all of the balance sheet accounts as of June 22, 2013?

6. Submit your reports based on the guidelines provided by your instructor.

7. Choose the appropriate option for your situation:

   ■ If you are continuing on to Lesson 6 or the Critical Thinking exercises, leave QuickBooks open.

   ■ If you are finished working in QuickBooks for now, choose **File→Exit**.

Critical Thinking

In the course of working through the following Critical Thinking exercises, you will be utilizing various skills taught in this and previous lesson(s). Take your time and think carefully about the tasks presented to you. Turn back to the lesson content if you need assistance.

5.1 Sort Through the Stack

Before You Begin: Restore the **Monkey Business, Lesson 5 (Portable)** *file from your storage location. (Remember that you are to leave the password field blank for Mary.) You also have the option of opening either the final file from Critical Thinking 4.1 or Monkey Business, Lesson 5 from your storage location.*

You have been hired by Mary Minard to help her with her organization's books. She is the owner of Monkey Business, a nonprofit organization that provides low-income students with help in preparing for college placement exams and applying for scholarships. You have just sat down at her desk and found a pile of papers. It is your job to sort through the papers and make sense of what you find, entering information into QuickBooks whenever appropriate, and answering any other questions in a word processing document saved as **Critical Thinking 5.1**. Remember, you are digging through papers on a desk, so it is up to you to determine the correct order in which to complete the tasks.

- Scribbled on a scrap of paper: I looked at QuickBooks and saw money in an account called "Undeposited Funds." Why isn't it in the Checking account? Can you move it for me? I deposited those funds into the Checking account on 7/11/2013!

- New credit card document on desk: From Jasper State Credit Union, number 7777 2222 0000 2938, $7,500 credit limit.

- Note: Opened a new Money Market bank account at Jasper State Credit Union on 7/10/13. Transferred $10,000 from Savings to fund the new account. Need QuickBooks account set up.

- Bank deposit slip: Check #2323 dated 7/14/2013 for a $2,500 deposit to Checking. Handwritten message on slip reads, "From Hanson Family Trust."

- Credit card receipt: Dated 7/15/2013; for cups, cookies, and napkins; $24.11; paid to Cherry City Supermart.

- Note: Would you please create a report that shows all of the activity in the Checking account for July 2013 and save it as a PDF file so I can email it to the accountant?

- Bank deposit slip: Dated 7/30/2013 for $500; handwritten on slip, check #3889 from Lakeside Christian School for payment toward invoice for College 101 seminar on 7/27/2013.

- Credit card receipt: Dated 7/23/2013; payable to Casey's Service Station; for auto fuel; amount of $35.61. (Hint: This is for travel to a school site.)

- Scribbled note from Mary: Can you produce a report for me that shows the balances for all of the asset, liability, and equity accounts as of 7/31/2013?

5.2 Tackle the Tasks

Now is your chance to work a little more with Chez Devereaux Salon and Spa and apply the skills that you have learned in this lesson to accomplish additional tasks. Open or restore the **Critical Thinking 5.2** company or portable company file from your file storage location, or open the company file you used in the Develop Your Skills exercises for this lesson. Then, enter the following tasks.

Create banking accounts	Use the following information to create two new accounts:
	10400•Money Market; Rhinelander Credit Union
	22000•American Express
Make a deposit	On 6/1/13, provide a haircut and manicure to Holly Rose for cash (use a Sales Receipt). Deposit the funds from Undeposited Funds to Checking on the same day.
Transfer funds	On 6/3/13, transfer $1,000 from Checking to Money Market.
Enter credit card transactions	Enter the following American Express transactions:
	On 6/2/13, purchase a customer appreciation lunch from Home Place Pizzaria (add as a new vendor) for $65.11, using the 64300•Meals and Entertainment account.
	On 6/4/13, purchase bottled water and cookies from Cost Club for $25.67, using 61500•Client Refreshments as the account.
Produce reports	Display a summary previous reconciliation report for the Checking account.
	Display a balance sheet detail report as of 6/4/13.

You may use the company file from this exercise for the Develop Your Skills exercises in the next lesson if you wish.

5.3 Use the Web as a Learning Tool

Throughout this book, you will be provided with an opportunity to use the Internet as a learning tool by completing WebQuests. According to the original creators of WebQuests, as described on their website (WebQuest.org), a WebQuest is "an inquiry-oriented activity in which most or all of the information used by learners is drawn from the web." To complete the WebQuest projects in this book, navigate to the student resource center and choose the WebQuest for the lesson on which you are currently working. The subject of each WebQuest will be relevant to the material found in the lesson.

WebQuest Subject: Online banking with QuickBooks

Correcting and Customizing in QuickBooks

LESSON OBJECTIVES

After studying this lesson, you will be able to:

- Edit and correct errors
- Issue refunds and credit memos
- Deal with bounced checks and account for bad debt
- Customize reports and graphs
- Create custom templates

It is inevitable that mistakes will be made when entering data in QuickBooks. How you deal with those errors will affect what happens behind the scenes, so this lesson will show you how to correct some common errors to maintain the integrity of your data. The not-so-pleasant topics of issuing refunds, accounting for bad debt, and dealing with bounced checks will also be covered. Finally, the artist in you gets to have some fun! It's time to learn about customizing QuickBooks forms and reports to look good and work best for your company. In this lesson, you will learn to customize your reports to include pertinent information, to jazz them up, and to make them look more attractive. Once you finish working with reports, you will create your own custom invoice template.

Chez Devereaux Salon and Spa

With Lisa and Bill both being new to QuickBooks, they have realized that some transactions were not entered properly. Lisa will look at the correct way to deal with these errors. She will also look at how to deal with a couple of other unfortunate tasks, such as issuing refunds, accounting for bad debt, and processing bounced checks.

Lisa, as a designer by trade, is ready to add some finesse to Chez Devereaux Salon and Spa's company reports and templates as well.

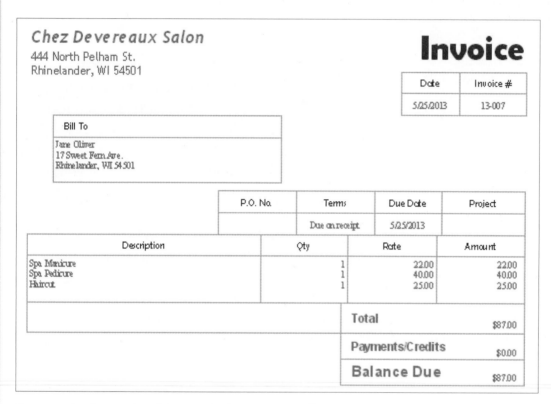

You can customize your templates to make them more appealing.

Dealing with Oops!

It is inevitable that you will need to deal with either errors or modifications to transactions in QuickBooks. It is very important that you do this properly to ensure that everything behind the scenes is correct.

Editing an Existing Transaction

To edit an existing transaction in QuickBooks, you simply open the window where the transaction is recorded and make the changes. You do need to think about the implications of any modifications that you make, though. Many transactions are tied to others, and a change to one can affect another. For instance, if a bill has been paid, both the bill and the bill payment are linked in QuickBooks.

Voiding vs. Deleting Transactions

QuickBooks allows you to either void or delete a transaction you no longer need recorded. In most cases, you will want to void a transaction so that you can keep a record of it. This will remove everything from behind the scenes and yet leave evidence that the transaction existed.

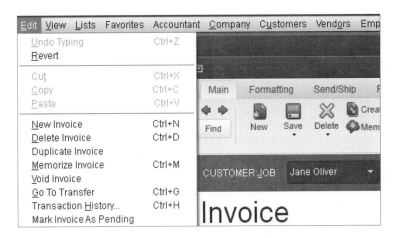

The Edit menu on the Create Invoices window provides options that allow you to work with the currently active transaction (in this case, an invoice).

Locating Transactions in QuickBooks

QuickBooks provides two methods for you to choose from in order to locate transactions in your company file.

QuickBooks Find Feature

QuickBooks provides a Find feature that helps you locate a transaction if you don't know all of the information about it. This can help save you a lot of time when you have a company file with a large number of transactions. The two options within Find are:

FROM THE KEYBOARD
Ctrl+f to open the Find window

- **Simple** to perform basic searches
- **Advanced** to perform more complex searches, utilizing filters to help sort through all of your data

QuickBooks Search Feature

With QuickBooks, you have the ability to perform searches based on text you enter throughout your company file and the menu commands. This feature is much more powerful than the Find feature and is similar to a search that you might perform on the Internet with any search engine. QuickBooks search allows you to find the following types of information:

- Forms/transactions (invoices, estimates, and so on)
- People and companies (customers, vendors, employees, and other names)
- List entries (items, tax items, and so on)
- Amounts and dates
- Menu commands (QuickBooks opens the menu and highlights the command for you)
- Specific text within notes, descriptions, memos, and transactions

You learned about the search feature and how to access it through the persistent search bar in Lesson 2, Creating a Company. You will explore it more in this lesson, and you will use it to locate a transaction to edit.

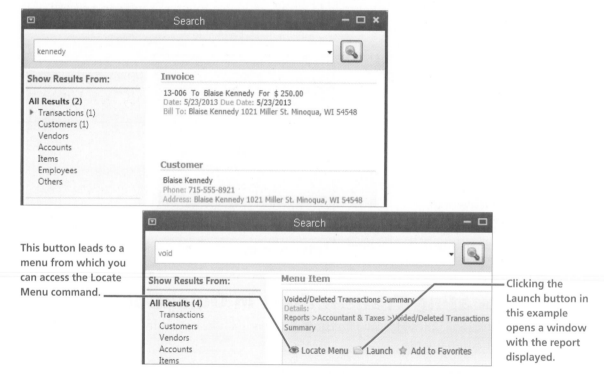

This button leads to a menu from which you can access the Locate Menu command.

Clicking the Launch button in this example opens a window with the report displayed.

A search on *kennedy* brings up the entry in the Customers & Jobs list and the customer invoice. A search on *void* brings up menu items (one displayed here). The buttons below the invoice and menu items appear when you move your mouse pointer over the entries.

Fixing Errors

The following table outlines a series of non-paycheck errors, the effects of the error behind the scenes, and how to correct the error.

Error	Effect Behind the Scenes	The Fix
An invoice is entered but the Receive Payments window is not used when the payment is deposited	Your income will be double-stated and Accounts Receivable for the customer is not "cleared out"	Delete the deposit and then enter the transaction properly using the Receive Payments window
A bill is entered but the Pay Bills window is not used when the payment is made	Your expenses will be double-stated and Accounts Payable for the vendor is not "cleared out"	Delete the check or credit card payment for the expense and then enter the transaction properly using the Pay Bills window
A "regular" check was cut to pay payroll or sales tax liabilities	The liability accounts are not cleared out; QuickBooks payroll essentially has a second set of books that are affected only when you pay the liabilities through the proper method	Void the "regular" check and then process the payment through the proper method (Pay Payroll Liabilities or Pay Sales Tax)
The wrong account type was chosen when creating a new account in the Chart of Accounts	The types of accounts involved will determine what the damage will be behind the scenes (but there will be damage!)	Edit the account through the Chart of Accounts, choosing the correct account type

FLASHBACK TO GAAP: PRUDENCE

Remember that if you need to choose between two solutions, pick the one that is less likely to overstate assets and income.

Dealing with errors in payroll will be covered in Lesson 9, Using QuickBooks for Payroll, as they must be treated differently since QuickBooks keeps a separate set of books behind the scenes for payroll.

QUICK REFERENCE	FINDING AND SEARCHING FOR INFORMATION
Task	**Procedure**
Find a transaction in QuickBooks	▪ Choose Edit→Find. ▪ Choose either the Simple or the Advanced tab. ▪ Enter as much information as possible about the transaction; click Find.
Search for text in the QuickBooks file and menu commands	▪ Choose Edit→Search. ▪ Type in the keyword on which you wish to base your search; tap ⎡Enter⎤.

DEVELOP YOUR SKILLS 6.1

Correct Errors in a QuickBooks File

In this exercise, you will search for and edit an invoice. Then you will execute a few tasks incorrectly and then fix them. The first step is to open QuickBooks, and then either open a company file or restore a portable company file.

1. Start **QuickBooks 2013**.

   If you downloaded the student exercise files in the portable company file *format, follow Option 1 below. If you downloaded the files in the* company file *format, follow Option 2 below.*

If you choose, you may use the final company file from Critical Thinking 5.2. In this case, open the Critical Thinking 5.2 company file from your default storage location in Option 2 below.

Option 1: Restore a Portable Company File

2. Choose **File→Open or Restore Company**.

3. Restore the **Chez Devereaux** portable file for this lesson from your file storage location, placing your name as the first word in the filename (e.g., Lisa's Chez Devereaux Salon and Spa, Lesson 6).
It may take a few moments for the portable company file to open. Once it does, continue with step 4.

Option 2: Open a Company File

2. Choose **File→Open or Restore Company**, ensure that **Open a regular company file** is selected, and then open the **Chez Devereaux** company file for this lesson from from your file storage location.
The QuickBooks company file will open.

3. Click **OK** to close the QuickBooks Information window. If necessary, click **No** in the Set Up External Accountant User window.

FROM THE KEYBOARD
[F3] to launch the Search feature

Use the Search Feature to Edit an Invoice

Now you will help Bill edit invoice 6 for Blaise Kennedy, who has said that he was incorrectly charged for two massages when he should have been charged for just one.

4. Choose **Edit→Search**; choose to update search information, if necessary.

5. Type **kennedy**, and then tap [Enter].

6. Move your mouse pointer over the invoice transaction displayed for **Blaise Kennedy** until the buttons appear, and then click **Open**.

7. Change the **quantity** on the massage line item to **1**.
Your screen should resemble the following illustration.

8. Click **Save & Close**; click **Yes** to record the transaction with the changes.

9. Close the **Search** window.

Do It the Wrong Way – Set the Account Type

The business has just received a Discover card that will be used for expenses. In this next example, you will set up the account incorrectly for the purpose of learning how to fix the error and do it correctly.

10. Choose **Lists→Chart of Accounts**.

11. Click the **Account** menu button, and then choose **New**.

12. Select **Expense** as the type of account, and then click **Continue**.

13. Type **62300** as the Number, tap Tab, and then type **Discover Card** as the Account Name.
    Your screen should resemble the following illustration.

14. Click **Save & Close**.
    No doubt you have already realized what the error is in this example! While you will be using the card to pay for expenses, you should not set it up as an expense account. This will have huge ramifications behind the scenes, so you need to fix it pronto!

Do It the Right Way – Set the Account Type

In order to fix the error of setting up an account as the wrong type, you need to open the Edit Account window. The Chart of Accounts should still be open from the last step.

15. Right-click **62300•Discover Card** in the Chart of Accounts window, and then choose **Edit Account** from the menu.

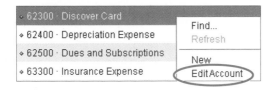

16. Follow these steps to fix the error:

    Ⓐ Click the **drop-down arrow,** and then choose **Credit Card.**   Ⓑ Tap Tab, and then type **23000.**   Ⓒ Click **Save & Close.**

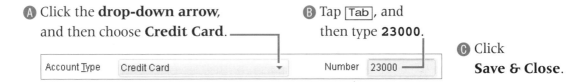

    You must change the account number when you change the account type.

17. Close the **Chart of Accounts** window.

Do It the Wrong Way – Receive Payment for an Invoice

Bill has just received a check from Blaise Kennedy for $165. Now you will enter the payment incorrectly *for the purpose of learning how to fix the error and do it correctly.*

18. Choose **Banking→Make Deposits**.

19. Follow these steps to enter the check:

Ⓐ Tap ⌈Tab⌉, and then type **060213**.

Ⓑ Tap ⌈Tab⌉, and then type **Check from B. Kennedy**.

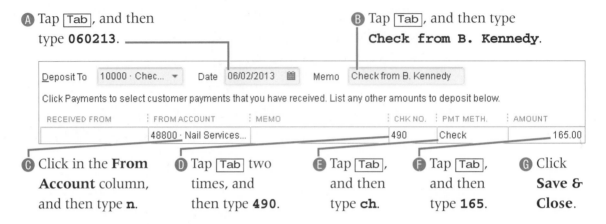

Ⓒ Click in the **From Account** column, and then type **n**.

Ⓓ Tap ⌈Tab⌉ two times, and then type **490**.

Ⓔ Tap ⌈Tab⌉, and then type **ch**.

Ⓕ Tap ⌈Tab⌉, and then type **165**.

Ⓖ Click **Save & Close**.

Think about this transaction. What is wrong with it? By entering the check for an invoice in the Make Deposits window, you have stated income twice and have not cleared the amount from Accounts Receivable.

BTS BRIEF

10000•Checking DR 165.00; 48800•Nail Services Income CR <165.00>

Do It the Right Way – Receive Payment for an Invoice

To fix the deposit that was handled improperly, you must delete it and reenter the payment using the Receive Payments window.

20. Choose **Banking→Make Deposits**.

21. Click the **Previous** button until the deposit you just made is displayed.
You can look for a transaction by using the Previous and Next buttons, if you believe the transaction to be easy to locate. If not, use the Find or Search feature.

22. Choose **Edit→Delete Deposit**; click **OK** in the Delete Transaction window.

23. Close the **Make Deposits** window.

24. Click the **Receive Payments** task icon in the Customers area of the Home page.

25. Follow these steps to enter the payment correctly:

A Type **b** for QuickBooks to fill **Blaise Kennedy** in for you.

B Tap Tab, and then type **165**.

C Tap Tab, and then type **060213**, if necessary.

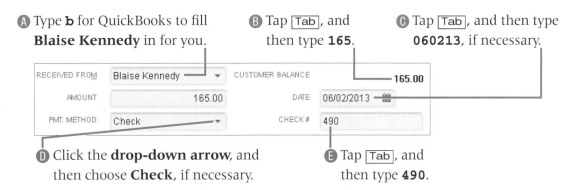

D Click the **drop-down arrow**, and then choose **Check**, if necessary.

E Tap Tab, and then type **490**.

BTS BRIEF

12000•Undeposited Funds DR 165.00; 12000•Accounts Receivable CR <165.00>

The Date and Pmt. Method should both be filled in for you based on information you have previously entered in QuickBooks.

26. Click **Save & Close**.

Before moving on, think about what you have just completed and make sure you understand the "why" behind it. You have deleted the overstated income by deleting the deposit and have "cleared out" Accounts Receivable for Blaise Kennedy by receiving the payment correctly.

Dealing with Bounced Checks

Unfortunately, virtually all business owners must deal with customers whose checks are returned for non-sufficient funds (NSF) at some time or another. Many people call these "bounced checks," and when Intuit briefly released a feature for certain editions of Quick-Books 2012 to deal with this issue, they also used that term. This book uses the terms *NSF* and *bounced check*, though the latter is used more often because it will likely be the term used in future versions/releases of QuickBooks.

In QuickBooks, you can deal with these NSF or "bounced" checks in either of two ways:

- You can re-invoice the customer, although this is not the preferred method if the original transaction involved sales tax.

- You can also generate a statement for the customer, which does not affect sales or sales tax reports.

In this lesson, we will examine how to generate a statement for a customer, which can be used for a returned check in any circumstance.

The bank may charge you a lesser amount than you choose to pass on to the customer for a bounced check. In this book, you will see that the bank charges $25. Lisa has chosen to charge $35 to the customer for the additional work of dealing with the bounced check.

Entering Statement Charges

If you wish to enter a charge for a customer without producing an invoice, you can use the Accounts Receivable register window. It is important that you choose the correct customer to whom you wish to apply the charge. Any transactions entered in a customer's accounts receivable register will show up on statements that you print for them.

Creating Statements for Customers

There are many instances when you may wish to send your customer a statement rather than an invoice. For instance, you may have one customer or job for which you do multiple projects within a billing period and you wish to bill them with an itemized statement. Another example, shown in this lesson, is to create a statement to bill a customer for a bounced check.

Statements can be produced for an individual customer or in a batch for multiple customers.

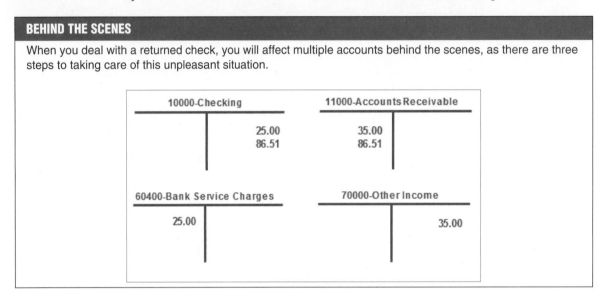

BEHIND THE SCENES

When you deal with a returned check, you will affect multiple accounts behind the scenes, as there are three steps to taking care of this unpleasant situation.

QUICK REFERENCE	DEALING WITH BOUNCED CHECKS
Task	**Procedure**
Generate a statement to account for a bounced check	▪ Create an Other Charge item for the service charge, directing it to the Other Income account. ▪ Record the bank's fee in your bank account register (Bank Service Charges as account). ▪ Record the check in your bank account register (customer/job as payee; Accounts Receivable as account). ▪ Enter a statement charge for the customer's fee. ▪ Send the customer a statement that shows the bounced check and fee.
Enter statement charges	▪ Choose Customers→Enter Statement Charges. ▪ Choose the customer whose Accounts Receivable register you wish to view. ▪ Enter the information for the statement charge; record the transaction.
Create a statement to send to a customer	▪ Choose Customers→Create Statements. ▪ Choose the date range for which you wish to create statements. ▪ Choose the customer(s) for whom you wish to create statements. ▪ Choose any additional options, as desired. ▪ (Optional) Click Preview to view the statement(s). ▪ Click Print or Email to deliver the statement(s) to the customer(s).

DEVELOP YOUR SKILLS 6.2
Handle a Bounced Check

In this exercise, you will account for a check that was returned to Chez Devereaux Salon and Spa for non-sufficient funds. The first step is to create an Other Charge item so you can pass the fee on to the customer. You will charge $35 to your customers for a returned check.

1. Click the **Items & Services** task icon in the Company area of the Home page.

2. Click the **Item** menu button, and then choose **New**.

Items & Services

3. Follow these steps to create the new item:

Ⓐ Click to choose **Other Charge** from the list.

Ⓑ Tap ⟨Tab⟩, and then type **Bounced Check Charge**.

Ⓒ Click in the **Description** field, and then type **Non-Sufficient Funds Service Charge**.

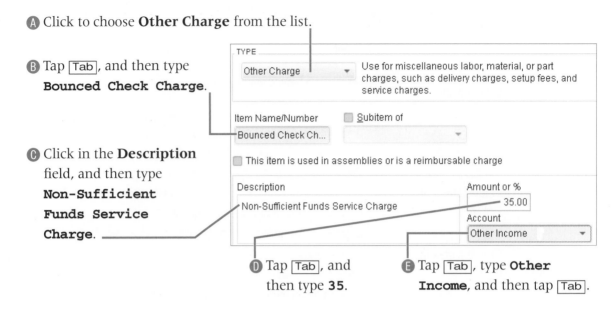

Ⓓ Tap ⟨Tab⟩, and then type **35**.

Ⓔ Tap ⟨Tab⟩, type **Other Income**, and then tap ⟨Tab⟩.

A window will appear informing you that Other Income is not in the Chart of Accounts.

Ⓕ Click **Set Up**.

A New Account window will appear.

Ⓖ Click the **drop-down arrow** and choose **Other Income**.

Ⓗ Tap ⟨Tab⟩, and then type **70000**.

Ⓘ Click **Save & Close**.

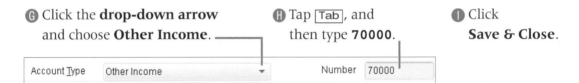

Other Income accounts are used to track income that is not the result of your regular business operations. Since you are not running a financial institution, customer fees are not a regular source of income for you.

4. Click **OK** to save the new item; close the **Item List** window.
   Notice that once you set up the new account, it will fill in to the Account field for you, account number and all.

Record the Fee and Check in the Register

In the following steps, you will record the transactions that affect your bank account balance. The bank charges you a $25 fee for handling the returned item.

5. Click the **Check Register** task icon in the Banking area of the Home page.

6. Click **OK** to choose **10000•Checking** as the account to use.

7. Follow these steps to record the NSF fee charged by the bank:

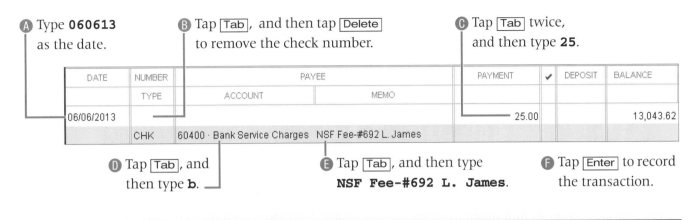

A Type **060613** as the date.

B Tap Tab, and then tap Delete to remove the check number.

C Tap Tab twice, and then type **25**.

D Tap Tab, and then type **b**.

E Tap Tab, and then type **NSF Fee-#692 L. James**.

F Tap Enter to record the transaction.

BTS BRIEF

60400•Bank Service Charges DR 25.00; 10000•Checking CR <25.00>

8. Follow these steps to record the NSF check in your checking register:

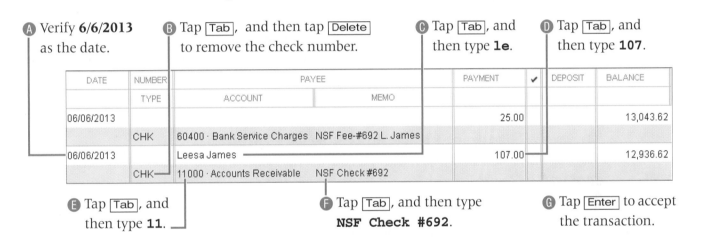

A Verify **6/6/2013** as the date.

B Tap Tab, and then tap Delete to remove the check number.

C Tap Tab, and then type **1e**.

D Tap Tab, and then type **107**.

E Tap Tab, and then type **11**.

F Tap Tab, and then type **NSF Check #692**.

G Tap Enter to accept the transaction.

BTS BRIEF

11000•Accounts Receivable DR 107.00; 10000•Checking CR <107.00>

9. Close the **Checking** register window.

In this last step, you took the funds received from Leesa James back "out" of your Checking account.

Enter a Statement Charge for the Customer's Fee

You have recorded the NSF fee that the bank charged to your register. Now it is time to record the fee that you will charge the customer.

10. Click the **Statement Charges** task icon in the Customers area of the Home page.

When you choose to enter a statement charge, you will view the Accounts Receivable register for a customer. It is important that you choose the correct customer, as is shown in the following step.

11. Click the **drop-down arrow** for the Customer:Job field and choose **Leesa James**.

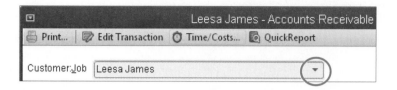

You will now be able to view the register for Leesa James.

12. Tap ⎡Tab⎤ to accept the date of 6/6/13 and move to the Item column.

13. Follow these steps to add the NSF charge:

Ⓐ Type **b**, and then tap ⎡Tab⎤.   Ⓑ Tap ⎡Enter⎤ to record the transaction.

06/06/2013				107.00		107.00
	CHK					
06/06/2013		Bounced Check Charge	35.00	35.00		142.00
	STMTCH	Non-Sufficient Funds Service Charge				

BTS BRIEF

11000•Accounts Receivable DR 35.00; 70000•Other Income CR <35.00>

---

14. Close the **Leesa James – Accounts Receivable** window.

Create a Statement to Send to the Customer

The final step in accounting for a NSF check is to create the statement for the customer that reflects the NSF check and NSF charge.

15. Click the **Statements** task icon in the Customers area of the Home page.

Statements

16. Follow these steps to prepare the statement for Leesa James:

Ⓐ Type **060613** in the Statement Date field.

Ⓑ Click in the circle to the left of **All open transactions as of Statement Date**.

Ⓒ Click in the circle to the left of **One Customer**.

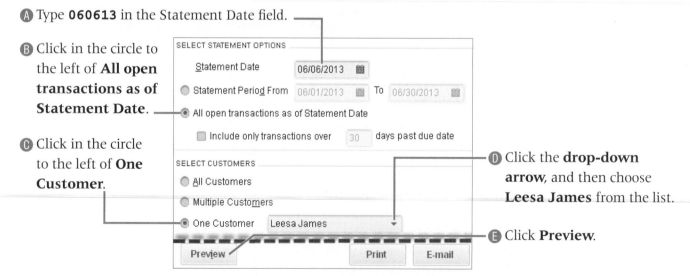

Ⓓ Click the **drop-down arrow**, and then choose **Leesa James** from the list.

Ⓔ Click **Preview**.

You will now see how the statement will look when printed.

17. Click **Zoom In** to see the information included in the statement better, if desired.

18. Close the **Print Preview** and **Create Statement** windows.

Writing Off Bad Debt

Virtually every business has to write off money owed as bad debt at some point or another. QuickBooks does allow you to do this via one of two methods: treating it as a discount or using a credit memo. Your sales tax liability will not be affected if you choose to treat bad debt as a discount, whereas it will be reduced if you use the credit memo method. It is for this reason that the credit memo is recommended when sales tax is involved. Regardless of the method selected, you will need to create an expense account in which to direct the bad debt.

Example: You learn that Leesa James has moved out of town. You believe it is unlikely that you will be able to collect for the amount of the returned check. You decide that it is time to write off the amount owed by this customer as a bad debt.

FLASHBACK TO GAAP: MATERIALITY

Remember that when an item is reported, its significance should be considered.

Treating Bad Debt as a Discount

In order to treat bad debt as a discount (not recommended for a debt that has sales tax associated with it), you would enter it as a discount in the Receive Payments window that you learned about in Lesson 4, Working with Customers. Make sure, though, that you use the proper expense account for the bad debt (e.g., Bad Debt Expense). If you receive a partial payment from a customer, you can also choose to "Write off the extra amount" in the Receive Payments window if you do not expect to ever receive the remaining balance.

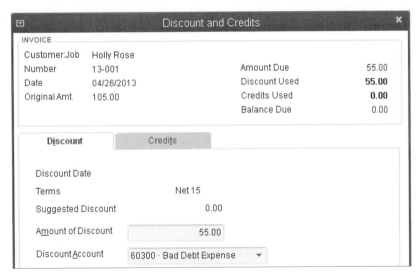

If you were to choose to use the discount method to write off the remainder of invoice #1 for Holly Rose, you would launch the Discount and Credits window from the Receive Payments window and choose 60300•Bad Debt Expense as the account.

Using a Credit Memo to Write Off a Bad Debt

In the next exercise, you will have the opportunity to create a credit memo in order to write off a bad debt. When you choose this method, you will use an Other Charge item to "route" the bad debt to the appropriate expense account (which will be debited), and Accounts Receivable will be credited. You can include both taxable and nontaxable bad debts on a single credit memo. You will finish the procedure by applying the credit memo to the original invoice.

BEHIND THE SCENES

When you write off a bad debt, you need to credit the Accounts Receivable account and the customer sub-register (which automatically occurs when you choose the customer) and debit the expense account you created to track bad debts, in this case Bad Debt Expense.

60300-Bad Debt Expense	11000-Accounts Receivable
121.51	121.51

QUICK REFERENCE	WRITING OFF BAD DEBT
Task	**Procedure**
Write off bad debt as a discount	▪ Create a new expense account called **Bad Debt Expense**.
	▪ Choose Customers→Receive Payments.
	▪ Select the customer and set the write-off date.
	▪ Click the Discounts & Credits button.
	▪ Enter the amount of the bad debt; choose Bad Debt Expense as the Discount Account.
	▪ Complete the transaction.
Write off bad debt using a credit memo	▪ Create a new expense account called **Bad Debt Expense**.
	▪ Create an Other Charge item called Bad Debt that is routed to the Bad Debt Expense account.
	▪ Choose Customers→Create Credit Memos/Refunds.
	▪ Select the customer and set the date.
	▪ Using the Bad Debt item, enter a line item for the total non-tax sales you are writing off; choose Non in the Tax column.
	▪ Using the Bad Debt item, enter a line item for the total taxable sales you are writing off; choose Tax in the Tax column.
	▪ Click Save & Close.
	▪ Choose to which invoice you wish to apply the credit (bad debt write-off).

DEVELOP YOUR SKILLS 6.3

Write Off Bad Debt

In this exercise, you will use the credit memo method to write off the amount owed by Leesa James. The first step is to create an expense account for the payment.

1. Click the **Chart of Accounts** task icon in the Company area of the Home page.

2. Click the **Account** menu button, and then choose **New**.

3. Choose **Expense** as the account type; click **Continue**.

4. Follow these steps to create the new account:

Chart of Accounts

Ⓐ Type **60300** as the **Number**. Ⓑ Tap ⎡Tab⎤, and then type **Bad Debt Expense**.

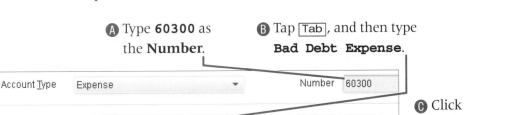

Ⓒ Click **Save & Close**.

5. Close the **Chart of Accounts**.

Set Up the Bad Debt Item

The next step in writing off a bad debt using a credit memo is to create the item.

6. Click the **Items & Services** task icon in the Company area of the Home page.

7. Click the **Item** menu button, and then choose **New**.

8. Follow these steps to create the new item:

Items & Services

Ⓐ Choose **Other Charge** as the type.

Ⓑ Tap ⎡Tab⎤, and then type **Bad Debt**.

Ⓒ Tap ⎡Tab⎤ three times, and then type **Bad Debt Write-Off**.

Ⓓ Tap ⎡Tab⎤ two times, and then type **b** to choose the Account.

Ⓔ Click **OK** to create the item.

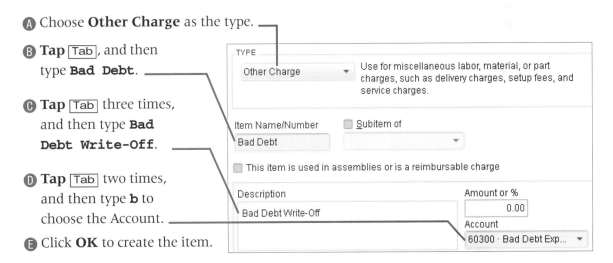

The amount is left blank here so you can fill in the correct amount for each transaction.

9. Close the **Item List** window.

Create the Credit Memo

Finally, you will create the credit memo to write off the bad debt and choose to which invoice(s) it should be applied.

10. Click the **Refunds & Credits** task icon in the Customers area of the Home page.

Refunds
& Credits

11. Follow these steps to complete the memo:

Ⓐ Click to remove the checkmark from this box.

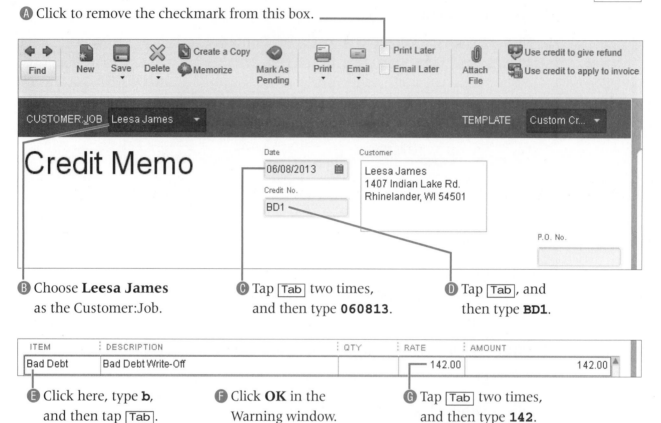

Ⓑ Choose **Leesa James** as the Customer:Job.

Ⓒ Tap Tab two times, and then type **060813**.

Ⓓ Tap Tab, and then type **BD1**.

Ⓔ Click here, type **b**, and then tap Tab.

Ⓕ Click **OK** in the Warning window.

Ⓖ Tap Tab two times, and then type **142**.

12. Click **Save & Close**.
An Available Credit window appears, from which you can decide what to do with the resulting credit.

13. Choose **Apply to an invoice**, and then click **OK**.
The Apply Credits to Invoice window appears, listing all open invoices for the customer. QuickBooks checked both invoices to which to apply the amount from the credit memo.

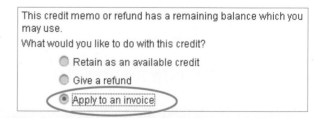

This credit memo or refund has a remaining balance which you may use.

What would you like to do with this credit?

⚪ Retain as an available credit

⚪ Give a refund

🔘 Apply to an invoice

BTS BRIEF

60300•Bad Debt Expense DR 142.00; 11000•Accounts Receivable CR <142.00>

14. Click **Done**.
The total amount owed by Leesa James has now been transferred to the Bad Debt Expense account.

Working with Refunds

There are many times when you may need to issue a refund to a customer. Once a credit memo has been created, you can choose to refund a customer by returning the payment in full. Or, your policy may be to issue a credit that can be applied to another purchase or to an invoice.

Issuing a Refund

There are a variety of reasons that you may wish to issue a refund to a customer, such as:

- For merchandise that has been returned
- For an order that was canceled
- To reimburse for an overpayment

If you wish to return a customer's payment, you can choose to issue a refund check or to return the funds to a credit card.

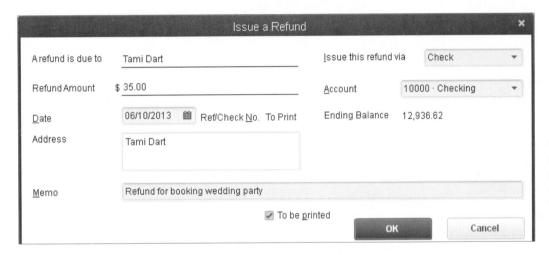

When you choose to issue a refund, the Issue a Refund window will appear. In this window, you can enter the information for the refund check.

Creating a Credit Memo

In the last section, you learned how to use a credit memo to write off bad debt. In this section, you will have the opportunity to create a credit memo as a refund for returned merchandise. Once a credit memo has been created you can choose to apply the credit to an invoice (as you did in the last exercise), or you can choose to issue a refund check to a customer.

Once you have processed a refund for a credit memo, the "Refunded" stamp will appear on the Credit Memo form.

One-Click Credit Memo

If you need to refund a customer for a purchase that was made on an invoice, you can use a feature in QuickBooks that allows you to convert an invoice to a credit memo with one click. This can save you time as you will not have to retype the information for the new transaction.

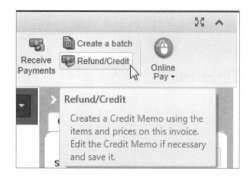

The Refund/Credit button on the Create Invoices window Ribbon allows you to easily create credit memos from invoices.

Applying a Credit as a Part of a Payment

Once a credit has been issued to a customer, you can apply it to payment(s) for future purchases. This is done through the Receive Payments window.

Entering a Credit from a Vendor

If you are on the receiving end of a credit memo, you will need to enter it in your QuickBooks company file as well. This is easily done through the Enter Bills window. Once you have recorded the credit, you can either pass it on to a customer (if you chose to do so in the Enter Bills window when you recorded it) or use it when you pay bills to this vendor in the future.

BEHIND THE SCENES

When you issue a refund, Accounts Receivable or Checking (depending on whether you have received the customer's payment or not), an income account, and Sales Tax Payable (if sales tax was charged in the original transaction) will be affected behind the scenes.

10000-Checking, or 11000-Accounts Receivable	48700-Hair Services Income	25500-Sales Tax Payable
36.93	35.00	1.93

QUICK REFERENCE	WORKING WITH REFUNDS AND CREDITS
Task	**Procedure**
Create a credit memo	▪ Choose Customers→Create Credit Memos/Refunds. ▪ Select the customer and set the date; enter the credit information.
Issue a refund check for returned merchandise	▪ Choose Customers→Create Credit Memos/Refunds. ▪ Choose the desired customer. ▪ Enter the items being returned as separate line items. ▪ Click the Use Credit button; choose Give Refund. ▪ Enter a memo (optional); click OK.
Issue a refund for overpayment on an invoice	▪ Choose Customers→Receive Payments. ▪ Enter payment information. (The overpayment box will appear.) ▪ Choose to refund the amount to the customer; save the transaction. ▪ Complete the customer information in the Issue a Refund window. ▪ Enter a memo as to the purpose of the refund (optional); click OK.
Issue a refund for a canceled prepaid order/deposit	▪ Choose Banking→Write Checks. ▪ Fill in the customer information in the top portion of the window. ▪ Choose Accounts Receivable; save the check. ▪ Choose Customers→Receive Payments. ▪ Choose the correct customer at the top of the window; leave the amount as zero. ▪ Click the Discounts & Credits button. The check you just wrote should be selected. If an invoice is selected, click to remove the checkmark. ▪ Save & Close the transaction.
Enter a credit from a vendor	▪ Choose Vendors→Enter Bills. ▪ Choose Credit, choose the vendor, and enter the credit amount. ▪ In the Account column, choose the account that you use to track vendor credits. ▪ Enter the amount of the credit; indicate whether to pass the credit on to a customer. ▪ Save & Close the credit.
Create a credit memo from an invoice	▪ Open the invoice from which you wish to create the credit memo. ▪ Click the Create button on the Create Invoices window toolbar; choose Credit Memo for this Invoice. ▪ Verify the information; click Save & Close.

Issue a Refund and Apply a Credit as a Partial Payment

In this exercise, you will create a credit memo and issue a refund to a customer. The first step is to create a credit memo for the customer. In this situation, Tami Dart came in for special event styling on 5/14/13. You have told her that if she books her entire wedding party with you, you will issue a refund for this service.

1. Click the **Refunds & Credits** task icon in the Customers area of the Home page.

Refunds
& Credits

2. Follow these steps to record the credit memo for Tami:

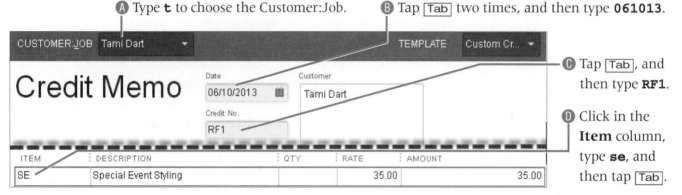

Ⓐ Type **t** to choose the Customer:Job.   Ⓑ Tap Tab two times, and then type **061013**.

Ⓒ Tap Tab, and then type **RF1**.

Ⓓ Click in the **Item** column, type **se**, and then tap Tab.

Leave the Create Credit Memos/Refunds window open. You will issue the refund from it in the next step.

Issue a Refund Check

3. Click the **Use credit to give refund** button on the Ribbon.

4. Click in the **Memo** field and type this text.

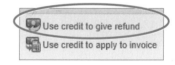

5. Review the information in the Issue a Refund window to ensure it is correct, and then click **OK**.

6. Click **Save & Close** to record the credit memo.

BTS BRIEF

60300•Hair Services Income DR 35.00; 10000•Checking CR <35.00>

Customizing Reports and Graphs

You have learned to create various reports throughout this book so far. Now you will customize the reports that you produce to make them work for you.

Customization takes place on many fronts. You may find yourself asking:

- Which accounts should I display?
- What information do I need to filter out?
- What header and footer information should I include?
- How do I want my fonts and numbers to look?

Display Properties

The Display tab of the Modify Report window allows you to change aspects of your report such as the dates it represents, your reporting basis (cash or accrual), the columns to display, and subcolumn preferences.

Report Date Range

Each preset report has a default date range displayed when the report is first created. The date can either be:

- When your reporting period ends, such as a balance sheet report created "As of June 30, 2013."
- For a range of days, such as a Profit & Loss report created for June 1-30, 2013.
  The type of date is determined by the type of report you produce.

Accrual vs. Cash Basis Reporting

If you recall from Lesson 1, Introducing QuickBooks Pro, there are two methods of accounting from which you can choose for your company. You enter data into QuickBooks the same way regardless of whether you use the cash or accrual basis of accounting. When you create your reports, you can easily switch between cash and accrual basis. And when you first create a QuickBooks company, the default will be for the reports to be displayed as the accrual basis. Of course, you will want to set your company's default report basis in the report section of the Edit Preferences window. Take a look at a review of both methods.

Accrual Basis

In the accrual basis of accounting, income is recorded when a sale is made, and expenses are recorded when accrued. This method is used often by firms and businesses with large inventories; it's required for publicly traded companies.

Cash Basis

In the cash basis of accounting, income is recorded when cash is received and expenses are recorded when cash is paid. This method is commonly used by small businesses and professionals.

If you operate using the cash basis, you will not need to display Accounts Receivable and Accounts Payable on your financial statements because cash has yet to change hands.

Columns

Each preset report displays certain default columns. You can change the columns to make your report much more useful. For instance, you can choose to display multiple months on a P&L report to compare income and expenses in different reporting periods. You can also specify subcolumns you want displayed if they are available for your specific report.

Subcolumns

Some reports allow you to add subcolumns to further analyze your data. Different subcolumns are available depending on the report you run. The entire list is shown in the following illustration.

The use of columns and subcolumns to stratify data can be a very valuable way to help you analyze and scrutinize your company's financial data.

Filtering Reports

In order to have reports display only essential data, you have the ability to apply a filter in QuickBooks. A filter will let you choose what information to include in your report, thereby "filtering out" the rest of it. Filters can be applied to any report, and the specific information that can be filtered is determined by the report you run. You are also able to filter transaction reports for text that is contained in custom fields if the fields are on the forms for the transactions included in the report.

Formatting

Formatting deals with the appearance of the report; it has nothing to do with the data contained within it. You can change the report's font(s) and the way numbers are displayed.

Fonts

QuickBooks displays its preset reports in the default font. You can make many choices as to the characteristics of the font in your report, such as the font name, style, color, and size.

Negative Numbers

When you have negative numbers in your report, they can be displayed in a variety of ways, as described in the illustration to the right.

All Numbers

You can also choose how QuickBooks will display all numbers in your report. The options available are displayed in the illustration to the right.

QUICK REFERENCE	CUSTOMIZING REPORTS
Task	**Procedure**
Change the default report basis	▪ Choose Edit→Preferences. ▪ Choose the Reports & Graphs category, and then the Company Preferences tab. ▪ Choose Accrual or Cash in the Summary Report Basis section; click OK.
Apply a filter to a report	▪ Create your report, and then click the Customize Report button. ▪ Click the Filters tab, apply the desired filter(s), and then click OK.
Change the font and number formatting on a report	▪ Create your report; click the Customize Report button. ▪ Click the Fonts & Numbers tab. ▪ Select any number formatting changes. ▪ Click on the report element to change; click Change Font. ▪ Make your changes; click OK twice.

DEVELOP YOUR SKILLS 6.5

Customize Your Reports

In this exercise, you will help Bill create and customize a Profit & Loss report for Chez Devereaux Salon and Spa. The QuickBooks default report basis is accrual. Lisa spoke with her accountant and determined that Chez Devereaux Salon and Spa would use the cash basis for reporting. You will begin by changing the default for the company file.

1. Choose **Edit→Preferences**.

2. Click the **Reports & Graphs** category on the left side of the window.

3. Click the **Company Preferences** tab, and then click in the circle to the left of **Cash** in the Summary Reports Basis section.

4. Click **OK** to save the new preference.

Add a Filter

Bill will first run the preset Profit & Loss Standard report. Then he will apply a filter to the report to show only income accounts.

5. Choose **Reports→Company & Financial→Profit & Loss Standard**.

6. Follow these steps to set a custom date range:

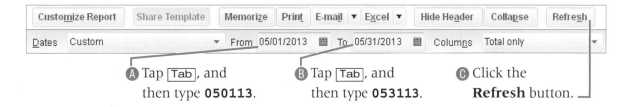

You will see the Profit & Loss by Class report displayed for May 2013.

7. Click the **Customize Report** button on the report toolbar.

8. Follow these steps to apply a filter that will include only income accounts on the report:

Ⓐ Click the **Filters** tab.

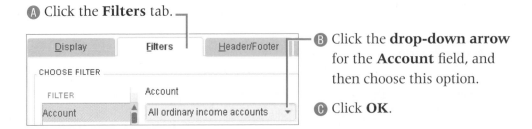

Ⓑ Click the **drop-down arrow** for the **Account** field, and then choose this option.

Ⓒ Click **OK**.

You will now see the report with no expense accounts shown.

Change the Font and Number Formatting

Bill wants to spruce up the report by changing the way the font and numbers appear.

9. Click the **Customize Report** button on the report toolbar.

10. Follow these steps to change the formatting:

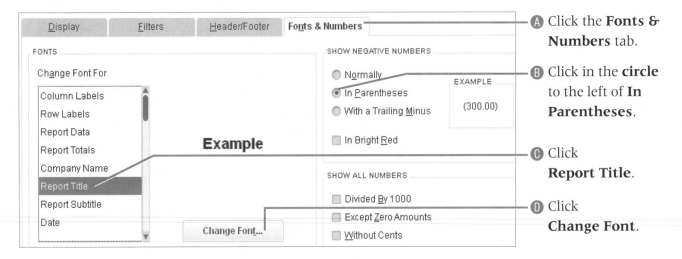

Ⓐ Click the **Fonts & Numbers** tab.

Ⓑ Click in the **circle** to the left of **In Parentheses**.

Ⓒ Click **Report Title**.

Ⓓ Click **Change Font**.

You will see a Report Title window similar to a Font dialog box that you may be familiar with from word-processing programs.

Ⓔ Type **t**; QuickBooks will bring Tahoma to the top of the list.

Ⓕ Click **Tahoma**.

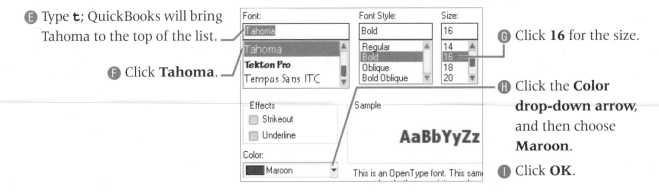

Ⓖ Click **16** for the size.

Ⓗ Click the **Color drop-down arrow**, and then choose **Maroon**.

Ⓘ Click **OK**.

11. Click **Yes** to change all related fonts.
    You will see the new font formatting displayed above the Change Font button.

12. Click **OK**.
    You will see the font formatting changes that you just made. Leave the report open; you will continue to customize it in the next exercise.

Working with Additional Formatting Options

You have learned to choose many report customization options. Now you will learn to create a header and footer to your specifications and to memorize and recall a report.

Header and Footer Options

All preset QuickBooks reports have default headers and footers. You can change the information included and how it is formatted on the Header/Footer tab of the Modify Report window.

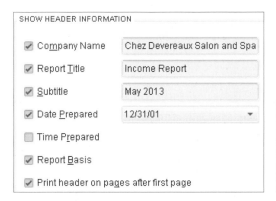

You have many options when it comes to customizing the header and footer of your report.

Page Layout

You can choose to use the default standard report layout or to use left, right, or centered alignment.

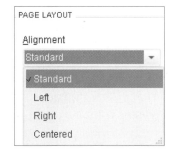

Memorizing Reports

Once you have created a report with your chosen settings, you may wish to save the report options so you can easily produce the same report again. The process of saving the settings of a report is called *memorizing* a report, and it is available for all reports. The memorizing feature memorizes the format of the report, not the data contained within it. This means that when you open a memorized report, it will contain your most recently entered data.

To recall the memorized report, you can choose it from the Memorized Report List.

Essential Skills

Memorized Report Groups

QuickBooks allows you to organize your memorized reports into groups. There are six preset groups (accountant, banking, company, customers, employees, and vendors) for you to use, or you can choose to create your own. When you memorize a report, you can place it into a group immediately or later.

When you choose to memorize a report, you have the opportunity to save it in a memorized report group.

Batch Processing of Reports

If you have a group of reports that you run together on a regular basis, you may wish to process them as a batch to save time. You will first need to set the reports you wish to process together as a memorized report group; then you will be able to process them all at once.

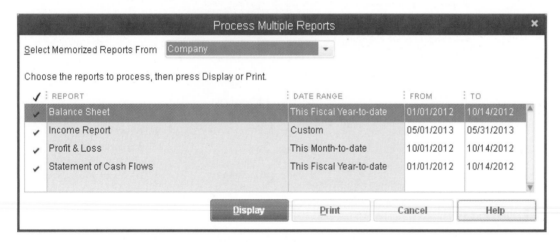

The Process Multiple Reports window allows you to choose which group of reports to process as a batch. You can set the date range in this window, too, if you need to change it from the range that was memorized.

QUICK REFERENCE	WORKING WITH AND MEMORIZING REPORTS
Task	**Procedure**
Change the report header/footer	■ Create your report; click the Customize Report button.
	■ Click the Header/Footer tab and make the desired changes; click OK.
Apply the % of row feature to a report	■ Create your report; click the Customize Report button.
	■ Click the Display tab and click in the box for % of row; click OK.

QUICK REFERENCE	WORKING WITH AND MEMORIZING REPORTS (continued)
Task	**Procedure**
Create a memorized report group	■ Choose Reports→Memorized Report List. ■ Click the Memorized Report menu button; choose New Group. ■ Type the name of the group; click OK.
Place a report in the memorized report group	■ Create and modify a report to your liking; click Memorize. ■ Type the name of the report. ■ Click in the checkbox to the left of Save in Memorized Report Group. ■ Click the drop-down arrow to choose the group; click OK.
Batch process a group of reports	■ Choose Reports→Process Multiple Reports. ■ Choose the group from which you wish to process the reports. ■ Choose the reports you wish to process; click either Display or Print.

DEVELOP YOUR SKILLS 6.6
Make Additional Report Customization Changes

In this exercise, you will help Bill make additional custom changes in the report and memorize the final product. The report that you were working on in the previous exercise should still be open. If not, repeat the steps in the previous exercise to produce the report needed to begin this exercise.

1. Click the **Customize Report** button on the report toolbar.

2. Follow these steps to make the changes to the header and footer:

Ⓐ Click the **Header/Footer** tab.

Ⓑ Replace the current Report Title with **Income Report**.

Ⓒ Click to uncheck the **Time Prepared** checkbox.

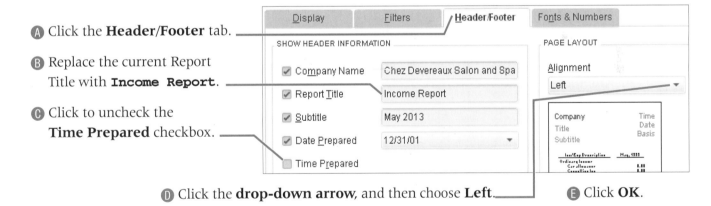

Ⓓ Click the **drop-down arrow**, and then choose **Left**.　　Ⓔ Click **OK**.

Look at the changes you have made to your report.

Change How Columns Are Displayed
Next you will help Bill modify the report so it separates the income by each two-week period.

3. Click the **Customize Report** button on the Report toolbar.

4. Click the **drop-down arrow** in the Columns section and choose **Two week**.

5. Click **OK**.

QuickBooks displays the Income Report that Bill has customized.

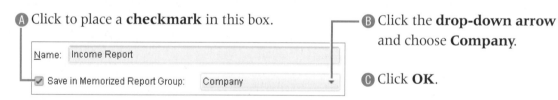

Chez Devereaux Salon and Spa

Income Report

May 2013   **Cash Basis**

	May 1 - 4, 13	May 5 - 18, 13	May 19 - 31, 13	TOTAL
▼ Ordinary Income/Expense				
▼ Income				
48700 · Hair Services Income ▶	0.00 ◀	385.00	225.00	610.00
48800 · Nail Services Income	0.00	44.00	122.00	166.00
48900 · Spa Services Income	0.00	0.00	85.00	85.00
Total Income	0.00	429.00	432.00	861.00
Gross Profit	0.00	429.00	432.00	861.00
Net Ordinary Income	0.00	429.00	432.00	861.00
Net Income	0.00	429.00	432.00	861.00

Memorize a Report

Now that Bill has the report just as he wants it, he will memorize it for easy recall.

6. Click the **Memorize** button on the report toolbar.

7. Follow these steps to memorize the report and place it in a group:

Ⓐ Click to place a **checkmark** in this box.

Ⓑ Click the **drop-down arrow** and choose **Company**.

Name:	Income Report
☑ Save in Memorized Report Group:	Company ▼

Ⓒ Click **OK**.

8. Close the **Income Report**.

Process Multiple Reports

Bill will now process a batch of reports from the Company group.

9. Choose **Reports→Memorized Reports→Memorized Report List**.

10. **Scroll down** until you see the group header **Company**.

11. Right-click **Company**, and then choose **Process Group**.

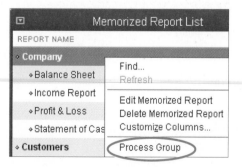

Take a look at the Process Multiple Reports window. You will see that the report that you just memorized, Income Report, is included in this group.

12. Click **Display** to process the batch of reports.
    QuickBooks will produce all of the reports in the Company group for the date ranges displayed.

13. Choose **Window→Close All**.

Creating Custom Forms

Before you customize your forms, think about what you want them to do for you:

■ Do you want to include custom fields?

■ Do you want to include a company logo?

■ What do you want the forms you will be sending out to your stakeholders to say about your company?

■ How much detail do you want to include?

■ What size fields will you need?

Templates

A template is a specific form format (with no data) on which you can base future forms. QuickBooks provides several templates, but you can also create custom templates to meet the needs of your unique company, or create templates for preprinted forms. All of the templates available for a particular type of form are available from the drop-down list at the top of the form. Changing templates for a transaction that has already been entered will not change the information recorded in the transaction, even if the field is not visible on the new form.

Creating a Custom Template

When you choose to create a custom template, you begin by specifying information in the Basic Customization window. This window also provides a preview of how the template looks as you make changes to the various fields and information.

Adding a Company Logo to Templates

QuickBooks allows you to further personalize your templates by including your company logo. When you choose to add a logo to your template, the image file will be stored in the folder where your company file is located.

 To add a logo or picture on a template, the company file must be located on the computer's hard drive or on a shared server. It will not work if your company file is located on a flash drive.

The Manage Templates Window

It is in the Manage Templates window where you will assign a name for your new template. You can also access additional templates online from this window. When you click the Download Templates button, QuickBooks launches a web browser and displays the QuickBooks website from which you can choose new templates.

Using Custom Fields in Forms and Reports

You need to create your own custom form template to utilize the custom fields you set up in Lesson 3, Working with Vendors. You can choose to add the custom field information for customers, jobs, vendors, and employees on the Header tab of the Additional Customization window. To add the custom fields for items, you must use the Columns tab. It is up to you to determine whether the various fields will be displayed on the screen, on the printed form, on both, or in neither place.

If you wish to display custom fields on reports, you can choose to display them in the Columns box on the Display tab of the Modify Report window.

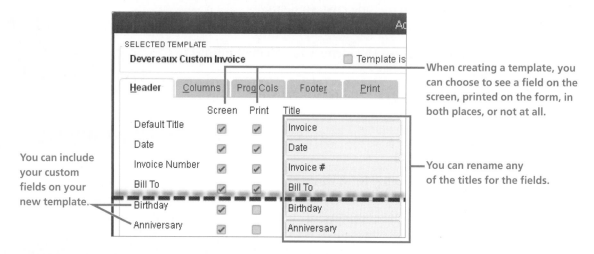

You can include your custom fields on your new template.

When creating a template, you can choose to see a field on the screen, printed on the form, in both places, or not at all.

You can rename any of the titles for the fields.

Working with the Layout Designer Window

QuickBooks allows you not only to determine what is included on a template, but also where it will be located. You can move fields and labels around your template and change the size of fields in the Layout Designer window. Each element on the template is termed an "object" in the Layout Designer window, and you can use some standard techniques to select, move, and resize all objects. The Snap to Grid feature ensures that all of your objects line up to a grid for which you can specify the spacing. In addition, you will see two shadows where the standard envelope windows are located so you can make sure to line up the addressees and return addresses properly.

QUICK REFERENCE	CREATING AND MODIFYING TEMPLATES
Task	**Procedure**
Create and name a new template	■ Choose Lists→Templates.
	■ Click the Templates menu button, choose New, and then choose the desired template type.
	■ Click the Manage Templates button; enter a name for the new template.
	■ Click OK twice to accept the new name and save the new template.
Modify a template	■ Choose Lists→Templates; single-click on the desired template.
	■ Click the Templates menu button; choose Edit.
	■ Make any desired changes; click OK.
Open layout designer for a template	■ Open the template you wish to modify further.
	■ Click the Layout Designer button.
	■ Make any necessary changes; click OK twice.

Set Up a New Template

In this exercise, you will help Bill create a template for the company.

1. Choose **Lists→Templates**.

2. Click the **Templates** menu button, and then choose **New**.

3. Ensure Invoice is the type of template selected; click **OK**.

4. Click the **Manage Templates** button.

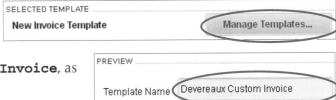

5. Replace the default Template Name with **Devereaux Custom Invoice**, as shown at right.

6. Click **OK** to return to the Basic Customization window.

Change the Color Scheme of the Template

You will now help Bill change the template and company name color.

7. Click the **drop-down arrow** to choose **Green** in the Select Color Scheme field.

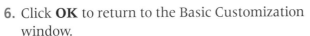

8. Click the **Apply Color Scheme** button.
You will now be able to view the new color in the preview area of the window to the right.

Add Customization

Now it is time to decide which customer and item fields you wish to include on the new template.

9. Click the **Additional Customization** button at the bottom of the window.

10. Click to place a checkmark in the **Due Date** checkbox in the **Print** column.
A Layout Designer window appears to let you know how you can make changes to how the new field will be laid out on the template.

11. Click in the box to the left of **Do not display this message in the future**; tap Enter.

12. Follow these steps to continue to customize your template:

Ⓐ Click to place checkmarks in the **Screen** column for both **Birthday** and **Anniversary**.

Ⓑ Click the **Columns** tab.

Ⓒ Click to place a checkmark in the **Screen** column for **Hold**.

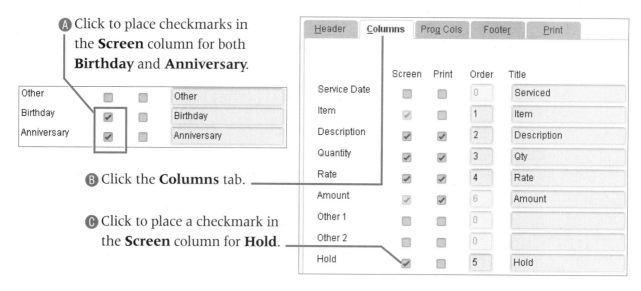

Notice the order column; it shows the order in which the columns will appear on the invoice from left to right.

13. Click **OK** in the Additional Customization window.

14. Feel free to play around and customize your template further, including using the Layout Designer!

15. When you are finished customizing your template, click **OK** in the Basic Customization window.

16. Close the **Templates** window.

17. Choose the appropriate option for your situation:

- If you are continuing on to the next lesson or to the end-of-lesson exercises, leave QuickBooks open.
- If you are finished working in QuickBooks for now, choose **File→Exit**.

Concepts Review

Concepts Review   http://labyrinthelab.com/qb13

To check your knowledge of the key concepts introduced in this lesson, complete the Concepts Review quiz by going to the URL listed above.

Reinforce Your Skills

Before you begin the Reinforce Your Skills exercises, complete one of these options:

- *Open* **[Your name]'s Tea Shoppe at the Lake, Lesson 5** *or Tea Shoppe at the Lake, Lesson 6 from your file storage location that you used for Lesson 5.*
- *Restore* **Tea Shoppe at the Lake, Lesson 6 (Portable)** *from your file storage location. If you need to review how to restore a portable company file, take a peek at Develop Your Skills 3.3. Make sure to place your name as the first word in the company filename (e.g., Susie's Tea Shoppe at the Lake, Lesson 6).*

REINFORCE YOUR SKILLS 6.1
Find and Edit a Transaction

Susie received an adjusted amount for the May water bill. Rather than clicking the Previous button over and over again, in this exercise, you will use the QuickBooks Find feature to locate the transaction.

1. Choose **Edit→Find**.

2. Choose **Bill** as the Transaction Type, and **City of Lake San Marcos** as the Vendor.

3. Enter the date range as **5/1/2013** to **5/31/2013**, and then click **Find**.
   The bill you are looking for will be displayed in the bottom of the window.

4. Double-click the bill dated **5/17/2013** in the bottom portion of the window.
   The Enter Bills window will open; leave it open for the next step.

Edit a Transaction

5. Change the amount of the bill to **97.37** and choose to **record the change** to the transaction.

6. **Save and close** the transaction; close the **Find** window.

Enter a Credit from a Vendor

Susie has received a credit from Vista Insurance Company to be applied to a future payment. In this exercise, you will record this credit.

1. Choose **Vendors→Enter Bills**; then, choose the **Credit** option at the top of the window.

2. Enter **6/7/2013** as the date; choose **Vista Insurance Company** as the Vendor.

3. Enter **106.94** as the Credit Amount; type **Refund on premium paid** as the Memo.

4. Ensure **Insurance Expense** is the account displayed.

5. Click **Save & Close** to enter the credit.

Apply the Credit When Paying a Bill

6. Choose **Vendors→Pay Bills**.

7. Click to the left of the **5/28/2013** bill for Vista Insurance Company to select it.

8. Click the **Set Credits** button in the middle portion of the window.
   The Discount and Credits window will appear.

9. Ensure that the credit of **$106.94 from 6/7/2013** is checked, and then click **Done**.

10. Set the date to **6/7/2013** if necessary, and then choose for the **check to be printed**.

11. Click **Pay Selected Bills**; click **Done** in the Payment Summary window.

Customize a Profit & Loss Report

In this exercise, you will help Susie create a customized P&L report for Tea Shoppe at the Lake.

1. Choose **Reports→Company & Financial→Profit & Loss Standard**.

2. Tap [Tab], type **050113**, tap [Tab] again, and then type **053113**.

3. Click the **Refresh** button on the Report toolbar.

Change the Columns Displayed

You will now display the columns by week across the top of the report.

4. Click the **Customize Report** button on the toolbar.

5. Choose the **Display** tab, if necessary.

6. Locate the **Columns** section of the window and choose to display the columns across the **top by week**; click **OK**.
   This report will allow you to compare the income and expenses from week to week.

Change the Formatting for the Header

Susie doesn't like the look of the default header, and she needs your help to get it just right.

7. Click the **Customize Report** button on the toolbar.

8. Display the **Header/Footer** tab.

9. Change the report title to **Profit & Loss by Week**.

10. Change the Alignment to **Left**.

11. Display the **Fonts & Numbers** tab.

12. Make any changes you like to the formatting of the fonts and numbers.

13. Click **OK** to save your changes.

14. Memorize the report, naming it **Profit & Loss by Week**; finally, close the report.

Modify the Custom Sales Report

In this exercise, you will create an appealing sales receipt for Tea Shoppe at the Lake. You can make changes to a template directly from an open form, and that is the approach you will use to modify the sales receipt template.

1. Choose **Customers→Enter Sales Receipts**.

2. Click the **Formatting** tab of the Ribbon, and then click **Manage Templates**. Click **OK** in the Manage Templates window.
   The Basic Customization window displays.

3. In the **Company & Transaction** area of the window, choose to **print the company phone number**.

4. Close the **Layout Designer** window, choosing to not have it appear again in the future.

5. Choose to print the **company fax number**.

6. Change the font and color scheme of the template to your liking.

7. Click the **Additional Customization** button.

8. On the **Footer** tab, add a long text that is to be printed:

   `We stand behind everything we sell. Please let us know if you are`
   `not fully satisfied so that we can have a chance to make you happy.`

Use Layout Designer

Finally, you will open the form in Layout Designer and make a few more changes.

9. Click the **Layout Designer** button.

10. **Scroll down**; select and move the **Phone #** and **Fax #** objects to the top of the form. (Hint: Select all four objects and move them simultaneously.)

11. Move any other objects around as you see fit.

12. When you have the template just right, click **OK** to save your changes.

13. Click **OK** in both the Additional Customization and the Basic Customization windows to save the changes to the template.

14. Close the **Enter Sales Receipt** window.

15. Choose the appropriate option for your situation:
    - If you are continuing on to the next lesson or the rest of the end-of-lesson exercises, leave QuickBooks open.
    - If you are finished working in QuickBooks for now, choose **File→Exit**.

Apply Your Skills

Before you begin the Apply Your Skills exercises, complete one of these options:

- *Open* **[Your name] Wet Noses Veterinary Clinic, Lesson 5** *or* **Wet Noses Veterinary Clinic, Lesson 6** *from your file storage location.*
- *Restore* **Wet Noses Veterinary Clinic, Lesson 6 (Portable)** *from your file storage location. Make sure to place your name as the first word in the company filename (e.g., Sadie's Wet Noses Veterinary Clinic, Lesson 6). If you need to review how to restore a portable company file, see Develop Your Skills 3.1.*

APPLY YOUR SKILLS 6.1
Deal with a Returned Check

In this exercise, you will help Dr. James account for check #6666 from Mary Ann Gulch for $145.65 that was returned for non-sufficient funds.

1. Create an **Other Income** account in the Chart of Accounts.
   Hint: You will find the account type in the Other Account Types drop-down list.

2. Create an **Other Charge** item for the service charge for $35, directing it to the Other Income account that you just created.

Enter the Checking Register Transactions

3. Open the **Checking** register, and record a service charge of $25 from the bank for the bounced check on 6/6/2013 using **Bank Service Charges** as the account. Leave the Payee and Number fields blank and type a message stating the customer name and check number for the NSF fee. Leave the Checking register open for the next step.

4. On 6/6/13, record the bounced check in your Checking register, filling in Mary Ann Gulch as the Payee, $145.65 as the Payment amount, and Accounts Receivable as the account. Leave the Number field blank and record a Memo of NSF Check #6666. Close the Checking register when you are finished.

Enter a Statement Charge and Create a Statement

5. Open the **Accounts Receivable** window (Hint: **Customers→Enter Statement Charges**), and then choose Mary Ann Gulch as the Customer:Job.
   Notice that the last transaction in the register is the "other side" of what you entered in the Checking register and that it increases the balance owing.

6. Enter a transaction for the Bounced Check Charge on 6/6/2013, choosing the other charge item you created.
   Once you choose the Bounced Check Charge item, all of the rest of the information will fill in from the Item List.

7. Click **Record**; close the **Accounts Receivable** register window.

8. Open the **Create Statements** window, and then choose to create a statement dated 6/6/2013 for Mary Ann Gulch with the All open transactions as of Statement Date option selected.

9. Preview the statement, printing it only if your instructor requests you to do so.

10. Close the **Print Preview** and **Create Statement** windows.

Deal with Bad Debt

Dr. James has learned that Natalie Sheehan moved out of town. You do not expect to receive payment for the two invoices (27 for $399.50 and 117 for $148.10, for a total of $547.60) she has outstanding. In this exercise, you will help Dr. James write off the amount as bad debt using a credit memo.

1. Create a new **expense** account called **Bad Debt Expense**.

2. Create a new **Other Charge** item called **Bad Debt** and route it to the Bad Debt Expense account you just created. Leave the amount as zero.

Create the Credit Memo and Apply It to the Invoices

3. Open the **Create Credit Memos/Refunds** window, and then choose **Natalie Sheehan:Dog-Sandy** as the Customer:Job.
   You must choose the Customer:Job just as it appears on the invoice to which you will be applying the credit.

4. Set the date to **6/13/2013**, enter **BD1** as the Credit No., choose **Bad Debt** as the Item, and then type **547.60** as the amount.

5. Choose for the credit memo to not be printed; click to **Save & Close** the window.

6. Choose to apply the amount of the credit to an invoice, and then click **OK**.

7. Click **Done** in the Apply Credit to Invoices window, ensuring both invoices are checked first.

Issue a Credit and a Refund Check

In this exercise, you find Dr. James realizing that she overcharged the City of Seattle K-9 Unit on invoice 148, as Duke did not receive a nail trim. You will help her to issue a credit memo and a refund check to the city.

1. Open the **Create Credit Memos/Refunds** window, and then choose **City of Seattle K-9 Unit:Dog-Duke** as the Customer:Job.

2. Set the date to **6/14/2013**, enter **RF1** as the Credit No., and then choose **Nails** as the Item.

3. Click **Save & Close**; then, choose to **Give a refund** in the Available Credit window.

4. Verify that the information is correct in the Issue a Refund window, making sure that the check is set to be printed, and then click **OK**.
   The refund check is now in the queue waiting to be printed.

Answer Questions with Reports

In this exercise, you will answer questions for Dr. James by running reports. You may wish to display the Report Center in List View to help you answer the questions. Ask your instructor if you should print the reports, print (save) them as PDF files, export them to Excel, or simply display them on the screen.

1. Would you create a Profit & Loss report that shows the income and expenses by week for the month of May 2013? Title it **Profit & Loss by Week** and add some color to spice it up a bit.

2. Can you show me a list of all items set up for the company, now that you have created new ones for NSF checks and bad debt?

3. Is it possible to display a report showing all transactions for each of the customers you worked with in this lesson's exercises: Mary Ann Gulch, Natalie Sheehan, and City of Seattle K-9 Unit? (Make sure to specify the correct job.)

4. Submit your reports based on the guidelines provided by your instructor.

5. Choose the appropriate option for your situation:

   ■ If you are continuing on to the next lesson or the Critical Thinking exercises, leave QuickBooks open.

   ■ If you are finished working in QuickBooks for now, choose **File→Exit**.

Critical Thinking

In the course of working through the following Critical Thinking exercises, you will be utilizing various skills taught in this and previous lesson(s). Take your time and think carefully about the tasks presented to you. Turn back to the lesson content if you need assistance.

6.1 Sort Through the Stack

Before You Begin: Restore the **Monkey Business, Lesson 6 (Portable)** *file from your storage location. (Remember that you are to leave the password field blank for Mary.) You also have the option of opening either the final file from Critical Thinking 5.1 or Monkey Business, Lesson 6 from your storage location.*

You have been hired by Mary Minard to help her with her organization's books. She is the owner of Monkey Business, a nonprofit organization that provides low-income students with help in preparing for college placement exams and applying for scholarships. You have just sat down at her desk and found a pile of papers. It is your job to sort through the papers and make sense of what you find, entering information into QuickBooks whenever appropriate, and answering any other questions in a word processing document saved as **Critical Thinking 6.1**. Remember, you are digging through papers on a desk, so it is up to you to determine the correct order in which to complete the tasks.

- Scribbled on a piece of paper: The price on the invoice for Lakeside Christian School for the College 101 seminar was incorrect; it should have been $885. Please make this correction in QuickBooks. The customer has already been notified.

- Note: The invoice that we send out is so boring looking…Would you please fancy it up a bit, add a picture (as a logo) that relates to education, and make it a bit more colorful? Also, please include our phone number on the invoice.

- NSF notice from bank: Dated 7/18/2013, check #552 for $425 from Polk Community Center was returned for non-sufficient funds. The bank charged a $30 fee for the item. Mary wrote the following message on the notice, "Please figure out how to account for this in Quick-Books. We need to charge Polk CC a $40 NSF fee and rebill for the service!"

- Printed copy of Balance Sheet report: A note on the report reads, "Please change the font on this report and make the title align to the right. Make the color of the heading match the color on the new invoice template. Memorize it or something so it will be easy for you to run it next time with the same look."

6.2 Tackle the Tasks

Now is your chance to work a little more with Chez Devereaux Salon and Spa and apply the skills that you have learned in this lesson to accomplish additional tasks. Open or restore the **Critical Thinking 6.2** company or portable company file from your file storage location, or open the company file you used in the Develop Your Skills exercises for this lesson. Then, enter the following tasks.

Correct errors	Jane Oliver's friend joined her for a manicure on May 25. Change invoice 13-007 to reflect two manicures.
Write off bad debt	You have had no luck collecting from Curtis Balando for invoice 13-002. Write it off as bad debt as of 6/16/13. (Hint: Look at the source invoice first.)
Customize a report	Create a Balance Sheet Standard report and choose for it to display only assets. Set the date as of June 30, 2013. Customize it as you like, and then memorize it as **Assets Report**.
Create a custom form	Create a new template for sales receipts. Save it as **Devereaux Cash Sales**, and then customize it as you see fit.

6.3 Use the Web as a Learning Tool

Throughout this book, you will be provided with an opportunity to use the Internet as a learning tool by completing WebQuests. According to the original creators of WebQuests, as described on their website (WebQuest.org), a WebQuest is "an inquiry-oriented activity in which most or all of the information used by learners is drawn from the web." To complete the WebQuest projects in this book, navigate to the student resource center and choose the WebQuest for the lesson on which you are currently working. The subject of each WebQuest will be relevant to the material found in the lesson.

WebQuest Subject: Shared reporting and custom templates

U N I T

2

Advanced Skills

UNIT OUTLINE

Advanced Skills

Now that you have mastered the basics, it's time to learn a little more about what really happens behind the scenes and dive deeper into the accounting knowledge that will help you to be more efficient and accurate in your bookkeeping. Lesson 7 will allow you to review the Generally Accepted Accounting Principles and begin to explore the accounting cycle. You will learn about all of the steps of the accounting cycle as you progress through Unit 2. In Lesson 12, you will properly close the books and wrap up a fiscal period. In between Lessons 7 and 12 you will learn about how QuickBooks deals with inventory and how to use QuickBooks to run payroll. Before wrapping up the accounting cycle, you will work with estimates and time tracking as well as asset, liability, and equity accounts.

Introducing the Accounting Cycle and Using Classes

LESSON OBJECTIVES

After studying this lesson, you will be able to:

- Work with the accounting cycle and GAAP
- Turn on class tracking
- Use classes in transactions
- Create an invoice for billable costs
- Set price levels
- Create a Statement of Cash Flows

In this lesson, you will learn about the accounting cycle and review generally accepted accounting principles (GAAP) before taking on the use of classes in QuickBooks. Throughout this lesson, you will work in depth on the first two steps of the accounting cycle while exploring classes and how to invoice for billable costs. Using classes in QuickBooks allows you to classify transactions to give you more data with which to manage your business. Wrapping up this lesson, you will have the opportunity to learn about and produce a Statement of Cash Flows.

Rock Castle Construction

In this lesson you will begin working with a new company file for a construction company called Rock Castle Construction. It is a sample company that comes with the QuickBooks software.

Rock Castle Construction is an S corporation and the chief financial officer of the company is Alan Sun. In this lesson, you will help Alan's office manager, Zoe Minch, go a step past "behind the scenes" and look at the steps of the accounting cycle. You will have a chance to work closely with the first two steps as well as with classes and invoicing for billable costs. Finally, you will examine the cash flow for the business as well as the net income by class by using QuickBooks reports.

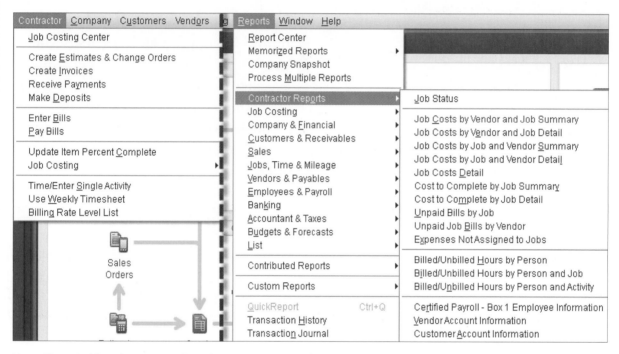

You will use QuickBooks Pro to perform the accounting tasks for a construction company. Here you can see the benefits of the Premier version of QuickBooks that is specialized for contracting businesses and provides additional reports and a special menu option with extra tools to work with your contracting business.

For the Develop Your Skills and Critical Thinking "Tackle the Tasks" exercises, you will be working with a QuickBooks sample file from this point forward. This QuickBooks file operates a bit differently from your own company file (or any non-sample file). The date will always be 12/15/2014 when you open a window to enter a new transaction, rather than the last date you used. The company file will close when you exit QuickBooks, which will require you to open it each time you launch QuickBooks. There are also certain features not available in a sample file. With all of that being said, it is a great tool to use to learn the more advanced features of QuickBooks as it has a year's worth of data entered and is set up with a sample payroll subscription so the payroll lesson will resemble what you will see in your own company file.

Exploring the Accounting Cycle and GAAP

Now we will dive deeper into what occurs behind the scenes in QuickBooks. So far you have had a glimpse of this through the Behind the Scenes and Flashback to the GAAP features of this book. Now we will look at how the accounting cycle and GAAP apply to QuickBooks users. If you are interested in a text that provides full coverage of these concepts and will help you develop a strong understanding of accounting, you should check out *The ABCs of Accounting, 2nd Edition* published by Labyrinth Learning. Much of the following information is borrowed from this text, and it is a great supplementary text for any QuickBooks class.

Time to Review the Generally Accepted Accounting Principles (GAAP)

If you recall from Lesson 1, Introducing QuickBooks Pro, the generally accepted accounting principles (GAAP) are rules used to prepare, present, and report financial statements for a wide variety of entities.

As GAAP attempts to achieve basic objectives, it has several basic assumptions, principles, and constraints. These are outlined in the following table.

Principle	Description
Business entity principle	The business is separate from the owners and from other businesses. Revenues and expenses of the business should be kept separate from the personal expenses of the business owner.
The assumption of the going concern	The business will be in operation indefinitely.
Monetary unit principle	A stable currency is going to be the unit of record.
Time-period principle	The activities of the business can be divided into time periods.
Cost principle	When a company purchases assets, it should record them at cost, not fair market value. For example, an item worth $750 bought for $100 is recorded at $100.
Revenue principle	Publicly traded companies (sole proprietorships can operate using either basis) record when the revenue is realized and earned (accrual basis of accounting), not when cash is received (cash basis of accounting)
Matching principle	Expenses need to be matched with revenues. If a contractor buys a specific sink for a specific bathroom, it is matched to the cost of remodeling the bathroom. Otherwise, the cost may be charged as an expense to the project. This principle allows a better evaluation of the profitability and performance (how much did you spend to earn the revenue?).
Objectivity principle	The statements of a company should be based on objectivity.
Materiality principle	When an item is reported, its significance should be considered. An item is considered significant when it would affect the decision made regarding its use.
Consistency principle	The company uses the same accounting principles and methods from year to year.
Prudence principle	When choosing between two solutions, the one that will be least likely to overstate assets and income should be selected.

Introducing the Accounting Cycle

Accounting records are kept and used to produce financial information. The records are kept for a period of time called a *fiscal period*. A fiscal period can be any length of time. It may be a month or even a quarter of the year. Most businesses use a year as their fiscal period. A business does not need to use the dates January 1 through December 31 as its fiscal period. Many businesses start their fiscal period in February and end in January. Government and educational institutions often use a fiscal period that begins July 1 and ends June 30.

The Steps of the Accounting Cycle

The accounting cycle is a series of steps that help the business keep its accounting records properly during the fiscal period.

1. Collect source documents; verify the financial information.
2. Analyze the business transactions.
3. Record the business transactions (both debit and credit parts) in a journal.
4. Post each journal entry to the ledger accounts.
5. Prepare the trial balance.
6. Prepare a worksheet.
7. Generate the financial statements.
8. Journalize and post closing entries.
9. Prepare the post-closing trial balance.

Who uses this information? Many people do. Business owners need to know how the business is doing. Banks, when they consider lending money to a business owner, need to know what is happening. The government, when assessing taxes on small businesses, needs to know how much revenue the business is generating.

If you took a careful look at the steps of the accounting cycle, you probably saw that Quick-Books takes care of a lot it behind the scenes for you. But, remember that if you leave too much to QuickBooks and don't exercise some common sense, you will be in trouble.

Throughout this lesson, we will look at the first two steps of the accounting cycle and how, together, you and QuickBooks can work as a team to ensure your books accurately document what is happening behind the scenes.

Cycle Step 1: Collect and Verify Documents

Source documents take many forms. Whether it is a receipt, check stub, utility bill, memo documenting the transaction, or another document, it is up to you to verify the information on it because QuickBooks can't do it for you. But, as you learned in Lesson 5, Banking with QuickBooks, QuickBooks does make it easy for you to keep track of source documents through the Doc Center feature.

The QuickBooks Doc Center

The Doc Center feature provides you with the ability to store your source documents electronically, attaching them to the transactions or list entries to which they belong. QuickBooks allows you to enter documents into the Doc Center through a variety of methods, including:

- Drag and drop from Windows Explorer or Outlook
- From a scanner
- From another storage location accessible to your computer

While it is very convenient and affordable to utilize the Doc Center, the files contained within it are not secure, so you need to take additional precautions when storing documents with sensitive information. You may wish to consider a third-party secure document management service (such as SmartVault™) that interfaces well with the QuickBooks Doc Center and provides security features to protect sensitive information.

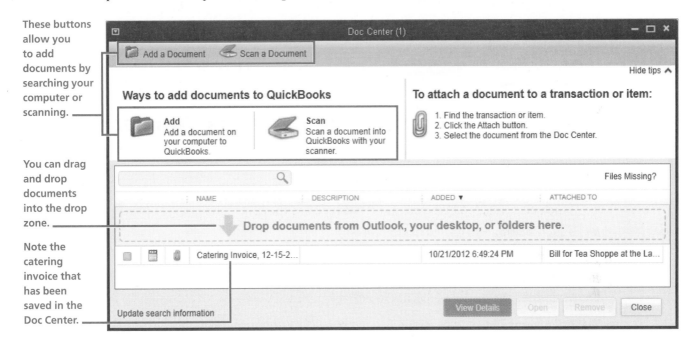

These buttons allow you to add documents by searching your computer or scanning.

You can drag and drop documents into the drop zone.

Note the catering invoice that has been saved in the Doc Center.

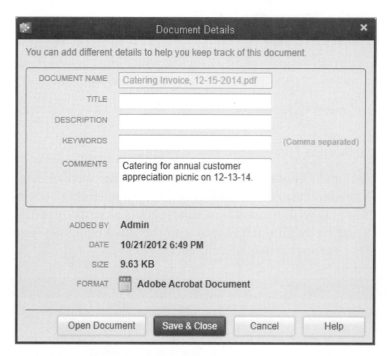

The Document Details window allows you to view and add details for a file in the Doc Center. The Date that displays in your company file will be different as it is captured from your computer's clock when the document is added.

Cycle Step 2: Analyze the Business Transactions

After you have taken care of the first step of compiling and verifying the source documents, you should analyze the transaction, QuickBooks style. When you perform this analysis, you will need to answer the following questions:

- Which accounts are involved and what type are they?
- Is each account increased or decreased?
- Which account is debited and for what amount?
- Which account is credited and for what amount?
- What does the completed entry look like?

The good news here is that in the Behind the Scenes feature throughout this book, you have been seeing this analysis in action. You will just now have the opportunity to perform it for yourself!

QUICK REFERENCE	USING THE DOC CENTER
Task	**Procedure**
Open the Doc Center	▪ Choose Company→Documents→Doc Center.
Add a file located on your computer to the Doc Center	▪ Open the Doc Center; click the Add a Document button. ▪ Navigate to and click the desired file; click Open.

Task	Procedure
Add a file to the Doc Center by scanning	■ Make sure your computer is connected to the scanner. ■ Open the Doc Center; click the Scan a Document button. ■ Choose a scan profile; click Scan.
Drag and drop a file from Outlook into the Doc Center	■ Open Outlook and display the message with the attachment you wish to add to the Doc Center. ■ Open the Doc Center. ■ Move windows as needed to ensure that you can see both the Outlook attachment and the drop zone in the Doc Center. ■ Drag and drop the attachment from Outlook to the Doc Center.
Attach a document to a transaction or item	■ Open the transaction or item to which you wish to attach a document. ■ Click the Attach button. ■ Choose the document from the Doc Center.

Advanced Skills

DEVELOP YOUR SKILLS 7.1

Work with the Accounting Cycle

In this exercise, you will work with the Doc Center and analyze transactions. The first step is to open Quick-Books, and then either open a company file or restore a portable company file.

1. Start **QuickBooks 2013**.

If you downloaded the student exercise files in the portable company file *format, follow Option 1 below. If you downloaded the files in the* company file *format, follow Option 2 below.*

Option 1: Restore a Portable Company File

2. Choose **File→Open or Restore Company**.

3. Click in the circle to the left of **Restore a portable file**, and then click **Next**.

4. Follow these steps to restore your file:

Ⓐ Navigate to your file storage location.

Ⓑ Click to select the **Rock Castle Construction** portable file for this lesson.

Ⓒ Click **Open**.

5. Click **Next**, and then follow these steps to determine where the resulting company file will be located:

Ⓐ Navigate to your file storage location.

Ⓑ Replace Zoe's name with your own (e.g., the author's filename would be Trish's Rock Castle Construction, Lesson 7).

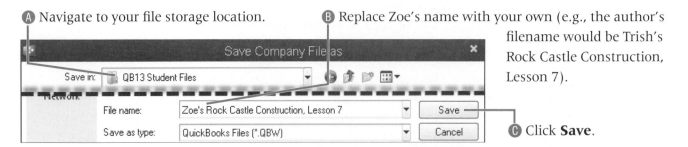

Save Company File as

Save in: QB13 Student Files

Network

File name: Zoe's Rock Castle Construction, Lesson 7   Save

Save as type: QuickBooks Files (*.QBW)   Cancel

Ⓒ Click **Save**.

It may take a few moments for the portable company file to open. Once it does, continue with step 6.

Option 2: Open a Company File

2. Choose **File→Open or Restore Company**.

3. Ensure that **Open a regular company file** is selected.

◉ Open a **c**ompany file
  • Open a regular company file (.qbw)

4. Follow these steps to open the company file:

Ⓐ Navigate to your file storage location.

Ⓑ Click the **Rock Castle Construction, Lesson 7** filename.

Open a Company

Look in: QB13 Student Files

Rock Castle Construction, Lesson 7

Network

File name: Rock Castle Construction, Lesson 7   Open

Files of type: QuickBooks Files (*.QBW,*.QBA)   Cancel

5. Click **Open**.
   The QuickBooks company file opens.

6. Click **OK** to close the QuickBooks Information windows.

7. Click **No** in the Set Up External Accountant User window, if necessary.

Explore and Use the Doc Center

You will copy move a document from your file storage location into the Doc Center.

8. Choose **Company→Documents→Doc Center**.
   The Doc Center window will be displayed.

9. Click the **Add a Document** button.
   The Select Documents to add to Inbox window will be displayed.

10. Follow these steps to select the file to add:

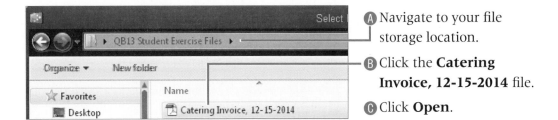

Ⓐ Navigate to your file storage location.

Ⓑ Click the **Catering Invoice, 12-15-2014** file.

Ⓒ Click **Open**.

The Catering Invoice file will be displayed in the Doc Center.

View and Edit the Details of a File in the Doc Center

Now you will view the details for a file in the Doc Center and add a comment.

11. Follow these steps to open a file for viewing:

Ⓐ Click in the **checkbox** to select the catering invoice.

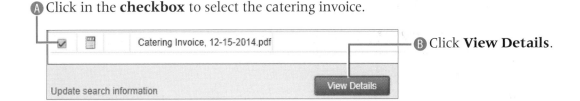

Ⓑ Click **View Details**.

The Document Details window will appear.

12. Click in the **Comments** field.

13. Type the comment as displayed in the figure below.

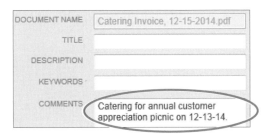

14. Click **Save & Close**.
    The information will be added to the details for the document, and the Doc Center will be displayed.

15. Close the **Doc Center**.

Advanced Skills

Enter a Bill and Attach a Document

You will now enter a bill into QuickBooks and attach the source document (catering invoice) to it.

16. Choose **Vendors→Enter Bills**.

17. Follow these steps to enter the information for the bill:

A Type **Tea Shoppe at the Lake**.   **B** Tap Tab, and then Quick Add as a **Vendor**.

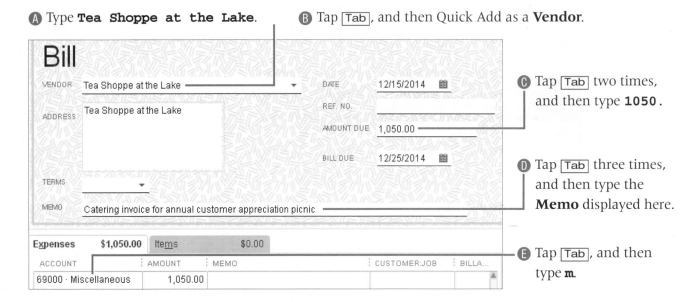

C Tap Tab two times, and then type **1050**.

D Tap Tab three times, and then type the **Memo** displayed here.

E Tap Tab, and then type **m**.

18. Click the **Attach File** button on the Ribbon.

19. Click **Yes** in the Recording Transaction window.

20. Click the **Doc Center** button in the Attachments window.

21. Click in the **checkbox** to the left of the Catering Invoice document, and then click **Attach**.

The document will appear in the Attachment – Bill for Tea Shoppe at the Lake on 12/15/2014 window.

22. Close the **Attachment** windows.

23. Click **OK** in the Attachment Successful window, and then click **Save & Close** in the Enter Bills window.

BTS BRIEF
69000•Miscellaneous DR 1,050.00; 20000•Accounts Payable CR <1,050.00>

Analyze Business Transactions

You will now take a look at a variety of transactions and analyze each one in the table displayed below. You may print a copy of this table from the student resource center if you do not wish to write in the book.

24. Complete the following table by answering the questions about each transaction in the space provided.

	Invoice #1093	Sales Receipt #3008	Bill dated 12/15/14, for Thomas Kitchen and Bath, Ref. No. 8059	Payment received on invoice #1087, dated 12/15/14	Deposit made to checking on 12/14/14
Which accounts are involved and what type are they?					
Is each account increased or decreased?					
Which account is debited and for what amount?					
Which account is credited and for what amount?					

The last question of "What does the completed entry look like?" is not included because you will be using the completed entry in order to answer the rest of the questions!

Working with Classes

Classes provide an additional way to track information about transactions. They allow you to keep an eye on particular segments of your business (such as new construction vs. remodel), tracking income and expenses for each. This way, if you wanted to evaluate which segment of the business was most profitable, it would be easy to do since your transactions contain class information that can easily be displayed on reports. Class tracking is a tool for you to use with your unique business, so you really need to think about what you want to see on your reports and base your class tracking on that.

What Are Classes?

You use classes to track income and expenses for different areas of your company; they classify transactions. Classes are not tied to any particular customer, vendor, or item. If you want to track types of customers, jobs, or vendors, use the profile lists QuickBooks provides. You use these "type" lists to classify customers, jobs, and vendors. An important rule about classes to remember is that you should use them to track only *one* particular aspect of your business. For instance, you should not use classes to track both locations and team performance; you will need to choose one aspect of your business and create classes only for that aspect.

Common Uses for Classes

There are many ways to use classes. The following table provides some examples of how classes are used by various types of companies.

Industry	Class Examples
Construction	Crews of workers, locations of jobs
Not-for-profit	Specific programs, administrative overhead
Restaurant	By business segment (bar, food, catering)
Retail	By department (accessories, ready to wear, shoes)
Consulting	Locations (North County, South County)

Do not use classes to track types of customers or vendors because QuickBooks already provides profile lists for these purposes. Since you can only use classes to track one aspect of your business, you will have eliminated this valuable tool if you use it to duplicate a specific list provided by QuickBooks.

A Class Example

Originally, Rock Castle Construction considered using classes to track residential versus commercial customers. Once this matter was discussed with the company's CPA, it was understood that QuickBooks already provides a list to track types of customers and that classes are meant to track an aspect of the business for which QuickBooks doesn't provide a list. It was then decided to use the class feature to track new construction versus remodel (realize that one customer can have both a job involving new construction and one that is a remodel), with overhead as the class that is the "catch all" for income and expenses that are not easily attributed to one of the "main" classes. Alan had also thought about using classes to track jobs by location, but it was decided that it would be more meaningful to the business to use classes as shown in the following illustration.

Classes are set up in the Class List in QuickBooks and are used to track a specific aspect of the business. They are flexible in that you can choose how to (and whether to!) use the feature for your unique company.

Setting Up and Managing Classes

Before you can use class tracking in QuickBooks, you must turn on the preference. The Class List looks and functions similarly to some of the other lists you have worked with thus far. For example, QuickBooks won't allow you to delete a class that has been used in any transaction. Once you turn on this preference, class fields will appear on sales forms and in other locations. You can edit classes much the same way that you have edited other list entries.

Planning for Class Tracking

As you may recall from Lesson 2, Creating a Company, when you create a new company in QuickBooks, you should take time to plan what you need the company to do for you. Before you begin to track classes in QuickBooks, think about what type of reporting you need for your company and exactly what information you need to display on your reports.

When you are setting up classes for your own company, make sure to also create a class for any type of transaction that doesn't apply to one of your named classes (such as "Overhead" or "Administrative"). This is important because you want to make sure that you apply a class to every transaction involving an income and/or expense once you set up your company to track classes.

Using Classes for Profit Center Reporting

Many businesses use classes for profit center reporting. A profit center is a sector of a business for which income and expenses are tracked separately so that its individual profitability can be determined. One type of business that often relies on profit center reporting, in order to ensure that the entire business is operating efficiently, is farming.

Utilizing Subclasses

Even though you are only allowed to use classes to track a single aspect of your business, you can use subclasses to further classify your data. For instance, a restaurant can set up "main" classes to track income and expenses by location, and then list food, bar, and catering as subclasses under each location (main class).

Some Examples of Subclasses in Action

The following table lists examples of subclasses that might be used with a class.

Industry	Class	Subclasses
Construction	Crews of workers	Location
Restaurant	Location	Bar, food, catering

Do *not* use classes to track more than one aspect of your business. If you need additional tracking, use subclasses. If you use classes to track more than one aspect, it will render the class data meaningless.

Task	Procedure
Turn on class tracking	■ Choose Edit→Preferences. ■ Click the Accounting category, and then the Company Preferences tab. ■ Click to check the Use Class Tracking box; click OK.
Create a new class	■ Choose Lists→Class List. ■ Click the Class menu button; choose New. ■ Type the name of the new class; click OK.
Edit a class	■ Choose Lists→Class List; click to select the class you wish to edit. ■ Click the Class menu button; choose Edit. ■ Make any desired changes; click OK.
Delete a class	■ Choose Lists→Class List. ■ Click to select the desired class, click the Class menu button, and then choose Delete. ■ Click OK to confirm the deletion.
Create a subclass	■ Choose Lists→Class List. ■ Click the Class menu button; choose New. ■ Type the name of the subclass; click to choose Subclass Of. ■ Choose the class to which you wish to assign it; click OK.

DEVELOP YOUR SKILLS 7.2
Turn On Class Tracking

In this exercise, you will turn on the class tracking feature of QuickBooks.

1. Choose **Edit→Preferences**.

2. Follow these steps to turn on the class tracking preference:

Ⓐ Click the **Accounting** category.

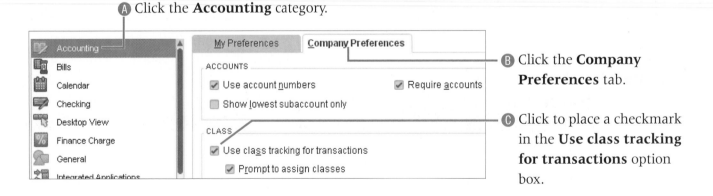

Ⓑ Click the **Company Preferences** tab.

Ⓒ Click to place a checkmark in the **Use class tracking for transactions** option box.

3. Click **OK** to activate the new preference.

Once you turn on this preference, QuickBooks will add class fields to many forms and registers such as the Create Invoices form, Enter Bills form, and customer Accounts Receivable reports. You can also run reports such as the Profit & Loss by Class now.

View the Class List

The sample company with which we are working was previously set up to track classes, so you just reactivated the preference. We will now take a look at the existing Class List.

4. Choose **Lists→Class List**.
   Notice the classes that have been set up to track based on the type of work.

5. Close the **Class List**.

Applying Classes to Transactions

You should apply classes to all transactions involving an income and/or expense account once the preference is set up. You can enter the class information on forms, registers, or journal entries. Once you have used classes in transactions, you can display them in reports and create budgets based on them. You can also apply classes to payroll transactions—either to a whole paycheck or to individual earning items.

Consistent Class Applications

Once you begin using class tracking, it is important to consistently apply a class to *every* transaction that deals with income and expense accounts so that your data, and therefore your reporting, are meaningful. If you apply classes to only some transactions and then create a report to show the profitability by class, the information will be skewed. This is why it is important to create a class (such as "Overhead") for transactions that don't fit one of your main classes.

Choosing Classes on Forms

Once you have set up your classes in QuickBooks, you can choose them on forms. You can find the class field in windows such as Create Invoices, Create Purchase Orders, and Pay Bills.

A class entered here will apply to the entire invoice.

You can also choose to apply classes by line item.

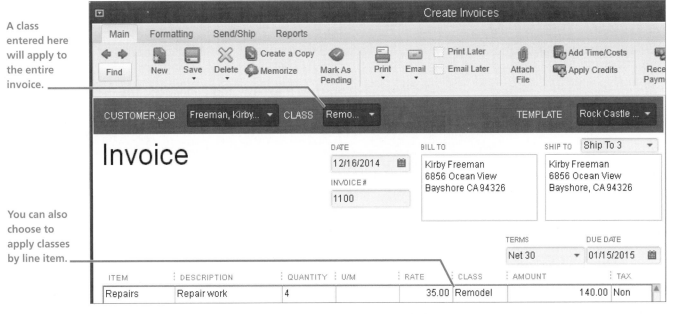

Notice that the class field is now available in the Create Invoices window.

Task	Procedure
Use a class on an invoice	■ Choose Customers→Create Invoices; enter all of the sales information. ■ Enter the appropriate class for each line item or the entire invoice. ■ Click Save & Close or Save & New.

DEVELOP YOUR SKILLS 7.3
Work with Classes

In this exercise, you will help Zoe utilize classes in transactions.

1. Click the **Create Invoices** task icon in the Customers area of the Home page.

Create
Invoices

2. Follow these steps to create an invoice:

Ⓐ Click the **drop-down arrow**, scroll down, and then click to choose the **Repairs** job for **Freeman, Kirby**.

Ⓑ Tap Tab, and then type **r**.

Ⓒ Tap Tab twice, and then tap + to set the date to **12/16/14**.

Ⓓ Click in the **Item** column, and then type **rep**.

Ⓔ Tap Tab two times, and then type **4**.

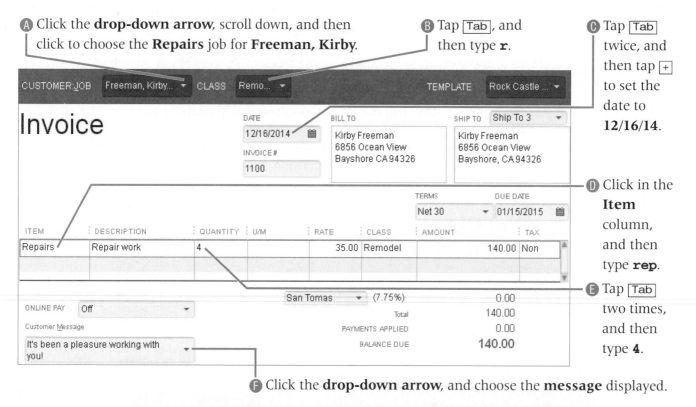

Ⓕ Click the **drop-down arrow**, and choose the **message** displayed.

BTS BRIEF

11000•Accounts Receivable DR 140.00; 40130•Labor Income CR <140.00>

3. Click **Save & Close**.

Apply Classes to a Credit Card Charge

Zoe needed to pick up some batteries for the main office as well as some materials for customer Anton Teschner for some finishing work on the sunroom you built. You will pass on the expense to Anton in an invoice in a later lesson. You will now apply two classes to a credit card transaction to document this purchase.

4. Click the **Enter Credit Card Charges** task icon in the Banking area of the Home page.

Enter Credit Card Charges

5. Follow these steps to complete the transaction:

Ⓐ Ensure the **QuickBooks Credit Card** is chosen.

Ⓑ Tap Tab three times, and then type **pat**.

Ⓒ Tap Tab, and then type **121614**.

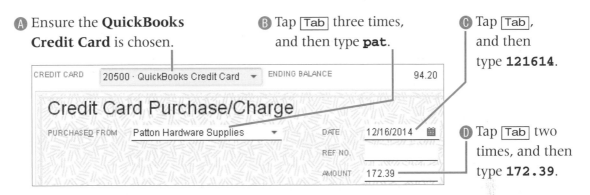

Ⓓ Tap Tab two times, and then type **172.39**.

Notice that 54300•Job Materials automatically filled in as the Account for this vendor.

Ⓔ Tap Tab three times, and then type **145.02**.

Ⓕ Click in the **Customer:Job** column, and then click the **drop-down arrow** and choose the job displayed.

Ⓖ Tap Tab two times, and then type **n**.

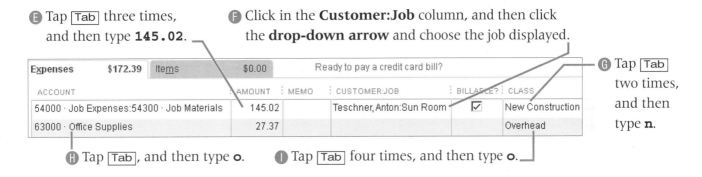

Ⓗ Tap Tab, and then type **o**.

Ⓘ Tap Tab four times, and then type **o**.

The amount for the second line will fill in for you by subtracting the amount in the first line from the total.

> **BTS BRIEF**
>
> **54300•Job Materials DR 145.02; 63000•Office Supplies DR 27.37; 20500•QuickBooks Credit Card CR <172.39>**

6. Click **Save & Close**.

Running Class Reports

QuickBooks provides preset reports that help you view your company data by class. For instance, The Profit & Loss by Class report shows you the net income or loss by class. If a column called "Unclassified" appears on your report, it will display all amounts that have not been assigned a class.

The Profit & Loss Unclassified Report

As you learned earlier in this lesson, once you begin to use class tracking, it is very important that you apply a class to each transaction. In order to ensure that you have done this, you can run the P&L Unclassified report, which will show you any amounts that do not have a class associated with them. It is then easy to use QuickBooks' QuickZoom feature to drill to the unclassified transactions and assign a class to them.

The Balance Sheet by Class Report

A new feature in QuickBooks 2011 was the Balance Sheet by Class report. It is available for those who are using a Premier or Enterprise version of QuickBooks. In this report, each class appears as a column. This is not a basic report for novice users to use, as it may display unexpected results at times and the ability to understand and fix these anomalies requires a solid accounting background.

QUICK REFERENCE	PRODUCING CLASS REPORTS
Task	**Procedure**
Run a Profit & Loss by Class report	▪ Choose Reports→Company & Financial→Profit & Loss by Class.
Run a Profit & Loss Unclassified report	▪ Choose Reports→Company & Financial→Profit & Loss Unclassified.
Run a Balance Sheet by Class report	▪ Choose Reports→Company & Financial→Balance Sheet by Class (only if you are using a Premier or Enterprise version of QuickBooks).

Create Class Reports

In this exercise, you will first create a report that will allow you to make sure that all transactions have been assigned a class. Then you will fix one that was entered without a class. Once you have cleared it up, you will produce a Profit & Loss by Class report for the month.

1. Choose **Reports→Company & Financial→Profit & Loss Unclassified**.
   Notice that there is income on the report that is not attributed to a class. You will now use QuickZoom to find the source of this amount.

2. Place your mouse pointer over the Labor Income amount until you see the zoom pointer, and then double-click.

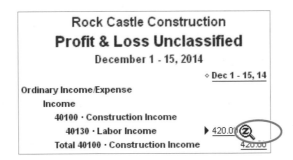

A Transaction Detail By Account report appears, on which you will see that the amount is from Sales Receipt 3009.

3. Place your mouse pointer over the sales receipt line in the report until you see the zoom pointer, and then double-click.

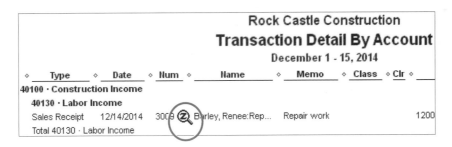

The source transaction will be displayed.

Add a Class to an Existing Transaction

Now that Zoe has the unclassified transaction displayed, she will assign a class to it.

4. Follow these steps to assign a class to the transaction:

Ⓐ Click in the **Class** column, and then type **r** to fill in **Remodel** as the class. ⎯ Ⓑ Click **Save & Close**.

ITEM	DESCRIPTION	QTY	U/M	RATE	CLASS	AMOUNT	TAX
Repairs	Repair work	12		35.00	Remodel	420.00	Non

You must choose the class for each line item when you are applying a class to an existing transaction. If you just indicate the class in the field at the top of the window, QuickBooks will not apply a class to the Repairs line item since it already existed before the invoice was edited.

5. Click **Yes** to confirm the changes and record the transaction.
   The Transaction Detail by Account report will once again be displayed, but it will contain no data as there are no unclassified transactions affecting the account.

6. Close the **Transaction Detail by Account** and **Profit & Loss Unclassified** windows.

Display a Profit & Loss by Class Report

Now that you know that all transactions have classes assigned to them, you will produce a report to show the net income (loss) by class and overall for December 2014.

7. Choose **Reports→Company & Financial→Profit & Loss by Class**.
   The report will be displayed with the default date range of This Fiscal Year-to-date.

8. Click the **Dates field drop-down arrow** and choose **This Month-to-date**.

You will now see the Profit & Loss by Class report for December 1–15, 2014.

9. Close the report window.

Invoicing for Billable Costs

As you may recall, you decided to pass on expenses for Anton Teschner's Sun Room job in the previous section. Now you will learn how to create an invoice based on a job that has outstanding billable costs that were passed on in a previous transaction. Once you create the invoice from the billable costs, you can add additional expenses as well.

After you have indicated that an expense is to be passed on to a customer in the Write Checks, Enter Credit Card Charges, or Enter Bills window, you will be prompted to indicate whether you wish to pass on the billable time or costs each time you create an invoice for the customer (until all expenses have been passed on). When you see the Billable Time/Costs window, you have the opportunity to either add the outstanding billable time or costs to the invoice or exclude them to be invoiced at a later date. There is also an option to set your preference for this feature in the window.

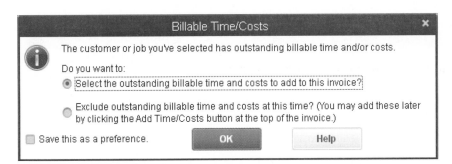

This window appears when you create an invoice for a customer who has outstanding billable time or costs. If you typically choose one option over the other, you may want to set a preference so it appears by default.

Working with Different Price Levels

There are many instances when a business may wish to charge different price levels for different customers or jobs. Once a price level is set and associated with a customer or job, it will automatically fill in for you in future transactions (although you can manually change what fills in, if needed). With all versions of QuickBooks, the price level can be set by a fixed percentage. If you are working with a Premier or higher version of QuickBooks, you can also set price levels per item. Before setting up price levels, you need to make sure that the preference is turned on in QuickBooks.

Using Fixed Percentage Price Levels

The fixed percentage price level allows you to decrease or increase the items being charged to a customer or job by a specific percentage amount. For instance, you may wish to decrease all items charged to Kristy Abercrombie by 8 percent.

Using Per Item Price Levels

If you use this Premier version or above option, you are able to create specific dollar amounts for items or groups of items that you can associate with selected customers or jobs. For instance, you may wish to charge Sonya Bristol $30 per hour for repair work rather than the standard $35 per hour rate.

Notice the two different types of price levels displayed on the Price Level List.

BEHIND THE SCENES

The accounting involved when you pass on an expense to a customer will reverse the debiting of the expense account (by crediting it) that occurred in the Enter Bills, Enter Credit Card Charges, or Write Checks window. Accounts receivable will be debited for the expense passed on to the customer, and an income account will be credited for any additional line items added to the invoice. Note that the total debits ($475.02) equal the total credits ($145.02+330=$475.02) in this transaction.

54300-Job Materials	40130-Labor Income	11000-Accounts Receivable
145.02	330.00	475.02

QUICK REFERENCE	WORKING WITH BILLABLE COSTS AND PRICE LEVELS
Task	**Procedure**
Create an invoice based on billable costs	▪ Open the Create Invoices window; choose the desired customer or job. ▪ Make your selection regarding what costs you wish to pass on. ▪ Complete the rest of the invoice information; click Save & Close.
Turn on the price level preference in QuickBooks	▪ Choose Edit→Preferences. ▪ Choose the Sales & Customers category, and the Company Preferences tab. ▪ Click to select the checkbox for Use price levels; click OK.
Create a price level in QuickBooks	▪ Choose Lists→Price Level. ▪ Click the Price Level menu button; choose New. ▪ Enter the name and type of the new price level. ▪ If you are creating a fixed percentage price level, enter whether it will be an increase or a decrease, and then enter the percentage. ▪ If you are creating a price level by item(s), enter the custom price for the item(s) or group of items. ▪ Click OK.

Set a Price Level and Create an Invoice for Billable Costs

In this exercise, you will first set a fixed percentage price level of 10 percent less than the "normal" price for Anton Teschner. Then you will create an invoice for costs you are passing on to a customer.

1. Choose **Lists→Price Level List**.

2. Click the **Price Level** menu button, and then choose **New**.

3. Follow these steps to set a new price level:

Ⓐ Click here, and then type **Repeat Customer**.

Ⓑ Ensure **Fixed %** is selected.

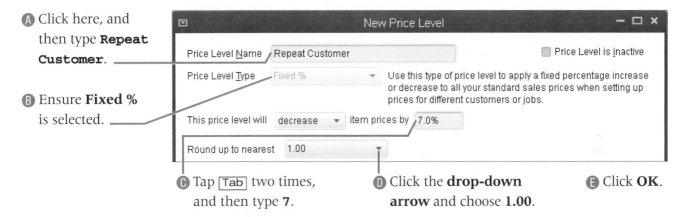

Price Level Name	Repeat Customer
Price Level Type	Fixed % — Use this type of price level to apply a fixed percentage increase or decrease to all your standard sales prices when setting up prices for different customers or jobs.
This price level will	decrease ▾ item prices by 7.0%
Round up to nearest	1.00 ▾

☐ Price Level is inactive

Ⓒ Tap Tab two times, and then type **7**.

Ⓓ Click the **drop-down arrow** and choose **1.00**.

Ⓔ Click **OK**.

4. Close the **Price Level List**.

Assign a Price Level to a Customer

5. Click the **Customers** button on the Icon Bar.

6. Scroll down the Customers & Jobs List until **Teschner, Anton** is displayed, and then double-click the entry.

Customers & Jobs	Transactions	
Active Customers ▾		>
NAME	BALANCE TOT...	ATTACH
◦ Teschner, Anton	565.95	▲
◦ Sun Room	565.95	

The Edit Customer window displays.

You can also type a "t" to move down the list to the first entry that starts with that letter.

7. Close the **New Feature** window if necessary, and then follow these steps to assign a price level to Anton Teschner:

Ⓐ Click the **Payment Settings** tab.

Ⓑ Click the **drop-down arrow**, and then choose **Repeat Customer**.

Ⓒ Click **OK**.

8. Close the **Customer Center**.

Add Billable Costs to an Invoice

You first need to start the process of creating an invoice. Then you will assign a billable cost to it.

9. Click the **Create Invoices** task icon in the Customers area of the Home page.

10. Click the **drop-down arrow**, and then scroll down to choose **Anton Teschner's Sun Room** job from the list.

Create
Invoices

QuickBooks displays a prompt because you have billable costs for this job.

11. Ensure that **Select the outstanding billable time and costs to add to this invoice?** is selected; click **OK**.

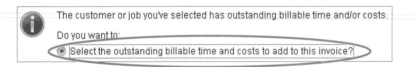

12. Follow these steps to invoice for billable costs:

Ⓐ Click the **Expenses** tab. ⎯⎯⎯

Ⓑ Click here to place a **checkmark**. ⎯

Ⓒ Click **OK**.

QuickBooks displays the Create Invoices window with the billable cost as the first line item.

13. Follow these steps to complete the invoice:

Ⓐ Click the **drop-down arrow**, and then choose **New Construction**.

Ⓑ Tap `Tab` two times, and then use `+` to change the date to **12/18/2014**.

Ⓒ Click here, and then type **Job Materials**.

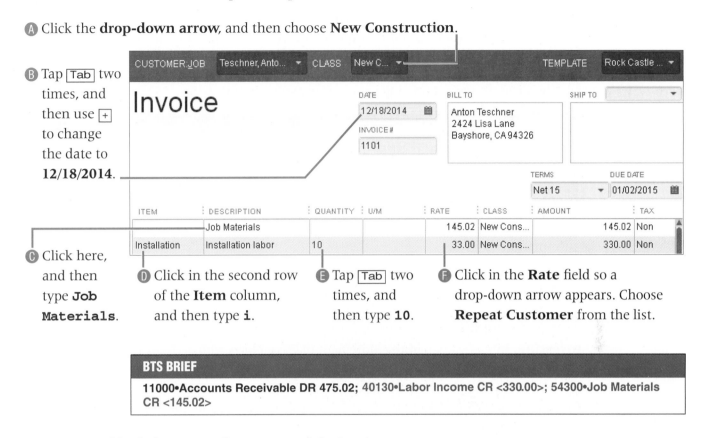

Ⓓ Click in the second row of the **Item** column, and then type **i**.

Ⓔ Tap `Tab` two times, and then type **10**.

Ⓕ Click in the **Rate** field so a drop-down arrow appears. Choose **Repeat Customer** from the list.

> **BTS BRIEF**
>
> 11000•Accounts Receivable DR 475.02; 40130•Labor Income CR <330.00>; 54300•Job Materials CR <145.02>

14. Click **Save & Close** to record the invoice.

Producing a Statement of Cash Flows

The Statement of Cash Flows is a financial report that has been required under GAAP since 1987. You have already seen balance sheet and profit and loss reports, but this report plays an important part in showing how viable the company is in the short term. This helps a variety of stakeholders see whether the company will be able to pay its bills, payroll, and other expenses. It also indicates the financial health of the company.

While the Profit & Loss report looks at the total amount of income coming in and the expenses going out, the Statement of Cash Flows specifically looks at the cash inflows and outflows during a period of time. If you remember from GAAP, corporations are required to use the accrual basis of accounting that records when income and expenses are accrued rather than when cash is exchanged. The Statement of Cash Flows essentially translates the company's data from accrual to cash basis so that an understanding of how the company is operating and how cash is being handled can be reached.

> **FLASHBACK TO GAAP: REVENUE PRINCIPLE**
>
> Remember that publicly traded companies must record when revenue is realized and earned (accrual basis of accounting), not when cash is received (cash basis).

Method of Reporting

QuickBooks uses the indirect method when creating a Statement of Cash Flows. This means that net income is the starting point for the report; you make adjustments for the non-cash transactions from there. So, basically, what happens is that you will take a net income generated using the accrual basis of accounting and convert it to the cash basis by adding increases to liability accounts and subtracting increases to asset accounts.

> **FLASHBACK TO GAAP: CONSISTENCY**
>
> Remember that this means that the company uses the same accounting principles and methods from year to year.

Sections of the Statement of Cash Flows Report

There are three sections of the Statement of Cash Flows that organize your company's financial information:

- **Operating:** In this section of the Statement of Cash Flows, you take the activities that result from the normal operation of the business and convert them to the cash basis. These types of activities may include such things as sales receipts, production costs, advertising, payroll, and expenses for services performed.

- **Investing:** In this section of the Statement of Cash Flows, you account for assets that are bought or sold, loans that you have issued, and other payments that are not related to the normal operation of the business (e.g., payments related to a merger).

- **Financing:** In this section of the Statement of Cash Flows, you take into account such items as cash from investors (company stock and bond transactions) and dividends that are paid.

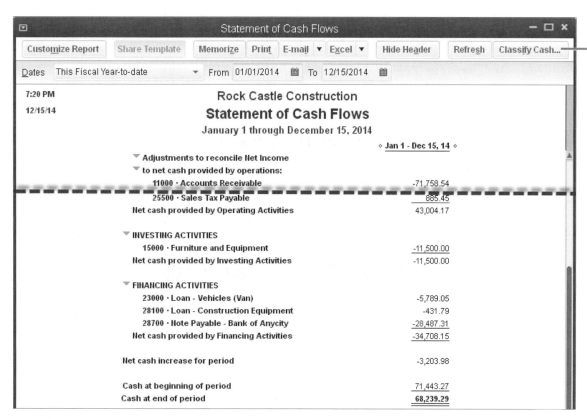

Clicking the Classify Cash button opens the Edit Preferences window with the Company Preferences tab of the Reports & Graphs category displayed.

The Statement of Cash Flows allows you to view the company financials "as if" you were using the cash basis of accounting. In QuickBooks, this report will be produced using the indirect method as shown above.

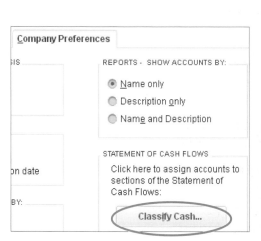

On the Company Preferences tab of the Reports & Graphs category, you will see a Statement of Cash Flows section. The Classify Cash window will launch if you click the button. The window allows you to assign accounts to different sections of the report.

Forecasting Cash Flow

As an average QuickBooks user, you may be wondering why this report is important. It is one of the main financial statements used to get approved for a loan, to attract shareholders, or to demonstrate the financial health of your company. You can also use it internally to help guide decisions that you have to make for your company by giving you a tool by which you can forecast the cash that is and will be flowing into and out of your company.

QuickBooks actually provides a separate report for you that will show you a forecast of cash flow, the Cash Flow Forecast report. The date range for this report will be in the immediate future.

8:19 PM 12/15/14	Rock Castle Construction Cash Flow Forecast December 14, 2014 through January 10, 2015				
	◇ Accnts Receivable ◇	Accnts Payable ◇	Bank Accnts ◇	Net Inflows ◇	Proj Balance
Beginning Balance	4,223.00	3,459.20	68,683.14		69,446.94
Week of Dec 14, 14 ▶	12,420.98 ◀	0.00	-9,443.85	2,977.13	72,424.07
Week of Dec 21, 14	0.00	1,050.00	0.00	-1,050.00	71,374.07
Week of Dec 28, 14	475.02	0.00	0.00	475.02	71,849.09
Week of Jan 4, 15	0.00	0.00	0.00	0.00	71,849.09
Dec 14, '14 - Jan 10, 15	12,896.00	1,050.00	-9,443.85	2,402.15	
Ending Balance	17,119.00	4,509.20	59,239.29		71,849.09

The Cash Flow Forecast report gives you a glimpse of what you can expect your cash flow to look like in the near future based on the data in your company file now.

QUICK REFERENCE	PRODUCING CASH FLOWS REPORTS
Task	**Procedure**
Produce a Statement Cash Flows report	▪ Choose Reports→Company & Financial→Statement of Cash Flows.
Produce a Cash Flow Forecast report	▪ Choose Reports→Company & Financial→Cash Flow Forecast.
Classify the accounts on a Statement of Cash Flows report	▪ Choose Edit→Preferences.
	▪ Display the Reports & Graphs category and the Company Preferences tab.
	▪ Click the Classify Cash button in the Statement of Cash Flows section.
	▪ Make changes to any account classifications; click OK.

Display Cash Flow Reports

In this exercise, you will help Zoe produce a Statement of Cash Flows for Alan to share at a management meeting. She will also create a report that will be used internally to make some decisions for the company.

1. Choose **Reports→Company & Financial→Statement of Cash Flows**.
   QuickBooks will display the Statement of Cash Flows report with default date range of This Fiscal Year-to-date.

2. Take a look at what the report tells you, and then close the **report window**.

Run a Cash Flow Forecast Report

The next report will look at the cash flow in the immediate future.

3. Choose **Reports→Company & Financial→Cash Flow Forecast**.
   QuickBooks will display the Cash Flow Forecast report with default date range of Next 4 Weeks.

4. Take a look at what the report tells you, and then close the **report window**.
   You will now have a chance to practice what you have learned in more depth.

5. Choose the appropriate option for your situation:
   - If you are continuing on to the next lesson or to the end-of-lesson exercises, leave QuickBooks open.
   - If you are finished working in QuickBooks for now, choose **File→Exit**.

Concepts Review

Concepts Review	http://labyrinthelab.com/qb13

To check your knowledge of the key concepts introduced in this lesson, complete the Concepts Review quiz by going to the URL listed above.

Reinforce Your Skills

Before you begin the Reinforce Your Skills exercises, complete one of these options:

- *Open* **[Your name]'s Tea Shoppe at the Lake, Lesson 6** *or Tea Shoppe at the Lake, Lesson 7 from your file storage location that you used for Lesson 6.*

- *Restore* **Tea Shoppe at the Lake, Lesson 7 (Portable)** *from your file storage location.*

REINFORCE YOUR SKILLS 7.1
Work with the Accounting Cycle

In this exercise, you will help Susie add a file to the Doc Center (step 1 of the accounting cycle). Then you will classify accounting transactions (step 2 of the accounting cycle).

Susie realizes that she should be organizing the source documents for her business a bit better, so she has decided to electronically store them using QuickBooks. You will begin by helping Susie add an invoice for some remodel work to the Doc Center by attaching it to a bill.

1. Choose **Vendors→Enter Bills**.

2. Enter `Rock Castle Construction` as the Vendor and **Quick Add** it to the Vendor List.

3. Set the date to **7/10/2013**, and then enter **$1,292.81** as the amount.

4. Choose **Repairs and Maintenance** as the expense account.

5. Click the **Attach File** button on the toolbar, and then click **Yes** to record the transaction.
   The Attachments window for the bill will open.

6. Choose to attach from your **computer**, and then navigate to your file storage location.
   Notice that you don't have to add a document to the Doc Center before adding it to a transaction.

7. Click the **Remodel Invoice** file, and then click **Open**.
   The file will be added to the Doc Center and attached to the bill.

8. Close the **Attachments** window, and then click **OK** in the Attachment Successful window.

9. Click **Save & Close**.

Classify Accounting Transactions

You will now take a look at a variety of transactions and analyze each one in the table displayed below. You may print a copy of this table from the student resource center if you do not wish to write in the book.

10. Complete the following table by answering the questions about each transaction in the space provided.

	Invoice #1	Sales Receipt #17	Bill dated 5/19/2013, for San Marcos Gas & Electric for $173.54	Payment received on invoice #1, dated 6/11/2013	Deposit made to checking on 5/21/2013
Which accounts are involved and what type are they?					
Is each account increased or decreased?					
Which account is debited and for what amount?					
Which account is credited and for what amount?					

REINFORCE YOUR SKILLS 7.2

Track and Use Classes

In this exercise, you will help Susie set up QuickBooks to track classes for her business based on category of item sold. She will begin class tracking for all transactions as of July 1, 2013. You will begin by turning on the preference and setting up the new classes in the Class List.

1. Choose **Edit→Preferences**.

2. Choose the **Accounting** category, and then the **Company Preferences** tab.

3. Turn on **class tracking**, and then click **OK**.

4. Choose **Lists→Class List**, click the **Class** menu button, and then choose **New**.

5. Create five new classes: **Food**, **Beverages**, **Crafts**, **Catering**, and **Other**. Use the **Next** button to move to each New Class window.
   The Crafts class will be used in the next lesson, when Tea Shoppe at the Lake begins to stock and sell inventory.

6. Close the **Class List** window.

Use Classes in Transactions

Now that Susie has set up the classes, she will begin to use them in all transactions. In this section of the exercise, make sure to identify the correct class for each transaction.

7. Enter the following transactions, using the appropriate class(es) for each:

- On **7/2/13**, your weekly sales were **$797** for food and **$1,637** for beverages. (Hint: Choose Customers→Enter Sales Receipts.)

- On **7/3/13**, you purchased paper goods for the beverages that you serve at **Priceco**. You paid the **$498.64** charge with your American Express card. (Hint: Choose Banking→Enter Credit Card Charges and clear the Splits on the Expenses tab.)

- On **7/5/13**, you received a bill from High Tec Mktg for **$349** for July's advertising and marketing. The terms for the bill are Net 15. (Hint: Choose Vendors→Enter Bills.)

- On **7/6/13**, **Peggy Oceans** (new customer) came in and booked a catering event for a total of **$350**. You created an invoice for her with Net 15 terms. (Hint: Choose Customers→Create Invoices.)

- On **7/9/13**, your weekly sales were: **$839** for food and **$1,642** for beverages. (Hint: Choose Customers→Enter Sales Receipts.)

- On **7/11/13**, **Rachel Geller** (new customer) came in and booked a catering event for **$972**. She paid the entire amount with check number **1992**. (Hint: Choose Customers→Enter Sales Receipts.)

- On **7/16/13**, your weekly sales were: **$870** for food, and **$1,623** for beverages.

- On **7/17/13**, you purchased a new computer printer table for your office from Priceco. The table cost **$79.87** and will be treated as an expense, not a fixed asset. You used your American Express card for the purchase. (Hint: Choose Banking→Enter Credit Card Charges.)

- On **7/21/13**, you received a bill from **San Marcos Gas & Electric** for **$200.13** for your gas and electric service. The terms for the bill are Net 15. (Hint: Choose Vendors→Enter Bills.)

- On **7/23/13**, your weekly sales were: **$849** for food, and **$1,526** for beverages.

REINFORCE YOUR SKILLS 7.3

Set Price Levels

In this exercise, you will create a price level to use for repeat catering customers. The first step is to set the preference.

1. Choose **Edit→Preferences**.

2. Click the **Sales & Customers** category, and then the **Company Preferences** tab.

3. Ensure that the **Use price levels** checkbox is selected; click **OK**.

Create a New Fixed Percentage Price Level

Now that you have verified that QuickBooks is set to track price levels, you will create a new fixed percentage price level. You will have to first set a price for Catering.

4. Choose **Lists→Item List**, and then double-click **Catering** to open it for editing.

5. Change the **Rate** for the Catering item to **$500**; click **OK**.
   This will be your new base rate that you can edit on sales forms, as needed, for each customer.

6. Close the **Item List**; then, choose **Lists→Price Level List**.

7. Click the **Price Level** menu button, and then click **New**.

8. Name the fixed % price level `Catering Repeat Customer`.

9. Choose to decrease item prices by fixed amount of **10 percent**.

10. Click **OK** to save the new price level, and then close the **Price Level List**.

Create an Invoice for a Repeat Catering Customer

Karen was so happy with the catering job that Susie did that she has returned to book her next event. You will help Susie to apply the price level discount for Karen's next job.

11. Choose **Customers→Create Invoices**.

12. Choose **Karen Douglas** as the Customer:Job, and then choose **Catering** as the Class.

13. Set the date as **7/25/2013**, and then choose **Catering** as the Item.

14. Click the **drop-down arrow** in the Rate column, choose the **Catering Repeat Customer** rate for Karen, and then click **Save & Close**.

Create a Cash Flow Report

In this exercise, you will help Susie to look at how her company's cash flow has been for February – May 2013.

1. Choose **Reports→Company & Financial→Statement of Cash Flows**.

2. Tap [Tab], type **020113**, tap [Tab] again, and then type **053113**.

3. Take a look at the **cash flow** for Tea Shoppe at the Lake for the period.

4. Close the **Statement of Cash Flows** window, choosing to not memorize the report.

5. Choose the appropriate option for your situation:
   - If you are continuing on to the next lesson or the rest of the end-of-lesson exercises, leave QuickBooks open.
   - If you are finished working in QuickBooks for now, choose **File→Exit**.

Apply Your Skills

Before you begin the Apply Your Skills exercises, complete one of these options:

- *Open* **[Your name] Wet Noses Veterinary Clinic, Lesson 6** *or* **Wet Noses Veterinary Clinic, Lesson 7** *from your file storage location.*

- *Restore* **Wet Noses Veterinary Clinic, Lesson 7 (Portable)** *from your file storage location. Make sure to place your name as the first word in the company filename (e.g., Sadie's Wet Noses Veterinary Clinic, Lesson 7). If you need to review how to restore a portable company file, see Develop Your Skills 7.1.*

APPLY YOUR SKILLS 7.1

Use Classes to Track Why Customers Visit

Dr. James has decided that she wishes to know a bit more about what brings her customers through her doors. In this exercise, you will help her use classes to track this aspect of her business.

1. Turn on the **class tracking** preference.

2. Set up four new classes: **Routine/Scheduled**, **Emergency**, **Product Sales**, and **Overhead**.

3. Enter the following transactions, using the new classes that have been established:

   - On 7/1/13, enter a bill for the monthly rent for $2,300 payable to Oberg Property Management.

   - On 7/1/13, Chris Lorenzo brought in his cat, Jaguar, who was having a hard time breathing. Create invoice #175 for the visit and charge him for an Exam, a Venipuncture, and a CBC Chem.

   - On 7/2/13, you received bill #77-9-57 from Seattle Vet Supply for $3,787.49 ($1,946.72 for medical supplies, $994.22 for medicines, and $846.55 for vaccines). The terms for the bill are Net 15. All of these items are used in the practice for a variety of procedures and ailments.

   - On 7/2/13, Krista Reinertson brought in her dog, Pansie, for her annual exam, a rabies shot, and a small dog dose of Revolution. She paid with check number 2627.

   - On 7/5/13, your received a bill from Brian's Pet Taxi for $56 for transporting an injured dog to your office (you will need to create a new expense account called Pet Transportation). You will pass on this expense to the dog's owner later in this exercise, so you need to choose Steve Gaines:Dog-Jasper as the Customer:Job and indicate that the expense is billable.

   - On 7/5/13, Toni Wagner brought in her dog, Arizona, for a checkup and to see if he can go off of his meds. Charge her for an Exam; she paid cash.

Set Price Levels

As QuickBooks is already set up to track price levels for Wet Noses, in this exercise you will create a new price level for the police dogs.

1. Open the **Price Level** List.

2. Create a new price level named **Police Dogs**.

3. Choose to decrease item prices by **10 percent**.

4. Click **OK** to save the new price level and then close the **Price Level List**.

Use the Price Level in an Invoice

One of the Snohomish K-9 Unit handlers brought in Admiral for a scheduled Exam because he has been limping a bit.

5. Open the **Create Invoices** window, and then choose **Snohomish County K-9 Unit:Dog-Admiral** as the Customer:Job.

6. Set the date to **7/8/2013**, and the Class to **Routine/Scheduled**.

7. Choose **Exam** as the first Item, and then **2 XRay films** as the second item.

8. Click the **Rate drop-down arrow** for both lines, and then choose the **Police Dogs** rate for each.

9. Click **Save & Close** for the invoice.

Create an Invoice for Billable Costs

In this exercise, you will pass on the Brian's Pet Taxi fee to Steve Gaines.

1. Open the **Create Invoices** window, and choose **Steve Gaines:Dog-Jasper** as the Customer:Job.

2. Choose to select the **outstanding billable time and costs** in the Billable Time/Costs window; then click **OK**.

3. Click the **Expenses** tab, click to the left of the **7/5/13** charge to place a checkmark, and then click **OK**.

4. Set the date of the invoice to **7/9/2013** and the class to **Emergency**.

5. Click in the Description column, and then type **Emergency transport of Jasper to clinic on 7/5/13**.

6. Set the Terms as **Due on receipt**; then, click **Save & Close**, choosing to not save the new terms for Steve.

Advanced Skills

Answer Questions with Reports

In this exercise, you will answer questions for Dr. James by running reports. You may wish to display the Report Center in List View to help you answer the questions. Ask your instructor if you should print the reports, print (save) them as PDF files, export them to Excel, or simply display them on the screen.

1. What is the forecasted cash flow for the month of July 2013, displayed in one week periods?

2. What does a Profit & Loss by Class report look like? I would like to see an example of what to expect once we have more class data entered.

3. Are there any unclassified transactions for the month of July 2013?

4. What is the per item price for each item for the Police Dogs price level?

5. Submit your reports based on the guidelines provided by your instructor.

6. Choose the appropriate option for your situation:

   - If you are continuing on to the next lesson or the Critical Thinking exercises, leave QuickBooks open.

   - If you are finished working in QuickBooks for now, choose **File→Exit**.

Critical Thinking

In the course of working through the following Critical Thinking exercises, you will be utilizing various skills taught in this and previous lesson(s). Take your time and think carefully about the tasks presented to you. Turn back to the lesson content if you need assistance.

7.1 Sort Through the Stack

Before You Begin: Restore the **Monkey Business, Lesson 7 (Portable)** *file from your storage location. (Remember that you are to leave the password field blank for Mary.) You also have the option of opening either the final file from Critical Thinking 6.1 or Monkey Business, Lesson 7 from your storage location.*

You have been hired by Mary Minard to help her with her organization's books. She is the owner of Monkey Business, a nonprofit organization that provides low-income students with help in preparing for college placement exams and applying for scholarships. You have just sat down at her desk and found a pile of papers. It is your job to sort through the papers and make sense of what you find, entering information into QuickBooks whenever appropriate and answering any other questions in a word-processing document saved as **Critical Thinking 7.1**. Remember, you are digging through papers on a desk, so it is up to you to determine the correct order in which to complete the tasks.

- Credit card receipt: From Woods Publishing Company, dated 8/2/2013 in the amount of $397 for the purchase of SAT prep guides for training at Lakeside Christian School. Choose to pass on the expense to the customer and indicate the correct class for the transaction.

- Message from Mary: "Can you set up a way for us to easily give a 10 percent discount to certain customers on a per-invoice basis?"

- Note from accountant: "Please develop a system to keep better track of source documents. You can do it electronically or 'physically,' but we need the backup documentation organized."

- Scribbled on a scrap of paper: Can we keep track of the funds that come in and go out for the different types of services we provide? Is there some sort of feature that would let us track income and expense by, let's say, College 101, FAFSA preparation, Scholarships, Exam Prep?

- Handwritten invoice: For SAT Test Prep workshop to be held at Lakeside Christian School on 8/14/2013 for $775. Due Net 15. Make sure you indicate that it is for exam prep on the invoice and include the test prep books you purchased by credit card.

- Scribbled note from Mary: "I would like to see what our cash flow is for July. Is there a report that will provide me with this information? What if I wanted to see what a prediction of cash flow for September 2013 might look like? Is there an easy way to do that in QuickBooks?"

7.2 Tackle the Tasks

Now is your chance to work a little more with Rock Castle Construction and apply the skills that you have learned in this lesson to accomplish additional tasks. Open or restore the **Critical Thinking 7.2** company or portable company file from your file storage location, or open the company file you used in the Develop Your Skills exercises for this lesson. Then, enter the following tasks.

Analyze transactions	Answer the following questions on a separate sheet of paper about invoice 1101 that you produced in this lesson.
	■ Which accounts are involved and what type are they?
	■ Is each account increased or decreased?
	■ Which account is debited and for what amount?
	■ Which account is credited and for what amount?
Apply classes to transactions	Write a check on 12/17/14 to **East Bayshore Tool & Supply**, using the next check number, for job materials that you need for repairs on Sonia Bristol's back porch in the amount of **$56.29**. Choose to pass on the expense to the customer and indicate the class as Remodel.
Produce a class report	Produce a Profit & Loss by Class report for December 2014.
Enter an invoice with a price level and billable expense included	Create an invoice for **Sonia Bristol** on 12/17/14 for eight hours of repairs that you did on her back porch. Use Remodel as the class, pass on the job materials expense, and set the price level for the labor as Repeat Customer.
Create a Statement of Cash Flows	Create a Statement of Cash Flows for the date range of 1/1/14 through 12/18/14.

You may use the company file from this exercise for the Develop Your Skills exercises in the next lesson if you wish.

7.3 Use the Web as a Learning Tool

Throughout this book, you will be provided with an opportunity to use the Internet as a learning tool by completing WebQuests. According to the original creators of WebQuests, as described on their website (WebQuest.org), a WebQuest is "an inquiry-oriented activity in which most or all of the information used by learners is drawn from the web." To complete the WebQuest projects in this book, navigate to the student resource center and choose the WebQuest for the lesson on which you are currently working. The subject of each WebQuest will be relevant to the material found in the lesson.

WebQuest Subject: Diving into the accounting cycle

Dealing with Physical Inventory

LESSON OBJECTIVES

After studying this lesson, you will be able to:

- Create and use items to track inventory
- Create purchase orders and receive items
- Adjust quantity/value on hand
- Sell items and process sales discounts
- Collect, track, and pay sales tax
- Work with reports to manage your inventory, sales, and receivables

In Lesson 4, Working with Customers, you learned to create service and non-inventory items. In this lesson, you will examine the inventory features available in QuickBooks. When you turn on the inventory features, QuickBooks allows you to create inventory items and purchase orders, receive items into inventory, sell inventory items, and run inventory-related reports. QuickBooks also creates accounts that you did not need until you began tracking inventory—Inventory Assets and Cost of Goods Sold. You can also create subaccounts for each of these new accounts to track your assets and costs for individual products or product types, if you choose. In addition, you will learn how to set up, track, and pay sales tax in QuickBooks. This lesson will conclude with a look at common inventory, sales, and collection reports.

Student Resources   http://labyrinthelab.com/qb13

Rock Castle Construction

In this lesson, you will help Zoe learn how to work with inventory items in QuickBooks. This will include the creation of inventory items, as well as their sales to customers. You will also learn how to set up and receive payments when sales discounts are involved. Finally, you and Zoe will explore reports in QuickBooks that will help Rock Castle manage inventory, report on sales, and make collection calls.

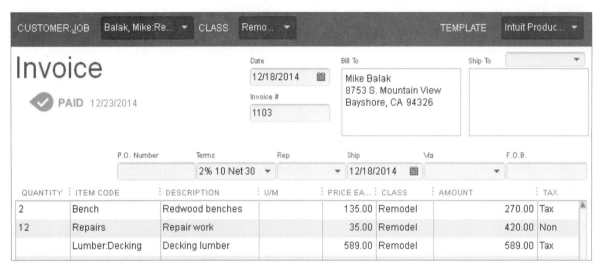

The product invoice template provides fields that are useful when you are dealing with the sale of physical inventory. You can sell inventory and service items on both the product and service invoice templates.

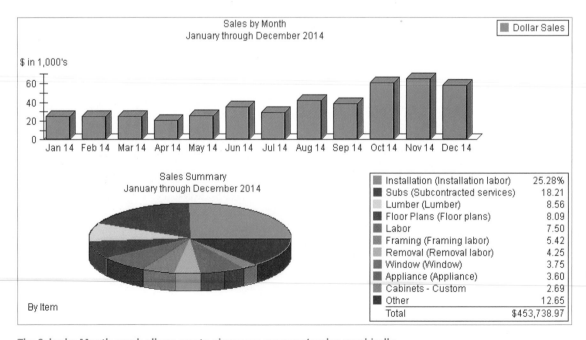

The Sales by Month graph allows you to view your company's sales graphically.

Tracking Inventory in QuickBooks

A useful feature in QuickBooks is inventory tracking. It must be turned on in the Preferences window. Once activated, it will add links to the Home page and options to the menu bar.

Should I Use QuickBooks to Track My Company's Inventory?

Not all companies are perfectly aligned to use QuickBooks to track their inventory. There are several factors that you should consider before deciding to use QuickBooks to track your company's inventory items:

- **How many types of products do I sell?** QuickBooks Pro and Premier work well for companies that have up to a few hundred items. If you have more items, you may want to consider using QuickBooks' Point-of-Sale edition.

- **Does my inventory include perishable items?** The bookkeeping for perishable items can be a bit tedious due to differences between your on-hand quantities and what you have recorded in QuickBooks.

- **Do I sell unique, one-of-a-kind products?** If you sell items such as antiques, you will have to create a new QuickBooks item for each product you sell.

- **Do I manufacture the products that I sell?** If you purchase raw materials and assemble them into products, QuickBooks Pro is not the most compatible software for your company. You may want to look at purchasing QuickBooks: Premier Manufacturing & Wholesale Edition or QuickBooks Enterprise Solutions: Manufacturing & Wholesale Edition, which address the unique needs of manufacturing businesses.

- **How fast do my inventory items become obsolete?** If this time frame is quite short, you may find that updating your inventory in QuickBooks is tedious.

- **How do I value my inventory?** QuickBooks uses the average cost method of inventory valuation. If you are using LIFO, FIFO, or another method, you may want to look at using a different tool to track your inventory.

Beginning with the Enterprise edition of QuickBooks 2012, users are now able to use the FIFO method of inventory valuation.

Inventory Center

In some Premier versions of QuickBooks, there is a new feature called the Inventory Center. This center looks similar to the Customer and Vendor centers. It provides a convenient place for you to manage your inventory items.

Advanced Skills

Setting Up the Item List

If you want to see anything on a sales form or a purchase order, it must be set up as an item first. Before you can create an inventory item, you must turn on QuickBooks' inventory features in the Preferences window.

Inventory vs. Non-Inventory Parts

In Lesson 4, Working with Customers, you learned about non-inventory parts. Once you turn on the QuickBooks inventory feature, you'll see both inventory and non-inventory parts. Inventory parts are tracked and sold by quantity. Examples of inventory parts might be vitamins that a doctor purchases and sells to her patients or lamps that an interior decorating company buys and resells.

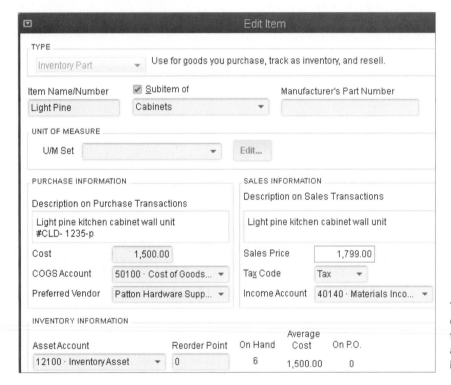

The Inventory Parts window consists of two "sides," one for the purchase information and one for the sales information.

QuickBooks allows you to classify non-inventory parts as well as inventory parts. Examples of items that should be created as non-inventory parts include:

- Items you don't track as inventory, such as nails used by a contractor or thread used by a seamstress
- Items you purchase for a particular customer
- Items you sell but don't first purchase, such as livestock that you breed and sell

Add/Edit Multiple List Entries

As you learned in Lesson 4, Working with Customers, there is a feature in QuickBooks that allows you to easily record multiple entries in your lists.

You can quickly update several entries in your lists by right-clicking and choosing either the Clear Column or Copy Down command.

Using Units of Measure

In the Premier and higher versions of QuickBooks, there is a feature that allows you to convert units of measure. With this feature, QuickBooks users can either work with single units of measure (e.g., buy a pound, sell a pound) or multiple units of measure (e.g., buy a yard, sell a foot).

The unit of measure feature is especially useful to companies that distribute or manufacture items. However, all companies that track inventory could find it handy if they purchase and sell in different units of measure or need to indicate units on purchase or sales forms.

Cost of Goods Sold

When you purchase items at wholesale to resell to your customers, the purchase price you pay is the cost of goods sold (COGS). Your profit is the difference between your sales and COGS.

Inventory Valuation

There are three inventory valuation methods allowed by GAAP:

■ **Last-In, First-Out (LIFO):** With this method, the value of the last inventory brought in is used to determine the COGS, whereas the value of the inventory is based on the inventory purchased earlier in the year.

■ **First-In, First-Out (FIFO):** With this method, the value of the first inventory brought in is used to determine the COGS, whereas the value of the inventory is based on the inventory purchased last (which more closely resembles the actual replacement cost).

■ **Average Cost (or Weighted Average):** With this method, the value of the inventory is determined by dividing the total value of the inventory by the total number of inventory items.

QuickBooks Pro and Premier use the average cost method of inventory valuation; the Enterprise edition uses the FIFO method as well.

> **FLASHBACK TO GAAP: CONSISTENCY**
> Remember that the company should use the same accounting principles and methods from year to year.

Show Lowest Subaccount Preference

It is often difficult to see the name and number of the subaccount you use in a transaction while working with the narrow account fields in the QuickBooks windows. QuickBooks has a way to help you overcome this problem by allowing you to choose to see only the lowest subaccount in these fields. For example, if you need to choose the Materials Income subaccount, it would normally be displayed as:

40100•Construction Income:40140•Materials Income

By choosing the show lowest subaccount preference, it will simply be displayed as:

40140•Materials Income

QUICK REFERENCE	PREPARING TO TRACK AND SELL INVENTORY
Task	**Procedure**
Turn on QuickBooks' inventory features	■ Choose Edit→Preferences.
	■ Choose the Items & Inventory category, and the Company Preferences tab.
	■ Click in the box to the left of Inventory and purchase orders are active; click OK.
Turn on the Show Lowest Subaccount preference	■ Choose Edit→Preferences.
	■ Choose the Accounting category, and then the Company Preferences tab.
	■ Click in the box to the left of the Show Lowest Subaccount Only option; click OK.
Create an inventory part item	■ Open the Item List; choose to create a new item.
	■ Choose Inventory Part as the type of item.
	■ Enter all required information in both the purchase and sales sides of the window; click OK to record the new item.

DEVELOP YOUR SKILLS 8.1
Prepare to Track and Sell Inventory

In this exercise, you will first help Zoe confirm that the inventory features are turned on in QuickBooks. Then you will set the show lowest subaccount preference and create inventory items.

In this exercise, you will first confirm that inventory features are turned on. Then you will set the show lowest subaccount preference and create inventory items. The first step is to open QuickBooks, and then either open a company file or restore a portable company file.

1. Start **QuickBooks 2013**.
   If you downloaded the student exercise files in the portable company file *format, follow Option 1 below. If you downloaded the files in the* company file *format, follow Option 2 below.*

If you choose, you may use the final company file from Critical Thinking 7.2. In this case, open the Critical Thinking 7.2 final company file from your default storage location in Option 2 below.

Option 1: Restore a Portable Company File

2. Choose **File→Open or Restore Company**.

3. Restore the **Rock Castle Construction** portable file for this lesson from your file storage location, placing your name as the first word in the filename (e.g., Zoe's Rock Castle Construction, Lesson 8).
It may take a few moments for the portable company file to open. Once it does, continue with step 4.

Option 2: Open a Company File

2. Choose **File→Open or Restore Company**, ensure that **Open a regular company file** is selected, and then open the **Rock Castle Construction** company file for this lesson from your file storage location.
The QuickBooks company file will open.

3. Click **OK** to close the QuickBooks Information windows. If necessary, click **No** in the Set Up External Accountant User window.

Set Inventory and Show Lowest Subaccount Preferences

Zoe believes that the QuickBooks file has been set up to track inventory, but she will open the Preferences window in order to confirm this, and while she is at it, she will set the show lowest subaccount preference.

4. Choose **Edit→Preferences**.

5. Follow these steps to determine the status of the inventory feature:

Ⓐ Click the **Items & Inventory** category. — Ⓑ Click the **Company Preferences** tab.

Ⓒ Ensure that the **Inventory and purchase orders are active** box is checked.

Ⓓ Click **OK**.

Before you can set the show lowest subaccount option, you must ensure that all accounts have a number assigned.

6. Choose **Lists→Chart of Accounts**.

7. Scroll through the **Chart of Accounts** to see if there are any that do not have an account number assigned.
You will find that Subcontracted Federal WH does not have an account number assigned.

8. Right-click **Subcontracted Federal WH**, and then choose **Edit Account**.

9. Type **22000**, and then click **Save & Close**.

10. Close the **Chart of Accounts** window.

11. Choose **Edit→Preferences**, and then follow these steps to turn on the show lowest subaccount option:

Ⓐ Click the **Accounting** category.   Ⓑ Click the **Company Preferences** tab.

Ⓒ Click the **Show lowest subaccount only** checkbox.   Ⓓ Click **OK**.

Create Multiple Inventory Items

Now you will help Zoe create additional inventory items for the company by utilizing the Add/Edit Multiple List Entries feature.

12. Choose **Lists→Add/Edit Multiple List Entries**.

13. Follow these steps to begin creating your inventory part items (if the Time Saving Tip window appears, click **OK**):

Ⓐ Click the **drop-down arrow**, and then choose **Inventory Parts**.

Ⓑ Click in the **Item Name** column below the last entry, and then type **Int Lights**.

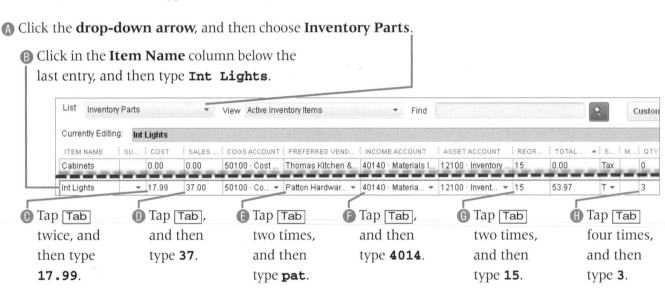

Ⓒ Tap Tab twice, and then type **17.99**.

Ⓓ Tap Tab, and then type **37**.

Ⓔ Tap Tab two times, and then type **pat**.

Ⓕ Tap Tab, and then type **4014**.

Ⓖ Tap Tab two times, and then type **15**.

Ⓗ Tap Tab four times, and then type **3**.

14. Tap Tab, and then follow these steps to add a second item:

Ⓐ Type **Bench**.

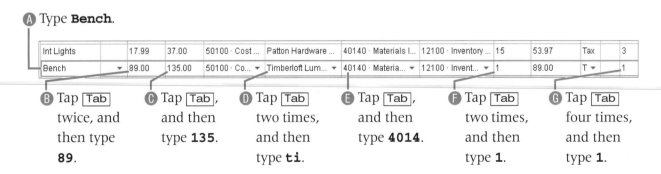

Ⓑ Tap Tab twice, and then type **89**.

Ⓒ Tap Tab, and then type **135**.

Ⓓ Tap Tab two times, and then type **ti**.

Ⓔ Tap Tab, and then type **4014**.

Ⓕ Tap Tab two times, and then type **1**.

Ⓖ Tap Tab four times, and then type **1**.

15. Click the **Save Changes** button at the bottom of the window and click **OK** in the Record(s) Saved window.

16. Close the **Add/Edit Multiple Entries List** window.

In this exercise you entered the basic, required information for your physical inventory items. You can add more information by customizing the columns and adding that information in the Add/Edit Multiple Entries List window or individually in the form where you select the item or in the Edit Item window available through the Item List.

Dealing with Sales Tax in QuickBooks

QuickBooks makes it easy to charge and collect sales tax for items. You can also choose whether to charge tax for individual customers who resell merchandise to their customers and charge sales tax on the final sale rather than pay the tax to you. How you set up sales tax in QuickBooks depends entirely on which state(s) you conduct business in. There are some states that do not collect sales tax at all (yay, Oregon!), and there is variation among the others regarding what is taxed. Some states tax service that is performed, while others do not (charging sales tax on services is the exception rather than the rule). Some tax grocery food items; others do not. You must know the sales tax laws in your state before you set up sales tax for your company.

When dealing with sales tax, take some time to learn about how the sales tax laws are set up in your jurisdiction. How you display items on invoices, in both structure and whether items are stated separately or grouped together, can affect the amount of tax due on a transaction. Taking time up front can save you and your customers money in the long run.

Behind the scenes, the sales tax collected will be directed to a Sales Tax Liability account that QuickBooks automatically creates for you. The funds will be held there until you pay them to the appropriate governing authority.

Sales Tax Items and Groups

To include sales tax on a sales form, you must set up the tax as an item. An interesting situation arises, though, when you have to pay the tax collected to multiple tax agencies. QuickBooks helps you deal with this situation by allowing you to combine multiple sales tax items into a sales tax group. This is necessary, as you can apply only one sales tax item or group to a sales form. Before you can collect sales tax, you must turn on the preference and create a sales tax item or group.

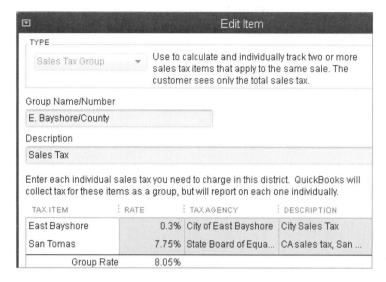

Notice that the sales tax group in this example comprises two sales tax items payable to two separate tax agencies.

Default Tax Rate

Once you have created your sales tax item(s) and group(s), you should set up a default tax rate in your preferences. This rate will appear when you create a sales form for a customer for whom a tax rate is not specified. You should choose the tax rate that you use most of the time as the default; you can change it on a sale-by-sale basis.

Dealing with Multiple Sales Tax Rates

Some companies conduct business in multiple areas. As such, the company must set up different sales tax items and/or groups with the different rates and taxing agencies. You can set one default tax rate for the company or default tax rates for each customer. Do this on the Additional Info tab of the New Customer and Edit Customer windows.

QUICK REFERENCE	SETTING UP SALES TAX IN QUICKBOOKS
Task	**Procedure**
Turn on the QuickBooks sales tax feature	▪ Choose Edit→Preferences.
	▪ Click the Sales Tax category; click the Company Preferences tab.
	▪ Click in the circle to the left of Yes in the "Do you charge sales tax?" section.
	▪ Select your most common sales tax item. If necessary, create the item.
	▪ Click OK to record the new preference.
Create a sales tax item	▪ Open the Item List; choose to create a new item.
	▪ Choose Sales Tax Item as the type of item (the sales tax preference must be set up first).
	▪ Type the name and description for the item.
	▪ Set the tax rate agency to which you pay the tax; click OK.

Task	Procedure
Create a sales tax group	■ You must first set up the items for the group following the above steps. ■ Open the item list, and then choose to create a new item. ■ Choose Sales Tax Group as the type. ■ Type the group name and description. ■ Choose each sales tax item that is to be included in the group; click OK.
Set your company's default tax rate	■ Choose Edit→Preferences. ■ Click the Sales Tax category, and then click the Company Preferences tab. ■ Choose your default tax rate from the "Your most common sales tax item" field drop-down button; click OK.
Set a customer's default tax rate	■ Open the Customer Center, and then double-click the customer whose default tax rate you wish to set. ■ Choose the Additional Info tab. ■ Choose the correct tax rate from the Tax Item field drop-down arrow; click OK.

Advanced Skills

Set Up Sales Tax for a New Area

In this exercise, you will help Zoe create a new sales tax item, since the company is doing business with Tea Shoppe at the Lake in San Diego County, which has a different tax rate. Before you can create any sales tax items or groups, you must have the preference turned on. Your first step is to help Zoe verify that the preference is on.

1. Choose **Edit→Preferences**.

2. Follow these steps to view the sales tax preference status:

Ⓐ Click the **Sales Tax** category.

Ⓑ Click the **Company Preferences** tab.

Ⓒ Verify that **Yes** is selected.

Ⓓ Click **OK**.

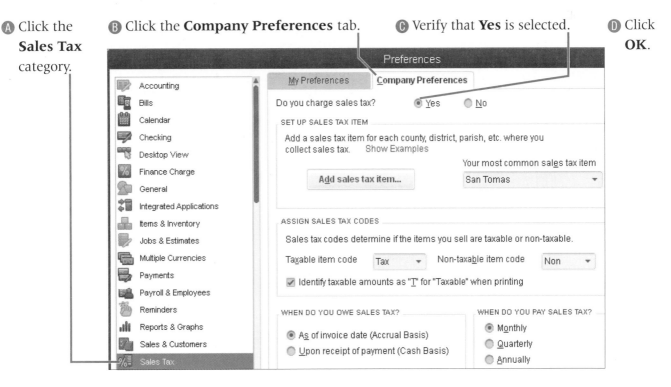

Create a New Sales Tax Item

Now that you have verified that the sales tax preference is correct, you can set up the new item to track sales tax from San Diego County.

3. Click the **Items & Services** task icon in the Company area of the Home page.

4. Click the **Item** menu button, and then choose **New** from the menu.

5. Follow these steps to create the new sales tax item:

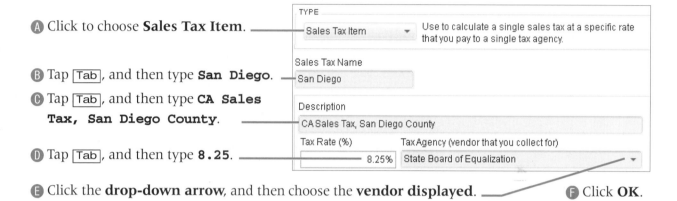

Ⓐ Click to choose **Sales Tax Item**.

Ⓑ Tap Tab, and then type **San Diego**.

Ⓒ Tap Tab, and then type **CA Sales Tax, San Diego County**.

Ⓓ Tap Tab, and then type **8.25**.

Ⓔ Click the **drop-down arrow**, and then choose the **vendor displayed**.

Ⓕ Click **OK**.

6. Close the **Item List**.

Use the New Sales Tax Item in a Transaction

Since you have only one customer in San Diego County, you will not set that as the default sales tax item. Instead, you will choose it only when selling to that customer.

7. Choose **Customers→Enter Sales Receipts**.

8. Follow these steps to record a sales transaction for a customer in San Diego County:

Ⓐ Type **The Tea Shoppe at the Lake**, and Quick Add it as a vendor.

Ⓑ Choose **Remodel** as the Class.

Ⓒ Tap Tab twice, and then tap + to set the date to **12/17/2014**.

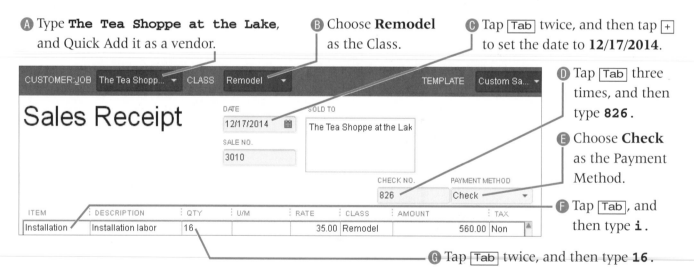

Ⓓ Tap Tab three times, and then type **826**.

Ⓔ Choose **Check** as the Payment Method.

Ⓕ Tap Tab, and then type **i**.

Ⓖ Tap Tab twice, and then type **16**.

Tea Shoppe at the Lake already exists on the Vendor list, and we cannot duplicate the entry. Therefore, in sub-step A above, you added the word "The" to the business name for the Customers & Jobs List entry.

H Click below Installation, and then type **cou**.

I Click the **drop-down arrow**, and then choose **San Diego**.

J Click **Save & Close**.

ITEM	DESCRIPTION	QTY	U/M	RATE	CLASS	AMOUNT	TAX
Installation	Installation labor	16		35.00	Remodel	560.00	Non
Counter	Custom made counter top			1,899.98	Remodel	1,899.98	Tax

San Diego ▾ (8.25%) 156.75

Total 2,616.73

9. Click **Yes** in the Name Information Changed window.
This will change the default sales tax item for Tea Shoppe at the Lake, if necessary.

BTS BRIEF

12000•Undeposited Funds DR 2,616.73; 40130•Labor Income CR <560.00>; 40140•Materials Income CR <1,899.98>; Sales Tax Payable CR <156.75>

Creating Purchase Orders

Many businesses use purchase orders for ordering items into inventory. When a purchase order is created, nothing occurs "behind the scenes," as you have done nothing yet to debit or credit an account.

Non-Posting Accounts

When you create your first purchase order, QuickBooks creates a non-posting account (an account that *does not* affect your P&L report or your balance sheet report), called Purchase Orders. Non-posting accounts appear at the end of your Chart of Accounts. By creating these accounts for you, QuickBooks allows you to create reports based on them.

QUICK REFERENCE	WORKING WITH PURCHASE ORDERS
Task	**Procedure**
Create a purchase order	■ Choose Vendors→Create Purchase Orders; choose the desired vendor. ■ Enter the items you are ordering; click Save & Close.
Produce an open purchase orders report	■ Choose Lists→Chart of Accounts; scroll to the bottom of the list. ■ Double-click the Purchase Orders account; set the correct date range for the report (if necessary).

Work with Purchase Orders

In this exercise, you will help Zoe create purchase orders for Rock Castle Construction and view the purchase orders report.

1. Click the **Purchase Orders** task icon in the Vendors area of the Home page.

2. Follow these steps to create a purchase order:

Ⓐ Type **ti**, and then tap ⌑Tab⌑ to choose the vendor.   Ⓑ Tap ⌑Tab⌑ four more times, and then type **121914**.

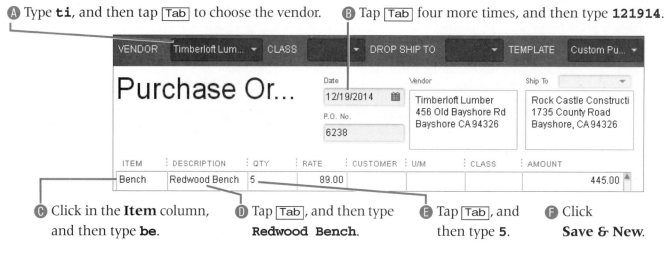

Ⓒ Click in the **Item** column, and then type **be**.   Ⓓ Tap ⌑Tab⌑, and then type **Redwood Bench**.   Ⓔ Tap ⌑Tab⌑, and then type **5**.   Ⓕ Click **Save & New**.

3. Click **Save Anyway** in the Items not assigned classes window.
In this case, a class was not assigned. It will be assigned later when you know if it is for a new construction or remodel job. Remember that purchase orders do not affect what occurs behind the scenes.

4. Follow these steps to create the second purchase order:

Ⓐ Type **pat**, and then tap ⌑Tab⌑ to choose the vendor.   Ⓑ Tap ⌑Tab⌑ three more times, and then type **121914**.

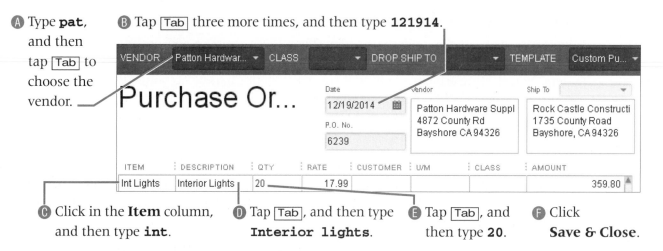

Ⓒ Click in the **Item** column, and then type **int**.   Ⓓ Tap ⌑Tab⌑, and then type **Interior lights**.   Ⓔ Tap ⌑Tab⌑, and then type **20**.   Ⓕ Click **Save & Close**.

5. Click **Save Anyway** in the Items not assigned classes window.

View the Open Purchase Orders Report

Next you will take a look at the Purchase Orders account QuickBooks created for Rock Castle Construction when the first purchase order was created.

6. Click the **Chart of Accounts** task icon in the Company area of the Home page.

7. Scroll to the bottom of the list and notice the non-posting **90100•Purchase Orders** account.

8. Double-click the **Purchase Orders** account.
   QuickBooks creates a QuickReport showing open purchase orders.

9. Type **a** to set the date range to all; then, scroll to the bottom of the report to view the purchase orders you just created.

10. Choose **Window→Close All**.

Receiving Items

When you receive the items on a purchase order, you need to enter them into inventory. You can carry this transaction out in either one or two steps, depending on how your vendor delivers the accompanying bill.

The Two Methods of Receiving Items

If a vendor sends the inventory items and the bill together, you can record them as one transaction. On the other hand, if you receive the items first and the bill later, you will enter them in two separate steps.

By clicking the drop-down arrow next to the Receive Inventory link on the Home page, you can choose how to enter the receipt of your items, either with or without the bill.

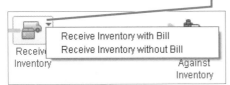

If you received the inventory items and later received the bill, click the Enter Bills Against Inventory link on the Home page to enter the bill for the items at a later date.

If you are going to pay a bill that is attached to a purchase order with a credit card, use the Enter Credit Card Charges window so QuickBooks will prompt you to receive against open purchase orders.

When you receive the items, QuickBooks will use the Items tab rather than the Expenses tab in the Enter Bills window. If you recall from Lesson 3, Working with Vendors, the Items tab is used to enter items into an inventory asset account rather than record an expense.

Including Expenses on a Bill for Items

You may incur additional shipping and handling charges when you order inventory items. These charges should not be entered on the Items tab but rather as an expense on the Expenses tab. Once QuickBooks enters the information on the Items tab, you can click on the Expenses tab to enter any additional expenses due with the bill.

Expenses	$35.00	Items	$305.83
ACCOUNT	AMOUNT	MEMO	
63100 · Postage	35.00		

Expenses	$35.00	Items		$305.83	
ITEM	DESCRIPTION	QTY	U/M	COST	AMOUNT
Int Lights	Interior Lights	17		17.99	305.83

Notice how the delivery charges are displayed on the Expenses tab of the Enter Bills window while the inventory items are displayed on the Items tab.

Discount Payment Terms

Your vendors may offer you discount payment terms in an attempt to get you to pay your bills earlier, which in turn improves their cash flow. Payment terms are created in the Terms List, which is one of the Customer & Vendor Profile Lists. You can change the terms on an individual invoice as needed without permanently changing them for the customer.

You will use the payment terms of 1% 10 Net 30 when entering a bill in this section. This means that if you pay the bill within 10 days of receipt, you will receive a 1 percent discount. But, if you don't pay within the first 10 days, the full bill is due in 30 days.

> **FLASHBACK TO GAAP: COST**
>
> Remember that when a company purchases assets, it should record them at cost, not fair market value. For example, if you bought an item worth $750 for $100, it should be recorded at $100.

> **BEHIND THE SCENES**
>
> Regardless the path you take, the behind the scenes action is the same: An Inventory Asset will be debited, and Accounts Payable will be credited.

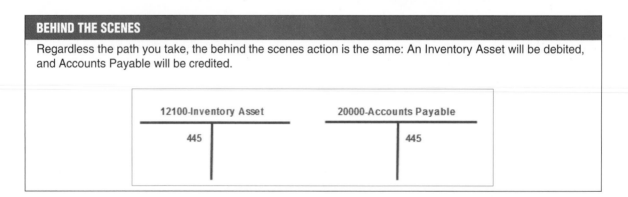

12100-Inventory Asset	20000-Accounts Payable
445	445

Task	Procedure
Receive the inventory and the bill together	■ Choose Vendors→Receive Items and Enter Bill; choose the desired vendor. ■ Click Yes in the Open PO's Exist window. ■ Click in the checkmark column to the left of the PO against which you are receiving items; click OK. ■ Make any necessary changes to the Enter Bills window; click Save & Close or Save & New.
Receive the inventory and the bill separately	Task 1: Update inventory when you receive the items: ■ Choose Vendors→Receive Items; choose the desired vendor. ■ Click Yes in the Open PO's Exist window. ■ Click in the checkmark column to the left of the PO against which you are receiving items; click OK. ■ Make any necessary changes to the Item Receipt window; click Save & Close. Task 2: Enter the bill after you receive it: ■ Choose Vendors→Enter Bill for Received Items; choose the desired vendor. ■ Click within the line of the proper item receipt; click OK. ■ Make any changes to the Enter Bills window; click Save & Close.
Include an expense on a bill for items	■ After the Item information is entered in the Enter Bills window, click the Expenses tab. ■ Choose the correct expense account in the Expense column; tap `Tab`. ■ Type the amount of the expense and correct the total amount due for the bill; click Save & Close.

DEVELOP YOUR SKILLS 8.4

Receive Inventory

In this exercise, you will receive the benches and later receive the bill for them. Following the receipt of the bill for the benches, you will receive the light fixtures and the bill for them together.

1. Choose **Company→Home Page**.

2. Click the **Receive Inventory drop-down arrow** in the Vendors area of the Home page, and then choose **Receive Inventory without Bill**.

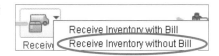

3. Type **ti**, and then tap `Tab`.
   QuickBooks fills in Timberloft Lumber, and the Open PO's Exist window appears.

4. Click **Yes** in the Open PO's Exist window.

5. Click to place a checkmark in the first column for PO number **6238** dated 12/19/14, and then click **OK**.
   QuickBooks displays the Create Item Receipts window with the information from the purchase order filled in. Notice that the items appear on the Items tab at the bottom of the window, not on the Expense tab!

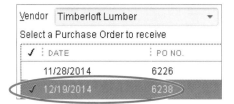

Advanced Skills

6. Tap ⊞ on the keyboard to change the date to **12/22/2014**.

7. Click **Save & Close** to record the item receipt; then, click **Save Anyway** in the Items not assigned classes window.
The class will be assigned to the items when they are sold to a customer for either new construction or a remodel.

Receive the Bill

The benches were entered into inventory when you received them. Now the bill for the items has arrived and you need to enter it.

8. Click the **Enter Bills Against Inventory** task icon in the Vendors area of the Home page.

9. Follow these steps to choose the correct Item Receipt:

Ⓐ Type **ti**, and then tap Tab.

Ⓑ Click anywhere within the line for the **Item Receipt** dated **12/22/2014**.

Ⓒ Click **OK**.

QuickBooks will display the Enter Bills window.

10. Tap Tab, type **122314** as the date, and then tap Tab again.

> **BTS BRIEF**
> **12100•Inventory Asset DR 445.00; 20000•Accounts Payable CR <445.00>**

11. Click **Save & Close** to record the new bill; click **Yes** to record your changes.

12. Click **Save Anyway** in the Items not assigned classes window.

Receive Inventory Items with a Bill and Add an Expense to the Bill

The interior light fixtures and the bill for them arrived at the same time. The bill also included a shipping fee of $35 that must be accounted for on the bill.

13. Click the **Receive Inventory drop-down arrow** in the Vendor area of the Home page, and then choose **Receive Inventory with Bill**.

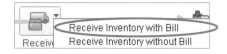

14. Type **pat**, and then tap Tab.
QuickBooks fills in Patton Hardware Supplies as the vendor and the Open PO's Exist window appears.

15. Click **Yes** in the Open PO's Exist window.

16. Click to place a checkmark in the first column for PO number **6239**.

17. Click **OK** to move to the Enter Bills window; click **OK** in the Warning window.
Patton Hardware Supplies was short by three lights for your order, so you need to record a receipt of only 17 interior light fixtures.

18. Follow these steps to complete the bill:

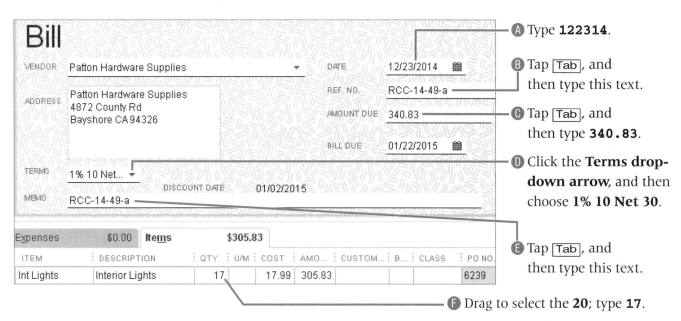

A Type **122314**.

B Tap Tab, and then type this text.

C Tap Tab, and then type **340.83**.

D Click the **Terms drop-down arrow**, and then choose **1% 10 Net 30**.

E Tap Tab, and then type this text.

F Drag to select the **20**; type **17**.

You will receive a 1% discount if you pay the bill by the discount date (01/02/2015).

Enter an Expense on the Bill for Inventory Items

When you received the bill for the interior lights, there was also a shipping charge of $35. You will now enter that as an expense on the bill.

19. Follow these steps to enter the shipping expense:

A Click to display the **Expenses** tab.   **B** Type **po** to choose 63100•Postage.

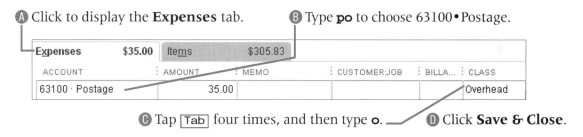

C Tap Tab four times, and then type **o**.   **D** Click **Save & Close**.

BTS BRIEF

12100•Inventory Asset DR 305.83; 63100•Postage DR 35.00; 20000•Accounts Payable CR <340.83>

---

20. Click **No** to reject changing the current terms for Patton Hardware Supplies; click **Save Anyway** in the Items not assigned classes window.

Selling Inventory Items

Once you have created, ordered, and received your items, it is time to start selling them! You will use the same Create Invoices window you used in Lesson 4, Working with Customers. You learned about customizing form templates in Lesson 6, Correcting and Customizing in QuickBooks, and in this lesson you will use a custom invoice template that has been specially created for Rock Castle Construction. In the last section, you learned about discount payment terms as they relate to your payables. In this section, you will apply them to a receivable transaction.

Emailing Invoices

For the majority of companies, email is one of the primary ways they do business nowadays. QuickBooks allows you to easily email invoices to customers, rather than having to send them via "snail mail" or fax. To indicate that you wish to send invoices and other forms to your customers via email, use the Additional Info tab of either the New or Edit Customer window. If you choose to email an invoice to a customer, that customer will receive it as a PDF file attached to the email along with a message that you set in the Preferences window.

Customer Send Method

The customer send method is the way that you primarily send invoices and other forms to a customer. You can change this on each transaction for the customer if it is not always the same method. In the Preferences window, you can customize both personal and company preferences for this feature.

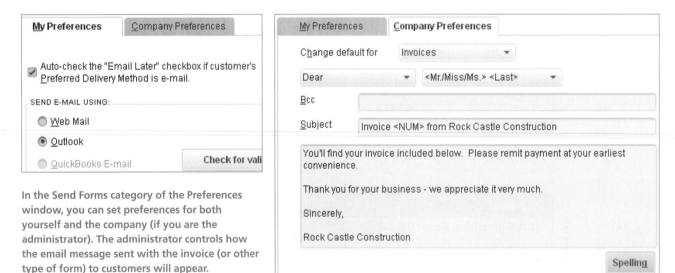

In the Send Forms category of the Preferences window, you can set preferences for both yourself and the company (if you are the administrator). The administrator controls how the email message sent with the invoice (or other type of form) to customers will appear.

Batch Invoicing

The batch invoicing feature allows you to fill out the invoice just once for the customers in the "batch" and then create invoices for all of them. In order to complete this task, you should first create a billing group of the customers for whom you wish to create a batch invoice (although you can add customers one at a time as well).

Make sure that the terms, sales tax code, and preferred delivery method are set for any customer you wish to include in the batch.

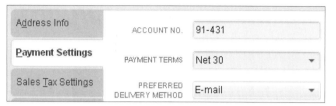

On each customer record, the payment terms and preferred delivery method are on the Payment Settings tab, and the sales tax code is on the Sales Tax Settings tab. To make changes, go to edit the customer from the Customer Center.

Batch Invoices Summary

Once you have created a batch of invoices for customers, you will see the Batch Invoices Summary window. Here you can choose to either print or email the invoices (based on the preferred send method for each customer).

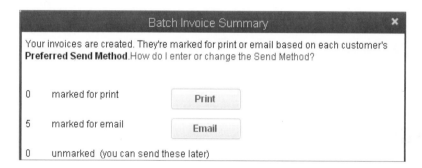

Send a Batch of Forms

You can send more than just invoices from QuickBooks. In the Preferences window, you have the ability to set the default message for eleven different types of forms and reports.

When you are ready to send all of the forms and reports that you have indicated you wish to send, issue a command from the File menu that displays the Select Forms to Send window. From this window, you can choose to send any form listed in the queue.

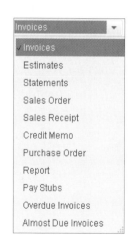

Note the types of forms and reports that you can choose to send from QuickBooks.

Producing Sales Orders

If you have the Premier or Enterprise edition of QuickBooks, there is a sales order feature available that allows you to manage customer orders for both products and services. You can track items that have been ordered by a customer but are currently out of stock, schedule work to be done, plan costs for labor, and estimate future revenue based on the work that has been scheduled.

Benefits of Sales Orders

There are certain benefits to using the sales order feature in QuickBooks:

- You can create one invoice for multiple sales orders.
- You can create multiple invoices for one sales order if you can only partially fulfill an order.
- You can track items that are on backorder.
- You can print a Sales Order Fulfillment Worksheet, which gives you a "big picture" and allows you to determine which orders to fill with the current inventory.

Once a sales order has been created, you can print a pick list that will assist you in fulfilling the order from inventory. If the order is for a service, you can schedule the service.

Tracking Sales Orders

Sales orders will not affect what goes on behind the scenes because no money has changed hands. You can track open sales orders the same way you track open purchase orders, by creating a QuickReport from the non-posting account called 90200 • Sales Orders, which is located at the bottom of the Chart of Accounts. Remember that, in order for you to complete the sale and for things to happen correctly behind the scenes, you must invoice the customer from the sales order.

Cycle Step 3: Record the Business Transaction

Since QuickBooks does the work behind the scenes for you, by entering a transaction in a QuickBooks form correctly you will include the necessary general journal information. If you were doing this by hand, you would need to enter:

- The date of the transaction
- The account names and amounts of each of the debit and credit parts
- A reference to the source document or a brief explanation

In QuickBooks, you need to ensure that your items are set up properly (i.e., routed to the right accounts) so the proper accounts will be debited and credited in the journal that is kept behind the scenes for you.

The following Behind the Scenes feature shows the account names and amounts for the debit and credit parts of this transaction.

The accounting that occurs for product sales is different from what occurs when you sell services. Take a look behind the scenes.

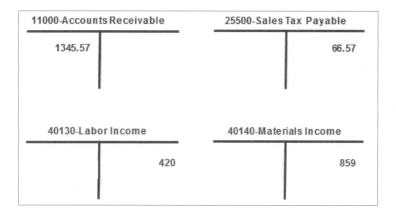

When an inventory item is sold, it "moves" the value of the item from the Inventory Asset account to the Cost of Goods Sold account.

Don't forget our friend sales tax… The rest of what happens behind the scenes looks similar to what happens when service items are sold. Notice that the credits (Materials Income + Labor Income + Sales Tax Payable) equal the debits (Accounts Receivable).

Advanced Skills

Task	Procedure
Create a batch of invoices and a new billing group	■ Choose Customers→Create Batch Invoices. ■ Click the Billing Group drop-down arrow; choose Add New. ■ Type the name of the new group; click Save. ■ Click to select a customer; click Add. Continue as necessary. ■ Click Save Group; click Next. ■ Enter the item information for the invoice and a customer message; click Next. ■ Review the list of invoices that you will create; click Create Invoices. ■ Choose to print or email invoices from the Batch Invoices Summary window.
Email an invoice from the Create Invoices window	■ Open the Create Invoices window and display the desired invoice. ■ Click the Send button drop-down arrow; choose E-mail Invoice. ■ Review the email message in your email program and make any changes. ■ Choose to send the email from your email program.
Send a batch of forms	■ Choose File→Send Forms. ■ Click to deselect any forms you do not wish to send. ■ Edit any emails you wish; click Send Now.
Create a sales order	■ Choose Customers→Create Sales Orders. ■ Fill in all relevant information; click Save & Close. ■ If the order is for a product, you can print a pick list to assist in fulfilling it. ■ If the order is for a service, you should schedule the service at this time.
Create an invoice from a sales order	■ Choose Customers→Create Invoices. ■ Choose the customer for whom you wish to create the invoice. ■ Mark the appropriate order in the Available Sales Orders window; click OK. ■ Choose whether the invoice is for all sales orders or only selected items. ■ Verify all of the information that has been filled in, adding any additional items if desired; click Save & Close.

DEVELOP YOUR SKILLS 8.5
Sell Inventory Items

In this exercise, you will first help Zoe create an invoice for a customer with discount payment terms. Then you will assist her in creating a batch of invoices for maintenance services.

Mike Balak has asked Rock Castle Construction to repair the deck at the back of his house and install two redwood benches. You will need to create a new job for the customer.

1. Click the **Customers** button on the Icon Bar.

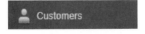

2. Single-click **Balak, Mike** on the Customers & Jobs List.

3. Click the **New Customer & Job** button, and then choose **Add Job**.

4. Type **Repair Deck**, and then click **OK**.

Create an Invoice with Discount Payment Terms

Now that the job has been created, you will create an invoice with discount payment terms that will be emailed for it. The job you just created should still be selected in the Customers & Jobs List.

5. Click the **New Transactions** button, and then choose **Invoices**.
   The Create Invoices window will appear with the Customer:Job entered.

6. Follow these steps to complete the invoice for Mike Balak's deck repair job:

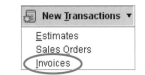

Ⓐ Tap [Tab], and then type **r**.

Ⓑ Tap [Tab] twice, and then type **121814**.

Ⓒ Click the **Terms drop-down arrow** and choose **2% 10 Net 30**.

Ⓓ Tap [Tab] two times, and then type **be**.

Ⓔ Tap [Tab], and then type **Redwood benches**.

Ⓕ Tap [Tab], and then type **2**.

Ⓖ Click below *Bench* here, and then type **rep**.

Ⓗ Tap [Tab] two times, and then type **12**.

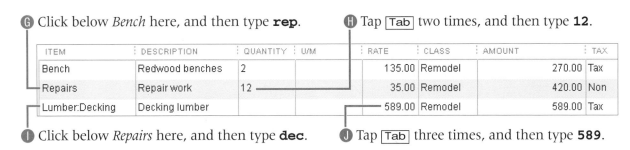

Ⓘ Click below *Repairs* here, and then type **dec**.

Ⓙ Tap [Tab] three times, and then type **589**.

Ⓚ On the Ribbon, click to choose to **Email Later**.

Notice that this is when you apply a class to the benches.

7. Click **Save & Close**; click **No** in the Name Information Changed window.

8. Close the **Customer Center**.

Create a Batch of Invoices and a New Billing Group

Now it is time to create a batch of invoices for several customers who subscribe to a monthly repair service fee. These customers pay a flat fee for repairs for the month.

9. Choose **Customers→Create Batch Invoices**; then, click **OK** in the "Is your customer info set up correctly?" window.
   The Batch Invoice window will appear.

10. Follow these steps to create a new billing group:

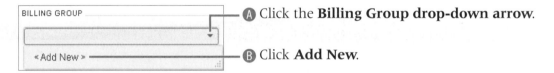

Ⓐ Click the **Billing Group drop-down arrow**.

Ⓑ Click **Add New**.

The Group Name window appears.

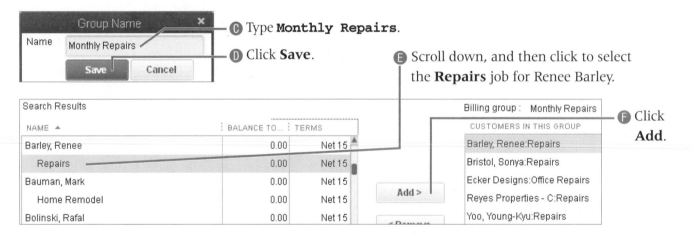

Ⓒ Type **Monthly Repairs**.

Ⓓ Click **Save**.

Ⓔ Scroll down, and then click to select the **Repairs** job for Renee Barley.

Ⓕ Click **Add**.

11. Scrolling down as you go, repeat **steps E and F** above until your list looks like the Customers in This Group list displayed to the right in the illustration above.
   You can also double-click on an item in the list on the left to add it to the group on the right.

12. Click the **Save Group** button located below the Customers in This Group list, and then click **Next**.

13. Follow these steps to set the item information for the invoice:

Ⓐ Tap the ⊞ key until the date is displayed as **12/22/2014**.

Ⓑ Click in the **Item** column, and then type **rep**.

Ⓒ Tap ⎣Tab⎤ three times, and then type **200**.

Ⓓ Tap ⎣Tab⎤, and then type **r**.

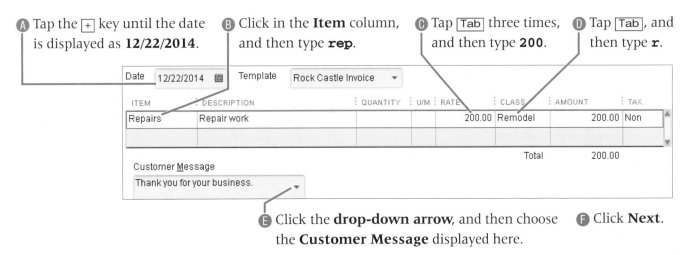

Ⓔ Click the **drop-down arrow**, and then choose the **Customer Message** displayed here.

Ⓕ Click **Next**.

14. Review the list of invoices that you are preparing to create.

	Batch Invoice								
Step 3 of 3: Review the list of invoices to be created for this batch and click **Create Invoices**.									
Invoice Date: 12/22/2014									
SELECT	CUSTOMER	TERMS	SEND METHOD	AMOUNT	TAX CODE	TAX RATE	TAX	TOTAL	STATUS
✔	Barley, Renee:...	Net 15	Email	200.00	Tax	7.75%	0.00	200.00	OK
✔	Bristol, Sonya:...	Net 30	Email	200.00	Tax	7.75%	0.00	200.00	OK
✔	Ecker Designs...	Net 30	Email	200.00	Tax	7.75%	0.00	200.00	OK
✔	Reyes Properti...	Net 30	Email	200.00	Tax	7.5%	0.00	200.00	OK
✔	Yoo, Young-Ky...	Net 30	Email	200.00	Tax	7.75%	0.00	200.00	OK

You will see a screen that shows all of the invoices to be created. If you were to choose to not create an invoice for a member of the group, you could deselect it at this step.

15. Click **Create Invoices**.
The Batch Invoice Summary window displays.

BTS BRIEF

11000•Accounts Receivable DR 1,000.00; 40130•Labor Income CR <1,000.00>

16. Close the **Batch Invoice Summary** window because you will choose to send all six of the invoices you have created in this exercise in the next few steps.

Choose to Send Forms from QuickBooks

In the final section of this exercise, you will send the invoice for Mike Balak that you marked to be sent by email as well as the five invoices you created as a batch.

17. Choose **File→Send Forms**.
The Select Forms to Send window will be displayed.

18. Follow these steps to email the six invoices you just created:

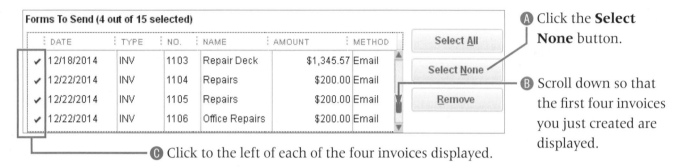

(A) Click the **Select None** button.

(B) Scroll down so that the first four invoices you just created are displayed.

(C) Click to the left of each of the four invoices displayed.

QuickBooks displays only four forms at a time in the Select Forms To Send window, so you will have to continue scrolling to view the other two invoices you just created.

(D) Scroll down to display the last two invoices you just created.

(E) Click to the left of the two additional invoices.

19. Click **Send Now,** and then click **OK** in the Warning window.
You cannot send invoices from a sample file. This exercise took you through all of the steps so that you will be able to do it in your own company file in the future.

20. Close the **Select Forms To Send** and **Customer Service** windows.

Processing Sales Discounts and Electronic Payments

In Lesson 4, Working with Customers, you learned how to receive customer payments for the entire invoice amount. Now you will deal with a discounted customer payment. The procedure for receiving a discounted payment is almost identical to receiving a "regular" payment, except that you must identify the account to be debited for the discount amount.

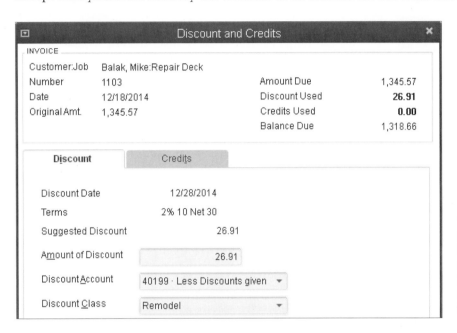

You can easily apply the discount in the QuickBooks Discount and Credits window. QuickBooks calculates the discount based on the payment terms.

Working with Electronic Customer Payments/Wire Transfers

In some instances, you may receive payments from your customers electronically. One method of dealing with this situation is to use a new payment type called Electronic Payment. When the bank notifies you that you have received an electronic payment, you enter the receipt in the Receive Payments window, noting Electronic Payment as the payment type. You will then be able to run reports, filtering by payment type, if you need to track electronic customer payments.

Online Invoice Payments

With QuickBooks 2013, you can now accept invoice payments through an online service. You can even choose to have these payments automatically recorded in your QuickBooks file. This feature is free for your customers, and costs businesses a small fee per transaction.

Invoice payments can be collected online by QuickBooks users with the 2013 version of the software.

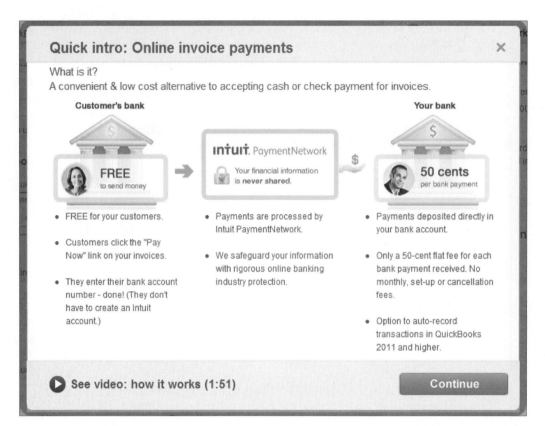

Quick intro: Online invoice payments ✕

What is it?
A convenient & low cost alternative to accepting cash or check payment for invoices.

Customer's bank

FREE
to send money

Intuit. PaymentNetwork
Your financial information is **never shared.**

$

Your bank

50 cents
per bank payment

- FREE for your customers.
- Customers click the "Pay Now" link on your invoices.
- They enter their bank account number - done! (They don't have to create an Intuit account.)

- Payments are processed by Intuit PaymentNetwork.
- We safeguard your information with rigorous online banking industry protection.

- Payments deposited directly in your bank account.
- Only a 50-cent flat fee for each bank payment received. No monthly, set-up or cancellation fees.
- Option to auto-record transactions in QuickBooks 2011 and higher.

▶ See video: how it works (1:51)   Continue

 To learn more, Choose Customers→Create Invoices, click the Online Pay button on the Ribbon, and then click the "See video: how it works" link at the bottom of the Quick Intro window.

The Shipping Manager

You can ship a package right from QuickBooks from both the Create Invoices and Enter Sales Receipt windows using FedEx, UPS, and now the United States Postal Service (through Stamps.com). You can use either your existing account(s) for any of these services, or you can sign up right from QuickBooks. QuickBooks will process the shipment and create a shipping label for you with the customer information that you have stored in QuickBooks. In addition, you can track your shipments from within QuickBooks.

The Customer Snapshot

You learned about the Company Snapshot in Lesson 5, Banking with QuickBooks. In this lesson, you will have a chance to take a tour of the Customer Snapshot.

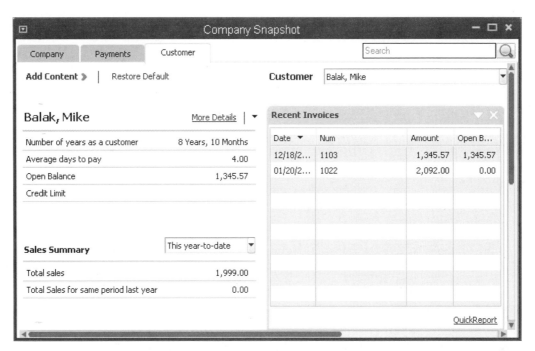

On the Customer tab of the Company Snapshot window, you can select a customer at the top and then view information about that customer in the rest of the window. Adding, moving, and removing content from this window is easy, as is restoring it to how it first appeared by restoring the default view.

BEHIND THE SCENES

When you receive a discounted payment, you need to credit the customer's Accounts Receivable account for the full amount even though you are not receiving the full amount in cash. The additional debit will be recorded in an expense account called 40199•Less Discounts Given.

11000-Accounts Receivable	12000-Undeposited Funds	40199-Less Discounts Given
1345.57	1318.66	26.91

QUICK REFERENCE	PROCESSING SALES DISCOUNTS AND ELECTRONIC PAYMENTS
Task	**Procedure**
Receive a discounted payment	■ Choose Customers→Receive Payments; choose the customer/job from whom/which you received the payment.
	■ Enter the payment information.
	■ Click to choose the invoice to which the discount applies; click Discount & Credits.
	■ Enter the discount amount and account.
	■ Click Done; click Save & Close or Save & New.

Task	Procedure
Receive an electronic payment	■ Choose Lists→Customer & Vendor Profile Lists→Payment Method List; create a new payment method called **Electronic Payment**.
	■ Choose Customers→Receive Payments; choose the desired customer/job.
	■ Enter the payment information; enter **Electronic Payment** as the payment type.
	■ Click Save & Close to record the payment.
	■ Choose Banking→Make Deposits; click to choose the electronic payment.
	■ Click OK to move to the Make Deposits window; enter the desired account.
	■ Enter the date of the deposit; click Save & Close.
Display the Customer Snapshot	■ Choose Company→Company Snapshot.
	■ Click the Customer tab.

DEVELOP YOUR SKILLS 8.6

Receive a Discounted Payment Electronically

In this exercise, you will help Zoe record a discounted payment and process an electronic payment for Rock Castle Construction.

1. Choose **Lists→Customer & Vendor Profile Lists→Payment Method List**.

2. Click the **Payment Method** menu button, and then choose **New**.

3. Follow these steps to set up the new payment method:

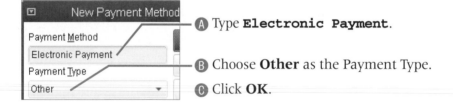

A Type **Electronic Payment**.

B Choose **Other** as the Payment Type.

C Click **OK**.

4. Close the **Payment Method List** window.

Process a Discounted Electronic Payment

Mike Balak has decided to take advantage of the early payment option, and he is paying electronically. You will help Zoe to record this transaction.

5. Click the **Receive Payments** task icon in the Customers area of the Home page.

Receive Payments

6. Follow these steps to record the discounted payment:

Ⓐ Choose **Balak, Mike:Repair Deck** from the list.

Ⓑ Tap Tab, and then type **1318.66** as the amount.

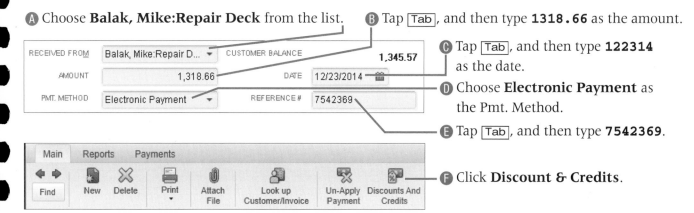

Ⓒ Tap Tab, and then type **122314** as the date.

Ⓓ Choose **Electronic Payment** as the Pmt. Method.

Ⓔ Tap Tab, and then type **7542369**.

Ⓕ Click **Discount & Credits**.

Notice the Underpayment section of this window. Whenever you enter a payment amount that is less than the total amount due, you will see this section. You can then choose how to handle the underpayment. You will apply a discount to the invoice to take care of the underpayment in this case.

7. Click the **drop-down arrow** to choose **Remodel** as the Discount Class.

A<u>m</u>ount of Discount	26.91
Discount <u>A</u>ccount	40199 · Less Discounts given ▾
Discount <u>C</u>lass	Remodel ▾

8. Click **Done** to return to the Receive Payments window.

BTS BRIEF

12000•Undeposited Funds DR 1,318.66; 40199•Less Discounts Given DR 26.91; 11000•Accounts Receivable CR <1,345.57>

---

9. Click **Save & Close** to complete the payment receipt.

Deposit an Electronic Payment

The last step is to record the deposit of the electronic payment into your bank account.

10. Click the **Record Deposits** task icon in the Banking area of the Home page. *The Payments to Deposit window will appear.*

Record Deposits

11. Click the **Electronic Payment** you just entered to select it, and then click **OK**.

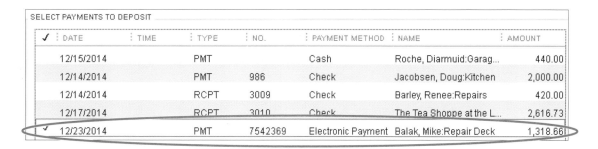

✓	DATE	TIME	TYPE	NO.	PAYMENT METHOD	NAME	AMOUNT
	12/15/2014		PMT		Cash	Roche, Diarmuid:Garag...	440.00
	12/14/2014		PMT	986	Check	Jacobsen, Doug:Kitchen	2,000.00
	12/14/2014		RCPT	3009	Check	Barley, Renee:Repairs	420.00
	12/17/2014		RCPT	3010	Check	The Tea Shoppe at the L...	2,616.73
✓	12/23/2014		PMT	7542369	Electronic Payment	Balak, Mike:Repair Deck	1,318.66

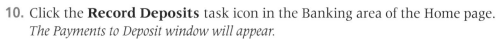

12. Tap Tab , and then type **122314** as the date.

> **BTS BRIEF**
>
> **10100•Checking DR 1,318.66; 12000•Undeposited Funds CR <1,318.66>**

13. Click **Save & Close** to record the deposit to 10100•Checking.

Adjusting Quantity/Value on Hand

There may be times when you have inventory that is no longer in sellable condition. You should remove these items from inventory and expense the amount. Other times you may need to adjust the value of your inventory due to obsolescence or some other reason. Or, you may need to adjust both the quantity and the value of your inventory.

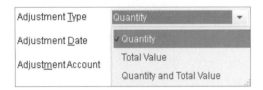

In the Adjust Quantity/Value on Hand window, you can choose the type of the adjustment via a drop-down list.

Adjusting the Quantity of Your Inventory

You can either enter the new quantity on hand (if you have just conducted an annual inventory, this may be the best choice) or the quantity difference (this option works well if you know how many items you have to remove). If you choose to enter the quantity difference, make sure to enter a minus sign in front of the number to show a decrease in the number of items.

Adjusting the Value of Your Inventory

If you don't need to adjust the quantity of your inventory but rather need to adjust the value of your inventory, you can use the same window. As was discussed earlier in this lesson, Quick-Books Pro and Premier use the average cost method of inventory valuation. You can adjust the average cost per inventory item by adjusting the total value of the inventory. Obsolescence or an incorrect beginning cost for inventory may require you to take this step.

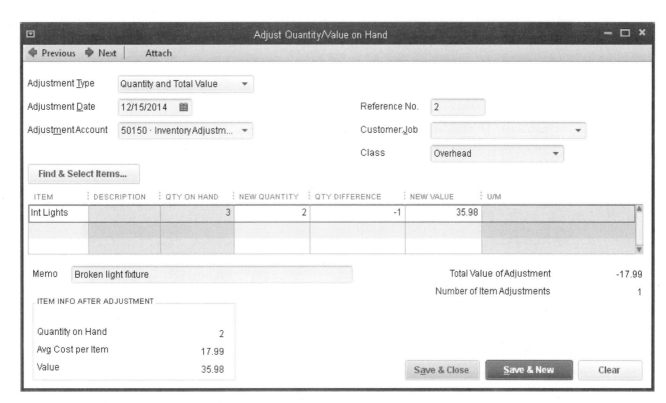

The Adjust Quantity/Value on Hand window

BEHIND THE SCENES

Behind the scenes, you remove the items from the Inventory Asset account and enter them as an Inventory Adjustment to Cost of Goods Sold for the company.

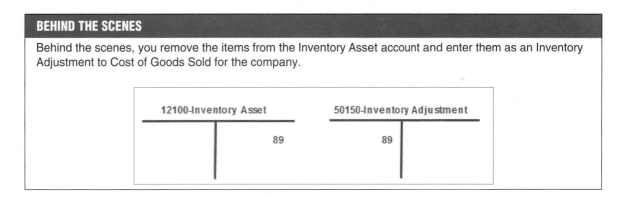

12100-Inventory Asset		50150-Inventory Adjustment	
	89	89	

QUICK REFERENCE	ADJUSTING QUANTITY/VALUE ON HAND
Task	**Procedure**
Adjust quantity or value of inventory items	▪ Choose Vendors→Inventory Activities→Adjust Quantity/Value on Hand. ▪ Choose the adjustment type and date. ▪ Choose Inventory Adjustment as the Adjustment Account; choose an adjustment class. ▪ Choose the desired items, indicate the new quantities and/or values, and type any memos. ▪ Click Save & Close or Save & New.

Make an Inventory Adjustment

When delivering one of the benches to a job site, the bench fell off of the truck and was damaged beyond repair. You will help Zoe to mark this inventory item out of inventory.

1. Click the **Inventory Activities drop-down arrow** in the Company area of the Home page, and then choose **Adjust Quantity/Value On Hand**.

2. Follow these steps to make an inventory adjustment:

Ⓐ Ensure **Quantity** is the Adjustment Type.

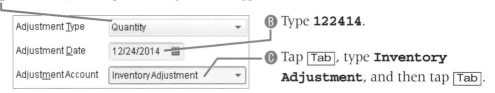

Ⓑ Type **122414**.

Ⓒ Tap Tab, type **Inventory Adjustment**, and then tap Tab.

Inventory Adjustment is a new account, so QuickBooks will prompt you to set it up.

Ⓓ Click **Set Up**.

Ⓔ Type **50150** as the Number.

Ⓕ Click **Save & Close** to create the new account.

Ⓖ Click the **drop-down arrow**, and then choose **Overhead** as the Class.

Ⓗ Click in the **Item** column, and then type **be**.

Ⓘ Tap Tab, and then type **3**.

Ⓙ Click in the **Memo** field and type **Dropped bench off of truck**.

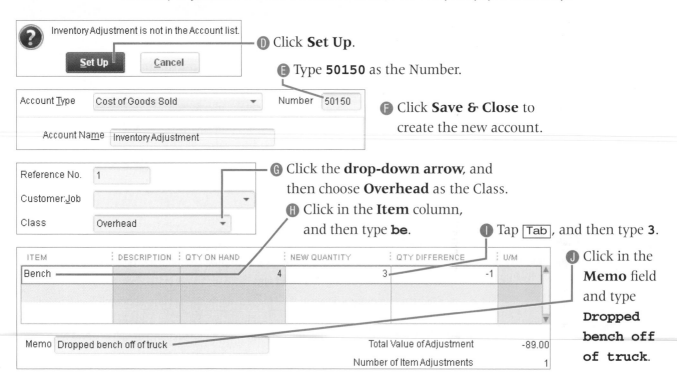

3. Click **Save & Close** to record the inventory adjustment.

Paying Sales Tax

You have been collecting sales tax for your inventory sales. Now it is time to learn how to pay the collected tax to the appropriate tax agencies.

Sales Tax Payable

As you have seen, when you bill a customer and collect sales tax, QuickBooks holds the funds in a current liability account. These taxes are never actually the property of your business (an asset), so you have been using a liabilities payable account as a place to "store" the taxes until it is time to remit them.

When you are ready to pay your sales tax, it is *imperative* that you do so through the Pay Sales Tax window. This is to ensure that the proper liability account is affected behind the scenes when the payment is processed.

When you are ready to pay sales tax, you must use the proper procedure, or you will not "empty" the Sales Tax Payable account behind the scenes.

The Sales Tax Liability Report

You can choose to run a sales tax liability report to see what funds you are holding in your sales tax payable account. This report will give you the values you need to file your sales tax return: total sales, taxable sales, nontaxable sales, and the amount of tax collected.

Advanced Skills

The Manage Sales Tax Window

The Manage Sales Tax window helps you manage all of your sales tax activities and reports easily by providing links to all of the tasks you will be performing when working with sales tax, from setting it up to paying it.

Dealing with Adjustments in Sales Tax

There are many situations that could result in an incorrect amount in the Pay Sales Tax window or on the sales tax liability report. You may have charged a customer a tax rate for the wrong jurisdiction or tax may have been charged for a nontaxable item. There could also be rounding errors, penalties, or credits/ discounts that you need to take into account.

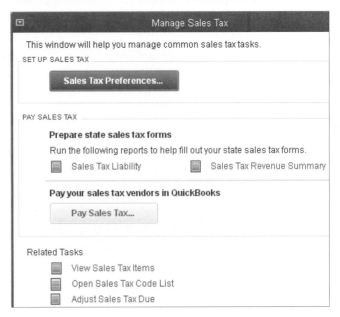

The Manage Sales Tax window helps you deal with all QuickBooks preferences, activities, and reports related to sales tax.

You can make an adjustment to the tax owed through the Pay Sales Tax window or by choosing Adjust Sales Tax Due from the Vendors menu. Make sure that you don't use Sales Tax Payable as the "pay from account." Instead, you should use the following types of accounts:

- **For a rounding error:** You can set up a special account or use the Miscellaneous Expense. Some businesses opt to create a special income account for a negative error or a special expense account for a positive error.
- **For a credit or to apply a discount:** Use an income account such as Other Income.
- **For interest due, fines, or penalties:** Use an expense account such as Interest Expense or Non-deductible Penalties.

If you make an adjustment to the sales tax liability account, you will need to choose the adjustment the next time you pay sales tax in order to get the correct amount to pay.

Changing a Tax Jurisdiction

If a customer is charged sales tax for the wrong jurisdiction, you need to go back to the original transaction and choose the correct sales tax item or group. If you charged tax on a nontaxable item (or vice versa), you need to adjust the invoice or sales receipt where the sale was made. This may require you to issue a credit to the customer if they overpaid or reissue the invoice/receipt (or a statement) if they underpaid.

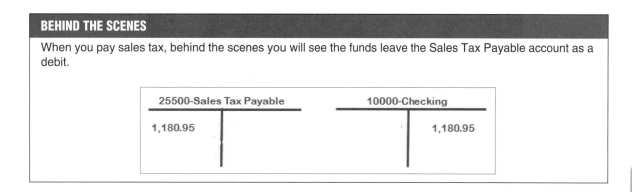

QUICK REFERENCE	PAYING SALES TAX
Task	**Procedure**
Pay sales tax	▪ Choose Vendors→Sales Tax→Pay Sales Tax.
	▪ Choose the bank account from which you will be paying the taxes.
	▪ Enter the date of the check and the date through which to show sales taxes.
	▪ Choose which taxes to pay by clicking in the Pay column; click OK.
Run a sales tax liability report	▪ Choose Reports→Vendors & Payables→Sales Tax Liability.
	▪ Set the correct date range for the report.
Adjust the amount of sales tax owed	▪ Choose Vendors→Sales Tax→Adjust Sales Tax Due.
	▪ Enter the date, vendor, account, amount, and memo; click OK.

DEVELOP YOUR SKILLS 8.8

Pay Sales Tax

In this exercise, you will help Zoe pay to the appropriate tax agencies all the tax collected that is due December 31, 2014. The first step is to run a report to determine how much sales tax is owed and to whom.

1. Click the **Manage Sales Tax** task icon in the Vendors area of the Home page. *QuickBooks displays the Manage Sales Tax window.*

Manage Sales Tax

2. Click the **Sales Tax Liability** link in the Manage Sales Tax window.

3. Click the **Dates drop-down arrow**, and then choose **This Month**.

Take a look at the information this report contains. The information you need to pay and file your taxes is in the last column, Sales Tax Payable as of Dec 31, 2014, which is $1,180.95.

4. Close the **Sales Tax Liability** report.

Pay the Sales Tax

From the report you just ran, you know that Rock Castle owes $1,180.95 as of 12/31/14 to the State Board of Equalization and $0.29 to City of East Bayshore.

5. Click the **Pay Sales Tax** button in the Manage Sales Tax window.

6. Ensure that **10000•Checking** is the Pay From Account.

7. Follow these steps to pay the taxes due:

Ⓐ Tap ⌷Tab⌷, and then type **123114**.

Ⓑ Tap ⌷Tab⌷, and then type **123114** again.

Ⓒ Click the **Pay All Tax** button (note that the button name changes after it has been clicked).

Ⓓ Ensure that the **To be printed** checkbox is checked.

Ⓔ Click **OK**.

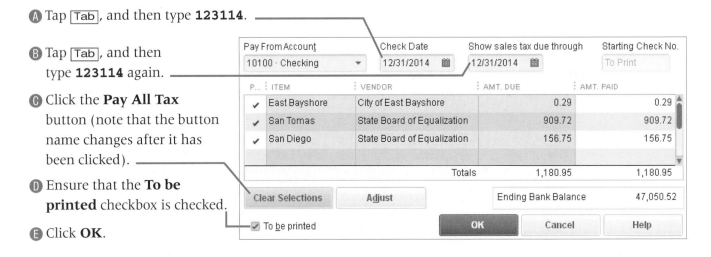

The liability check has now been entered into the queue of checks to be printed.

BTS BRIEF

25500•Sales Tax Payable DR 1,180.95; 10100•Checking CR <1,180.95>

8. Close the **Manage Sales Tax** window.

Producing Inventory, Sales, and Receivables Reports and Graphs

QuickBooks features many preset reports to help you efficiently manage inventory, sales, and receivables. You will produce these reports in much the same way as you have created reports for other aspects of your business.

Physical Inventory Worksheet

Periodically, it is important to physically count your inventory items and to make sure that what is "on the books" is actually what you have in stock. Many businesses do this type of procedure annually and adjust their books accordingly. QuickBooks provides a great report that can aid in this process—the Physical Inventory Worksheet. It shows the name, description, preferred vendor, and on-hand quantity of each item you have in inventory. It also provides a column with blank lines, where you can record what you actually have during a physical inventory count.

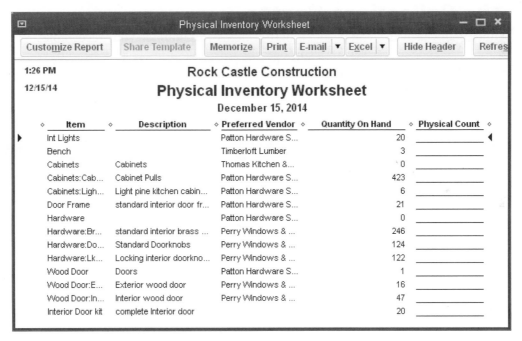

Notice that there is no Description for the inventory items entered earlier. This is because we did not enter that information in the Add/Edit Multiple List Entries window, but you can do so by going back there and adding columns or by editing in the Edit Item window.

The following table lists many reports useful when you work with inventory items.

Inventory Report Name	What it will tell you...
Inventory Valuation Summary	The value of your inventory by item
Inventory Valuation Detail	The details of the transactions that affect the value of inventory
Inventory Stock Status by Item	The inventory items you need to reorder and the current number in stock of each item
Inventory Stock Status by Vendor	Similar to the Inventory Stock Status by Item but arranged by vendor
Physical Inventory Worksheet	A printable worksheet used to count physical inventory or to compare physical quantity to the number QuickBooks has recorded

Receivables Reports

In the Customers & Receivables category of the Report Center, you can see all of the reports designed to help you track and collect the money owed to your company. In addition, you will be able to view a brief description of each of these reports.

The Collections Center

QuickBooks provides you with a tool that helps you manage your receivables—the Collections Center. You can access this tool through the Customer Center and, from it, you can send a batch email to customers with either overdue or almost due invoices. QuickBooks also makes it easy for you to contact customers with overdue invoices by providing the phone number as a part of the Collections Center.

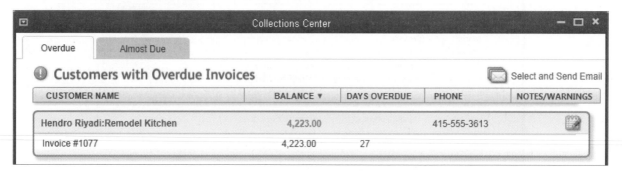

The Collections Center window. Notice the tabs at the top that allow you to switch between Overdue and Almost Due invoices.

Tracking Sales

The Sales area of the Report Center features reports and graphs that help you stay on top of your company's sales. You can choose from reports grouped by Sales by Customer, Sales by Item, and Sales by Rep (if sales reps have been set up). You can also view sales information by job if you have jobs set up for your company. The Sales Graph can graphically display your sales by item, customer, and rep.

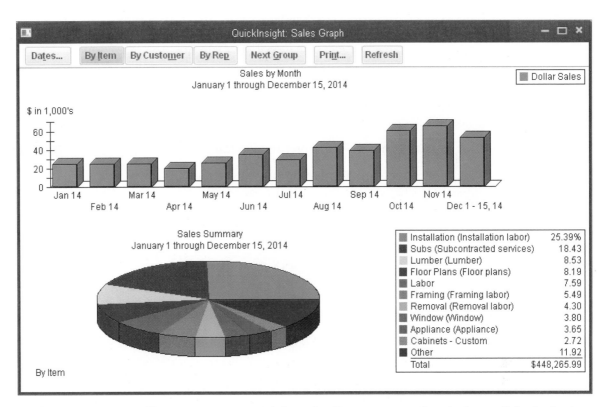

Graphs are a great way to illustrate your company's information. Here, you can see the sales by month for the fiscal year to date as well as the sales by item. Remember that if QuickBooks doesn't provide a preset graph that works for you, you can export your data to Excel and create your graphs there.

QUICK REFERENCE	PRODUCING INVENTORY, RECEIVABLES, AND SALES REPORTS AND GRAPHS
Task	**Procedure**
Display an inventory, receivable or sales report or graph	▪ Open the Report Center. ▪ Choose the category of the report you wish to run. ▪ Click the report; click the Display button.
Display the Collections Center	▪ Open the Customer Center. ▪ Click the Collections Center button on the toolbar.

Display the Collections Center and Create Inventory and Sales Reports

In this exercise, you will help Zoe run a variety of reports and graphs and take a look at the Collections Center. You will begin by taking a look at the Collections Center to see what is owed to the company.

1. Click the **Customers** button on the Icon Bar.

2. Click the **Collections Center** button on the toolbar.

The Collections Center opens with the Overdue tab selected.

3. Click the **Almost Due** tab.
You can now see the invoice that is close to being due.

4. Close the **Collections Center**, and then the **Customer Center**.

Determine the Inventory Value

This report will show Zoe the dollar value (based on purchase price) of the company's inventory.

5. Choose **Reports→Inventory→Inventory Valuation Summary**.

6. Tap ⓐ to set All as the date range for the report.
The report will show the number of items you have in inventory as well as their asset value (cost) and retail value.

7. Close the report.

Determine Which Items to Reorder

This report will help Zoe determine when she needs to order additional items.

8. Choose **Reports→Inventory→Inventory Stock Status by Item**.

9. Tap ⓐ to set the date range to All.

Rock Castle Construction
Inventory Stock Status by Item
All Transactions

	Item Description	Pref Vendor	Reorder Pt	On Hand	U/M	Order	On PO	Next Deliv	Sales/Week
Inventory									
Int Lights	▸	Patton Hard...	15	20			3	12/19/2014	0 ◂
Bench		Timberloft L...	1	3			0		1.4
Cabinets									
Cabinet Pulls	Cabinet Pulls	Patton Hard...	15	423	ea		0		0.6
Light Pine	Light pine kitchen c...	Patton Hard...	0	6			0		0.1
Cabinets - Other	Cabinets	Thomas Kitc...	15	0		✓	0		0
Total Cabinets				429	ea		0		0.7

Notice that a checkmark appears in the Order column when it is time to place an order.

10. Close the **Inventory Stock Status by Item** window.

Create a Sales Graph

Finally, you will create a graph that will show you all of the sales by month and the sales by customer for the fiscal year to date.

11. Choose **Reports→Sales→Sales Graph**.

12. Click the **By Customer** button on the toolbar.

Notice the sales graph in the lower area of the window by customer. There are so many customers for the company that you will have to use QuickZoom to drill down to those classified as "Other."

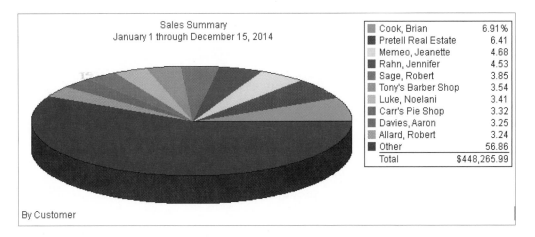

13. Close the **Sales Graph** window.

14. Choose the appropriate option for your situation:

   ■ If you are continuing on to the next lesson or to the end-of-lesson exercises, leave QuickBooks open.

   ■ If you are finished working in QuickBooks for now, choose **File→Exit**.

Concepts Review

Concepts Review   http://labyrinthelab.com/qb13

To check your knowledge of the key concepts introduced in this lesson, complete the Concepts Review quiz by going to the URL listed above.

Reinforce Your Skills

Before you begin the Reinforce Your Skills exercises, complete one of these options:

- *Open* **[Your Name]'s Tea Shoppe at the Lake, Lesson 7** *or Tea Shoppe at the Lake, Lesson 8 from your file storage location.*

- *Restore* **Tea Shoppe at the Lake, Lesson 8 (Portable)** *from your file storage location. Make sure to place your name as the first word in the company filename (e.g., Susie's Tea Shoppe at the Lake, Lesson 8).*

REINFORCE YOUR SKILLS 8.1
Set Up Inventory and Sales Tax Items

In this exercise, you will set up sales tax and inventory items for Susie. The first step is to turn on the sales tax preference and set up a sales tax item.

1. Choose **Edit→Preferences**.

2. Display the **Company Preferences** tab of the Sales Tax category.

3. Turn on the **sales tax preference**.

4. Set up a new sales tax item using the following information.

Sales Tax Name	`SD County`
Description	`San Diego County Sales Tax`
Tax Rate	`8.25%`
Tax Agency	`San Diego County Treasurer` (Quick Add as a vendor)

5. Click **OK** to add the new sales tax item.

6. Choose **SD County** as the most common sales tax item.

7. Click **OK** to close the Preferences window and accept the new preference.

8. Click **OK** in the Updating Sales Tax window; then, click **OK** to acknowledge the closing of all open windows.

Turn On Inventory Preferences

Susie has decided to start offering custom-built woodworking items for sale to her customers. You will now help her set up her QuickBooks file to deal with her inventory along with the new income and expenses involved.

9. Choose **Edit→Preferences**.

10. Click the **Items & Inventory** category, and then click the **Company Preferences** tab.

11. Click in the box to the left of **Inventory and purchase orders are active**.

12. Click **OK** to close the Preferences window; click **OK** to close the Warning window, if necessary.

Create a New Income Account

The next step for Susie to take is to set up a separate income account for her product sales.

13. Choose **Lists→Chart of Accounts**.

14. Click the **Account** menu button, and then choose **New**.

15. Choose **Income** as the account type, and then click **Continue**.

16. Type **Craft Sales**, and then click **Save & Close**.

17. Close the **Chart of Accounts**.

Create a New Inventory Item

Now Susie needs to set up an inventory item to be able to sell her product using the sales forms.

18. Choose **Lists→Item List**, click the **Item** menu button, and then choose **New**.

19. Choose **Inventory Part** as the item type.

20. Use the following illustration to create the new item; click **OK** when you are finished.

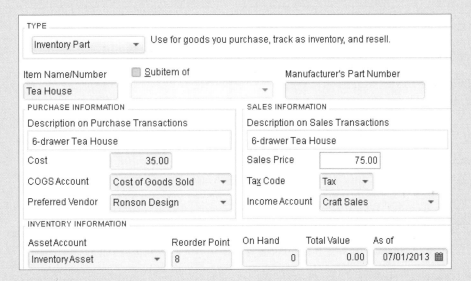

21. Close the **Item List**.

Create Purchase Orders and Receive Items

In this exercise, you will help Susie order and receive inventory items. You will begin by creating a purchase order for the tea houses.

1. Choose **Vendors→Create Purchase Orders**.

2. Use the following illustration to enter the information into the purchase order.

3. Click **Save & Close**.

Receive the Items

The items have arrived without the bill, so Susie needs to receive them into QuickBooks.

4. Choose **Vendors→Receive Items**.

5. Choose **Ronson Design** as the vendor, tap ⟦Tab⟧, and then click **Yes** to receive against an open purchase order.

6. Click in the **checkmark** column to the left of the purchase order dated 7/1/2013, and then click **OK**.

7. Change the date of the **Item Receipt** to **7/5/2013**, and then click **Save & Close**.

Receive the Bill

The bill for the houses has just arrived, so it is time to enter it into QuickBooks.

8. Choose **Vendors→Enter Bill for Received Items**, and then choose **Ronson Design** as the vendor.

9. Click on the Item Receipt dated **7/5/13** to select it, and then click **OK**.

10. Tap ⟦Tab⟧, and then tap ⟦+⟧ until the date reads **7/8/2013**.

11. Enter **Inv. #TSL-1** as the Ref. No. and Memo, and then enter **Net 15** as the terms.

12. Click **Save & Close**, clicking **Yes** to agree to change the transaction.

13. Click **Yes** to permanently change the information for Ronson Designs.

Sell Inventory Items

Once the products have been entered into inventory, it is time to start selling! In this exercise, you will record inventory sales.

1. Choose **Customers→Enter Sales Receipts**.

2. Use the following illustration to enter the information for the sales receipt.

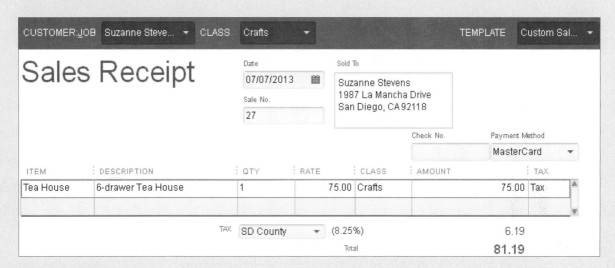

3. Click **Save & New** to record the sale.

Record Sales from a Craft Fair

Susie rented a booth at a local craft fair and sold her tea houses. You will now help her to enter the sales.

4. Choose **Crafts** as the Class.

5. Enter **7/10/2013** as the date of the sale, and then **Cash** as the Payment Method.

6. Choose **Tea House** as the Item, with a quantity of **5**.

7. Enter **Craft Fair Sales** as the memo.

8. Click **Save & Close** to record the sale.

Process Payments and Pay Sales Tax

In this exercise, you will help Susie deposit all of the payments received into the Checking account and then pay the sales tax due.

1. Choose **Banking→Make Deposits**.
   The Payments to Deposit window will appear.

2. Click the **Select All** button, and then click **OK**.

3. Change the date of the deposit to **7/23/2013**, and then click **Save & Close**.
   All of the payments waiting in the Undeposited Funds account have now been deposited into the Checking account.

Pay Sales Tax

4. Choose **Vendors→Sales Tax→Pay Sales Tax**.

5. Ensure **Checking** is the account from which the payment will come.

6. Set the **Check Date** and **Show sales tax due through** to **7/31/13**.

7. Choose for the check to be **printed** and to **pay all tax due**.

8. Click **OK** to send the liability check to the queue to be printed.

REINFORCE YOUR SKILLS 8.5
Adjust Inventory

In this exercise, you will help Susie make an adjustment to her inventory because she provided a tea house to a silent auction in exchange for advertising for her business.

1. Choose **Vendors→Inventory Activities→Adjust Quantity/Value on Hand**.

2. Set the Adjustment Type to **Quantity**, and the date to **7/26/2013**.

3. Choose **Advertising and Promotion** as the Adjustment Account, and then **Other** as the Class.

4. Click in the **Item** column, and then type **t**.

5. Tap ⌜Tab⌝, and then type **8** in the New Quantity column.

6. Click in the **Memo** field, and then type **Donation to Lake San Marcos Elementary silent auction**.

7. Click **Save & Close**.

REINFORCE YOUR SKILLS 8.6
Produce Reports

In this exercise, you will create an inventory report that details the quantity and value of inventory on hand. Then you will change information on a source transaction using QuickZoom.

1. Choose **Reports→Inventory→Inventory Valuation Detail**.

2. Tap ⌞a⌟ to set the date range to All.

3. Using **QuickZoom**, go to the bill for the tea houses.

4. Change the terms of the bill to **Net 30**.

5. **Save the bill** with the changes, choosing to have the new terms appear next time and become a permanent change to the vendor record.

6. Click **Yes** to refresh the report.

7. **Close the report**, choosing not to memorize it.

8. Choose the appropriate option for your situation:

   ■ If you are continuing on to the next lesson or the rest of the end-of-lesson exercises, leave QuickBooks open.

   ■ If you are finished working in QuickBooks for now, choose **File→Exit**.

Apply Your Skills

Before you begin the Apply Your Skills exercises, complete one of these options:

■ *Open* **[Your name] Wet Noses Veterinary Clinic, Lesson 7** *or* **Wet Noses Veterinary Clinic, Lesson 8** *from your file storage location.*

■ *Restore* **Wet Noses Veterinary Clinic, Lesson 8 (Portable**) *from your file storage location. Make sure to place your name as the first word in the company filename (e.g., Sadie's Wet Noses Veterinary Clinic, Lesson 8).*

APPLY YOUR SKILLS 8.1
Set Up Sales Tax and Inventory Items

In this exercise, you will help Sadie set up sales tax and inventory items that she will begin selling to her customers. You will help Dr. James to set up to collect sales tax on inventory items. Service items will remain not taxable.

1. Open the **Preferences** window and set the preference to collect sales tax.

2. Set up a new sales tax item (**King County Sales Tax** for **10%**, payable to **King County Treasurer**), and then set it as the **most common sales tax item**.

3. Click **OK** to close the Preferences window and accept the new preference.

4. Choose to make **all existing customers taxable** but not all existing non-inventory and inventory parts.

Turn On the Preference and Create a New Income Account

Before you can set up inventory items, you must turn on the preference and have an income account for the item sales to flow into.

5. Open the **Preferences** window, and then turn on the **Inventory and purchase order** feature; click OK in the Preferences window.

6. Choose **Company→Home Page**.

7. Open the **Chart of Accounts**, and then create a new income account called **Sales**. Close the **Chart of Accounts** when finished.

Create New Inventory Items

Now you will set up the new items that will be sold.

8. Using either the **Item List** or the **Add/Edit Multiple List Entries** window, create the following inventory part items.

Item Name	Toothbrush	Chew Toy	Cat Collar
Purchase/Sales Description	Dog toothbrush and paste kit	The great indestructible ball!	Designer cat collar
Cost	6.49	3.71	8.00
Preferred Vendor	Seattle Vet Supply	Bothell Pet Supply Co.	Take a Walk
Sales Price	14.99	8.99	19.99
Income Account	Sales	Sales	Sales
Reorder Point	15	20	10

9. Close the **Item List** or **Add/Edit Multiple List Entries** window.

APPLY YOUR SKILLS 8.2

Purchase and Receive Inventory Items

In this exercise, you will help Dr. James purchase and receive her new inventory items in order to have them in stock.

Create Purchase Orders

First you must create the purchase orders.

1. Open the **Create Purchase Orders** window.

2. Order 25 toothbrushes from Seattle Vet Supply on 7/1/13 using Product Sales as the Class.

3. Click **Save & New**.

4. Order 40 chew toys from Bothell Pet Supply Co. on 7/2/13 using Product Sales as the Class.

5. Click **Save & New**.

6. Order 15 cat collars from Take a Walk on 7/2/13 using Product Sales as the Class.

7. Click **Save & Close**.

Receive the Items

You will now receive the items into inventory.

8. You received all 25 toothbrushes from Seattle Vet Supply on 7/7/2013, along with the bill. Receive the items and enter the bill, making sure to receive against the purchase order you created. Click **Save Anyway** when the Items not assigned classes window appears. (It will appear as you have accounts prefilled on the Expenses tab with no amounts allocated to them.)

9. You received 33 of the chew toys from Bothell Pet Supply Co. The rest are on backorder, so you did not receive the bill yet. Receive these 33 items into inventory on 7/8/2013. Click **Save Anyway** when the Items not assigned classes window appears. (It will appear as you have accounts prefilled on the Expenses tab with no amounts allocated to them.)

10. You received all 15 of the cat collars from Take a Walk on 7/12/2013, along with the bill. Included on the bill was a shipping charge of $12.95. Receive the items into inventory and enter the bill. Create a new Postage and Delivery expense account for the shipping charge, and use **Product Sales** as the class.

11. On 7/14/2013, you received a bill for the chew toys you received on 7/8/2013, along with a shipping charge of $13.50 and a note stating that they would not be charging you a shipping charge for the backordered chew toys.

12. Receive the seven chew toys that were on backorder, along with the bill, on 7/25/2013.

APPLY YOUR SKILLS 8.3

Sell Inventory

In this exercise, you will help Sadie process sales for the new inventory items.

Sell Inventory

Jill Ann Tank came in to pick up two of the new cat collars she heard you talking about.

1. Using an **Enter Sales Receipts** window, sell Jill Ann Tank two of the new designer cat collars on 7/14/2013, choosing Product Sales as the Class. She pays with cash.

Sell Inventory with Discount Payment Terms

One of the dog handlers from King County Sheriff decided to get toothbrushes and chew toys for the dogs. You will create an invoice using the Police Dog price level and discount payment terms.

2. Sell seven toothbrushes and seven chew toys to King County Sheriff K-9 Unit on 7/15/2013. The Terms should be 2% 10 Net 30 and the class Product Sales. Use the Police Dog price level for both line items. Choose to not make the change in Terms permanent.

Sell Inventory with Service and Non-Inventory Items

Inventory items can be sold on invoices with any other type of item. You will create an invoice that includes service, inventory, and non-inventory items.

3. Stacy LiMarzi brought in his cat, Reagan, for a scheduled new-patient exam on 7/19/2013. Create an invoice for him for the New Patient Exam, a FIV/FeLV test, and a dose of Revolution for a cat. Stacy noticed the new cat collars in the lobby and decided to get one for Reagan as well. Only the collar is taxable.

Receive Payments for Inventory Sales

Now you will receive payment on the two invoices you just created.

4. Open the **Receive Payments** window, and then choose King County Sheriff K-9 Unit as the customer. Receive check 7796 for $162.87 to pay for invoice 178 on 7/21/2013, applying the 2 percent discount of $3.32 since the payment was received within 10 days. Create a new income account called Less Discounts Given as the Discount Account, and Product Sales should be the Discount Class, clicking Save & New when you have entered all of the information correctly.

5. Choose Stacy LiMarzi as the customer and 7/22/2013 as the Date. Stacy has paid the entire amount of invoice 179 with check 448. **Save & Close** the transaction.

Pay Sales Tax

You will now help Sadie to pay the sales tax that she collected.

6. Choose **Vendors→Sales Tax→Pay Sales Tax**.

7. Set the **Check Date** and **Show sales tax due through** to **7/31/13**, ensuring that **Checking** is the payment account.

8. Choose for the check to be **printed**, and to **pay all tax due**.

9. Click **OK** to send the liability check to the queue to be printed.

Answer Questions with Reports

In this exercise, you will answer questions for Dr. James by running reports. You may wish to display the Report Center in List View to help you answer the questions. Ask your instructor if you should print the reports, print (save) them as PDF files, export them to Excel, or simply display them on the screen.

1. How many inventory items do we currently have in stock?

2. How much is the inventory that we have in stock worth?

3. What is the sales amount for each customer during the month of July 2013?

4. What item have we "sold" the most of during the month of July 2013?

5. Who should we be making collections calls on as of 6/30/2013? Can the phone number be included on the report?

6. Submit your reports based on the guidelines provided by your instructor.

7. Choose the appropriate option for your situation:

   ■ If you are continuing on to the next lesson or the Critical Thinking exercises, leave QuickBooks open.

   ■ If you are finished working in QuickBooks for now, choose **File→Exit**.

Advanced Skills

Critical Thinking

In the course of working through the following Critical Thinking exercises, you will be utilizing various skills taught in this and previous lesson(s). Take your time and think carefully about the tasks presented to you. Turn back to the lesson content if you need assistance.

8.1 Sort Through the Stack

Before You Begin: Restore the **Monkey Business, Lesson 8 (Portable)** *file from your storage location. (Remember that you are to leave the password field blank for Mary.) You also have the option of opening either the final file from Critical Thinking 7.1 or Monkey Business, Lesson 8 from your storage location.*

You have been hired by Mary Minard to help her with her organization's books. She is the owner of Monkey Business, a nonprofit organization that provides low-income students with help in preparing for college placement exams and applying for scholarships. You have just sat down at her desk and found a pile of papers. It is your job to sort through the papers and make sense of what you find, entering information into QuickBooks whenever appropriate and answering any other questions in a word-processing document saved as **Critical Thinking 8.1**. Remember, you are digging through papers on a desk, so it is up to you to determine the correct order in which to complete the tasks.

- Sticky note from Mary: We are going to start stocking SAT Prep guides and College 101 texts. I would like to see if we can set them up in QuickBooks. Our accountant told me that we should use the "average cost" method to keep track of our inventory. Will we be able to track this in QuickBooks? (Explain your answer.)

- Packing slip and bill from Woods Publishing: Enter items into inventory and enter the bill for payment on 8/4/2013. Monkey Business received 40 copies of The Ultimate SAT Prep Guide, and a $35 shipping charge was included in the bill.

- Note from Mary: We had a water leak on 8/10/2013 and three copies of College 101 were damaged and cannot be resold. Please figure out a way to take them out of inventory in QuickBooks.

- Scribbled on a scrap of paper: If we can track inventory in QuickBooks, please set up "The Ultimate SAT Prep Guide" as an inventory item, the cost from Woods Publishing is $15.34 and the resale price is $29.95. (There is no sales tax in Oregon.) Also, please set up another inventory item to track "College 101" texts. The cost from Woods Publishing is $18.73 and the resale price is $32.95. As of 8/1/2013, order 40 copies of the SAT Prep text and 50 copies of College 101.

- Handwritten invoice: Four copies of "The Ultimate SAT Prep Guide" for a semiprivate prep session at Achievement, Inc., dated 8/6/2013, due 2% 10 Net 30.

- Packing slip from Woods Publishing: Dated 8/5/2013 for receipt of 23 copies of College 101; the rest are on backorder.

- Photocopy of a check: Check 2007 from Achievement, Inc. dated 8/10/2013 for $117.40 and with a memo stating the company took advantage of the 2 percent discount.

- Scribbled note from Mary: Can you produce a report for me that shows the value of the inventory we currently have in stock? How about the number of each item?

8.2 Tackle the Tasks

Now is your chance to work a little more with Rock Castle Construction and apply the skills that you have learned in this lesson to accomplish additional tasks. Open or restore the **Critical Thinking 8.2** company or portable company file from your file storage location, or open the company file you used in the Develop Your Skills exercises for this lesson. Then, enter the following tasks.

Create Inventory Item	Item Name: Porch Light; Description: Standard Porch Light; Cost: 23.87; Sales Amt.: 40.00; COGS: 50100•Cost of Goods Sold; Pref. Vendor: Patton Hardware Supplies; Income Acct: 40140•Materials Income; Asset Acct.: 12100•Inventory Asset; Reorder: 10; Qty on Hand: 0.
Create Purchase Order	Create a PO to purchase 12 of the porch lights you just entered as an inventory item on 12/19/14.
Receive Items	Receive the porch lights with the bill on 12/23/14. Add a $30 shipping charge to the bill with Overhead as the Class.
Sell Items	Sell two porch lights to Mike Balak for his deck repair job on 12/24/14, terms 2% 10 Net 30. Class is remodel and terms are only for this invoice.
Receive Payment	Receive an electronic payment, 758946, from Mike Balak for the porch lights on 12/28/14. Mike has taken advantage of the early payment discount; use Overhead as the class for the discount amount. Deposit the payment to Checking on the same day.
Adjust Inventory	An interior light was dropped on a job, so you need to mark one interior light out of inventory on 12/27/14, using Overhead as the class.
Run Reports	Create a report that shows a summary of the aging for Rock Castle's receivable (i.e., A/R Aging Summary).

You may use the company file from this exercise for the Develop Your Skills exercises in the next lesson if you wish.

8.3 Use the Web as a Learning Tool

Throughout this book, you will be provided with an opportunity to use the Internet as a learning tool by completing WebQuests. According to the original creators of WebQuests, as described on their website (WebQuest.org), a WebQuest is "an inquiry-oriented activity in which most or all of the information used by learners is drawn from the web." To complete the WebQuest projects in this book, navigate to the student resource center and choose the WebQuest for the lesson on which you are currently working. The subject of each WebQuest will be relevant to the material found in the lesson.

WebQuest Subject: Learning about sales tax where you do business

Using QuickBooks for Payroll

LESSON OBJECTIVES

After studying this lesson, you will be able to:

- Set up QuickBooks to run payroll
- Manage the Employees List
- Create paychecks
- Track and pay payroll liabilities
- Process payroll forms
- Input information from an outside payroll service into QuickBooks

Payroll is a very sensitive subject as it affects people's livelihoods. As an employer, you should be well-informed of all the payroll options and well-equipped to efficiently run payroll for your business. In this lesson, you will examine how QuickBooks deals with payroll, how to manage the Employees List so you can create paychecks and track payroll liabilities, and how to process payroll forms. In addition, you will look at how to deal with payroll if you choose to use an outside service to handle it for you.

Rock Castle Construction

Rock Castle Construction has been doing so well that it needs to hire two more employees to help out. Zoe knows that Alan has been using QuickBooks to run the company's payroll, so she will enter the new employees into the Employees List and create paychecks for them. She will also pay the payroll liabilities and examine payroll options to make sure that the company is using the option that is right for it.

The Employees area of the Home page provides task icons that will help you with payroll and time-tracking tasks.

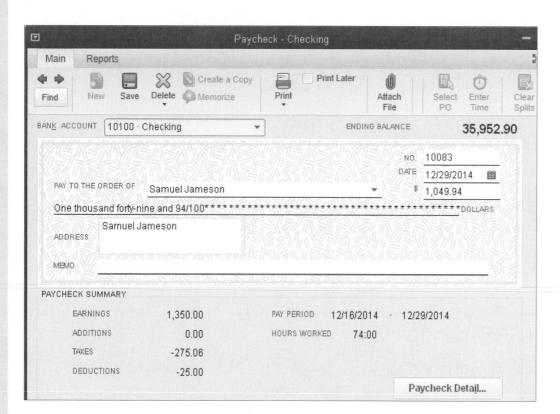

 This lesson teaches how to use QuickBooks to run payroll for a company using a basic service. You must contact your local tax agency to determine what tax laws apply to you and to whom you should submit your taxes. Do not use the specific percentages, vendors, or amounts shown, even if it is from your local jurisdiction, because tax laws change all the time! It is your responsibility to stay informed, either on your own or through a paid service (such as those offered by Intuit).

Setting Up QuickBooks to Run Payroll

In this section, you will look at the payroll options in QuickBooks and learn how to properly set up payroll items.

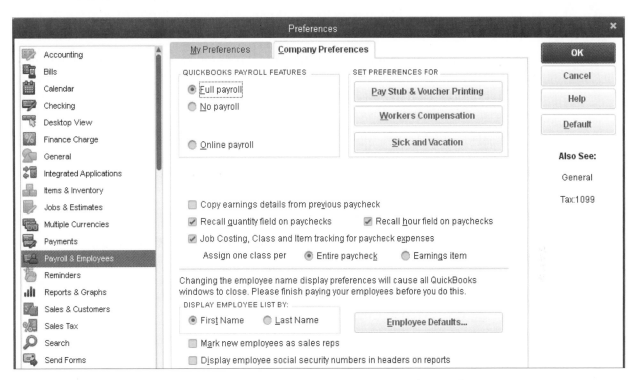

Notice all of the preferences the company administrator has the opportunity to set for payroll.

Payroll Recordkeeping in QuickBooks

In order to produce all of the required federal, state, and local payroll forms and reports, QuickBooks keeps a separate set of records for payroll. This separate set of records tracks payroll liabilities, paychecks (and the items listed on them), and taxes. Due to this method of payroll recordkeeping, only those transactions entered via QuickBooks' payroll features will affect payroll reporting.

Evaluating Payroll Options

QuickBooks payroll offers five options: Manual, Basic, Enhanced, Enhanced for Accountants, and Assisted Payroll. Each option has its pros and cons, and all but the Manual option have an associated fee for the service. Intuit does not recommend the Manual option, as it requires you to stay on top of all tax law changes and there is a higher likelihood of errors and resulting penalties when you have to enter everything yourself. If you choose to use the Assisted Service option, QuickBooks has a "No Penalties" Guarantee in which Intuit will pay any penalties you incur if you provide proper information in a timely manner and have sufficient funds in your bank account.

You may be wondering if it makes sense for you to do your own payroll. The last section in this lesson will provide you with information regarding how you can use QuickBooks for payroll that is run by an outside service and then entered into your QuickBooks company.

 If you are using QuickBooks for a Canadian company, Intuit produces a separate line of products for the Canadian market that addresses multiple currencies and Canadian payroll regulations. Find more information at http://quickbooks.ca/.

If you would like to learn more about the payroll options available through QuickBooks, check out the link on the student resource center. QuickBooks can change its payroll options at any time, so it is advised that you check out the website to ensure that you are dealing with the most current information.

QuickBooks is not ideal for all companies' payroll needs. If multiple states require you run payroll for an individual employee, or you withhold a certain percentage of wages on paychecks, using QuickBooks for payroll may not be the best solution for you.

The Payroll Setup Interview

In order to set up payroll in QuickBooks, you are provided with a Payroll Setup Interview that will walk you through all of the steps to make sure you set up taxes, compensation, and benefits correctly. After the interview leads you through the steps to set up your payroll items, it will help you to set up your employees and enter historical amounts so you can begin doing your company's payroll in QuickBooks.

Payroll Items

Anything you wish to include on a paycheck—such as wages, taxes, employee loans, and 401(k) withholdings—must first be set up as a payroll item. The majority of payroll mistakes are made due to payroll items not being set up properly.

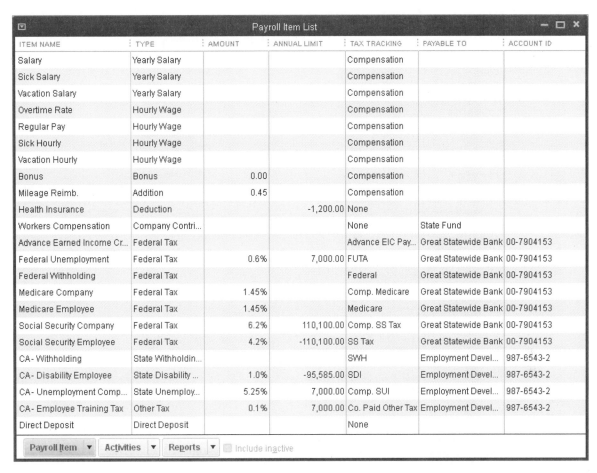

ITEM NAME	TYPE	AMOUNT	ANNUAL LIMIT	TAX TRACKING	PAYABLE TO	ACCOUNT ID
Salary	Yearly Salary			Compensation		
Sick Salary	Yearly Salary			Compensation		
Vacation Salary	Yearly Salary			Compensation		
Overtime Rate	Hourly Wage			Compensation		
Regular Pay	Hourly Wage			Compensation		
Sick Hourly	Hourly Wage			Compensation		
Vacation Hourly	Hourly Wage			Compensation		
Bonus	Bonus	0.00		Compensation		
Mileage Reimb.	Addition	0.45		Compensation		
Health Insurance	Deduction		-1,200.00	None		
Workers Compensation	Company Contri...			None	State Fund	
Advance Earned Income Cr...	Federal Tax			Advance EIC Pay...	Great Statewide Bank	00-7904153
Federal Unemployment	Federal Tax	0.6%	7,000.00	FUTA	Great Statewide Bank	00-7904153
Federal Withholding	Federal Tax			Federal	Great Statewide Bank	00-7904153
Medicare Company	Federal Tax	1.45%		Comp. Medicare	Great Statewide Bank	00-7904153
Medicare Employee	Federal Tax	1.45%		Medicare	Great Statewide Bank	00-7904153
Social Security Company	Federal Tax	6.2%	110,100.00	Comp. SS Tax	Great Statewide Bank	00-7904153
Social Security Employee	Federal Tax	4.2%	-110,100.00	SS Tax	Great Statewide Bank	00-7904153
CA- Withholding	State Withholdin...			SWH	Employment Devel...	987-6543-2
CA- Disability Employee	State Disability ...	1.0%	-95,585.00	SDI	Employment Devel...	987-6543-2
CA- Unemployment Comp...	State Unemploy...	5.25%	7,000.00	Comp. SUI	Employment Devel...	987-6543-2
CA- Employee Training Tax	Other Tax	0.1%	7,000.00	Co. Paid Other Tax	Employment Devel...	987-6543-2
Direct Deposit	Direct Deposit			None		

The Payroll Item List displays all of the payroll items, from compensation to taxes and other deductions.

If you need to add payroll items at a later date, you can always return to the QuickBooks Payroll Setup Interview or access the Payroll Item List from the menu bar.

Making Payroll Data More Meaningful

When you turn on the payroll preference in QuickBooks, the payroll expense and liability accounts are created for you. QuickBooks then automatically routes payroll items set up through the QuickBooks Payroll Setup to these accounts. If you wish to provide more meaningful information in your reports and make troubleshooting more user-friendly, you may want to consider setting up subaccounts for the payroll accounts QuickBooks creates for you. Once you create these subaccounts, you must remap each payroll item to the correct one through the Payroll Item List.

Verifying Correct Payroll Item Setup

To verify that payroll items are set up correctly and mapped to the correct accounts, you need to run a payroll item listing report. If you see either Payroll Liability-Other or Payroll Expense-Other displayed on a balance sheet or P&L, you know that you have a payroll item mapped to a parent account rather than to a subaccount.

Rock Castle Construction
Payroll Item Listing

Payroll Item	Type	Amount	Limit	Expense Account	Liability Account	Tax Tracking
Salary	Yearly Salary			62710 · Gross Wages		Compensation
Sick Salary	Yearly Salary			62710 · Gross Wages		Compensation
Vacation Salary	Yearly Salary			62710 · Gross Wages		Compensation
Overtime Rate	Hourly Wage			62710 · Gross Wages		Compensation
Regular Pay	Hourly Wage			62710 · Gross Wages		Compensation
Sick Hourly	Hourly Wage			62710 · Gross Wages		Compensation
Vacation Hourly	Hourly Wage			62710 · Gross Wages		Compensation
Bonus	Bonus	0.00		62710 · Gross Wages		Compensation
Mileage Reimb.	Addition	0.45		62710 · Gross Wages		Compensation
Health Insurance	Deduction		1,200.00		24100 · Emp. Health Ins Pa...	None
Workers Compensation	Company Contrib...			62130 · Work Comp	24080 · Worker's Compens...	None
Advance Earned Income C...	Federal Tax				24030 · AEIC Payable	Advance EIC Paym...
Federal Unemployment	Federal Tax	0.8%	7,000.00	62730 · FUTA Expense	24040 · FUTA Payable	FUTA
Federal Withholding	Federal Tax				24010 · Federal Withholding	Federal
Medicare Company	Federal Tax	1.45%		62720 · Payroll Taxes	24020 · FICA Payable	Comp. Medicare
Medicare Employee	Federal Tax	1.45%			24020 · FICA Payable	Medicare
Social Security Company	Federal Tax	6.2%	106,800.00	62720 · Payroll Taxes	24020 · FICA Payable	Comp. SS Tax
Social Security Employee	Federal Tax	6.2%	106,800.00		24020 · FICA Payable	SS Tax
CA - Withholding	State Withholding...				24050 · State Withholding	SWH
CA - Disability Employee	State Disability Tax	1.1%	93,316.00		24070 · State Disability Pay...	SDI
CA - Unemployment Comp...	State Unemploym...	5.25%	7,000.00	62740 · SUTA Expen...	24060 · SUTA Payable	Comp. SUI
CA - Employee Training Tax	Other Tax	0.1%	7,000.00	62740 · SUTA Expen...	24060 · SUTA Payable	Co. Paid Other Tax
Direct Deposit	Direct Deposit				24090 · Direct Deposit Liab...	None

Notice that the Payroll Item Listing report shows you what happens behind the scenes with expense and liability accounts when you use a payroll item.

Common Mistakes When Using QuickBooks for Payroll

Two very common mistakes people make when using QuickBooks for payroll are:

- Making a payroll liabilities adjustment with a journal entry
- Paying the liabilities with a "regular check" rather than a liability check similar to what you used when paying sales tax

In both cases, the Chart of Accounts will be affected but the separate payroll records that QuickBooks keeps will not be. If you have used a regular check for payroll liabilities, you will need to make an adjustment in the Liability Adjustment window, from where you can choose for QuickBooks to not affect the Chart of Accounts.

Another very common error is for people to set up their payroll items incorrectly. If you do choose to use subaccounts and remap your payroll accounts manually, be very careful to map the payroll items correctly!

Entering Historical Amounts

If you are beginning to use the QuickBooks payroll feature for existing employees who have received at least one paycheck from you (and it is not the first day of January), you must enter the payroll history amounts. This will ensure that QuickBooks properly calculates taxes with thresholds. It also ensures that you will be able to produce accurate W-2s at the end of the year.

QuickBooks offers step-by-step help to assist you in entering the required payroll history. Before you begin setting up historical amounts, make sure you have:

- Prior-period paychecks
- Prior liability payments

Step-by-step help for this task is accessible through the QuickBooks Payroll Setup Interview. Once you have entered the information, you will have the opportunity to reconcile and verify your data to ensure it is correct.

 Visualize!

Tab: Other Topics
Topic: Payroll overview

QUICK REFERENCE	PREPARING TO USE QUICKBOOKS TO RUN PAYROLL
Task	**Procedure**
Turn on QuickBooks payroll preferences	■ Choose Edit→Preferences. ■ Click the Payroll & Employees category; click the Company Preferences tab. ■ Click in the circle to the left of Full Payroll; click OK.
Sign up for a QuickBooks payroll service	■ Choose Employees→Payroll Service Options→Order Payroll Service. ■ Click the Learn More button or dial the indicated phone number.
Access the Payroll Setup Interview	■ Choose Employees→Payroll Setup. ■ Follow the interview to complete the process by answering questions and clicking the Continue button.
Create subaccounts for payroll accounts	■ Choose Lists→Chart of Accounts, right-click the desired item, and then choose New Account. ■ Create Other Current Liability subaccounts for your Payroll Liabilities account. ■ Create Expense subaccounts for your Payroll Expenses account.
Edit payroll items	■ Choose Lists→Payroll Item List; double-click the desired item. ■ Follow the steps on the screen, making any necessary changes. ■ Ensure you have the items mapped to the correct accounts.
Enter payroll year-to-date amounts	■ Complete steps 1–4 of the QuickBooks Payroll Setup Interview. ■ Choose Employees→Payroll Setup (if you are not still viewing the interview). ■ Complete step 5 "Payroll History" of the interview.
Make an adjustment to a payroll liability	■ Choose Employees→Payroll Taxes and Liabilities→Adjust Payroll Liabilities. ■ Enter the adjustment information; click OK.
Run a payroll item listing report	■ Choose Reports→Employees & Payroll→Payroll Item Listing.

Set Up QuickBooks to Run Payroll

In this exercise, you will view how to set the payroll preference for a company. The first step is to open Quick-Books, and then either open a company file or restore a portable company file.

1. Start **QuickBooks 2013**.

    If you downloaded the student exercise files in the portable company file *format, follow Option 1 below. If you downloaded the files in the* company file *format, follow Option 2 below.*

 If you choose, you may use the final company file from Critical Thinking 8.2. In this case, open the Critical Thinking 8.2 company file from your default storage location in Option 2 below.

Option 1: Restore a Portable Company File

2. Choose **File→Open or Restore Company**.

3. Restore the **Rock Castle Construction** portable file for this lesson from your file storage location, placing your name as the first word in the filename (e.g., Zoe's Rock Castle Construction, Lesson 9).

    It may take a few moments for the portable company file to open. Once it does, continue with step 4.

Option 2: Open a Company File

2. Choose **File→Open or Restore Company**, ensure that **Open a regular company file** is selected, and then open the **Rock Castle Construction** company file for this lesson from your file storage location.

    The QuickBooks company file will open.

3. Click **OK** to close the QuickBooks Information windows. If necessary, click **No** in the Set Up External Accountant User window.

View the Payroll Preference

If you are setting QuickBooks up to run payroll for the first time in your company file, you will need to set the preference. In this case, you will help Zoe to verify that it is set correctly.

4. Choose **Edit→Preferences**.

5. Click the **Payroll & Employees** category on the left, and then the **Company Preferences** tab.

6. Notice that **Full payroll** is turned on for this company file.

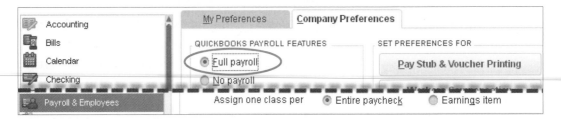

7. Click **Cancel** to close the Preferences window.

Working with Employees in QuickBooks

Just as you used the Vendor Center to track vendors and the Customer Center to track customers and jobs, you will use the Employee Center to track employees. If you recall, QuickBooks defines a customer as someone who pays you money. Well, the QuickBooks definition of an employee is someone to whom you issue a W-2 at the end of the year. Subcontractors are *not* to be entered into the Employees List; remember from Lesson 3, Working with Vendors that subcontractors are included in the Vendor List.

Setting Up Employees Through the Payroll Setup Interview

QuickBooks allows you to set up your employees in two ways. You can enter them through the payroll setup interview process, or you can enter them directly into the Employees List accessed via the Employee Center.

Managing the Employees List

Managing the Employees List is similar to managing the Customers & Jobs List and the Vendors List. You will edit, delete, and create new employees the same way you did for customers and vendors. New employees can also be set up as part of the QuickBooks Payroll Setup Interview.

Clicking the Payroll tab displays the Payroll Center, which helps guide you through payroll activities.

The Employee Center looks very similar to the Vendor and Customer Centers with which you have already worked.

Setting Up a New Employee

To run payroll, you need to enter important tax information for each employee. If you don't have your employees' W-4s handy, you can always add the information later—as long as it is entered before you first run payroll. (This is not optional!)

Advanced Skills

It is very important to have all of your employees' W-4 and I-9 forms filed neatly with all personnel records. Workman's Compensation companies are very thorough when they review company payroll records. Even though you do not treat independent contractors as employees in QuickBooks, it is important that you have a I-9 form on file for each contractor as well.

Gather Your Employee Information

Before you can set up employees in QuickBooks, regardless of which approach you take, you need to have certain information handy. If you don't have all of the information from the W-4 forms when you set up your employees, you will need to ensure that it is entered before you first run payroll.

Following is a list of necessary employee information required for payroll setup:

- Name
- Address
- Social security number
- Birthday
- Federal and state exemption information

Setting Employee Defaults

Before you set up your employees, you should set the employee defaults. These preferences will be applied to each new employee you create, and you can change them as needed. When setting employee defaults, choose the options that you assume will apply to the majority of employees you will create.

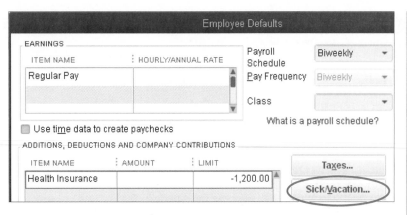

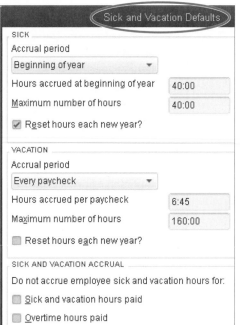

One of the default items you can set deals with how (and if) sick and vacation time is tracked for employees.

Visualize! **Tab:** Other Topics
Topic: Paying employees

Task	Procedure
Create a new employee	▪ Choose Employees→Employee Center; click the New Employee button. ▪ Enter all applicable information on each of the tabs; click OK.
Edit an existing employee	▪ Choose Employees→Employee Center; double-click the desired employee. ▪ Make any necessary changes; click OK.
Set employee defaults outside of the Payroll Setup Interview	▪ Choose Employees→Employee Center; click the Manage Employee Information button at the top of the window. ▪ Choose Change New Employee Default Settings, enter the new settings, and then click OK.

Set Up and Manage Employees

In this exercise, you will help Zoe set up two new employees for Rock Castle Construction (they began on 12/16/2014) after she has modified the employee defaults for payroll.

1. Click the **Employees** button in the Employees area of the Home page.
   The Employee Center will be displayed.

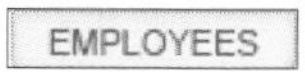

   EMPLOYEES

2. Click the **Manage Employee Information** button, and then choose **Change New Employee Default Settings**.

QuickBooks displays the Employee Defaults window.

Advanced Skills

3. Follow these steps to edit the new employee default settings (you must click in the Item Name column to see a drop-down arrow displayed that will allow you to choose the items from a list of payroll items):

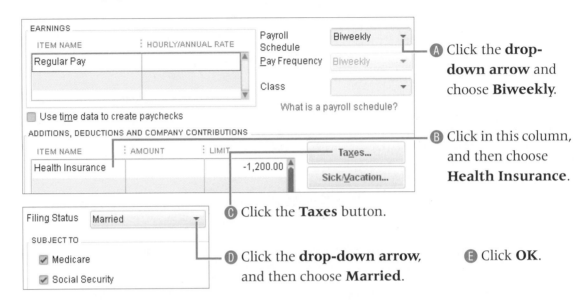

Ⓐ Click the **drop-down arrow** and choose **Biweekly**.

Ⓑ Click in this column, and then choose **Health Insurance**.

Ⓒ Click the **Taxes** button.

Ⓓ Click the **drop-down arrow**, and then choose **Married**.

Ⓔ Click **OK**.

Take a look at any of the other defaults that you have the option of setting, if you wish, making sure to not make any changes to them.

4. Click **OK** in the Employee Defaults window.
   You will once again be viewing the Employee Center window.

Set Up a New Employee Using the Employees List
The next task you will help Zoe with is setting up a new employee.

5. Click the **New Employee** button on the Employee Center toolbar.

6. Follow these steps to set up the personal information for Stephen:

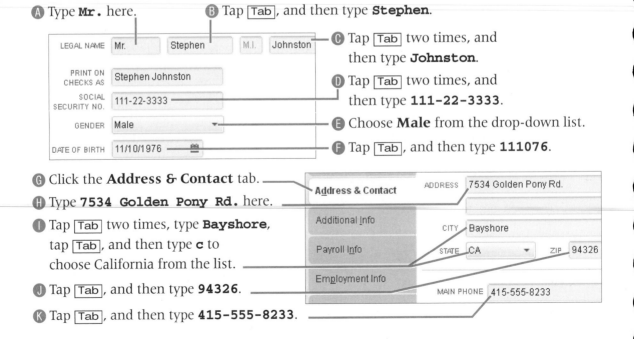

Ⓐ Type **Mr.** here.

Ⓑ Tap Tab, and then type **Stephen**.

Ⓒ Tap Tab two times, and then type **Johnston**.

Ⓓ Tap Tab two times, and then type **111-22-3333**.

Ⓔ Choose **Male** from the drop-down list.

Ⓕ Tap Tab, and then type **111076**.

Ⓖ Click the **Address & Contact** tab.

Ⓗ Type **7534 Golden Pony Rd.** here.

Ⓘ Tap Tab two times, type **Bayshore**, tap Tab, and then type **c** to choose California from the list.

Ⓙ Tap Tab, and then type **94326**.

Ⓚ Tap Tab, and then type **415-555-8233**.

7. Follow these steps to set up the payroll information for Stephen:

Ⓐ Click **the Payroll Info** tab.　　**Ⓑ** Click here, and then type **18.5**.

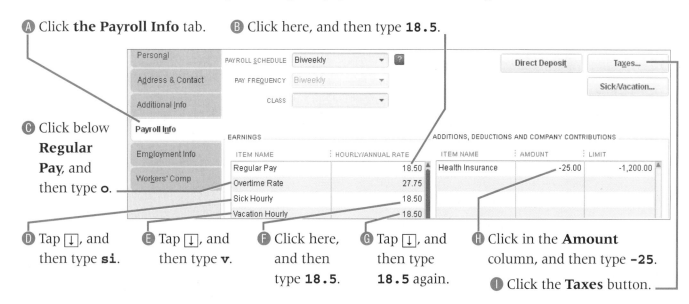

Ⓒ Click below **Regular Pay**, and then type **o**.

Ⓓ Tap ↓, and then type **si**.

Ⓔ Tap ↓, and then type **v**.

Ⓕ Click here, and then type **18.5**.

Ⓖ Tap ↓, and then type **18.5** again.

Ⓗ Click in the **Amount** column, and then type **−25**.

Ⓘ Click the **Taxes** button.

Don't forget to type the minus sign for the Health Insurance amount!

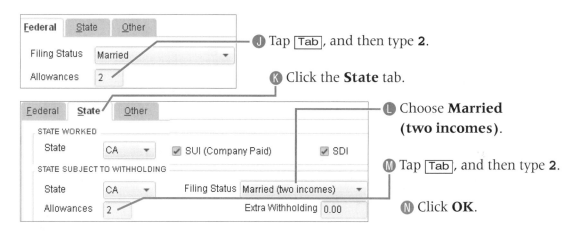

Ⓙ Tap Tab, and then type **2**.

Ⓚ Click the **State** tab.

Ⓛ Choose **Married (two incomes)**.

Ⓜ Tap Tab, and then type **2**.

Ⓝ Click **OK**.

Notice how the various employee defaults that you set were set up filled in for you and that you can change any of them as you set up each individual employee.

8. Click **OK** again to save Stephen's information.

9. Click **Leave As Is**.
   By choosing to leave the sick/vacation information "as is," you are applying the employee defaults to Stephen.

Add an Additional Employee

You will now help Zoe to add one more employee, Sam Jameson.

10. Use the following information and the steps outlined in the previous section to add one more employee.

Remember to choose the Payroll Info tab when you are ready to enter the pay rate and exemptions information.

Advanced Skills

Name	Mr. Samuel Jameson
Address	303 McMurray Place Middlefield, CA 93210
Phone	415-555-8791
SS No.	999-88-7777
Gender	Male
Date of Birth	013078
Hourly Rate	18.00
Overtime Rate	27.00
Sick and Vacation Rate	18.00
Filing Status and Allowances	Single, 1
Health Insurance	-25

11. Click **Leave As Is** to apply the sick/vacation defaults to Sam.

12. Close the **Employee Center**.

Dealing with Payroll Deductions

You have learned about two of the three main tasks associated with setting up QuickBooks to run payroll—setting up payroll items and employees. Now you will need to let QuickBooks know which taxes and deductions to collect and to whom they need to be paid. You can use the QuickBooks Payroll Setup Interview to take a quick whirl through the taxes you have set up to make sure they are correct. In addition, you can view the Payroll Item Listing report to verify that the taxes and deductions are being routed to the right expense and liability accounts as well as the actual Payroll Item List to make sure the vendors to whom you pay them are correct.

You must have your Federal Employer Identification Number listed in your company file in order for payroll to be processed correctly. If you did not enter this correctly or at all when you created your company file, you can make that change at any time.

Workers Compensation Insurance

QuickBooks can process Workman's Comp insurance in much the same way that it processes payroll taxes. To track this payroll expense, the preference must be turned on in QuickBooks.

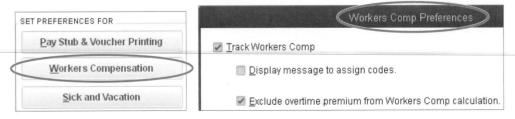

The Workers Compensation button in the Set preferences for area of the Company Preferences tab of the Payroll & Employees category leads to a window that allows you to choose whether to track workers comp in QuickBooks.

Task	Procedure
Enter your company's FEIN	■ Choose Company→Company Information. ■ Click in the Federal Employer Identification No. field, and then type your FEIN. ◆ If you are a sole proprietor and don't have a FEIN, click in the Social Security Number field, type your SSN, and then click OK.
Choose to track workers comp in QuickBooks	■ Choose Edit→Preferences. ■ Click the Payroll & Employees category; choose the Company Preferences tab. ■ Click the Workers Compensation button; click in the checkbox to the left of Track Workers Comp. ■ Click OK two times to set the new preference.
Create a Payroll Item Listing report	■ Choose Reports→Employees & Payroll→Payroll Item Listing.
View the Payroll Item List	■ Choose Lists→Payroll Item List.

DEVELOP YOUR SKILLS 9.3

Set Up Payroll Taxes

In this exercise, you will make sure that the company's Federal Employer Identification Number is entered properly and that the company is set up correctly to account for payroll taxes.

You will begin by helping Zoe make sure that the company's FEIN is entered correctly in QuickBooks.

1. Choose **Company→Company Information**.

2. Verify that **00-7904153** is the FEIN entered for Rock Castle Construction.

3. Click **OK**.

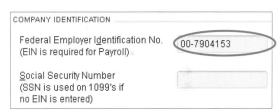

Verify Correct Payroll Tax Setup

You will now use the QuickBooks Payroll Setup Interview as a tool to make sure the payroll taxes are set up properly. If there is an obvious error, QuickBooks will alert you and ask you to make a change.

4. Choose **Employees→Payroll Setup**.

5. Click in the box to the left of **Taxes**.

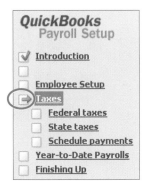

6. Click **Continue**.

You will see a screen that lists all of the federal taxes that have been set up for you. Notice that both Medicare and Social Security have two separate entries; they are paid by both the company and employee.

7. Click **Continue**.

On this next screen, you will see the state taxes that QuickBooks has set up for you. Remember that this book is meant to be a training tool only. You must contact your local tax agency to know how to set up taxes for your jurisdiction!

8. Click **Continue**.

In this next screen, you will see how and when you pay each of your withholding taxes.

9. Click the **Finish Later** button at the bottom left of the QuickBooks Payroll Setup window; click **OK** in the Finish Later window.

Notice that even after your payroll is set up you can use the QuickBooks Payroll Setup feature to examine the information you have entered for it.

Create a Payroll Item Listing Report to Verify Accounts

It is very important for your payroll items to link to the proper accounts in your Chart of Accounts! You will now review a report that shows how the items are linked so you can ensure you are doing payroll properly.

10. Choose **Reports→Employees & Payroll→ Payroll Item Listing**.

The Payroll Item Listing report will be displayed.

11. Note the **Expense Account** and the **Liability Account** columns.

The expense accounts indicate the payroll expenses for your company, from salaries and benefits to employer taxes that you are required to pay. The liability accounts are where you "hold" the funds until you have to pay them to the proper taxing authority. Remember that QuickBooks keeps a separate set of records for payroll behind the scenes, so when you choose to pay your payroll liabilities with a special Liability Check window, it will "empty" these accounts properly.

Expense Account	Liability Account
62710 · Gross Wages	
62710 · Gross Wages	
62710 · Gross Wages	
62710 · Gross Wages	
62710 · Gross Wages	
62710 · Gross Wages	
62710 · Gross Wages	
62710 · Gross Wages	
62710 · Gross Wages	
	24100 · Emp. Health Ins Payable
62130 · Work Comp	24080 · Worker's Compensation
	24030 · AEIC Payable
62730 · FUTA Expense	24040 · FUTA Payable
	24010 · Federal Withholding
62720 · Payroll Taxes	24020 · FICA Payable
	24020 · FICA Payable
62720 · Payroll Taxes	24020 · FICA Payable
	24020 · FICA Payable
	24050 · State Withholding
	24070 · State Disability Payable
62740 · SUTA Expense	24060 · SUTA Payable
62740 · SUTA Expense	24060 · SUTA Payable
	24090 · Direct Deposit Liabilities

12. Close the **Payroll Item Listing** window.

Verify Vendors and Edit a Payroll Item

The final step you will take to verify that your payroll taxes are set up properly is to make sure that you are paying the taxes to the proper vendors.

13. Choose **Lists→Payroll Item List**, resizing the window as necessary so you can see all columns clearly.
    Look in the Payable To column. This shows to whom you must pay each tax that you are holding in your liability accounts. Notice that there is no vendor listed for Health Insurance in the Payable to column. You will help Zoe add this information now.

14. Double-click **Health Insurance** to open it for editing.

An Edit Payroll Item window displays. You will be clicking Next to move through the screens to modify this item.

15. Click **Next** as the name for the item is correct.

16. Follow these steps to set up the vendor to whom you will pay the insurance premiums:

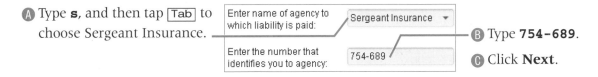

Ⓐ Type **s**, and then tap Tab to choose Sergeant Insurance.

Ⓑ Type **754–689**.

Ⓒ Click **Next**.

The Liability account is correct, so you do not need to edit it.

17. Type **o** in the Tax tracking type screen to choose **Other**; click **Next**.

18. Click **Next** in the Taxes screen; click **Next** in the Calculate based on quantity screen.

19. Click **Next** in the Gross vs. net window.

20. Click **Finish** in the Default rate and limit window.
    You will enter the deduction amount when you set up each new employee, rather than entering a default here.

Create a Payroll Item

You will now help Zoe create a new payroll item to track court-mandated child support deductions as well as payments to a charity the company has adopted, Niños del Lago. The Payroll Item List should still be displayed from the previous step, but if not, Choose Lists→Payroll Item List.

21. Click the **Payroll Item menu button**, and then choose **New**.

22. Click **Next** to choose EZ Setup.

23. Click in the circle to the left of **Other Deductions**, and then click **Next**.

24. Click in the boxes to the left of **Wage garnishment** and **Donation to charity**, and then click **Next**.

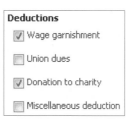

25. Follow these steps to set up the payment schedule for the charity donations:

Ⓐ Type **Ninos del Lago**.

Ⓑ Tap Tab, and then type **RCC**.

Ⓒ Click in the circle to the left of **Quarterly**.

Ⓓ Click **Next**.

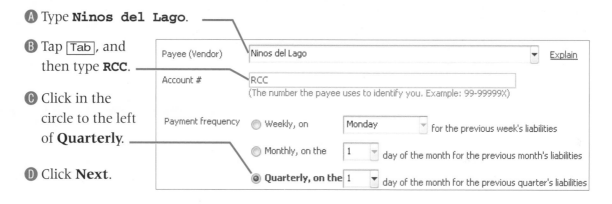

26. Follow these steps to set up the payment schedule for the child support deductions:

Ⓐ Type **County Family Services**.   Ⓑ Tap Tab, and then type **00-7904153**.

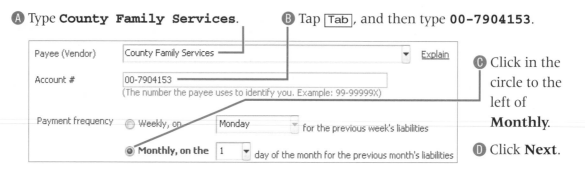

Ⓒ Click in the circle to the left of **Monthly**.

Ⓓ Click **Next**.

27. Click **Finish**.
You will now see the Payroll Item List displayed with your two new payroll items added to it. If you wish, you can rename the items from this list.

28. Close the **Payroll Item List**.

Creating Paychecks

Once you have chosen your payroll method, made sure your payroll items are set up properly, and set up your employees and payroll tax information, you can begin to create paychecks for your employees. When you first choose to pay employees, you will see an Enter Hours window displayed. Once you have entered the paycheck information for each employee, you will see all of the data displayed in the Review and Create Paychecks window.

We are using the QuickBooks sample file. If you use a QuickBooks payroll service, your subscription status will appear here.

The Pay Employees area of the window helps you process payroll for employees. The Related Payroll Activities button gives you the option to edit or void paychecks, add or edit payroll schedules, and create a termination check.

The Pay Scheduled Liabilities area helps you make sure that you pay all of the funds you are holding in your payroll liability accounts on time.

The File Tax Forms area guides you through creation of W-2s and other payroll forms.

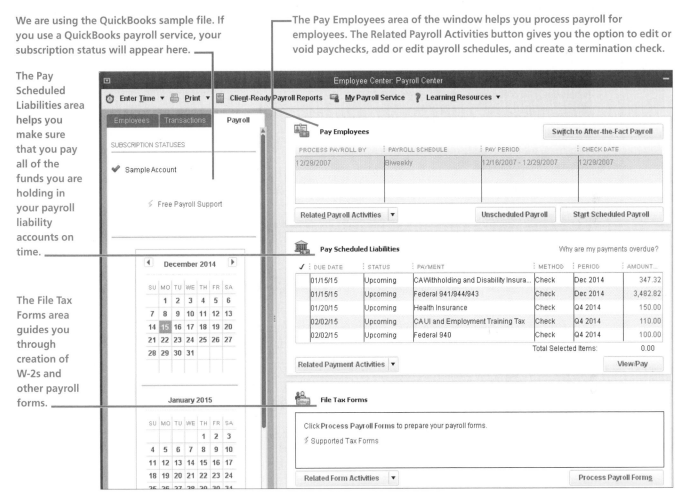

The Payroll Center window. Notice that it helps guide you through all of your payroll tasks.

You will have the opportunity to enter information for each employee in a Review or Change Paycheck window, moving from one employee to another using the Next and Previous buttons.

Working with Payroll Schedules

When you choose to use QuickBooks for payroll, you have the option to set up payroll schedules in order to more efficiently run payroll. Payroll schedules allow you to set how often you pay employees, the date on which the paycheck is due, the date on which you will run payroll, all the while taking into account holidays and weekends to ensure that you pay your employees on time. Another benefit of using scheduled payroll is that you can choose to pay your employees by group or by batch.

Payroll schedules are created from the Payroll Center after the payroll setup is complete. You will have an opportunity to run a scheduled payroll for Rock Castle Construction. In the Reinforce Your Skills exercise, you will run payroll without using a payroll schedule.

Using scheduled payroll does not limit you from creating a paycheck for an employee "off schedule." This can be completed by clicking the Unscheduled Payroll button in the Payroll Center.

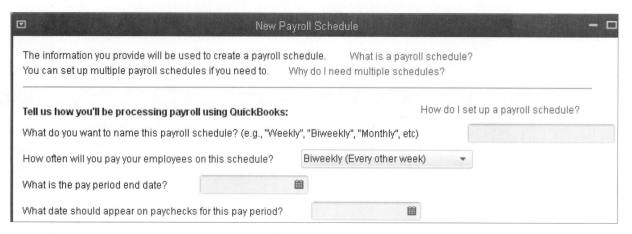

In the New Payroll Schedule window, you can set the vital information that will apply to the payroll schedule being created for a group of employees.

Passing On Billable Time to Customers

In Lesson 7, Introducing the Accounting Cycle and Using Classes, you learned that it was possible to pass on expenses to customers. In this section, you will learn to pass on billable payroll expenses to customers. When you create a paycheck for an employee who has billable hours, make sure to choose the correct customer or job to which to pass on the expense.

Assigning Sick or Vacation Hours

You learned how to set QuickBooks up to track sick and vacation hours for employees previously in this lesson. To document an employee's use of "banked" paid time off, you will assign the time to payroll items that specifically track the banked time.

Notice the separate Sick Hourly and Vacation Hourly items that you would use to track the sick and vacation hours used by an employee.

QuickBooks makes it easy for you to ensure that an employee has sick and/or vacation hours available to use before you include them on a paycheck.

If you include a Customer:Job in this column, then the payroll expense can be easily passed on to a customer.

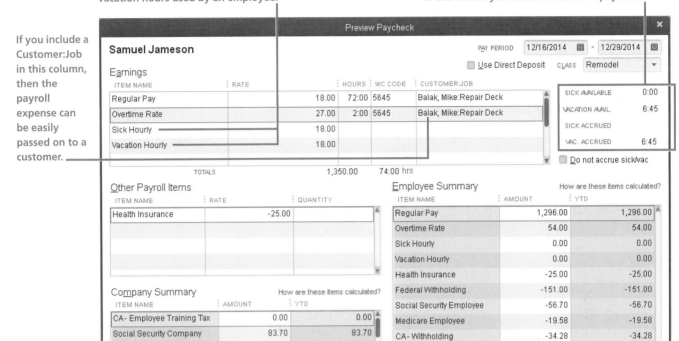

In the Preview Paycheck window, you will set the number of hours worked for an employee. This information will be used to calculate the payroll taxes for you (providing you subscribe to a QuickBooks payroll service).

BEHIND THE SCENES

When you create paychecks, you will pay employees, pay taxes, and withhold taxes from employee paychecks. In this example, we will look at Samuel Jameson's paycheck, which you will create in the next exercise. You will issue a net paycheck for $1,029.33, with $320.67 of employee deductions going to the Payroll Liability subaccounts (only the parent accounts of Payroll Liabilities and Payroll Expenses are shown in this example) and $184.96 of company-paid taxes going from the Payroll Expenses subaccounts to the Payroll Liability subaccounts. The gross pay is $1,350.

10400-Checking	24000-Payroll Liabilities	62700-Payroll Expenses
1,029.33	184.96 320.67	1,350.00 184.96

   CREATING PAYCHECKS AND PAYROLL SCHEDULES

Task	Procedure
Create employee paychecks	■ Choose Employees→Pay Employees; set the check date and the last day of the pay period.
	■ Set the bank account and paycheck options.
	■ In the Enter Hours window, click the first employee for whom you wish to enter paycheck information.
	■ Enter the hours in the Review or Change Paycheck window; click Next.
	■ Repeat the previous step for all of the employees you will be paying, clicking OK after entering the last employee's information.
	■ Verify that the information is correct; click Create Paychecks.
Print paychecks	■ Choose File→Print Forms→Paychecks; choose the correct bank account.
	■ Select the checks you wish to print; click OK.
	■ Select the type of checks you use; click Print.
Print pay stubs	■ Choose File→Print Forms→Pay Stubs; set the correct date range.
	■ Select the desired statements, click OK, and then click Print.
Pass billable payroll expenses on to a customer	■ Choose Customers→Create Invoices.
	■ Choose the customer to whom you will be passing on the expense.
	■ Click the Time/Costs button on the toolbar, and then click the Expenses tab.
	■ Choose the hours you wish to pass on; click OK.
	■ Finish entering invoice information; click Save & Close.
Create a payroll schedule	■ Choose Employees→Payroll Center.
	■ Click the Related Payroll Activities button; choose Add or Edit Payroll Schedules.
	■ Click the Payroll Schedule menu button; click New.
	■ Enter a name for the schedule, how often the payroll will run, and the pay period end date as well as the paycheck date; click OK.
	■ Assign the payroll schedule to all employees with the same pay frequency.
Edit a payroll schedule	■ Choose Employees→Payroll Center.
	■ Click the Related Payroll Activities button; choose Add or Edit Payroll Schedules.
	■ Click to select the payroll schedule you wish to edit.
	■ Click the Payroll Schedule menu button; click Edit.
	■ Make any desired changes; click OK.

DEVELOP YOUR SKILLS 9.4

Create Paychecks for Employees

In this exercise, you will help Zoe run payroll for all employees for the period ending 12/29/2014.

1. Choose **Company→Home Page**.

2. Click the **Pay Employees** task icon in the Employee area of the Home page.
   The Employee Center: Payroll Center window opens. We are using the QuickBooks sample company file for this exercise, and it shows the scheduled payroll as being in the year 2007. We will change the pay period dates as we move through the payroll process. When you do the payroll for your own company, the dates should show up correctly in this window once you have issued the first paycheck—if the payroll schedule is set up properly.

3. Click the **Start Scheduled Payroll** button in the Pay Employees area of the window.

The Enter Payroll Information window displays with the Check Date field selected.

4. Follow these steps to select which employees to pay and when to pay them:

Ⓐ Type **122914**.　　Ⓑ Tap Shift + Tab, and　　Ⓒ Click **Samuel Jameson**.
　　　　　　　　　　　　　　then type **122914**.

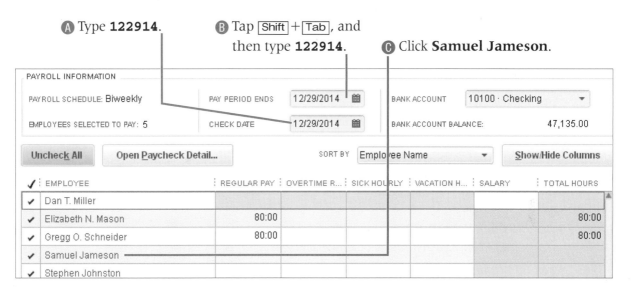

The Preview Paycheck window for Samuel Jameson will appear.

You will be creating paychecks for all employees. Since all employees are checked by default, you do not have to make changes in this area. You have already created paychecks in the past for Dan, Elizabeth, and Gregg, so you can choose to use the information that was used the last time a check was created for each of them. If you choose to use previous information, you will have a chance to see what it looks like before you issue the paycheck.

FROM THE KEYBOARD
Shift + Tab to "back tab" or go back one field on a form

5. Follow these steps to create a paycheck for Samuel:

Ⓐ Type **72**.　Ⓑ Click the **drop-down arrow**, and　Ⓒ Click the **drop-down arrow**, and then
　　　　　　then choose **5645** for Carpentry.　　choose **Balak, Mike: Repair Deck**.

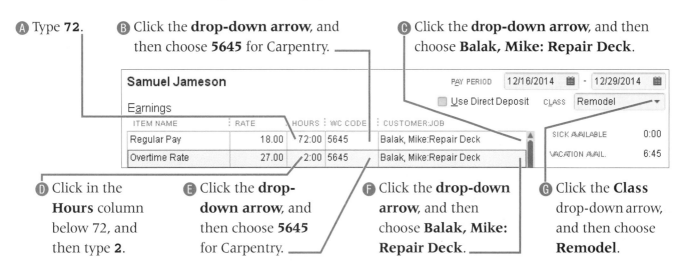

Ⓓ Click in the **Hours** column below 72, and then type **2**.

Ⓔ Click the **drop-down arrow**, and then choose **5645** for Carpentry.

Ⓕ Click the **drop-down arrow**, and then choose **Balak, Mike: Repair Deck**.

Ⓖ Click the **Class** drop-down arrow, and then choose **Remodel**.

Advanced Skills

Notice that once you filled in the hours worked for Samuel, the tax amounts automatically filled in for you. This will happen for you as well as long as you have subscribed to a QuickBooks payroll service. You can choose to do paychecks manually, but that will require you to enter each amount manually and to stay on top of all tax law changes. It results in a much greater chance for error.

6. Click **Save & Next**.

   The Preview Paycheck window for Stephen Johnston displays. Stephen is working on a new home that you are building and has just finished the roofing.

7. Follow these steps to create a paycheck for Stephen:

   Ⓐ Type **64**.　　Ⓑ Click the **drop-down arrow**, and then choose **5552** for Roofing.　　Ⓒ Click the **drop-down arrow**, and then choose **New Construction**.

8. Click **Save & Close**.

   The Enter Payroll Information window will again be displayed.

9. Click **Continue**; then, click **OK**.

   The Review and Create Paychecks window displays, summarizing all of the information for you regarding the paychecks you are choosing to create. If you need to make any changes to a paycheck, simply click on the employee's name. The Preview Paycheck window for that employee will display, from where you can make any changes necessary.

Create Paychecks

In the next step, you will see the Review and Create Paychecks window, which summarizes the payroll information for this pay period.

10. Ensure that **Print paychecks from QuickBooks** is the Paycheck Option selected.

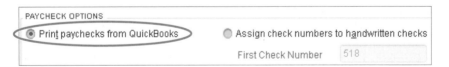

11. Click **Create Paychecks**.

The Confirmation and Next Steps window will be displayed. Notice that this window shows you the "flow" for payroll. It provides buttons for you to make printing paychecks and pay stubs easy.

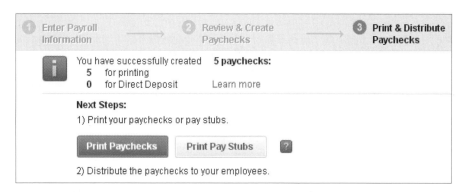

In the following BTS Brief section, the numbers reflect all five paychecks created in the previous steps, including those that you did not edit for three of the employees. You are also viewing the "parent accounts" in this case, not the various subaccounts.

BTS BRIEF

62700•Payroll Expenses DR 7,350.20; 24000•Payroll Liabilities CR <1,658.23>; 10100•Checking CR <5,691.97>

Print Paychecks and Pay Stubs

Once you have created paychecks, you need to print them. You will help Zoe print the paychecks from the Confirmation and Next Steps window and then help her print the pay stubs using the menu bar command that is always available.

12. Click the **Print Paychecks** button in the Confirmation and Next Steps window.
    The Select Paychecks to Print window displays. At this point, you would place preprinted checks into the printer. Of course, for this exercise there are no preprinted checks. You will print them on blank sheets of paper or as a PDF file.

13. Click **OK** to choose to print all five paychecks, using **10080** as the first check number.
    The Print Checks dialog box displays. When you are dealing with your own company, look at the checks you place in the printer to verify that the first check number is correct.

14. Follow the desired step, depending on whether you wish to physically print the paychecks:

    ■ Click **Print**. You can also choose this option if you wish to print the checks as an electronic PDF file. Click **OK** to verify that all checks printed correctly.

    ■ Print choosing ***.pdf** as the printer, and then choose where to save the PDF file. Click **OK** to verify that all checks printed correctly.

15. Close the **Confirmation and Next Steps** window.
    Yes, you could have printed the pay stubs from that window, but it is important for you to know how to print paychecks and pay stubs from the menu bar as well!

16. Choose **File→Print Forms→Pay Stubs**.

17. Tap $\boxed{\text{Tab}}$, and then type **122914**.

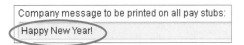

Now only the pay stubs for the paychecks you just created display. You do not need to worry about changing the "thru" date, as the checks dated 12/29/14 are the latest ones created.

18. Click in the **Company message** field, and then type the following: **Happy New Year!**

19. Click **Preview** to view what the employee pay stubs will look like. Close the **Print Preview** window when you are finished.

20. Close the **Select Pay Stubs** window and the **Employee Center: Payroll Center** window.

Tracking and Paying Payroll Liabilities

In Lesson 8, Dealing with Physical Inventory, you collected sales tax and held it in a current liability account until it was time to pay the tax agencies. When you run payroll, you must collect taxes and other deductions and hold them in a payroll liabilities account until you are required to pay them.

Knowing How Much to Pay

QuickBooks has preset reports that you can run to determine how much you need to pay from what you hold in Payroll Liabilities. Remember that you hold taxes along with other deductions in the payroll liabilities account.

If you have your bank send in your federal payroll taxes electronically, clear the Print Later checkbox and enter EFTPS (Electronic Federal Tax Payment Service) into the check number field.

The Pay Payroll Liabilities Window

Just as you used the Pay Sales Tax window to pay your sales tax liabilities, you will use a special Pay Liabilities window to pay your payroll taxes and deductions. You should never just "write a check" for your payroll taxes because QuickBooks will not properly debit the liability accounts.

One of the top errors made by new users is to use the Write Checks window for paying payroll liabilities rather than the QuickBooks Pay Liabilities window.

Tab: Other Topics
Topic: Pay taxes and other liabilities

BEHIND THE SCENES

When you pay your payroll liabilities, you decrease the amount in both your checking (by crediting) and payroll liabilities (by debiting) accounts. In the following example, you can see the three liability payments you will make in the next exercise on 12/29/2014. Only the parent account, Payroll Liabilities is used in this example.

10400-Checking	24000-Payroll Liabilities
568.71	568.71
262.50	262.50
5,013.42	5,013.42
5,844.63	5,844.63

QUICK REFERENCE	PAYING PAYROLL LIABILITIES
Task	**Procedure**
Run a payroll liability report	▪ Choose Reports→Employees & Payroll→Payroll Liability Balances. ▪ Set the proper date range, and then click Refresh.
Pay payroll liabilities	▪ Choose Employees→Process Payroll Liabilities→Pay Payroll Liabilities. ▪ Set the date range for the liabilities; click OK. ▪ Set the bank account and the check date. ▪ Select the payroll liabilities you need to pay; click Create.

DEVELOP YOUR SKILLS 9.5
Pay the Payroll Liabilities

In this exercise, you will assist Zoe with the task of paying the payroll liabilities that have been collected.

Zoe first wants to see exactly how much she needs to pay to the various payroll vendors, so she will run a report that shows all of the taxes and deductions being held in the payroll liabilities account. You received a notice that you overpaid the liabilities in November, so you will run a report that shows the balance owed based on the adjustments from November and the total collected in December.

1. Choose **Reports→Employees & Payroll→Payroll Liability Balances**.

2. Follow these steps to set the date range for the report:

Ⓐ Tap Tab, and then type **110114**.   Ⓑ Tap Tab, and then type **123114**.   Ⓒ Click **Refresh**.

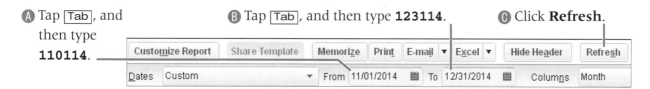

Your report should resemble the illustration below.

Rock Castle Construction
Payroll Liability Balances
November through December 2014

	◇ Nov 14 ◇	Dec 14 ◇	BALANCE ◇
▼ **Payroll Liabilities**			
Advance Earned Income Credit ▶	0.00 ◀	0.00	0.00
Federal Withholding	-8.00	1,956.00	1,948.00
Medicare Employee	0.00	297.82	297.82
Social Security Employee	0.00	965.03	965.03
Federal Unemployment	0.00	115.20	115.20
Medicare Company	0.00	297.82	297.82
Social Security Company	0.00	1,273.40	1,273.40
CA - Withholding	-4.00	426.09	422.09
CA - Disability Employee	-17.20	90.67	73.47
CA - Unemployment Company	0.00	233.04	233.04
CA - Employee Training Tax	0.00	10.00	10.00
Health Insurance	0.00	212.50	212.50
Workers Compensation	0.00	1,948.91	1,948.91
Total Payroll Liabilities	**-29.20**	**7,826.48**	**7,797.28**

3. Close the **Payroll Liability Balances** report.

Pay the Payroll Liabilities

Zoe is now ready to pay the payroll liabilities due in January. You will help her pay them by using a liability check. Note that if you are paying liabilities for your own company, you need to pay them based on the schedule that applies to your business.

4. Click the **Pay Liabilities** task icon in the Employees area of the Home page.
   The Employee Center: Payroll Center will be displayed again.

Pay
Liabilities

5. Follow these steps to pay the liabilities due in January:

Ⓐ Click to the left of the **three payments** due in January.

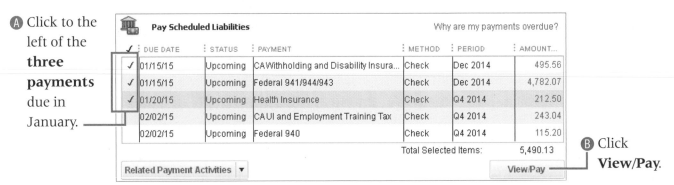

Ⓑ Click **View/Pay**.

The Liability Payment – Checking window will be displayed (notice that it is not *the Write Checks window!), with the check information for the first payroll vendor filled in.*

6. Change the date on the check to **12/29/2014**, and then click **Save & Next**.
   Since this is a sample company file, QuickBooks loads 12/15/2014 as the date each time you go to create a new transaction. In your own company file, the date that would be displayed is the last date you used in another transaction.

   The second liability payment information displays in the window.

7. Change the date on the second payroll liability check to **12/29/2014**, and then click **Save & Next**.

8. Change the date on the third liability check to **12/29/2014**, and then click **Save & Close**. *A Payment Summary window displays. Notice that you can choose to print the checks right from this window. If you choose to print them at a later date, they will be placed in the queue of checks waiting to be printed. You can access that from the menu bar.*

   In the following BTS Brief section, you are viewing the "parent account" for Payroll Liabilities, not the various subaccounts.

BTS BRIEF
24000•Payroll Liabilities DR 5,490.13; 10100•Checking CR <5,490.13>

9. Close the **Payment Summary** and **Employee Center: Payroll Center** windows.

Dealing with Errors in Payroll

When you encounter a situation that needs to be corrected in payroll, you must be very careful and ensure that you handle it in the proper manner. Remember that QuickBooks keeps a separate "set of books" for payroll, so you must make changes via the payroll features in QuickBooks.

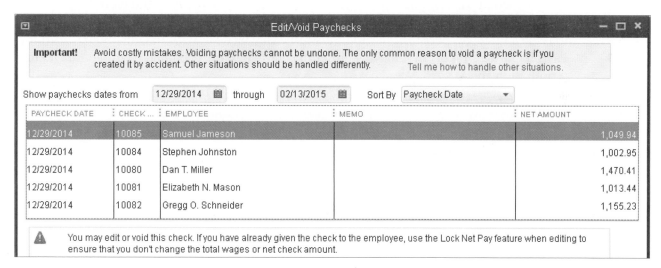

The Edit/Void Paychecks window allows you to choose which paycheck to void or edit and provides guidance. Note the important message at the top of the window regarding voiding paychecks and the message at the bottom of the window that refers to the selected paycheck (Samuel Jameson's).

Fixing a Paycheck

It is only on rare occasions that you should void a paycheck. Two such times that it would be warranted are when you accidentally created a paycheck or when you have to correct a paycheck from a prior year.

Correcting a Paycheck Error from a Prior Year

If you need to change the date of a paycheck from one year to another, you must void the paycheck and reissue it. (In previous versions, you could change a paycheck in a prior year without re-creating it.) Voiding a paycheck is done in basically the same way as voiding any transaction in QuickBooks. Just remember that when you re-create the paycheck, you must do it through the proper method in QuickBooks. In other words, you cannot just create a new check in the Write Checks window.

Lock Net Pay Feature

If you need to make changes to a paycheck and want to make sure that you don't change the amount of the check (which would need to be dealt with in a different way), you can use the QuickBooks Lock Net Pay feature that ensures you don't change the amount of the paycheck or the total wages. When this feature is activated, you will only be able to make changes that do not affect the amount of the check, such as the Class to which it is assigned, vacation or sick time accrual, or select/deselect to use a direct deposit.

Unscheduled Payroll Checks

There may be times when you need to issue a paycheck to an employee, and it is not at the end of a pay period. For instance, you may have underpaid an employee and do not want that employee to have to wait until the next payday to receive the compensation, or you may need to issue a final paycheck. These situations can easily be dealt with in QuickBooks from the Payroll Center window by choosing either to conduct an unscheduled payroll or to create a termination check.

Related Payroll Activities ▼	Unscheduled Payroll	Start Scheduled Payroll
Edit or Void Paychecks		
Add or Edit Payroll Schedules		
Create Termination Check		

Notice the additional options available in the Pay Employees area of the Payroll Center.

Let's take a look at how to correct some common paycheck errors that may occur.

The Error	The Fix
You have to replace a paycheck that was lost or damaged	Reprint and reissue the check with the next check number; document the event by creating and then voiding a check
You find out that the pay period dates are wrong but still within the same calendar year	Edit the pay period dates in the Review Paycheck window and create a memo in the check register
You discover that an employee was overpaid	Correct the overpayment on the next payroll (rather than reissuing the paycheck)
You discover that an employee was underpaid	Issue an unscheduled payroll check or correct the underpayment on the next payroll
You realize that a paycheck item is incorrect and that the error will not affect the amount of the check	Edit the paycheck information while in Lock Net Pay mode

Depending on the type of payroll service you subscribe to, there may be limitations on how you will be able to correct certain payroll errors.

Making Corrections to a Payroll Liability Payment

Paying a payroll liability with a regular check rather than a liability check will create issues for you behind the scenes, as you learned about in Lesson 6, Correcting and Customizing in QuickBooks. To set things right, you need to void the regular check and then process the payment through the pay payroll liabilities feature in QuickBooks.

QUICK REFERENCE	DEALING WITH PAYROLL ERRORS
Task	**Procedure**
Replace a lost or damaged paycheck	Reissue the check: ■ Choose Banking→Use Register; choose the desired account. ■ Find the applicable check; record the check number and net pay amount. ■ Double-click the paycheck entry in the check register; click in the To be printed checkbox. ■ Click the print button at the top of the window (use the next check number). ■ Click Save & Close; close the register. Document the lost check: ■ Choose Banking→Write Checks. ■ Create a check using the same check number and day as the one that was lost, payable to the employee. ■ Enter the net amount from the original check; note in the memo field that this check was replaced. ■ Choose Payroll Expenses as the Account on the Expenses tab; click Save & Close. ■ Choose Banking→Use Register; choose the same account into which you just entered the check. ■ Right-click on the check that you just created using the lost check number and date; choose to Void Check.
Issue an unscheduled payroll check	■ Choose Employees→Pay Employees→Unscheduled Payroll. ■ Choose the employees for whom you wish to create a paycheck. ■ Create the paycheck(s) using the same procedure you used to issue scheduled paychecks.
Void a regular check and replace it with a payroll liabilities check	■ Open the Checking register, and locate the check you wish to void. ■ Right-click the check; choose Void Check. ■ Choose Employees→Process Payroll Liabilities→Pay Payroll Liabilities. ■ Set the date range for the liabilities to be paid; click OK. ■ Set the bank account and the check date. ■ Select the payroll liabilities you need to pay; click Create.

Fix Payroll Errors

In this exercise, you will help Zoe take care of two paycheck "issues." She first needs to replace the paycheck for Samuel Jameson and issue an unscheduled payroll check to Stephen Johnston for an underpayment on the paycheck just produced.

1. Click the **Check Register** task icon in the Banking area of the Home page.

Check Register

2. Click **OK** to choose to **10100•Checking** as the account to use.

3. Scroll up until you see **Samuel Jameson's paycheck, 10083**; double-click anywhere within the transaction.
   The Paycheck – Checking window displays.

4. Write down the check number (**10083**) and net amount (**$1,029.33**) for future reference.

5. Follow these steps to reprint the check:

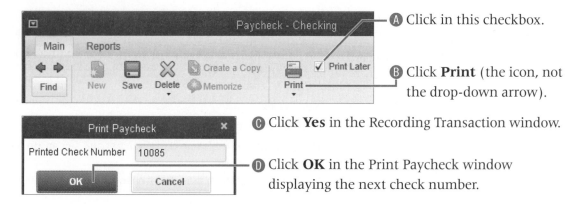

Ⓐ Click in this checkbox.

Ⓑ Click **Print** (the icon, not the drop-down arrow).

Ⓒ Click **Yes** in the Recording Transaction window.

Ⓓ Click **OK** in the Print Paycheck window displaying the next check number.

6. Ensure that the correct printer is selected (or choose to print to PDF), and then click **Print**.

7. Click **OK** in the Print Checks Confirmation window.
   This is the check you will give Samuel.

8. Click **Save & Close** in the Paycheck – Checking window.
   Leave the 10100•Checking register window open; you will need to use it again.

9. Choose **Banking→Write Checks**.

10. Click to choose for the check not to be printed later.

11. Follow these steps to create a check matching the one that was lost:

Ⓐ Enter **10083** as the No.

Ⓑ Tap Tab, and then type **122914**.

Ⓒ Tap Tab, type **sam**, and then **tap** Tab again.

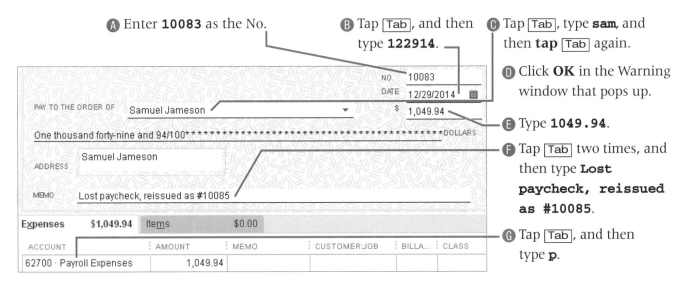

Ⓓ Click **OK** in the Warning window that pops up.

Ⓔ Type **1049.94**.

Ⓕ Tap Tab two times, and then type **Lost paycheck, reissued as #10085**.

Ⓖ Tap Tab, and then type **p**.

12. Click **Save & Close**; click **Save Anyway** in the Items not assigned classes window.
    You will be voiding the check in a moment, and the original transaction had a class assigned, so there is no reason to assign one here. The 10100•Checking window should be displayed.

13. Locate the check you just created (**10083**) in the 10100•Checking window, scrolling if necessary.

14. Right-click anywhere within the two lines of the **check 10083 transaction**, and then choose **Void Check**.
    You will see VOID: preceding the memo you entered into the check, and the dollar amount will be zero.

15. Click **Record**; click **Yes** to record the transaction.

16. Click **No, just void the check**, and then close the **Checking register window**.

Issue an Unscheduled Payroll Check

To pay Stephen for the eight regular pay hours he worked, you will help Zoe create a special paycheck.

17. Click the **Payroll Center** task icon in the Employees area of the Home page.

18. Click the **Unscheduled Payroll** button in the Pay Employees area of the Payroll Center.

19. Follow these steps to create the paycheck for Stephen:

Ⓐ Type **123014**.

Ⓑ Tap Shift + Tab, and then type **122914**.

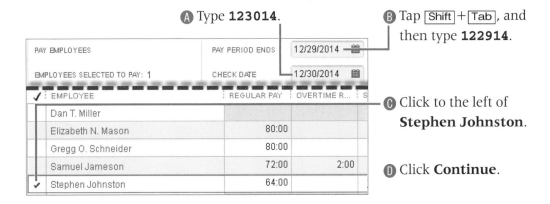

Ⓒ Click to the left of **Stephen Johnston**.

Ⓓ Click **Continue**.

20. Click **OK** in the window indicating some items may not have been assigned a class (you will assign it next).

21. Click on **Stephen Johnston's** name in the Review and Create Paychecks window.
    The Preview Paycheck window appears with the Hours field selected.

Employee

Stephen Johnston

22. Follow these steps to set up the paycheck:

Ⓐ Type **8**, and then tap Tab.

Ⓑ Click **OK** in the Special Calculation Situation window.

Ⓒ Click the **drop-down arrow**, and then choose **5645** for Carpentry.

Ⓓ Click the **drop-down arrow**, and then choose **Balak, Mike: Repair Deck**.

Ⓔ Click the **Class** drop-down arrow, and then choose **Remodel**.

Ⓕ Click in this **checkbox**.

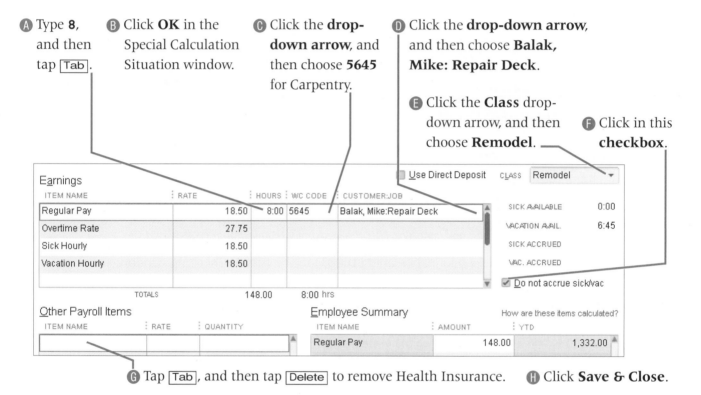

Earnings				
ITEM NAME	RATE	HOURS	WC CODE	CUSTOMER:JOB
Regular Pay	18.50	8:00	5645	Balak, Mike:Repair Deck
Overtime Rate	27.75			
Sick Hourly	18.50			
Vacation Hourly	18.50			

☐ Use Direct Deposit   CLASS Remodel ▼

SICK AVAILABLE 0:00
VACATION AVAIL. 6:45
SICK ACCRUED
VAC. ACCRUED

TOTALS 148.00 8:00 hrs

☑ Do not accrue sick/vac

Other Payroll Items		
ITEM NAME	RATE	QUANTITY

Employee Summary		
ITEM NAME	AMOUNT	YTD
Regular Pay	148.00	1,332.00

How are these items calculated?

Ⓖ Tap Tab, and then tap Delete to remove Health Insurance.   Ⓗ Click **Save & Close**.

23. Click **Create Paychecks**.
    The Confirmation and Next Steps window will be displayed.

24. Click **Print Paychecks**; click **OK** in the Select Paychecks to Print window.

> **BTS BRIEF**
>
> 62700•Payroll Expenses DR 167.97; 24000•Payroll Liabilities CR <29.80>; 10100•Checking CR <138.17>

25. Ensure the correct printer is selected, and then click **Print**.

26. Click **OK** in the Print Checks – Confirmation window, and then close the **Confirmation and Next Steps** window.

27. Close the **Employee Center: Payroll Center**.

Working with 1099s and Processing Payroll Forms and Reports

The forms you are able to produce through QuickBooks depend on the payroll option you select. Look at a few basic payroll forms used in the United States and how QuickBooks supports each of them. If you live in Canada, check out www.quickbooks.ca to learn about payroll solutions and Intuit products available for the Canadian market.

W-2s and W-3s

W-2s are provided to each employee. They summarize earnings and deductions for the year. A W-3 form is what you prepare and submit to the government. It summarizes the W-2 information you provided to employees.

If you subscribe to one of the Enhanced payroll services you can print W-2s and W-3s on blank paper right from QuickBooks. If you subscribe to the Payroll Assisted Service, QuickBooks will provide the completed forms to you.

If you have chosen the Basic payroll service or will manually run payroll in QuickBooks, you can still purchase blank W-2 and W-3 forms and print them in QuickBooks.

940 and 941

Form 941 is the Employer's Quarterly Federal Tax Return. QuickBooks will fill in the appropriate amounts. You can edit the amounts if the IRS rules instruct you to do so.

Form 940 is the Employer's Annual Federal Unemployment (FUTA) Tax Return. QuickBooks stores forms for only one year at a time. You will need to subscribe to a payroll service to download the correct year's form. QuickBooks will fill in the appropriate amounts, which you can edit if necessary.

1099-MISC and 1096

When you have vendors who you subcontract work to, you will report their earnings on a 1099-MISC form that is provided to them. The 1096 form is something you prepare for the federal government. It summarizes the 1099 information you provided to subcontractors.

If you subscribe to the Enhanced payroll service, you can print 1099-MISC forms for your subcontractors right from QuickBooks. If you subscribe to the Payroll Assisted Service, Intuit will prepare the 1099-MISC forms for you.

If you have chosen the Basic payroll service or will manually run payroll in QuickBooks, you can purchase 1099-MISC and 1096 forms and print them in QuickBooks.

Before you can run 1099-MISC forms, you must turn on the preference in QuickBooks and properly set up your 1099 vendors. A wizard will walk you through 1099 and 1096 form preparation and filing.

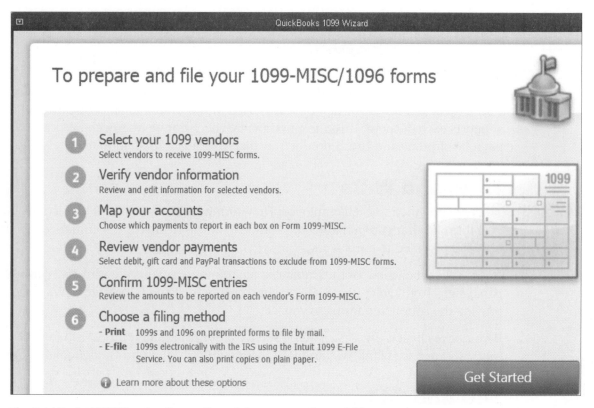

The QuickBooks 1099 Wizard walks you through form preparation and filing.

 Tab: Other Topics
Topic: File payroll tax forms

Other Payroll Reports

In addition to the reports you have already seen that deal with payroll, QuickBooks provides a variety of additional reports, including a number of them that can be run in Excel. All of these reports can be found in the Employees & Payroll category in the Report Center.

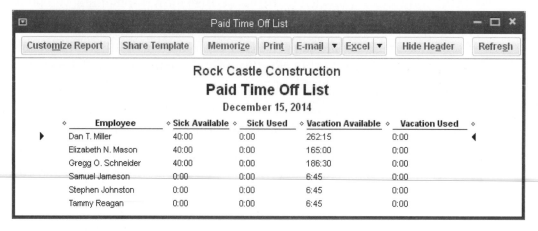

Employee	Sick Available	Sick Used	Vacation Available	Vacation Used
Dan T. Miller	40:00	0:00	262:15	0:00
Elizabeth N. Mason	40:00	0:00	165:00	0:00
Gregg O. Schneider	40:00	0:00	186:30	0:00
Samuel Jameson	0:00	0:00	6:45	0:00
Stephen Johnston	0:00	0:00	6:45	0:00
Tammy Reagan	0:00	0:00	6:45	0:00

The Paid Time Off List report is just one report available when you use QuickBooks for payroll. It shows the amount of sick and vacation hours both available to and used by employees.

Task	Procedure
Turn on the 1099 preference	▪ Choose Edit→Preferences.
	▪ Click the Tax:1099 category, and then the Company Preferences tab.
	▪ Click to choose Yes, that you file 1099-MISC forms; click OK.
Produce annual W-2 and W-3 reports	▪ Choose Employees→Payroll Forms→Process Payroll Forms.
	▪ Click in the circle to the left of Federal Form; click OK.
	▪ Click Annual Form W-2/W-3 and enter the year for which you wish to create the forms; click OK.
	▪ Select the employees for whom you wish to produce W-2s, and then click the Review/Edit button so you can make sure the information is correct before printing. Continue to click Next through the screens displaying the company and employee W-2 information.
	▪ After reviewing the W-2s, click Next to view the W-3 form; click Next to view the Filing and Printing Instructions.
	▪ Check to make sure there are no errors; click Submit Form.
	▪ Use perforated paper or preprinted forms in the printer and choose to print the W-2s.
	▪ Choose to print the W-3 form.
Produce 1099-MISC and 1096 forms	▪ Choose Vendors→Print 1099s/1096.
	▪ Work through the first three steps of 1099 production.
	▪ Click the Print 1099s button and specify the date range; click OK.
	▪ Click Print 1099 and ensure your printer settings are correct; click Print.
	▪ Click the Print 1096 button; enter your contact information.
	▪ Preview how the form will print; click Print.
Produce Form 940	▪ Choose Employees→Payroll Forms→Process Payroll Forms.
	▪ Click in the circle to the left of Federal Form; click OK.
	▪ Click Annual Form 940/940EZ and enter the year; click OK.
	▪ Follow the series of steps to verify your data and print the forms.
Produce Form 941 and Schedule B	▪ Choose Employees→Payroll Forms→Process Payroll Forms;.
	▪ Click in the circle to the left of Federal Form; click OK.
	▪ Click Annual Form 941/Schedule B, set the filing period, and then click OK.
	▪ Follow the series of steps to verify your data and print the forms.
Make adjustments to W-2 and 941 forms	▪ Right-click the box that requires an adjustment; choose Override from the pop-up menu.
Produce a Paid Time Off List report	▪ Choose Reports→Employees & Payroll→Paid Time Off List.
	▪ Set the correct date range.

Advanced Skills

Run 1099 Forms and W-2s

In this exercise, you will help Zoe print 1099-MISC forms for the subcontractors and W-2s for the employees for the 2014 tax year.

1. Choose **Vendors→Print/E-file 1099s→1099 Wizard**.
   The QuickBooks 1099 Wizard will launch.

2. Click the **Get Started** button.
   You will be asked to select your 1099 vendors.

3. Click **Continue** five times.
   You will move through several screens. Make sure to look at each as you continue through the wizard.

4. Click **Print 1099s**.

5. Choose **This Calendar Year** as the date range, and then click **OK**.
   The Select 1099s to Print window will appear.

6. Click the **Preview 1099** button, page through the forms, and then close the Print Preview window.

View the 1096 Form Which Is Submitted to the Government

The 1096 Form is what you provide to the government. It summarizes the information contained in all of the 1099s you issued.

7. Click the **Print 1096** button.

8. Type your name in the **Contact Name** field, and then click **OK**.

9. Click **Preview** to see how the form will print, and then close the **Print Preview** window.

10. Click **Cancel** in the Print 1096 window, close the **Select 1099s to Print** window, and then save and close the **QuickBooks 1099 Wizard** window.

Prepare to Print W-2s for Employees and a W-3 for the Government

You will wrap up employee payroll for the year next by producing W-2s for employees and then a W-3 for the government.

11. Click the **Process Payroll Forms** task icon in the Employees area of the Home page.

Process Payroll Forms

12. Click **OK** in the Select Form Type window to choose the default of **Federal** form.

13. Follow these steps to prepare to issue W-2s:

Ⓐ Click to select **Annual Form W-2/W-3**.

Form	Quarterly Form 941/Sch. B - Employer's Quarterly Federal Tax Return
	Quarterly Form 941-X - Adjusted Employer's Quarterly Federal Tax Return
	Annual Form 940/Sch. A - Employer's Annual Federal Unemployment (FUTA) Tax Return
	Annual Form W-2/W-3 - Wage and Tax Statement/Transmittal

Process W-2s for: ● All Employees (5 Employees)   Which option should I choose?

Ⓑ Delete **2011**, and then type **2014**.

○ Employee's Last Name - From: ▼ To: ▼

SELECT FILING PERIOD

Year 2014

Ⓒ Click **OK**.

14. Click **OK** in the Warning window, as we will work with the 2011 form for instructional purposes. Make sure you always have an up-to-date payroll service and forms when you do your own company's payroll!
The Payroll Tax Form window and the Select Employees for Form W-2/W-3 launch.

15. Click the **Review/Edit** button in the Select Employees for Form W-2/W-3 window.
Now you can see the Payroll Tax Form window a bit better. Notice that it functions as an interview, walking you through a series of steps to produce the W-2s and W-3.

Verify and Modify Company and Employee Information

16. Click **Next**; verify the company information in the next screen.
Since Zoe is doing all of the bookkeeping for Rock Castle now, she will replace Alan's name with her own.

17. Right-click **Alan Sun** in the Contact person field, and then choose **Override**.

18. Type **Zoe Minch**, and then tap Tab.

19. Click the **Next** button; take a look at the W-2 information for **Samuel**.

20. Click the **Next** button five more times, viewing each employee's information along the way.
You will now see a checklist that you can print and use for your own records, if you wish.

21. Click **Next**; take a look at the **W-3 form information** that is displayed.

22. Click **Next**; view the **Filing and Printing Instructions** that are displayed.

23. Click **Submit Form**, choosing to **Skip** viewing the errors.
Obviously, when working with your own company file, you would work through each error. The errors in this case are due to the fact that we are using a sample file and tax forms for an incorrect year.

Print W-2s

24. Click the **Print** button; click **Yes** in the Warning window.

25. Place the correct perforated paper in your printer, and then click the **Print** button to print the W-2 forms for your employees. (Print to PDF, if applicable.)
If you need to change the printer settings, you would click the Printer Setup button before clicking Print.

Print W-3

26. Click in the circle to the left of **W-3, 1 per page**, and then click **Print**.
This will print the form you need to file with the federal government for you.

27. Close the **Print W-2 and W-3 forms** window.

28. Click **Save & Close** in the Payroll Tax Form window; click **OK** in the Next Steps window.

29. When you are finished learning about Working with an Outside Payroll Service, choose the appropriate option for your situation:
    - If you are continuing on to the next lesson or to the end-of-lesson exercises, leave QuickBooks open.
    - If you are finished working in QuickBooks for now, choose **File→Exit**.

Working with an Outside Payroll Service

Some companies choose to go with an outside payroll service. If this is the case, you still need to enter the information into QuickBooks so you can create meaningful financial statements. The level of information you track in QuickBooks does not have to be as detailed when you use an outside service.

Information to Track

You will not need to worry about setting QuickBooks up for payroll or using the payroll features of the software, since you are not tracking specific withholdings and deductions. Your intent when working with an outside service is to track expenses, cash flow, and balances being held in liability accounts so that your balance sheet, profit & loss, and cash flow reports are accurate.

Do not turn on the QuickBooks payroll features to track payroll from an outside source.

Track Employees

You should enter your employees into the Employees List in QuickBooks. You will not need to enter information on the Payroll and Compensation Info tab, though, as that will be tracked by the service.

Track Expenses

To account for the payroll expenses for your company, you will need to set up an expense account, such as Payroll Expenses, and appropriate subaccounts for each type of payroll expense. Examples of subaccounts that you may wish to create are Gross Wages, Company-Paid Taxes, and Company-Paid Benefits.

Notice the subaccounts that are set up for Payroll Expenses and used to track information from an outside payroll service.

Track Liabilities

You will still be holding deductions and withdrawals from employees that have to be paid to the appropriate agency at some time in the future. This means that you need to set up an Other Current Liability account, such as Payroll Liabilities, to track this information.

Enter Information from the Outside Service into QuickBooks

When you receive a report from the payroll service that shows the payroll activity for your company, you will need to enter it in to QuickBooks. You will see payments going to employees and then out to the agencies for which you are currently holding funds in the Payroll Liabilities account.

Enter Employee Paychecks

Employee paychecks should be entered in the Write Checks window since you are not worried about keeping the "other set of books" for payroll in QuickBooks. You will enter gross wages on the first line of the Expenses tab. All deductions will be entered on the second line with a minus sign and will flow to the Payroll Liabilities account.

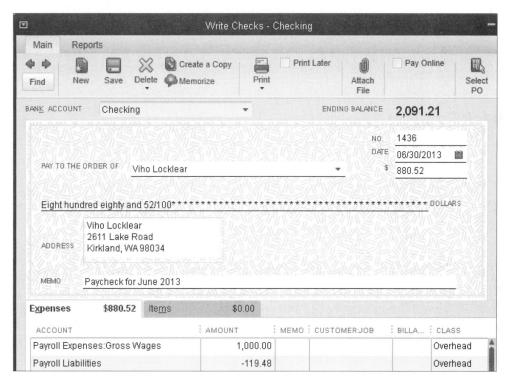

When entering paychecks from an outside payroll service, you use the Write Checks window and enter the gross wages as a positive amount and the payroll liabilities as a negative amount.

Enter Tax and Benefit Payments

When you use an outside payroll service, you will also use the Write Checks window to enter payments when you pay the payroll liabilities. On the Expense tab, you will enter the employee-paid taxes/deductions being held in Payroll Liabilities. Company-paid taxes and benefits will be entered on separate lines using the appropriate Payroll Expenses subaccounts.

Remember that, in this section, what we are talking about applies *only* when a company is using an outside payroll service! You should *never* use the Write Checks window for payroll transactions if you are completing your own payroll in QuickBooks!

QUICK REFERENCE	USING AN OUTSIDE PAYROLL SERVICE WITH QUICKBOOKS
Task	**Procedure**
Set up to track payroll expenses	▪ Choose Lists→Chart of Accounts.
	▪ Set up the following expense account: Payroll Expenses.
	▪ Set up the following subaccounts for Payroll Expenses: Gross Wages, Company-Paid Taxes, and Company-Paid Benefits.
Set up to track payroll liabilities	▪ Choose Lists→Chart of Accounts.
	▪ Inactivate the Payroll Liabilities account that was created for you.
	▪ Set up the following other current liability account: Payroll Liabilities-OS.
Enter an employee paycheck from an outside payroll service	▪ Choose Banking→Write Checks.
	▪ Set the date of the check and fill in the employee in the Pay to the Order of field.
	▪ Enter the amount of the check.
	▪ On the Expenses tab, enter the total wages on the first line using the Payroll Expenses:Gross Wages account.
	▪ On the second line of the Expenses tab, enter the total taxes and deductions held from the employee's gross wages as a negative number using the Payroll Liabilities account.
Enter tax and benefit payments	▪ Choose Banking→Write Checks.
	▪ Set the date of the check; fill in the vendor to whom you are paying the taxes or benefits in the Pay to the Order of field.
	▪ Enter the amount of the check.
	▪ On the Expenses tab, enter the employee deductions being paid on one line using Payroll Liabilities as the account.
	▪ On a separate line of the Expenses tab, enter the company-paid portion of the taxes or benefits using the appropriate subaccount, either Payroll Expenses:Company – Paid Taxes or Payroll Expenses Company – Paid Benefits.

You will have the opportunity to work with an outside payroll service in the Apply Your Skills exercise at the end of this lesson since payroll is already set up for Rock Castle Construction.

Concepts Review

Concepts Review   http://labyrinthelab.com/qb13

To check your knowledge of the key concepts introduced in this lesson, complete the Concepts Review quiz by going to the URL listed above.

Reinforce Your Skills

Before you begin the Reinforce Your Skills exercises, restore **Ginger's Gift Shop, Lesson 9 (Portable)** *from your file storage location.*

To complete payroll exercises in QuickBooks, we will be leaving Susie and Tea Shoppe at the Lake and switching to a QuickBooks sample file for Ginger's Gift Shop, which is also run as a sole proprietorship. This company file will always assume that the current date is 12/15/14, just as you have experienced with Rock Castle Construction.

REINFORCE YOUR SKILLS 9.1
Enter a New Employee

In this exercise, you will help add a new employee that Ginger just hired.

1. Choose **Employees→Employee Center**.
   The Employee Center will be displayed with three current employees.

2. Click the **New Employee** button.

3. Use the following information to set up Aiyana Harrison as a new employee.

Name	**Ms. Aiyana Harrison**
Address	**503 Oregon Place** **Bayshore, CA 92333**
Phone	**415-555-2134**
SS No.	**999-88-6666**
Gender	**Female**
Date of Birth	**04/13/86**
Hourly/Sick/Vacation Rate	**20.00**
Overtime Rate	**30.00**
Filing Status and Allowances	**Single, 0**
Vacation and Sick Leave	Use defaults

4. Close the **Employee Center** window.

Create Paychecks for Employees

In this exercise, you will create a paycheck for all of the employees for the period of 12/16/14–12/31/14.

1. Choose **Employees→Payroll Center**.

2. Click the **Pay Employees** button in the Pay Employees area of the Payroll Center.
   No scheduled payrolls have been set up for this company, so there is no Unscheduled Payroll button. Instead, you see a Pay Employees button.

3. Set the **Check Date** and the **Pay Period Ends** date both to **12/31/2014**.

4. Click the **Check All** button to choose to pay all employees; then, click **Aiyana Harrison's** name.
   The Preview Paycheck window for Aiyana appears.

5. Type **63** as the number of hours for Aiyana at the Hourly Regular Rate, and then tap Tab.
   Notice that all of the payroll tax information fills in for you once you move to the next field. You have no other entries for Aiyana, so her paycheck information is complete.

6. Click **Save & Next**.
   In this case, you are viewing the paycheck information for a salaried employee.

7. Click **Save & Next** two more times to view the paycheck information for the rest of the employees.
   Notice that QuickBooks fills in the information from the previous paycheck for you.

8. Change the number of hours worked by Regina French to **55**, and then click **Save & Close**.

Create and Print Paychecks

You will now review the information entered for each employee, and then create the paychecks.

9. Click **Continue**.
   The Review and Create Paychecks window will be displayed.

10. Click **Create Paychecks**.
    The Confirmation and Next Steps window will appear, showing a summary of how many paychecks were created as well as providing you with a shortcut to printing paychecks and pay stubs.

11. Click **Print Paychecks**, tap Tab, and then type **10733** as the First Check Number.

12. Click **OK** in the Select Paychecks to Print window; then, follow the desired step, depending on whether you wish to physically print the paychecks:

    - Click **Print**, and then retrieve the printout from the printer. You can also choose this option if you wish to print the checks as an electronic PDF file. Click **OK** to verify that all checks printed correctly.
    - Print choosing ***.pdf** as the printer, and then choose where to save the PDF file. Click **OK** to verify that all checks printed correctly.

13. Click the **Print Pay Stubs** button.

14. Tap Tab, type **123114**, tap Tab again, and then type **123114** (if necessary).

15. Click **Preview** to view how the pay stubs will print, and then close the **Print Preview** window.

16. Close the **Select Pay Stubs** window and the **Confirmation and Next Steps** window.

17. Close the **Payroll Center**.

REINFORCE YOUR SKILLS 9.3
Pay the Payroll Liabilities

In this exercise, you will pay all of the payroll liabilities due in January 2015.

1. Choose **Employees→Payroll Taxes and Liabilities→Pay Scheduled Liabilities**.

2. Click to the left of the two liability payments due in **January** to place checkmarks.

✓	DUE DATE	STATUS	PAYMENT	METHOD	PERIOD	AMOUNT D...
✓	01/15/15	Upcoming	CA Withholding and Disability Insur...	Check	Dec 2014	1,003.42
✓	01/15/15	Upcoming	Federal 941/944/943	Check	Dec 2014	2,464.54
	02/02/15	Upcoming	CA UI and Employment Training Tax	Check	Q4 2014	637.84
	02/02/15	Upcoming	Federal 940	Check	Q4 2014	143.56

3. Click the **View/Pay** button in the Pay Scheduled Liabilities area of the Payroll Center. *A Liability Payment – Checking window will be displayed for the first payment.*

4. Change the date to **12/31/14**, and then click **Save & Next** to view the next payment.

5. Change the date to **12/31/14**, and then click **Save & Close** to record the liability check.

6. Close the **Payment Summary** window, and then close the **Payroll Center**.

Process Form 941

In this exercise, you will follow the steps to produce the required Form 941 for Ginger's Gift Shop for this quarter.

1. Choose **Employees→Payroll Tax Forms & W-2s→Process Payroll Forms**.

2. Click **OK** to choose to prepare Federal forms.

3. Click **Quarterly Form 941/Sch. B**, set the filing period to **This Calendar Quarter ending 12/31/2014**, and then click **OK**.

4. Click **OK** in the Warning window.

5. Click **Next**.

6. Click **Submit Form**; click **Skip** in the Warning window.

You will receive warnings for a variety of reasons. You will skip them in this instance, but if there are errors discovered in your own company's federal tax forms, you must take the time to resolve them!

7. Click **Close** in the Submit Form window, close the **Payroll Tax Form** window, and then click **OK** in the Next Steps window.

8. Choose the appropriate option for your situation:

   ■ If you are continuing on to the next lesson or the rest of the end-of-lesson exercises, leave QuickBooks open.

   ■ If you are finished working in QuickBooks for now, choose **File→Exit**.

Apply Your Skills

Before you begin the Apply Your Skills exercises, complete one of these options:

- *Open* **[Your name] Wet Noses Veterinary Clinic, Lesson 8** *or* **Wet Noses Veterinary Clinic, Lesson 9** *from your file storage location.*

- *Restore* **Wet Noses Veterinary Clinic, Lesson 9 (Portable)** *from your file storage location. Make sure to place your name as the first word in the company filename (e.g., Sadie's Wet Noses Veterinary Clinic, Lesson 9).*

APPLY YOUR SKILLS 9.1

Set Up QuickBooks to Track Payroll from an Outside Service

Dr. James has been using an outside payroll service. In this exercise, you will help her verify that the correct accounts are set up to track expenses and liabilities properly. Then you will enter a new employee. You will need to have accounts set up in your Chart of Accounts to track your payroll expenses and liabilities.

The QuickBooks payroll features should not be turned on when entering payroll from an outside source.

1. Open the **Chart of Accounts**.

2. Verify that **Payroll Liabilities** is set up as an **Other Current Liability**.

3. Scroll down, and then verify that **Payroll Expenses** is set up as an **Expense** account.
   Dr. James has learned that she should set up subaccounts for the Payroll Expenses account, so you will help her to do this now.

4. Set up three subaccounts for Payroll Expenses: **Gross Wages**, **Company-Paid Taxes**, and **Company-Paid Benefits**.

Enter a New Employee

When you are entering a new employee and using an outside payroll service, you do not need to set up tax information.

5. Create a new employee for Wet Noses using the following information.

Name	**Mr. Viho Locklear**
Address	**2611 Lake Road** **Kirkland, WA 98034**
Phone	**425-555-1066**
SS No.	**111-33-5555**
Gender	**Male**
Date of Birth	**04/24/83**

6. Close the **Employee Center** window.

Create Paychecks Based on Information from an Outside Payroll Service

Dr. James has received a statement from the payroll service showing the amount to pay each employee (see below) and the amount that has been deducted. In this exercise, you will help her create the paychecks for the employees.

WET NOSES VETERINARY CLINIC JUNE 2013 PAYROLL					
Employee	Gross Wages	Employee Federal Taxes Withheld	Net Pay	Company Federal Taxes Owed	Company Benefits Owed
Bentley Batson	$1,500.00	$234.62	$1,265.38	$174.55	$450.00
Carrie Jones	$2,166.00	$395.72	$1,770.28	$243.19	$450.00
Samantha Reese	$2,166.00	$324.21	$1,841.79	$228.61	$450.00
Viho Locklear	$1,000.00	$119.48	$880.52	$87.37	$225.00
Totals	$6,832.00	$1,074.03	$5,757.97	$733.72	$1,575.00

1. Create paychecks for the employees listed above dated 6/30/2013 using the Write Checks window. Look at the example below as a hint regarding how to create the checks.

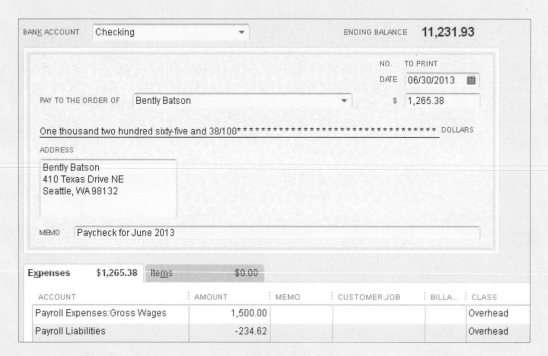

Remember, you only use the Write Checks window to create paychecks if you use an outside payroll service. *Never* use it if you are running payroll through QuickBooks!

Pay the Payroll Liabilities and Print Checks

In this exercise, you will use the information in the table shown in Apply Your Skills 9.2 to create a payroll liability check for June 2013.

1. Open the Write Checks window, and then set the date to 6/30/2013.

2. Create a liability check to the U.S. Treasury (Quick Add as a vendor) for all federal taxes owed. Use the illustration below as a guide.

	NO.	TO PRINT	
	DATE	06/30/2013	

PAY TO THE ORDER OF U.S. Treasury $ 1,807.75

One thousand eight hundred seven and 75/100********************************DOLLARS

U.S. Treasury

ADDRESS

MEMO   June 2013 Federal Taxes, FEIN# 99-9999999

Expenses   **$1,807.75**   Items $0.00

ACCOUNT	AMOUNT	MEMO	CUSTOMER:JOB	BILLA...	CLASS
Payroll Liabilities	1,074.03				Overhead
Payroll Expenses:Company-Paid Taxes	733.72				Overhead

3. Create a second check dated 6/30/2013, made payable to Kellerman Insurance, for the company-paid medical benefits owed.

4. Enter June 2013 Medical/Dental Insurance for Employees as the Memo, Company-Paid Benefits subaccount as the Account, and Overhead as the Class.

5. Choose to print all checks in the queue waiting to be printed, using 1431 as the first check number.

Advanced Skills

Answer Questions and Correct Information with Reports

In this exercise, you will answer questions for Dr. James by running reports. You may wish to display the Report Center in List View to help you answer the questions. Ask your instructor if you should print the reports, print (save) them as PDF files, export them to Excel, or simply display them on the screen.

1. How much has been paid in payroll to each employee? (Hint: Use a Quick Report for the Checking account, and then filter by Name, choosing All Employees.) Leave this report open for the next step.

   As you are creating this report, you realize that you just set up the Payroll Expenses subaccounts and that the 5/31/2013 payroll checks did not use the correct account. You will use QuickZoom to change the account on each of the three checks from 5/31/2013.

2. Double-click on each of the 5/31/2013 checks, using QuickZoom to open the transaction in the Write Checks window, and change the Payroll Expenses account to Payroll Expenses:Gross Wages, as indicated in the following illustration. Save the transactions without a class (you did not begin class tracking until after May).

Expenses	$1,265.38	Items	$0.00	
ACCOUNT			AMOUNT	MEMO
Payroll Expenses:Gross Wages			1,500.00	
Payroll Liabilities			-234.62	

3. How much was paid in Gross Wages from 5/1/2013–6/30/2013?

4. Would it be possible for you to print a list of all of the employees with their name, phone number, and address? Please make sure there is no information such as social security number or birthday displayed on the list, for privacy reasons. After the report is displayed, you notice that phone numbers were not entered for three employees. Using QuickZoom, add the following phone numbers to the employee records:

   ■ Bently Batson (206) 555-8789

   ■ Carrie Jones (425) 555-2052

   ■ Samantha Reese (425) 555-1742

5. Submit your reports based on the guidelines provided by your instructor.

6. Choose the appropriate option for your situation:

   ■ If you are continuing on to the next lesson or the Critical Thinking exercises, leave QuickBooks open.

   ■ If you are finished working in QuickBooks for now, choose **File→Exit**.

Critical Thinking

In the course of working through the following Critical Thinking exercises, you will be utilizing various skills taught in this and previous lesson(s). Take your time and think carefully about the tasks presented to you. Turn back to the lesson content if you need assistance.

9.1 Sort Through the Stack

Before You Begin: Restore the **Monkey Business, Lesson 9 (Portable)** *file from your storage location. (Remember that you are to leave the password field blank for Mary.) You also have the option of opening either the final file from Critical Thinking 8.1 or Monkey Business, Lesson 9 from your storage location.*

You have been hired by Mary Minard to help her with her organization's books. She is the owner of Monkey Business, a nonprofit organization that provides low-income students with help in preparing for college placement exams and applying for scholarships. You have just sat down at her desk and found a pile of papers. It is your job to sort through the papers and make sense of what you find, entering information into QuickBooks whenever appropriate and answering any other questions in a word-processing document saved as **Critical Thinking 9.1**. Remember, you are digging through papers on a desk, so it is up to you to determine the correct order in which to complete the tasks.

- Sticky note from Mary: Hired two part-time employees to provide training on 7/31/2013. Will use an outside payroll service. How will we enter the payroll information into QuickBooks? (Explain your answer.)

- Completed W-4 and I-9: Chelsea Sathrum; 8213 NW College Ct., Salem, OR, 97304; 503-555-2003; SS# 111-22-3333; Female; DOB 05/21/1988.

- Sticky note from Mary: Please prepare a check to pay all federal payroll liabilities that are owed. The amount in Payroll Liabilities that is owed to the U.S. Treasury is $80, but don't forget to pay the company's share!

- Note from accountant: Enter the accounts and subaccounts necessary to track an outside payroll service in QuickBooks.

- Statement from payroll service, dated 8/15/2013.

MONKEY BUSINESS AUGUST 15, 2013 PAYROLL					
Employee	Gross Wages	Employee Federal & State Taxes Withheld	Net Pay	Company Federal Taxes Owed	Company Unemployment Owed
Andy Martinez	$450.00	$78.00	$372.00	$34.42	$16.28
Chelsea Sathrum	$420.00	$48.71	$371.29	$32.13	$15.35

- Completed W-4 and I-9: Andy Martinez; 16932 SE Freedom Way, Salem, OR 97306; SS# 333-22-1111; Male; DOB 07/04/1987.

- Scribbled note from Mary: Can you produce a report for me that shows how much has been paid in payroll for each employee?

9.2 Tackle the Tasks

Now is your chance to work a little more with Rock Castle Construction and apply the skills that you have learned in this lesson to accomplish additional tasks. Open or restore the **Critical Thinking 9.2** company or portable company file from your file storage location, or open the company file you used in the Develop Your Skills exercises for this lesson. Then, enter the following tasks.

Add an employee	Add the following new employee:
	Tammy Reagan; 14896 Highridge Estates, Bayshore, CA 94326; 415-555-4004; SS# 333-22-1111; Female; DOB 6/17/1969; Hourly, sick, and vacation rate $20; Overtime rate $30; Filing status-Single with one exemption; Health insurance $25/paycheck.
Process a paycheck	Create a paycheck for Tammy as an unscheduled payroll for the pay period ending 12/29/2014. Date the paycheck 12/31/2014 for 56 hours of work, using Overhead as the Class, and 8810-Clerical as the WC Code.
Print a paycheck and pay stub	Print the paycheck you just created for Tammy; print a pay stub to go with it.
Pay liabilities	Run a Payroll Liabilities Report for December 2014 to view what is currently being held. Pay the payroll liabilities from Tammy's check as well as the extra paycheck that you issued Stephen that are due anytime in January 2015 on 12/31/2014.
Run a report	Create a report showing all of your employees and their withholding information.
Create a W-2	Create a W-2 for Tammy for the time worked in 2014.

You may use the company file from this exercise for the Develop Your Skills exercises in the next lesson if you wish.

9.3 Use the Web as a Learning Tool

Throughout this book, you will be provided with an opportunity to use the Internet as a learning tool by completing WebQuests. According to the original creators of WebQuests, as described on their website (WebQuest.org), a WebQuest is "an inquiry-oriented activity in which most or all of the information used by learners is drawn from the web." To complete the WebQuest projects in this book, navigate to the student resource center and choose the WebQuest for the lesson on which you are currently working. The subject of each WebQuest will be relevant to the material found in the lesson.

WebQuest Subject: Researching payroll regulations and determining the best payroll option

Working with Estimates and Time Tracking

LESSON OUTLINE

Creating an Estimate for a Job

Converting an Estimate to an Invoice

Dealing with Customer Deposits

Using QuickBooks' Time-Tracking and Mileage Features

Using Time-Tracking Hours to Create a Paycheck

Assessing Finance Charges

Reporting for Estimates, Time Tracking, and Mileage

Concepts Review

Reinforce Your Skills

Apply Your Skills

Critical Thinking

LESSON OBJECTIVES

After studying this lesson, you will be able to:

- Create an estimate for a job or customer and convert it to a progress invoice
- Apply the time-tracking feature and create a paycheck based on tracked time
- Work with customer deposits on account
- Assign finance charges to overdue accounts
- Work with reports for estimates and time tracking

QuickBooks allows you to create estimates for your jobs or for your customers if you don't have jobs assigned to them. Once you are awarded a job based on an estimate, QuickBooks makes it easy to convert the estimate to an invoice, saving you the time of having to reenter the information. Job costing is an important aspect for many businesses. In this lesson you will learn how to use jobs in QuickBooks to track profitability by those jobs. Also covered is the time-tracking feature, which allows you to track the time spent by each employee on each job. This feature allows you to track payroll expenses for each job much more accurately.

Rock Castle Construction

The president of Rock Castle Construction will be bidding for a job with the City of Bayshore to remodel the city's Lionello Community Center. Zoe has been asked to create an estimate in QuickBooks to be submitted with the bid.

Once the job is awarded, Zoe will need to convert the estimate to an invoice and bill the city for a portion of the amount using QuickBooks' progress invoicing feature. Zoe will receive the payment from the city and take some time to learn about how to deal with customer deposits for unearned income.

Time tracking allows a company to track employee time and create paychecks and invoices based on the data collected. You will look at how this QuickBooks feature works and help Zoe to create an invoice and a paycheck using the time data.

Finally, Zoe will assess finance charges for the customer and produce reports that will allow Alan to analyze job costing, estimate, and time-tracking data for the company.

You will continue to learn about the accounting cycle in this lesson, specifically the fourth step—how QuickBooks posts to ledger accounts.

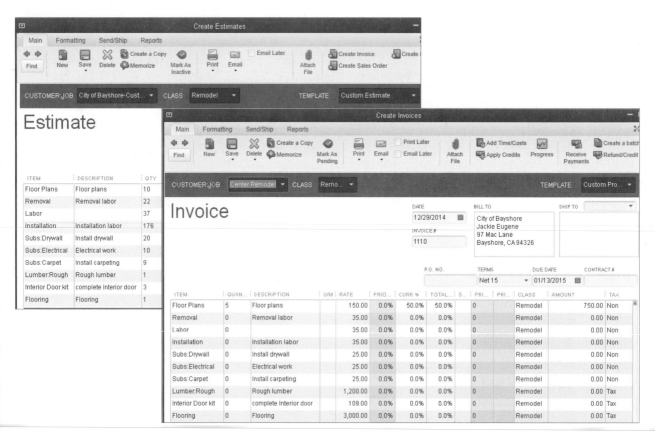

Notice that when you create a progress invoice from an estimate, the invoice includes all items on the estimate and shows the progress in regards to how much has been billed.

Creating an Estimate for a Job

When you create an estimate, QuickBooks creates a non-posting account that allows you to track your outstanding estimates. This account is displayed at the bottom of your Chart of Accounts. The non-posting account is created because estimates, like purchase orders, do not affect anything behind the scenes and, therefore, do not affect actual QuickBooks accounts.

You can create estimates for either customers or jobs. You can also create multiple estimates for a customer or a job. If a customer has no jobs created for it, there will be a Job Info tab available in the Edit Customer window with which you can work, but if at least one job has been created for a customer, that tab is no longer available. Before you can create any estimates, you must turn on the estimates feature in your Preferences window.

Job Costing in QuickBooks

In Lesson 4, Working with Customers, you learned that job information is stored with your customer data in the Customers & Jobs List, which is a component of the Customer Center. If you have multiple projects for an individual customer, you can create separate jobs for that customer. If you will perform just one job for a customer, you can track that information in the customer's record on the Job Info tab.

For Rock Castle Construction, all customers have a job associated with them, so you must always choose a job on a form, not just the customer.

> **FLASHBACK TO GAAP: MATCHING**
>
> Remember that expenses need to be matched with revenues. If a contractor buys a specific sink for a specific bathroom, it is matched to the cost of remodeling the bathroom. If there is no connection, then the cost may be charged as an expense to the project. This principle allows a better evaluation of the profitability and performance.

Preparing for Job Costing

For companies that deal with jobs, especially businesses such as construction companies, it is important to be able to look at the profitability of each job. To conduct job costing in QuickBooks, you need to take three basic steps.

1. Set up your data in the Customers & Jobs List.
2. Enter all job revenues and expenses.
3. Use QuickBooks reports to analyze job data.

The first two steps are covered as long as you set up your customers and jobs correctly and then enter them properly on sales and purchase forms. We will look at the job costing reports available in QuickBooks later in this lesson.

Task	Procedure
Add a job to a customer	■ Open the Customer Center; single-click the desired customer. ■ Click the New Customers & Jobs button; click Add Job. ■ Enter the information for the job; click OK.
Turn on estimating and progress invoicing	■ Choose Edit→Preferences. ■ Click the Jobs & Estimates category, and the Company Preferences tab. ■ Choose Yes to create estimates and do progress invoicing; click OK.
Create an estimate for a job	■ Choose Customers→Create Estimates. ■ Enter all of the information for the estimate; click Save & Close.

Create an Estimate

In this exercise, you will help Zoe create an estimate for a new customer. The first step is to open Quick-Books, and then either open a company file or restore a portable company file.

1. Start **QuickBooks 2013**.

   If you downloaded the student exercise files in the portable company file *format, follow Option 1 below. If you downloaded the files in the* company file *format, follow Option 2 below.*

 If you choose, you may use the final company file from Critical Thinking 9.2. In this case, open the Critical Thinking 9.2 company file from your default storage location in Option 2 below.

Option 1: Restore a Portable Company File

2. Choose **File→Open or Restore Company**.

3. Restore the **Rock Castle Construction** portable file for this lesson from your file storage location, placing your name as the first word in the filename (e.g., Zoe's Rock Castle Construction, Lesson 10).

   It may take a few moments for the portable company file to open. Once it does, continue with step 4.

Option 2: Open a Company File

2. Choose **File→Open or Restore Company**, ensure that **Open a regular company file** is selected, and then open the **Rock Castle Construction** company file for this lesson from your file storage location.

   The QuickBooks company file will open.

3. Click **OK** to close the QuickBooks Information windows. If necessary, click **No** in the Set Up External Accountant User window.

Verify the Estimates and Progress Invoicing Preferences

Now you need to make sure that the preferences are set up correctly for Rock Castle to use estimates and progress invoicing.

4. Choose **Edit→Preferences**.

5. Follow these steps to turn on the estimates and progress invoicing features:

Ⓐ Click the **Jobs & Estimates** category.   Ⓑ Click the **Company Preferences** tab.   Ⓒ Verify that **Yes** is selected for both estimates and progress invoicing.   Ⓓ Click **OK**.

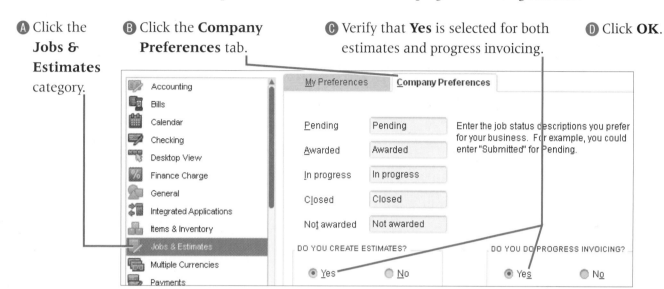

Advanced Skills

Create a New Customer

The City of Bayshore is not yet set up as a customer, so you will help Zoe create a new customer and a job for the customer.

6. Click the **Customers** button on the Icon Bar.

7. Tap ⎡Ctrl⎤+⎡n⎤ to open a New Customer window.

8. Type **City of Bayshore-Cust**, and then tap ⎡Tab⎤ three times.

The City of Bayshore is already an entry on the Vendors List and you cannot have the same name in multiple lists. Therefore, you need to modify how the name will be displayed in one list or the other. In this case, adding "-Cust" to the end will differentiate the customer and vendor list entries.

9. Follow these steps to create the new customer:

Ⓐ Type **City of Bayshore**.   **Ⓑ** Type this text, tapping Tab to move from field to field.

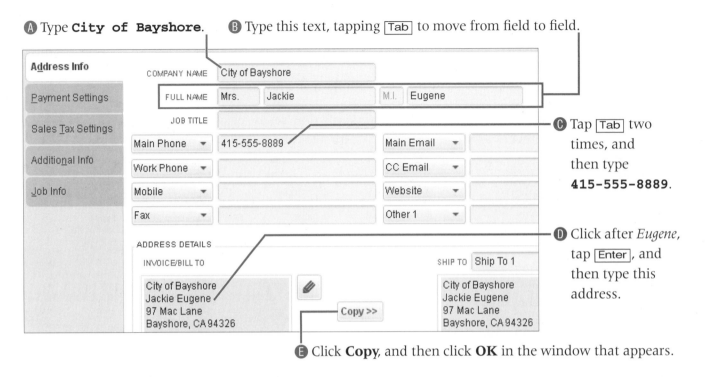

Ⓒ Tap Tab two times, and then type **415-555-8889**.

Ⓓ Click after *Eugene*, tap Enter, and then type this address.

Ⓔ Click **Copy**, and then click **OK** in the window that appears.

10. Click the **Payment Settings** tab, and then follow these steps to add information:

Ⓐ Click the **drop-down arrow**, and then choose **Net 15**.

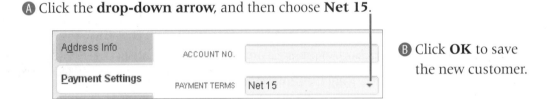

Ⓑ Click **OK** to save the new customer.

You will see your new customer displayed on the list; it is selected.

Create a New Job for the Customer

11. Click the **New Customer & Job** button, and then choose **Add Job**.

12. Follow these steps to add information for the new job:

Ⓐ Type **Comm Center Remodel**.

Ⓑ Click the **Job Info** tab.　　Ⓒ Type **Remodel Community Center** here.

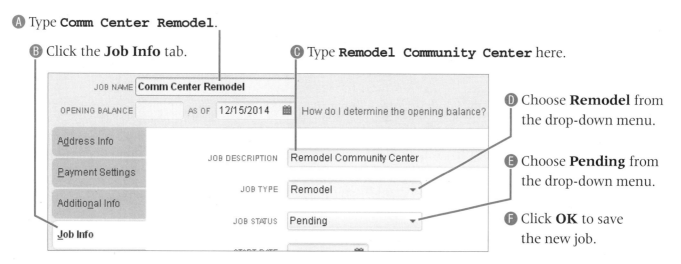

Ⓓ Choose **Remodel** from the drop-down menu.

Ⓔ Choose **Pending** from the drop-down menu.

Ⓕ Click **OK** to save the new job.

Advanced Skills

Create an Estimate for a Job

The newly created job now appears in the Customers & Jobs List and is selected, ready for you to create a new transaction for it.

13. Click the **New Transactions** button, and then choose **Estimates**. *The Create Estimates window opens with the Community Center Remodel job already filled in.*

14. Follow these steps to complete the estimate:

Ⓐ Tap `Tab`, and then type **r**.

Ⓑ Tap `Tab` two times, and then type **122214**.

Ⓒ Choose each **Item** listed, and then enter the **quantity** and **cost** displayed.

Ⓓ Click **Save & Close**.

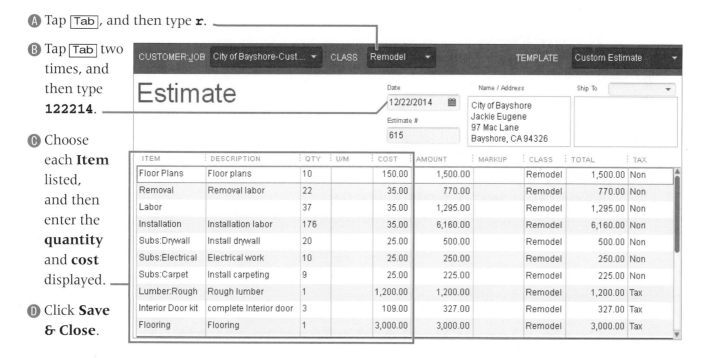

The estimate is created. Now you will wait to hear if you have been awarded the job before doing anything else with it. Remember that nothing happens behind the scenes here!

15. Close the **Customer Center**.

Converting an Estimate to an Invoice

QuickBooks makes it very easy for you to convert an estimate to an invoice once a job has been awarded. When you choose a customer or job with an existing estimate in the Create Invoices window, you have the opportunity to choose to create the invoice based on the estimate.

Progress Invoicing

QuickBooks allows you to invoice from an estimate in stages rather than for the entire estimate amount. You can either invoice a customer for the entire amount or for a percentage of the entire amount. You can even specify different percentages for each line item or which items to include. You must turn on the progress invoicing feature in the Preferences window before you can use it.

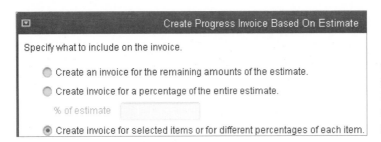

When the progress invoicing feature is turned on, you will see the Create Progress Invoice Based On Estimate window appear after you choose the estimate on which you will base an invoice.

Once you have chosen how much you wish to include on the invoice, you will see an invoice based on the Progress Invoice template. You will see new columns included on this invoice template: Est Amt, Prior Amt, and Total %.

Using Estimates for Change Orders

If you are using the contractor or accountant version of QuickBooks Premier, you can use estimates to track change orders. If you are using a different version, you can make changes to estimates, but they will not be called out as change orders. The change order feature will detail the amount of each change, exactly what changed, and the net change to the amount of the estimate. It will also document the change order for you in the description field of the estimate window.

Working with Sales Reps

For many businesses, being able to track sales by employee or representative is important, and QuickBooks provides a way to track this information by providing a Sales Rep List as one of the Customer & Vendor Profile Lists that you learned about in Lesson 3, Working with Vendors. Sales Reps may be employees, a partner in the business, or independent contractors to whom you issue 1099s.

Cycle Step 4: Post to Ledger Accounts

In the fourth step of the accounting cycle, you find the entries that were entered into the general journal posted to the individual ledger accounts. This step is done entirely behind the scenes for you. (Thank you, QuickBooks!) If you recall in Lesson 5, Banking with QuickBooks, you can double-click to view a register for a balance sheet account and a QuickReport for any income or expense account to see the transactions affecting the account. Viewing these registers and QuickReports will show you that the amounts have been properly posted from transactions to the underlying accounts.

You will be creating a progress invoice based on the estimate for 50 percent of the design work on the floor plans. Take a look at the following T-accounts to see what is happening behind the scenes in this transaction.

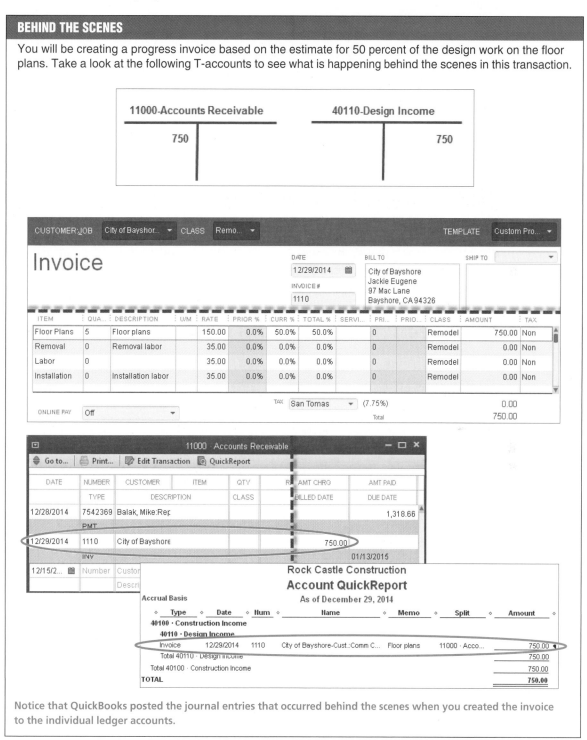

Notice that QuickBooks posted the journal entries that occurred behind the scenes when you created the invoice to the individual ledger accounts.

| CREATING AN INVOICE FROM AN ESTIMATE

Task	Procedure
Use an estimate to create an invoice	■ Open the Create Invoices window; choose the desired customer/job.
	■ Select the desired estimate; choose whether to use progress invoicing.
	■ Enter any additional information, including selecting a price level if appropriate; click Save & Close.
Add a new sales rep	■ Choose Lists→Customer & Vendor Profile Lists→Sales Rep List.
	■ Click the Sales Rep menu button; choose New.
	■ Click the drop-down arrow; choose the name from the Vendors, Employees, or Other Names List.
	■ Enter the initials of the sales rep and the sales rep type; click OK.

DEVELOP YOUR SKILLS 10.2

Create a Progress Invoice Based on an Estimate

Zoe has just learned that Rock Castle Construction has been awarded the job for the remodel of the Community Center. In this exercise, you will update the job information and create a progress invoice based on the estimate. The first step is to open the Edit Job window for the Community Center Remodel and change the status of the job on the Job Info tab.

1. Click the **Customers** button on the Icon Bar.

2. Double-click the **Comm Center Remodel** job for the **City of Bayshore** to open it for editing.

3. Follow these steps to edit the job:

Ⓐ Click the **Job Info** tab.   Ⓑ Choose **Awarded** from the drop-down menu.

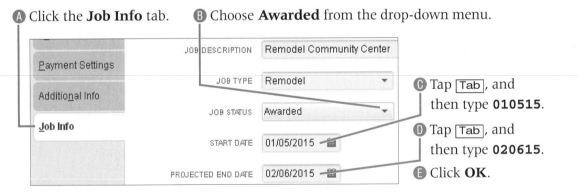

Ⓒ Tap [Tab], and then type **010515**.

Ⓓ Tap [Tab], and then type **020615**.

Ⓔ Click **OK**.

The Edit Job window closes after recording the changes to the job information.

4. Close the **Customer Center** window.

Create a Progress Invoice Based on an Estimate

Now you will create a progress invoice based on the estimate. Rock Castle will bill the city for 50 percent of the cost of the floor plans upfront.

5. Click the **Create Invoices** task icon in the Customers area of the Home page.

6. Choose the **Comm Center Remodel** job as the Customer:Job, and then tap [Tab].
The Available Estimates window appears, displaying all of the available estimates for the job.

7. Single-click to select **Estimate 615** in the Available Estimates window, and then tap Enter.
The Create Progress Invoice Based on Estimate window appears.

8. Click to the left of **Create invoice for selected items or for different percentages of each item**, and then click **OK**.

The Specify Invoice Amounts for Items on Estimate window appears.

9. Follow these steps to identify what should be included on the invoice:

Ⓐ Click in the checkbox to deselect **Show Quantity and Rate**.

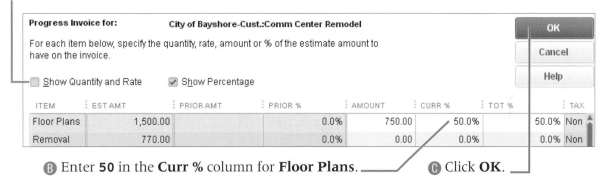

Ⓑ Enter **50** in the **Curr %** column for **Floor Plans**. ————— Ⓒ Click **OK**. —

The Create Invoices window displays with 50 percent of the Floor Plans charge filled in for you.

10. Follow these steps to complete the invoice:

Ⓐ Click the **drop-down arrow** and choose **Custom Progress Invoice**.

Ⓑ Tap Tab, and then type **122914**.

BTS BRIEF

11000•Accounts Receivable DR 750.00; 40110•Design Income CR <750.00>

11. Click **Save & Close**.
The progress invoice is recorded. The next time you choose to create an invoice based off of the estimate for the Community Center Remodel job, the 50 percent that you just invoiced for will show as a prior amount.

Dealing with Customer Deposits

When you collect money from a customer as a deposit or sell a gift certificate, you need to record the receipt as unearned income, since no work has been performed and no product has been sold.

Unearned Income

If you receive funds before they are earned, they are considered unearned income or unearned revenue. You may also hear this called customer deposits or deferred revenue. You shouldn't credit unearned income to an income account. The proper way to deal with it is to hold it in a liability account such as Customer Deposits or Unearned Revenues. Once you have delivered the goods or performed the service, you can then decrease the liability account and credit, or increase, an income account.

Customer Deposits or Gift Certificates, Oh My!

No worries! Both customer deposits and gift certificates are tracked the same way in Quick-Books. And they both require you to go through the three steps of setting up, collecting, and recording. In this lesson, we will deal specifically with customer deposits, but you can apply the same principles if you need to account for gift certificates.

Set Up to Track Customer Deposits

The first step in dealing with unearned income is to set up an Other Current Liability account and two items (an Other Charge and a Payment type) because, by accepting a customer deposit or a payment for a gift certificate, you essentially are accepting the liability to turn the deposit into a payment or to redeem the gift certificate for goods or services. By setting up a liability account, you will be able to show that you are holding the funds in a separate account until the income becomes "earned."

Receiving a Customer Deposit

You will use an invoice to record the receipt of the deposit, but you will use the item that you created to direct the funds to a liability account. In essence, you are "liable" for doing something in return for the funds you are receiving, and you will hold onto the funds in a special account until you have done what is promised. You will not record the income until the service is performed, the product is delivered, or the gift certificate is redeemed.

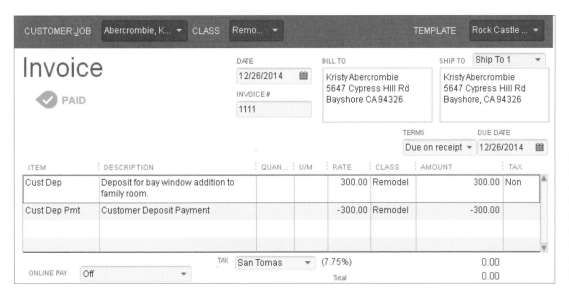

Notice the invoice created when a customer deposit is received. It does not affect an income account or Accounts Receivable (since the balance owing on the invoice is zero).

Presto! Turning a Deposit into a Payment

Once you have delivered on your promise and have traded goods or services for the gift certificate, you will use an invoice to record the income. The invoice will increase an income account and then reduce the liability account when the income becomes "earned" and you are no longer liable to perform or deliver.

BEHIND THE SCENES

When you receive the customer deposit or issue a gift certificate, you will increase both Undeposited Funds (by debiting it) and Customer Deposits (by crediting it).

Once the gift certificate is redeemed or the goods/services are delivered, you will remove the funds from the Customer Deposits liability account and realize the earned income. In the exercise you are about to complete, the cost of the service was more than the deposit amount, so the remainder will go into Accounts Receivable.

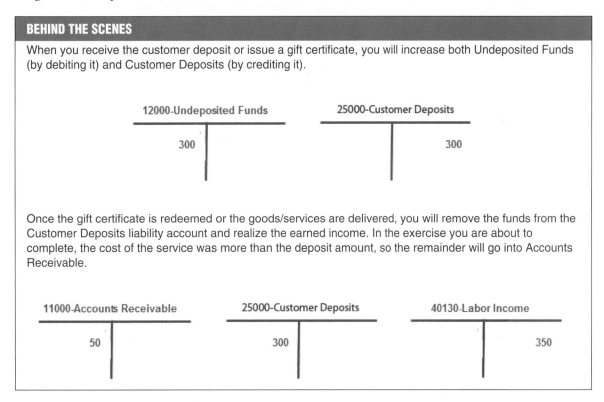

Task	Procedure
Set up to track customer deposits	Create a liability account:
	▪ Choose Lists→Chart of Accounts.
	▪ Create a new Other Current Liability account named Customer Deposits with the proper account number (if applicable).
	Create two new items:
	▪ Choose Lists→Item List.
	▪ Create a new Other Charge item named Cust Dep.
	▪ Direct the item to Customer Deposits (amount is blank; item is nontaxable).
	▪ Create a new Payment item named Cust Dep Pmt.
Collect a customer deposit	▪ Choose Customers→Create Invoices.
	▪ Enter the Customer:Job, Date, Class, and Terms in the top area of the invoice.
	▪ First line: Enter the Cust Dep Other Charge and deposit amount; fill in the Description field.
	▪ Second line: Enter the Cust Dep Pmt item and the deposit amount.
	▪ Click Save & Close; the net amount of the invoice should be zero.
Turn a customer deposit into a payment	▪ Choose Customers→Create Invoices.
	▪ Enter the Customer:Job, Date, Class, and Terms in the top area of the invoice.
	▪ Enter all of the sales items, line by line, into the invoice.
	▪ Enter the Cust Dep Other Charge item in the next line of the invoice after the sales items. If the deposit is for more than the amount of the invoice, enter only the total invoice amount for the deposit. If the deposit is for less than the amount of the invoice, then enter the full amount of the deposit.
	▪ Click Save & Close.

Account for a Customer Deposit

In this exercise, you will assist Zoe in preparing to track customer deposits, receiving a deposit from a customer, and turning the deposit into a payment.

Before you can even think about dealing with unearned income and, in Rock Castle's case, customer deposits, you must set up the proper account and items.

1. Click the **Chart of Accounts** task icon in the Company area of the Home page.

2. Click the **Account** menu button, and then choose **New**.

Chart of
Accounts

3. Follow these steps to create the new account:

Ⓐ Click in the circle for **Other Account Types**.

Ⓑ Click to choose **Other Current Liability**.

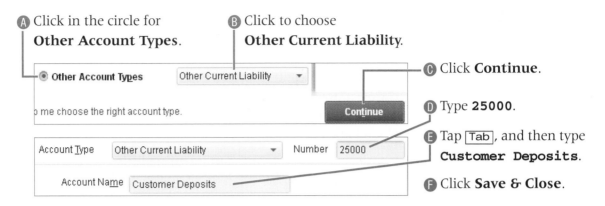

Ⓒ Click **Continue**.

Ⓓ Type **25000**.

Ⓔ Tap ⎡Tab⎤, and then type **Customer Deposits**.

Ⓕ Click **Save & Close**.

4. Close the **Chart of Accounts**.

5. Click the **Items & Services** task icon in the Company area of the Home page.

6. Click the **Item** menu button, and then choose **New**.

7. Follow these steps to create the first item:

Items & Services

Ⓐ Click to choose **Other Charge** as the type of item.

Ⓑ Tap ⎡Tab⎤, and then type **Cust Dep**.

Ⓒ Tap ⎡Tab⎤ three times, and then type **Customer Deposit**.

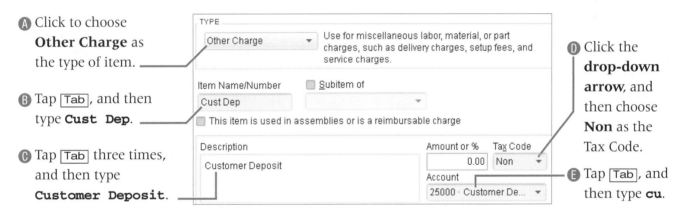

Ⓓ Click the **drop-down arrow**, and then choose **Non** as the Tax Code.

Ⓔ Tap ⎡Tab⎤, and then type **cu**.

The Amount field is left as 0.00; you will fill that in at the time of sale.

8. Click **Next**.

9. Follow these steps to create the second new item:

Ⓐ Type **p**.

Ⓑ Tap ⎡Tab⎤, and then type **Cust Dep Pmt**.

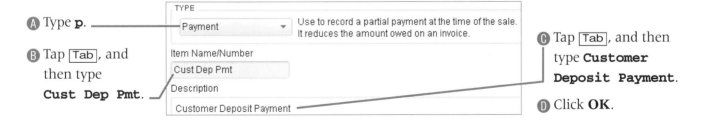

Ⓒ Tap ⎡Tab⎤, and then type **Customer Deposit Payment**.

Ⓓ Click **OK**.

10. Close the **Item List** window.

Collect a Customer Deposit

Kristy Abercrombie just called and asked for a bay window to be installed in the family room that you remodeled for her earlier in the year. Alan asked for a deposit to be made before the work begins. You will help Zoe record this deposit.

11. Click the **Create Invoices** task icon in the Customers area of the Home page.

12. Click the **Customer:Job field drop-down arrow**, and then choose **Abercrombie, Kristy:Family Room** from the list.
    The Billable Time/Costs window will appear.

13. Click to the left of the option to **Exclude outstanding billable time and costs**, and then click **OK**.

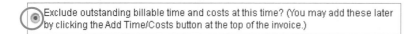

Exclude outstanding billable time and costs at this time? (You may add these later by clicking the Add Time/Costs button at the top of the invoice.)

14. Follow these steps to complete the invoice:

Ⓐ Click the **drop-down arrow**, and then choose **Remodel**.

Ⓑ Tap Tab two times, and then type **122614**.

Ⓒ Click on the **Terms drop-down arrow**, and then choose **Due on receipt**.

Ⓓ Click the **drop-down arrow** in the first line of the Item field, and then choose **Cust Dep**.

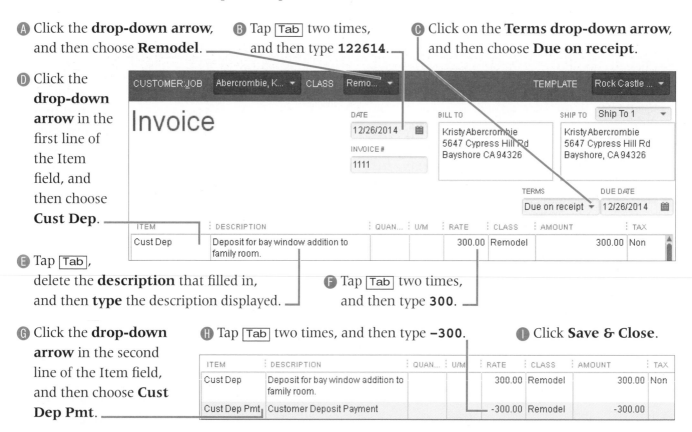

Ⓔ Tap Tab, delete the **description** that filled in, and then **type** the description displayed.

Ⓕ Tap Tab two times, and then type **300**.

Ⓖ Click the **drop-down arrow** in the second line of the Item field, and then choose **Cust Dep Pmt**.

Ⓗ Tap Tab two times, and then type **–300**.

Ⓘ Click **Save & Close**.

ITEM	DESCRIPTION	QUAN...	U/M	RATE	CLASS	AMOUNT	TAX
Cust Dep	Deposit for bay window addition to family room.			300.00	Remodel	300.00	Non
Cust Dep Pmt	Customer Deposit Payment			-300.00	Remodel	-300.00	

The total due for the invoice should be 0.00 because the net effect to Accounts Receivable is 0.00. In other words, the customer doesn't owe anything as a result of the transaction. What you have accomplished behind the scenes, though, is that you collected $300 that debited Undeposited Funds and credited Customer Deposits.

BTS BRIEF

12000•Undeposited Funds DR 300.00; 25000•Customer Deposits CR <300.00>

---

15. Click **No** in the Name Information Changed window.
You changed the terms to Due upon receipt for this one transaction, but you want the default terms you have set for the customer to remain the same.

Turn a Deposit into a Payment

The final step when working with customer deposits is to do a little magic and turn the deposit into a payment!

16. Click the **Create Invoices** task icon in the Customers area of the Home page.

Create Invoices

17. Click the **Customer:Job field drop-down arrow**, and then choose **Abercrombie, Kristy:Family Room** from the list.
The Billable Time/Costs window will appear.

18. Click to the left of the option to **Exclude outstanding billable time and costs**, and then click **OK**.

19. Follow these steps to complete the invoice:

Ⓐ Click the **drop-down arrow**, and then choose **Remodel**.

Ⓑ Tap Tab two times, and then type **123114**.

Ⓒ Click the **drop-down arrow** in the first line of the Item field, and then choose **Installation**.

Ⓓ Tap Tab, delete the default description, and then type **Installation of bay window**.

Ⓔ Tap Tab, and then type **10**.

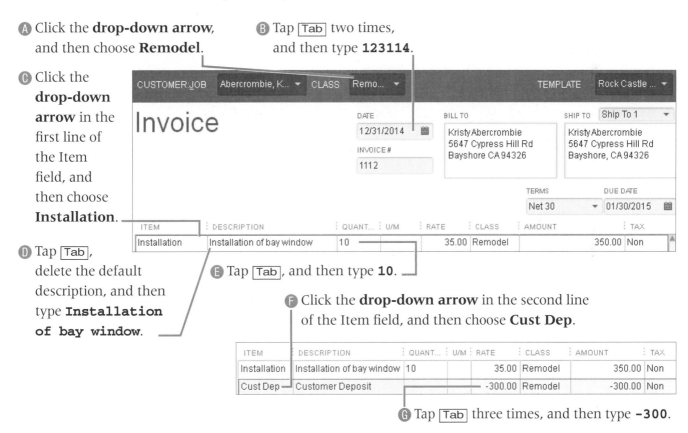

Ⓕ Click the **drop-down arrow** in the second line of the Item field, and then choose **Cust Dep**.

Ⓖ Tap Tab three times, and then type **–300**.

Note that it is up to you to type in the amount of the deposit that will apply to the invoice. In this case, the invoice was for more than the deposit, so the customer owes $50 (see the following illustration) and Accounts Receivable will be debited for this net amount owing on the invoice. If the deposit was for more than the total invoice amount, you would only enter that amount for the Customer Deposit on the invoice; the rest would remain in the liability account.

ITEM	DESCRIPTION	QUAN...	U/M	RATE	CLASS	AMOUNT	TAX
Installation	Installation of bay window	10		35.00	Remodel	350.00	Non
Cust Dep	Customer Deposit			-300.00	Remodel	-300.00	Non

TAX San Tomas ▼ (7.75%) 0.00

ONLINE PAY Off ▼ Total 50.00

BTS BRIEF

25000•Customer Deposits DR 300.00; 11000•Accounts Receivable DR 50.00; 40130•Labor Income CR <350.00>

---

20. Click **Save & Close**.

The invoice is recorded. There are no longer funds on deposit in the liability account for this customer.

Using QuickBooks' Time-Tracking and Mileage Features

The Time-Tracking feature allows you to create weekly timesheets so you can break down the hours by customer/job or to record single activities for a customer/job. In addition to these payroll benefits, time tracking also allows you to:

- Invoice customers for number of hours worked (If you recall, in Lesson 9, Using Quick-Books for Payroll, the billable costs were classified as expenses rather than time; with this feature, you can bill customers based on time)
- Automatically fill in the hours worked on paychecks
- Track time for subcontractors by automatically filling in time data on bills and checks
- Track payroll costs by job, class, or type of work performed
- Track billable versus non-billable time

Once you have used time data, you can run reports such as the Time by Job Summary to view how many man-hours you are putting into each job. Time tracking also allows you to allocate the appropriate payroll costs to a job, making your job costing reports more accurate and meaningful.

Methods of Entering Time

When you enter a single activity, it is recorded on that employee's weekly timesheet. A single activity can be entered by typing in the amount of time or by using the timer feature to actually track the exact amount of time on a task. If you choose to use the timer feature, you can use it only for timed activities on the current day.

There are two methods by which you can enter time data in QuickBooks:

- **As a single activity when it occurs:** You can either type the amount of time in the single activity window or use the built-in timer to record the exact amount of time.

Notice the Timesheet button. It allows you to toggle to the Weekly Timesheet window.

The check in the Billable checkbox shows that you intend to use this time data in the future to bill a customer.

You can either type in the duration of a task or click Start to record the actual time.

Advanced Skills

- **On a weekly timesheet:** The weekly timesheet allows you to enter time data for multiple customer/jobs, service items, and payroll items for a single employee. You can use this information to create paychecks when you process payroll.

The column to the far right is the "billable" column. If a checkmark is in this field, you can bill the customer for the time. If an invoice icon appears, it means the time has already been invoiced.

Fields Available in Both Time Data Entry Windows

Regardless of whether you choose to enter time as single activities or on a weekly timesheet, notice that each window provides the following fields:

- **Customer:Job:** Information entered in this field allows you to bill a customer for the time and to keep track of information required for accurate job costing.
- **Service Item:** Information entered in this field allows you to track services performed.
- **Payroll Item:** Information entered in this field allows you to create paychecks from your time data.
- **Billable:** If you choose this field, the information is made available for you to bill the customer for the time.
- **Notes:** Information entered in this field is displayed in the description field on reports and invoices.

Batch Timesheets

Some businesses may find that they have employees or vendors who work the same hours for a job, for instance, if you are a construction company with crews who work together on the same jobs each day. These businesses can create one timesheet for multiple payroll names (employees for whom you have chosen to use time data to create paychecks) or multiple non-payroll names (can be vendors and/or employees). Something to keep in mind if you choose to work with batch timesheets, though, is that all workers for whom you are creating a timesheet must have the following criteria in common: job, number of hours worked per day, payroll item(s), and service item(s).

Notice that when you go to choose a name for a weekly timesheet, you have the option to choose multiple payroll or multiple non-payroll names in order to create a batch timesheet.

Tracking Mileage

The mileage tracking feature in QuickBooks allows you to track mileage for your business vehicle—but not for the purpose of reimbursing your employees. If you do track mileage, you can use the data to bill customers for the expense or for tax reporting purposes. It will be up to you to keep on top of the IRS mileage reimbursement rates, and QuickBooks will calculate the mileage expense based on the approved rate on the specific day. To track mileage for a particular vehicle, you need to enter the vehicle into the Vehicle List first.

To view your mileage information once you have start tracking it, QuickBooks provides mileage reports from which you can choose to display your data. You can also choose to pass on the mileage expense to your customers and create reports to view the amount that has been billed.

Rock Castle Construction
Mileage by Vehicle Summary
January through December 2014

	Jan - Dec 14	
	Miles	Mileage Expense
1998 Saturn	379	183.84
2001 Chevy Minivan	471	228.47
2002 Ford Truck	289	140.20
TOTAL	1,139.00	552.51

Rock Castle Construction
Mileage by Job Summary
January 1 through December 15, 2014

	Jan 1 - Dec 15, 14	
	Miles	Billable Amount
Abercrombie, Kristy		
Family Room	371	135.44
Total Abercrombie, Kristy	371.00	135.44
Barley, Renee	224	81.78

The Mileage by Vehicle Summary displays the total number of miles and the expense based on the approved IRS mileage rate. If you choose to track the mileage by customer and/or job, you can also view the mileage expense billed to each customer and job.

Task	Procedure
Create a single time activity	■ Choose Employees→Enter Time→Time/Edit Single Activity.
	■ Choose the desired Name; enter the Date, Customer:Job, Service Item, and Payroll Item information.
	■ Enter the of time spent, and any appropriate note; click Save & Close.
Enter hours on a weekly timesheet	■ Choose Employees→Enter Time→Use Weekly Timesheet.
	■ Choose the desired Name.
	■ Click the Set Date button, and then type the appropriate week; enter the Customer:Job, Service Item, and Payroll Item for each line.
	■ Enter the time worked for each day; click Save & Close.
Create a batch timesheet for multiple people	■ Choose Employees→Enter Time→Use Weekly Timesheet.
	■ Choose to select from either Payroll or Non-Payroll multiple names.
	■ Choose the desired Names.
	■ Click the Set Date button, and then type the appropriate week; enter the Customer:Job, Service Item, and Payroll Item (if appropriate) for each line.
	■ Enter the time worked for each day; click Save & Close.
Enter vehicle mileage	Enter the current mileage rate:
	■ Choose Company→Enter Vehicle Mileage.
	■ Click the Mileage Rates button.
	■ Type in the Effective Date and the Rate; click Close.
	Add a vehicle to the list:
	■ Choose Lists→Customer & Vendor Profile Lists→Vehicle List.
	■ Click the Vehicle menu button; choose New.
	■ Enter the vehicle's name and description; click OK.
	Add an item, if you wish to pass mileage expenses on to customers:
	■ Choose Lists→Item List.
	■ Create a new service or other charge item called Mileage or Delivery Charges, leaving the rate field as zero.
	■ Choose the appropriate expense account; click Save & Close.
	Enter mileage:
	■ Choose Company→Enter Vehicle Mileage.
	■ Choose the Vehicle; enter the start and end dates for the trip.
	■ Type in the odometer readings from the start and end of the trip.
	■ If passing this expense on to a customer or job, mark the Billable checkbox, choose the appropriate Customer:Job, and choose Mileage or Delivery Charges as the Item.
	■ Enter any appropriate notes, if desired; click Save & Close.

Advanced Skills

Track Time for a Job

In this exercise, you will help Zoe record the time spent on the Lionello Community Center job for the City of Bayshore and track the mileage for the job.

1. Click the **Enter Time** task icon in the Employees area of the Home page, and then choose **Time/Enter Single Activity**.

2. Follow these steps to enter Stephen's billable time:

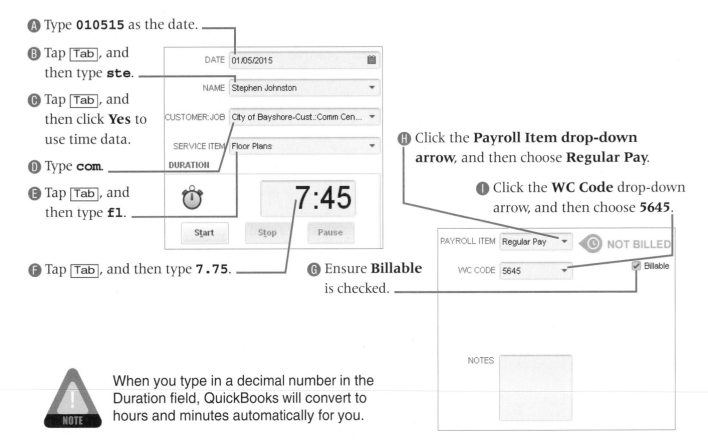

A Type **010515** as the date.

B Tap [Tab], and then type **ste**.

C Tap [Tab], and then click **Yes** to use time data.

D Type **com**.

E Tap [Tab], and then type **f1**.

F Tap [Tab], and then type **7.75**.

G Ensure **Billable** is checked.

H Click the **Payroll Item drop-down arrow**, and then choose **Regular Pay**.

I Click the **WC Code** drop-down arrow, and then choose **5645**.

DATE 01/05/2015

NAME Stephen Johnston

CUSTOMER:JOB City of Bayshore-Cust.:Comm Cen...

SERVICE ITEM Floor Plans

DURATION

7:45

Start   Stop   Pause

PAYROLL ITEM Regular Pay   NOT BILLED

WC CODE 5645   ☑ Billable

NOTES

NOTE When you type in a decimal number in the Duration field, QuickBooks will convert to hours and minutes automatically for you.

3. Click **Save & Close**.

Enter Time Using a Weekly Timesheet

You will now enter the rest of Stephen's time for the week.

4. Click the **Enter Time** task icon in the Employees area of the Home page, and then choose **Use Weekly Timesheet**.

5. Type **ste**, and then tap [Tab] to fill in Stephen Johnston as the Name.

6. Follow these steps to set the time frame for the timesheet:

Ⓐ Click this **button** to display a calendar.

Ⓑ Click the **right arrow** to display **January 2015**.

Ⓒ Click the **5** on the calendar.

QuickBooks sets the week of Jan 5 to Jan 11, 2015 as the date range for the timesheet. Notice that the time data you just entered as a single activity appears on the weekly timesheet for the week of 1/5/2015.

7. Follow these steps to enter the rest of Stephen's time data for the Community Center job:

Ⓐ Click in the first line under **7**, and then type **2**.

Ⓑ Click under **City of Bayshore**, and then type **com**.

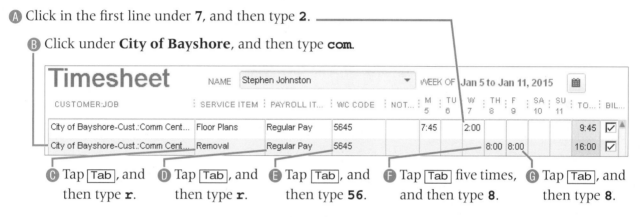

Ⓒ Tap Tab, and then type **r**.

Ⓓ Tap Tab, and then type **r**.

Ⓔ Tap Tab, and then type **56**.

Ⓕ Tap Tab five times, and then type **8**.

Ⓖ Tap Tab, and then type **8**.

Ⓗ Click here, and then click the **drop-down arrow** and choose the **Barley, Renee: Repairs** job.

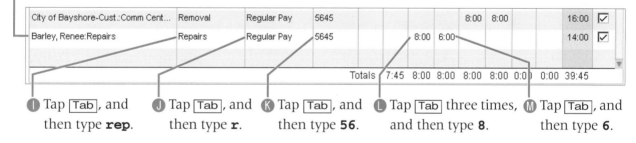

Ⓘ Tap Tab, and then type **rep**.

Ⓙ Tap Tab, and then type **r**.

Ⓚ Tap Tab, and then type **56**.

Ⓛ Tap Tab three times, and then type **8**.

Ⓜ Tap Tab, and then type **6**.

8. Click **Save & Close**.

Enter Vehicle Mileage

Finally, you will enter the mileage Stephen put on the Ford truck while doing some repair work for Renee Barley. You will need to update the mileage rate before you enter the miles driven.

9. Choose **Company→Enter Vehicle Mileage**.

10. Click the **Mileage Rates** button on the toolbar.

11. Follow these steps to enter a new mileage rate:

Ⓐ Click in the second line of the **Effective Date** column, and then type **010114**.

EFFECTIVE DATE	RATE
01/01/2007	0.485
01/01/2014	0.515

Ⓑ Tap [Tab], and then type **.515**.

Ⓒ Click **Close**.

Do not use this mileage rate for your own company—unless it is the rate that is currently being used by the IRS!

12. Follow these steps to enter the mileage driven:

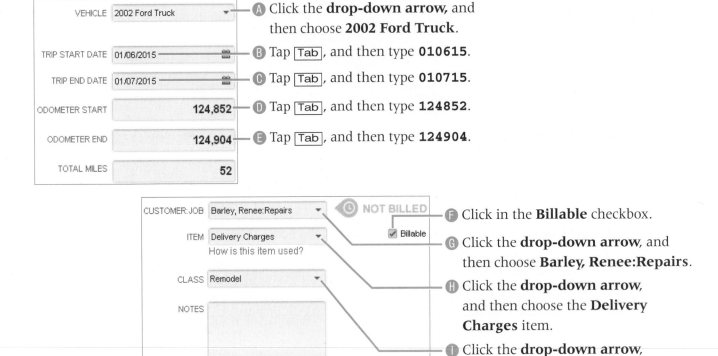

Ⓐ Click the **drop-down arrow,** and then choose **2002 Ford Truck**.

Ⓑ Tap [Tab], and then type **010615**.

Ⓒ Tap [Tab], and then type **010715**.

Ⓓ Tap [Tab], and then type **124852**.

Ⓔ Tap [Tab], and then type **124904**.

Ⓕ Click in the **Billable** checkbox.

Ⓖ Click the **drop-down arrow**, and then choose **Barley, Renee:Repairs**.

Ⓗ Click the **drop-down arrow**, and then choose the **Delivery Charges** item.

Ⓘ Click the **drop-down arrow**, and then choose **Remodel**.

13. Click **Save & Close**.

Using Time-Tracking Hours to Create a Paycheck

You can use time data for employees to create their paychecks. If you recall from the last exercise, the first time you entered time data for Stephen Johnston, you were prompted to set him up to use time data during paycheck creation.

There are two ways to use class tracking when it comes to payroll. You can choose a class for an entire paycheck or for each earning item. The default setting is a class for an entire paycheck. You should determine which option works best for your company based on what you track with classes.

Allocating Salaried Pay to an Individual Customer or Job

To accurately determine the cost of a job, you need to account for the time spent by salaried employees, too. You can record their time using the time-tracking features and choosing to "use time data to create paychecks" in the Preview Paycheck window.

Invoicing a Customer for Time Spent on a Job

In Lesson 9, Using QuickBooks for Payroll, you learned how to pass on billable payroll expenses to customers. You can also use the time-tracking feature to pass on billable time to customers. In addition, you can use the same procedure to include the billable mileage. Regardless of what type of cost you are passing on to the customer, the process is virtually the same—and you can even choose to specify a markup amount for the hours.

QUICK REFERENCE	USING TIME DATA TO CREATE A PAYCHECK
Task	**Procedure**
Use time tracking to create a paycheck	■ Choose Employees→Pay Employees. ■ Enter the check date, pay period end date, and the payee; click Create. ■ Enter any Class information or modifications, if appropriate; click Create.
Create an invoice for a customer using time and mileage information	■ Choose Customers→Create Invoices. ■ Choose the Customer:Job you wish to bill; indicate that you wish to include the outstanding billable time and costs to the invoice. ■ Click the Time tab and select any time data; click the Mileage tab and select any mileage data.

Create a Paycheck and Invoice from Time and Mileage Data

In this exercise, you will help Zoe create a paycheck for Stephen based on the time data that was entered. The first step is to set the preference that will allow you to assign classes by earnings item rather that just for an entire paycheck.

1. Choose **Edit→Preferences**.

2. Follow these steps to set the preference:

Ⓐ Click the **Payroll & Employees** category.   Ⓑ Click the **Company Preferences** tab.

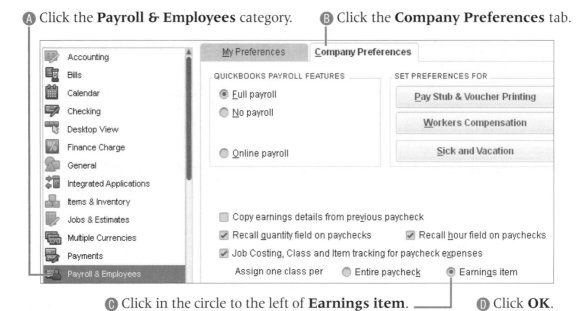

Ⓒ Click in the circle to the left of **Earnings item**. ——— Ⓓ Click **OK**.

3. Click the **Pay Employees** task icon in the Employees area of the Home page.

4. Click the **Unscheduled Payroll** button in the Pay Employees area of the window.

The Enter Payroll Information window displays. Look at the Regular Pay column for Stephen Johnston and notice that the amount is in blue, which indicates it is for the amount of billable time that you have entered.

5. Follow these steps to choose to pay Stephen:

Ⓐ Type **011215**.

Ⓑ Click to the left of **Stephen Johnston**.

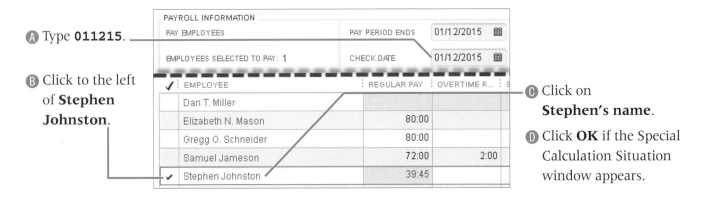

Ⓒ Click on **Stephen's name**.

Ⓓ Click **OK** if the Special Calculation Situation window appears.

The Preview Paycheck window appears. Stephen also worked in the office while another staff member was on vacation, so you will add that time to his paycheck.

6. Follow these steps to complete the paycheck for Stephen:

Ⓐ Click below the last entry in the **Item Name** column, and then type **r**.

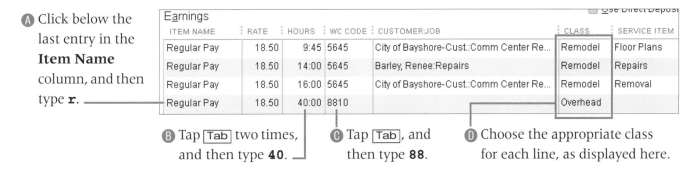

Ⓑ Tap Tab two times, and then type **40**.

Ⓒ Tap Tab, and then type **88**.

Ⓓ Choose the appropriate class for each line, as displayed here.

The following BTS Brief section shows the "parent accounts," not the various subaccounts.

BTS BRIEF

62700•Payroll Expenses DR 1,674.55; 24000•Payroll Liabilities CR <457.52>; 10100•Checking CR <1,217.03>

7. Click **Save & Close**; then, click **Continue**.

8. Click **Create Paychecks**; then, close the **Confirmation and Next Steps** window as well as the **Payroll Center**.

Create an Invoice from Time and Mileage Data

You will now create an invoice for Renee Barley that includes the time and mileage costs for the repair work Stephen completed for her.

9. Click the **Create Invoices** task icon in the Customers area of the Home page.

10. Click the **Customer:Job field drop-down arrow** and choose the **Repairs** job for Renee Barley.
The Billable Time/Costs window appears.

Create Invoices

11. Click **OK** in the Billable Time/Costs window to choose the default of selecting outstanding billable time and costs to add to the invoice.
The Time tab of the Choose Billable Time and Costs window displays.

12. Follow these steps to choose the billable time and costs to pass on:

Ⓐ Click the **Select All** button.

Ⓑ Click the **Mileage** tab.

Ⓒ Click the **Select All** button.

Ⓓ Click **OK**.

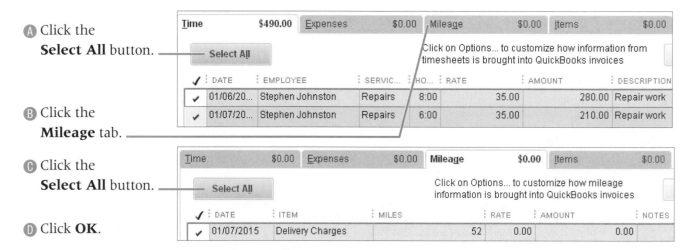

The Create Invoices window displays.

13. Follow these steps to complete the invoice:

Ⓐ Tap ⌜Tab⌟ three times, and then type **010715**.
Ⓑ Choose **Remodel** as the class.

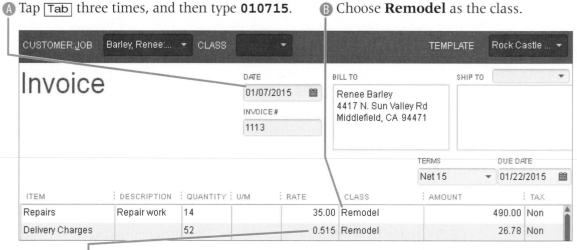

Ⓒ Drag to select **0.00**, and then type **.515** as the rate for the Delivery Charges.

BTS BRIEF

11000•Accounts Receivable DR 516.78; 40130•Labor Income CR <490.00>; 40530•Reimbursed Freight & Delivery CR <26.78>

---

14. Click **Save & Close**.

Assessing Finance Charges

If you are invoicing customers, you will inevitably find that not all of your customers pay their invoices on time. You may wish to assess finance charges for these late-paying customers.

Lending laws vary by jurisdiction, so you will need to research those applicable to you regarding whether you can assess finance charges on overdue balances. After you've performed this research, you are ready to set your preferences in QuickBooks.

 Finance charge laws are different in different locations! Do *not* use the specifics provided in this book; rather, find out the laws that apply to you and apply them to the principles you have been taught.

QuickBooks allows you to set several finance charge preferences in the Finance Charge category on the Company Preferences tab. The following illustration shows an example of the types of preferences you can control.

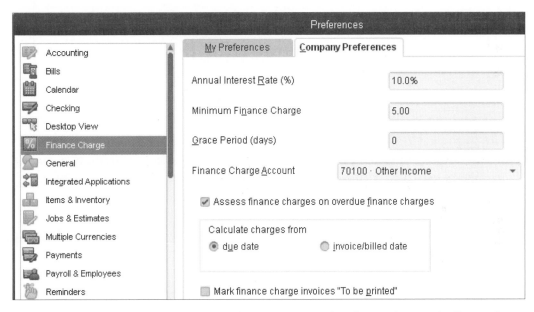

Note the preferences that you are responsible for setting in regards to finance charges. The finance charge account is an Other Income account as the income received is not the result of your normal business practices (unless you are a bank!). Before you set whether you will assess finance charges on overdue finance charges or when to calculate charges from, understand the laws where you do business.

The Assess Finance Charges Window

The Assess Finance Charges window does more than provide you with a means to determine which customers are overdue and should be charged a finance charge. It also calculates the charge due (based on the preferences set) and gives you a quick way to view the preferences and customize the finance charge invoice template.

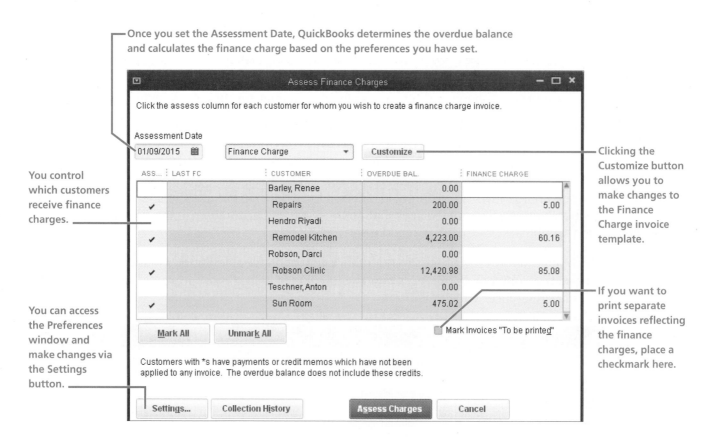

Once you set the Assessment Date, QuickBooks determines the overdue balance and calculates the finance charge based on the preferences you have set.

You control which customers receive finance charges.

You can access the Preferences window and make changes via the Settings button.

Clicking the Customize button allows you to make changes to the Finance Charge invoice template.

If you want to print separate invoices reflecting the finance charges, place a checkmark here.

Once you view the Assess Finance Charges window, you may also see customers that need friendly collections calls or may need to have their balances written off as bad debt. You learned how to deal with collections in Lesson 8, Dealing with Physical Inventory and bad debt in Lesson 6, Correcting and Customizing in QuickBooks.

Using a Batch of Statements to Bill for Finance Charges

You can send an invoice reflecting assessed finance charges to your customers. To do this, you need to ensure that there is a checkmark in the "To be printed" checkbox in the Preferences window.

The more common way to alert customers to finance charges that they owe is to produce a statement that reflects the finance charge, outstanding invoices, and aging information. You can produce a statement for just one customer, if you wish (as you did in Lesson 6, Correcting and Customizing in QuickBooks, when dealing with a NSF check). In the following exercise, you will produce a batch of statements for multiple customers, though.

When you assess finance charges, you need to debit Accounts Receivable and the appropriate accounts receivable customer subregister (you can see the example for Dr. Darci Robson below), as well as indicate the account credited by the charge (in this case, 70000•Other Income).

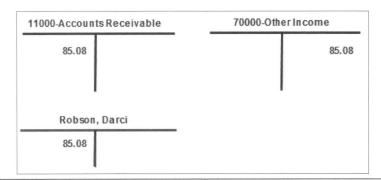

QUICK REFERENCE	SETTING UP AND ASSESSING FINANCE CHARGES
Task	**Procedure**
Set a company's finance charge preferences	▪ Choose Edit→Preferences. ▪ Click the Finance Charge category, and then the Company Preferences tab. ▪ Enter the appropriate finance charge preferences; click OK.
Assess finance charges	▪ Choose Customers→Assess Finance Charges. ▪ Set the date from which to assess the charges; choose which customers should be assessed charges. ▪ Verify and modify, if necessary, the information; click Assess Charges.
Produce a batch of statements	▪ Choose Customers→Create Statements. ▪ Choose the appropriate date range and customers, as well as any additional options. ▪ Click Print or Email to deliver the statements.

DEVELOP YOUR SKILLS 10.6

Assess Finance Charges

In this exercise, you will help Zoe assess finance charges for any customers who have overdue balances. The finance charge preferences have already been set, but Zoe wants to take a look at them to make sure they match what she just looked up for the jurisdiction in which Rock Castle Construction operates.

1. Choose **Edit→Preferences**.

2. Click the **Finance Charge** category on the left, and then the **Company Preferences** tab. *You will see the finance charge preferences that have been set up for Rock Castle Construction.*

3. Click **Cancel** to close the Preferences window without making any changes.

Assess Finance Charges

Now that you have verified that the finance charge preferences are correct, you will choose to assess finance charges on all overdue invoices.

4. Click the **Finance Charges** task icon in the Customers area of the Home page.
   The Assess Finance Charges window will be displayed.

5. Type **010915** as the Assessment Date, and then tap ⌈Tab⌋.
   All customers with open invoices that are past due as of January 9 display, along with the calculated finance charge.

6. Click **Assess Charges** and then click **Yes** in the Assess Finance Charges window.
   The finance charges are now reflected in Accounts Receivable for each customer assessed.

> **BTS BRIEF**
>
> 11000•Accounts Receivable DR 155.24 (each customer's subregister is also debited for the finance charge amount); 70000•Other Income CR <155.24>

Produce a Batch of Statements

You will now help Zoe create statements for the four customers to whom you just assessed finance charges (Renee Barley, Riyadi Hendro, Darci Robson, and Anton Teschner).

7. Click the **Statements** task icon in the Customers area of the Home page.

8. Follow these steps to produce a batch of statements:

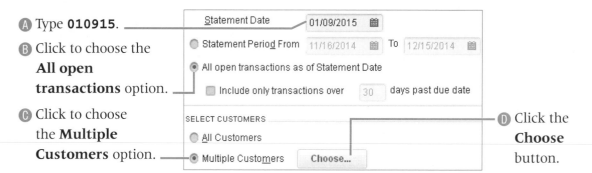

Ⓐ Type **010915**.

Ⓑ Click to choose the **All open transactions** option.

Ⓒ Click to choose the **Multiple Customers** option.

Ⓓ Click the **Choose** button.

The Print Statements window appears.

Ⓔ Use the **scroll down button** until you see each customer for whom a finance charge was assessed.

Ⓕ Click to select the customers (Renee Barley, Riyadi Hendro, Darci Robson, and Anton Teschner).

Ⓖ Click **OK**.

9. Click the **Preview** button at the bottom left of the Create Statements window.
   You can now see what each statement will look like printed.

10. Click the **Close** button at the top of the Print Preview window.
    At this point, you would choose to print or email the statements by clicking the appropriate button at the bottom of the window.

11. Close the **Create Statements** window, unless your instructor wishes for you to print the statements for review.

Reporting for Estimates, Time Tracking, and Mileage

QuickBooks' job costing, estimating, mileage, and time-tracking features include many preset reports that you can run to learn more about your business. Notice in the figure below the reports available in the QuickBooks Pro version for the Jobs, Time & Mileage category on the Reports menu. Many other reports are available for your use if you use a Premier version of QuickBooks that is specialized for your type of company.

There are a large number of standard reports available to QuickBooks users to help with tracking jobs, time, and mileage.

Task	Procedure
Produce a report to show the amount of an estimate invoiced	■ Choose Reports→Jobs, Time & Mileage→Job Progress Invoices vs. Estimates. ■ Set the date range.
Produce a report to show time tracked for each job	■ Choose Reports→Jobs, Time & Mileage→Time by Job Summary. ■ Set the date range.
Produce a report to show the profitability of all jobs	■ Choose Reports→Jobs, Time & Mileage→Job Profitability Summary.
Produce a report to show the detailed mileage expenses for all vehicles	■ Choose Reports→Jobs, Time & Mileage→Mileage by Vehicle Detail.

Produce Job, Estimate, Mileage, and Time-Tracking Reports

In this exercise, you will work with Zoe to produce a variety of reports for Rock Castle Construction.

1. Choose **Reports→Jobs, Time & Mileage→Job Progress Invoices vs. Estimates**.

2. Click the **Dates drop-down arrow**, and then choose **This Fiscal Year**.

   The Job Progress Invoices vs. Estimates report for 2014 displays.

3. Take a look at the first entry on the report and notice the result of the **estimate and progress invoice** that you entered in this lesson.

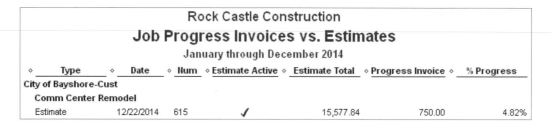

	Rock Castle Construction					
	Job Progress Invoices vs. Estimates					
	January through December 2014					
◇ Type	◇ Date	◇ Num	◇ Estimate Active	◇ Estimate Total	◇ Progress Invoice	◇ % Progress
City of Bayshore-Cust						
Comm Center Remodel						
Estimate	12/22/2014	615	✓	15,577.84	750.00	4.82%

4. Close the **Job Progress Invoices vs. Estimates** window.

Report on Time Tracking

The next report will show the time spent on each job.

5. Choose **Reports→Jobs, Time & Mileage→Time by Job Summary**.

6. Tap $\boxed{a}$ to set the date range to All.
   The Time by Job Summary report displays for all dates. Take a look down the report and notice the time for which you invoiced Renee Barley, as shown in the following illustration.

Rock Castle Construction	
Time by Job Summary	
All Transactions	
	◇ Jan 12, 15
Barley, Renee:Repairs	
Repairs	14:00
Total Barley, Renee:Repairs	14:00

7. Close the **Time by Job Summary** window.

Report on Job Costing

The third report will show the profitability of each job.

8. Choose **Reports→Jobs, Time & Mileage→Job Profitability Summary**.
   The Job Profitability Summary report displays with the default date range of all dates.

9. Take a look at the **profitability** so far for the Lionello Community Center remodel for the City of Bayshore.

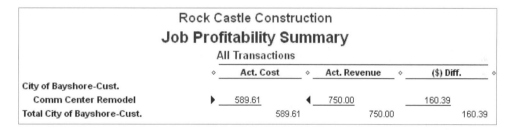

Rock Castle Construction			
Job Profitability Summary			
All Transactions			
	◇ Act. Cost	◇ Act. Revenue	◇ ($) Diff.
City of Bayshore-Cust.			
Comm Center Remodel	▶ 589.61	◀ 750.00	160.39
Total City of Bayshore-Cust.	589.61	750.00	160.39

10. Close the **Job Profitability Summary** window.

Advanced Skills

Report on Mileage

The final report that you will produce in this exercise will detail the mileage expenses for all vehicles.

11. Choose **Reports→Jobs, Time & Mileage→Mileage by Vehicle Detail**.

12. Tap ⓐ to set the date range to All.
    The Mileage by Vehicle Detail report displays for all dates. Scroll down to see the entries for the Ford truck and notice the mileage expense that you entered on 1/7/2015, as displayed in the following illustration.

Rock Castle Construction
Mileage by Vehicle Detail
All Transactions

◇ Vehicle	◇ Trip End Date	◇ Total Miles	◇ Mileage Rate	◇ Mileage Expense
2002 Ford Truck				
2002 Ford Truck	06/15/2014	18	0.515	9.27
2002 Ford Truck	06/17/2014	35	0.515	18.03
2002 Ford Truck	06/22/2014	71	0.515	36.57
2002 Ford Truck	06/22/2014	15	0.515	7.73
2002 Ford Truck	07/02/2014	44	0.515	22.66
2002 Ford Truck	07/07/2014	11	0.515	5.67
2002 Ford Truck	08/14/2014	31	0.515	15.97
2002 Ford Truck	08/19/2014	7	0.515	3.61
2002 Ford Truck	09/06/2014	9	0.515	4.64
2002 Ford Truck	09/23/2014	48	0.515	24.72
2002 Ford Truck	01/07/2015	52	0.515	26.78
Total 2002 Ford Truck		341		175.65
TOTAL		**1,191**		**613.46**

13. Close the **Mileage by Vehicle Detail** window.

14. Choose the appropriate option for your situation:

    ■ If you are continuing on to the next lesson or to the end-of-lesson exercises, leave QuickBooks open.

    ■ If you are finished working in QuickBooks for now, choose **File→Exit**.

Concepts Review

Concepts Review   http://labyrinthelab.com/qb13

To check your knowledge of the key concepts introduced in this lesson, complete the Concepts Review quiz by going to the URL listed above.

Reinforce Your Skills

Before you begin the Reinforce Your Skills exercises, complete one of these options:

- *Open* **[Your name]'s Tea Shoppe at the Lake, Lesson 8** *from your file storage location that you used for Lesson 8 (not Lesson 9, as we used a different company file to learn about payroll). Or, open Tea Shoppe at the Lake, Lesson 10 if you are working with company files instead of portable company files.*

- *Restore* **Tea Shoppe at the Lake, Lesson 10 (Portable)** *from your file storage location.*

REINFORCE YOUR SKILLS 10.1

Create a Job and an Estimate for a Customer

In this exercise, you will produce a job for Lisa Silvers and then create an estimate for her. Lisa is getting married and has asked Susie for an estimate to cater her reception. Before Susie can create estimates and conduct progress invoicing, the preferences must be set.

1. Choose **Edit→Preferences**.

2. Click the **Jobs & Estimates** category, and then the **Company Preferences** tab.

3. Click in the circle to the left of **Yes** to turn on both the estimate creation and progress invoicing features, and then click **OK**. Click **OK** to close all windows to set the preference.

Create a Job for a Customer

Next you will create a job for Lisa Silvers for her reception.

4. Choose **Customers→Customer Center**.

5. Right-click on **Lisa Silvers**, and then choose **Add Job** from the pop-up menu.

6. Type **Wedding Catering** as the Job Name, and then click **OK**.
   The new job appears on the Customers & Jobs List; it is selected.

Create an Estimate for a Job

Now that you have a job set up for Lisa's wedding reception, you will create an estimate for it. The Wedding Catering job should still be selected.

7. Click the **New Transactions** button, and then choose **Estimates**.

8. Enter Catering as the **Class**, and then **7/16/2013** as the **Date**.

9. Choose Catering as the **Item**, and then tap ⎡Tab⎤.

10. Delete the displayed description, and then **type the description and cost** displayed in the following illustration.

ITEM	DESCRIPTION	QTY	COST	CLASS	TOTAL	TAX
Catering	Catering for wedding on Lady of San Marcos boat for 65 people. Buffet-style with appetizers, salads, entree, side dish, non-alcoholic beverages, and champagne toast.		3,575.00	Catering	3,575.00	Non

11. Click **Save & Close** for the estimate.

12. Close the **Customer Center**.

Create a Progress Invoice Based on an Estimate

In this exercise, you will create a progress invoice to collect a down payment for the catering job for Lisa's wedding reception, as she liked your quote. Susie has decided to collect 25 percent up front.

1. Choose **Customers→Create Invoices**, and then choose **Lisa Silvers:Wedding Catering** as the Customer:Job.

2. Click the estimate for **7/16/2013** in the Available Estimates window, and then click **OK**.

3. Click to choose to create the invoice based on a percentage of the estimate, enter **25%** as the percent of estimate, and then click **OK**.
   Note that once that selection is made, everything will fill into the Create Invoices window, including the Class.

   > Specify what to include on the invoice.
   >
   > ○ Create invoice for the entire estimate (100%).
   >
   > ● Create invoice for a percentage of the entire estimate.
   >
   >   % of estimate   25.0%

4. Choose **Due on receipt** as the Terms, and set the date to 7/22/2013.

5. Click **Save & Close**, choosing to not have the Terms permanently changed.

Enter Mileage for a Job

In this exercise, you will help Susie enter a car in the Vehicle List and track mileage for a catering job. You will first enter the current IRS-approved mileage rate. Susie has chosen to not pass on mileage expenses to customers, so you will not set up a separate item.

1. Choose **Lists→Customer & Vendor Profile Lists→Vehicle List**.

2. Click the **Vehicle** menu button, and then choose **New**.

3. Type **Honda CR-V** as the vehicle name, and then click **OK**.

4. Close the **Vehicle List**.

Enter the Current Mileage Rate

Now you will enter the current mileage rate.

5. Choose **Company→Enter Vehicle Mileage**, and then click the **Mileage Rates** button.

6. Click below the last **Effective Date** entry, and then type **070113**.

7. Tap ⌷Tab⌷, and then type **.515** as the Rate.

8. Close the **Mileage Rates** window, leaving the **Enter Vehicle Mileage** window open for the next step.

Enter Mileage for a Vehicle

Now you will help Susie enter mileage for the catering job for Peggy Oceans on 7/4/2013.

9. Type **h**, and then tap Tab to choose **Honda CR-V** as the Vehicle.

10. Type **070413**, tap Tab, and then type **070413** again.

11. Tap Tab, and then type **22167** as the Odometer Start.

12. Tap Tab, and then type **22302** as the Odometer End.

13. Choose **Catering** as the Class, tap Tab, and then type `Catering for 4th of July party` in the **Notes** field.

14. Click **Save & Close**.
    In this case, you have not indicated a customer as you do not plan to pass on the expense.

Display Reports for Estimates and Mileage Tracking

In this exercise, you will help Susie create estimate and mileage reports.

1. Choose **Lists→Chart of Accounts**.

2. Scroll to the bottom of the list, right-click on **Estimates**, and then choose **QuickReport: Estimates** from the pop-up menu.
   Take a look at the report to view the estimate you created.

3. Set the date range to **All**, and then close the **Account QuickReport** and the **Chart of Accounts** windows.

View the Progress of Invoicing an Estimate

You will now run a report that will show you the percentage of the estimate that has been invoiced.

4. Choose **Reports→Jobs, Time & Mileage→Job Progress Invoices vs. Estimates**.

5. Tap a to set the date range to All.
   Notice that this report shows the 25 percent of the estimate that you have invoiced.

6. Close the **Job Progress vs. Estimates** window, choosing not to memorize report.

Create a Vehicle Mileage Report

Finally, you will create a report that shows the details of the mileage for the Honda CR-V.

7. Choose **Reports→Jobs, Time & Mileage→Mileage by Vehicle Detail**.

8. Tap a to set the date range to All.
   You will see a report that displays the mileage for the catering job that you just entered.

9. Close the **Mileage by Vehicle Detail** report, choosing to not memorize the report.

10. Choose the appropriate option for your situation:
    - If you are continuing on to the next lesson or the rest of the end-of-lesson exercises, leave QuickBooks open.
    - If you are finished working in QuickBooks for now, choose **File→Exit**.

Advanced Skills

Apply Your Skills

Before you begin the Apply Your Skills exercises, complete one of these options:

- *Open* **[Your name] Wet Noses Veterinary Clinic, Lesson 9** *or* **Wet Noses Veterinary Clinic, Lesson 10** *from your file storage location.*
- *Restore* **Wet Noses Veterinary Clinic, Lesson 10 (Portable)** *from your file storage location. Make sure to place your name as the first word in the company filename (e.g., Sadie's Wet Noses Veterinary Clinic, Lesson 10).*

APPLY YOUR SKILLS 10.1

Set the Preferences and Create a New Job

In this exercise, you will set the necessary preferences to be able to use QuickBooks' estimating and progress invoicing features. Then you will create a new "job" for Amy Ridgeway's new kitten, Autumn.

1. Open the **Preferences** window, and display the **Company Preferences** tab for the Jobs & Estimates category.

2. Choose to both create estimates and do progress invoicing.

3. Click **OK** in the **Preferences** window to save the changes.

Create a New Job

Now that the preferences have been set, you will create the job for Amy's new kitten.

4. Create a new job for Amy Ridgeway called **Cat-Autumn**.

5. On the **Additional Info** tab, enter the following information into the custom fields: **Feline**, **DMH** (for domestic medium hair), **Tortoise Shell**, and **Female**.

6. Click **OK**.
   Dr. James has decided that it is not important for her to track "job status" for her customers, so you will leave the fields on the Job Info tab blank.

APPLY YOUR SKILLS 10.2

Create an Estimate for a Job

Amy knows that she needs to bring in her new kitten to be spayed, tested for FIV and feline leukemia, and vaccinated, but she is concerned about the total cost and needs to budget the services. In this exercise, you will create an estimate for her so she can see the full cost for all of the services. Remember that all service and non-inventory items are not taxable; only inventory items are taxable.

ITEM	DESCRIPTION
New Patient	New Patient Exam
Vaccine	Vaccine Injection Fee
Pre-A Blood Wk	Pre-Anesthesia Blood Work
Spay Cat	Feline Spay Procedure
IV Fluids	Intravenous Fluids
Pain Meds	Pre- & Post-Surgical Pain Medication
FIV/FeLV	FIV/Feline Leukemia Test
F Leuk	Feline Leukemia Vaccine
Feline DHC	Feline DHC Vaccine
Rabies	Rabies Vaccine
Rev-Cat/Sm Dog	Revolution-Cat/Small Dog

1. Create an estimate on 7/15/2013 for Amy Ridgeway: Cat-Autumn, using Routine/Scheduled as the class for the items displayed in illustration to the right.

2. Click **Save & Close**.

APPLY YOUR SKILLS 10.3

Create an Invoice from the Estimate

Amy Ridgeway has decided to get Autumn the care she needs in phases. In this exercise, you will create a progress invoice for the first set of items.

1. Open the **Create Invoices** window, and choose **Amy Ridgeway:Cat-Autumn** as the Customer:Job. Set the date to **7/17/13**.

2. Choose to create the invoice based on the estimate created on 7/15/2013, and then to create an invoice for selected items.

3. In the Specify Invoice Amount for Items on Estimate, click in the Show Percentage checkbox, and then choose the following items to include on the invoice: New Patient, FIV/FeLV, Vaccine, and Rabies by typing **100%** in the Curr % column. Click **OK** when you are finished.

Once you enter 100 in the Curr % column for the first item, you can use the ↓ key to move down the column to enter the percentage for the other three items.

4. Read the warning message; click **OK** in the Zero Amount Items window.

5. Click **Save & Close** on the invoice.
   The invoice is created for the customer. The rest of the estimate will still be available, from which you can create future invoices.

APPLY YOUR SKILLS 10.4

Answer Questions with Reports

In this exercise, you will answer questions for Dr. James by running reports. You may wish to display the Report Center in List View to help you answer the questions. Ask your instructor if you should print the reports, print (save) them as PDF files, export them to Excel, or simply display them on the screen.

1. What is the balance still outstanding on the estimate created for Amy Ridgeway?

2. How much does each customer currently owe?

3. Is it possible to see a pie chart that shows the income by account for May 2013?

4. Will you please show me, graphically, the income by class for Wet Noses for July 2013?

5. Submit your reports based on the guidelines provided by your instructor.

6. Choose the appropriate option for your situation:
   - If you are continuing on to the next lesson or the Critical Thinking exercises, leave QuickBooks open.
   - If you are finished working in QuickBooks for now, choose **File→Exit**.

Critical Thinking

In the course of working through the following Critical Thinking exercises, you will be utilizing various skills taught in this and previous lesson(s). Take your time and think carefully about the tasks presented to you. Turn back to the lesson content if you need assistance.

10.1 Sort Through the Stack

Before You Begin: Restore the **Monkey Business, Lesson 10 (Portable)** *file from your storage location. (Remember that you are to leave the password field blank for Mary.) You also have the option of opening either the final file from Critical Thinking 9.1 or Monkey Business, Lesson 10 from your storage location.*

You have been hired by Mary Minard to help her with her organization's books. She is the owner of Monkey Business, a nonprofit organization that provides low-income students with help in preparing for college placement exams and applying for scholarships. You have just sat down at her desk and found a pile of papers. It is your job to sort through the papers and make sense of what you find, entering information into QuickBooks whenever appropriate and answering any other questions in a word-processing document saved as **Critical Thinking 10.1**. Remember, you are digging through papers on a desk, so it is up to you to determine the correct order in which to complete the tasks.

- Handwritten receipt: Dated 8/19/2013 for a $329.50 donation from Matthew Drill to provide College 101 books to ten children who are not able to afford them. Sticky note from Mary on the receipt: Can you please figure out a way to account for this donation since the books have not been distributed to the kids yet?

- Handwritten estimate: Dated 8/17/2013 for a series of workshops (College 101, FAFSA preparation, SAT preparation, and Searching for Scholarships) for a local home-school group, Expanding Opportunities Together. (They are asking for bids from three different groups before choosing a provider.) Each of the four workshops was on a separate line: College 101 $875; FAFSA $450; SAT $895; Scholarships $370. Also included were 35 College 101 texts and 35 SAT Prep books, both at 10 percent off regular retail.

- Message from Mary: "We should probably think about what we should do if customers do not pay their bill on time…Can we assess finance charges in QuickBooks? If so, please set it up so we charge 12 percent interest on overdue invoices. I think we need to have a nice grace period, though, so please set that at 30 days. Don't worry about charging a minimum finance charge or charging interest on overdue finance charges."

- Printed email: Received the contract from Expanding Opportunities Together. Could you please bill them for 50 percent up front?

- Scribbled note from Mary: Is there a report you can create for me that will show how much of the estimate has been invoiced?

10.2 Tackle the Tasks

Now is your chance to work a little more with Rock Castle Construction and apply the skills that you have learned in this lesson to accomplish additional tasks. Open or restore the **Critical Thinking 10.2** company or portable company file from your file storage location, or open the company file you used in the Develop Your Skills exercises for this lesson. Then, enter the following tasks.

Create an estimate for a new job	Create a new job for Paula Easley called Family Room, as you will be bidding on the opportunity to remodel it.
	Create an estimate for the remodel job on 01/05/2015 for 8 hours of removal labor, 40 hours of labor at $25/hour, 20 hours of installation labor, 12 hours of sub-drywall work, 8 hours of sub-electrical work, 8 hours of sub-carpeting work, flooring in the amount of $1,000, and rough lumber in the amount of $850.
Create a progress invoice based on an estimate	You have been awarded the family room remodel job for Paula Easley, so edit the job to show this. The dates for the job will be 1/19/2015 to 2/13/2015.
	Create an invoice dated 1/12/2015 for 50 percent of the entire estimate. Set the terms for the invoice as Net 15 (do not make the change permanent).
Receive a customer deposit	Chris Baker would like you to install some cabinetry that he has purchased for his garage. Receive a deposit from Chris using the Garage Repair job on 1/7/2015 for $500 for the work.
Apply a customer deposit as a payment	The garage cabinets for Chris Baker were installed on 1/15/2015 and 1/16/2015. The job took 16 hours. Create an invoice on 1/19/2015 for the work, using Installation as the item. Apply the $500 customer deposit to the invoice.
Enter time worked on a job	Samuel worked on the City of Bayshore's Lionello Community Center job for 8 hours a day from 1/12/2015 to 1/16/2015. Enter the time using a weekly timesheet. The first 22 hours were spent on removal labor; the last 18 hours were for regular labor. Choose to use time data for Samuel and use 5645 as the WC code. The class is New Construction.

 You may use the company file from this exercise for the Develop Your Skills exercises in the next lesson if you wish.

10.3 Use the Web as a Learning Tool

Throughout this book, you will be provided with an opportunity to use the Internet as a learning tool by completing WebQuests. According to the original creators of WebQuests, as described on their website (WebQuest.org), a WebQuest is "an inquiry-oriented activity in which most or all of the information used by learners is drawn from the web." To complete the WebQuest projects in this book, navigate to the student resource center and choose the WebQuest for the lesson on which you are currently working. The subject of each WebQuest will be relevant to the material found in the lesson.

WebQuest Subject: Working with gift certificates

Working with Balance Sheet Accounts and Budgets

LESSON OUTLINE

Working with Other Current Assets

Transferring Funds Between Accounts

Tracking Petty Cash

Working with Fixed Asset Accounts

Setting Up a Long Term Liability

Working with Equity Accounts

Creating Budgets & Forecasts in QuickBooks

Concepts Review

Reinforce Your Skills

Apply Your Skills

Critical Thinking

LESSON OBJECTIVES

After studying this lesson, you will be able to:

- Work with other current assets and transfer funds between accounts
- Track petty cash
- Work with fixed asset accounts and items
- Set up a long term liability
- Work with equity accounts
- Set up and use QuickBooks budgets

In previous lessons you learned to work with banking and credit card accounts, along with two current liabilities—sales tax payable and payroll liabilities. Also, you worked with an Other Current Liability account when dealing with customer deposits in the last lesson. In this lesson, you will tackle the other balance sheet accounts in QuickBooks: Other Current Assets, Fixed Assets, Long Term Liabilities, and Equity. These other balance sheet accounts allow you to track the various assets owned by your business, loans that span more than one year, prepaid expenses, and owner/shareholder investment in a company. Finally, you will learn how to use the budgeting feature in QuickBooks.

Rock Castle Construction

Rock Castle Construction has decided to rent a new office space in Millbrae. The landlord has approached Alan and offered a discount on the monthly rent amount if the company will pay six months of rent up front. Alan has decided to take advantage of this offer and has asked Zoe to set QuickBooks up to track this rent prepayment.

The president of the company has decided to purchase a new truck that will be located at the Millbrae office since business is doing so well. Zoe will be setting up a fixed asset item for the truck and a long term liability to track the loan for it.

Finally, Zoe will explore how to work with budgets in QuickBooks, creating a budget for 2015 and running a budget vs. actual report for 2014.

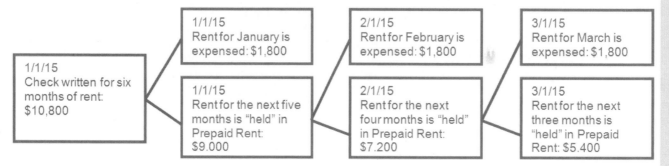

Notice how the Prepaid Insurance account "holds" funds that you have prepaid so you can expense them in the month they are actually used.

Rock Castle Construction
Profit & Loss Budget vs. Actual
January through December 2014

	Jan - Dec 14	Budget	$ Over Budget	% of Budget
Ordinary Income/Expense				
Income				
40100 · Construction Income				
40110 · Design Income	▶ 37,479.25 ◀			
40130 · Labor Income	211,149.42	93,500.00	117,649.42	225.8%
40140 · Materials Income	120,859.67	110,400.00	10,459.67	109.5%
40150 · Subcontracted Labor Income	82,710.35	192,500.00	-109,789.65	43%
40199 · Less Discounts given	-76.98	1,100.00	-1,176.98	-7%
40100 · Construction Income - Other	0.00			
Total 40100 · Construction Income	452,121.71	397,500.00	54,621.71	113.7%

The Profit & Loss Budget vs. Actual shows you how the company performed in relation to the budget prepared at the beginning of the year. This illustration displays only the income aspect of the budget.

Working with Other Current Assets

Companies use other current assets to help them match their expenses to income within the same reporting period. This is a particularly important aspect when you use the accrual basis of accounting. You will recall from Lesson 1, Introducing QuickBooks Pro that a company using the accrual basis of accounting records expenses when accrued, not when cash is paid. This means that even if you pay a six-month insurance policy up front, you must expense it during the month that it covers.

Balance Sheet Accounts

Remember, the balance sheet accounts are the asset, liability, and equity accounts. You have already learned about many balance sheet accounts: bank, credit card, current liabilities (sales tax payable and payroll liabilities), Accounts Receivable, and Accounts Payable. Now you will focus on the remaining balance sheet accounts. Refer to the following table to learn more about these other accounts.

ADDITIONAL TYPES OF BALANCE SHEET ACCOUNTS

Account Type	Description	Examples
Other Current Asset	Assets you plan to either use or convert to cash within one year	■ Prepaid Insurance ■ Security Deposit
Fixed Asset	Assets you do not plan to convert to cash within one year; they are usually depreciable	■ Vehicle ■ Equipment
Long Term Liabilities	Liabilities (loans) you do not plan to pay off within the next year	■ Mortgage ■ Auto Loan
Equity	The owner's equity in the company, whether it is a sole proprietor, a partner, or shareholders	■ Owner's Equity ■ Retained Earnings

BEHIND THE SCENES

When writing a check for six months of rent, you expense the current month's coverage and hold the rest in the Prepaid Rent account.

10400-Checking	63900-Rent Expense	13200-Prepaid Rent
10,800	1,800	9,000

QUICK REFERENCE	USING OTHER CURRENT ASSET ACCOUNTS
Task	**Procedure**
Create an Other Current Asset account	■ Choose Lists→Chart of Accounts.
	■ Click the Account menu button, and choose New.
	■ Choose Other Account Types, select Other Current Asset from the drop-down list, and then click Continue.
	■ Type the account number and the name of the new account.
Fund an Other Current Asset account	■ Choose Banking→Write Checks.
	■ Choose Checking as the bank account; complete the rest of the vendor information.
	■ Enter the amount for the current month as an expense and the remaining amount as a debit to the other current asset account you created to track it (such as Prepaid Rent).

DEVELOP YOUR SKILLS 11.1

Create and Fund a Prepaid Rent Account

In this exercise, you will help Zoe set QuickBooks up to be able to track the prepayment of rent for the company. The first step is to open QuickBooks, and then either open a company file or restore a portable company file.

1. Start **QuickBooks 2013**.

   If you downloaded the student exercise files in the portable company file *format, follow Option 1 below. If you downloaded the files in the* company file *format, follow Option 2 below.*

 If you choose, you may use the final company file from Critical Thinking 10.2. In this case, open the Critical Thinking 10.2 company file from your default storage location in Option 2 below.

Option 1: Restore a Portable Company File

2. Choose **File→Open or Restore Company**.

3. Restore the **Rock Castle Construction** portable file for this lesson from your file storage location, placing your name as the first word in the filename (e.g., Zoe's Rock Castle Construction, Lesson 11).

   It may take a few moments for the portable company file to open. Once it does, continue with step 4.

Option 2: Open a Company File

2. Choose **File→Open or Restore Company**, ensure that **Open a regular company file** is selected, and then open the **Rock Castle Construction** company file for this lesson from your file storage location.

   The QuickBooks company file will open.

3. Click **OK** to close the QuickBooks Information windows. If necessary, click **No** in the Set Up External Accountant User window.

Create a Prepaid Rent Account

Now you will create a prepaid rent account.

4. Click the **Chart of Accounts** task icon in the Company area of the Home page.

5. Click the **Account** menu button and then choose **New**.

6. Follow these steps to create the new account:

Chart of Accounts

Ⓐ Click to choose **Other Account Types**.

Ⓑ Click to choose **Other Current Asset**.

Ⓒ Click **Continue**.

Ⓓ Type **13200** as the Number.

Ⓔ Tap ⌄Tab⌄, and then type **Prepaid Rent**.

7. Click **Save & Close**; close the **Chart of Accounts** window.

Fund the Prepaid Rent Account

Zoe will now write the check for the rent payment, expensing the current month and placing the rest in the prepaid rent account.

8. Click the **Write Checks** task icon in the Banking area of the Home page.

9. Follow these steps to write the rent check:

Write Checks

Ⓐ Set the date to **01/01/2015**.

Ⓑ Tap ⌄Tab⌄, and then type **re**.

Ⓒ Tap ⌄Tab⌄, and then type **10800**.

Ⓓ Tap ⌄Tab⌄ two times, and then type **Rent for January-June 2015**.

Ⓔ Tap ⌄Tab⌄ two times, and then type **1800**.

Ⓕ Tap ⌄Tab⌄ three times, and then type **o**.

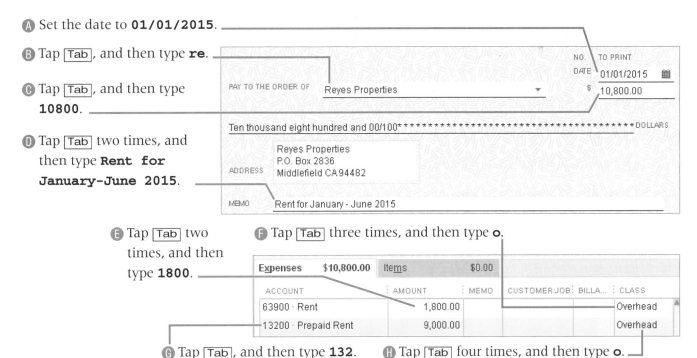

Ⓖ Tap ⌄Tab⌄, and then type **132**.

Ⓗ Tap ⌄Tab⌄ four times, and then type **o**.

Advanced Skills

10. Click **Save & Close**.

Transferring Funds Between Accounts

Once you place funds in an Other Current Asset account, you must be able to expense them when they are used. This is important, as you need to make sure to match expenses to income during the period in which they are utilized. Another term for this transfer of funds from the asset to the expense account is *amortization*. Amortization is likely familiar to you; it is simply the process of a balance decreasing over time. For instance, if you have a home mortgage, the way that the balance that you owe decreases over, say 30 years, is amortization. You can accomplish this transfer in the register window of the asset; you do not have to use a formal journal entry.

Memorizing Transactions

FROM THE KEYBOARD

Ctrl+t to open the Memorized Transactions List

There are many transactions (such as the expensing of other current assets) that you have to repeat over and over again. You can choose to have QuickBooks memorize these transactions to increase your efficiency. When QuickBooks memorizes a transaction, you can choose:

■ To be reminded about the transaction

■ To not be reminded and simply have it listed on the Memorized Transaction List

■ To have QuickBooks automatically enter it as frequently as you wish

By default, QuickBooks will choose for you to be reminded of the memorized transaction. You must make sure to choose one of the other options if you want the transaction to be listed or to occur automatically.

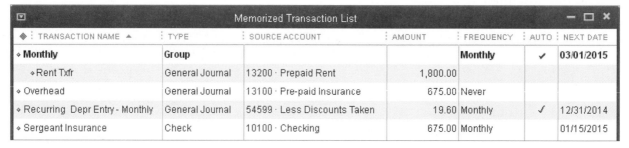

TRANSACTION NAME ▲	TYPE	SOURCE ACCOUNT	AMOUNT	FREQUENCY	AUTO	NEXT DATE
◆ **Monthly**	**Group**			**Monthly**	✔	**03/01/2015**
◆ Rent Txfr	General Journal	13200 · Prepaid Rent	1,800.00			
◆ Overhead	General Journal	13100 · Pre-paid Insurance	675.00	Never		
◆ Recurring Depr Entry - Monthly	General Journal	54599 · Less Discounts Taken	19.60	Monthly	✔	12/31/2014
◆ Sergeant Insurance	Check	10100 · Checking	675.00	Monthly		01/15/2015

The Memorized Transaction List keeps track of all of your memorized transactions for you. Access it via the Lists option
on the menu bar.

Recurring Transactions

When you are creating a new memorized transaction that you want QuickBooks to enter automatically for you, you can now group it with other transactions you have memorized.

The Enter Memorized Transactions window appears whenever you open QuickBooks and have transactions that are scheduled to be entered. This detailed list of automatic transactions helps you stay on top of which transactions are slated to be entered. And, if you enter all of them, you will have a reminder of exactly what QuickBooks is doing for you behind the scenes when entering automatic transactions.

Using Memorized Transactions for Common Transactions

You can also use the Memorized Transaction List for transactions that you complete on a regular basis. For instance, if you often pay bills electronically you can memorize a Write Checks window with BPOL (Bill Pay Online) in the check number field, and then just double-click it from the Memorized Transaction List when you need to enter another online bill payment.

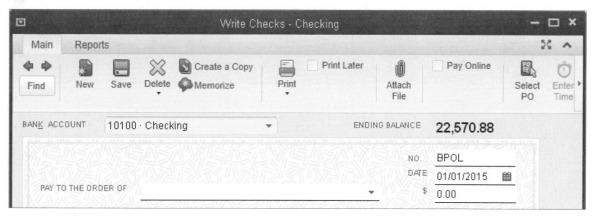

To set up a common transaction to be memorized, add the entries in the correct transaction window. Here, note that "BPOL" has been entered as the check number.

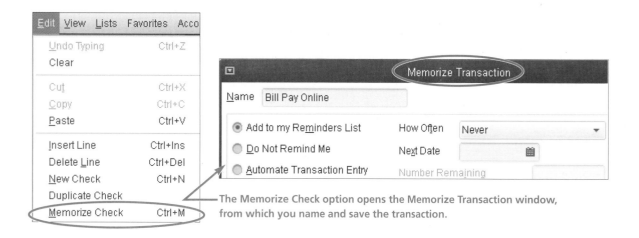

The Memorize Check option opens the Memorize Transaction window, from which you name and save the transaction.

Each month the amount for the current month's rent should be expensed.

13200-Prepaid Rent		63900-Rent	
	1,800	1,800	

Task	Procedure
Transfer funds between accounts using a register	■ Choose Lists→Chart of Accounts.
	■ Double-click the desired account; enter the date and amount of the transfer.
	■ Choose the desired account; record the transaction.
Memorize a transaction	■ Ensure that the desired transaction is currently displayed, and then single-click within it to select it.
	■ Choose Edit→Memorize General Journal (or whatever type of transaction it is).
	■ Enter the information regarding how you want QuickBooks to deal with the memorized transaction; click OK.

DEVELOP YOUR SKILLS 11.2

Make and Memorize a Transfer of Funds

In this exercise, you will help Zoe record the first transfer of funds from Prepaid Rent to Rent Expense. Once the transfer is set up, you will memorize it to occur automatically.

Before you set up your first recurring monthly transaction in your Memorized Transaction List, you will create a group called "Monthly" for this list entry. You can then add new monthly transactions as they are created.

1. Choose **Lists→Memorized Transaction List**.
   The Memorized Transaction List window will appear.

2. Click the **Memorized Transaction menu button**, and then choose **New Group**.
   The New Memorized Transaction Group window will be displayed.

3. Follow these steps to create the new group:

Ⓐ Type **Monthly**.

Ⓑ Click to the left of **Automate Transaction Entry**.

Ⓒ Click the **drop-down arrow** and choose **Monthly**.

Ⓓ Tap Tab, and then type **030115**.

4. Click **OK** to record the new memorized group.

Record Next Month's Insurance Expense

5. Choose **Lists→Chart of Accounts**.

6. Double-click the **13200•Prepaid Rent** account.
   The register for the asset will open. Notice that QuickBooks has registered an increase in the Prepaid Rent account for $9,000.

7. Follow these steps to record a transfer of $1,800 from Prepaid Rent to the Rent expense account:

Ⓐ Type **020115** as the date.　　Ⓑ Tap Tab three times, and then type **1800**.　　Ⓒ Tap Tab, and then type **ren**.

DATE	REF	PAYEE		DECREASE	✔	INCREASE	BALANCE
	TYPE	ACCOUNT	MEMO				
01/01/2015		Reyes Properties				9,000.00	9,000.00
	CHK	10100 · Checking [s					
02/01/2015	FAM2012			1,800.00			7,200.00
	GENJRN	63900 · Rent					

BTS BRIEF

63900•Rent Expense DR 1,800.00; 13200•Prepaid Rent CR <1,800.00>

---

8. Click **Record** at the bottom right of the register window.

Memorize the Transaction

So that Zoe will not have to sit down at the computer at the first of each month and record this transfer, she will memorize it and choose for QuickBooks to include it in the Enter Memorized Transactions window.

9. Click anywhere within the two lines of the transaction you just recorded.

10. Choose **Edit→Memorize General Journal**.
    This transaction is considered a general journal entry because it is a basic transfer between accounts.

11. Follow these steps to memorize the transaction in the Monthly group:

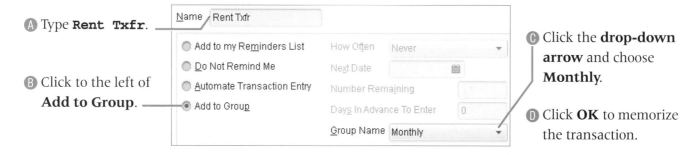

Ⓐ Type **Rent Txfr**.

Ⓑ Click to the left of **Add to Group**.

Ⓒ Click the **drop-down arrow** and choose **Monthly**.

Ⓓ Click **OK** to memorize the transaction.

12. Close the **Prepaid Insurance** account register and the **Chart of Accounts** window.
    Take a look at the Memorized Transaction List and notice the new group and rent transfer entries.

13. Close the **Memorized Transaction List** window.

Tracking Petty Cash

Most businesses keep cash around for small expenditures. This is known as petty cash. In QuickBooks, you set up Petty Cash as a bank account in your Chart of Accounts. You fund it by transferring money from another account or by keeping cash back when you make a deposit.

Recording Methods

QuickBooks offers two methods to record petty cash expenditures:

- **Write Checks Method:** You can choose Petty Cash as the account and use the Write Checks window to record your petty cash expenses.
- **The Register Method:** You can enter petty cash expenditures directly into the register.

The register method allows you to enter your petty cash expenditures more quickly, as you can tab through it faster.

BEHIND THE SCENES

When you use the checking account to fund the petty cash account, you debit Petty Cash and credit Checking.

10100-Checking		10400-Petty Cash	
	200	200	

When you use petty cash for a purchase, you debit the expense account (in this example Postage) and credit Petty Cash.

63100-Postage		10400-Petty Cash	
44			44

TRACKING PETTY CASH

Task	Procedure
Create a Petty Cash account	▪ Choose Lists→Chart of Accounts. ▪ Click the Account menu button; choose New. ▪ Choose Bank as the account type; click Continue. ▪ Type the account number, and then name the account Petty Cash.
Fund the Petty Cash account	▪ Choose Banking→Write Checks. ▪ Enter a check to cash for the amount, with Petty Cash as the account, and then record the transaction.
Enter petty cash expenditures	▪ Choose Banking→Write Checks. ▪ Choose Petty Cash as the Bank Account, enter the details, and then record the transaction.

Advanced Skills

DEVELOP YOUR SKILLS 11.3
Work with a Petty Cash Account

In this exercise, you will help Zoe fund and use a petty cash account.

Rock Castle already has a Petty Cash account on the books, so you do not need to create it before transferring funds into it.

1. Click the **Write Checks** task icon in the Banking area of the Home page.

2. Tap Tab once you have ensured that Checking is the account; then, follow these steps to complete the check:

Write Checks

Ⓐ Type **010215** as the Date.

Ⓑ Tap Tab, type **Cash**, and then tap Tab, Quick Adding it as a vendor.

Ⓒ Type **200** as the amount.

Ⓓ Click in the **Account** column, and then type **pe**.

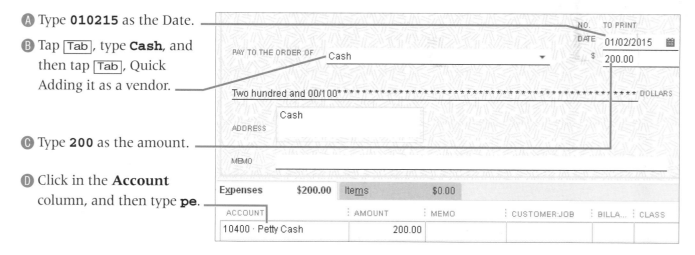

BTS BRIEF

10400•Petty Cash DR 200.00; 10100•Checking CR <200.00>

3. Click **Save & Close**, and then click **Save Anyway**.

Pay for Stamps Using the Petty Cash Register

Zoe will now purchase a roll of stamps with petty cash and record the transaction in the Petty Cash register.

4. Click the **Chart of Accounts** task icon in the Company area of the Home page.

Chart of
Accounts

5. Double-click the **Petty Cash** account in the Chart of Accounts window.

6. Follow these steps to record the charge to petty cash:

Ⓐ Type **010515** as the Date.

Ⓑ Tap Tab, and then tap Delete to remove the check number.

Ⓒ Tap Tab, type **USPS** as the Payee, and then tap Tab and Quick Add it as a vendor.

Ⓓ Type **44** as the amount.

Ⓔ Tap Tab, and then type **po**.

DATE	NUMBER	PAYEE		PAYMENT	✔	DEPOSIT	BALANCE
	TYPE	ACCOUNT	MEMO				
01/02/2015		Cash				200.00	700.00
	CHK	10100 · Checking					
01/05/2015		USPS		44.00			656.00
	CHK	63100 · Postage					

BTS BRIEF

63100•Postage DR 44.00; 10400•Petty Cash CR <44.00>

7. Click **Record**; close the **Petty Cash** register window.

8. Close the **Chart of Accounts** window.

Working with Fixed Asset Accounts

As you saw in the Additional Types of Balance Sheet Accounts table on page 443, a fixed asset is one that you don't plan to use up or turn into cash within the next year. A business uses fixed assets in a productive capacity to promote the main operations of the company. Fixed assets are also depreciable, which means that you don't expense the assets when you purchase them but rather over the useful life of the asset.

Look at the following list to see the main types of fixed assets:

- Land
- Furniture & Equipment
- Buildings
- Vehicles
- Leasehold Improvements

Setting Up Fixed Assets in QuickBooks

There are many correct ways to set up your fixed assets in QuickBooks. You should ask your accountant which method she prefers that you use. In this lesson, you will look at one method that involves creating a fixed asset account for each major type of fixed asset and then an account to track accumulated depreciation for all fixed assets. This is displayed in the following illustration.

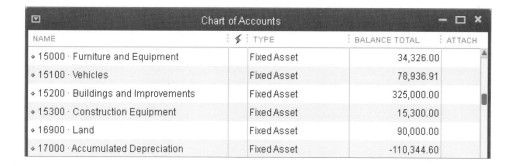

NAME	$	TYPE	BALANCE TOTAL	ATTACH
◆ 15000 · Furniture and Equipment		Fixed Asset	34,326.00	
◆ 15100 · Vehicles		Fixed Asset	78,936.91	
◆ 15200 · Buildings and Improvements		Fixed Asset	325,000.00	
◆ 15300 · Construction Equipment		Fixed Asset	15,300.00	
◆ 16900 · Land		Fixed Asset	90,000.00	
◆ 17000 · Accumulated Depreciation		Fixed Asset	-110,344.60	

Depreciation

Depreciation provides a business with a way to match income to expenses. A fixed asset is used to produce income over a period of time, and depreciation allows you to record the appropriate expense for the same period. Many small businesses record depreciation transactions just once a year, but they can be entered monthly or quarterly if the business produces financial statements for those periods. You will learn how to enter the annual depreciation transaction in Lesson 12, Reporting, Closing the Books, and Adjusting Entries.

> **FLASHBACK TO GAAP: MATCHING**
> Remember that expenses need to be matched with revenues.

Accumulated Depreciation

Each accounting period, a business records a depreciation expense for the fixed asset(s). These depreciation expenses "accumulate" in an account called Accumulated Depreciation, which is also a fixed asset account. Accumulated Depreciation is a *contra account*, which means it offsets the balance of the related fixed asset accounts by entering a negative amount so that the book value is displayed rather than the original cost on the balance sheet report.

Fixed Asset Items

Fixed asset items provide a convenient way to track your fixed assets. After creating your fixed asset account and subaccounts, you should set up the fixed asset item. These items help you consolidate all of the important information about each fixed asset in a convenient place. In addition, your accountant can transfer the information from your Fixed Asset List to the Fixed Asset Manager, if they use that feature of QuickBooks.

In the Fixed Asset Item List QuickBooks allows you to track the following information:

- Purchase information/cost basis
- Sales information
- Corresponding asset account
- Serial number
- Warranty information
- Notes and descriptions

NAME	LOCATION OF FI...	PURCHASE ...	ACCOUNT ▲	COST	COST/BASIS	ACCUMULAT...	BOOK VALUE	SAL...	PRI...	A...
◈ Desktop PC (5) - 8		05/01/2010	15000 · Furniture a...	13,000.00	13,000.00	2,600.00	10,400.00		0.00	
◈ Copier/Printer - 15	Main Office	04/26/2010	15000 · Furniture a...	5,000.00	5,000.00	1,000.00	4,000.00		0.00	
◈ Chairs - 3		11/15/2009	15000 · Furniture a...	475.00	475.00	247.00	228.00		0.00	
◈ Conference Table - 4		11/15/2009	15000 · Furniture a...	3,500.00	3,500.00	1,820.00	1,680.00		0.00	
◈ Desks - 5		12/20/2009	15000 · Furniture a...	2,100.00	2,100.00	1,092.00	1,008.00		0.00	
◈ Desktop computer - 6	MV	10/15/2009	15000 · Furniture a...	2,000.00	2,000.00	1,040.00	960.00		0.00	
◈ Desktop PC - 7		10/01/2009	15000 · Furniture a...	5,000.00	5,000.00	2,600.00	2,400.00		0.00	
◈ Laser Printer - 9		10/01/2009	15000 · Furniture a...	2,001.00	2,001.00	1,040.52	960.48		0.00	
◈ Metal filling cabinets - ...		10/29/2009	15000 · Furniture a...	1,250.00	1,250.00	484.69	765.31		0.00	
◈ Server - 13		10/01/2009	15000 · Furniture a...	6,500.00	6,500.00	3,380.00	3,120.00		0.00	
◈ 2015 Ford Truck - 18	Millbrae, CA	01/02/2015	15100 · Vehicles	30,649.00					0.00	
◈ Lexus - 16		04/26/2010	15100 · Vehicles	75,000.00	75,000.00	15,000.00	60,000.00		0.00	
◈ 2005 pickup - 2	Bayshore, CA	02/14/2007	15100 · Vehicles	28,602.91	28,602.91	12,585.00	16,017.91		0.00	
◈ 2005 Van - 14		10/15/2007	15100 · Vehicles	26,000.00	26,000.00	21,507.20	4,492.80		0.00	
◈ Utility Truck - 1	Bayshore, CA	06/01/2007	15100 · Vehicles	24,334.00	24,334.00	12,585.00	11,749.00		0.00	
◈ Office Building - 11	1735 County Ro...	09/22/2007	15200 · Buildings a...	325,000.00	325,000.00	27,430.54	297,569.46		0.00	
◈ Equipment - 17		12/31/2009	15300 · Constructio...	15,300.00	15,300.00	5,932.65	9,367.35		0.00	
◈ Office Land - 12	1735 Country R...	09/22/2007	16900 · Land	90,000.00	90,000.00		90,000.00		0.00	

The Fixed Asset Item List helps you to track your fixed assets and compile all of the essential information for them in one convenient place.

Creating Fixed Asset Items

There are two ways that a new fixed asset item can be set up:

- Create the new item when entering the purchase transaction
- Open the Fixed Asset Item List and create a new item

When you enter fixed assets upon creation of a new company, you will debit the fixed asset account and credit Opening Balance Equity. If you recall from Lesson 2, Creating a Company, this account is created by QuickBooks when the first balance sheet account is created so you have an accurate balance sheet from the beginning. If a loan is associated with the fixed asset, the loan amount will be entered in a Long Term Liability account and the difference in an equity account.

When you set up a fixed asset item, you indicate the account into which it has been entered. This does not enter it into the account or affect what happens behind the scenes. You must also complete the appropriate transaction to make sure and enter the fixed asset properly.

Accountant Tool: Fixed Asset Manager

If your accountant uses the Premier Accountant version of QuickBooks, he can pull the fixed asset information from your Fixed Asset Item list into the Fixed Asset Manager in order to work with your fixed assets. This tool will help him determine how to depreciate the fixed assets as well as the amount that needs to be posted back to the company file as an adjusting entry.

QUICK REFERENCE	DEALING WITH FIXED ASSET ITEMS
Task	**Procedure**
Create a fixed asset item from a transaction	▪ Enter the purchase transaction information; click the Items tab. ▪ Click the Item column drop-down arrow; choose <Add New>. ▪ Enter all of the fixed asset information, choosing the correct fixed asset account, and then click OK.
Create a fixed asset item using the Fixed Asset Item List	▪ Choose Lists→Fixed Asset Item List. ▪ Click the Item menu button; choose New. ▪ Enter all of the fixed asset information, choosing the correct fixed asset account, and then click OK.

DEVELOP YOUR SKILLS 11.4

Create a Fixed Asset Item

In this exercise, you will help Zoe create a new fixed asset item for the new truck that was purchased.

1. Choose **Lists→Fixed Asset Item List**.

2. Click the **Item** menu button, and then choose **New**.

3. Follow these steps to create the new item:

Ⓐ Type **2015 Ford Truck – 18**.

Ⓑ Tap Tab three times, and then type **Ford F-150 Truck**.

Ⓒ Tap Tab, and then type **010215**.

Ⓓ Tap Tab, and then type **30649**.

Ⓔ Tap Tab, and then type **Bayshore Ford**.

Ⓕ Tap Tab, and then type **v**.

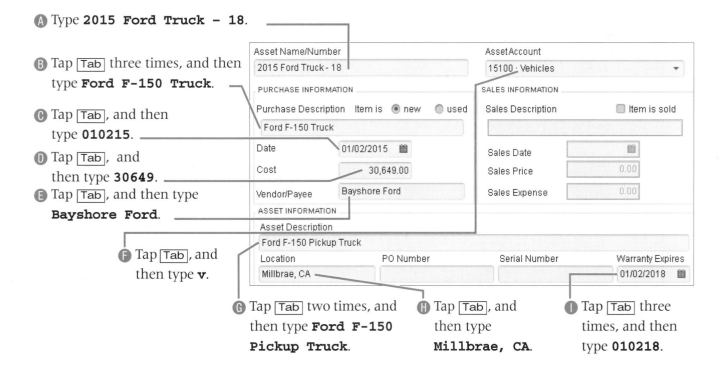

Ⓖ Tap Tab two times, and then type **Ford F-150 Pickup Truck**.

Ⓗ Tap Tab, and then type **Millbrae, CA**.

Ⓘ Tap Tab three times, and then type **010218**.

4. Click **OK**.

5. Close the **Fixed Asset Item List**.

   You did not affect anything behind the scenes in this exercise, but in the next exercise you will see how the purchase of the new fixed asset is entered behind the scenes.

Setting Up a Long Term Liability

Most companies have to take out a loan for a fixed asset (or a loan for some other item for a period longer than a year) at some time or another. In this section, you will create a Long Term Liability account to track the new truck loan. A company uses a Long Term Liability to track a loan that is scheduled to take longer than a year to pay off.

The QuickBooks Loan Manager

QuickBooks provides a tool for you to track your loans, similar to the Fixed Asset Item List that allows you to track your fixed assets. The Loan Manager allows you to set up loans based on information that you have entered in a long term liability or other current liability account. The Loan Manager tracks the principle and interest payments without having to set up separate amortization schedules. You can also use the Loan Manager to compare different loan scenarios. In addition, you have the opportunity to print loans from the Loan Manager.

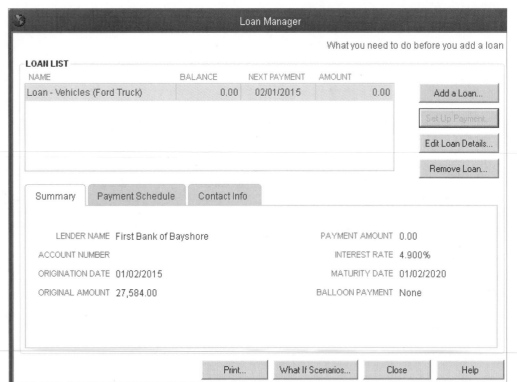

The Loan Manager provides you with a place to track your long term liabilities. You can even click the What If Scenarios button to explore possible loan situations before you make a decision.

Preparing to Use the Loan Manager

There are a number of items you should prepare before you set up a loan in the Loan Manager:

■ **Set Up Your Accounts:** Make sure to set up any liability (i.e., 23300•Loan – Vehicles (Ford Truck)), expense (i.e., 62420•Loan Interest), and escrow (only if required) accounts that will be affected by the loan.

■ **Check Previous Transactions:** If you are working with an existing (rather than new) loan, you will also need to confirm that all of the transactions related to it are entered into QuickBooks before setting up the loan in the Loan Manager.

■ **Gather Loan Documents:** Make sure you have all of your original loan documents handy before you begin to set up the loan. It is important that you enter the opening balance and other information properly.

Once all transactions are up to date and the loan has been entered into the Loan Manager, you will be able to record future loan payments in the Set Up Payment window.

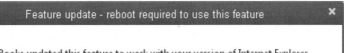

If this window appears when you use the Loan Manager, you will have to reboot your computer in order for the feature to work.

BEHIND THE SCENES

When you pay for the truck with your new loan and down payment, the offsetting account will be the fixed asset account.

10100-Checking	15100-Vehicles	23300-Loan - Vehicles (Ford Truck)
3,065	30,649	27,584

Making a payment affects three accounts (unless you have a 0 percent interest loan): the loan account, the bank account, and the interest expense account.

10100-Checking	62420-Loan Interest	23300-Loan - Vehicles (Ford Truck)
519.28	112.63	406.65

Task	Procedure
Enter the funds for the loan	▪ Choose Lists→Chart of Accounts.
	▪ Double-click the desired Long Term Liability account.
	▪ Enter the transaction date and the amount.
	▪ Choose the correct fixed asset to debit; click Record.
Enter a loan in the Loan Manager	▪ Gather all of your loan documents and information.
	▪ Set up the liability and expense accounts required to track the loan.
	▪ Choose Banking→Loan Manager; click the Add a Loan button.
	▪ Enter the information on each screen, clicking Next to move through the setup screens and clicking Finish once all information has been entered.
Set up a loan payment with the Loan Manager	▪ Choose Banking→Loan Manager.
	▪ Click to select the loan for which you need to set up a payment; click Set Up Payment.
	▪ Make any necessary changes in the Set Up Payment window; click OK.
	▪ Look over the bill or check to ensure its accuracy; click Save & Close.

DEVELOP YOUR SKILLS 11.5

Create a Long Term Liability

In this exercise, you will assist Zoe with setting up the loan account for the new truck, funding the loan, and setting up the loan in the Loan Manager.

First, you will create the new liability account.

1. Click the **Chart of Accounts** task icon in the Company area of the Home page.

2. Click the **Account** menu button, and then choose **New**.

3. Follow these steps to create the new Long Term Liability account:

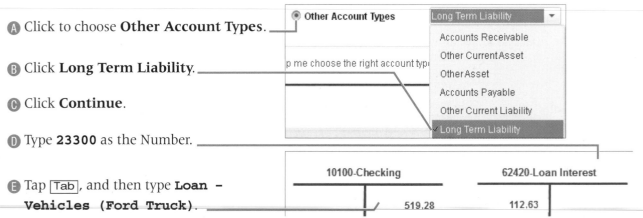

Ⓐ Click to choose **Other Account Types.**

Ⓑ Click **Long Term Liability.**

Ⓒ Click **Continue**.

Ⓓ Type **23300** as the Number.

Ⓔ Tap Tab, and then type **Loan – Vehicles (Ford Truck)**.

4. Click **Save & Close** to record the new account.

Fund the Long Term Liability Account

Rock Castle has just received the new truck and the First Bank of Bayshore has issued the funds on your behalf to Bayshore Ford. It's now time for Zoe to record the starting balance for the loan and the cost of the truck.

5. Double-click the **Loan – Vehicles (Ford Truck)** account in the Chart of Accounts window.

6. Follow these steps to record the funding of the loan:

Ⓐ Type **010215** as the Date.

Ⓑ Tap `Tab` three times, and then type **27584** as the amount.

Ⓒ Tap `Tab`, and then type **v** to choose the Vehicles account.

Ⓓ Click **Record**.

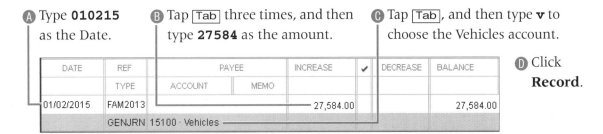

DATE	REF	PAYEE		INCREASE	✔	DECREASE	BALANCE
	TYPE	ACCOUNT	MEMO				
01/02/2015	FAM2013			27,584.00			27,584.00
	GENJRN 15100 · Vehicles						

BTS BRIEF

15100•Vehicles DR 27,584.00; 23300•Loan – Vehicles (Ford Truck) CR <27,584.00>

7. Close the **register** window; close the **Chart of Accounts** window.

Write a Check for the Down Payment

Alan has asked Zoe to prepare a check for the 10 percent that the company put down on the new truck.

8. Click the **Write Checks** task icon in the Banking area of the Home page.

9. Check **Print Later** from the Ribbon, and then follow these steps to create the check for the down payment:

Write Checks

Ⓐ Tap `Tab`, and then type **010215**.

Ⓑ Tap `Tab`, type **First Bank of Bayshore**, tap `Tab`, and then **Quick Add** it as a vendor.

Ⓒ Type **3065** as the amount.

Ⓓ Tap `Tab` two times, and then type **Down payment, Ford F-150 truck**.

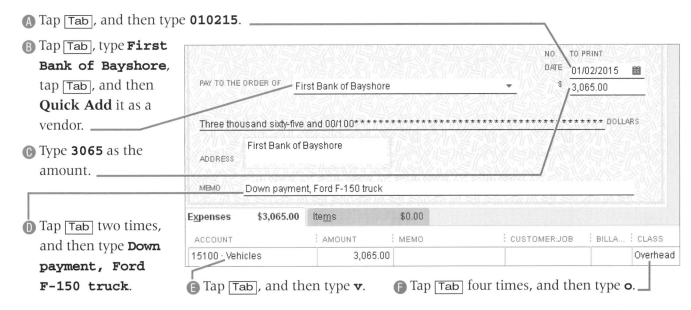

Ⓔ Tap `Tab`, and then type **v**.

Ⓕ Tap `Tab` four times, and then type **o**.

Advanced Skills

10. Click **Save & Close** to record the transaction.

The 15100 • Vehicles account will be increased by total cost of the truck ($27,584 from the loan and $3,065 from the down payment).

Enter a Loan in the Loan Manager

11. Choose **Banking→Loan Manager**.

12. If the Feature update window appears, click **OK**, and then reboot your computer.

 If you had to reboot your computer, you will need to launch QuickBooks, open [Your name]'s Rock Castle Construction, Lesson 11 company file, and then choose Banking→Loan Manager before continuing.

13. Click the **Add a Loan** button ⟨ Add a Loan... ⟩.

14. Follow these steps to enter the account information for the loan:

Ⓐ Choose this account from this drop-down menu. ────────

Ⓑ Choose First Bank of Bayshore from this drop-down menu. ────

Ⓒ Tap ⟨Tab⟩, and then type **010215**. ────

Ⓓ Tap ⟨Tab⟩, and then type **27584**. ────

Ⓔ Tap ⟨Tab⟩, and then type **60**. ────

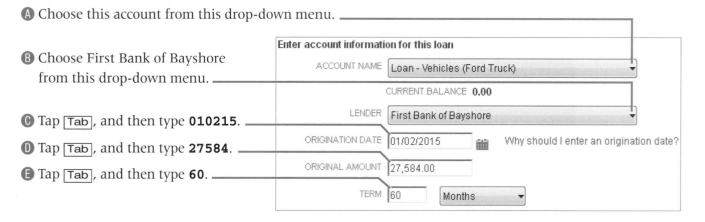

15. Click **Next**, and then follow these steps to enter the payment information:

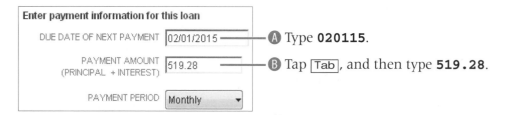

Ⓐ Type **020115**.

Ⓑ Tap ⟨Tab⟩, and then type **519.28**.

16. Click **Next**, and then follow these steps to enter the interest information:

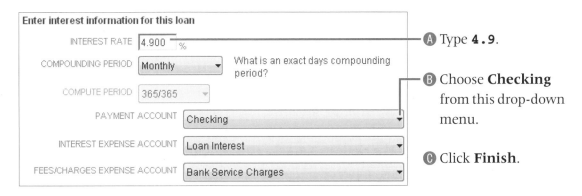

Ⓐ Type **4.9**.

Ⓑ Choose **Checking** from this drop-down menu.

Ⓒ Click **Finish**.

The loan is now set up in the Loan Manager, ready for you to track.

17. Close the **Loan Manager** window.

Working with Equity Accounts

Equity accounts reflect the net worth of a company. Take another look at Appendix A, Need to Know Accounting and notice that the accounting equation teaches that the sum of the equity accounts is equal to assets (what you own) less liabilities (what you owe):

Equity = Assets – Liabilities

An equity account has a credit normal balance. It represents how viable your company is since it shows how much you would have left if you sold all of your assets and then paid off the liabilities.

Owner's Equity / Capital Stock

In a sole proprietorship, the equity is what the owner has invested in the company. In a corporation, the equity is what the shareholders have invested in the company. An owner's investment occurs when an owner deposits funds into the company or shareholders purchase stock. An owner's withdrawal of funds from the company is known as a draw; if it is a corporation you will see shareholder distributions.

Retained Earnings

At the end of the fiscal year, a business will show either a net income or a net loss. When the books are closed, this amount is transferred into the Retained Earnings account to clear out all income and expense accounts for the next year. When the fiscal year ends, QuickBooks automatically makes this transfer.

Opening Balance Equity

QuickBooks creates the Opening Balance Equity account when you first create your company. As you enter opening balances into the accounts, QuickBooks uses Opening Balance Equity as the offset account so you can have a working balance sheet right from the beginning. You may need to enter a transfer between accounts if there is a balance in the Opening Balance Equity account once all of your new accounts are entered into QuickBooks. In addition, there are other times when QuickBooks may use the Opening Balance Equity account and an adjustment must be made. For instance, when you set QuickBooks up to track inventory in Lesson 8, Dealing with Physical Inventory and entered a beginning number of inventory items on hand, you debited 12100•Inventory Asset, and 30000•Opening Bal Equity was credited behind the scenes.

Equity transactions can be a bit tricky. You should talk to your accountant about how to deal with them for your unique company. Dealing with the transfer of funds from the Opening Balance Equity account will be covered in Lesson 12, Reporting, Closing the Books, and Adjusting Entries.

FLASHBACK TO GAAP: BUSINESS ENTITY

Remember that the first assumption of GAAP is that the business is separate from the owners and from other businesses. Revenues and expenses of the business should be kept separate from the personal expenses of the business owner.

QUICK REFERENCE	DEALING WITH EQUITY TRANSACTIONS
Task	**Procedure**
Record an Owner's Investment	▪ Choose Banking→Make Deposits. ▪ Choose the account into which the deposit will be made, and the owner's equity account in the From Account field. ▪ Enter the payment information and amount; click Save & Close.
Record an Owner's Draw	▪ Choose Banking→Write Checks. ▪ Enter the owner as the payee, as well as the date and amount of the check. ▪ Choose Owners draw in the Account column on the Expenses tab. ▪ Choose whether to print the check; click Save & Close.

Creating Budgets & Forecasts in QuickBooks

QuickBooks includes a budgeting feature that allows you to create account-based budgets for Balance Sheet or Profit & Loss accounts. Budgets can be created based on a previous year's budget or from scratch—or, if you have been using QuickBooks for a year, the actual figures from the previous year.

Forecasting the Future

In addition to budgets, QuickBooks also supplies you with a forecasting feature that assists you with making predictions about the future; for instance, it allows you to conduct "what-if" analyses as well as look at future cash flow or revenue. Forecasts can be based on actual figures from the last year or from scratch.

Once you have created a budget or a forecast, you will run a report to view the information. QuickBooks provides several reports that will allow you to use the information in your budget(s) or forecast(s).

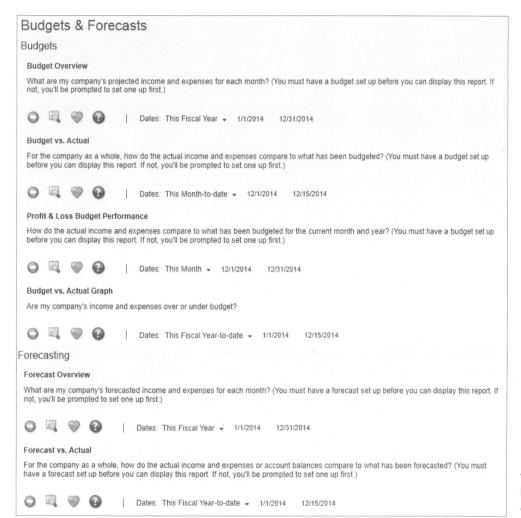

The Report Center lists all of the budget and forecast reports available for you to create.

Email Functionality in Reports

QuickBooks allows you to email reports from any report window. You have a chance to choose whether the recipient will receive the report as an Adobe Acrobat (PDF) or Microsoft Excel file. The report will appear the same as it would as if you printed it from QuickBooks.

When you click the Email button on the toolbar, you can choose the type of file that will be attached to your email message.

You cannot send a report by email when using a sample company file, but you will have a chance to explore this feature in the Reinforce Your Skills exercises at the end of this lesson.

Task	Procedure
Create a budget in QuickBooks	■ Choose Company→Planning & Budgeting→Set Up Budgets.
	■ Click the Create New Budget button.
	■ Choose the budget year and type; click Next.
	■ Choose to base the budget on a customer:job or class, or neither; click Next.
	■ Choose whether you wish to create the budget from scratch or by using the previous year's actual data, and then click Finish.
Create a forecast in QuickBooks	■ Choose Company→Planning & Budgeting→Set Up Forecast.
	■ Click the Create New Forecast button.
	■ Choose the year for the forecast; click Next.
	■ Choose whether the forecast will use customer:job, class, or neither of them as additional criteria; click Next.
	■ Choose whether you wish to create the forecast from scratch or by using the previous year's actual data, and then click Finish.
Email a report from QuickBooks	■ Produce the report you wish to email.
	■ Click the Email button, and choose to send it as a PDF or an Excel file.
	■ Using your email program, enter the recipients and make any desired modifications to the message.
	■ Send the email.

DEVELOP YOUR SKILLS 11.6

Produce a Budget and a Budget Report

In this exercise, you will help Zoe create a budget for 2015 based on the actual figures from 2014.

1. Choose **Company→Planning & Budgeting→Set Up Budgets**.
   The Set Up Budgets window appears with the FY2014-15 Profit & Loss by Account budget displayed.

2. Click the **Create New Budget** button.

   > Create New Budget

3. Ensure that **2015** and **Profit and Loss** are selected; click **Next**.

4. Ensure that **No additional criteria** is selected; click **Next**.
   Your budget will be based on all classes and all customers:jobs, so you do not need to add additional criteria at this time.

5. Click to the left of **Create budget from previous year's actual data**; click **Finish**.

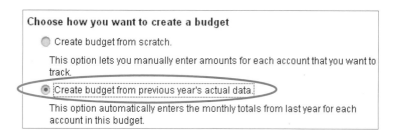

The new budget that you just created displays. Alan has told you that based on projections, the company plans to increase the labor income by 25 percent. You will make a change to Jan 15 reflecting this increase and then copy the amount across to every month.

6. Follow these steps to make the change to the budget:

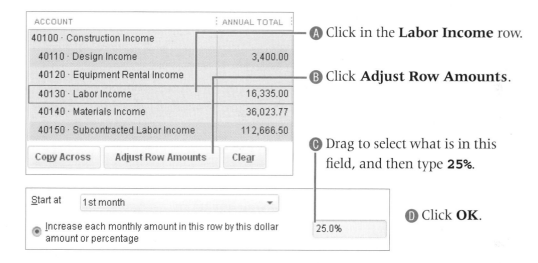

Ⓐ Click in the **Labor Income** row.

Ⓑ Click **Adjust Row Amounts**.

Ⓒ Drag to select what is in this field, and then type **25%**.

Ⓓ Click **OK**.

7. Click **OK** to save the budget with the changes.
   The Set Up Budget window closes with the changes you made intact.

Produce a Budget Report

Now that the budget for 2015 has been produced, Alan would like to see a report showing the amount budgeted for 2014 compared to the actual amount earned or spent.

8. Choose **Reports→Budgets & Forecasts→Budget vs. Actual**.
   A Budget Report "wizard" will appear to walk you through selections that will help you create the report you desire.

9. Click the **drop-down arrow**, and then choose to use the **FY2014-15** budget; click **Next**.

10. Click **Next** to choose for the layout to be Account by Month.

11. Click **Finish** to create the report.
    Now you will modify the report so that it shows the information for the entire year.

12. Follow these steps to view the actual vs. budget for all of 2014:

Ⓐ Click the **Dates drop-down arrow**, and then choose **This Fiscal Year**.

Ⓑ Click the **Columns drop-down arrow**, and then choose **Year**.

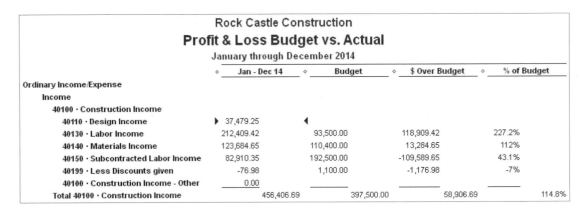

The top portion of your report should resemble the following illustration.

Rock Castle Construction
Profit & Loss Budget vs. Actual
January through December 2014

	Jan - Dec 14	Budget	$ Over Budget	% of Budget
Ordinary Income/Expense				
Income				
40100 · Construction Income				
40110 · Design Income	▶ 37,479.25 ◀			
40130 · Labor Income	212,409.42	93,500.00	118,909.42	227.2%
40140 · Materials Income	123,684.65	110,400.00	13,284.65	112%
40150 · Subcontracted Labor Income	82,910.35	192,500.00	-109,589.65	43.1%
40199 · Less Discounts given	-76.98	1,100.00	-1,176.98	-7%
40100 · Construction Income - Other	0.00			
Total 40100 · Construction Income	456,406.69	397,500.00	58,906.69	114.8%

13. Close the **budget report** window.

14. Choose the appropriate option for your situation:

- ▪ If you are continuing on to the next lesson or to the end-of-lesson exercises, leave QuickBooks open.
- ▪ If you are finished working in QuickBooks for now, choose **File→Exit**.

Concepts Review

Concepts Review   http://labyrinthelab.com/qb13

To check your knowledge of the key concepts introduced in this lesson, complete the Concepts Review quiz by going to the URL listed above.

Reinforce Your Skills

Before you begin the Reinforce Your Skills exercises, complete one of these options:

- *Open* **[Your name]'s Tea Shoppe at the Lake, Lesson 10** *or Tea Shoppe at the Lake, Lesson 11 from your file storage location that you used for Lesson 10.*

- *Restore* **Tea Shoppe at the Lake, Lesson 11 (Portable)** *from your file storage location.*

REINFORCE YOUR SKILLS 11.1
Use a Prepaid Rent Account

In this exercise, you will help Susie set up and use a Prepaid Rent account. The first step is to set up an Other Current Asset account.

1. Choose **Lists→Chart of Accounts**.

2. Click the **Account** menu button, and then choose **New**.

3. Create a new **Other Current Asset** account called `Prepaid Rent`.

Write the Rent Check
The next step is to write the check for the rent.

4. Choose **Banking→Write Checks**.

5. Write a **$6900** check to **Palomar Property Management** on **6/1/13** for six months of discounted rent ($1,150/month).

6. Choose for the check to be printed and enter a Memo of **Rent for June–November 2013**; expense the first month (**$1,150**) to Rent Expense and the rest (**$5,750**) to Prepaid Rent.

7. Enter **Other** as the Class for both lines of the transaction.

8. Save the **check** and close the **Write Checks** window.

Memorize a Funds Transfer
Now you will help Susie make the first transfer from Prepaid Rent to Rent Expense. The Chart of Accounts should still be open. If it isn't, choose Lists→Chart of Accounts.

9. Double-click the **Prepaid Rent** account to open the register.

10. Record a transfer of **$1,150** to Rent Expense on **7/1/13**.

11. Click within the transaction and choose **Edit→Memorize General Journal**.

12. Create a memorized transaction called **Rent Transfer** that is a monthly automated transaction entry. The next transfer will be on **8/1/13** and there are **4** remaining.

13. Close the **Prepaid Rent** register window.

Track Petty Cash

In this exercise, you will help Susie set up and use a petty cash account for her minor expenses, and to make a purchase with it.

If necessary, choose Lists→Chart of Accounts.

1. Click the **Account** menu button, and then click **New**.

2. Create a new **Bank** account called **Petty Cash**; choose to not set up online services.

3. Choose **Banking→Write Checks**, and then choose **Checking**.

4. Enter the next check number, **1109**, and then set the date to **7/06/13**.

5. Write the check to **Cash** (Quick Add as a vendor) for **$200**, choose **Petty Cash** as the account, and then choose **Other** as the Class.

Make a Purchase with Petty Cash

Now that the Petty Cash account is set up, you will use it to purchase whipped cream. (You ran out with many more drinks to make!)

6. Double-click **Petty Cash** from the Chart of Accounts window.

7. Enter **7/08/13** as the date, tap [Tab], and then tap [Delete] to remove the Number.

8. Tap [Tab] again, and then type **Grissom's Grocery** as the Payee.

9. Tap [Tab] and choose to **Quick Add** it as a vendor, type **$21.87** as the Payment, and then choose **Food Purchases** as the Account.

10. Enter **whipped cream** as the Memo; save the transaction, and then close the **Petty Cash** window.

Deal with a New Fixed Asset Item

Susie purchased a new milk steamer machine for Tea Shoppe at the Lake so she can make her famous Earl Grey non-fat misto with sugar-free vanilla syrup en masse. In this exercise, you will set up this purchase as a fixed asset item in her QuickBooks company file.

1. Choose **List→Fixed Asset Item List**.

2. Create a new **Fixed Asset Item** for the equipment using the following information:
   - Asset Name: **Espresso Steamer**
   - Purchase Description: **New Standalone Steamer**
   - Date: **7/8/2013**
   - Cost: **$2,569**
   - Vendor: **Poway Restaurant Supply**
   - Asset Account: Furniture and Equipment
   - Asset Description: **BUNN 35800.0401 Standalone Steamer Unit**

3. Save the new **Fixed Asset Item**; close the **Fixed Asset Item List**.
   Leave the Chart of Accounts open for the next exercise.

Track a Long Term Liability

Susie took out a loan for a portion of the cost of the new steamer unit. In this exercise, you will help her set up the Long Term Liability account and record the purchase transaction. The Chart of Accounts window should still be open. If it is not, choose Lists→Chart of Accounts.

1. Click the **Account** menu button, and then choose **New**.

2. Choose to create a new **Long Term Liability** account (which is an Other Account Type), and then click Continue.

3. Type **Steamer Loan** as the Account Name.

4. Click **Save & Close**.

Enter the Down Payment Transaction

You will now enter the two transactions to account for the full purchase price of the steamer unit.

5. Choose **Banking→Write Checks**, and then choose **Checking** as the account.

6. Choose for the **check to be printed later**, and then set the date to **7/8/13**.

7. Enter **Poway Restaurant Supply** as the payee, and **$569** as the amount of the down payment.

8. Type **Steamer Unit Down Payment** as the Memo, and then choose **Furniture and Equipment** as the Account.

9. Choose **Beverages** as the Class; click **Save & Close**.

Enter the Loan Transaction

The loan has been funded, so now you need to account for it in QuickBooks. The Chart of Accounts should still be open. If it is not, choose Lists→Chart of Accounts.

10. Double-click the **Steamer Loan** Long Term Liability account.
    The Steamer Loan register window opens.

11. Ensure that the date is set to **7/8/2013**, and then tap Tab three times.

12. Type **$2,000** as an Increase and choose **Furniture and Equipment** as the Account; **record** the transaction.

13. Close the **Steamer Loan** and **Chart of Accounts** windows.

Email a Report

In this exercise, you will help Susie create a report that shows all of the accounts in her Chart of Accounts to send to her accountant, who has requested it since she created the new asset and liability accounts. You will take the steps necessary to email the report but will not be able to hit send unless your computer is set up with email capability.

1. Choose **Reports→List→Account Listing**.

2. Click the **Email** button on the report toolbar, and then choose **Send report as PDF**.

3. Click **OK** in the Email Security box after reading the message.
   The report will be saved for you as a PDF file and attached to an email message. What happens at this point will depend on how the computer on which you are working is set up for email. At this stage, if you were working with your own company file, you would enter the email address of the recipient, make any edits to the message, and then click Send.

4. Close the email window that may have appeared; choose **Window→Close All**.

5. Choose the appropriate option for your situation:
   - If you are continuing on to the next lesson or the rest of the end-of-lesson exercises, leave QuickBooks open.
   - If you are finished working in QuickBooks for now, choose **File→Exit**.

Apply Your Skills

Before you begin the Apply Your Skills exercises, complete one of these options:

- *Open* **[Your name] Wet Noses Veterinary Clinic, Lesson 10** *or* **Wet Noses Veterinary Clinic, Lesson 11** *from your file storage location.*

- *Restore* **Wet Noses Veterinary Clinic, Lesson 11 (Portable)** *from your file storage location. Make sure to place your name as the first word in the company filename (e.g., Sadie's Wet Noses Veterinary Clinic, Lesson 11).*

APPLY YOUR SKILLS 11.1
Deal with Prepaid Web Hosting

Dr. James has decided that her business needs a website, and she has found a company to host it. She can get a deal if she pays for a year in advance, so she has decided to take that option. In this exercise, you will set up an Other Current Asset account for her to track the prepaid web hosting expense.

1. Open the **Chart of Accounts,** and then choose to create an **Other Current Asset** account.

2. Name the account **Prepaid Web Hosting**, and then **save** it.

Pay for the Prepaid Expense

You will now pay for the entire year, expensing one month's worth and placing the rest in the prepaid expense account you just created.

3. Open the **Write Checks** window, ensure that it is set for the **check to be printed later**, and then set the date to **7/22/2013**.

4. Type **Zoom Web Services** as the payee (Quick Add it as a vendor), and then **$1,068** as the amount (the deal is for $89/month).

5. Type **One year web hosting, July 2013-June 2014** as the Memo.

6. Choose to expense **$89** to Computer and Internet Expenses, and the rest to Prepaid Web Hosting. Choose **Overhead** as the Class for each line. Finally, save the transaction.

Make and Memorize a Transfer of Funds

You will now enter the transfer of $89 from the other current asset account to the expense account for August and set it up to happen automatically for the rest of the 12-month period.

7. Open the **Prepaid Web Hosting** register window from the Chart of Accounts.

8. Enter **8/22/2013** as the date and **89** in the Decrease field. Set **Computer and Internet Expenses** as the Account.

9. Choose to **memorize the transaction**.

10. Type **Web Host Txfr** as the Name.

11. Choose to have the transaction entry automated every month, with the next transfer occurring on **9/22/2013** and **10** more remaining.

12. Save the **memorized transaction** and the **register entry**; close the **Prepaid Web Hosting** window.

Leave the Chart of Accounts window open for the next exercise.

APPLY YOUR SKILLS 11.2

Track and Use Petty Cash

In this exercise, you will create a petty cash account and use it to pay for an expense.

1. Open the **Chart of Accounts**, and then create a new bank account called **Petty Cash**.

2. Write a check to fund the **Petty Cash** account on **7/8/13** for **$300**. Enter the next check number, **1440**, and indicate **Overhead** as the class.

3. Purchase an appetizer platter for **$44.95** from Laura's Café for an office party on **7/12/13**. Use **Petty Cash** to pay for it.

4. Close the **Write Checks** or **Petty Cash** register window.

APPLY YOUR SKILLS 11.3

Buy a New Ultrasound Machine (Fixed Asset)

In this exercise, you will help Sadie enter a new ultrasound machine into the Fixed Asset Item List.

1. Open the **Fixed Asset Item List**.

2. Use the following information to create a new fixed asset item:
   - Asset Name: **Ultrasound Machine**
   - Purchase Description: **New Health Power Ultrasound Machine**
   - Date: **7/21/2013**
   - Cost: **$2,050**
   - Vendor: **Seattle Vet Supply**
   - Asset Account: Furniture and Equipment
   - Asset Description: **High Performance +7.5 MHz Vet Ultrasound**

3. Save the new **Fixed Asset Item**; close the **Fixed Asset Item List**.

Create and Fund a Long Term Liability Account

In this exercise, you will use the Loan Manager to track the loan that you took out for the x-ray machine.

1. Create a new **long term liability** account called **Ultrasound Loan**.

2. Fund the loan by entering an increase to the Ultrasound Loan account for **$2,050** on 7/22/13.

3. Open the **Loan Manager**.

4. Create a new loan using the following information:
   - Account Name: Ultrasound Loan
   - Lender: Bank of Bothell
   - Origination Date: **7/21/2013**
   - Original Amount **$2,050**
   - Term: **36** months
   - Due Date of Next Payment: **8/21/2013**
   - Payment Amount: **$64.05**
   - Payment Period: Monthly
   - Interest Rate: **7.8%**
   - Payment Account: Checking
   - Interest Expense Account: Interest Expense
   - Fees/Charges Expense Account: Bank Service Charges

5. Close the **Loan Manager** and the **Chart of Accounts**.

Answer Questions with Reports

In this exercise, you will answer questions for Dr. James by running reports. You may wish to display the Report Center in List View to help you answer the questions. Ask your instructor if you should print the reports, print (save) them as PDF files, export them to Excel, or simply display them on the screen.

1. Will you please print a list of all of the accounts that are set up in the Chart of Accounts for the accountant?

2. If we were to take out a five-year loan at 8.75 percent interest for a new piece of equipment for $5,000, what would the monthly payments be? (Hint: The Loan Manager has a feature that can help with this! If the Loan Manager is not working for you, go online and use a free loan calculator.)

3. Create a report that shows the entries of the Fixed Asset Item List.

4. Prepare a report that shows all transactions affecting the Prepaid Web Hosting account.

5. Submit your reports based on the guidelines provided by your instructor.

6. Choose the appropriate option for your situation:

   ■ If you are continuing on to the next lesson or the Critical Thinking exercises, leave QuickBooks open.

   ■ If you are finished working in QuickBooks for now, choose **File→Exit**.

Critical Thinking

In the course of working through the following Critical Thinking exercises, you will be utilizing various skills taught in this and previous lesson(s). Take your time and think carefully about the tasks presented to you. Turn back to the lesson content if you need assistance.

11.1 Sort Through the Stack

Before You Begin: Restore the **Monkey Business, Lesson 11 (Portable)** *file from your storage location. (Remember that you are to leave the password field blank for Mary.) You also have the option of opening either the final file from Critical Thinking 10.1 or Monkey Business, Lesson 11 from your storage location.*

You have been hired by Mary Minard to help her with her organization's books. She is the owner of Monkey Business, a nonprofit organization that provides low-income students with help in preparing for college placement exams and applying for scholarships. You have just sat down at her desk and found a pile of papers. It is your job to sort through the papers and make sense of what you find, entering information into QuickBooks whenever appropriate and answering any other questions in a word-processing document saved as **Critical Thinking 11.1**. Remember, you are digging through papers on a desk, so it is up to you to determine the correct order in which to complete the tasks.

- Receipt from USPS: Dated 8/15/2013, $44.00 for 100 first-class stamps, paid for with petty cash.

- Deposit slip: Check #578 for $5,000 from the House Foundation, deposited in the Checking account on 8/12/2013; $200 was kept back for petty cash.

- Bill from landlord for six months of rent at a discount: Mary wrote a note on the bill stating she wants to take advantage of a discounted rent by prepaying it for six months. The amount per month is $875, payable to Keely Amaral Properties, LLC. Pay the rent for August 2013 on 8/5/2013 and then set it up for the remaining months of rent to automatically transfer the on the fifth of each month for the remainder of the six-month term.

- Note from the accountant: Need to set up account for loan for new computer equipment. Total financed is $3,029. Loan was funded on 8/10/2013. Please set up the equipment as a fixed asset item as well, using Furniture & Equipment as the account. Description of equipment is two new Sony desktop computers, two 21-inch dual monitors, and a new laser printer. The vendor is Lancaster Computer Sales. It was financed by Cherry City Finance.

- Scribbled note from Mary: I would like to set up a budget for the rest of the fiscal year (September 2013–June 2014) based on the amounts spent and received in July and August. Is that something you could do in QuickBooks for me? If so, please create the budget for me and save it for me as a PDF file so I can send it by email.

11.2 Tackle the Tasks

Now is your chance to work a little more with Rock Castle Construction and apply the skills that you have learned in this lesson to accomplish additional tasks. Open or restore the **Critical Thinking 11.2** company or portable company file from your file storage location, or open the company file you used in the Develop Your Skills exercises for this lesson. Then, enter the following tasks.

Create and fund a prepaid utilities account	Rock Castle has decided to prepay the water bill for the next six months. Create 13300•Prepaid Utilities as an Other Current Asset account. Write a check to City of Bayshore on 1/1/15 for $1,200, expensing $200 in January to 65130•Water, placing the rest in the Prepaid Utilities account. Use Overhead as the Class.
Record and memorize a transfer of funds	Record a transfer of $200 from 13300•Prepaid Utilities to 65130•Water on 2/1/15. Memorize the transaction in the Monthly group.
Make a petty cash expenditure	Use 10400•Petty Cash to purchase a birthday cake on 1/30/15 for Samuel's birthday. The total amount is $33.75, payable to Billy's Bakery, expensed to 69000•Miscellaneous.
Create a new fixed asset item	Rock Castle Construction purchased furniture for the Millbrae office on 1/8/15 for $2,639 from Pa's Custom Furniture. Create a new fixed asset item called Millbrae Office Furniture – 19, and use 15000•Furniture and Equipment as the Asset Account.
Create a long term liability	Create a long term liability account for the new furniture for the Millbrae office called 28300•Loan – Furniture (Millbrae). On 1/8/15, enter the total amount of the furniture as an increase in the new liability account you just created, using 15000•Furniture and Equipment as the Account.
Create a forecast	Create a forecast for Rock Castle Construction for FY2015, based on last year's actual amount. Increase the amount for design income by 35 percent for the year.

You may use the company file from this exercise for the Develop Your Skills exercises in the next lesson if you wish.

11.3 Use the Web as a Learning Tool

Throughout this book, you will be provided with an opportunity to use the Internet as a learning tool by completing WebQuests. According to the original creators of WebQuests, as described on their website (WebQuest.org), a WebQuest is "an inquiry-oriented activity in which most or all of the information used by learners is drawn from the web." To complete the WebQuest projects in this book, navigate to the student resource center and choose the WebQuest for the lesson on which you are currently working. The subject of each WebQuest will be relevant to the material found in the lesson.

WebQuest Subject: Learning about the depreciation of fixed assets

Reporting, Closing the Books, and Adjusting Entries

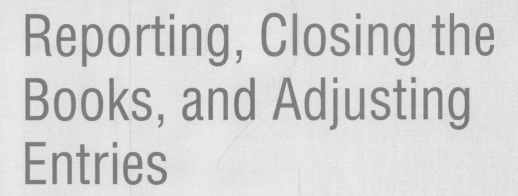

LESSON OBJECTIVES

After studying this lesson, you will be able to:

- Prepare a Trial Balance report
- Make general journal entries
- Create financial statements
- Integrate QuickBooks with Microsoft Excel
- Close the books in QuickBooks

It is now time to wrap up all you have learned and finish out the accounting cycle. In this lesson, you will work through the last five steps of the cycle as you close out the fiscal period. You will have the opportunity to dive in and look a bit closer at what's behind the scenes by learning how to make general journal entries. You will also take a stroll through the major end-of-period financial reports—Trial Balance, Worksheet, Income Statement, Statement of Owner's Equity, and Balance Sheet. In addition to closing the books, you will take a look at another way QuickBooks integrates with Microsoft Office by learning how to export reports to Excel. Finally, you will learn what closing the books looks like in QuickBooks.

Rock Castle Construction

Alan has asked Zoe to close Rock Castle Construction's books for the fiscal year 2014. She will begin the process by creating a Trial Balance report, which will tell her whether the debits and credits are equal and will display the balances of each account. Then it will be time to take a look at what a "pen-and-paper" worksheet includes and how the information flows from column to column through it.

Zoe will next dive behind the scenes and take a look at the Make General Journal Entries window, where she will enter adjusting entries for depreciation and the Opening Balance Equity account.

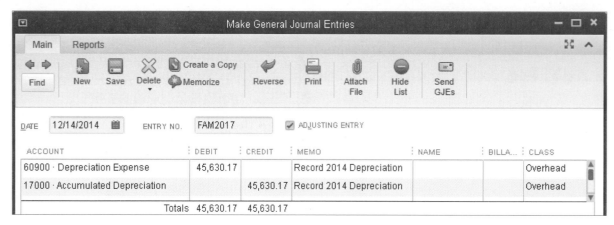

Adjusting entries are made in the Make General Journal Entries window.

Once the adjusting entries have been posted, it will be time for Zoe to create Rock Castle Construction's financial statements for 2014 and export a report to Microsoft Excel so she can use Excel's advanced features to work with the company's QuickBooks data.

Rock Castle Construction
Income Statement
January through December 2014

	Jan - Dec 14
Ordinary Income/Expense	
Income	
40100 · Construction Income	
40110 · Design Income	▶ 37,479.25
40130 · Labor Income	212,409.42
40140 · Materials Income	123,684.65
40150 · Subcontracted Labor Incom.	82,910.35
40199 · Less Discounts given	-76.98
40100 · Construction Income - Oth...	0.00
Total 40100 · Construction Income	456,406.69

The Income Statement is one of the main financial statements.

Closing the Books in QuickBooks

The last five steps of the accounting cycle deal with "closing" the books at the end of a fiscal period. You have probably figured out by now that QuickBooks makes things easy for you in many ways by what it performs behind the scenes. The same is true when it comes to the end of the fiscal year. QuickBooks knows when your fiscal year has ended based on the information you entered when you first created your company or that is displayed in the Report Information area of the Company Information window in QuickBooks.

The fiscal year information is set in the Report Information area of the Company Information window.

Behind the Scenes with Closing the Books

You can set a closing date in QuickBooks, although QuickBooks will perform year-end adjustments automatically based on your fiscal year. You will learn how to set a closing date in QuickBooks at the end of this lesson, once you have explored the rest of the accounting cycle.

The Final Steps of the Accounting Cycle

This lesson will take you through the final five steps of the accounting cycle, which results in your company books being closed for the past fiscal period and ready for the next one. For many companies, the last steps of the accounting cycle are carried out by an accountant. You will learn about the final steps, but it will be up to you to determine if it will be wiser for you to complete them yourself for your company or to trust them to your accountant. So far, in your path through the accounting cycle, you have ensured that source documents are available and organized as well as analyzed and recorded transactions (QuickBooks posted them in a journal and to ledger accounts behind the scenes for you). Now you will prepare reports to show how your company performed for the fiscal period and close out temporary accounts. As you explore these final steps, you will be doing so "QuickBooks style" in that you will look at each step and how it is addressed in QuickBooks.

Permanent Accounts

Accounts for which the ending balance for one fiscal period is the opening balance for the next are called permanent accounts. These are also the balance sheet accounts. Think about it a bit...You don't zero out your checking account at the end of each year; it continues on from one accounting period to the next!

Temporary (a.k.a. Nominal) Accounts

No doubt you have figured out that not all accounts are permanent! The opposite of permanent accounts are temporary, or nominal, accounts. These accounts are zeroed out at the end of each fiscal period, with the amounts from them moving into an equity account as either a net income (if income was greater than expenses) or a net loss (if expenses exceeded income for the period).

The Income Summary Account

If you were doing paper-based accounting, you would use an Income Summary account to "clear out" the temporary account balances and move the lump sum to an equity account. QuickBooks doesn't actually create an Income Summary account, but it takes the net income or loss resulting from the balances in your income and expense accounts and moves it to the capital/equity account for you. You will learn more about this temporary capital/equity account as we progress through this lesson.

QuickBooks Automatic Year-End Adjustments

As you learned earlier, QuickBooks performs adjustments automatically for you behind the scenes at the end of your fiscal year. Specifically, QuickBooks will:

- Close out the temporary accounts by moving the balances to a "virtual" income summary account

- Determine a net income or loss for the company to be displayed on the balance sheet for the last day of the fiscal year, after transferring the balances from the temporary accounts

- Automatically transfer the net income or loss from the last day of the fiscal period to the Retained Earnings account on the first day of the new fiscal period

The result of this behind the scenes action is that you will start off the new fiscal year with a net income of zero (and a zero balance in each of the temporary accounts).

QUICK REFERENCE	SETTING A COMPANY'S FISCAL YEAR IN QUICKBOOKS
Task	**Procedure**
Set the company's fiscal period in QuickBooks	▪ Choose Company→Company Information. ▪ In the Report Information area, click the Fiscal Year drop-down arrow to choose the correct first month of the company's fiscal year.

Verify Fiscal Period

In this exercise, you will verify that the correct month is set as the first month of the fiscal period for Rock Castle Construction. The first step is to open QuickBooks, and then either open a company file or restore a portable company file.

1. Start **QuickBooks 2013**.

   If you downloaded the student exercise files in the portable company file *format, follow Option 1 below. If you downloaded the files in the* company file *format, follow Option 2 below.*

 If you choose, you may use the final company file from Critical Thinking 11.2. In this case, open the Critical Thinking 11.2 company file from your default storage location in Option 2 below.

Option 1: Restore a Portable Company File

2. Choose **File→Open or Restore Company**.

3. Restore the **Rock Castle Construction** portable file for this lesson from your file storage location, placing your name as the first word in the filename (e.g., Zoe's Rock Castle Construction, Lesson 12).

   It may take a few moments for the portable company file to open. Once it does, continue with step 4.

Option 2: Open a Company File

2. Choose **File→Open or Restore Company**, ensure that **Open a regular company file** is selected, and then open the **Rock Castle Construction** company file for this lesson from your file storage location.

   The QuickBooks company file will open.

3. Click **OK** to close the QuickBooks Information windows. If necessary, click **No** in the Set Up External Accountant User window.

Verify the Fiscal Period Information

Next you will verify that January is set up as the first month of the fiscal period for Rock Castle Construction.

4. Choose **Company→Company Information**.

5. Ensure that **January** is displayed as the first month in the company's Fiscal Year.

6. Close the **Company Information** window.

Preparing for Year-End Reporting

When you are doing pen-and-paper accounting, you must prepare a Trial Balance report to ensure that the debits and credits are equal. Preparing a Trial Balance report involves taking all of the ledger accounts and their balances and displaying them on one report to ensure debits equal credits. When you use QuickBooks, though, you cannot record a transaction if the debits and credits are not equal, so a more useful purpose for the Trial Balance report is to use it to prepare for adjusting entries.

QuickBooks Reporting Capabilities

QuickBooks provides users with a large number of reports organized into eleven categories. These reports can be used to tell the story about your business in many ways.

Contributed Reports

As a QuickBooks user, you can use reports contributed by other users that may help you better tell your company's story. You can sort for reports by report category and by industry sector. If you find a report that may be beneficial to you and your business, simply download it into your QuickBooks software.

Custom Reports

QuickBooks allows users to create custom summary and detail reports. The software provides a window that guides you through the decision of what custom report to create.

> Company & Financial
> Customers & Receivables
> Sales
> Jobs, Time & Mileage
> Vendors & Payables
> Purchases
> Inventory
> Banking
> Accountant & Taxes
> Budgets
> List

The eleven categories into which QuickBooks reports are organized

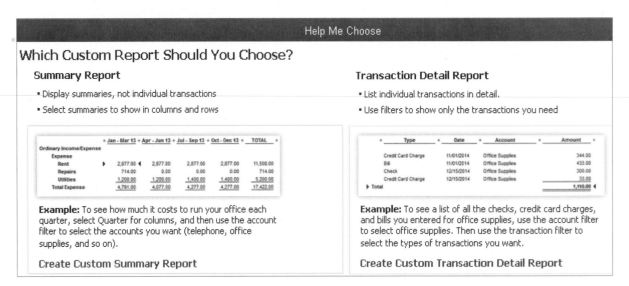

The Help Me Choose window that aids QuickBooks users in determining the desired custom report

Industry-Specific Reports

The industry-specific premiere editions of QuickBooks also provide reports that are specialized for industry sectors. You can access all of these reports through the Accountant edition of the software as well.

<table>
<tr><td>Contractor Reports
Manufacturing and Wholesale Reports
Professional Services Reports
Retail Reports
Nonprofit Reports</td><td>Industry-specific reports are available in these QuickBooks editions of QuickBooks Premiere, as well as in the Accountant edition.</td></tr>
</table>

Cycle Step 5: Prepare the Trial Balance

In the fourth step of the accounting cycle, QuickBooks posted the amounts from the journal that documents all transactions to individual account ledgers behind the scenes for you. The next step of the accounting cycle involves creating a Trial Balance report. QuickBooks Pro allows you to create a Trial Balance report and if you have the Premier Accountant edition, you can create a Working Trial Balance report as well.

In traditional accounting, a Trial Balance is a report that adds up all the debits and credits so mistakes can be traced if debits don't equal credits. Because QuickBooks always adds correctly, you do not need to do a trial balance. Nevertheless, QuickBooks provides a Trial Balance report if you want to see your data in this format.

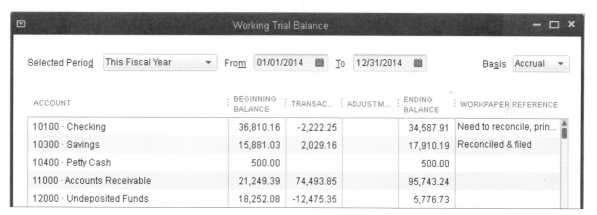

When working with the Premier Accountant edition of QuickBooks, you can display a Working Trial Balance report, which allows you to view the beginning and ending balances of all accounts as well as the transactions and adjustments that affect each one.

What the Trial Balance Report Tells You

The Trial Balance report lets you look at the ending balance of every account in the Chart of Accounts for a chosen period of time. You can use it to help guide you as you create adjusting entries. If you are curious as to what transactions comprise a figure on the Trial Balance report, you can use the Quick Zoom feature to find the source of the amount.

Advanced Skills

Cycle Step 6: Prepare a Worksheet

In pen-and-paper accounting, a worksheet is a report that you create to assist you with preparing the year-end financial statements. The worksheet has five sets of debit and credit columns that represent the following sections (displayed from left to right):

- Trial Balance
- Adjustments
- Adjusted Trial Balance
- Income Statement
- Balance Sheet

The information from the Trial Balance report is displayed in the Trial Balance section. You would work across the worksheet as adjustments are made and then recorded in the Adjusted Trial Balance section. Finally, the amounts from the Adjusted Trial Balance would be transferred to the Income Statement and Balance Sheet sections, based on which accounts would be found on each one.

It is probably evident to you by now that QuickBooks does this behind the scenes for you, so there is no worksheet for you to physically produce in QuickBooks. Just realize that the steps performed in the preparation of a worksheet are being completed for you behind the scenes.

QUICK REFERENCE	PRODUCING A TRIAL BALANCE REPORT
Task	**Procedure**
Create a Trial Balance report	■ Choose Reports→Accountant & Taxes→Trial Balance.
	■ Set the date range for the report.
Create a Working Trial Balance report (QuickBooks Premier Accountant Edition)	■ Choose Accountant→Working Trial Balance.
	■ Set the date range for the report.

DEVELOP YOUR SKILLS 12.2
Run a Trial Balance Report

In this exercise, you will create a Trial Balance report for Rock Castle Construction.

1. Choose **Reports→Accountant & Taxes→Trial Balance**.

2. Click the **Dates field drop-down arrow**, and then choose **This Fiscal Year**.

Take a look at the information contained in this report. It displays all of the accounts in your Chart of Accounts and the current balance for each.

3. Close the **Trial Balance** report.

Digging in "Behind the Scenes" with Adjusting Entries

Throughout this book, you have had the opportunity to take a glimpse at the accounting QuickBooks does behind the scenes. Now you will take a step further to see how QuickBooks records journal entries and how you can create your own journal entries.

Rule #1: Debits and Credits Must Always Be Equal

When you venture into the General Journal Entry window, you will see a debit column and a credit column. As you create your journal entries, you must make sure that the debits equal the credits. (Don't worry, though. QuickBooks will not let you record a transaction until you get this right!)

Depending on the version of QuickBooks you are using, the Make General Journal Entries window may look a bit different. The images in this text are from the Pro version.

Making Journal Entries

You already learned how to record a journal entry when you recorded the prepaid insurance transfer in the last lesson; you just used a register to accomplish the task rather than the Make General Journal Entries window. If you are familiar with pen-and-paper accounting, you will see that the Make General Journal Entries window looks like a journal you would use in manual accounting.

Rock Castle Construction
Journal
December 2014

Trans #	Type	Date	Num	Adj	Name	Memo	Account	Debit	Credit
184	Check	12/01/2014	476		Abercrombie, Kri...		10100 · Checking		711.15
					Abercrombie, Kri...		11000 · Accounts...	711.15	
								711.15	711.15
185	Cred...	12/01/2014	4002		Abercrombie, Kri...		11000 · Accounts...		711.15
					Abercrombie, Kri...	Whirlpool ...	40140 · Materials I...	660.00	
					State Board of Eq...	CA sales ...	25500 · Sales Tax...	51.15	
								711.15	711.15
248	Bill	12/01/2014			Fay, Maureen Ly...		20000 · Accounts...		250.00
					Overhead	Pre-tax w...	63610 · Accounting	250.00	
								250.00	250.00
253	Bill P...	12/01/2014	477		Larson Flooring		10100 · Checking		2,700.00
					Larson Flooring		20000 · Accounts...	2,700.00	
								2,700.00	2,700.00

You can produce a report in QuickBooks that shows the entries as they would appear in a pen-and-paper journal.

Adjusting Entries

Adjusting entries are made at the end of an accounting period in order to bring some of the general journal account balances up to date so they will be correct on the financial statements. Some examples of adjusting entries that are often made are:

- Updating the book value of fixed assets by recording depreciation for the fiscal period
- Updating prepaid accounts (other current assets) by transferring the amount used in the fiscal period to an expense account
- Transferring balances out of the Opening Balance Equity account to their correct "resting place"

Accounting for Depreciation

In the last lesson, you learned about fixed assets and the fact that you don't expense them when purchased, but rather over the life of the asset. You should enter a depreciation transaction for your fixed assets for every fiscal period in which you produce financial statements. For small businesses, this is typically at the end of a fiscal year.

The depreciation adjusting entry can be made in the Make General Journal Entries window. It affects the expense account that tracks depreciation and the accumulated depreciation fixed asset contra account. When you make this transfer the current book value of your fixed assets will be displayed correctly, meaning that the credit amount in the accumulated depreciation contra account will decrease the total value of the company's fixed assets (which have a debit normal balance).

Adjusted Trial Balance Report

If you are using the Premier Accountant edition of QuickBooks, once the adjusting entries have been entered into QuickBooks, you can create an Adjusted Trial Balance report if you wish. This report will show the beginning balance, the adjustments, and the ending balance for each account. It will be these final, ending balances that will be used for the financial statements. This report also represents one of the sections of the worksheet that represents the sixth step of the accounting cycle.

For those using the Pro version of QuickBooks, after adjusting entries are made you can create another Trial Balance report, which reflects the adjusted amounts.

BEHIND THE SCENES

When making an adjusting entry for depreciation, you will debit the Depreciation Expense account and credit the Accumulated Depreciation account. Remember that Accumulated Depreciation is a fixed asset contra account. By crediting it, you are decreasing the value of the fixed assets.

17000-Accumulated Depreciation	60900-Depreciation Expense
45,630.17	45,630.17

QUICK REFERENCE	WORKING WITH GENERAL JOURNAL ENTRIES
Task	**Procedure**
Make a general journal entry	■ Choose Company→Make General Journal Entries.
	■ Set the correct date.
	■ Enter the first account, and then the debit or credit amount.
	■ Continue entering accounts and their debit or credit amounts as needed.
Create an Adjusting Journal Entries report	■ Choose Reports→Accountant & Taxes→Adjusting Journal Entries.
	■ Set the date range.

DEVELOP YOUR SKILLS 12.3
Make Adjusting Entries

In this exercise, you will help Zoe make two adjusting entries: one to transfer funds from the Opening Balance Equity account and another to account for the depreciation for the fiscal year.

The first general journal entry you will make will move $142.97 from the Opening Balance Equity account that was posted there when you entered the opening balance for inventory items.

1. Choose **Company→Make General Journal Entries**.

2. Click the **Previous** button a few times to take a look at how transactions that you have entered are displayed in the general journal; click **Next** until you come to an empty window where no transaction is displayed.

3. Set the date to **12/14/2014**.
   Due to the fact that we are using a sample file that perpetually sets the date to 12/15/2014, we will be using 12/14/2014 as the closing date for our company file so we can perform the closing entries.

4. Follow these steps to record the journal entry:

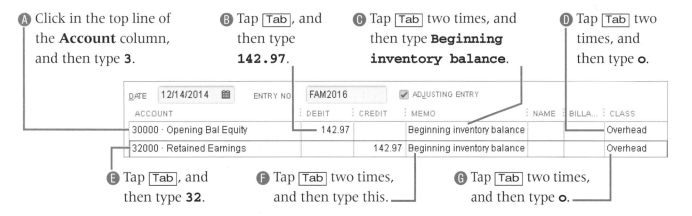

Ⓐ Click in the top line of the **Account** column, and then type **3**.

Ⓑ Tap Tab, and then type **142.97**.

Ⓒ Tap Tab two times, and then type **Beginning inventory balance**.

Ⓓ Tap Tab two times, and then type **o**.

Ⓔ Tap Tab, and then type **32**.

Ⓕ Tap Tab two times, and then type this.

Ⓖ Tap Tab two times, and then type **o**.

BTS BRIEF

30000•Opening Bal Equity DR 142.97; 32000•Retained Earnings CR <142.97>

---

5. Click **Save & New** to record the journal entry.

6. Click **OK** to post to the Retained Earnings account.

Record the Depreciation Entry for the Fiscal Year

The entry you are about to record will expense the depreciation for the year and decrease the book value of Rock Castle's fixed assets. Remember that there are a variety of ways to track depreciation. You should use the value your accountant has provided to you for a transaction such as this.

The Make General Journal Entries window should still be displayed. If it is not, choose Company→Make General Journal Entries.

7. Type **121414** as the Date.

8. Follow these steps to record the journal entry for depreciation:

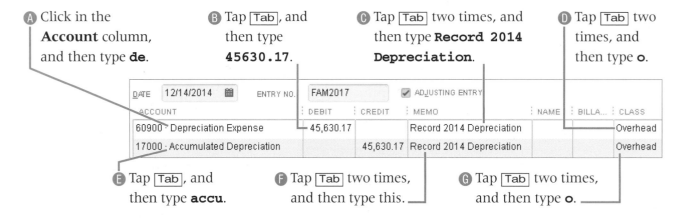

Ⓐ Click in the **Account** column, and then type **de**.

Ⓑ Tap Tab, and then type **45630.17**.

Ⓒ Tap Tab two times, and then type **Record 2014 Depreciation**.

Ⓓ Tap Tab two times, and then type **o**.

Ⓔ Tap Tab, and then type **accu**.

Ⓕ Tap Tab two times, and then type this.

Ⓖ Tap Tab two times, and then type **o**.

BTS BRIEF

60900•Depreciation Expense DR 45,630.17; 17000•Accumulated Depreciation CR <45,630.17>

---

9. Click **Save & Close**.

Preparing Financial Statements

Once the adjusted entries have been made, it is time to move on to producing the financial statements for the company. Financial statements are very important in that they can be used both internally and externally to learn about the financial health of a company. Internally, reports are used by management to make decisions in regards to operations. It is beneficial to not only look at the current year's statements, but also to compare them to the statements from the previous fiscal year. Externally, the financial statements are used in a variety of capacities such as to determine if money should be lent to a company, whether a business is profitable, and whether to purchase stock in a company.

FLASHBACK TO GAAP: OBJECTIVITY

Remember that the statements of a company should be based on objectivity.

Cycle Step 7: Generate the Financial Statements

The next step in the accounting cycle requires that financial statements be produced. The statements you must produce are the income statement, the statement of owner's equity, and the balance sheet. You have seen two of these reports already in the first part of this book. Now you will look at them in more depth.

The Income Statement

The Income Statement (a.k.a the Profit & Loss report) is a report that displays the income and expenses generated over a specific period of time. In this case, the net income or net loss will tell a story about the financial health of the company. When using pen-and-paper accounting, the values to be displayed on the Income Statement will come from the Income Statement section of the worksheet.

The Income Statement will have either two or three sections, depending on whether the company deals with inventory or not. If inventory is involved, then a Cost of Goods Sold section will be displayed along with the Income and Expense sections.

> **FLASHBACK TO THE GAAP: MATCHING**
>
> Remember that you are to match the expenses to revenues within the same fiscal period. The Income Statement helps you to make sure this happens.

The Income Statement is made up of temporary accounts. Therefore, it will begin each fiscal year with all accounts displaying a zero balance because the previous period's amounts will have been transferred to the Retained Earnings account as either a net income or a net loss.

Analyzing the Income Statement

There are different measures used to analyze a company's health using the income statement, and the measure used will depend on the purpose of the analysis. As you learned in Lesson 7, Introducing the Accounting Cycle and Using Classes, the Statement of Cash Flows is a more reliable report in many instances, but the Income Statement can still be a useful tool for analyzing aspects of the business such as:

- Ratios to measure profitability (gross margin %, net income %)
- Growth trend analysis (earnings vs. expenses)
- Comparison to similar businesses
- Return on investment

The Balance Sheet

The Balance Sheet is a report that displays the permanent accounts, which make up the elements of the accounting equation (Assets = Liabilities + Equity). It reflects the financial condition of a business on a particular date. In pen-and-paper accounting, the values for the Balance Sheet come from the Balance Sheet section of the worksheet.

> **FLASHBACK TO GAAP: TIME PERIOD**
>
> Remember that the activities of the business can be divided into time periods.

Analyzing the Balance Sheet

Just as the Income Statement is not a perfect tool for analyzing a business, the Balance Sheet is not always the right tool. It can, though, be useful for looking at:

- Ratios to measure profitability, liquidity, and financial strength in the long run (current ratio, quick ratio, return on assets, and return on equity)
- Comparison of assets to liabilities over time
- Working capital (current assets less current liabilities)
- Leverage (debt/worth)

The Statement of Owner's Equity

The Statement of Owner's Equity is a report that shows the capital at the beginning of the fiscal period, any additional investments as well as draws, the net income or loss, and the ending amount.

The amounts on the Statement of Owner's Equity come from two sections of the pen-and-paper worksheet. The net income or loss comes from the Income Statement section, and the beginning capital, investments, and draws come from the Balance Sheet section.

QuickBooks does not provide this as a report for you. One way to look at the change in owner's equity from one fiscal period to another is to customize a balance sheet previous year comparison report by filtering it to show only equity accounts.

Creating Reports to Compare Data from Previous Fiscal Periods

QuickBooks provides ready-made reports to help you compare company financial information from the current and previous fiscal periods easily. The Profit & Loss Previous Year Comparison and Balance Sheet Previous Year Comparison reports show the dollar values for each year and detail the change in amount and percentage.

In addition to the preset reports available in QuickBooks to compare data, you can also customize summary reports to show the same previous period information.

Exporting QuickBooks Reports to Excel

While there are many reports provided for you in QuickBooks, even templates provided by other users, you may find that you would like more control over how you manage and display your QuickBooks data. To analyze your QuickBooks data more effectively, you may wish to export it to a spreadsheet program such as Microsoft Excel so you can use the advanced features available in that program. QuickBooks makes it very easy to export and now update a report.

In this book, we will export to Excel. You may want to experiment with exporting to other programs.

QuickBooks allows you to easily export a report or update an existing spreadsheet by clicking the Excel button on a report's toolbar.

Updating Excel Reports

One of the most exciting new features in QuickBooks 2012 was the ability for a user to update reports exported to Excel without having to reformat all of the data each time a new entry has been made in QuickBooks. What this means is that most of the formatting changes that you make to your QuickBooks data in Excel will be "memorized," so when you export that same report in the future, you will be able to update an existing worksheet rather than having to go in and change all of the formatting each time. Some of the formatting options that will be memorized for you are report titles, new formulas, row and column headers (both font changes and new header names), and inserted columns and rows.

You have two options for updating QuickBooks reports that have been exported to Excel. You can either initiate it from the report window in QuickBooks or from the Excel window while viewing the report.

When you click the Excel button and choose Create a New Worksheet, the Send Report to Excel window will be displayed.

When you click the Advanced button, you will be provided with options that help you to control how your data is exported to Excel.

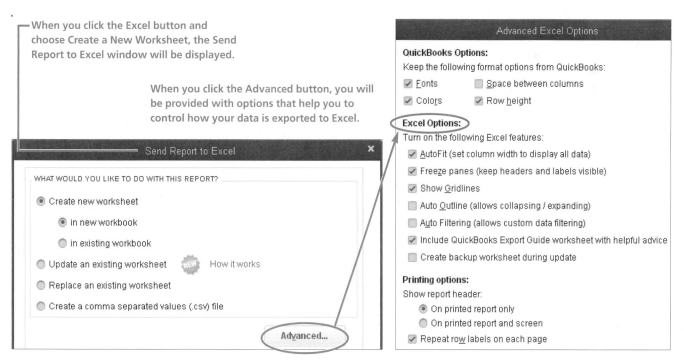

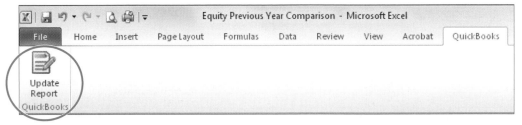

When you are working in Excel with a spreadsheet containing data that has been exported from QuickBooks, you can update the spreadsheet using the QuickBooks tab from within Excel.

QUICK REFERENCE	PRODUCING FINANCIAL STATEMENTS AND EXPORTING TO EXCEL
Task	**Procedure**
Produce an Income Statement report	■ Choose Reports→Company & Financial→Profit & Loss Standard. ■ Set the date range for the report.
Produce a balance sheet report	■ Choose Reports→Company & Financial→Balance Sheet Standard. ■ Set the "as of" date for the report.
Produce a report showing the change in owner equity from one period to the next	■ Choose Reports→Company & Financial→Balance Sheet Prev Year Comparison. ■ Click the Modify Report button; set the date range for the report. ■ Click the Filters tab, choose to filter by Account, and then choose All equity accounts. ■ Click the Header/Footer tab, and then change the Report Title to **Equity Previous Year Comparison.**
Modify a summary report to show previous period comparison data	■ Create a summary report with the data you wish to compare to a prior period. ■ Click the Modify Report button on the toolbar; set the desired date range. ■ Click to choose to Add subcolumns for Previous Period and/or Previous Year. ■ Choose if you want to see the % Change and/or $ Change for each subcolumn.
Export a report to Excel	■ Create the report you wish to export. ■ Click the Export button on the report toolbar. ■ Choose the desired options; click Export.
Update an Excel spreadsheet with new QuickBooks data	■ Display the report you wish to update in QuickBooks. ■ Click the Excel button on the toolbar; choose Update Existing Worksheet. ■ Choose the worksheet you wish to update with new data; click Export. *or* ■ Display the Excel spreadsheet created from QuickBooks data. ■ Click the QuickBooks tab on the Excel Ribbon; click Update Report.

Create Financial Statements and Export a Report to Excel

In this exercise, you will help Zoe create financial statements for Rock Castle Construction. The first report you will create is the Income Statement for the fiscal year 2014.

1. Choose **Reports→Company & Financial→Profit & Loss Standard**.

2. Tap ⎡Tab⎤, type **010114**, tap ⎡Tab⎤ again, and then type **121414**.

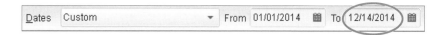

3. Click the **Customize Report** button on the toolbar; click the **Header/Footer** tab.

4. Tap ⎡Tab⎤ three times, and then type **Income Statement** as the new Report Title.

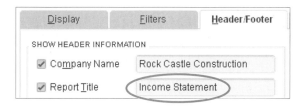

5. Click **OK** in the Modify Report window.
   You will now see the report that you have just modified.

6. Close the **Profit & Loss** window.

Run a Balance Sheet Report

The next financial statement to be produced is the Balance Sheet report for the period ending December 31, 2014.

7. Choose **Reports→Company & Financial→Balance Sheet Standard**.

8. Click the **Dates drop-down arrow**, and then choose **This Fiscal Year** as the date range.

You will now see a basic Balance Sheet report.

9. Close the **Balance Sheet** window.

Create a Report That Shows the Equity Account Information from Two Periods

Next, you will create a report that shows the change in equity information from one period to the next.

10. Choose **Reports→Company & Financial→Balance Sheet Prev Year Comparison**.

11. Click the **Dates drop-down arrow**, and then choose **This Fiscal Year** as the date range.

Advanced Skills

12. Click the **Customize Report** button.

13. Follow these steps to further modify the report:

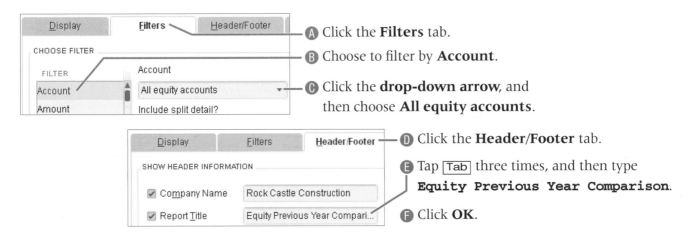

Ⓐ Click the **Filters** tab.

Ⓑ Choose to filter by **Account**.

Ⓒ Click the **drop-down arrow**, and then choose **All equity accounts**.

Ⓓ Click the **Header/Footer** tab.

Ⓔ Tap [Tab] three times, and then type **Equity Previous Year Comparison**.

Ⓕ Click **OK**.

The report displays the balances for the equity accounts on 12/31/2013 and 12/31/2014 as well as the dollar and percentage change. You have not made the closing entries yet, so the net income/loss has not yet been added to the equity accounts. The only change (e.g., the difference between last year and this year) you will see at this point is the addition of the starting inventory that you recorded in the last exercise.

Export a Report to Excel

Now you will export the report you just produced to Excel. To complete this task, you will need to have Microsoft Excel 2003 or later installed on your computer.

14. Click the **Excel** button on the report toolbar, and then choose **Create New Worksheet**.

15. Ensure that your report data will be used to **create a new worksheet in a new workbook**.

16. Click **Export**.

17. Choose **File→Save As** from the Excel Ribbon.

18. Navigate to your file storage location, and then save the report as **Equity Previous Year Comparison**.

 To learn more about how to work with your report in Excel, you may want to utilize a Labyrinth Learning Excel textbook for the version you are using (2013, 2010, 2007, etc.).

19. Close the **Microsoft Excel** window.

20. Close the **Balance Sheet Prev Year Comparison** report window in QuickBooks.

Wrapping Up the Accounting Cycle and Closing the Books

To wrap up the accounting cycle, you need to "zero out" the temporary accounts and move the resulting net income or net loss to a permanent account (specifically an equity account) to begin the next fiscal year. In addition to moving the net income or net loss to the equity account, you also need to bring the account that tracks owner's draw or shareholder distributions to zero.

Cycle Step 8: Journalize and Post Closing Entries

In pen-and-paper accounting, there are four tasks involved in the eighth step of the accounting cycle.

1. Transfer the ending amounts from all of the income accounts to the Income Summary account
2. Transfer the ending amounts from all of the expense accounts to the Income Summary account
3. Transfer the amount in the Income Summary account to the capital account
4. Transfer the amount in the owner's draw account to the capital account

Each of these tasks results in journal transactions that close out the temporary accounts and move the amounts to Income Summary. Then a transaction is recorded that transfers the amount from Income Summary to the capital account. Take note of the following:

- If the balance in the Income Summary account is a credit, then you will need to debit it and credit the capital account. This signifies that the company has experienced a net income.

- If the balance in the Income Summary account is a debit, then you will need to credit it and debit the capital account. This signifies that the company has experienced a net loss.

In QuickBooks, all of this is done for you behind the scenes when you close the books. This step will result in either an increase or decrease in the capital account balance based on whether the company saw a net income or a net loss and the amount of funds the owner(s) drew from the company.

Setting a Closing Date

As you know, you are not required to close the books in QuickBooks, but you can choose to if you like. When you close the books by setting a closing date, QuickBooks does the following for you:

- Transfers the net income or net loss to Retained Earnings
- Restricts access to transactions prior to the closing date by requiring a password
- Allows you to clean up your data

Only the company file administrator can set a closing date and allow or restrict access to prior-period transactions by user.

Pros and Cons of Setting a Closing Date

Since QuickBooks automatically performs some closing actions at the end of your fiscal year (as you learned about earlier in this lesson), you may wonder if you should set a closing date for your file. Take a look at the following pros and cons of setting a closing date in QuickBooks.

SETTING A CLOSING DATE IN QUICKBOOKS

Pros	Cons
▪ You can restrict access to prior-period transactions by setting a password.	▪ You can't easily access all of the details from previous-period transactions
▪ You can create a closing date exception report that displays any modified transactions that are dated on or before the closing date.	▪ You can't create reports that compare transaction data from prior periods.

BEHIND THE SCENES

Following is an example of the eighth step of the accounting cycle in action. In this case, you can see that $100,000 of income will move into the Income Summary account as well as $50,000 of expenses. That results in a $50,000 credit balance that, when transferred to the capital account, will represent a net income of $50,000. In addition, you can see how the owner draw of $10,000 affects the capital account.

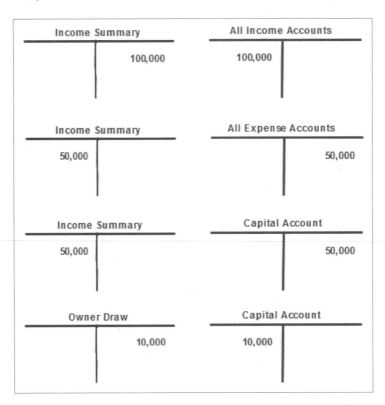

The net effect behind the scenes in this example is a zero balance in the Income Summary account, all the income accounts, all the expense accounts, and the owner draw account. There will be a net increase (credit) in the capital account of $40,000.

Task	Procedure
Set a company closing date	▪ Choose Company→Set Closing Date. ▪ Click the Set Date/Password button in the Closing Date area of the window. ▪ Enter the closing date and password; click OK.

DEVELOP YOUR SKILLS 12.5

Set the Closing Date in QuickBooks

In this exercise, you will set a closing date and password for the Rock Castle Construction QuickBooks company file.

1. Choose **Company→Set Closing Date** and then click the **Set Date/Password** button in the Preferences window.
   The Set Closing Date and Password window appears.

2. Follow these steps to set the closing date and password:

Ⓐ Click here to exclude some transactions.

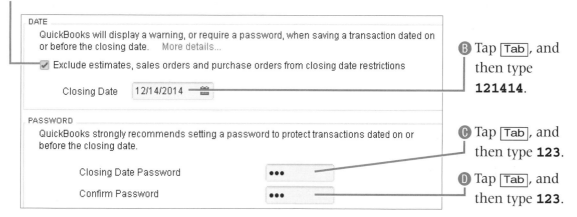

DATE
QuickBooks will display a warning, or require a password, when saving a transaction dated on or before the closing date.   More details...

☑ Exclude estimates, sales orders and purchase orders from closing date restrictions

Closing Date   12/14/2014

Ⓑ Tap Tab, and then type **121414**.

PASSWORD
QuickBooks strongly recommends setting a password to protect transactions dated on or before the closing date.

Closing Date Password   •••

Confirm Password   •••

Ⓒ Tap Tab, and then type **123**.

Ⓓ Tap Tab, and then type **123**.

When closing the books, you can choose to not include transactions that do not affect what happens "behind the scenes" by excluding estimates, sales orders, and purchase orders. If you are not sure what decision to make for your own company, check with your accountant. Also, remember that "123" is not a good password to use in your own company file. It is used here as a basic example.

We are dealing with a sample file that perpetually sets the date to 12/15/2014, so we needed to set the closing date before this date in order to be able to perform the rest of the exercises for this lesson. With your own company, you will choose the last date of your fiscal period!

3. Click **OK** in the Set Closing Date and Password window; close the **Preferences** window.

Working with a Company File After Closing

Once you have set a closing date, there is one additional step to the accounting cycle; it has to do with creating another Trial Balance report. You also may choose to clean up your company's data after you close the books.

Cycle Step 9: Prepare the Post-Closing Trial Balance

The final step of the accounting cycle is to produce another Trial Balance report that shows all of the temporary accounts with a zero balance. This step also allows you to check for one last time that debits and credits are equal. You should have only permanent accounts displayed in the Post-Closing Trial Balance.

Correcting Transactions from a Closed Period

As you learned in the last section, you can set a password when you set a closing date. If a password was set, you will need to enter it if you wish to change any of the transactions from the prior period.

The Closing Date Exception Report

If you are using the Premier Accountant edition of QuickBooks, you can choose to produce a report that shows any transactions dated on or before the closing date that were entered after you set the closing date.

The Audit Trail

The audit trail feature of QuickBooks allows you to track every entry, modification, or deletion to transactions in your file. The audit trail feature is always on to make sure that an accurate record of your QuickBooks data is kept. The audit trail does not track changes to lists, only to transactions. This can help you research transaction history and determine whether certain types of fraudulent activity are occurring. To view the audit trail, you can run a QuickBooks report called "Audit Trail," which is available from the Accountant & Taxes category of the Report Center. In fact, the QuickBooks Audit Trail report has even been reported to have helped determine a fraud case in court!

Cleaning Up Your Data

Once you have closed the books, you have the opportunity to clean up your data. During this process, QuickBooks will delete transactions from before the company closing date that are no longer needed and create "summary" transactions to take their places. Types of transactions that will not be summarized are:

- Those with open balances or that are linked to others with open balances
- Any that have not been reconciled or cleared
- Any that are marked "to be printed"

QuickBooks will not remove any payroll transactions for the current calendar year due to payroll tax reporting requirements.

Cleaning up your company data has huge implications, so make sure you understand what you are doing before you perform this operation.

Preparing for Clean Up

Before QuickBooks begins the clean-up process, it will do three things.

1. Create a backup copy of your file so you can restore your company to its "before clean up" state if necessary.
2. Create an archive copy of your file that will allow you to examine the information that was cleaned up.
3. Verify the integrity of your company file.

Once these three steps are complete, QuickBooks will continue on with the clean-up process. Remember that transactions dated after your company closing date will not be affected by the clean-up process.

List Clean Up

An advantage to cleaning up your file is that you will be able to clean up your lists as well. As you know, when a list entry has been used in a transaction, you cannot delete it. After the clean-up process, if all of the transactions for a particular list entry have been deleted or summarized, you can then delete the list entry.

 Make sure that you have completed all year-end activities before you clean up your company file, such as producing W-2s, W-3s, and 1099 MISC forms.

Working with an Accountant's Copy

If your accountant needs to make adjustments to your QuickBooks file but you do not want to lose access to it while it is being adjusted, you may want to create an accountant's copy file. Your accountant can make the needed adjustments, and you can at least keep up with your daily transactions.

However, there are some tasks that you *cannot* do while your accountant is working on your file, such as:

■ Edit or delete accounts
■ Add, edit, or delete transactions dated on or before the dividing date
■ Reconcile an account

Just as with setting a closing date, only the company file administrator can create an accountant's copy.

The Dividing Date

When you create an accountant's copy, you must set a dividing date. The dividing date determines the point up to which your accountant can work on the file and the point from which you can work in your company file. Be careful when setting this date to ensure that your accountant will have the access needed and that you will still be able to modify recent transactions, if necessary. If your accountant is making adjusting entries, it makes sense to set the dividing date as the last day of the previous fiscal year.

Advanced Skills

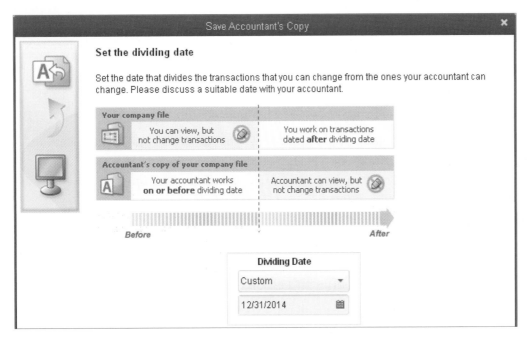

The dividing date will determine the date from which your accountant can make changes to your company file. It also dictates your own access to your company file.

Managing Accountant's Copies

There are four different tasks you will encounter when working with accountant's copies: saving, sending, importing, and removing restrictions. All of these are accessible through the File option on the menu:

- **Saving the file:** This task allows you to create a file, similar to a portable company or backup file, with which your accountant will be able to work while you continue with many of your daily tasks.

- **Sending the file:** You can email the file or save it to a CD or other storage media in order to provide your accountant with the file. Beginning with QuickBooks 2009, Intuit also provides a service called Intuit's Accountant's Copy File Transfer service. This option, found under the File menu, is available if you have Internet access. It does not require that you save a copy of the file (it is done for you when you upload it to the Intuit web server). Your accountant will receive an email with a link that can be used to access your file for download.

- **Importing the file:** Once you receive the file back from your accountant, you must import it into your company file. When you import your accountant's changes, you will be prompted to create a backup copy of your file. This is important in case the import is not successful—you will still have a workable copy of your company file. During the import process, it will be up to you to accept all or none of the changes into your company file and to view the notes left for you from your accountant.

- **Removing restrictions on your file:** To cancel an accountant's copy, you must choose to remove restrictions. If you do this, though, you will not be able to import the accountant's copy changes. On the other hand, if you accidentally create an accountant's copy file, just cancel it to work with your file in normal mode.

WORKING WITH ACCOUNTANT REPORTING, ACCOUNTANT'S COPIES, AND QUICKBOOKS' CLEAN-UP FEATURES

Task	Procedure
Produce a closing date exception report (Premier Accountant edition)	■ Choose Reports→Accountant & Taxes→Closing Date Exception Report.
Run an audit trail report	■ Choose Reports→Accountant & Taxes→Audit Trail. ■ Set the desired date or date range.
Create an accountant's copy	■ Choose File→Accountant's Copy→Save File. ■ Choose Accountant's Copy; click Next. ■ Set the dividing date, click Next, and then click OK. ■ Choose the save location; click Save.
Import an accountant's copy	■ Choose File→Accountant's Copy→Import Accountant's Changes. ■ Locate the QuickBooks Accountant Change File; click Open. ■ Click Import; click OK to let QuickBooks close all windows. ■ Click OK to allow QuickBooks to create a backup file; set the location and complete the backup steps. ■ Once the backup is complete, click OK to acknowledge it; click Close in the Import Accountant's Changes window.
Cancel an accountant's copy	■ Choose File→Accountant's Copy→Remove Restrictions. ■ Click in box to the left of Yes, I want to remove the Accountant's Copy restrictions; click OK.
Send file via Intuit server	■ Choose File→Accountant's Copy→Send to Accountant. ■ Click Next to confirm; choose your dividing date. ■ Enter your and your accountant's email addresses and names. ■ Enter a password for your accountant's copy, enter any notes for your accountant (do not include the password here!), and then click Send.
Clean up a company file	■ Choose File→Utilities→Clean Up Company Data. ■ Choose whether to remove all transactions or those as of a certain date; click Next. ■ Select any additional criteria for removing transactions; click Next. ■ Choose whether you want unused list entries removed for you; click Next. ■ Click Begin Cleanup; follow the steps displayed. ■ Once the backup copy is created, QuickBooks will automatically continue with the archive copy, the data validation, and the clean-up process. When the cleanup is completed, click OK.

Advanced Skills

Correct a Transaction from a Closed Period and Run an Audit Trail Report

In this exercise, you will help Zoe correct a transaction from a closed period and produce an audit trail report. She realized that invoice #1093, dated 12/12/2014, should have been dated 12/15/2014. You will first help Zoe to make this change.

1. Choose **Edit→Find**, and then click the **Simple** tab.

2. Click in the **Invoice #** field, type **1093**, and then click **Find**.

3. Click the **Go To** button.
   Invoice #1093 was already selected, so when you clicked Go To, QuickBooks opened the Create Invoices window with invoice #1093 displayed.

4. Tap [Tab] three times, type **121514**, and then tap [Tab] again.

5. Click **Save & Close** to record the new date for the invoice; click **Yes** to make the change to the transaction.
   A QuickBooks window appears that lets you know that you are making a change to a transaction from a closed period. To bypass this window and make the change, you need to enter the closing date password.

6. Type **123**, and then click **OK**.

7. Close the **Find** window.

Create an Audit Trail Report

You will now take a look at the Audit Trail report, which will show you the change that you just made to invoice #1093.

8. Choose **Reports→Accountant & Taxes→Audit Trail**.

9. Scroll down until you can see the documentation of the change that you just made to invoice **#1093**.

10:29 AM
12/15/14

Rock Castle Construction
Audit Trail
Entered/Last Modified December 15, 2014

Num	Entered/Last Mod...	Last m...	State	Date	Name	Memo	Account	Split	Debit	Credit
Invoice 1093										
1093	12/15/2014 10:28:35	Admin	Latest	*12/15/2014*	Lew Plumbing - C:...		11000 · Acco...	-SPLIT-	220.00	
					Lew Plumbing - C:...	Framing l...	*40130 · Labo...*	11000 · ...		220.00
					State Board of Equ...	CA sales...	25500 · Sales...	11000 · ...	0.00	
1093	12/14/2013 21:20:12	Admin	Prior	*12/12/2014*	Lew Plumbing - C:...		11000 · Acco...	-SPLIT-	220.00	
					Lew Plumbing - C:...	Framing l...	40100 · Cons...	11000 · ...		220.00
					State Board of Equ...	CA sales...	25500 · Sales...	11000 · ...	0.00	

The Audit Trail report shows the prior and most current "version" of a transaction.

10. Close the **Audit Trail** report window.

11. Choose the appropriate option for your situation:

   ■ If you are continuing on to the end-of-lesson exercises, leave QuickBooks open.

   ■ If you are finished working in QuickBooks for now, choose **File→Exit**.

Concepts Review

Concepts Review   http://labyrinthelab.com/qb13

To check your knowledge of the key concepts introduced in this lesson, complete the Concepts Review quiz by going to the URL listed above.

Reinforce Your Skills

Before you begin the Reinforce Your Skills exercises, complete one of these options:

- *Open* **[Your name]'s Tea Shoppe at the Lake, Lesson 11** *or Tea Shoppe at the Lake, Lesson 12 from your file storage location that you used for Lesson 11.*

- *Restore* **Tea Shoppe at the Lake, Lesson 12 (Portable)** *from your file storage location. Make sure to place your name as the first word in the company filename (e.g., Susie's Tea Shoppe at the Lake, Lesson 12).*

You will work with a six-month reporting period (February–July 2013) for Tea Shoppe at the Lake.

REINFORCE YOUR SKILLS 12.1
Work with the Trial Balance Report

In this exercise, you will create a Trial Balance report for Tea Shoppe at the Lake.

1. Choose **Reports→Accountant & Taxes→Trial Balance**.

2. Tap ⎡Tab⎤, type **020113**, tap ⎡Tab⎤ again, and then type **073113**.

3. Click the **Refresh** button.
   The trial balance report for the six month period of February – July 2013 displays.

4. Close the **Trial Balance** report, choosing not to memorize it.

REINFORCE YOUR SKILLS 12.2
Create Adjusting Entries

Susie realized that she created entries in the fixed asset item list for the equipment she purchased just prior to starting her business, but she never entered the value of the equipment into her Chart of Accounts. In this exercise, you will create adjusting entries and record the fixed asset depreciation for the fiscal period.

The first journal entry you will create is one to record the fixed assets (Business computer $743, Espresso machine $3,989, Furniture $3500, Office Furniture $459, and Register $429 = $9,120) that Susie "invested" in the company when it started on 2/1/2013.

1. Choose **Company→Make General Journal Entry**; click **OK** in the Assigning Numbers to Journal Entries window.

2. Type **020113** as the date.

3. Follow these steps to enter the journal transaction:

Ⓐ Click in the first line of the **Account** column, and then type **fu**.

Ⓑ Tap ⎡Tab⎤, and then type **9120**.

Ⓒ Tap ⎡Tab⎤ two times, and then type **Record fixed asset investment**.

Ⓓ Tap ⎡Tab⎤ two times, and then type **o**.

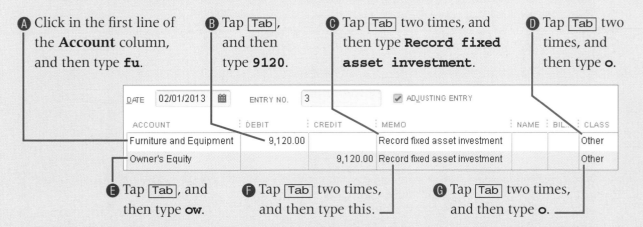

Ⓔ Tap ⎡Tab⎤, and then type **ow**.

Ⓕ Tap ⎡Tab⎤ two times, and then type this.

Ⓖ Tap ⎡Tab⎤ two times, and then type **o**.

4. Click **Save & New** to record the transaction and leave the window open.

5. Click in the **checkbox** to not display the message in the future; click **OK** in the Tracking Fixed Assets on Journal Entries window.

Record the Depreciation Transaction

Next you will help Susie record the depreciation transaction for the fiscal period. The total depreciation she will record is $560. The Make General Journal Entries window should still be open. If it is not, choose Company→Make General Journal Entries.

6. Type **073113** as the date, and then tap ⎡Tab⎤.

7. Follow these steps to record the journal entry:

Ⓐ Click in the first line of the **Account** column, and then type **de**.

Ⓑ Tap ⎡Tab⎤, and then type **560**.

Ⓒ Tap ⎡Tab⎤ two times, and then type **Record depreciation 2/13-7/13**.

Ⓓ Tap ⎡Tab⎤ two times, and then type **o**.

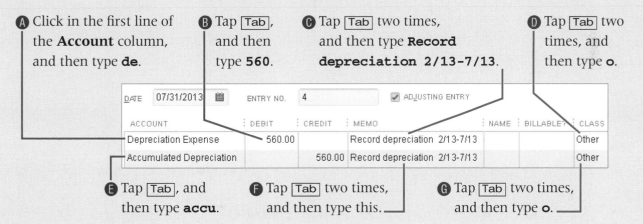

Ⓔ Tap ⎡Tab⎤, and then type **accu**.

Ⓕ Tap ⎡Tab⎤ two times, and then type this.

Ⓖ Tap ⎡Tab⎤ two times, and then type **o**.

8. Click **Save & Close**.

Produce Financial Statements and Export to Excel

In this exercise, you will produce an Income Statement and a Balance Sheet for Tea Shoppe at the Lake. Then you will export the Balance Sheet to Excel

1. Choose **Reports→Company & Financial→Profit & Loss Standard**.

2. Tap Tab, type **020113**, tap Tab again, and then type **073113**.

3. Click **Refresh**.

   The Profit & Loss report displays for February –July 2013. You will now change the report title to Income Statement.

4. Click the **Customize Report** button, and then click the **Header/Footer** tab.

5. Change the Report Title to **Income Statement**, and then click **OK**.

6. Click the **Memorize** button on the toolbar, type **Income Statement, Feb - Jul 2013**, and then click **OK**.

7. Close the **report window**.

Create a Balance Sheet Report and Export It to Excel

You must have Excel installed on your computer for this section of the exercise.

8. Choose **Reports→Company & Financial→Balance Sheet Standard**.

9. Tap Tab, type **073113**, and then tap Tab again.

   Note that QuickBooks has added a line to the Balance Sheet to show the Net Income of $31,597.10 and that the Owner Draw is $8,000.

10. Click the **Excel** button on the report toolbar, and then choose **Create New Worksheet**. Ensure that the report will be exported to a new Excel workbook, and then click **Export**.

    You can now use Excel to calculate various ratios to analyze your company data.

11. Close the **Excel** window, choosing to save the workbook as **Balance Sheet, 7-31-2013** in your default storage location.

12. Click the **Memorize** button on the report toolbar, type **Balance Sheet, 7/31/13**, and then click **OK**.

13. Close the **report** window.

Close the Books

In this exercise, you will now help Susie set a closing date for her QuickBooks company file.

1. Choose **Company→Set Closing Date**.

2. Click the **Set Date/Password** button.

    The Set Closing Date and Password window appears.

3. Click in the **checkbox** to choose to exclude estimates, sales orders, and purchase orders from closing date restrictions.

4. Tap ⌐Tab¬, and then type **073113**.

5. Tap ⌐Tab¬, type **123**, tap ⌐Tab¬ again, and then type **123**.

6. Click **OK** to set the closing date and password, click **No** in the No Password Entered window, and then click **OK** in the Preferences window.

Make a Correction to a Transaction from a Prior Period

In this exercise, you will make a correction to a transaction from a closed period. Susie realized that she needs to change the Terms of the bill dated 7/5/2013 for High Tec Mktg to Net 30. You will help her to make that change now.

1. Choose **Edit→Find**.

2. Choose **Bill** as the Transaction Type and choose **High Tec Mktg** as the Vendor; click **Find**.
   You will see all of the bills for the vendor displayed at the bottom of the window.

3. Double-click the bill for **7/5/2013**.
   The Enter Bills window will open with the selected bill displayed.

4. Change the Terms on the bill to **Net 30** and click **Save & Close**; click **Yes** to record the transaction.
   A QuickBooks window appears, asking for you to enter the closing date password in order to make the change.

5. Type **123** and click **OK**; click **Yes** to permanently change the terms for the vendor.

6. Close the **Find** window.

7. Choose the appropriate option for your situation:

   ■ If you are continuing on to the rest of the end-of-lesson exercises, leave QuickBooks open.

   ■ If you are finished working in QuickBooks for now, choose **File→Exit**.

Advanced Skills

Apply Your Skills

Before you begin the Apply Your Skills exercises, complete one of these options:

- *Open* [Your name] **Wet Noses Veterinary Clinic, Lesson 11** *or* **Wet Noses Veterinary Clinic, Lesson 12** *from your file storage location.*

- *Restore* **Wet Noses Veterinary Clinic, Lesson 12 (Portable)** *from your file storage location. Make sure to place your name as the first word in the company filename (e.g., Sadie's Wet Noses Veterinary Clinic, Lesson 12).*

You will work with a one-month (May 2013) reporting period for Wet Noses Veterinary Clinic.

APPLY YOUR SKILLS 12.1
Create a Trial Balance Report

In this exercise, you will help Dr. James create a Trial Balance report for Wet Noses.

1. Choose **Reports→Accountant & Taxes→Trial Balance**.

2. Set the date range to cover **May 2013**.
   The trial balance report for the one month period of May 2013 displays.

3. Close the **Trial Balance report**, choosing not to memorize it.

APPLY YOUR SKILLS 12.2
Work with Journal Entries

In this exercise, you will create adjusting entries. Dr. James has realized that she needs to enter the equipment that she invested into the company. She will then need to enter the depreciation transaction for the fixed assets.

Record a Fixed Asset Investment

You will first help Sadie enter a general journal entry to record the furniture and equipment that she provided to the company.

1. Open the **Make General Journal** Entries window.

2. Create a transaction dated **5/1/2013** that debits Furniture and Equipment and credits the Partner 1 Equity account for **16,320**. Use **Overhead** as the class and **Record fixed asset investment** as the Memo.

Record a Depreciation Transaction

You will now help Sadie record the depreciation for the month.

3. Create a transaction dated **5/31/2013** that debits Depreciation Expense and credits the Accumulated Depreciation account for **$128**. Use **Overhead** as the class and **Record May 2013 Depreciation** as the Memo.

4. Click **Save & Close** when you are finished to save the transaction and close the window.

Close the Books

In this exercise, you will close the books and create an Accountant's Copy of the file.

1. Open the **Preferences** window with the Accounting category and the Company Preferences tab displayed.

2. Choose to set the closing date and password; choose to exclude estimates, sales orders, and purchase order from closing date restrictions.

3. Enter **5/31/2013** as the Closing Date, and then use **123** as the Closing Date Password. Choose to not add or edit users.

Create an Accountant's Copy

Next you will create an accountant's copy that your accountant can use to view your company data and make adjusting entries.

4. Choose **File→Accountant's Copy→Save File**.
   If using the Premier Accountant edition, the menu command will be File→Accountant's Copy→Client Activities→Save File.

5. Choose **Accountant's Copy**, and then click **Next**.

If you are completing this exercise prior to 5/31/2013, you will not be allowed to set the closing date (since it is in the future). In that case, click Cancel.

6. Set the dividing date as **5/31/2013**, click **Next**, and then click **OK**.

7. Choose your default file storage location, and then click **Save**.
   Now you have a file that you can send to your accountant.

Advanced Skills

Answer Questions with Reports

In this exercise, you will answer questions for Dr. James by running reports. You may wish to display the Report Center in List View to help you answer the questions. Ask your instructor if you should print the reports, print (save) them as PDF files, export them to Excel, or simply display them on the screen. This exercise requires you to create some basic formulas in Excel. If you do not have Excel on your computer, or do not know how to use it, you may skip this exercise.

1. What is the net profit margin for the business during the month of May 2013? (Hint: Create a Profit & Loss Standard report and edit the report title to **Income Statement**. Export the report to Excel and then calculate the net profit margin by taking the net income and dividing it by the revenue.) Memorize the report as **Income Statement, May 2013**.

2. What is the current ratio of the company as of May 31, 2013? (Hint: Create a Summary Balance Sheet report as of **5/31/2013**. Export the report to Excel and then calculate the current ratio by dividing the current assets by the current liabilities.) Memorize the report as **Balance Sheet, 5/31/2013**.

3. Create a report showing the change in owner's equity from **5/1/2013** to **6/1/2013**.

4. Submit your reports based on the guidelines provided by your instructor.

5. Choose the option that is appropriate for your situation:
   - If you are continuing on to the Critical Thinking exercises, leave QuickBooks open.
   - If you are finished working in QuickBooks for now, choose **File→Exit**.

Critical Thinking

12.1 Sort Through the Stack

In the course of working through the following Critical Thinking exercises, you will be utilizing various skills taught in this and previous lesson(s). Take your time and think carefully about the tasks presented to you. Turn back to the lesson content if you need assistance.

Before You Begin: Restore the **Monkey Business, Lesson 12 (Portable)** *file from your storage location. (Remember that you are to leave the password field blank for Mary.) You also have the option of opening either the final file from Critical Thinking 11.1 or Monkey Business, Lesson 12 from your storage location.*

You have been hired by Mary Minard to help her with her organization's books. She is the owner of Monkey Business, a nonprofit organization that provides low-income students with help in preparing for college placement exams and applying for scholarships. You have just sat down at her desk and found a pile of papers. It is your job to sort through the papers and make sense of what you find, entering information into QuickBooks whenever appropriate and answering any other questions in a word-processing document saved as **Critical Thinking 12.1**.

■ Note from Mary: I know that the end-of-period accounting for not-for-profits is a bit different than that what is done for "regular" for-profit businesses. Will you please go to **http://labyrinthelab.com/qb13** and complete the WebQuest that will help you to learn more about what we need to know about not-for-profit accounting?

■ Scribbled note from Mary: Please create a Balance Sheet report as of 8/31/2013, change the name of it to **Statement of Financial Position**, and export it to Excel. Save the Excel file as **SFP, 8-31-13**.

12.2 Tackle the Tasks

Now is your chance to work a little more with Rock Castle Construction and apply the skills that you have learned in this lesson to accomplish additional tasks. Open or restore the **Critical Thinking 12.2** company or portable company file from your file storage location or open the company file you used in the Develop Your Skills exercises for this lesson, create the report indicated, export it to Excel, and then perform the calculations associated with each. If you wish to not write in the book, you can print a worksheet from the student resource center.

CREATE A BALANCE SHEET REPORT AS OF 12/31/2014	
Calculation	**Answer**
Quick ratio: (current assets − inventory)/current liabilities	
Return on assets: net income/total assets	
Working capital: current assets − current liabilities	

CREATE AN INCOME STATEMENT REPORT FOR THE PERIOD 1/1/2014–12/31/2014	
Calculation	**Answer**
Gross profit margin: (revenue − COGS)/revenue	
Operating profit margin: revenue − expenses related to day-to-day operations of the business	
Net profit margin: net income/revenue	

12.3 Use the Web as a Learning Tool

Throughout this book, you will be provided with an opportunity to use the Internet as a learning tool by completing WebQuests. According to the original creators of WebQuests, as described on their website (WebQuest.org), a WebQuest is "an inquiry-oriented activity in which most or all of the information used by learners is drawn from the web." To complete the WebQuest projects in this book, navigate to the student resource center and choose the WebQuest for the lesson on which you are currently working. The subject of each WebQuest will be relevant to the material found in the lesson.

WebQuest Subject: End-of-period reporting

Need to Know Accounting

E ven though QuickBooks does everything for you "behind the scenes," it is important that you have a basic understanding of what is happening to your books.

In this appendix, you will learn about the basic financial statements important to any business and the accounts that appear on these reports. You will also learn about the double-entry accounting system and the debits and credits that must always be equal.

Working with Financial Statements

There are two main reports that a company will produce periodically to illustrate its financial well-being.

- A **Balance Sheet** report displays all of the holdings of the company along with the debts as of a particular date.
- An **Income Statement**, otherwise known as a Profit & Loss Report, displays the income and expenses for a specified period of time.

Understanding the accounts that make up each of these reports is key to understanding your company's books.

The Accounting Equation and the Balance Sheet

The first equation you need to learn when it comes to accounting is simply termed the accounting equation:

$$\text{Assets} = \text{Liabilities} + \text{Equity}$$

This means that if you take all of your company's debt and add any investments (equity), you will have a value equal to all of the assets that your company owns.

A balance sheet is a financial statement that displays all asset, liability, and equity accounts (the balance sheet accounts). Take a look at the following illustrations to see how the accounting equation works and is represented in a balance sheet.

The upper section represents the left side of the accounting equation and displays all assets.

The lower section represents the right side of the accounting equation and displays all liability and equity accounts.

The Tea Shoppe at the Lake
Balance Sheet
As of July 31, 2013

	◇ Jul 31, 13 ◇
▼ ASSETS	
▼ Current Assets	
▼ Checking/Savings	
Checking	▶ 22,847.58 ◀
Money Market	10,000.00
Petty Cash	178.13
Total Checking/Savings	33,025.71
▼ Accounts Receivable	
Accounts Receivable	1,767.48
Total Accounts Receivable	1,767.48
▼ Other Current Assets	
Inventory Asset	280.00
Prepaid Rent	4,600.00
Total Other Current Assets	4,880.00
Total Current Assets	39,673.19
▼ Fixed Assets	
Accumulated Depreciation	-560.00
Furniture and Equipment	11,689.00
Total Fixed Assets	11,129.00
TOTAL ASSETS	50,802.19

Notice that the amount for Total Assets is $50,802.19.

Notice that the amount for Total Liabilities & Equity is also $50,802.19.

The Tea Shoppe at the Lake
Balance Sheet
As of July 31, 2013

	◇ Jul 31, 13 ◇
▼ LIABILITIES & EQUITY	
▼ Liabilities	
▼ Current Liabilities	
▼ Accounts Payable	
Accounts Payable	2,818.85
Total Accounts Payable	2,818.85
▼ Credit Cards	
American Express	578.51
ROP CU Visa	120.00
Total Credit Cards	698.51
▼ Other Current Liabilities	
Sales Tax Payable	73.73
Total Other Current Liabilities	73.73
Total Current Liabilities	3,591.09
▼ Long Term Liabilities	
Steamer Loan	2,000.00
Total Long Term Liabilities	2,000.00
Total Liabilities	5,591.09
▼ Equity	
Owner's Equity	19,120.00
Owner Draw	-8,000.00
Retained Earnings	2,494.00
Net Income	31,597.10
Total Equity	45,211.10
TOTAL LIABILITIES & EQUITY	50,802.19

The Income Statement

The accounts that you find on the Income Statement (or Profit & Loss report) are income and expense. In the following illustration you can view an Income Statement and the accounts that appear on it.

The Tea Shoppe at the Lake

Profit & Loss

February through July 2013

	◇ Feb - Jul 13 ◇
▼ Ordinary Income/Expense	
▼ Income	
Beverage Sales	▶ 38,150.00 ◀
Catering Sales	4,215.75
Craft Sales	450.00
Food Sales	20,496.00
Total Income	63,311.75
▼ Cost of Goods Sold	
Cost of Goods Sold	210.00
Food Purchases	13,270.87
Restaurant Supplies	2,458.71
Total COGS	15,939.58
Gross Profit	47,372.17
▼ Expense	
Advertising and Promotion	1,780.00
Bank Service Charges	40.00
Business Licenses and Permits	125.00
Computer and Internet Expenses	312.73
Depreciation Expense	560.00
Insurance Expense	1,556.00
Office Supplies	407.25
Professional Fees	575.00
Rent Expense	5,900.00
Repairs and Maintenance	1,539.81
Uniforms & Linens	374.97
Utilities	1,511.25
Vendor Credits	-106.94
Total Expense	14,575.07
Net Ordinary Income	32,797.10
Net Income	**32,797.10**

The total of all your income accounts will result in your Gross Profit.

The Total Expense is totaled below the Gross Profit.

The difference between the Gross Profit and Total Expense results in the Net Income (or Net Loss if the expenses are greater than the income).

Debits and Credits: The Double-Entry Accounting System

There is another equation in accounting that is paramount for us to keep in mind: Debits must always equal credits! Most people who do not work in the accounting field are confused about debits and credits, though.

Accounts are often displayed in a "T" format in accounting (which you can see in all of the Behind the Scenes sections of this book). The T accounts allow you to place the name of the account on the top, account debits on the left side, and account credits on the right side. This means that the left side (debits) must always equal the right side (credits) when entering accounting transactions (hence the term "double-entry").

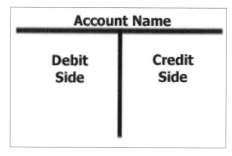

A simple way to view an account is to use the T format.

In order to understand debits and credits a bit better, we will now look at the types of accounts and their normal balances.

Types of Accounts and Normal Balances

We have looked at the two main financial statements and the types of accounts included in each. The balance sheet is composed of asset, liability, and equity accounts. The income statement is composed of income and expense accounts. Before we look deeper into each account type, it is important to understand normal balances.

Take a look at Lesson 2, Creating a Company, to view all of the account sub-types that you can create in QuickBooks.

About Normal Balances

Each type of account must have a normal balance of either a debit or a credit. The normal balance is the side that will increase the amount of the account. Assets and expenses both have debit normal balances and will increase when debited and decrease when credited. Liabilities, equity, and income all have credit normal balances and will increase when credited and decrease when debited.

The concept of normal balances makes sense if you think of the balance sheet. Assets with a debit normal balance must equal the sum of the liabilities and equity, which both have a credit normal balance. Think of this as the marriage of the accounting equation and the fact that debits must equal credits!

The following table describes the primary account types and their normal balances.

Account Type	Description
Assets	An asset is anything that a company owns or monies that are owed to the company. Examples of assets are checking accounts, accounts receivable, and autos. Assets have a debit normal balance.
Liabilities	A liability is something that a company owes such as an auto loan or a credit card balance. Liabilities have a credit normal balance.
Equity	Equity accounts are both investments into the company (Owner's Equity or Stockholder's Equity) and the net income or loss from the operation of a business (Retained Earnings). Equity accounts have a credit normal balance.
Income	Income accounts reflect the sales and fees earned during an accounting period. Income accounts have a credit normal balance.
Expenses	Expense accounts record the expenditures that a company accrues while conducting business. Expense accounts have a debit normal balance.

The Trial Balance Report

At the end of an accounting cycle a trial balance is prepared that shows all accounts affected during the cycle. The balance of each account is entered in the appropriate column based on its normal balance. The net income or net loss is the difference between income and expenses. If the income is greater than the expenses, an excess credit balance will result and will increase the equity account (a net income). If the expenses are greater than the income, an excess debit balance will result and will decrease the equity account (a net loss).

The Tea Shoppe at the Lake
Trial Balance
As of July 31, 2013

| | Jul 31, 13 | |
	Debit	Credit
Checking	22,847.58	
Money Market	10,000.00	
Petty Cash	178.13	
Accounts Receivable	1,767.48	
Inventory Asset	280.00	
Prepaid Rent	4,600.00	
Undeposited Funds	0.00	
Furniture and Equipment	2,569.00	
Accounts Payable		2,818.85
American Express		578.51
ROP CU Visa		120.00
Sales Tax Payable		73.73
Steamer Loan		2,000.00
Owner's Equity		10,000.00
Owner Draw	8,000.00	
Retained Earnings		2,494.00
Beverage Sales		38,150.00
Catering Sales		4,215.75
Craft Sales		450.00
Food Sales		20,496.00
Cost of Goods Sold	210.00	
Food Purchases	13,270.87	
Restaurant Supplies	2,458.71	
Advertising and Promotion	1,780.00	
Bank Service Charges	40.00	
Business Licenses and Permits	125.00	
Computer and Internet Expenses	312.73	
Insurance Expense	1,556.00	
Office Supplies	407.25	
Professional Fees	575.00	
Rent Expense	7,100.00	
Repairs and Maintenance	1,539.81	
Uniforms & Linens	374.97	
Utilities	1,511.25	
Vendor Credits		106.94
TOTAL	**81,503.78**	**81,503.78**

—The debits and credits in a Trial Balance must be equal.

Finding Additional Accounting Resources

Want to learn more about what happens to your company's books behind the scenes in QuickBooks? Visit the student resource center to explore a variety of online learning resources or purchase a copy of *The ABCs of Accounting, 2nd Edition*, which is also published by Labyrinth Learning.

Glossary

Accountant's Copy
A special copy of your QuickBooks file that can be created if your accountant needs to make adjustments to your Quick-Books file, but you do not want to lose access to it while it is being adjusted

Accounting Cycle
A series of steps to help a business keep its accounting records properly during the fiscal period

Accrual Basis
In the accrual basis of accounting, income is recorded when the sale is made and expenses recorded when accrued; often used by firms or businesses with large inventories

Activities
Affect what is happening behind the scenes; can be easily input into forms such as invoices or bills

Administrator
QuickBooks user who controls the access of all users of a Quick-Books file; administrator also controls all company preferences in the Edit Preferences window

Advanced Setup
This method of company creation takes you through a series of questions; your answer to each question determines how your company is set up

Assets
Anything owned by a company or that is owed to a company; items such as a checking account, a building, a prepaid insurance account, or accounts receivable

Audit Trail
Allows you to track every entry, modification, or deletion to transactions in your file; accessed through the Accounting category in the Report Center or the Report option on the menu bar

Average Cost
A method of inventory tracking where the value of the inventory is determined by dividing the total value of the inventory by the total number of inventory items

Backup
The process of creating a condensed copy of your QuickBooks file to ensure you don't lose your data or to allow yourself or another person the ability to view your company file on another computer

Bad Debt
Funds owed to you that are not collectable and need to be written off

Balance Sheet Accounts
The asset, liability, and equity accounts, such as bank, credit card, current liabilities (sales tax payable and payroll liabilities), accounts receivable, accounts payable, and retained earnings

Balance Sheet by Class Report
Balance sheet report on which each class appears as a separate column; should be used only by expert users

Balance Sheet Report
A report that displays all assets, liabilities, and equity as of a specific date

Batch Invoicing
Feature that lets a user create invoices that are basically the same for multiple customers at one time

Batch Timesheets
Feature that allows you to create timesheets for multiple employees who work the same hours on the same jobs and using the same payroll item(s)

Behind the Scenes
The accounting that QuickBooks performs for you when you enter transactions

Bounced Check
A check returned by the bank due to non-sufficient funds in the account; also called a "NSF" check

Browser
A software application used to locate and display web pages, such as Netscape Navigator and Microsoft Internet Explorer

Budget
In QuickBooks, create a budget for your company either from scratch or based on actual values from a previous period

Cash Basis
In the cash basis of accounting, income is recorded when cash is received and expenses recorded when cash is paid; commonly used by small businesses and professionals

Cash Flow Forecast
A report that gives you a glimpse of what you can expect a company's cash flow to look like in the near future based on current data in the company file

Centers
QuickBooks has four centers: Customer, Employee, Report, and Vendor; centers allow you to view the Customers & Jobs, Employee, and Vendor lists, access QuickBooks reports, and view snapshots of information (of an individual customer, vendor, or employee)

Classes
Classes are used to rate; not tied to any particular customer, vendor, or item; used to track only one particular aspect of your business, such as location or individual programs

Closing the Books
During this process at the end of your fiscal year, QuickBooks transfers the net income or net loss to Retained Earnings, restricts access to transactions prior to the closing date (unless you know the password), and allows you to clean up your company data; you are not required to "close the books" in QuickBooks

Collections Center
Feature that helps users easily identify customers who have overdue balances; also provides contact information

Company File
The QuickBooks file you use when working with your company's day-to-day operations

Company Setup
Takes you through the steps necessary to set up a new company in QuickBooks

Company Snapshot
A window that offers a quick view of your company's bottom line in one convenient place

Contributed Reports
Feature that allows you to look for a report submitted by another user so you don't have to "reinvent the wheel"; you can also share your custom reports with this feature

Customers & Jobs List
A list in QuickBooks that stores all information related to your customers and the jobs associated with them

Customer & Vendor Profile Lists
Lists QuickBooks provides to track customer and vendor information

Depreciation
Provides a business with a way to match income to expenses; a fixed asset is used to produce income over a period of time, and depreciation allows you to record the appropriate expense for the same period; many small businesses record depreciation transactions just once a year, but they can be entered monthly or quarterly if the business produces financial statements for those periods

Doc Center
Feature that allows you to store your source documents electronically, attaching them to the transactions or list entries to which they belong

Draw
An owner's withdrawal of funds from the company

Edition
Intuit creates a multitude of editions of QuickBooks to choose from: QuickBooks Online, QuickBooks Pro, QuickBooks Premier, and QuickBooks Enterprise

Electronic Payments
Some companies receive payments from customers electronically; they can be handled by using a new payment type called Electronic Payment

Employees List
A list in QuickBooks that helps you to keep track of your employee data; can be used as a source of information to run payroll in QuickBooks; accessed through the Employee Center

Equity Accounts
Reflect the owner's investment in the company and have a credit normal balance; in a Sole Proprietorship, equity is what the owner has invested in the company and in a corporation, the equity is what the shareholders have invested in the company

Estimates
Feature that allows a user to create a proposal for a customer or job

Express Start
In this method of company creation, QuickBooks asks you for your basic company information, and it will be up to you to set up certain items such as payroll and inventory later

Field
A box into which data is entered

File Storage Location
Location where you store files for this course (USB flash drive, the My Documents folder, or a network drive at a school or company)

Filtering
Filtering allows you to include only the essential data in your report; choose to filter out many types of data such as accounts, dollar amounts, and types of customers; allows you to closely examine and report on a specific group of data

Finance Charge
A charge assessed to an overdue customer balance

Fixed Asset
An asset you don't plan to use up or turn into cash within the next year; businesses use fixed assets in a productive capacity to promote the main operations of the company; are depreciable, which means that you don't expense the assets when you purchase them, but rather over the useful life of the asset

Fixed Asset Account
Type of account that tracks the activities associated with a fixed asset

Fonts
QuickBooks displays its preset reports in a default font; you can make many changes to the characteristics of the font in your report, such as the font name, style, color, and size

Forecast
A feature that allows you to make predictions about the future; they can be created based on actual figures from the last year or from scratch

Formatting
Formatting deals with the appearance of the report; it has nothing to do with the data contained within it

Generally Accepted Accounting Principles (GAAP)
Rules used to prepare, present, and report financial statements for a wide variety of entities

Graphs
Graphs in QuickBooks allow you to display your information in a more illustrative way

Header and Footer
Default headers and footers appear on all preset QuickBooks reports; change the information included along with how it is formatted on the Header and Footer tabs of the Additional Customization window

Homepage
A web page that serves as an index or table of contents to other documents stored on the site; the main page for a large website; the web page that comes up by default when you open your browser

Hypertext Markup Language (HTML)
A text-based language that any computer can read; used to organize pages with devices such as headings, paragraphs, lists, etc.

Income Statement
Financial report that can be found in the Company & Financial category of the Report Finder window; P&L reports reflect all transactions that have affected income and expense accounts within a specified time period; also called a Profit & Loss Report

Internet
A collection of computers all over the world that send, receive, and store information; access is gained through an Internet Service Provider (ISP); the web is just a portion of the Internet

Investment
Occurs when an owner deposits funds into the company

Job Costing
Allows a users to determine the profitability of each job for a customer

Joint Photographic Experts Group (JPG)
Committee that designed the graphics format; JPG images support 16 million colors and are best suited for photographs and complex graphics

Just in Time Transaction History
Allows you to see summary information when entering a transaction for a customer or vendor

Layout Designer
The Layout Designer window provides rulers to line up objects, and toolbar buttons to help manipulate your template objects

Lead Center
Feature that allows you to track information about potential customers

Link
Also called hyperlink; provides navigation through a website; displayed on the QuickBooks Home page to provide navigation throughout the QuickBooks program

List (Database)
Allows you to store information about customers, vendors, employees, and other data important to your business

Live Community
A place where a user can collaborate with other QuickBooks users to get advice or to provide insights

Logo
QuickBooks allows you to personalize your templates by including your company logo

Long Term Liabilities Account
A QuickBooks account that tracks a liability (loan) you do not plan to pay off within the next year

Nominal Account
Accounts are zeroed out at the end of each fiscal period, with the amounts from them moving into an equity account as either a net income (if income was greater than expenses) or a net loss (if expenses exceeded income for the period); also called a temporary account

One-Click Tasks
Feature that allows you to create credit memos, payments, letters, or memorized transactions from invoices with just one click

Online Backup
QuickBooks offers an online backup option for a monthly fee that is determined based on the amount of room you wish to have available for your backup work

On the Fly
When you type a new entry into a field that draws from a list, QuickBooks gives you the opportunity to add the record to the list "on the fly" as you create the transaction

Opening Balance Equity Account
An equity account created by QuickBooks when you start your first balance sheet account; it allows you to have an accurate balance sheet from the start

Other Current Assets Account
An account that tracks the transactions related to an asset that you plan to either use up or convert to cash within one year

Outside Payroll Service
A service that runs payroll for a company outside of QuickBooks; the company inputs the information into QuickBooks without using the payroll features

Passing an Expense On to Customers
The process of identifying an expense in a transaction for which you plan to charge a customer and invoicing the customer for the expense

Payroll Liabilities
The account in which you hold payroll taxes and other deductions until you are required to pay them

Payroll Options
Intuit provides a variety of options to run your payroll; to view and compare these options, visit the book's website at http://labyrinthelab.com/qb13

PDF File
PDF stands for "portable document format;" it is a type of file that preserves formatting, data, and graphics; saves in a portable file

Permanent Account
An account for which the ending balance for one fiscal period is the opening balance for the next

Petty Cash
Cash kept by businesses for small expenditures; in QuickBooks, Petty Cash is set up as a bank account in the Chart of Accounts

Portable Company File
A type of QuickBooks file that contains all company data in a compressed format; it must be restored to be utilized; it is much smaller in size than a company or backup file

Preferences
The way you interact with QuickBooks is controlled by the preferences you select; the Preferences window has 19 categories; company preferences are controlled by the administrator and determine how the entire company interacts with QuickBooks; personal preferences are controlled by individual users and dictate interactions between QuickBooks and only that one user

Price Level List
Allows a user to set and charge different price levels for different customers or jobs

Profit and Loss (P&L) Report
A financial report that can be found in the Company & Financial category of the Report Finder window; P&L reports reflect all transactions that have affected income and expense accounts within a specified time period; also called an Income Statement

Progess Invoicing
Allows you to invoice from an estimate in stages rather than for the entire estimate amount

Purchase Order
A form utilized by many companies to enter items into inventory; it does not affect anything "behind the scenes"

Quick Reference Tables
Tables that summarize the tasks you have just learned. Use them as guidelines when you begin work on your own QuickBooks company file.

Quick Report
A report that shows all the transactions recorded in QuickBooks for a particular list record, which can be run from the various list windows

QuickBooks Shipping Manager
Allows you to use your USPS, FedEx, or UPS account to ship directly from QuickBooks; allows you to create a shipment and shipping label (with all of the information pre-filled) right from the Create Invoices and Enter Sales Receipts windows; can be used to track your shipments

QuickZoom
A QuickBooks report and graph feature that allows you to zoom through underlying sub-reports until you reach the form where the data were originally entered; this can be extremely useful if you have questions about where a figure in a report or graph comes from

Reconciliation
The process of matching your QuickBooks accounts to the bank and credit card statements you receive. It is important to make sure that your account records in QuickBooks match those of the bank or credit card company

Report
A way to display your company information in various ways such as printed, onscreen, or as a PDF file

Resize
To change the height or width of an image, window, or object

Restoring
The process of decompressing a QuickBooks backup or portable company file; when you restore a file in the same location with the same name as another file, it will replace that file

Sales Orders
Allows you to manage customer orders of both products and services; available in the Premier and Enterprise editions

Search Feature
Allows a user to perform searches based on text entered throughout a company file and menu commands

Starter Chart of Accounts
During the setup process, QuickBooks asks you to choose the business type that your company most closely resembles; QuickBooks uses your choice to create a Chart of Accounts close to what you need (it will take you less time to edit it to fit your unique business than to start from scratch); you cannot change the business type option later

Statement of Cash Flows
Report that shows how viable a company is in the short term; demonstrates whether a company will be able to pay its bills, payroll, and other expenses; also indicates the financial health of the company

Statement of Owner's Equity
Report that shows the capital at the beginning of the fiscal period, any additional investments, as well as draws, the net income or loss, and the ending amount

Subaccounts

Help you keep precise records; to track expenses more closely, you may want to have separate accounts for your office phone, office fax, cellular phone, etc.; subaccounts are a great way to track these separate expenses while keeping the number of expense accounts down

Template

A specific form format (with no data) on which you can base all of your future forms; QuickBooks provides several templates, but you can also create custom templates

Temporary Account

Accounts are zeroed out at the end of each fiscal period, with the amounts from them moving into an equity account as either a net income (if income was greater than expenses) or a net loss (if expenses exceeded income for the period); also called a nominal account

Time Tracking

Allows you to create weekly timesheets so you can break down the hours by customer/job or to record single activities for a customer/job

Trial Balance

Report that adds up the debits and credits at the end of an accounting period so mistakes can be traced if debits don't equal credits

Unearned Income

Funds received from a customer as a deposit or for a gift certificate; these funds should be held in a liability account until they are "earned"

Uniform Resource Locator (URL)

A web address used to identify a unique page on the Internet

Units of Measure

Feature that allows you to convert units of measure; useful for companies that purchase and sell in different units of measure or need to indicate units on purchase or sales forms; available in the Premier and higher versions of QuickBooks

Users

You can set up an unlimited number of users for your QuickBooks company and assign a password for each person; users can only change their own personal preferences (the administrator controls the access each user has to the QuickBooks file)

Vendor

Anyone (except employees) to whom you pay money; could be the electric company, the organization to which you pay taxes, a merchandise supplier, or subcontractors you pay to do work for your customers

Vendor List

A list in QuickBooks that stores all information related to your vendors

Version

Intuit creates a new version of QuickBooks each year (such as QuickBooks 2011, 2012, or 2013) and each new version provides additional features that are new for that year

Website

Refers to a collection of related web pages and their supporting files and folders.

World Wide Web (WWW)

Also called the web; organized system of Internet servers that support HTML documents; the fun part of the Internet

Year-to-Date Amounts

If you begin to use the QuickBooks payroll feature for existing employees who have received at least one paycheck from you (and it is not the first day of January), you must enter year-to-date amounts for them to ensure that QuickBooks calculates taxes with thresholds properly and you will be able to print accurate W-2s at the end of the year

Index